THE POWER AND SECRET
OF
THE JESUITS

BY RENE FULOP-MILLER

TRANSLATED BY

F.S. FLINT AND D.R. TAIT

Tsun Su
Art of War

Ignatius Loyola

Engraving after a painting by Rubens.

Copyright 2014 by Gerald E. Greene

ISBN: 978-1494939250

The content of this book from the 1930 edition has been retyped and edited for the benefit of the reader. Few words have been changed, and certain spellings have been modified. The pictures were scanned from the published book and not from the original photographs.

Gerald E. Greene

Never before in the course of the world's history had such a Society appeared. The old Roman Senate itself did not lay schemes for world domination with greater certainty of success. Never had the carrying out of a greater idea been considered with greater understanding. For all time this Society will be an example to every society which feels an organic longing for infinite extension and eternal duration—but it will also be a witness to the fact that unregarded Time alone brings to naught the cleverest undertakings, and that the natural growth of the whole race inevitably suppresses the artificial growth of a part."

NOVALIS.

PREFACE

Writings concerning the Society of Jesus may be numbered by thousands; from the foundation of the order to the present day, every epoch, and almost every people and every tongue has produced an extensive literature relating to the Jesuits. Of all these works, few indeed attempt to treat the subject objectively, while the remainder are all concerned either with reviling and accusing or with praising and defending.

Nevertheless, anyone who in our days seeks the truth about Jesuitism will find more valuable help in these partisan, controversial writings than in the guaranteed information of the historians. For, however important in many respects verified data and documents may be, such dry compilations never reveal to us the whole, or, indeed, the most essential part. Of the truth. Incomparably deeper insight into the being and the meaning of Jesuitism is afforded by all the hate-filled pamphlets, the highly colored apologies, distorted representations, doctored reports, the slanderings and glorifications of the order's history. They show us the attitude of living men to the Jesuit idea, disclose how deeply this idea has influenced emotions, thoughts and actions at every period, to what a passionate degree of rage and enthusiasm it has driven the mind of man.

In these writings, we see the combatants in the midst of the conflict, accusing or conciliatory, arrogant or humble, entreating or triumphing, cunning or open-hearted; we hear the cadence of their speech, see their actions and their plottings. In consequence, the judgment to which such controversial literature leads us is not derived from colorless, historical material, reduced to dry data, but grows from the evidence of living witnesses and from direct observation.

The author, therefore, could scarcely have wished for more valuable or suggestive material relating to his subject than that which is to hand. It introduces us to the salons of Paris society, the observatories of great astronomers, the primeval forests of South America, the ceremonial halls of China, the palace of the *Sacrum Officium*, the lodges of the Freemasons, into churches, conspirators' conventicles and hermits' cells; we pass through every town and country of the inhabited earth, through every epoch of recent times. We find ourselves involved in theological, philosophical, scientific, political, sociological and literary controversies until we at last realize that the four hundred years we have explored are the most significant in the development and culture of modern humanity and are filled with its most decisive problems.

The present volume, therefore, does not profess to be the contribution of a professional historian to the history of the Jesuit order, so much as a picture of those human passions and dreams, achievements and failures, which have decided our modern culture, and a picture no

Preface

less of those factors of cunning, infamy, heroism, intrigue, power of persuasion, despotism, sagacity and deception which have played their part in shaping the present.

For this reason, the method of presentation of the professional historians, with its esoteric language, its impartial dryness and objectivity, for the sake of which the stupid and the wise, the sublime and the ridiculous are treated with equal respect, seemed unsuitable to the author's purpose.

In the author's opinion, subjective appraisement, enthusiastic affirmation and denial, awe-struck reverence, indulgent humor and malicious mockery, as the subject at the moment demands, are no less valid means of representation than the objectivity of impersonal relation. It seems to him that the striving after true understanding should never compel a limitation of the means of expression, that, on the contrary, every conceivable faculty should be called into play, if the truth is to be rendered even approximately.

The author here wishes to express his sincerest and most heartfelt thanks especially to his esteemed friend, Mr. Johannes von Guenther, literary editor of the German publishers, for encouraging him to do justice to the problems of Catholicism in a modern study and for the sympathy and understanding that were always forthcoming for the author and his work. He also thanks all those persons, authorities and societies whose help has been of the utmost value to him in his travels and in the collection of the documentary and illustrative material required; here it should be remarked that Jesuits and other Catholic groups, as well as their opponents, Protestants, Socialists and Freemasons, have placed their services at his disposal in the most amicable way.

In Spain, the author has had the help of Mr. M. Velasco y Aguirre, Curator of the Department of Prints and Engravings of Madrid, Mr. F. de P. Amat, General Secretary of the University, of the editors of Razón y Fé, Father Z.G. Villada, Mr. G. Fernandez-Shaw, Mr. E. Lucas, professor M.G. Morente, Professor Don Anizeto Sardo y Villar and of Mr. M. Ullmann in Madrid, of Fathers P. Pastella, and J. Villar at Manresa, J.M. de Estefania and l. Frias at Loyola, Father A. Tobella of the Benedictine Abbey of Montserrat, Mr. J. de Urquito, President of the Basque society at San Sebastian, Dr. Rubio of the Catalonian Library at Barcelona, of the eminent authority on Loyola, Father J. Creixel, and of Mr. C.B. Plata, Director of Indian Archives at Seville.

The author's thanks are likewise due to Messrs. A. Bebelon, A. Linzeler and M. Aubry of the Bibliothèque Nationale in Paris, Professor J. Baruzzi and Mr. M. Bonnerot of the Sorbonne, Mr. F. Calot of the Ste.-Geneviève Library, Mr. F. Boucher of the Carnavalet Museum, Mrs. Horn and Mr. Rondel of the Arsenal Library, the editor-in-chief of *Études*, Father Dudon, and to Fathers Chambeau and Rouet in Paris.

Their support in the work has also been given by Fathers P. Tacchi-Venturi, C. Bricarelli, F. Busnelli and E. Rosa, Professor A. Petrucci, Professor F. X. Zimmerman, Professor Galassi-Paluzzi, Fathers Schulien and Schnidt, the directors of the Lateran Mission Exhibition, and Dr. J. Jorda of the Austrian Embassy at the Quirinal.

The author's grateful thanks are also due to Dr. Joseph Gregor, the famous historian of dramatic art and director of the dramatic section of the National Library at Vienna, for rare works and engravings, to Mr. Franz Hanaczek, the director of Herder and Co. of Vienna and

Preface

to Dr. Hermann Leber of Munich for valuable references. In procuring the necessary photographic reproductions, help has been given by Merrsr. Vaule in Paris, Lagos in Madrid, Sarda at Manresa, Korty in Vienna, and Alinari, Calderisi and San Saini in Rome.

Finally, special thanks are due to Mr. Percy Eckstiein the author's friend, who has given him the most valuable assistance in this work.

Rene Fülöp-Miller

Vienna, August, 1929.

CONTENTS

Part I: Page

- Mystical Ecstasy and the Natural Way — 19
- The "Application of the Senses" — 24
- The Militant Saviour of the Jesuits — 26
- Examination of Conscience by the Schedule System — 30
- The "Living Art" of the Exercises — 33
- The "Corpse-Like Obedience" — 34
- The Pyramid to God — 41

Part II:

- His Personality and Work — 47
- "Given Up to the Vanities of the World" — 49
- His Visions on the Rack — 58
- From Philanderer to a "Master of the Affects" — 63
- At the Tables of the Pious Ladies — 70
- The Travels and Adventures of a Fool — 73
- Salvation and perplexity — 81
- The Work of Conversion in the Students' Room — 84
- The Founding of the Society of Jesus — 89
- Up Against Modern Problems — 93
- The Way to World Domination — 100
- Physical Asceticism and Discipline of the Will — 103
- Death and the Post for Spain — 105

Part III:

- Grace and Salvation through Good Works — 111
- Perplexities from Stagira to Trent — 114
- The Pope's Comma — 118
- The Uproar Among the Theologians — 122
- Grace in the Salons — 124
- "Novelists and Dramatists are Poisonmongers" — 131
- The Fateful Five Propositions — 133
- Signs and Wonders — 142
- Doubt, the Source of Knowledge — 148
- Descartes and the Jesuits — 149

Contents

Part III: (Cont'd)   Page

Leibniz, the Friend of the Jesuits	153
Free Will in the Light of the Newer Philosophy	156
The Dispute between the Jesuits and the Experimental Psychologists	158
"Behaviourism," Plant-Lice and Pavlov's Dog	160

PART IV:

Free Will and Responsibility	165
The Jesuits and Absolution	167
"The End Justifies the Means"	172
Aristotle, the Progenitor of Jesuit Moral Philosophy	176
The Atomization of morality	183
Problems of Confessional Practice	186
The Judge in the Confessional	190
The Moral Philosophy of the Talmud and of the Stoics	198
Probabilism	202
The "Certain" and the "Uncertain" Conscience	205
"Austere and Morbid Pascal"	208

PART V:

Merchant Among Merchants and Soldier Among Soldiers	213
With the Pearl-Fishers and Rajahs	217
The Dream of "Chinquinquo"	222
At the Court of the Great Voo	228
"Deus" Against "Dainichi"	230
Before the Gates of China	232
Jesuits as Brahmins and Yogis	235
At the Court of the Great Mogul	238
From the Tea Ceremonial to Martyrdom	243
Father Ricci—Doctor Li	248
Conversion through Clock and Calendar	255
Teachers and Diplomats at the Peking Court	262
The Order of Gardeners and "Lightning Artists"	268
The Triumph of the Fountain and the Mechanical Lion	275
Profanation or Toleration?	277

Contents

	Page
PART V: (Cont'd)	
The Fish-Hook Mission	282
Father Marquette, the Explorer of the Mississippi	284
Friends of the Red Men	287
The Jesuits' Musical Kingdom	292
A Benevolent Dictatorship	298
The Armed Forces of the Jesuit Republic	302
A Forest Utopia	305
PART VI:	
The Struggle with the English Police Agents	311
The Theologian on the Royal Throne	317
The "Sovereignty of the People" and Tyrannicide	320
Comedy of the Disguises	326
The Mediator of War and Peace	330
A Jesuit at the Court of Ivan the Terrible	334
The "False Demetrius"	340
The Success and the End of the Jesuit Kings"	344
The Struggle Against the German Reformation	348
The Jesuits in the thirty Years' War	351
The Conscience of Kings	360
The Confessors of Louis XIV	365
The Tribulations of Madame de Pompadour	373
"Enlightened Despotism"	376
The "Mutiny of the Hats"	381
Dominus ac Redemptor	383
PART VII:	
The Resurrection of the Order	387
The Catholicization of Thought	392
The Jesuits and Galileo	397
Scholars Among Scholars	400
The Educational Work of the Fathers	403
The Jesuit Theatre	407
Jesuit Opera and Jesuit Ballet	413
The Stage Management of the Jesuits	414

Contents

PART VII: (Cont'd)	**Page**
The Society of Jesus and the Arts	417
The Revolt of the Scholars	422
The Freemasons and the Jesuits	432
The Return in Spirit	434
Kant and Neo-Scholasticism	439
Jesuitism and Psychoanalysis	445
The Conflict Over Modern Political Ideals	448
Dostwievsky's Grand Inquisitor	457

PART VIII:

Gloria Dei and Gloria Mundi	463
Jesuit Methods in the Light of Modern Times	466
True to the Earth	473
The Service of the Order to Civilization	475
The Way of Knowledge and the Way of Faith	477

Bibliography   481

Index   513

ILLUSTRATIONS

1. Examen particulare
2. Examination of the conscience
3. The torments of hell
4. The seven deadly sins
5. The election
6. The two standards
7. The followers of Christ
8. The evil spirits
9. The circles of purification
10. The Last Supper
11. The Resurrection
12. The sepulcher of the Virgin
13-14. Nuns and mendicant monks before the appearance of the Jesuits
15. The Jesuit Martini as a Chinese mandarin pays a ceremonial visit to the Emperor
16. Ignatius as the Knight Iñigo
17. Queen Germaine
18-21. Woodcuts from the Tale of Chivalry, *Amadis of Gaul*
22. Ignatius dedicates his life to the Queen of Heaven
23. Ignatius, weakened by his penances, is cared for by the ladies of the house of Amigrant in Manresa
24. Montserrat
25. The court of the cloister at Montserrat
26. The Senator Trevisano finds Ignatius
27. Ignatius on the voyage to Jerusalem
28. Jerusalem
29. The Doctors of the University of Salamanca
30. Ignatius, at the age of thirty-three, attends the school for boys in Barcelona
31. Ignatius in prison suspected of heresy
32. The almshouse St.-Jacques de l'Hôpital where Ignatius lived in Paris
33. Collège de Montaigu, Paris
34. The chapel of St. Mary on Montmartre
35. The University Quarter in Paris
36. La Storta
37. The house on the Piazza Margana where Ignatius lived in Rome
38. Rome in the sixteenth century
39. The pope dispensing his blessing from the benediction balcony of St. Peter's
40. Pope Paul III

Illustrations

41. The life of Ignatius: Pope Paul III sanctions the Society of Jesus. Ignatius composes the *Constitutions*. He sends his first missionaries into the world.
42. Copy of a letter by Ignatius
43. Ignatius Loyola (*Lavater*)
44. Ignatius Loyola (*Titian*)
45. Ignatius Loyola (*Coello*)
46. The work of Ignatius: the order and its establishments over the whole world
47. Session of the Council of Trent
48. Cardinal Bellarmine: the famous Jesuit controversialist
49. Luis Molina: the originator of Molinism
50. Bishop Cornelius Jansen
51. Du Vergier de Hauranne, Abbot of Saint-Cyran
52. Port Royal des Champs
53. Port Royal de Paris
54. The nuns of Port Royal in the convent garden
55. Procession of the nuns of Port Royal
56. Angélique Arnauld
57. Catherine Agnès Arnauld
58. Princesse de Conti: the protectress of Port Royal
59. Mock procession against Jansenism instituted by the students of the Jesuit college of Mâcon
60. Jean Racine
61. Blaise Pascal
62. "While the shepherds quarrel the wolves devour the herd:" Contemporary caricature on the clerical strife
63. Jansenist satirical drawing against the Jesuits
64. François de Paris doing penance in his cell
65. François de Paris on his deathbed
66. Ladies of rank at the wonder-working grave of François de Paris
67. Francisco Suarez
68. Antonio Escobar y Mendoza
69. Symbolical painting from the Jesuit church at Billom, representing the work of salvation of the order
70. Confession
71. The Jesuit Girard and his confessant, "la bella Cadière"
72. The death of Francis Xavier
73. Street life in Goa
74. Portuguese galley manned by natives of Malabar
75. The King of Cochin and his retinue
76. State galley of the King of Tonking
77. A Japanese preacher
78. The Jesuits in Japan
79. Daimyo Nobunaga: the friend of the Christians

Illustrations

80. Dainyo Hideyoshi: the enemy of the Christians
81-82. The martyrs of the Jesuit mission to Japan
83. The Jesuit missionary Robert de Nobili
84. The Jesuit missionary Ricci and a Chinese converted by him
85. A Jesuit representation of Confucius
86. The astronomical observatory erected in Peking by the Jesuits
87. The Jesuit Court astronomers of the Emperor of China, two Chinese converted by them, and the Chinese cross they used
88. Chinese Festival
89. A Jesuit representation of the gods of China
90. The first map of the Mississippi
91. The torture of the Jesuits Brébeuf and Lalemant by the Canadian Indians
92. Indians of the Jesuit Republic of Paraguay
93. The Jesuit Republic of Paraguay
94. the Castle of San Augustin de Arecutagua in Paraguay
95. The plan of a Jesuit reduction in Paraguay
96. Ruins of the mission church of San Miguel
97. King James I of England
98. The Jesuit theologian Mariana: Educator of Philip III of Spain
99. The controversial work of James I against the pope
100. The "League": procession of armed crowds under the leadership of priests
101. The assassination of Henry III by the monk Clément
102. Execution of the Jesuit Guigard
103. King James II of England
104. The Jesuit school, Heythorpe College, in Oxfordshire, England
105. Vienna
106. Peter Canisius
107. Peter Faber
108. Expulsion of the Jesuits from Paris under Henry IV
109. Henry IV's heart being transferred to the Jesuit college of La Flèche
110. Louis XIV and his court ride in state to the Jesuit church
111. King Louis XIV of France
112. Marquise de Montespan
113. Madame de Maintenon
114. Mademoiselle de La Vallière
115. Louis XV of France
116. Marquise de Pompadour
117. Father-confessor Perusseau
118. The expulsion of the Jesuits from Portugal
119. The expulsion of the Jesuits from Spain
120. The professed house of the Jesuits in Vienna
121. The Jesuit college of La Flèche

Illustrations

122. Pope Clement XIV 108. Expulsion of the Jesuits from Paris under Henry IV
109. Henry IV's heart being transferred to the Jesuit college of La Flèche
110. Louis XIV and his court ride in state to the Jesuit church
111. King Louis XIV of France
112. Marquise de Montespan
113. Madame de Maintenon
114. Mademoiselle de La Vallière
115. Louis XV of France
116. Marquise de Pompadour
117. Father-confessor Perusseau
118. The expulsion of the Jesuits from Portugal
119. The expulsion of the Jesuits from Spain
120. The professed house of the Jesuits in Vienna
121. The Jesuit college of La Flèche
122. Pope Clement XIV (Ganganelli), who abolished the Jesuit order
123. Galileo Galilei
124. Scenery from the Jesuit theater at Clermont
125. Grand festival in the Collège de Clermont in celebration of the birth of Louis XIII
126. Scene from the Jesuit festival play *Pietas Victrix* in Vienna (Ganganelli), who abolished the Jesuit order
123. Galileo Galilei
124. Scenery from the Jesuit theater at Clermont
125. Grand festival in the Collège de Clermont in celebration of the birth of Louis XIII
126. Scene from the Jesuit festival play *Pietas Victrix* in Vienna
127. Sketch of a scene for the Jesuit theater in Vienna by Ludovico Burnacini
128. Jesuit festival in Vienna to celebrate the averting of the plague
129. Carnival procession of the Jesuits in Mexico, 1647
130-133. Sketches for festivals and games by the Jesuit Menestrier
134. Sketch for a church festival by Pozzo
135. Jesuit church in Courtray
136. Ignatius healing the possessed
138. Ignatius Loyola (*Montañes*)
139. Francisco Borgia
140. The magic lantern invented by the Jesuit Father Kircher
141. Astrologic medicine
142. The glory of St. Ignatius

THE POWER AND SECRET OF

THE JESUITS

PART I

THE SPIRIT OF JESUITISM

Mystical Ecstasy and the Natural Way

The attainment of a state of perfection, that goal which has hovered from time immemorial before man's eyes, has never been desired with such passionate ardor as in the Christian Middle Ages. But, until far into modern times, Christendom was scarcely aware of any other perfection possible in this life than that of "union with God" in mystical ecstasy.

It was thought, however, that this could not be attained by human endeavor, however fervent, but that the *visio Dei* was accorded only to those enlightened by the grace of God. "To this state of blessedness," said Bernard of Clairvaux, the famous preacher of the twelfth century, "man never attains by his own efforts; it is a gift of God and not the desert of mean."

Man's endeavor to raise himself through spiritual exercises above the ordinary standard to a higher degree of achievement was, indeed, considered praiseworthy and meritorious; but the "acquired illumination" which might be attained by this method was regarded mostly as a low, preparatory degree of purification. According to prevailing mediaeval belief, the difference between this and the true perfection, which was accorded to the elect in the ecstasy of "infused illumination," was one not merely of degree, but of kind.

Even the ascetic, mystical school of the "Brothers of Common Life," who were the first to preach a practical way of purification by means of ascetic exercises, as opposed to purely passive mysticism, taught at the same time that such a *via purgative* could at best render a man more fit for the reception of illumination, but that this itself was always a *donum extraordinarium*, a free gift of God to the elect.

Therefore, it is also impossible to apprehend the circumstances of this "union with God" with the natural senses. All the mystics teach that reason is impotent, memory dies away, images, forms and likenesses vanish before this perfection *sine forma corporea, sine specie imaginaria et sine ommi luce creata*. Only when every sensible perception is extinguished can the soul behold the brightness of God, "in blindness and nescience, without form or sound, and without the powers of reason."

"Good people are often hindered by this," says the German mystic Master Eckhart, "that they rely too much on sight and see things as images in their minds, and thereby hinder their true perfection, in that they remain dependent in their mental affections upon the image of the humanity of Our Lord." True enlightenment, on the other hand, is far removed from everything that might be compared to anything in the common world of the senses.

Accordingly the gulf separating the ordinary man from the supernatural state appeared unbridgeable: there was no likeness, no image, nothing that could give even an inkling of that state. Every word of the mystics seemed designed to throw the great mass of those who had not received divine grace into the depths of despair, and to make them feel how vain must be all their endeavors, and how impotent these were to lead them to perfection.

The Jesuits, however, in direct opposition to such opinions, made themselves the exponents of another doctrine, according to which perfection could not only be experienced in supernatural ecstasy, but also could be attained by the exercise of the natural human capacities. If the mystics maintained, with St. Dionysius, that perfection consisted solely in a *divina pati*, in "suffering the Divine," the Jesuits, in accordance with the teaching of the founder of their order, Ignatius Loyola, taught that even those who did not possess the supernatural illumination, infused into the soul, of which the mystics though so highly, could achieve perfection by their own efforts and pains.

According to this teaching, man was no longer condemned to wait in patience until the *visio Dei* was vouchsafed to him; on the contrary, to the human will was attributed that same power which had hitherto been sought only in supernatural illumination.

"I can find God at all times, whenever I will," Ignatius Loyola said once to Manares, one of the brothers of his order. Man, he taught, had only to strive after God in the right way, in order to attain to him; all that was necessary was zeal and the right use of natural capacities. As the body can be exercised "by going, walking and running," so by exercises the will may be disposed "to find the divine will."

These fundamental principles formulated by Ignatius became the guiding principle of the Jesuit order. Thus, in later days, the Jesuit theologian, Francisco Suarez, wrote that holiness consisted in nothing but "the conforming of our will to the will of God"; this conformity, however, could quite well be attained "without the grace of illumination." The Spanish Jesuit, Godinez, went yet further when he said that in general the man who lived in a state of intense contemplation was not to be regarded as the more perfect, but he whose will strove the more eagerly after perfection.

Through their tireless advocacy of this teaching, the Jesuits brought about a complete revolution in Catholic thought, especially after they had succeeded in inspiring with their principles prominent churchmen outside the Society of Jesus. Thus, under Jesuit influence, Vincent de Paul, could be attained "in an ordinary manner," by will and purpose more surely than by contemplative mysticism. The great bishop of Geneva, Francis of Sales, frequently emphasized the fact that many canonized saints had never had "visions," but had reached holiness merely by their ardent efforts.

In his *Book of the Spiritual Exercises*, Ignatius Loyola has endeavored to show how man may develop his natural powers to the highest degree by systematic exercises. He starts from the fundamental assumption that perfection, in the last resort, consists solely in this: that man, who from his ordinary standpoint views life in a false, earthly and transitory perspective, and consequently often goes astray, should struggle forward to a free way of life and thought leading straight to the highest goal.

In the very first introductory paragraph of the *Spiritual Exercises*, known as the "Foundation," this point of view is plainly expressed. In it, the purpose of man is defined as conforming to the will of God and thereby adapting himself to the highest moral order. All other creatures on the earth were created solely for the sake of man, so that he may use them as far as they are of use to him in the attainment of the end appointed for him by God.

The introductory meditation of the *Exercises* demands "inner freedom in respect of temporal possessions, troubles and affections." It is necessary "that we make ourselves indifferent in regard to all created things, so that we shall not wish for health rather than sickness, for riches rather than poverty, for honor rather than reproach, for a long life rather than a short one." We must desire only that "which may better lead us to the end for which we were created."

This "indifference" does not, however, signify with Ignatius an end in itself, like the *ataraxia* of the ancient Stoics or the "detachment" of the mediaeval mystics; it is merely a necessary pre-condition, so that the will may free itself from all disturbing, confusing attachments and inclinations, and may learn to act solely in accordance with the divine will.

For, according to Jesuit teaching, God is not to be found only in inactive transports of ecstasy, but above all in a clear recognition of the divine will, and in an activity directed by this recognition: man attains to perfection when all his actions are directed "to the greater glory of God."

This point of view destroyed the hitherto prevalent belief in the special vocation of the few, elect persons. Hosts of pious people, who had never received a "revelation," now saw before them a way by which they might reach a perfection, with no less certainty than those whom God elevated to himself in the fire of mystical ecstasy.

In his *Exercises*, Ignatius has accurately delineated this way, describing carefully all the regions, the valleys, heights and depths to be traversed. He has indicated the places where the pilgrim may take his ease, and those other places where a steep ascent is to be expected, the side tracks that lead astray, the threatening precipices and dangerous abysses. Here and there are signposts and milestones, so that the wanderer may know how great a distance he has put behind him, and how near of far is the goal.

Everywhere along the way there are familiar pictures, bathed in a light which is the very light of earth. To the end, the disciple is allowed the use of his earthly senses, and he is never required to divest himself of his humanity. For the *Exercises*—unlike the mystical writings which taught that to reach to God is was necessary to extinguish seeing and hearing, images and likenesses—endeavor to lead man to the highest goal with the aid of his natural capacities and senses.

Ignatius avails himself in especial, of the power of imagination; he tries to awaken in his pupils quite definite pictorial representations, all with the object of intensifying the power of distinguishing between right and wrong conduct. For man's progress to perfection must be based on this ability to distinguish right from wrong; but we are perpetually halting between two possibilities, right or wrong, good or bad, Christ or Satan, usually unable to be sure of always choosing what is right.

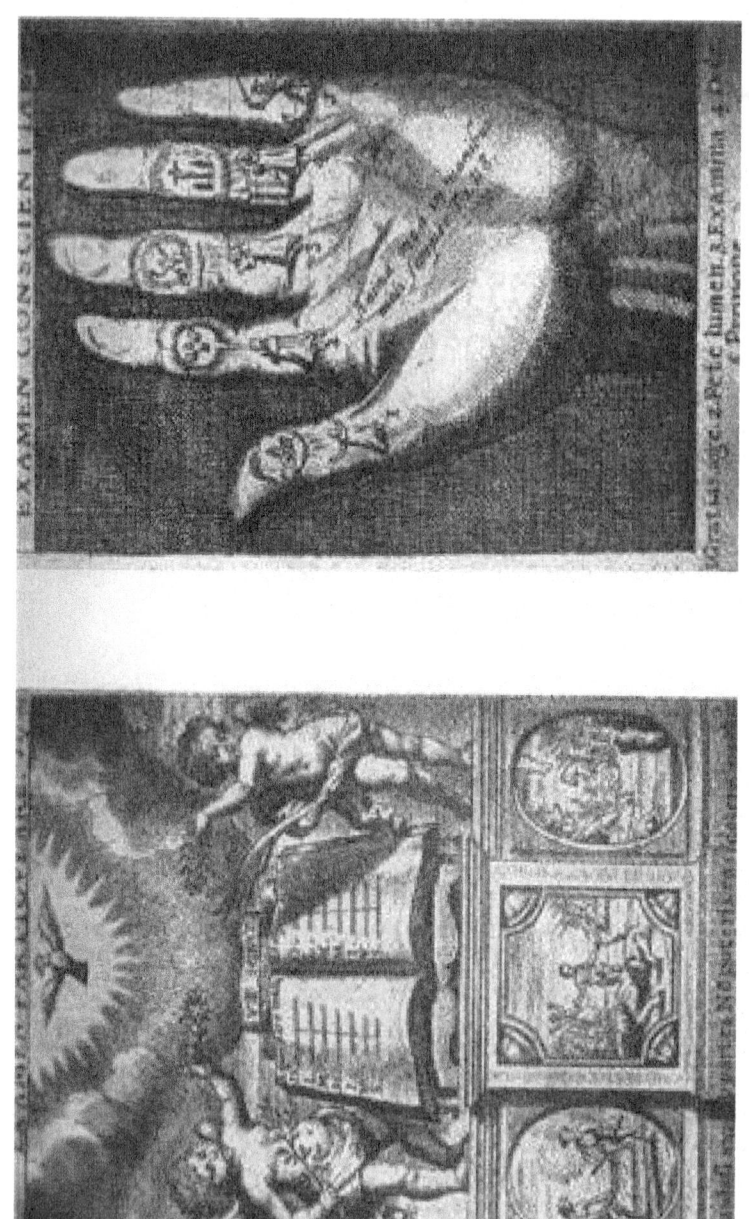

1. EXAMEN PARTUCULARE   2. EXAMINATION OF THE CONSCIENCE

From the first illustrated edition of the Spiritual Exercises.

3. THE TORMENTS OF HELL

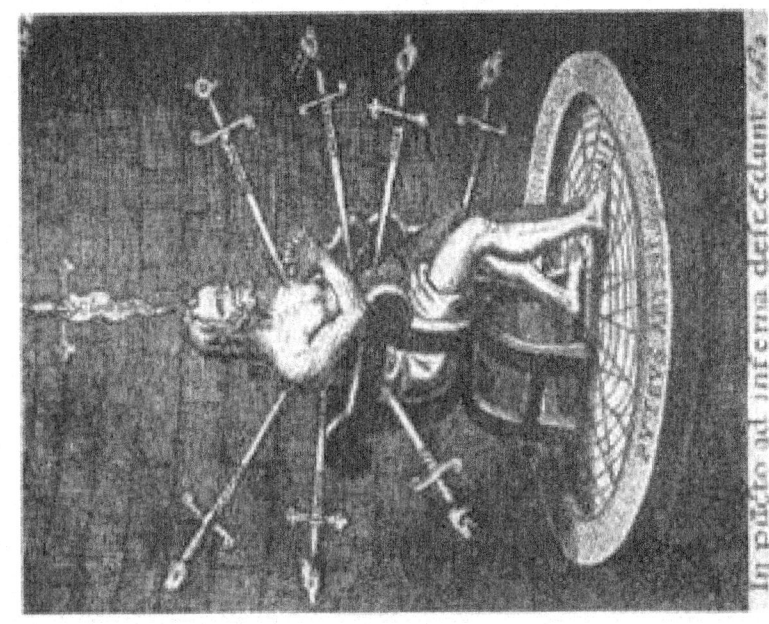

4. THE SEVEN DEADLY SINS

From the first illustrated edition of the Spiritual Exercises.

He who goes through Loyola's *Spiritual Exercises* has to experience hell and heaven with all his senses, to know burning pain and blessed rapture, so that the distinction between good and evil is forever indelibly imprinted in his soul. With this preparation, the exercitant is brought to the great "election," the choice between Satan and Christ; it is to this election that actual life will bring him again and again, and it is on this that his good or bad conduct will constantly depend.

It is through images that Ignatius strives to assist mankind towards perfection; for every day and for every hour of the day the *Exercises* prescribe exactly what representations the exercitant has to evoke, and of what aids to this end he has to make use. Today, four hundred years after the birth of the *Exercises*, the modern psychologist will no doubt regard many of these late mediaeval representations as antiquated and consequently ineffective; but he will not be able to withhold admiration from the deep psychological knowledge with which understanding, imagination and will have been made to co-operate in the *Exercises*. From this point of view, the *Exercises* of Ignatius is acclaimed to this day as a psychological masterpiece.

The "Application of the Senses"

The vivid representation of Evil is achieved in the *Spiritual Exercises* by terrible pictures of hell, while Good is symbolized by the earthly life of Christ, which the exercitant must represent to himself stage by stage, as if it were a realistic Passion play. The final "election" is depicted dramatically as two belligerent armies: the militant hordes of Satan oppose the "standard of Christ."

First of all, hell is represented in all its horror, filled with the wailing crowds of the damned. In this exercise, the pupil has in the first place "to see with the eye of the imagination the length, breadth and depth of hell"; but the other senses must co-operate, for it is written in these peculiar directions with their precise division into "points":

"The first point consists in this, that I see with the eye of imagination those enormous fires, and the souls as it were in bodies of fire.

"The second point consists in this, that I hear with the ears of the imagination the lamentations, howlings, cries, the blasphemies against Christ Our Lord and against all His saints.

"The third point consists in this, that I smell with the sense of smell of the imagination the smoke, brimstone, refuse and rotting things of hell.

"The fourth point consists in this, that I taste with the sense of taste of the imagination the bitter things, the tears, sorrows and the worm of conscience in hell.

"The fifth point consists in feeling with the sense of touch of the imagination how these fires fasten upon and burn souls."

The exercitant, therefore, experiences hell with all his senses; he sees, hears, smells, tastes and feels it until he is overwhelmed with horror of the terrors of the inferno, and shuddering fear of the judgment of God.

Catholic doctrine has always seen in the "fear of God" a means of purification of peculiar

The "Application of the Senses"

potency. "Blessed is he to whom it is given to know the fear of God!" exclaims Anselm of Canterbury, and Bernard of Clairvaux asserts that the soul first tastes of God "when he moves it to fear, not when he leads it to knowledge." According to Cassiodorus, too, fear is "the portal of conversion," through which man goes to God "as through an open door."

Although the great scholastics Peter Lombard and Thomas Aquinas distinguished between a "servile fear" and a higher "filial fear of God" born of true love, they emphasize at the same time that servile fear, the sinner's fear of death and the pains of hell, is the prelude to filial fear.

Bonaventura, the "Seraphic Doctor" of scholasticism, even gives instructions how to stimulate servile fear; "Consider the way and manner in which man dies, and put yourself sometimes in the position of one in the throes of death, then will you be able to picture more vividly the circumstances of death. . . How reluctantly will the soul quit this life, when at its departure it first looks upon an unknown country and sees how whole hordes of evil spirits are lying in wait for it!"

The books which exercised the strongest influence on Ignatius Loyola likewise contained vivid descriptions of eternal damnation. "It will be profitable to you, dear brother," it is written in the *Book of Exercises* of Spanish abbot, Garcia de Cisneros, "to picture to yourself the torments of hell, as well as hell itself. . . Picture to yourself therefore: an exceedingly desolate confusion, a place deep under the earth like a fiery crater or a gigantic town, shrouded in terrible darkness, blazing with dreadful flames. Cries and lamentations which pierce to the very marrow fill the air. The unhappy inhabitants, whose pains and torments no human tongue can describe, are burning in raging despair."

The inferno is similarly described in Thomas à Kempis's *Imitation of Christ:* "There shall the slothful be pricked forward with burning goads, and the gluttons be tormented with vast thirst and hunger. There shall the luxurious and lovers of pleasure be bathed in burning pitch and stinking brimstone. . . There one hour of pain shall be more severe than a hundred years of the severest penance here."

Just at the beginning of the sixteenth century, when the *Exercises* were being composed, the general delineation of death, hell and purgatory had reached its zenith; the *memento mori* forced its way upon man's attention from every direction. Even on articles of ornament, skeletons or flaming jaws of hell were engraved, and rosary beads were made in the shape of skulls. Priests preached impressively from every pulpit on eternal damnation, and the numerous tracts on the *ars bene moriendi*, the books of hours, primers and breviaries of the time dealt with the same subject; scientific works gave minute details the pains of death, and full topographical descriptions of the situation, dimensions and organization of the Satanic kingdom.

The material for Ignatius's representation of hell was, therefore, ready to his hand, in a thousand different forms, in the spiritual artistic world of the time; but, in his *Exercises*, these pictorial images were for the first time systematically employed to produce a quite definite psychological effect, and to contribute to a process of inner purification. The pictures of death and hell are intended to alarm and terrify the mind of the exercitant, so that, clearly recognizing his own sinfulness and the eternal damnation which threatens him, he may decide to change his way of life and thought.

When this has been achieved, the exercitant is shown the ideal which he is to imitate: Ignatius admonished him to steep himself in the life and passion of Christ. As with the previous representations of hell, here again all the senses are employed to evoke visible images, and here again Ignatius insists on an exact "representation of the place."

"I am to picture to myself, as if I saw with the eye of the imagination, the synagogues, villages and towns which Christ Our Lord passes through and in which he preaches. . . If the Blessed Virgin is the subject, the method of meditation is that I picture to myself a little house, and then in particular the house and the apartment of Our Blessed lady in the city of Nazareth in the country of Galilee."

In the contemplation of the birth of Our Lord, Ignatius gives the command "to see with the eye of the imagination the road leading from Nazareth to Bethlehem"; its length and breadth "are to be considered as well as the circumstance whether the road is flat or whether it leads through valleys and over heights." The exercitant has also "to picture the cave of the nativity, how broad or how narrow, how low or how lofty it is and how constructed."

The exercitant is always directed to see the persons "with the eye of the imagination" and "to hear with the hearing what they say"; with the sense of smell and taste he must perceive "the immeasurable fragrance and sweetness of the Godhead" and "with the sense of touch of the imagination" must touch the places where Christ has set foot.

The Last Supper is to be pictured as vividly as if the exercitant were himself sitting at the table, seeing the actions of Christ and hearing the speech of those present. The exercitant must taste the loaves and fishes with which Jesus feeds the multitude; he must smell the Magdalene's ointment, and with her must anoint the Savior's feet, wipe them and kiss them. But he must also suffer with Christ the scourging and the pains of the Crucifixion; with Him he must descend into the grave and ascend at last to heaven. Thus Loyola's disciple is himself drawn into the mystery play which presents, with holy awe, the life of the Son of God from His birth to His transfiguration.

Even in the meditation of the night in the Garden of Gethsemane, a precise *repraesentatio loci* is prescribed: "Here the road from Mount Sion to the Valley of Jehoshaphat must be contemplated, and likewise the Garden, whether it is broad or long, whether of one style or of another."

Edgar Quinet, one of the great Catholic opponents of the Ignatian teaching, says with indignation, of this part of the *Exercises*, that it is quite incomprehensible that here, where a divine mystery is being considered, the prelude should consist in this: that, in the first place, a materialistically conceived place should be described, its area measured in a trivial manner, the path methodically marked out. "Christ stands at the foot of Mount Tabor, at the inexpressible moment of transfiguration and—the exercitant has to occupy himself with the form of the mountain, its height, its breadth and vegetation!"

The Militant Saviour of the Jesuits

The meditations on the earthly life, the crucifixion and resurrection of the Saviour had been embodied in Catholic religious life long before the days of Ignatius, both in the liturgi-

6. THE TWO STANDARDS

5. THE ELECTION

From the first illustrated edition of the Spiritual Exercises.

7. THE FOLLOWERS OF CHRIST 8. THE EVIL SPIRITS

From the first illustrated edition of the Spiritual Exercises.

The Militant Saviour of the Jesuits

cal worship of the Church itself and in a great number of prayers and mystical meditations, such as had been in use from the early days of Christianity.

Augustine himself had proclaimed that the way of purification leads *per Christum hominem ad Christum Deum*, and Thomas Aquinas had taught that man truly belongs to Christ only when, penetrated by the spirit of Jesus, he does his sins to death in the imitation of the Saviour. This idea of the *imitation Christi*, however, finds its most beautiful expression in Francis of Assisi, for whom Jesus was the Example of voluntary self-abasement, humility and self-abnegation. It is, indeed, reported of Francis that he felt the sufferings of Christ so intensely that at last the stigmata of the Crucified appeared on his body.

After Bernard of Clairvaux, in particular, had made the life and sufferings of Christ the basis of his famous preaching, a great part of mediaeval piety stood under the spell of Bernard's mysticism of the Passion. It is in this spirit that the Christ of the German mystic, Heinrich Suso, proclaims: "No one can attain to divine heights and to unaccustomed sweetness, unless he is drawn thither by the picture of my human sufferings."

Even Martin Luther wrote: "Whether I am to hear it or think of it, it is inevitable that I make an image of it in my heart. Whether I will or not, there projects itself in my heart the image of a Man hanging on the Cross, just as my countenance is projected in water when I gaze therein."

Yet, it is in the very contemplations on the Passion that the fundamental difference between the Ignatian exercises and former methods of religious meditation is most clearly shown. In all other forms of Catholic devotion, Jesus appears as the Lord of heaven, enthroned in sublime heights, to Whom man can only pray, in all humility. In this way had the Son of God been always reverenced hitherto: by nocturnal prayer and solemn changes, and, as is written in the Benedictine formula, "with praise, glory, honor and service of the Divine Majesty." Even Francis's "imitation of Christ" consists for the most part in a self-forgetting mystical submersion, remote from the world, of which the *"Poverello"* had given the first example.

The relation of the Jesuit to his Saviour is something entirely different. For, in the *Exercises*, Christ is not merely the object of reflective contemplation; here, He approaches the exercitant, speaks to him, and requires of him decision and action. Here, Jesus is not by any means the Lord of Heaven, peacefully enthroned in His glory; on the contrary, He appears as a militant King, fighting for His kingdom. He turns to man, and requires his service in the great battle against Lucifer.

The *"Meditation of the Reign of Christ"* in the Exercises begins by the exercitant's representing to himself an earthly king "to whom all princes and all Christian people pay reverence and obedience." This king speaks to his followers, saying that he desires to conquer the land of the infidel for the true faith, and requires the support of all his vassals. "Whoever wishes to come with me must labor as I do by day and watch by night, so that he may at last be made partaker of my victory."

Now the exercitant has to consider "what should be the answer of good subjects to so noble and generous a king." The answer can be nothing but an oath of fealty, and when the exercitant has clearly recognized this, the second part of the exercise presented by Ignatius consists "in applying the example of an earthly king to Christ our Lord." If the call of an earthly king inspires his subjects to follow him, how much the more should it inspire when the Son of God calls mankind to the fight against the Evil One!

This call to arms is repeated even more impressively in the famous "meditation on the Two Standards." Here, with the "application of all the senses," Jesus has to be represented "on the field before Jerusalem" as the supreme Captain of his army, while over against Him "in the region of Babylon" Satan calls together his demons for the last decisive battle.

"I picture to myself how Lucifer calls together an assembly of countless evil spirits, and then how he sends them out throughout the whole world, leaving out no land, nor place, nor race nor individual. . . In like manner, I must consider on the opposite side, the Supreme and True Captain, Our Lord Christ. . how he chooses His apostles and disciples, and sends them out into the whole world, so that they may spread the sacred doctrine among all mankind."

Ignatius, according to his disciples, regarded the meditations on the "Reign of Christ" and the "Two Standards" as the kernel of the *Exercises*, and in them indeed the fundamental principle of Jesuit teaching is expressed: the call to man to make a voluntary decision to join the side of Christ and to co-operate in increasing the glory of God: *ad marjoram Dei gloriam.*

The idea of the glory of God is not, indeed, peculiar to Jesuitism, but is found in the rest of the Catholic Church, and, yet more, in Calvinism. At the very time when Ignatius was attempting, with the help of his newly founded order, to bring the world "under the dominion of God," Calvin was making the same attempt in the narrow confines of the republic of Geneva. Just as the founder of the Society of Jesus called his efforts "military service for God," so Calvin called his work a "holy military service for the Supreme Captain," and the Genevan reformer, too, often spoke of the "glory of God" when he summoned his followers to the campaign against sin.

Yet, between the Jesuit and the Calvinist conception of the "glory of God" there is an abysmal difference. For Calvinism, dominated by the strict belief in predestination, everything in the world is pre-determined from all eternity; man's good deeds, therefore, cannot increase the glory of God, nor his ill deeds detract from it. In the splendor of God, there is no place for the co-operation of man, and the only link between mortal man and the unapproachable majesty of Christ is the word of God.

But, according to Jesuit teaching, the realization of the kingdom of God depends ultimately on the will of men, and it can be set up only by their help. In the *Exercises*, Jesus approaches man directly, seeks to guide him to the right "election," and commands him to contribute "to the greater glory of God." The very use of this comparative, always employed by Ignatius, indicates an idea of motion and increase peculiar to Jesuitism: the glory of God can be increased, and that by the co-operation of man.

Examination of Conscience by the Schedule System

Form the "Foundation" to the final meditations, the *Exercises* is carefully planned so that every impulse of the exercitant shall conform to a definite psychological system. The inner life, no less than the imagination, is put under the most severe discipline: sorrow and joy, despair and rejoicing, are not left to the arbitrary moods of the moment, but all emotions are placed under the control of a purposeful will.

The student is given precise instructions on what he has to feel from time to time during the exercises: so, at one place it is written: "The fifth point is a cry of wonder, with a flood of emotion." A stern warning is moreover given "that no foreign emotion, however noble, should interrupt the prescribed course, so that when lamentation over sin or the pains of death should be tasted, the consolation of redemption and resurrection should not intrude, out of its place."

The *Exercises* also teaches the student what he must do, to attain at all times the right mood: "if I desire to awaken in me heartfelt sorrow for the sufferings of Christ, then I must suffer no pleasant thoughts, however good and holy, to enter in, but I must rouse myself to sorrow, grief and pain, by calling constantly to mind the grieves, pains and sorrows of Our Lord from His birth to his passion."

The conscience likewise has to be disciplined and governed by the help of mechanical rules, and to this end Ignatius prescribes the use of a written system of control. The exercitant has from day to day to mark with points on a schedule the sins he has committed, and the comparison between the rows of dots at the beginning of the exercise and the rows, shortened as much as possible, at a later stage shows the progress made in the rooting out of sinful habits and tendencies.

Eberhard Gothein describes the manner of this peculiar *examen particulare* very aptly, when he says that it is undertaken "in the form of accurate book-keeping." "The number of sins is entered in a schedule, and from this the moral position can be reckoned from day to day with the accuracy of a calculating machine."

It is highly remarkable that the Puritan sage, Benjamin Franklin, arrived of his own accord at a system of examination of conscience which is the exact counterpart of the Ignatian *examen particulare*.

"I made myself a little book," writes Franklin in the memoirs of his life, "and ruled each page so as to have seven columns, one for each day of the week. In these columns I marked with a little black spot every fault which I had committed. . . I determined to give a week's strict attention to each of the virtues successively . . . I was surprised to find myself so much fuller of faults than I had imagined; but I had the satisfaction of seeing them diminish. . . It may be well my posterity should be informed that to this little artifice, with the blessing of God, their ancestor owed the constant felicity of his life."

Ignatius also gives full directions concerning the outward bearing of the exercitant during the performance of the exercises; he prescribes carefully the right way of breathing in and out during prayer, what bodily posture is desirable, when the cell must be darkened, when the exercitant should gaze upon dead men's bones, and again when the contemplation of fresh flowers may call to mind "the blossoming of the spiritual life."

But, in addition to this, the exercitant is given an experienced guide on his way to perfection, someone who has already trodden the road many times and knows its dangers well. "As man cannot well dispense with the external direction of superiors and spiritual fathers," writes Ignatius, "it is very necessary that he should discuss all his spiritual exercises with a wise person and always follow his advice." The exercises, therefore, are rarely performed by the exercitant alone, but are given him by a "master of the exercises." It is the task of this master to adapt the exercises to the particular individuality of the student, and in this way to make certain that the desired effect, the complete discipline of the will and of the inner life, shall be attained in every case.

"At last the passions have found their master!" cried Cochlæus, the humanistic opponent of Luther, when he learnt of the exercises through the Jesuit, Peter Faber. Nevertheless, Edgar Quinet declared that these spiritual exercises were a system which led "to ecstasy, by the yoke of method."

Yet, in this very thing perhaps lies the secret of the effectiveness of Loyola's work. For Rudolf Kassner, in his fine treatise on the *Elements of human Greatness*, has very rightly emphasized that the greatness of the mystic is ultimately invalidated "because he undertakes to live without measure," whereas historical greatness is "possible only be the application of a common standard." It is because the exercises brought the interior conversion of man within the bounds of a system within the reach of everybody, rationalized religious experience and adapted it to the general standard, that the small group of the elect gave place to the military-disciplined *Compañía de Jusús*.

He who peruses the *Exercises* for the first time will declare in astonishment that the book is a collection of contradictory rules, instructions, observations, annotations and additions. Even if you refrain from comparing this peculiar work with the inspired writings of the great mystics or with the skilled rhetoric of the humanists, it appears unusually dry and dull. The whole construction seems by no means clear; many parts entirely pass the comprehension, and, owing to the lack of style, the language fails to impress.

This judgment, however, holds good only so long as the *Exercises* is considered merely as a literary work. It is not until the exercises are performed that these contradictory provisions acquire their real meaning, and the diverse instructions with their countless additions unite to form a living whole.

In the exercises, everything depends on the "living art" of the master of the exercises; these rules must be "given" aright, and the practical delivery of the exercises must assist the written word. The first promulgator of the exercises could say with justice: "This" book is not intended for those who merely read, but for those who wish to do."

When the Jesuits began their activities, their Protestant opponents saw in the *Exercises* a work of the Devil: they spoke of "secret, magic arts, by which the Jesuits on certain days bring strange things to pass, in special apartments from which, after the performance of the magic, they return pale as though haunted by a spirit." At the same time, a Calvinistic preacher declared in all seriousness: "The Jesuits lead many astray to strange practices, which they call Exercises. The victims, so it is credibly reported, are intoxicated by steam and other means, so that they think they have seen the Devil in person, bellow like bulls, forswear Christ and serve the Devil."

Later, however, and especially in our time, even Protestant investigators have been unable to continue to ignore the historical significance of the *Exercises*. The Protestant scholar, Heinrich Boehmer, for instance, has said that the *Spiritual Exercises* of Loyola is to be regard-

The "Corpse-Like Obedience"

in such a way that the activities of the whole society of Jesus stand to the exercises of the individual exercitants in the same relation as the operations of an army stand to the exercises of the individual soldiers.

Constructed on the same principle, dominated by the same spirit, the *Exercises* and the *Constitutions* are the harmonious complements of each other.

In the *Exercises*, Christ appears to man as a world-conquering Captain calling His followers to battle. He who would obey this call must not remain a mere pious enthusiast, but must become a determined champion of the Kingdom of God. All the soldiers of Christ won over by the *Exercises* must join up in a strong, military formation, and Suarez was speaking in this sense when he said that the Society of Jesus represented a company of soldiers. Where "duty" in the military sense is concerned, as it is in the Society of Jesus, obedience becomes the highest virtue, as it is in the army. The Jesuit renders this obedience primarily to his superiors, for behind this superior, with all his human shortcomings, he sees the image of the Saviour, and he submits to him as if he were Christ Himself.

The thirty-first rule of the *Exercises* reads: "For progress, it is above all things profitable that everyone render complete obedience, regarding the superior, whoever he may be, as the representative of Our Lord Christ, and according him inward love and reverence."

In a letter to the members of his order, which has become famous, Ignatius wrote: "Through the man, regard Him to Whom you render obedience, that is to say Christ, the Supreme Wisdom, Eternal Good and Love, the Lord, of Whom you know that he can neither err nor be deceived."

It is because the Jesuit always perceives the Divine Person in his superior, that obedience is for him a kind of *unio mystica* with the will of God. Accordingly, when the Jesuits talk of obedience, their language recalls the terminology of mysticism. "He who will attain to true obedience must put off his own will, and put on the divine will, which will be placed upon him by his superior."

For, as the mystics see the highest form of perfection in union with God in the complete extinction of the ego, so the Jesuits seek to attain to God through "blind obedience" and the sacrifice of the will. St. John of the Cross says that in obedience the human will conforms to the divine will, and the human soul to the Divine.

The contradiction is, therefore, apparent rather than real, when the Jesuits preach on the one hand the saving might of free will and on the other unconditional obedience; for only he whose will is free is able to surrender it on his own account to the service of an ideal.

Belief in the saving might of obedience is rooted deep in a psychological principle of human nature: in it, the ancient tie between father and child finds a living embodiment. It is not for nothing that in all these religious relationships of authority and subordination, the superior is known as "father"; in obeying his superior, the man becomes a son, with a child's belief in authority. So, for the Jesuits too, the *Pater Superior* stands in the place of God the Father, the final and general "father-image." This explains the unconditional nature of the obedience required, commanded and practiced by the Jesuits.

Ignatius distinguishes carefully the various grades of obedience. The lowest stage, the

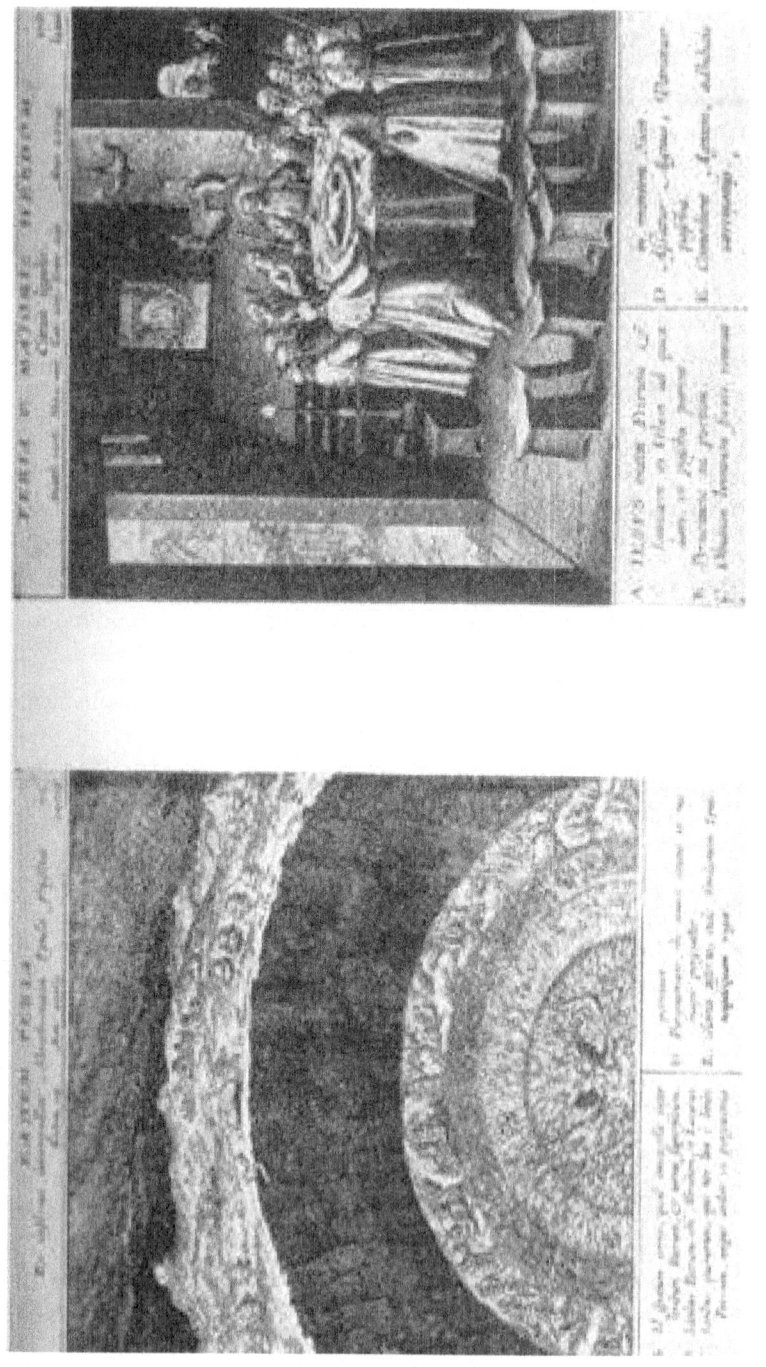

9. THE CIRCLES OF PURIFICATION   10. THE LAST SUPPER

From the gospel History, edition of H. Nodal, disciple of Ignatius, Rome, 1559.

13. THE SEPULCHER OF THE VIRGIN

11. THE RESURRECTION

From the Gospel History, edition of H. Nadal, disciple of Ignatius, Rome, 1559

purely external "obedience in deed," consists in this, that the subordinate confines himself to accomplishing what is required of him; this obedience Ignatius describes as "very imperfect." The second stage is distinguished by the subordinate's making his superior's will his own will: "at this stage there is already joy in obedience." But he who desires to offer himself wholly to the service of God must "bring not only his will but his intelligence." He must reach the stage where "he not only wishes the same, but thinks the same as the superior, and submits his judgment to that of his superior so far as only the surrendered will can sway the intellect."

Herein, Ignatius requires nothing less than the complete sacrifice of the man's own understanding, "unlimited obedience even to the very sacrifice of conviction"; it is significant that he adds here: "So may Abraham well have felt, when God commanded him to sacrifice his son Isaac."

Quite apart from overt opposition, the Jesuit must never indulge in any interior questionings whether his superior is in the right. He must be utterly convinced that whatever he is commanded to do will promote "the greater glory of God," and he must obey joyfully, with zealous enthusiasm.

The unconditional nature of Jesuit obedience immediately leads to a difficult problem: what is to happen when the superior demands the performance of a sinful action? Are his instructions to be carried out in that case? Almost all the opponents of the Jesuits maintain that "obedience unto sin" is actually enjoined by the Jesuits, while the apologists of the order categorically deny it.

Now it is the general teaching of the Catholic Church that in no case may a man commit a sin, not even if he should be commanded to do so by his temporal or ecclesiastical superior; and Ignatius, too, when he enjoins obedience, adds the proviso that manifest sin is excluded from the obligation. Suarez, the great theorist of Jesuitism, expressly declares that obedience always assumes "the lawfulness of the object."

The *Constitutions*, in common with the rules of all other religious orders, accords the subordinate the right "to make discreet remonstrances," when there appears to be a danger of sin. Ignatius himself made express provision for this, and at a later date the general of the order, Acquaviva, likewise laid down that the superior must always give his subordinate the opportunity to raise his objections, "so that everything may be done in a mild, paternal spirit."

These provisions, however, have not appeased the opponents of the order, who maintain that the fundamental suppression of private judgment does away with any possibility of seriously examining a command; Ignatius, indeed, utters a warning against questioning or doubting whether a command is expedient and will lead to good. Actually, the duty of "blind obedience" is limited only by such reservations as *ad quos potest cum caritate se oboedientia extendere*. The constitutions of the order expressly require that the subordinate should have the will and judgment of the superior as the standard for his own will and judgment"; perfect obedience is blind, and "in this blindness its wisdom and perfection" consist.

"Though the other religious orders," Ignatius writes, "may surpass us in fastings and night-watchings and other severities of food and raiment, our brothers must take precedence in true and perfect obedience, in the voluntary renunciation of private judgment."

The "Corpse-Like Obedience"

Great renown has been achieved by a pronouncement of Loyola which is found in a similar form in the *Exercises*, and from which the phrase the "corpse-like obedience" of the Jesuits has presumably been derived: "Altogether, I must not desire to belong to myself, but to my Creator and to his representative. I must let myself be led and moved as a lump of wax lets itself be kneaded, must order myself as a dead man without will or judgment, as a little crucifix which lets itself be moved without difficulty from one place to another, as a staff in the hand of an old man, to be placed where he will and where he can best make use of me. Thus I must always be ready to hand, so that the order may use me and apply me in the way that seems to it good. . ."

The command to blind obedience, which is emphasized so much in the Jesuit order, of itself signified no revolutionary innovation in the Catholic Church. Obedience was already numbered among the three "evangelical counsels" said to have been delivered to mankind by Christ Himself: poverty, chastity and obedience, according to the words of the New Testament, are virtues which although not necessary to salvation are certainly commendable.

In the early days of the Christian Church, obedience always formed the most important foundation of all monastic communities. Basil, the founder of Eastern monasticism, proclaims in his rule that the member of the order must be in the hand of his superior, "as an ax in the hand of a woodcutter"; Benedict of Nursia, again, requires his disciples to submit themselves obediently in all things to their superior. In the rule of the Carthusians, it is laid down that the monk must offer up his will "as a sheep to the slaughter," and the Carmelites hold any opposition to the command of a superior to be a grievous sin.

But it is Francis of Assisi, in particular, who enjoins unconditional obedience on his disciples; it was he who said that a brother must regard himself "like as a corpse, which receives life and spirit through the Spirit of God by harboring obediently the will of God."

Finally, those teachers of the late Middle Ages under whose influence Ignatius became the founder of an order, glorified obedience in nearly all their writings. "Is it any thing of account," writes Garcia de Cisneros, "that you, who are dust and a very nothing, should submit yourself to a man for God's sake, when I, the Almighty and the Supreme, Who created all things out of nothing, submitted Myself humbly to man for your sake? Learn therefore to obey and show yourself so submissive and small that everyone may walk over you and tread you down as mud in the street. . . ."

The idea that a man should see God Himself in his superior had already been expressed by Augustine and by Bernard of Clairvaux, while Bonaventura declared that it was "more meritorious for the sake of God to obey a man than God direct."

But while other orders insisted on obedience, obedience had always served with them merely as a means of ascetic discipline, of regulating penitential works for the mortification of man's earthly nature: prayer, watchings and flagellations.

Basil, in his Sermon *de institutione monachorum*, said that the intention of the monastic life was to give the monk the opportunity to concern himself, in quiet seclusion, with the salvation of his soul. In accordance with this conception, even the works of charity and brotherly love performed by the Benedictines and the Franciscans outside the walls of the cloister always remained merely *instrumenta bonorum operum*; they designed to facilitate the monk's own salvation.

The same thing holds good for the freer communities of the late Middle ages, such as the Flemish "Brothers of Common Life"; their most famous representative, Thomas à Kempis, says that he always felt a diminution of his spiritual purity so soon as he put his foot outside the cloister. All these men aspired to nothing except that withdrawal from the world which had been practiced by the very first monastic orders on the banks of the Nile.

The Jesuits, however, set themselves a totally different task: they were not satisfied with accomplishing their own salvation; their most fervent efforts were directed towards inspiring sinful humanity outside the cloister with the spirit of Christ, and winning them for God.

In consequence, obedience assumed with the Jesuits an entirely new meaning; it was concerned with external activities, united, clear-sighted action, and it played the same part as it plays in military service. The members of this order who went out into the world, to preach and to conduct their campaign in the most distant lands, had to be united with each other and with the central, directing power of the order, by a discipline of iron.

"When an army is widely scattered," it is written in the eight paragraph of the *Constitutions*, "the separate detachments must be in touch with one another and with the commander-in-chief . . . so that the same spirit, the same aim and the same endeavors may prevail throughout." Similarly, the paragraph continues, the Society of Jesus requires a corporate organization, based on obedience, if it is not to depart from its original spirit and lose its fighting powers.

The supreme leader of the Jesuit order, who bears the title of General, exercises an authority which is unique. It is true that the mendicant orders, the Franciscans and Dominicans, already had their generals; but the government of the friaries was actually left to the individual chapters, whereas the Society of Jesus it is the general alone who, at his own pleasure, appoints the other officers; he is answerable only to the General Congregation, which can depose him in case of grave misdemeanors.

There is a precisely graded hierarchy of officers between the simple novice and the commander-in-chief. There are the "professed of the four vows," who form the real kernel of the order; the newly admitted novices are under them, as are the lay brothers and the spiritual and temporal "coadjutors." The "professed houses" are governed by Superiors, who in their turn are under the head of the order in the province, the Provincial. The direction and supervision of the provincials falls to the general, who exercises control over the provinces from time to time by specially appointed Visitors.

A most active system of written reports unites the various colonies of Jesuits with headquarters. This lively correspondence is designed not least to keep headquarters constantly informed of the merits and demerits of every individual member; the superiors submit reports on the conduct of their subordinates, but the subordinates are empowered, and even obliged, to report any misdemeanor of their superiors to the highest quarter.

Without so stern a discipline and so rigid an organization, it would have been impossible to maintain the connection between all members of the order, working in the most diverse fields; it was the obedience of Jesuits that made it possible to oppose to the enemies of the Church a really trained and formidable army.

The Pyramid to God

The Pyramid to God

It is often asserted that Ignatius Loyola, who before his conversion was himself an officer in the Spanish army, transferred to his order the spirit of military subordination. Is not the unconditional obedience of the Jesuit identical with that military discipline which forbids the subordinate to question why this or that is commanded him?

Although it is true that in the organization of the order there are many features reminiscent of military organization, it would be wrong to suppose that Ignatius was a mere slavish imitator of the regulations with which he was familiar in his military service. The parallel between the Jesuit and the military subordination goes much deeper, and rests on certain fundamental similarities between Church and army.

Sigmund Freud, in his *Massenpsychologie und Ich-Analyse*, has explained this connection. He writes: "In the Church, as in the army, however different the two may be, the same pretense (illusion) holds good, that a Chief is present—in the Catholic Church, Christ, in the army, the General—who loves all the individuals of the mass with the same love. Everything lies in this illusion; if it were allowed to drop, Church and army, as far as outside forces permitted it, would fall to pieces at once... the general is the father loving equally each of his soldiers, who are therefore comrades together... Every captain is at once the general and the father of his company; every corporal that of his squad. A similar hierarchy is built up in the Church..."

Here, as there, exists the same idea of "identification," the same sentimental bond with the leader, and it would therefore be untrue to regard the blind obedience of the Jesuits simply as an imitation of military subordination. Its real spiritual source must be sought rather in a hierarchical view of the universe, in the idea of a cosmic order in which everything has its appointed place, and in which accordingly the inferior submits willingly to the superior.

The idea of a hierarchical world-order has its root deep in the foundations of human thought. Aristotle recognized that the forms of strict logic represented at the same time a kind of picture of the universe. All logical conclusions rest on the subordination of a particular minor proposition to a generally accepted major premise; so every part of the cosmos is subordinate to the more general and is superior to the more particular, and maintains thereby its one appointed place in the universe, its *locus naturalis*.

The introduction of Aristotelean philosophy and logic into mediaeval scholasticism, and their amalgamation with the world of Christian art, led to the acceptance of a peculiar hierarchical world system. The major premise of Aristotelean logic, becoming more and more general, led to a most general, an *ens generalissimum*, which could be nothing but God Himself. From God downwards, the universe descended from the particular to the more particular, and in this gradation, according to scholasticism, a man could, as Leopold Ziegler says in his *Gestaltwandel der Götter*, "always reckon and establish his position, its length, breadth and height, as exactly as a navigator."

"Hierarchy above hierarchy, in most wonderful gradation, the immortal inhabitants of the spheres rise to the empyrean where the eternal light of grace and truth shines like fire encircling the eternal round or worlds... While the murky airs of the sub-lunar spheres are fearfully, diabolically populated with the damned, the outcast and the fallen, there circle on the other side of the eight revolving heavens, the choirs who, again divided into three hierarchies as angels, archangels and principalities, as powers, virtues and dominations, and as thrones, cherubim and seraphim, soar nearer and nearer to the *Lumen gloriae*."

A man who was accustomed, in the manner of Dionysius the Areopagite, to regard the world as a hierarchical pyramid rising up to God, of necessity saw his ethical task to be the humble accommodation of himself to his own appropriate *locus naturalis*; indeed, everything in the universe from lifeless stone to archangels seemed filled with inner striving to attain its *locus naturalis*, and, having once attained it, never again to leave it.

But to accommodate and subordinate oneself is to obey; and thus the mediaeval view of the universe led quite naturally to voluntary recognition of authority, and called forth the readiness to obey. Men were still far from recognizing the "liberty of a Christian man," who should be "a free lord over all things, and subject to no one."

In Jesuitism, the traditional conceptions of scholasticism were to survive far beyond the Middle Ages, for Ignatius intended, through a system of obedience in which "the lower submits to the higher by means of a certain agreement and order," to imitate in his order this very harmonious hierarchical system of Creation.

It is, therefore, written in his *Letter on Obedience*, addressed to the Jesuits in Portugal, that only thus can "the present subordination and the consequent unity and love" rest secure, "without which, in our Society as in other spiritual communities, an ordered administration is impossible. It is in this way that Creation is sweetly and lovingly governed by the providence of God. God has appointed the lower beings under the higher, the higher under the highest, everything corresponding to its purpose. Thus even between the individual choirs of angels there is an ordered relation, thus with the stars and all moving bodies, the lower are appointed beneath the higher, and these again beneath a highest and final director, by immutable laws inherent in them. The same phenomenon may be seen in all well-ordered states, and not least in the ecclesiastical hierarchy, culminating in the pope as the Vicar of Christ..."

The rationalistic Catholic thinker of the nineteenth century utterly devoid of this enthusiasm for the hierarchical idea, necessarily regarded Loyola's work with entirely different eyes. So Edgar Quinet writes that he sees in Loyola's *Constitutions* "nothing but provincials, rectors, examiners, consulters, admonitors, procurators, prefects of spiritual things, prefects of health, prefects of library, of the refectory, attendants and stewards. Each of these officers has his especial, his clearly defined and appointed task... But show me among all these the Christian soul! In the midst of so many offices, titles and external occupations, the man escapes me, the Christian is submerged."

While this peculiar organization of the "militant disciples of Christ" required, on the one hand, the most rigid discipline and a carefully constructed administrative organization, yet, on the other, it could not attain success without considerable independence of each individual member. For often enough the Jesuit, in a dangerous post cut off from the headquarters of the order, had to make rapid decisions and to act on his own initiative.

13-14 NUNS AND MENDICANT MONKS BEFORE THE APPEARANCE OF THE JESUITS

15. THE FIRST JESUIT MARTINI AS A CHINESE MANDARIN PAYS A CEREMONIAL VISIT TO THE EMPEROR

The Pyramid to God

From the beginning, the Society of Jesus has known how to make use of the personal qualities of its members, and it is in this very combination of discipline and individualism that the novelty of the community founded by Ignatius lies.

A Jesuit might very well be "a staff in the hand of an old man" when his superior assigned to him a definite mission and imparted to him the necessary instructions; but within the limit of his instructions he could display his personal initiative. For, within a short time after the foundation of the order, the Jesuits were acting as spiritual directors at the courts of Europe, as preachers in the most remote primeval forests, as political conspirators, disguised and in constant danger of death; thus they had a thousand opportunities to employ their talents, their cleverness, their knowledge of the world, and even their cunning, "to the greater glory of God."

In his regard for personal performance, Ignatius expressed an important tendency of his time, for, with the Renaissance in Europe, individuality had acquired a completely new value. Whatever a man may think of the activities of the Society, it cannot be denied that the Society presents an unparalleled example of the organization of the will of every individual to obey, an organization scattered over the whole world whose members act independently in their own spheres of activity, and at the same time, when circumstances demand it. Are prepared humbly to obey commands. Only such an organization, combining the most rigid discipline with individual freedom of movement, could have made possible the inner unity of the order and its astonishing continuity throughout the centuries in the face of the widest geographical dispersal; and herein lies the secret of the power once exercised by the Jesuits, and which, to a considerable extent, they exercise today.

The Power and Secret of the Jesuits

PART II

IGNATIUS LOYOLA

His Personality and Work

Diego Laynez, Loyola's pupil and successor, said that few great men had so few ideas as the founder of Jesuitism but that still fewer had been more thoroughly earnest in the realization of these ideas.

The ideas preached by Ignatius, this one-time Spanish courtier, brought about almost a revolution in the whole Catholic world, and, further, they determined to a considerable extent the whole course of the development of European culture, religion as well as philosophy, education and art, either by direct influence, or indirectly by provoking violent opposition.

Prominent thinkers of modern times, such as Voltaire, Descartes and Diderot, in their youth were educated in the spirit of the Spanish cavalier; distinguished poets, such as Molière and Corneille, received their first theatrical impulses from Jesuit school dramas; great artists were urged on in their work by Jesuitism; and eminent scholars, in their zeal for the success of Loyola's teachings, have enriched science in all its branches by their research and discoveries.

More often than a superficial examination will reveal, we meet obvious traces of Jesuit influence in our present-day culture. Not only do the many monuments in the baroque style remind us of Jesuitism and its artistic endeavors, but many traces of Jesuitic influence also remain in the theatre and, above all, in the schools. It should not be overlooked that the advantages as well as the disadvantages of our humanist classical education are for the most part attributable to that pedagogic activity which, at one time, was spread by the Society of Jesus over all the countries of the world.

However we, in our day, may judge the teachings of Loyola, illuminating them by means of subtle psychological methods, in however great a degree our attitude towards religious questions may have changed since the sixteenth century, it cannot but be acknowledged, in any criticism of Jesuitism, that Loyola's work has played an important part in the history of modern times. Few people, since the beginning of history, have conceived and thought out an idea with such utter logic as Ignatius Loyola did, or carried it through with such extraordinary tenacity of will, or so deeply affected all human thought, feeling and actions.

In a certain sense, perhaps, our times have produced a kindred historical personality.

The Power and Secret of the Jesuits

Lenin, too, had few ideas, but these he sought to put into practice with an earnestness and a power equal to Loyola's. The doctrines of Lenin, in a manner similar to those of Loyola, seriously disturbed the peoples of Europe, Asia, Africa and America, affecting intellectual circles in no less a degree than the lower strata of society, and producing great armies of submissive and obedient followers as well as inexorable enemies.

These two men, the greatest zealot of the sixteenth and the greatest atheist of the twentieth century, approached the profound problems of human nature with an iron resolve, and were not contented with a few superficial changes, but compelled the complete subjugation and transformation, in accordance with their ideas, of the intellect, the beliefs, the perceptions and the desires of their followers. Both also knew the secret of historical efficacy, which consists in putting every theory to the test of practice, in creating an interplay of fancy, scientific knowledge, human nature can be mastered. No one else has ever understood to the same extent as Ignatius and Lenin the importance of that power which alone can unite thousands of people in all parts of the world into a uniform and exactly functioning organization: the importance of absolute obedience. Both men, moreover, possessed the inflexible courage to carry into effect, even to its utmost consequences, a principle which they had one acknowledged as right, against all the remonstrances of the rest of men, and without regard to the protests of powerful opponents.

Of course, an abyss separates Ignatius from Lenin. Neither the moral personalities nor the ideas and the aims of the two men have anything in common. What lies between the catholic saint and the Socialist revolutionary is an intellectual gap of no less than four centuries; what links them, however, is their insight into the deep foundations of human nature, which time does not change, and the immense driving-power of their thought.

The materialistic conception of history notwithstanding, it cannot be denied that Jesuitism is for the greater part the expression of Loyola's personality. Not only Jesuit writers, but also such Protestant investigators as Heinrich Boehmer and Eberhard Gothein, quite rightly point out that Ignatius built up his order on the basis of his personal experiences, and, indeed, that he first reformed himself by means of newly discovered psychological methods, before he began to convert the outer world to his beliefs and make it subject to his will.

Whatever Ignatius achieved, he attained as a result of much toil; it was the victory of a wonderful tenacity of will. His ideas, which later were to have so great an effect on the whole world, did not come to him freely and spontaneously or without the exercise of great mental power; they were not the result of the creative inspiration of genius, and, therefore, they lacked that stirring and illuminative power which so often characterizes other great doctrines of humanity. Loyola's inmost soul glowed steadily, but never burst into flame.

From a lowly beginning, Ignatius gradually, with great care and continual deliberation, elaboration and emendation, made his work what it finally became. The *Exercises* and *Constitutions* were in the same way the fruits of a laborious process, and testify to many decades of diligent and untiring industry. When Ignatius was about to introduce into the *Constitutions* of the order a new provision, he would generally withdraw to his cell and ponder over all the considerations for and against the proposed precept, and observe most strictly the effect on the state of his soul. Like a careful experimenter, he kept a detailed record of all his thoughts and perceptions. It was often a month before he was able to arrive at a decision in this way.

Afterwards, he referred to numerous books, and he further tested the new rule thoroughly in practice for a time; then finally he inserted it in the *Constitutions*.

He used to rewrite his letters as many as twenty times before he committed then to the post; he did this not only with important official letters, but also with harmless private epistles to his friends and relations.

Similarly, Ignatius deliberated over and considered the most trivial matter, even though it concerned only the engagement of a nurse, a porter or a cook. In regard to himself, he continued to the last to work at and extend his mastery of his feelings, his gestures, his outward appearances, his mode of speech and his learning. He was already a fully grown man when he realized that his education as a youth had been of such a nature as to hinder him in making serious progress; thereupon, despite his three-and-thirty years, he sat with children on the school benches, and sought to acquire the rudiments of Latin grammar. Once even he threw himself down before his teacher, and requested earnestly that he might be punished with the rod before the rest of the scholars if he should show any lack of necessary zeal for learning. Still later, when, on account of his sermons from the Roman pulpit, he had already excited much admiration, he did not disdain to request his youngest pupil, Ribadeneira, to call his attention to any errors in his use of the Italian language. "Watch me closely when I speak," he said humbly, "and take note of everything that is not correct, so that you may improve my knowledge."

Few great men in history have accomplished such great work as he, and few have so persistently disdained the fame which their work brought them. He did not, as most other founders have done, give his name to the order which, down to the smallest detail, was his work: unlike others, he withdrew behind the order he had created and merged himself in it completely, so that, in the end, the Society of Jesus was known, but he himself hardly at all.

This great modesty, this superiority to personal vanity, must be all the more admired because in it can be seen the result of a rigorous self-education, for only in the course of many decades and with the exercise of superhuman perseverance and patience, and, indeed, with the aid of inhuman means of self-castigation, had Ignatius been able to struggle through to this independence of worldly considerations.

"Given up to the Vanities of the World"

From his earliest youth, Iñigo de Loyola's mind was constantly being poisoned by unrestrained ambitions. In the days of his boyhood, every nobler experience was denied him, and until he reached manhood his life was spent in frivolous and meaningless dalliance at the court of Ferdinand the Catholic.

Iñigo's parents were noble, but impoverished and too abundantly blessed with children; they were delighted when their kinsman, Don Juan Velasquez de Cuellar, the governor of the royal summer residence at Arevalo, took the seven-year-old boy into his service as a page. Don Juan's wife was one of the queen's ladies-in-waiting, and, consequently, the constant talk that reached Iñigo's ears in this house was of ambitious hopes based on the greater or lesser favors shown by the reigning couple. Gradually, the belief must have become fixed in the child's mind that the only thing in the world worth striving for was the favor of the monarch.

This state of mind was probably at its tensest in the Cuellar household when King Ferdinand, after the death of Queen Isabella, married the young French princess, Germaine de Foix. It was scarcely a year after Isabella, garbed in a coarse Franciscan cowl in accordance with her own wished, had been lowered, almost without ceremony, into the royal vault at Granada, when the arrival in the harbor of Valencia of a fleet of thirty vessels laden with raiment, shoes, caps, linen, perfumes and cosmetics, proclaimed the presence of the new queen. Such changes must have caused the greatest excitement in the residence at Arevalo.

Up to the time of the death of Isabella, the wife of the governor had, in careful deference to the wishes of the queen, distinguished herself by her rigorous views on godliness and by an intense dislike of feminine finery and worldly conversation. Now, under the changed regime, she had to endeavor to maintain her position as first lady of the court, and this in turn called for a complete readjustment to the wishes, customs and humors of Queen Germaine.

Queen Germaine was the very antithesis of her predecessor; she was a gay young lady, eager for pleasure. Whereas, formerly, twenty ducats daily had sufficed for the frugal meals of the court, the new queen desired dishes which cost two hundred ducats or more. Expressly for her, rare fish, poultry, fruit, spices and wine had to be brought from Seville, and the recipes for most of the dishes by which Germaine set great store were not given in Nola's Catalonian manual of court cookery.

It appeared indeed, as if the Spaniards had only just become aware of the powerful position to which the kingdom had risen during the past few decades. Yet Spain had, almost without any defined period of transition, changed from a feudal state torn by continual internal strife into a world power; she had subjugated new continents and had driven her hereditary enemies, the Moors, from the country. So long, however, as the severe-minded Queen Isabella had lived, the work of building up the new kingdom had proceeded so actively that there had been no time to become aware of the important changes that had taken place.

The fruits of these achievements were only not to be enjoyed. The self-satisfied consciousness of might and of riches burst suddenly into a wild frenzy of vulgar sensuality and coarse voracity. At the court and in the houses of the grandees, one banquet followed another and at these enormous quantities of food were swallowed; more than once it happened that partakers of such feasts died as a result of their immoderate eating and drinking.

One man only remained aloof from the extravagant doings at the court of the new queen, and towered above it in the manner of a solitary witness to the strictness of former days. This person was the lean-faced monk, Francisco Jimenez de Cisneros, Primate of Spain, Grand Inquisitor, and Royal Chancellor. Unaffected by the change of times, he stood as a living emblem of the Middle Ages.

This Spain, to whose riches and power there appeared to be no limit, was not in the least of his making. While all about him were given up to a wild revel of luxury, the work, for Cisneros, was far from being completed, and he alone was not content to rest on achievements already won.

17. QUEEN GERMAINE
THE KNIGHT IÑIGO'S "QUEEN OF HEARTS"

16. IGNATIUS AS THE KNIGHT IÑIGO

18-21 WOODCUTS FROM THE TALE OF CHIVALRY, "AMADIS OF GAUL"

"Given up to the Vanities of the World"

He possessed an enormous fortune, and his income exceeded even that of the Crown, but for all that he made not the least use of his wealth for his personal needs. In the luxurious apartments which were always at his disposal in the royal palace, he slept wrapped in the rough mantle of his order on the floor or on hard boards; his clothing was so shabby that the pope had to admonish him by a personal breve not to expose the dignity of his high office to the public ridicule.

After the second marriage of King Ferdinand, the cardinal appeared less frequently at the court, for the gay, brilliant and extravagant life there displeased him. When he did come, everyone knew that a crisis of great moment was at hand.

With the versatility of an ambitious court lady Doña Maria Valasquez de Cuellar had immediately adapted herself to the character of the new queen. Just as devotedly as she had at one time listened by the side of Isabella to the sacred hymns of the choristers, she now amused herself with the frivolous French madrigals, and felt herself moved to boisterous applause at the spectacle of the dances introduced by the new queen.

She soon succeeded in making the stay of her young mistress at Arevalo very pleasant, and became her trusted and indispensable friend. Doña Germaine visited the Cuellar household more and more frequently, in order that she might talk undisturbed with Doña Maria, and it happened often enough that the page, Iñigo de Loyola, waited on her at table, on bended knee with goblets, and, on her departure, carried her mantle and lighted her way with candles.

At that time, Iñigo was fourteen years old. Under the influence of the household, in an atmosphere of unbounded ambition, the growing boy's first feelings of romance were directed towards the queen. Thus love for him became synonymous with constant diligence in the service of the court, his dreams of women were bound up in an empty longing to distinguish himself in her eyes and to win her favorer.

When, in due course, he became a knight, and, according to custom, must choose a "queen of hearts," he chose the queen. At festivities and tournaments, he carried her colors, and the greatest recompense for which he could hope was a lace kerchief thrown from her hand to him as victor in the joust. When he met her, he was careful not to remove his cap, as, according to the chivalry of the court, such a breach of etiquette was regarded as a sign of great and abject idolatry.

Thus his love sprang less from a genuine passion than from the foolish endeavor to bring himself before the notice of the highest lady in the land, yet this romantic idolatry of an unattainable "queen of hearts" went hand-in-hand with a complete disdain for the honor of those women whom he sacrificed to his lusts. For, like other young knights of his time, Iñigo pursued the most vulgar sensual pleasures and was constantly getting entangled in some dubious adventure or other.

Dissolute excesses in his little native town of Azpeitia brought him into conflict with the judicial authorities; he was, however, able to flee in time from the jurisdiction of the Corregidor, and to submit himself to the judgment of the episcopal court in the town of Pamplona; it was known that the excesses of young noblemen were dealt with by this tribunal with the greatest indulgence, and at the most were punished by a penance.

The Power and Secret of the Jesuits

How little he was distinguished in youth by sincerity of character is clearly indicated in his own confession. Many decades afterwards, when he had become the enlightened general of the order, he related penitently to one of his fellow-members that, as a young knight, he had not been ashamed to commit theft and to allow an innocent man to be punished in his stead.

At the time when Iñigo was in attendance at the Spanish court, the indolent life of the knights surrounding the reigning sovereigns had sapped them of the manly bravery and proud dignity that distinguished their ancestors. So too with Loyola, the eagerness for battle of his ancestors had dwindled to a cheap delight in all kinds of knavish tricks against defenseless citizens, men and women. All these young knights were arrogant and haughty when dealing with their social inferiors, humble and cringing towards their masters and their privileged favorites, but among themselves they observed a ceremonial courtesy which was almost ridiculous.

With this empty mode of life and these wretched ideals went a superficial and frivolous education. He had certainly learnt to read, but his reading consisted solely of romances of chivalry and tales of magic which at that time aroused general enthusiasm. Not much time had elapsed since the discovery of the art of printing, and this great achievement at first served almost entirely to spread the romances of chivalry among all classes and ranks of society. It was this period of history which soon afterwards was to produce Cervantes's grandiose travesty.

Iñigo too was absorbed for nights at a time in Johanot Martorell's *Tirant lo blanch* and in *Amadis of Gaul*, Montalvo's "sir Love-of-God," "the Knight of the Green Sword" who made the greatest impression on him,.

At that period all Spain was breathless over the wonderful deeds and adventures of this hero, who in thousands of perilous adventures proved himself the champion of oppressed virtue, rescued kings from crafty magicians, assisted beautiful queens to regain their lawful thrones, and finally, after endless dangers, succeeded in gaining hand of Oriana, his "queen of hearts." These heroic deeds completely captured Iñigo's interest.

The young knight spent his days in mock martial exercises, in hunting, gallant flirtations, excessive drinking and vulgar brawling. A contemporary official document, a minute of the correctional court of Guipuzcoa to the episcopal court in Pamplona of the year 1515, has preserved for us a description of the knight, Iñigo de Loyola. He is portrayed in this document as being bold and defiant, clothed in leather trousers and cuirass, armed with dagger and pistol, his long hair flowing from beneath his knight's cap of velvet; and the judge further describes his character as "cunning, violent and vindictive."

A court scandal unexpectedly brought about an estrangement between the queen and Doña Maria, and the Cuellars found themselves in disfavor and had to leave the court in great haste. The same fate befell Iñigo, as a member of Don Juan's household.

Thus ended for the time being his easy life, divided between tournaments and chivalrous deeds, and his ambitious expectations of a glorious career under the eyes of the queen. He was forced to look about for another calling, and decided to join the guard of the Duke of Najera, a relative, who had a short time before been appointed viceroy of Navarre.

"Given up to the Vanities of the World"

Once again, it was mainly his insatiable ambition which caused him to take this step. Navarre was frequently threatened by internal unrest and by the attacks of its French neighbors, and Iñigo hoped for an opportunity to distinguish himself by special heroism in this unsettled border province.

The military service which waited him in Pamplona must have come to him as an unpleasant surprise. Within the safe precincts of the court at Arevalo, the warlike exercises of the knights had been restricted to jousting, and the knights, clad in noble armor, with luxurious plumes and golden chain-mail for their arms, and encouraged by the glances and cheers of beautiful ladies, had endeavored by a skillful thrust with their blunted lances to unseat their opponents or to shatter their shields. Here in the border fortress at Pamplona, however, war service was quite a different matter.

Far beyond the walls of the town on a barren, desolate and rocky plateau, the infantry drilled to the monotonous commands of officers; they executed in endless repetition the same steps, holds and evolutions. Nowhere were there any beautiful women to gaze admiringly at their efforts.

After he had more or less settled down to these new conditions, Iñigo found that he had lost none of his burning ambition; on the contrary, it had grown. It was indeed, much more difficult to distinguish himself than it had been during the time he was at the royal court. There it had been sufficient to prove his skill in man-to-man encounters, but here he had to make himself conspicuous among thousands of men and dozens of officers. Feverishly he awaited an opportunity for some special deed for a while, it is true, in vain, since to his great disgust peace reigned in the country.

Finally, when, after long waiting, a revolt broke out in the town of Najera, Iñigo was permitted to take part as a company commander in the expedition sent to suppress the insurgents, but at the last moment, a malicious fate deprived him of his glory. As he was leading his men, his long sword in his hand, to attack the enemy over the old seven-arched bridge, the insurgents surrendered to the troops of the viceroy, who, in the meantime, had entered the town from another direction.

Only after waiting four years were his ambitious hopes to be at last fulfilled. A real war broke out. French troops, encouraged by serious risings in Castile, crossed the Spanish border, and Navarre then became a somewhat unimportant theatre of war in the first great world conflict between Charles the Fifth and Francis of France.

The Spanish governor was unable to offer any great resistance to the enemy, who were ten times superior in numbers, for all appeals to Castile for assistance had been in vain; there every man was needed to suppress the internal rising, and reinforcements for Navarre were not to be thought of. Thus the French advanced almost without meeting any hindrance.

In May, 1521, the French army stood before the walls of Pamplona. The viceroy had fled; the town council had willingly handed over the keys to the enemy, and the small Spanish garrison was forced to withdraw to the citadel. This, however, was not sufficiently strong to withstand a heavy attack; the bastions were unfinished, and there was a shortage of cannon, munitions and provender. The commandant called a council of war, and it was soon decided that to offer any resistance to the superior forces of the enemy would be hopeless

22. IGNATIUS DEDICATES HIS LIFE TO THE QUEEN OF HEAVEN — Spanish Painting.

23. IGNATIUS, WEAKENED BY HIS PENANCES, IS CARED FOR BY THE LADIES OF THE HOUSE OF AMIGNAT IN MANRESA —Painting, Manresa.

and that there was nothing to do but capitulate.

It was then that Iñigo's heroic career had to be decided. At first, he listened in silence to the arguments of his comrades, and then he suddenly sprang up and addressed them heatedly. He, the youngest of the officer, appealed to the honor of his comrades as hidalgos, and cried that it was the duty of them all to go to their death rather than lay down their arms in disgrace. His enthusiasm carried the other officers with him for the moment, and, heedless of their earlier and more rational views, they decided to resist the enemy to the last.

Aflame with the courage of battle, Iñigo hastened to the most dangerous point in the breastworks of the fortress against which the most violent attack of the enemy was directed, and brandishing his sword he encouraged his men valiantly to stand fast. But, after a brief struggle, the French entered the captured citadel, the hour of knightly and heroic courage was past, and the fiery bravery of one individual was in vain; success had followed the weight of numbers and the well-aimed work of nameless cannoneers.

The French soldiers found Iñigo de Loyola, weltering in blood, lying on the bastion with a shattered leg. What an object of derision he was, the daring and courageous knight, beaten by the impersonal machine of modern warfare, by a cannon ball fired from nowhere in particular and against which all heroism must remain impotent and without meaning!

His Visions on the Rack

When, after an agonizing journey, he was brought to the castle of his ancestors at Loyola, it was obvious that the shattered bones of the leg had been so clumsily set that it would be necessary to break the leg again. The result of this operation was a complete failure. The bones again knitted incorrectly, so that a stump of bone protruded from the leg.

The doctors informed the patient that this hideous protuberance could only be removed by sawing it off, an extremely painful operation, but Loyola agreed without hesitation that they should perform it. Without a single murmur of pain, he held his foot under the surgeon's saw.

As the leg was then too short, he underwent many weeks of painful torment on a surgical rack, on which he had to lie completely still. All this he suffered with patience in order that he might not become lame, for to him whose whole value of life was bound up in a determination to distinguish himself in tournaments before the eyes of the queen, a deformed leg would have seemed the greatest misfortune. A well-shaped leg at that time meant, in the eyes of women, more than the face or the figure, for in the tournaments which formed their whole interest, it was the leg now drawn up to the body, now extended, that was most in evidence in many feats of horsemanship. The admiring glances of the female spectators were attracted by the rhythmical play of shapely limbs, and, enraptured by these, they would throw into the tilting ground costly rings, plumes, perfumed gloves and lace kerchiefs.

However great the pain might be, Iñigo wished to avoid at all cost any deformity that would make it impossible for him to wear elegant and close-fitting knee-boots. His superhuman ambition, his boundless vanity caused him to suffer the most frightful torment willingly

His Visions on the Rack

and without a murmur.

"Up to my six-and-twentieth year, I was entirely given to the vanities of the world," he himself declared a few years before his death. "Above all, I found pleasure in the management of arms, and felt a keen and empty craving to excel."

After his leg had completely healed, he had to lie still for many weeks, and, now that he was free of pain, the endless hours lay heavily on his hands. He endeavored to pass the time with romantic thoughts of Queen Germaine, and in imagining how he could arrange it so that he might again reach her and attract her attention by further heroic deeds.

He lived in anticipation through every phase of his future happiness in her presence: how he would meet her, bow before her, speak to her in well-turned phrases, and once more display all his skill in the knights' games. He saw himself again in the riding school, flourishing his sword and galloping smoothly along, his plumed hat on his head, in close-fitting hose and knee-boots.

The picture, however, faded away, and as often as he endeavored to spur on his imagination he never got beyond the representation of the lists, nor beyond galloping round the riding enclosure; at this point, the imagination that had hitherto painted such a highly colored pictures always grew weak.

Then it occurred to him to assist his imagination by means of borrowed portraits, and he asked for *Amadis of Gaul*, a book he had been accustomed, since his days as a page, to refer to for counsel in his love torments. It was, however, not usual to read books at the castle of Loyola, and consequently the library consisted only of two works; the four folios of *The Life of Christ* by Ludolphus of Saxony and a collection of more or less authentic sacred legends under the title of *The Flowers of the Saints*. In place of the *Amadis* he yearned for, Iñigo finally turned towards the holy books, and began to read them. At first, he felt a violent dislike for the many "penances," "castigations" and "works of humility" which were the themes of these sacred tales. Frequently he put aside the heavy tomes in boredom, and then again took them up mechanically, until gradually the deeds of the saints began to appear to him in an intimate and chivalric light.

He fell upon the story of St. Dominic, who proposed to a mother that he should sell himself as a slave in order to procure for her the ransom for her son, who had been captured; he read of St. Francis, how he went unafraid into the camp of the cruel sultan, in order to shame the terrible heathens by his Christian courage. All this aroused in him memories of those chivalrous romances to which he was accustomed; St. Francis had even distinguished himself as a knight, and for that reason had drawn a red cross on his mantle.

Iñigo found more and more exciting adventures to interest him in these stories of the saints in the *Flos Sanctorum*, and he read them with the credulity

he had formerly bestowed on the wonderful journeys of Amadis the knight. Soon he even discovered that many of the deeds of the saints could be compared with the boldest adventures of that wandering hero. In astonishment, he read how St. Francis of Assisi had subdued wild animals with nothing more than a glance of the eye. St. Dominic was granted by God the gift of working strange miracles. When, with his face turned to heaven his hands clasped above his head, he devoted himself to prayer, his body would lose its earthly weight and begin to rise from the ground. Never before had Iñigo heard of such deeds.

But the strangest thing of all was that these knights of the faith set forth on their adventures clad only in a shabby cowl, without arms and decorative plumes, and, therefore, were deserving of the greatest praise and honor. Thus it was that an angel appeared each day to St. Onuphrius (who, naked and with long flowing hair, lived in the desert) and brought him food from heaven. In honor of St. Francis, the rocks and shone like rubies and sapphires, the heavens had opened and seraphic hosts had sung the most magnificent songs of praise. But the highest distinction came to those champions of the faith to whom the heavenly Lady had descended, and whom, with gracious smiles and soft words, she had inspired with courage and endurance. Compared with such rewards, lace kerchiefs were but a poor recompense, and so Iñigo soon ceased to be concerned about his shortened leg.

A new and irresistible longing had seized him, similar to that desire which had led the conquistadores to cross the seas to distant lands. Like these, he longed for an unknown world which had not yet been defiled by the bitterness of experience. His ambition had found a new outlet: he would join the band of great saints, and, one with them, armed with cowl and penitential girdle, gain the kingdom of heaven.

Iñigo had not lived his life in total ignorance of religious matters. As befitted a knight, he had attended church regularly and, in addition to many a madrigal beloved by the court, he had once composed a hymn to the Apostle Peter, the patron saint of knights. But it had never entered his head that there was another, higher sphere of religious experience beyond the formal piety of which he in his clinging to outward appearances was then alone capable.

Laboriously, he sought with all his unpracticed perceptions to see his way in this sphere which was totally strange to him. To begin with, he was able to distinguish between two classes of ideas only; those which produced in him pleasant and those which produced unpleasant feelings. Nothing seemed more simple than to regard all these fancies either as good or bad, according to their stimulating or depressing effect on the mind. Since, however, he was unable in any way to think in the abstract, he conjured up pictures of these matters in the light of experiences with which he had been well acquainted during his life as a knight; the comforting representations he regarded as the whisperings of good spirits, and the distressing as the temptations of demons, and these good and evil spirits appeared to him in the shape of knights who, divided into two great camps, fought continually for the human soul. Around the banner of Christ, the supreme Commander of the righteous, assembled the valiant angels and saints, who strove to lead the soul to heaven, whilst the Devil and the demons under the banner of Satan sought to throw men into hell.

Iñigo had no hesitation over the camp, of these two, in which he was to fight. His place was in the army of the heavenly King. Having recognized this, he gave up finally all idea of again submitting his shortened leg to the torture in his newly found career as a soldier of the Lord. From that day on, he had himself carried each evening by his servant to the window, and he sat there for of the rack, since he realized that his deformity could in no way hinder him hours at a time. Silently he would gaze at the firmament and dream of the kingdom above the start, a thousand times greater and mightier than the kingdom of Charles the Fifth, his former master, even though it extended to many parts of the earth. What a noble and proud feeling it must be to fight for that heavenly King, and to earn the favor of the

25. THE COURT OF THE CLOISTER AT MONTSERRAT

From Philanderer to a "Master of the Affects"

heavenly Queen!

One night he raised himself from his couch and knelt down before the picture of the Virgin in the corner of the room and solemnly promised from then on to serve as a faithful soldier under the banner of Christ.

From Philanderer to a "Master of the Affects"

It was, however, a long time before the vain courtier succeeded in attaining real sincerity, and even in the most subtle forms of the expression of Loyola's later piety there was some trace of that superficiality which had completely governed the conduct of the erstwhile frivolous knight.

When he resolved to renounce the glamour of the world, he imagined the act of his "conversion" and also every further attempt at a new life in the light of knightly ideas. Thus his departure from his native castle, after his recovery, to go out into the world as a champion of God, he regarded as nothing more than a chivalrous venture. He wished to become a saint in order to bring honor to his family, and, in answering his brother when he questioned him with regard to his intended destination, he said he knew what was due to the name of the Loyolas, and he would prove himself worthy of that name.

Like a crusader, he had himself escorted on the first stage of his journey by his brothers and sisters, his attendants and other domestic servants. Then he mounted his mule and set out on his way to Our Lady of Montserrat.

On the way, he met a "Morisco" a baptized Arab, and entered into conversation with him on the subject of the Virgin Mary. The Moor professed his belief in the immaculate conception of the Mother of God, but disputed that this virginity could have endured after the birth of Christ. Iñigo regarded this view as an affront to his new "queen of hearts," and in the manner of chivalry he took the Morisco sharply to task. The latter felt a premonition of danger, and rode away in great haste, while Iñigo was considering whether or not it was his duty to hasten after the slanderer and slay him.

This doubt was not dispelled by the workings of his conscience and innermost feelings. In accordance with an old and aristocratic superstition, he left the decision to an external "sign," in this case the wishes of his mule. He gave him free rein, and the Morisco owed his life to the fact that the animal scorned to trot after a baptized heathen.

Thus Iñigo's service as a "knight of the heavenly kingdom" began with a deed totally in keeping with the spirit of worldly chivalry, and similarly he completed his initiation as a spiritual knight. For the scene of this he had chosen Montserrat, where the legendary mount of the Holy Grail was situated. After he had changed clothes with a beggar, he made a vigil before the picture of our Lady of Montserrat, exactly in accordance with a description of such a ceremony which he had found in *Amadis of Gaul*. Then in the morning he descended from the mountain clad in the new garments of a soldier of God, a wretched beggar's coat, a calabash and a pilgrim's staff, and set forth to conquer the heavenly kingdom.

He turned towards the little town of Manresa, and there chose as his abode a damp cave at the foot of a rocky cliff; here, from then on, he practiced the severest austerities. Seven hours a day he spent on his knees praying, and the short time he devoted to sleep was passed on the damp ground, with a stone or a piece of wood for his pillow. Often he fasted for three or four days at a time, and, when he did finally take food, it was the hardest and blackest pieces of bread or some herbs which he ate; and then only after he had rendered them still less palatable by sprinkling them with ashes.

Occasionally, on his way to the little town of Manresa, he begged alms, and there he associated with the poor and the sick, and endeavored as far as possible to make himself like them in his clothing, speech and appearance. He neglected his body and allowed his hair and beard to grow; he never washed, and he covered himself with the dirtiest of rags. He did not, however, succeed in making the beggars regard him as one of themselves; on the contrary, they ridiculed him when he came among them in his shabby cowl, a bread-sack over his shoulder and a great rosary round his neck. In the streets the boys pointed at him and shouted after him the jeering words "Father Sack."

He scourged himself daily, and he often beat his breast with a stone until it was bruised, and once he went so far with this self-castigation that he became seriously ill and had to be taken unconscious to the house of Doña Angelica de Amigant, his patroness. The doctors who were called in on him despaired of his life, and some pious ladies even entreated the mistress of the house to present them with pieces of Iñigo's clothing as relics. Doña Angelica, wishing to gratify the desire of these ladies, opened Iñigo's cupboard in order to take out the clothes of him they believed dead; soon afterwards she returned terrified, for in the wardrobe hung the most terrible weapons of mortification: a girdle into which wire had been worked, heavy chains, nails strung together in the form of a cross, and an undergarment interwoven with small iron thorns. All these Iñigo had worn next hi skin!

Nevertheless, some of his old vanity still remained at this time. It was still that ambitious endeavor to distinguish himself in the service of the Lord by some special and glorious work which led him to torture himself with such frightful penances, and he wished to imitate and, whenever possible, even surpass the saints of whom he had read in *Flos Sanctorum*.

In later years, on looking back to those days, he openly confessed this himself. He related to the disciple Gonzales that at that time he always said to himself, "It will do what St. Francis or St. Dominic has done."

"He resolved," writes Gonzales, "to perform great penances, not on account of the sins he had committed, but in order to please God. He said himself that he did, indeed, feel at that time a positive abhorrence of his earlier sins, but the inordinate desire to do great deeds in the service of Christ was so great that in his penances he did not think particularly of his sins." During illness, according to his own statement, the vain thought came to him suddenly that he could now meet death happily as had "by his penances richly earned eternal salvation."

Even after he had fully subdued his body, and freed his soul of worldly vanity, Ignatius had a long and difficult path to tread before he could attain that balance of mind and deliberation which later distinguished the old general of the order in so high a degree, and made him an example for his disciples to follow. On the contrary, it was only now that his real troubles and torments began, since now he must search the depths of his inner being. At first, he ex-

26. THE SENATOR TREVISANO FINDS IGNATIUS   27. IGNATIUS ON THE VOYAGE TO JERUSALEM

Engravings from the first biography of Ignatius by Ribadeneira.

28. JERUSALEM
Woodcut, 1550.

From Philanderer to a "Master of the Affects"

perienced the most blissful feelings, such as he had never before known; soon, however, great chasms opened out before him and he learned such hopeless despair of the soul as is never experienced by those people concerned only with the outer world, and experienced that conflict which occurs only in the perilous course of spiritual transformation.

In Manresa strange "illuminations" had already begun to make their appearance. According to his own story, he felt, while walking along the bank of the river, a peculiar "condition" in that he was able to recognize and understand many things appertaining both to spiritual life and to faith; everything seemed suddenly new to him. It was a great "light of understanding," and he had the feeling that no natural experience could at any time have taught him so much as this single moment of divine knowledge.

On the steps of the church of Manresa, he states, he became aware of "a higher light," which showed him "how God had created the universe." Then he saw "the Catholic dogma so clearly that he was prepared to die for the doctrine which he had seen in such a manner."

But there was also no lack of strange visions. One day appeared to him "something white like three keys of a clavichord or an organ," and immediately he was convinced that this was the Holy Trinity. In the apparition of a white body "not very large and not very small," he believed he could see "the person of Christ"; in another similar vision he saw the Virgin Mary. Frequently he imagined he saw a great lighted sphere "a little larger than the sun," which he explained to himself as Jesus Christ.

Only thrice in the whole of his life did Ignatius have visions which were not light-phenomena: in the first, the celebrated vision of La Storta, he saw "Christ carrying the cross on His shoulder with the Eternal Father close beside him"; in the second, he saw the "soul of a disciple enter into heaven; and, in the third, "the Madonna with the Infant Jesus" appeared to him.

However dispassionately these apparitions may be judged in the light of modern psychology, it is certain that the penitent of Manresa, who was struggling for belief and for his spiritual welfare, saw in these visions weighty divine portents and indications. Certainly it was only seldom that he felt a pure joy in such "divine visitations," for he became terrified at the dangers of his inner life, which were only now plain to him. Soon he was tormented by the uncertainty whether these apparitions were actually of divine origin, or whether they arose from the whisperings of evil spirits. In this condition of fearful uncertainty, he once had a light-vision which resembled a serpent and which made him uneasy, in spite of its dazzling beauty. On his observing that the vision "appeared to lose some of its beauty when close to the cross," he decided that it was not God who appeared in this serpent, but Satan. He immediately took up his pilgrims staff and drove away this demon with heavy blows.

But even those visions about whose origin he had no doubt at all sometimes caused him some difficulty when they appeared at the wrong moment. This happened in the evenings, when he desired to rest after long penances, and, as a consequence, he was unable to sleep. When, at a later period, he was learning Latin, and especially during his zealous studies, he was attacked by all sorts and kinds of "new spiritual knowledge and sensations," which rendered him incapable of busying himself seriously with his words and phrases. By degrees, however, he became accustomed to interpret each inopportune apparition or illumination as a "temptation," for he was firmly convinced that God would never hinder one of his servants in the performance of a pious work or in the execution of a really useful project.

For a time in Manresa, he had to struggle against an agony of torments of conscience, against a sudden attack of scrupulousness, which almost reduced him to despair. In vain did he confess at frequent intervals, and included in the list of his transgressions sins he had already expiated; in vain did he delve and endeavor to remember trivial offences against the divine precepts. In spite of all this, he fell deeper into the most utter uncertainty.

One day, depressed and wearied by this continual conflict of mind, he cried out in despair: "Help me, O Lord, for there is no help in man, nor do I find succor in any creature! Show me where I might seek help and find it; even if I must run after a dog in order to be saved by him, I would certainly do it!"

He came to the verge of suicide, and once nearly threw himself over a precipice; resisting this mood at the last moment, however, he became conscious of the fact that God had forbidden suicide.

It was a long time before he was able to master this agony of conscience, but, when he did succeed, he was able, as no other has done, to command all the movements of his inner life and at all times to control his soul and regulate its working. His experience of perilous abysses during his stay in Manresa, together with his all-conquering will, finally led him to that knowledge of the human soul which made him appear so wonderful in his later years.

He was at last able to keep in check the creations of his imagination, once so unbridled, as well as his feelings of sorrow and jubilation; he succeeded in transforming himself so completely that, in the course of years, he became a quite different person with other thoughts and feelings.

Each action and each emotion had at last its prescribed period: mass should not occupy more than half an hour, and a sand-glass was at hand in order that this time should not be exceeded. He permitted himself "illuminations" only during mass, and even the tears of emotion and commotion were not to him simply an unchecked *gratia lacrimarum* as in the earlier days of his transformation; he wept now only when it appeared to him appropriate for reasons of inner discipline. In one of his diaries, he used to note down these torrents of tears, and, as it were, measure their intensity and duration, whether the tears were few or a "storm of tears with sobbing."

Each practical rule of the *Exercises*, each direction for the production of definite representations and for the removal of others, had its origin in Loyola's personal experience. The entirely subjective origin of the *Exercises* on the basis of his own knowledge shows itself all the more distinctly when a careful comparison is made between his life and his work; moreover, Ignatius himself expressly admitted this in a statement he made to his disciple Gonzales.

"He said to me," Gonzales writes, "that he had not written the *Exercises* all at the one time; he had kept a written record of some things which he had observed in his inner life, the usefulness of which he had recognized, and which appeared to him to be of value to others." Ribadeneira, too, Loyola's first biographer, reported that Loyola had compiled his *Spiritual Exercises* "on the basis of a precise observation of what had happened in himself."

From Philanderer to "Master of the Affects"

The writers of the order, especially the Spanish Jesuits, have often tried to represent the composition of the *Exercises* as a miracle which cannot be explained in a natural way, and to attribute the origin of the work to the direct inspiration of the Virgin Mary. They support this contention by the circumstance that in Manresa Ignatius had no kind of knowledge of theology, and, therefore, it cannot be understood how he could have been in a position to compose this masterpiece without heavenly aid.

On the other hand, many historians, especially in Benedictine and Protestant circles, have endeavored to prove that the *Exercises* were in the main little more than a copy of the writings of earlier ascetics and mystics. In particular, the book of spiritual exercises by the Benedictine abbot, Garcia de Cisneros, Ludolphus of Saxony's *Vita Christi* and the *Imitation of Christ* of Thomas à Kempis, have been cited, and obvious similarities in these works and in Loyola's *Spiritual Exercises* have been discovered.

But both legends of the supernatural origin of the *Exercises* and the critical examination of the text to prove its lack of originality are contradicted by the close relationship between Loyola's little book and his own personal experiences. Of course, books contributed much towards Loyola's particular development, but it would be erroneous to regard the *Exercises* merely as the fruits of his reading. The result of a life so rich in profound agitation can never be understood, if it is sought to attribute his work to the influence of a few books or documents.

On the other hand, however, a closer consideration of the history of the *Exercises* destroys all notion of its miraculousness: it is true that Ignatius at that time knew but few books, but it cannot therefore be maintained that he was totally in ignorance of mystic and spiritual matters, and that consequently he had to depend on supernatural inspiration.

The books which Iñigo read in his castle, on Montserrat and in Manresa, including both the *Vita Christi* of the Carthusian monk, Ludolphus of Saxony, and the *Imitatio Christi* of the Netherlander, Thomas à Kempis, were all nothing but compilations from the great works of the mystics. This was especially the case with the *Book of Exercises* of the Benedictine monk, Garcia de Cisneros, whose purpose had been to leave behind him for his brethren in the cloister at Montserrat an anthology of all the valuable thoughts of former masters on monastic asceticism.

Since Ignatius had thus studied these three books thoroughly, he acquired at the same time a knowledge of the whole mystical tradition, and, under these circumstances, there can be no question in his case of a "complete lack of education." The puzzle would appear to be solved if we consider, in addition to this, that the *Exercises* did not assume their final form in Manresa, but only much later, at a time when Ignatius was studying at the University of Paris. For in Paris he had every opportunity of consulting the great works of scholastic divinity, and, moreover, in the College of Montaigu he came into lose contact with the mystic school of the Brothers of Common Life.

Before the final version of the *Exercises* was completed, he had, therefore, already acquired the necessary familiarity with the spirit of ascetic mysticism, but he had hardly any need merely to copy his models, for in the *Exercises* at every turn can be discerned his own personal experiences and self-won knowledge. Each page of this work testifies to his own struggles and strivings, to his advance from an unbridled courtier and knight to the cold "master of affects" and to the calculating modern organizer.

At the Tables of the Pious Ladies

The beginnings of the Society of Jesus lay in a senseless and romantic fancy which must have seemed even to Loyola's contemporaries an impracticable and "pious folly." In the same way, the means used by Loyola to carry out his plan were foolish and unworldly, yet from these pitiable beginnings developed the first foundations of the future universal order.

As Iñigo, newly converted and feverishly inspired, meditated on how he could best join the forces of the knights of God, an alluring way was suddenly shown to his ignorant and clumsy soul, in which he could distinguish himself by specially heroic deeds in the service of heaven; this was the adventurous idea of undertaking a journey to the Holy Land and reconquering it for Christendom.

On his sick-bed in Loyola, he had read in the *Vita Christi* of the Carthusian monk, Ludolphus of Saxony, a glorification of the holy town of Jerusalem, and this passage had made a deep impression on him. "Let us deplore," writes Ludolphus, "the neglect of Christendom in our days, which is provided with so many sublime models, and yet hesitates to tear from the hands of the enemy the earth which Christ sanctified with his blood. . . ."

The great dream of the Middle Ages to win back Jerusalem, a dream which, since the days of Gregory the Seventh, had through centuries ruled Christian thought., no longer played a serious part in the higher politics of Loyola's time. Since Acre, the last stronghold of the crusaders, fell into the hands of the Arabs in 1291, the pope had never again been able to organize a new crusade. The secular princes, without whose support such an undertaking was impossible, now found themselves entangled in interests of quite a different nature; indeed, there were Christian rulers who, far from abhorring the heathen sultan as the "hereditary enemy of the Church," were much more concerned about winning him over as an ally in their wars.

Even in the notions of the people, the idea of the capture of the Holy Land had at that time lost all romantic attraction. Everywhere in Europe, there may, indeed, still have existed the lively craving for distant lands which had been awakened by the crusades, but the age of discoveries had turned this desire for adventure into quite different channels. The bands of people who had once been driven to Jerusalem by fatal plagues and by the economic needs of Europe now found a more alluring goal beyond the seas. Therefore the part which Jerusalem had played in the struggle for the Faith was finally at an end. The Christians who still went to Palestine were no longer warriors in search of conquest, but peaceful pilgrims, whose only concern was to obtain a share in the many ecclesiastical favors and indulgences associated with such pilgrimages.

But Ignatius Loyola dreamt of greater things. He wished to free the sanctuaries of the dominance of the false prophet, and, in this way, altogether alone, armed only with weapons of humility, to accomplish the work which the swords of the proud crusaders had not succeeded in doing. Poor and barefooted, defying all danger, he thought of journeying to Jerusa-

At the Tables of the Pious Ladies

lem as a "warrior knight of the faith" and there winning over the heathen with the weapon of the word and by an heroic example of martyrdom for the true Church.

Just as romantic and unreal as this proposal were also the means with which he sought to realize it. The journey of this belated crusader was nothing more than the adventurous voyage of a fool, and his experiences were like those of the young prince in the fairy tale, who, thanks to his awkwardness, was always falling into great danger, but who was always successful in getting out again unscathed. So it was that Ignatius, protected by his own foolishness, passed through encounters with pirates at sea, warlike Turks, cunning cheats, swindlers and footpads; scarcely would he leave a ship when it would run into difficulties at sea; invariably he would lag behind the other pilgrims only to avoid thereby the misfortune which befell those who arrived before him; and always he was certain to reach his destination safe and sound. Each stage of this strange pilgrimage shows Ignatius as a simpleton, who unsuspectingly groped his way through endless dangers and adventures to his final goal, only at the end to stand by like a clumsy dunce while the reward of victory slipped through his fingers. A strangely touching serenity and charity hover over this curious pilgrim, and transfigure everything that happened to him on his journey to and from Jerusalem.

He had scarcely arrived at Barcelona to embark thence for Italy when the port was closed on account of the plague; he was therefore forced to remain in a town alien to him and await the uncertain date when the sailings would be resumed.

As befitted a pious pilgrim, he spent this period of inaction in zealous mortifications, prayer and pious visits to the prisons, hospitals, poor-houses. He also appeared regularly in the cloisters, in order to engage in edifying conversation with the monks and nuns there; the Cloister de las Jeronimas attracted him particularly, and there he busied himself in delivering God-fearing and instructive discourses to the newly entered nun, Sor Antonia Estrada, who was well known on account of her piety. Like the other pious pilgrims he obtained his subsistence by begging in the streets, but he presented the greater portion of the alms he received in this way to the poor.

He had at that time already gathered round him a circle of women disciples, a host of leisured ladies from the higher ranks of society, who felt themselves drawn to him by pious curiosity. The first of these patronesses, Inez Pascual, he had met when he took the road to Manresa, after his nightly vigil before the image of the Holy Mother on the mount of Montserrat.

The peculiar appearance of the wanderer had immediately attracted the lively interest of this rich lady. She saw a young man of elegant build, clad in an excessively long sackcloth girdled with a coarse rope, with a calabash round his neck and a long staff in his hand. His youthful face, fresh and rosy, was in strange contrast to his pilgrims clothing; this circumstance immediately struck the pious lady as being unusual. Iñigo approached her with halting steps, cast his eyes modestly to the ground, and, in well-chosen words, which betrayed the manners of a court, inquired whether there was in the neighborhood a hospice where he could spend the night. From the time of this meeting, Inez Pascual was completely won over to the God-fearing pilgrim.

Doña Isabella Roser, his second patroness, made his acquaintance in a similar manner; she had likewise felt herself attracted by the peculiar appearance of the strange pilgrim.

The Power and Secret of the Jesuits

One day, absorbed in prayer in the cathedral at Barcelona, she had, on glancing up, suddenly noticed a beggar in the grey frock of a penitent, kneeling on the steps of the altar, his right foot in the hempen shoe of the country, his left foot bare. Some compulsion made her stare for so long at the strange man that she almost believed she saw a curious light above his head and heard a voice which murmured: "Speak to him—speak to him!"

Soon numerous other ladies of rank in the town associated themselves with Inez Pascual and Isabella Roser. On account of their attachment to Ignatius, this band were soon called in jest the "Iñigas." Inez Pascual gave Ignatius lodging; he slept at night in her house on the hard floor, after he had scourged himself bloodily the whole evening; during the day, he spent many hours in devout prayer; after that he went begging and returned towards evening with some money, and, if the wooden grill before Señora Pascual's cotton-goods shop was closed, he used to present his possessions through the grating to the poor people gathered outside.

Ignatius required very little for his own personal needs. His raiment consisted of his penitential garments, a gourd round his neck and shoes of bast on this feet; he scarcely ate or drank, and allowed the rich and pious ladies to supply him with those things which were necessary. As was customary in those days, these good souls competed for the presence of the pilgrim at their tables, in order to have devout discussions with him.

There he sat in the midst of the pious ladies, for the most part in silence, listening only to the conversation. Then he would speak of God, of salvation and of the thoughts that had come to him during his prayers or while he was reading devotional books. Thus he passed the whole of his stay in Barcelona, until the plague was at an end, and the sailings were resumed.

Then one day is casually told the host of ladies who crowded round him that he had to leave them for a time, as God had now shown him his way and he had already secured a place on a small brigantine for the voyage to Italy.

The devout women received this news in dismay, and implored him anxiously to give up his intention. They said that one so holy and so helpless in worldly matters ought not to expose himself to the dangers of such a journey. And when he replied to their objections that it was the immutable will of God that he should undertake the journey, they besought him to take with him a companion conversant with the Italian language.

He refused this request, however, declaring that he took as his companions only faith, hope and charity. The women wished at least to present the pilgrim with food, cushions and rugs, so that he should lack nothing on the way. Ignatius must, however, have noticed with pain, in the midst of these protestations of love which were being showered upon him on all sides, how little these good ladies understood him, and how difficult it was for rich women really to comprehend the omnipotence of God. Others, in their imperfect trust in God, might provide themselves with money for traveling and with pillows and rugs, but to him nothing more than a firm faith was necessary on his journey. With modest pride he refused all assistance for he desired to set out to reconquer the Holy Land in the manner of the saints of whom he had read—poor and barefooted, clad in penitential garments, with a pilgrim's staff and gourd.

The Travels and Adventures of a Fool

"For the mercy of God" the captain of the ship had given Iñigo his passage free, and the food for the voyage he begged in the streets of Barcelona.

The Travels and Adventures of a Fool

Without a groat in his pocket, sick and half-starved, Iñigo eventually arrived in Rome, after a stormy voyage and adventurous wanderings on foot. At Rome, he had to obtain the necessary papal passes for his journey to Jerusalem. His pale face and his ragged clothes made so pitiable an impression that the members of the Spanish colony in Rome were ashamed of their countryman, and, in order to avoid any scandal they energetically pressed their assistance on him.

When he departed for Venice a few days later, with the pope's blessing and the necessary documents, the Spaniards compelled him to accept some gold pieces to make his difficult journey easier. He was hardly out of sight of these hidalgos before he presented nearly the whole of this amount to the first beggar he met.

Now he had to wander about without food for days at a time. His was led through pest-ridden areas, through towns and villages which appeared totally deserted. Those who were unable to flee locked themselves in their houses, and if they went into the street, they hurried along with cloths soaked in vinegar before their noses. Iñigo's wan and emaciated features awakened suspicion everywhere. The people fled before him, and closed their houses to him, so that he often wandered for days without obtaining either alms or lodgings.

Notwithstanding this, he finally reached Chioggia, from which town he hoped to cross over to Venice. But, on his arrival, he was informed that nobody could enter the city of lagoons without a medical certificate. Such certificates, however, were only issued by the health authorities in Padua. The other travelers who were in Chioggia immediately hastened to Padua, while Iñigo gave up the idea of doing this owing to his weariness. Left behind by the others, he laid himself down in the open and fell asleep.

The next day, while the other travelers were waiting for their certificates in Padua, he set out on his way to Venice, and the plague guards allowed him to enter the town without any difficulty whatever. This seemed a miracle to him; actually, however, the Great Council had, in spite of the danger of infection, only that day suspended the quarantine for the period of the great spring fair, in order not to prejudice trade and foreign commerce.

The Venetian nobles were above all good business men and they knew that the existence of their town depended on unrestricted commerce. The pious pilgrims who came every year to Venice at the time of the fair, and thence travelled to the Holy Land, brought considerable business to the Venetian merchants. At such time, the hostels for foreigners increased the prices for their rooms, the provision dealers were able to dispose of their stocks and sausages, wine, cheese, sugar, aniseed and licorice, the drapers sold large quantities of sheets, rugs and pillows, and business in other trades was also brisk; travelers before leaving Venice had to provide themselves with all the things they required, from kettles, pots, pans and dishes to candles, tinder-boxes and pails.

The Power and Secret of the Jesuits

Particularly, however, the rich ship-owners did good business at this time. The pilgrims, ignorant of the ways of the world, with their indomitable and pious desire to reach the holy places with all possible speed, were by far the most acceptable passengers. They could be herded into the dark and fetid holds of great merchantmen overladen with bales of wares, and for such accommodation the ship-owners demanded the highest prices.

The pilgrims bargained eagerly with the ship-owners in the Piazza di San Marco and in the hostelries over the price of the voyage. One master required ninety ducats, another asked a lower figure, while, on vessels which were quite cheap, a place could be obtained for as little as sixty ducats.

For a while Iñigo listened in astonishment to the embittered arguments of his fellow-travelers, and then passed quietly on his way like one who was not concerned with all this. He had neither eighty nor sixty ducats; he and hardly any money at all, and he would need the aid of Providence to enable him to get to Jerusalem. Immediately on his arrival in Venice, God had provided a lodging for him; while the other pilgrims obtained shelter at high prices and were accommodated six at a time in the small and dirty rooms of the inns, he had quietly laid his bed under the arcades of the Piazza di San Marco and was found there by a rich senator, to whose palace he was taken and by whom he was given princely apartments and entertainment.

Now that he had left those pilgrims who were haggling over the cost of the voyage, he was not troubled as to how he was going to reach the Holy Land, and in fact he presently met among that throng of people an old acquaintance, a rich Spanish merchant, who immediately declared that he would use his influence with the doge in order to obtain for Ignatius a free passage for the journey. The doge received the merchant and his protégé with the greatest kindness, and, as the new Venetian governor was just about to depart in a large ship for Cyprus, the doge, without a moment's hesitation, permitted Iñigo to take a place in the following of this functionary, and so he set off at the cost of the state and on a stout and spacious vessel into the bargain.

The wise Caliph Haroun al-Raschid, despite his reverence for Mohammed the Prophet, had appreciated the advantages of foreign intercourse, and, consequently, he had concluded a treaty with Charlemagne, under which Christians were freely allowed to visit the holy shrines in Palestine on payment of suitable dues. And during the era of Christian domination, the order of the Templars had organized the pilgrim traffic, and had made fantastic profits out of money-changing. When the crusades had come to an end, the Turkish rulers again fell back on the old treaty, for the money of the pilgrims seemed of sufficient importance for then to allow the detested Christians to enter the country. The pilgrims, therefore, were again able to visit the holy places which were under Turkish rule, and there make their devotions; indeed, an intricate organization had been elaborated to deal with this influx of pilgrims and every step, every genuflexion and every devout motion was made to yield a profit for the local authorities.

When a ship had cast anchor at Jaffa, and the pilgrims, deeply affected by their first glimpse of the Holy Land, had sung their "Te Deum," a Turkish official , accompanied by several soldiers armed with guns and bows, immediately appeared on board to examine the

29. THE DOCTORS OF THE UNIVERSITY OF SALAMANCA

Painting, Madrid.

30 IGNATIUS, AT THE AGE OF 33, ATTENDS THE SCHOOL FOR BOYS IN BARCELONA

31. IGNATIUS IN PRISON SUSPECTED OF HERESY

Engravings from the first biography of Ignatius by Ribadeneira.

The Travels and Adventures of a Fool

papers of the travelers and to collect the taxes demanded, Scarcely had the pilgrims set foot on land, and, enraptured and overcome by the greatness of this moment, had fervently kissed the holy ground, when they were surrounded by mounted soldiers, and, like a herd, were driven into a filthy cellar; there they were forced to wait; closely penned, until such time as the dragoman had paid to the Emir of Ramleh the passenger dues required.

When this was done, they appeared before six aged Turks with flowing beards reaching to the floor, and there they each stated their rank, name, father's name and origin, and, after this, on payment of the appropriated fee, they were each supplied with an Arabian passport.

Mounted on mules which had been hired at excessive prices, and escorted by soldiers, who, on the way, acquired the stores of wine and food of the travelers, at first by entreaty and then by threatening with butts of their guns, the pilgrims set out for Jerusalem. In Ramleh, they were driven into a dirty stable, where they were handed over to a host of importunate dealers until the tax which would enable them to continue on their way had been paid.

Finally, at the gate of Jerusalem, there was a further examination of their belongings with a corresponding payment, and, from then on, the fate of the pilgrims was in the hands of the monks of the Franciscan monastery on Mount Zion; these monks had their arrangements with the Turkish governor, and made themselves responsible for the board, lodging and behavior of the pilgrims.

In the monastery, they were at once given a hearty breakfast, carpets, cushions and bread and wine. After the violent, heathen methods of collection of the well-armed Turks, the humble manner in which the monks asked for the customary five ducats a day must have seemed to the pilgrims like an expression of Christian charity.

At last, the great moment came, when, having arrived at the end of their difficult journey, they were to look upon the holy places; before this, however, a Franciscan came amongst them, and repeated in Latin, Italian and German a number of instructions which had already been impressed upon them on the ship. They must guard against going out alone, against entering Mohammedan tombs, against crowding forward unbecomingly when visiting sacred places, against disputes and laughter. They must abstain from scribbling on the walls of the Holy Sepulcher with red chalk or with charcoal, as the unbelievers looked upon this with dreadful scorn.

Together with some twenty pilgrims, Germans, Swiss, Dutchmen and Spaniards, Iñigo had succeeded in reaching Jerusalem. He had always, at the critical moment, found somebody to pay the dragoman, the emir, the soldiers, and passport examiners, the dealers, and the monks for him.

He was now in line with the others, and, holding his burning candle firmly in the hand, he accompanied them from one holy place to another. Everywhere he listened devoutly to the explanations of the monks, who at each place intoned an edifying song, and then rapidly explained the significance of the holy shrine, and how many indulgences it would bring to the pilgrims because they had visited it.

In accordance with a long-tried system, the Franciscans took those under their protection round the town and its environs, and showed them the post at which Christ was scourged, the house in which Mary died, the place where Abraham sacrificed Isaac, the houses of Simon the leper, of the beggar Lazarus, of Herod, and of Saint Anne, without mentioning numerous other remarkable sights of lesser interest.

The devout wonder of the pious pilgrims, however, reached its climax when they stood before the marble church which contained the Holy Sepulcher. One after the other, their candles burning in their hands, they entered the cone-shaped room through a low and narrow gateway; from this room the heavens could be seen through an opening in the roof in the form of a cross.

At last, Iñigo stood on that consecrated spot to which he had been so strongly attracted as he lay on his sick-bed in his native castle. In the glimmer of nine hanging lamps he saw the grey tomb of the Saviour rising from the rough rock; for this place the flower of Christian knighthood had shed its blood; to this place all true and pious people had of old made their pilgrimage.

To the other pilgrims who crowded round the Sepulcher with him and heard mass and received the holy communion on that night, this must have been the most significant and solemn event of the whole journey, which, when they had returned to their native lands, they would be able to recount to their devout and attentive relatives. Iñigo, however, intended never to leave this sacred place. He would remain there for the rest of his days in order to win the tomb for Christianity with the weapons of the apostles.

The pilgrims tarried in the holy shrine until the stars which were visible though the opening above the dome-shaped room had faded and the dawn broke. Then they opened the small gate again and proceeded from one object of interest to another; they were shown where the Jews erected the Cross, where the soldiers threw dice for the clothing of Christ; they saw the stone on which Christ sat while the crown of thorns was being placed on His head, and the fissure in the rock where the foot of the Cross had been fixed.

On the Mount of Olives, the Franciscans pointed out the place where an angel appeared to the Virgin Mary and the place where Christ had preached to the apostles on the subject of the day of judgment. On entering the church on the Mount of Olives, there was to be seen a stone on which the imprint of the foot of Christ was still visible; the monks explained that it was from this stone that the Lord had ascended into heaven.

While seeing all these sights and objects of interest, Iñigo had not for a moment forgotten the true purpose of his journey, and he had already taken the necessary steps. Every Christian who wished to stay in Jerusalem longer than the customary period had to obtain the consent of the Franciscans, and Iñigo, soon after his arrival, had sought permission to remain in the Holy Land and devote himself to the conversion of the heathens.

Up to that time, his request had not been granted, but he had no doubt that he would eventually receive the permission he sought. Consequently, he made no preparations for his departure, although the other pilgrims had already packed their belongings. The Franciscan provincial, Fra Angelo, however, sent for him, and informed him that he must immediately leave Jerusalem with the other pilgrims.

In a kindly manner, but with the grave explicitness of an experienced official, the provincial explained to him that his project was wholly impracticable. It was true that the Turks allowed the pilgrims to enter the Holy Land, but they would not countenance any attempt at

32. THE ALMSHOUSE ST.-JACQUES DE L'HÔPITAL
WHERE IGNATIUS LIVED IN PARIS

33. COLLÈGE DE MONTAIGU, PARIS

34. THE CHAPEL OF ST. MARY ON MONTMARTRE

35. THE UNIVERSITY QUARTER IN PARIS

Woodcut of the sixteenth century

conversion. Others before Iñigo had had similar intentions, and these had been either slain or taken prisoners by the fanatical Mohammedans. The provincial, who was responsible for peace between the Christians and the Turks, could neither approve nor allow this undertaking.

Iñigo was at first determined in his resolve, and cried with chivalrous impetuosity that he dreaded neither death nor slavery; he yielded immediately, however, when the provincial referred to a papal bull which gave him full authority over all Christians in Jerusalem. As an obedient warrior in the army of Christ, he could not do otherwise than comply with an order emanating from the pope, God's terrestrial commander.

Sadly he limped out through the Jaffa gate, his hempen shoes on his feet, his pilgrim's staff in his hand, and the calabash round his neck, each step taking him farther from the holy City and nearer to his native land. Defiantly he had once set out to capture Jerusalem's holy ground; now he was returning disconsolate, with a small wooden box under his arm, full of tiny chips of stone, small pieces of earth and flowers; these small souvenirs he had collected from the different holy places. This small box he was taking with him for the pious nun, Antonia Estrada, of the Convent of las Jeronimas, as a memento of his pilgrimage.

Salvation and Perplexity

Thus the campaign for the conquest of the Holy Land had proved itself to be an utter failure; but even the "band of devout souls" which he intended to form on his return from Jerusalem remained for a long time a company of immature visionaries, and still many years were to pass before a "Society of Jesus" was actually to arise from such romantic beginnings.

From the very start, Ignatius had not aimed merely at his own salvation; on the contrary, it was is constant preoccupation to bring about the "rescue" of other souls and in that way develop an apostolic activity.

This endeavor had already been prominent in Manresa shortly after his conversion, and, in fact, it was the stimulus that resulted in the *Exercises*. In order to be able to communicate his experiences to others, he had put them down in writing, and from then on, using these notes, he confided his exercises with a fanatical zeal for conversion to all those who appeared to him in any degree suitable.

Polanco, who was later his secretary, remarks that even in Manresa he had instructed others in the ways and means of "purging the soul by repentance and atonement, of meditating on the life of Christ, of making a good choice . . . of kindling in themselves a love of God and, finally, of practicing the various which was finally to become the noble and universally admired Jesuit school of the will, begins with a frivolous though distinguished circle of simple and hypocritical ladies.

He himself felt no satisfaction in this society of "converted souls," who, indeed, were bound to him only by an entirely superficial enthusiasm. He declared later that neither Manresa nor in Barcelona did he find anybody whom he had been able to advance in spiritual life.

Things became still worse when, shortly after his return from Jerusalem, he left Barcelona, and went to study at the celebrated University of Alcalá. Instead of strenuously applying his whole energy to that learning with which he was so unfamiliar, he spent the greater part of his time in gathering round him a group of disciples, for he was longing passionately to communicate to others the spiritual knowledge he had acquired in Manresa, and thereby to convert as many souls as possible.

In Alcalá, as elsewhere, it was chiefly the curiosity aroused by his strange means of the exercises appeared! The history of the practice of the exercises, and mysterious appearance which brought women disciples to him. He walked round the town barefooted and wrapped in a grey smock which reached to his feet, and behaved exactly like an apostle of a new holy sect.

He practiced the exercises with his newly acquired community in the chamber of the poor-house in which he and found lodgings or in a barn or the back room of a baker's shop. Poor women of the people it was who, burdened with by poor- lodgings or in a barn or the back people it was who, bur with sorrow, had sorrow, had gathered round him and followed his exercises, working women and girls, disillusioned wives, serving maids and prostitutes. Subsequently, when Ignatius's following was suspected of heresy, the authorities examined numerous witnesses, and their statements as recorded afford us some insight into the activity of this fanatical association.

"I have seen many married women and girls visit Iñigo," declared the caretaker of the hospice. "Among these were the seventeen-year-old daughter of the tax-collector Isidro, the daughter of Juan de la Perra, who is the same age, Isabel Sanchez, who prays, Beatriz Davila, and the wife of the saddler Juan. So many came each day that I am no longer able to recall them exactly. . . sometimes they appeared quite early in the morning, but occasionally at any hour up to nightfall. . ."

These women regarded Ignatius as a saint, and worshipped him with a profound devotion. "I arrived at the house behind the Church of St. Francis in which Beata Isabel Sanchez lives," the Franciscan monk Rubio told the inquisitor, "and when I looked in at the door I noticed several people in the courtyard on a straw mat. A young and barefooted man was sitting on a chair, and before him two or three people were kneeling as though praying. They looked up to the young man and spoke to him, but I could not hear what they said. . . Later the same evening, however, Beata Sanchez came to me and said: 'Father, do not take exception to what you have seen today; the young man is a saint!'"

Ignatius no longer restricted himself to edifying discourses on the fundamental ideas of his exercises; on the contrary, he began systematically to deal with individual women, and he induced then "to speak with him for a month," and in these conversations recall all the sins they had committed; they were to delve deeply into their souls and experience anew everything evil which they had thought or done, and in this way overcome evil for all time.

He had thus already discovered that method which made it possible to stir the human soul to its depths by means of systematic exercises; but he still lacked the power to curb the vague strivings so aroused and to subdue and master them by a judicious control.

"He told me himself," said Maria de la Flor, who was once a prostitute, "that I should feel depressed after the second week without knowing why. When after that a profound melancholy repeatedly came over me, and I learned from the other women that they suffered still greater dejection, I asked Iñigo: 'What is it? Where do these moods come from?' Thereupon he answered: 'The Devil does these things to us when we enter the service of God!' One of our number even maintains that she has seen the Devil incarnate in the shape of an enormous black body. When this happened to her, I saw her sink unconscious to the ground...."

There was much fainting among the women disciples, with the exception of those who were married; some became unconscious as many as twenty times, and one lost the power of speech "on catching a glimpse of the Devil." Young, happy girls who used to play at ball, dress themselves up and enjoy themselves without restraint, flung themselves convulsed in frightful torment on the floor almost as soon as they began to descend into the depths of their souls.

"At times, I fainted and lost consciousness," said the apprentice girl, Ana de Benavente, when she was examined. "Sometimes I felt such grief that I rolled all over the floor, and it was necessary for the others to hold me, and I would not be pacified. . . . Leonora, my mother's maid, had such fainting fits much more frequently than I, and I also saw Maria de la Flor, Ana Diaz and two other girls lose consciousness. . . ."

These little apprentice girls and unfortunate women were not attracted to Ignatius by mere superficial devotion like the rich ladies of Manresa; they readily allowed him to teach them, and humbly accepted all the torment of their descent into the "inferno of their sins." But scarcely one of them found a way out from that inferno, for although Ignatius knew already how the soul should be cultivated in order that it might, with all the senses, see, hear, smell, taste and touch hell, it was only at a much later stage in his mental advancement that he was to acquire the ability to restore lasting peace to feelings which had been so violently agitated. His activity in Alcalá thus had no other result than to produce in his women followers accesses of ecstasy and the symptoms of a very doubtful enthusiasm.

The effects on the feelings of the first male members of his following were not less confused. Shortly after his arrival in Alcalá, four eccentric young men, besides the many women, had gathered round the strange student; these were Calixto de Sa of Segovia, Juan de Arteaga of Estepa, Lope de Caceres of Catalonia, and Juan de Reinalde of Navarre.

These young men, under Ignatius's direction, practiced the spiritual exercises, and thereafter, so long as they kept in touch with him, they were his absolutely submissive tools; in Alcalá and later in Salamanca, they helped him assiduously in his "recruiting of souls." But this relationship did not lead so much to the formation of a true band of spiritual disciples as to a theatrical imitation of Loyola's external behavior.

Although they were all in a position to maintain themselves, under his influence they took pride in asking alms in the streets as beggars, and thus providing for their existence. Contrary to all the customs of the university, they wore the same striking garments as Iñigo, close-fitting grey smocks reaching to the feet and caps strangely shaped and colored. This small group of eccentric students were soon known to thee whole town, and the children in the streets nicknamed them *ensayalados*, "the men in wool."

Just as the relationship of these youths to their master rested on nothing more than an immature enthusiasm, so too was it of scant duration. When Ignatius left Spain in order to continue his studies in Paris, his disciples did not accompany him, and he waited in vain for them to follow him. Hardly had his personal influence been withdrawn when the whole association was dissolved.

Arteaga was successful in obtaining a lucrative benefice in the knightly order of San Iago; Reinalde became a monk; Caceres returned to his native town and there led the contented life of a well-to-do man. Calixto, however, who had at one time been the most enthusiastic of them all, later went to the West Indies as the courier of a foreign lady, established a profitable business there and ended his days in Salamanca as a rich merchant.

This strange circle of ecstatic youths and women must necessarily have excited the suspicion of the ecclesiastical authorities. The neighborhood of Alcalá was the seat of the "Alumbrados," a strange sect of Spanish mystics against whom the Inquisition was at that time energetically entering the field. Soon it was suspected that Ignatius was a member of the sect. Exhaustive investigations were made; Ignatius and his disciples were arrested more than once; finally, as he was totally lacking in theological knowledge, he was merely forbidden to acquire disciples, and allowed to continue on his way.

A similar fate befell him in Salamanca, to which place he had gone after his release in order to continue his studies. The authorities there also instituted an inquiry, and again, after an exhaustive examination, he was acquitted on condition that henceforth he refrain from preaching.

Nevertheless, as his ardent desire to "rescue souls" would not give him peace, he at last resolved to leave Spain altogether, and so, towards the end of the year 1527, he set out on foot for Paris, driving before him an ass laden with books.

The Work of Conversion in the Students' Room

He soon became a well-known figure among the Paris students for he was to be seen daily in the dirty, narrow "Dogs' Alley" between the colleges of Montaigu and St. Barbara. At that time, he gave the impression of being a haggard, oldish man with distinguished features, who, on account of his unhealthy and emaciated appearance, his tangled dark beard and his dirty, long black robe, had an unpleasant effect on those who came into contact with him.

While Ignatius was still studying the rudiments of grammar at the Collège de Montaigu, a Spaniard, Amador, who, up to that time, had been regarded as a model student, disappeared one day from the neighboring college in the company of two other Spanish students, Peralta and Doctor de Castro.

A change had already been observed in the manners of these three young men. For some time, they had been neglecting their studies, and had prayed and meditated unceasingly; in turn they sold their books, their clothes and their furniture, giving away the proceeds of the sale and living only on the money they obtained by begging. Immediately after their flight, it became known that they had in all this been persuaded by the Spanish student, Iñigo de Loyola, and that they were residing in the Hòpital St.-Jacques where the latter lived. Thereupon some hundreds of their fellow-students gathered in front of the hospice, stormed it, and

36. LA STORTA

From the Acta Sanctorum.

37. THE HOUSE ON THE PIAZZA MARGANA WHERE
IGNATIUS LIVED IN ROME

38. ROME IN THE SIXTEENTH CENTURY

From the Chronicle of Schelel.

The Work of Conversion in the Students' Room

seized the fugitives and forced them to return to the college.

Only after this new failure was Ignatius to find in Paris and draw to him those men who were in the future to form the nucleus of his order. When the excitement over the flight of the Spaniards had died down, Ignatius himself entered the Collège de Sainte-Barbe. He there shared a room with two other students who were preparing diligently for their examinations.; he subordinated himself quite calmly to these fellow-workers, but, from the first moment he set eyes on that room, he was seized by an overwhelming desire to possess those two souls for his own. Such an excellent opportunity of first minutely examining the objects of his passion for converting people in the narrow confines of a room shared in common with them and of testing the effect of each word on them had never before presented itself to him.

Peter Faber, one of his new roommates, was a man of profound learning; he had mastered the subtleties of Aristotle so well that even the teachers called upon him for his opinion in settling difficult points connected with the interpretation of that philosopher. Nevertheless, Ignatius soon noticed that behind the disciplined mind of this son of a Savoyard peasant there was hidden a soul embarrassed by distress and perplexity; the superstition of the erstwhile herdsman, the deep fear of evil and dangerous forces which had at one time claimed the boy on the Alpine pasture, had not even now been entirely dispelled by the logic of Aristotle.

A long time was to pass before Ignatius was certain that Faber was to be one of his followers. A small sum of money which he had begged from a rich Dutch merchant gave him his first opportunity of approaching him, for Peter Faber was poor and suffered much on account of his enormous appetite. Unobtrusively, Ignatius made it possible for him to eat his fill.

At last the moment came when Faber began to open his mind to his new roommate. Step by step during their studies, Ignatius had persuaded this taciturn peasant to begin to tell him of his past life, and finally everything hidden burst forth naïve and incoherent from his soul. Ignatius saw the twelve-year-old shepherd boy sitting in the midst of this flock, and, panic-stricken by a troubled conscience, taking a vow of chastity. Now the awakened man struggled in anguish to keep himself pure amid a thousand desires and temptations. "My temptations," said Faber himself later, "consisted of sinful representations which the angel of darkness aroused in me, and which were such as I could not understand, as I was deficient in the ability to distinguish between the spirits."

Faber soon surrendered wholly to the influence of his new preceptor. Led by Ignatius, he gradually emerged from a mental state of chaotic disorder to contented lucidity and order. For he had learned by the *Exercises* with its *examen particulare* to analyze into its constituent parts the generalized feeling of sin which had previously harassed and threatened to overwhelm him, and then to analyze each sin singly.

Francis Xavier, Loyola's second roommate, was one of those hilarious and cheerful young students who seem to overcome all difficulties with an easy grace. Learning gave him no trouble, and, consequently, he was able to spend much of his spare time on the islands in the Seine where, with other young people, he ran and fought for wagers. At night, he was seldom to be found in the small room at the college; it was mostly towards morning before he returned from these joyful expeditions by way of the doubtful taverns of the Latin Quarter. It was his life's ambition to acquire a rich living in his native Navarre, and his most zealous endeavors were directed to establishing in proper form his somewhat doubtful claim to noble rank. With this aim in view, he kept up a lively correspondence, and addressed numerous memorials to every possible office and authority.

Ignatius, who kept him under constant quiet observation, was able to perceive those otherwise unnoticed moments when Xavier, the apparently careless man of the world, became undecided, and stared vacantly before him, wearied by the empty monotony of his repeated excesses, terrified by the sight of faces bearing the threatening marks of the new venereal disease.

Xavier for a long time felt a strong aversion to Ignatius, and the bigotry of this older student repelled him. At every opportunity, Ignatius urged his colleagues to be converted to a "Christian life," and on Sundays allowed no occasion to pass without unctuously uttering a pious text; it was said of him in jest that, challenged to a billiard match by a fellow-student, he made the condition that, if he won, he should give spiritual exercises to his opponent. This all went towards arousing in Xavier a lively feeling of disapproval and antipathy.

As with Peter Faber, Ignatius called money to his aid in the conquest of Xavier's soul. The flighty student was never able to make both ends meet, was often in financial difficulties, and gladly accepted the assistance offered by Ignatius, whom he esteemed so little.

Once, however, when Xavier had boastingly unfolded his ambitious plans for the future, Ignatius, after a while, quite casually mentioned the words of the Gospel according to St. Matthew: "For what is a man profited if he shall gain the whole world and lose his own soul?"

His high-flown discussion interrupted by a scriptural text which sounded almost malicious, Xavier felt that the remark was out of place; later, however, the sentence of the "ridiculous hypocrite" constantly intruded upon him; as time went on, the words interrupted for a while his amusements and his dissipations, until at last he yielded. In vain did he struggle against the growing power of his conscience, and cling in spite of everything to his worldly life; the words of the Bible waxed within him and flourished on all his wicked diversions, his disappointments, his dull weariness, and on every trivial cause for mental reflection.

Xavier listened more and more attentively to Loyola's discourses on spiritual matters, and, in a short time, begged him outright for instruction and guidance; soon he had not only forgotten his boon companions, but had broken away from the men who were devoted to the new humanistic ideas, and whom hitherto he had regarded as his teachers and his models.

The religious feeling in Francis Xavier had become so overpowering that he was ready to lay down the instructorship he had lately acquired, and devote himself solely to spiritual meditations; Ignatius had to prevail upon him almost with force to continue for yet a while in his profession.

Xavier later became one of the most brilliant of the apostles of the Ignatian doctrine, and in him the spirit of Loyola reached its finest bloom. The former frivolous man of the world went out as the first Jesuit missionary to India and Japan, and there wrote poems which for their fervent strength of spiritual longing must be counted among the finest testimonies of Catholic sentiment:

> At such love, my love I kindle
> Were there no heaven, still must I love!
> Were there no hell, sin would I shun!
> Were heaven and hell to pass away,
> With their rewards and punishments,
> In me would love for love endure!

The Founding of the Society of Jesus

Shortly after Ignatius has won over Faber and Xavier, other followers from among the Parisian students gathered round him. The Spaniards, Laynez and Salmeron, had come to the French capital from Alcalá, and Ignatius had met them as they were dismounting from their horses in front of the inn; they immediately joined their countryman, of whom they had already heard in Alcalá. The Portuguese, Rodriguez, was also quickly gained, for he had a natural gift for religious dreaming, and for that reason was predestined to devoted discipleship. Finally he was joined by Bobadilla, an impoverished nobleman, who was able to pursue his studies only under conditions of the greatest privation; as in the case of Faber and Xavier, he was first of all made tractable by means of pecuniary assistance, until at last he was bound fast in spirit to Ignatius.

Each for himself, under Loyola's guidance they all practiced the spiritual exercises. The practice of the exercises still had something fanatical about it. In spite of the exceptionally cold winter, Faber disdained to warm his room, and did some part of the exercises in the open in the courtyard of his house, which was deeply covered with snow; at night he slept in his shirt on a wood-pile, and for fully six days he did not take a bite of food.

When that small but completely reliable band of fighters for God had gathered about him in Paris, Ignatius believed that he had almost completed his work. Actually, however, his real and most serious difficulties lay ahead of him.

It was now necessary for Ignatius to assign their tasks to this small band, but it became at once apparent that he still had no practical or definite end in view, for, on the formation of the Society on the day of the Feast of Assumption in the year 1534, what he discussed with his followers in glowing words was nothing else than the old fantastic dream of the conquest of Jerusalem.

Although, on his pilgrimage, he had had an opportunity of becoming personally acquainted with the actual conditions in the Holy Land, the difficult position of the Christians living there, and the power and fanatical zeal of the Turks, he nevertheless told his disciples that they should go to Jerusalem, and by the peaceful conversion of the unbelievers accomplish the great work in which the crusaders had failed. On their knees in the Chapel of St.

The Power and Secret of the Jesuits

Mary on Montmartre, they all took a vow of purity and poverty, and swore solemnly to set out at any appointed time for the Holy Land.

With all his enthusiasm, Ignatius was, nevertheless, not quite happy about the resolution they had made; even though he did not admit it., his bright hopes of establishing the kingdom of Christ in the Holy Land were already overshadowed by a great uncertainty. With the presentiment that his plan might prove impracticable, he added a second plank to his programme: if by a certain date the journey to Jerusalem had not proved possible, they would all go to Rome and offer their services to the pope.

Thus the solemn vow taken on Montmartre, which in fact was the real beginning of the Society of Jesus, contained from the first a strange inconsistency. Two eventualities were provide for, and instead of giving a fixed and inviolable form to a clearly stated intention, the vow provided, in its ambiguity, a peculiar combination of blind enthusiasm and pessimistic foreshadowing of difficulties. Loyola's uncertainty soon proved itself to be justified, for the crusade came to an end in Venice.

From Paris, they had all set out for the Venetian Republic, which they reached after great privation, animated only by the passionate desire to reach the Holy Land. From Venice, Ignatius dispatched three of his disciples to Rome, in order to ask the pope for the passports to Jerusalem.

The aged pope, Paul III, a follower and pupil of the humanist Pomponius Lætus, loved to hear, after the old custom, philosophical and theological discussions at his table; on these occasions, the doctors present put difficult and involved theological questions to the speakers and the pope found his pleasure in the subtleties of the answers.

Through the good offices of the imperial ambassador, Pedro Ortiz, the three disciples of Ignatius, soon after their arrival in Rome, were invited to one of these theological repasts. On this occasion, the young masters of the Paris faculty showed the profundity of their knowledge, and the pope graciously promised theme every assistance in their pilgrimage. Paul, who was well informed of the preparations the Venetians were making for a war against the Turks, remarked: "I give you my blessing freely, but I do not believe it will be possible for you to make an early departure!"

The pope was right. When Ignatius and his band were ready to start, the Turkish war broke out rendering impossible for a long while all journeys to Mohammedan countries.

Ignatius never again in his life saw the Holy Land, but his adventurous scheme of conquest was not forgotten. Decades later, when the Jesuit order had become the sober, definite and conscious organization which we know, when Ignatius himself had become the prudent and clear-thinking general of the order, the romantic idea of a new crusade seized him once again. While engaged in matters concerned with sober administrative measures, he elaborated a plan which he intended to put before the emperor, and which aimed at the capture of Jerusalem.

Naturally, the means he now wished to employ were quite different; in the meantime, he had learned that little was to be achieved in a struggle against the Turks, if pious humility alone were used, and so he explained quite coolly to the emperor how necessary it was to raise a fleet of some hundreds of vessels and obtain the money for this purpose by levying a

39. THE POPE DISPENSING HIS BLESSING FROM THE BENEDICTION BALCONY OF ST. PETER'S

Copperplate engraving from the Speculum Romaine magnificentiae of Lafreri.

40. POPE Paul III

Painting by Titian.

heavy special tax.

This plan was no more carried out than was the earlier idea of a peaceful conquest of the Mohammedans by preaching and martyrdom. Nevertheless, this endeavor of Loyola's to lead unbelievers into the bosom of the Church became of the utmost importance in relation to the further development of the order, for in it lay the germ of that apostolic missionary work which was to lead the Jesuits to great success.

When, in 1537, on account of the war, it at last became certain that it would be impossible to undertake the journey to Jerusalem for some time to come, the little band found it necessary to carry into effect the second part of the program conceived on Montmartre; a plan no less romantic than the first. They were to offer their services to the pope, but in what these services were actually to consist, they did not clearly understand.

The pope himself was quite embarrassed by the offer, which later was to prove to be the beginning of a new and magnificent era in the power of the Hole See. At the beginning of 1538, Ignatius, accompanied by Laynez and Faber, appeared at the Curia, and there, as he later declared, he found "the window shut." For Paul III, who was especially interested in international politics, was at that moment endeavoring to unravel the warlike entanglements of the emperor and the king of France; what could these scholars from Paris mean to him? They had nothing more to offer him than a devotion as enthusiastic as it was obscure!

As it happened Paul needed additional teachers for the university in Rome, and so he allotted to Laynez and Faber the task of delivering theological lectures at the "Sapienza"; he then departed for Nice to attend the peace conference between King Francis and Charles the Fifth, and, for the time being, troubled himself no further about his new auxiliary force.

Up Against Modern Problems

The long period of waiting in Venice had furnished the small Society for the first time with the opportunity for practical work. The whole structure of the band created by Ignatius contained a tendency towards external activity, for the forces of this association, organized on a military basis, of themselves urged it to some active employment. The members of the Society eagerly desired to do something or other to distinguish themselves, and to be active in every conceivable way in the fight for the Kingdom of Christ.

Of all other spiritual fellowships, the order of the Theatines, which had been established a short time before, was especially prominent. In it the new spirit of the Catholic Reformation made its appearance for the first time; strong in their principles, the Theatines strove to set the world an example of energy and sacrifice, and performed, to the general admiration of all, much good work in connection with the care of the sick in the hospitals. Those who still had hopes of a resuscitation of the almost degenerate Catholic piety turned their eyes expectantly to the Theatines.

It was inevitable that Ignatius and his comrades should seek to compete with the Theatines. They threw themselves into the business of tending the sick, assisting the poor, the imprisoned, and the dying, and in all this they exhibited a devotion which was almost superhuman. Their ambition to outshine the crusaders was gradually replaced by the striving to emu-

The Power and Secret of the Jesuits

late the order of the Theatines; this desire often misled them into doing things less with the idea of helping the sick than of making them subjects for the exercise of their own heroic self-control

Immediately after his conversion Ignatius had shown a similar pathetic heroism in the hospice at Manresa. He had come into contact with sick persons whose infirmities evoked the greatest disgust, and, when he felt his senses revolting against the stench, filth and everything around him, he had immediately forced himself to embrace tenderly the most repellent inmates of the hospital.

Wholly in this wise, tis followers now conducted themselves in the Venetian hospitals. Not only did they perform the most menial services, sweeping and scrubbing the filthy floors, cleaning the chamber utensils, putting the dead upon biers and digging graves, but they chose just those labors which were most calculated to produce loathing and horror.

When Xavier was once requested by one of the patients to scrape out an abscess and he felt rather squeamish about it, he put his hand which was covered with purulent matter, to his mouth, in order to put his self-control to the extreme test. Simon Rodriguez invited a leper who had been refused admission to the hospital into his room and shared his bed with him.

On another occasion, on the journey from Venice to Rome, Rodriguez spent the night in a hospital in Ravenna, and the bed-sheets which were offered to him were still wet with the puss of a sick man. Shaken with horror, Rodriguez would not at first make use of this resting place, but afterwards, in order to punish himself for his weakness, he laid himself down naked in a bed in which, immediately before, a man had died of pediculosis, and which still swarmed with vermin.

The whole mode of living of the small band was governed by such fanatical ideas of subduing the soul. They went about in rags, and lived in dilapidated houses without doors or windows, in which they were exposed to malaria mosquitoes. They starved, begged, and distributed the money they obtained in this way. Since, however, their privations and miseries were not the result of a pressing need, their attitude lacked true brevity and inner justification; there was always something artificial and theatrical about it. However, the fact that these zealots had begun to take an interest in the evils of their time and to think of suitable methods for combating them meant a decided turning-point in their ideas. Slowly the Jesuit organization developed from a group of immature visionaries to one that was to strive painstakingly after sober tasks.

Once the efforts of these first Jesuits had been turned from fantastic and remote ideals to practical needs, problems sprang up on all sides, for the solution of which the militarily disciplined "Compañía de Jusús" seemed to have been specially formed.

For in this sixteenth century, in the much-vaunted period of the florescence of the arts, of the cultivation of the serenity of classical antiquity, and of the free "Renaissance man," there were also innumerable helpless people, victims of the black death and of leprosy, about whom their corpses could be thrown into a common grave. While philosophers, individual, innumerable children, in whom nobody was interested, were completely neglected, and unnoticed thousands perished of hunger and privation.

41. THE LIFE OF IGNATIUS: POPE Paul iii SANCTIONS THE SOCIETY OF Jesus. IGNATIUS COMPOSES THE "CONSTITUTIONS." HE SENDS HIS FIRST MISSIONARIES INTO THE WORLD

42. COPY OF A PORTION OF A LETTER
BY IGNATIUS

43. IGNATIUS LOYOLA
Engraving from Lavater's Physiognomy.

44. IGNATIUS LOYOLA
Engraving after a painting by Titian.

The Power and Secret of the Jesuits

Shortly after their arrival in Rome, Ignatius and his disciples had occasion to show how they had learned to combat practical evils by practical means. At the latter end of the cold autumn of 1538, a severe famine afflicted the Holy City, and the people fell from exhaustion in great numbers in the streets. Night after night, the Jesuits went round with torches and stretchers gathered up the starving, and carried them to the house which their devoted admirer, Antonio Frangipani, had placed at their disposal for their residence. By means of systematic house-to-house collections, they begged for money, food, clothing, kindling and straw, and were thus able to provide their charges with sustenance and clothing and with straw beds beside a warm fire.

Soon, however, Ignatius began to realize how feeble such assistance devoted and self-sacrificing though it was, must be in relation to those social needs which, deeply rooted in the structure of society, had existed as permanent institutions from time immemorial. He could, therefore, no longer be content to hasten here and there with his small band in order to succor a few of the sick and the starving; what moved him now was a strong desire to combat the evil in its entirety, and the whole of society became the test of his powers and of those of his followers. The need of society was not, however, to be met by the benevolent succor of individuals, but by planned and organized assistance on a large scale.

Mediaeval Christian charity, based on spontaneous compassion, now for the first time broadened into well-thought-out social-welfare work, and the Jesuits striking into this path were the first who went far beyond the charitable activities as thitherto exercised by the spiritual brotherhoods.

The great, enthusiastic impulse, the unreserved surrender to a spiritual aim, of which only the mediaeval man was capable to such an extent, had, in more sober surroundings, been able to express itself only in absurd, romantic and theatrical poses; this energy was not gradually transformed, and was to continue its life in the form of a severely rationalistic organization of compelling power. Many of the plans conceived at that time were, indeed, abortive; they had beginnings, but miscarried and had finally to be abandoned. The intention behind all these endeavors, however, clearly revealed a new kind of social thought, which has developed more and more clearly right up to the present day.

The evils which the Jesuits took up the task of combating were in many ways similar to the social evils which exist at the present time: begging, unemployment, child neglect and prostitution. The plan devised by Ignatius to establish in all large districts, at the public expense, central offices for the supervision of beggars, employment exchanges for those able to work, and institutions for the aged and the sick could not be carried out; it has not, indeed, been fully realized even today, when the feeling of social responsibility is so much more highly developed, nor did the idea of providing proper homes for abandoned children get beyond an insignificant beginning.

Ignatius placed the greatest emphasis on the evils of prostitution, and he devoted his most earnest attentions to its prevention. In this, his religious conception of the sinfulness of carnal lust and of the duty of rescuing erring souls from the meshes of Satan played a great part, but his efforts to put an end to prostitution also testify to his solicitous regard for the social evils of those days.

For at that time venereal disease, which had been introduced from France and Spain, claimed many victims from among all classes of Roman society. Not only in the notorious districts near Saint' Angelo, the Tiber bridges, round about the cemeteries and behind the shops of the money-changers on the Via dei Bianchi did helpless and despised prostitutes wander about sick or shaking with the disease; but also in the salons of the great courtesans, decorated with heavy tapestries and brocades, costly pictures and gilded leathern curtains, round the tables richly covered with silver vessels, Venetian glassware and vases filled with flowers and among the cardinals, aristocrats, merchants, artists and savants gathered there, the amusing conversations seemed forced and the praises of "free love" and of the "great hetaerae" rang false and ungenuine. The trembling fear of infection was hidden behind all this wanton chatter and praise of the erotic and behind all these festivities, amusements and embraces; each day the names of new victims were on everybody's lips.

The courtesans who had formerly been honored as the reincarnation of the ancient ideal of love were now beginning to be cursed. In the presence of this disease, even many of the cardinals of the Renaissance had once more to believe that richly embroidered clothes and velvet slippers were a mockery and colored ribbons and costly necklaces the fetters of Satan; through the perfume of elegant gloves, there seemed suddenly to percolate a suspicious odor of brimstone, and, in the eyes of the dismayed clerics, the chambermaids, eunuchs, and black slave-women of the courtesans changed into grotesque servants of Satan.

While those who moved in distinguished circles were still concerned in gallantly concealing the prevailing consternation, the people of the streets cried out their indignation to the world at large. A revolt broke out against the cult of the hetaerae. From all sides responded bitter, satirical songs, in which the prostitutes were branded with the lewdest abuse as the carriers of the horrible disease, Ballad mongers and singers went through the town, collected groups of people round them, and taught them the new "syphilis songs."

When, therefore, Ignatius announced that he would give his life, if only to prevent the sins of a single prostitute on a single night, this statement was not received as a mere meaningless and sentimental utterance, for among both high and low alike, it touched the hearts of those who had once more begun to regard carnal pleasure as a sin. Thus the work of rescuing fallen women and girls undertaken by Ignatius in no wise appeared merely as the product of religious zeal, but as a step towards the removal of a glaring social evil, and, therefore, it came about that in this enterprise he received the guidance and support of all classes of society.

Ignatius was at especial pains to rescue married women who had succumbed to the enticements of procuresses, the women of whom Pietro Aretino complained: "Like bats or owls, they come at night from their nests and beat up the monasteries, the courts, the brothels and the hostelries; here they take away a nun, there a monk; to this one they bring a loose woman, to that one a widow, to one a wife, to another a virgin; the lackeys they satisfy with the waiting-women of their mistresses, the steward consoles himself with his lady. . ."

Ignatius and his colleagues soon became the terror of the procuresses. With the penetration of detectives, they investigated the haunts of these go-betweens; they lay in wait for hours at a time before the house doors and caught the women as they entered in order to admonish them. Should one of them be stricken with remorse, the Jesuits gave her shelter in a private dwelling, where lodging attention and a respectable livelihood were offered her. Ignatius himself collected money from rich people, and founded an asylum for fallen women;

in the "Martha House," former prostitutes lived under strict supervision, performed all kinds of work, and were permitted finally to leave the institution only when they had promised to return to the orderly life of a respectable citizen.

The Way to World Domination

Of all the aspects of social activity developed by the Jesuits in these early days, preaching alone, although in a different form, was to maintain in later years its importance for the Society of Jesus; indeed, it was to become one of the bases of the great success of the order.

In Venice, among those Catholics who enthusiastically favored a reform, and had gathered round the Benedictine abbot, Cortese, Ignatius had often heard talk of the horrifying condition of the Church. He had learned how completely secularized the clergy had become, and how they had lost much of their influence over the people.

The bishops lived at great distances from their dioceses, and were represented by paid deputies; the priests regarded their office merely as a sinecure and confined their spiritual activities to taking money for christening infants and performing the marriage and burial services; for the rest, they lived contentedly with their concubines, without troubling in the least about the spiritual welfare of their parish. The churches themselves were in many ways little more than places where people forgathered to talk business or to dally with pretty women; there were towns where the courts of law were held in the cathedral while mass was proceeding, and in other towns the church served as an exchange.

Even the monasteries, apart from a few exceptions, had become haunts of depravity. It was possible for Cardinal Contarini to declare in public that the convents had taken the place of the brothels. The distinguished orders such as the Benedictines, which had remained undefiled by the corruption of morals, lacked all contact with the people. The proud and learned monks led a life of refined culture and meditation, and exerted no kind of influence on the multitude.

In this way, the population was left almost entirely to its own resources, and it lost all respect for ecclesiastical authority. It sank into a scarcely comprehensible ignorance of religious matters; many people knew neither the Lord's Prayer nor the Ten Commandments; in many districts of southern Italy, the greater part of the population had reverted to paganism, and even in towns many half-educated people confused the Christian saints with the ancient gods. Those who were actuated by real piety turned in great numbers more or less openly towards Protestantism.

Of the clergy, the monks of the begging fraternities—the Franciscans, the Dominicans, and the Augustinians—alone maintained a certain contact with the people. They alone spoke to the masses and still preached. But even the members of these orders were not untouched by the general decadence in matters of faith. They often employed the crudest methods in order to direct towards themselves the attention of an indifferent populace, and, with the help of hired accomplices, they staged fraudulent "miraculous healings."

In opposition to this decadence, the Theatines, here too, as in the cases of the sick, set a good example. Cardinal Caraffa, who later became Pope Paul IV, appeared in person in the deserted pulpits of the Roman churches, in order to warn the people of the impending punishment of God.

The work of preaching to the nation, however, became systematic only when Ignatius and his disciples began to take part in it. In twos, they went from Venice to Vicenza, Monfelice, Bassano, Verona and Treviso, and, in the busy squares, they stood on a stone or on a bench, and, by animated gestures that the waving of their hats, they invited those around them to listen to them, and then delivered their sermons unheedful of the loud sneers of the scoffers. This they continued until their fiery rhetoric touched their audiences, and more and more listeners came who desired to confess and communicate.

This activity was extended to Rome. A few months after the small band had reached that city, Loyola's disciples distributed themselves as preachers among the most important churches, some in the center of the city and others in the poorer districts. The public soon flocked to them in ever-increasing numbers, for, according to the instructions issued by Ignatius, "they were to influence the people more by the glow of the spirit and eyes than by well-chosen words," and, consequently, as far as possible, they spoke forcibly, spiritedly and clearly.

At that time, they practiced a sudden and crude attack on the human soul, and sought to move their audiences either by an extravagant description of heavenly happiness or by arousing in them a fear of the punishments of hell. As time went on, however, they slowly began to realize that an enduring conversion could but seldom be attained by such methods. In order to gather together a circle of reliable followers, strong in their faith, they had gradually to abandon the theatrical playing on the emotions of their hearers, and they sought more and more for other means, in addition to preaching, which would give them a lasting guidance of souls.

For this purpose, it seemed to the Jesuits that confession was especially suited. Had it not at all times been one of the strongest means for the chastening of the faithful? It was not only by pious Catholics that confession was regarded as a prescriptive obligation; other religions and cultures had also recognized the extraordinary importance of intimate confession.

"Know ye," Seneca has said, "why we keep our vices secret? Because they are part of us. To acknowledge them, however, is a sure sign of healing." And in the thirty-second Psalm of David, we have: "I acknowledged my sin unto thee, and mine iniquity have I not hid. I said, I will confess my transgressions unto the Lord, and thou forgavest the iniquity of my sin."

The Indian laws of Manu say: "The more sincerely and freely a man confesses his sins, the better is he able to cast them from him, as a snake sloughs its skin." Similar commendations of voluntary confession are to be found among nearly all peoples, among the Peruvians, the Turks, the Tibetans and the Japanese. The great teachers of the Christian Church have given even more prominence to the extraordinary significance of confession; according to the Catholic doctrine, however, it is above all to be regarded as an indispensable preparation for the mystical act of communion.

In this sense, Ignatius in Manresa had also attributed especial importance to confession, for, under the influence of ancient mystical writings, he had striven to receive the communion sacrament as often as possible. Now, however, the idea of the examination of conscience, of the constant and systematic supervision of all the movements of the soul, stood out more and more strongly, for in every *examen conscientiæ* preceding absolution, the penitent was compelled to disclose his whole soul to the father-confessor, and to enumerate his offences against the laws of the Church; in this condition of more or less complete contrition, the father-confessor must appear as an all-powerful judge, endowed with the power to bind or to loose; if this judge then admonished or counselled the penitent, he might well acquire full ascendancy over the penitent's soul.

Therefore, wherever Ignatius and his disciples appeared, they began immediately a lively agitation in favor of confession, and from that time on their eloquence in the pulpit was concentrated on the task of urging as many or their hearers as possible to the confessional.

Ignatius himself set the example. When he preached in the church of Santa Maria della Strada in Rome, he was able, in spite of his defective knowledge of Italian, to so move his audience that, driven by repentance, they hastened in large numbers to the confessional to obtain there forgiveness for their sins.

But as the number of penitents won over the by the Jesuits grew larger and larger, so too grew up in them the knowledge that, though power over the souls of the masses was important, it was still more important to win the mastery of those few men in influential places on whom the fate of nations depended. The real political role of the Jesuits started only from the moment when they began to dominate the consciences of kings and princes. The way to world domination, which had first of all led them from direct charity to organized social-welfare work, now brought them up against new aims, in that the activity of the order was applied more and more to the spiritual guidance of princes, for the order of the Jesuits from now on recognized in the rulers the personification of the whole nation.

Ignatius soon perceived with great distinctness the historical mission of the Society he had created. When it first became the task of Ignatius and his disciples to act as confessors to princes, there was in the beginning some doubt whether the acceptance of such high positions was compatible with their vow of humility. Ignatius, however, soon rid himself of this scruple, and ordered his disciples in no case to decline the office of court confessor. In the year 1553, he wrote to Miron, the provincial of the order at Lisbon: "The public interest and the service of God can only gain by this, for the members participate in the well-being of the head, subjects in the well-being of the prince; therefore spiritual help is in no case so well applied as in this."

In the meantime, they continued with their preaching to the people, but only in those places, as, for example, on their missions, where it served to obtain for the Jesuits entry into a foreign territory and the confidence of the masses. In other countries, where they had already gained a footing, street and popular preaching was later practiced almost wholly for the purpose of training the young novices of the order.

When the Jesuits of Cologne spent too much time on popular missions such activity was only to be recommended as a beginning. Nothing was worse than to pursue trivial successes, and thereby to lose sight of the great tasks; the Jesuits had far higher aims to strive after than the mere conversion of peasants.

These higher aims consisted for the most part in the conquest and enduring guidance of secular and spiritual authorities on whom, in a time of ever stronger absolutism, finally depended every important decision even in matters of faith.

Physical Asceticism and Discipline of the Will

In the new order, there was no longer any place for monkish mortification, which belonged to a past age of religious life. The ascetics of the Middle Ages had endeavored to overcome the flesh by torture and privation, and by such means to free the spirit of all earthly hindrances, but Ignatius desired to create a "host of Christ" for the conquest of the world.

The severe asceticism of the Middle Ages, with its self-castigations and privations, was, moreover, in no wise suited to a military order of warriors eager for battle: the Society of Jesus needed powerful and healthy men, ever ready for any service or any work. Ignatius very soon, therefore, set his face against the mortification of the flesh by castigation which was practiced by Christian fraternities. Of course, Loyola's emancipation from the ascetic ideal did not take place suddenly; during the time he was studying in Paris, he had himself performed many special penances. But, when he perceived the physical injury resulting from self-castigations, he became more and more opposed to such severe exercises. The later version of the *Spiritual Exercises* consequently contains energetic prohibitions of the practice of excessive penances: the exercitant shall neither fast nor scourge himself heavily, for the necessary preparation for spiritual experiences is now the way of the spirit.

Even in the first statutes of the order, of the year 1539, it is stated that the brethren shall not have imposed upon them "fasts, scourgings, walking barefooted or bareheaded, particular colors for their clothes, particular foods, penances, hair shirts or other mortifications under penalty of grievous sin." Moreover, the final *Constitutions* of the society repeatedly emphasize the duty of the Jesuit to look after his body, and by suitable exercises to make it a fitting tool of the spirit.

Loyola's views on asceticism are most clearly expressed in his letter of September 20, 1548, to Duke Francisco Borgia. "As for fasts and abstinence," he says, "I would wish you to maintain your bodily powers in health for the service of our Lord, and to strengthen them instead of weakening them... We must look after the body and keep it healthy inasmuch as it serves the soul and fits it for the service and glorification of the Creator... Instead of weakening the body by excessive mortifications, it is more reasonable to honor God by inward devotions and other discreet exercises. Then will the soul be well and a healthy mind dwell in a healthy body. Without doubt there is more virtue and grace in being able to enjoy your God in various business at various places than at the praying stool..." Thus bodily asceticism gradually sank more and more to a mere discipline of the will; it became a test of strength a preparatory exercise, and lost all importance as an end in itself. Mortification of the body was refined into a mortification of the spirit; from asceticism gradually emerged discipline.

Ignatius and his disciples no longer dwelt in dilapidated and squalid houses. Although they clung to their modest way of living, they now had cleanly covered tables and plentiful meals; they must have had the appearance of "the poorer nobility," never sumptuous, but always orderly and clean. Ignatius was delighted when his guests ate heartily, and he frequently invited to his table a corpulent brother of his order, because the latter enjoyed his meals with such obvious pleasure. He now liked most of all to see happy faces round about him, and he once wrote in his notebook: "I see thee always laughing, my dearest! I am delighted about it, for he whom God has sanctified has no cause to sorrow, but every reason for being happy."

Perhaps nothing can better illustrate the great change in the spirit of the Society of Jesus than the dispute in which Ignatius and Simon Rodriguez, one of the first disciples, were involved.

At a time when they were all engaged in emotional itinerant preaching and self-castigation, Rodriguez had gone to Portugal, and there, at his isolated post, had remained untouched by the great change in the rest of the Society. In Lisbon, he had from the beginning labored at street preaching with the crudest methods, and had sought to move the population by songs of penitence and by nocturnal torchlight processions. In the college he directed at Coimbra, he had evolved a strange form of religious fanaticism, under the influence of which his students practiced the weirdest forms of self-castigation. Once Rodriguez reported to Rome that a young member of the college, in order to humiliate himself, had walked stark naked through the streets of the town, and he could not understand why Ignatius received such reports not only without praise but with ever sharper reproof.

Ignatius had finally to decide to recall Rodriguez from Portugal. The trustworthy Miron was appointed his successor, and he energetically reformed the College of Coimbra. There also senseless castigation was replaced by the spirit of organized discipline.

For Ignatius, with deepening understanding, had grasped that a really homogeneous fighting force, aiming at success under the most difficult internal and external conditions, needed discipline before all. Only in a union of men so trained could those forces be freed which until then had been weakened by mortifications, and which now, rightly directed, were united into a superior, all-compelling power.

But the introduction of such a discipline into the community founded by Ignatius proceeded but slowly and laboriously, for it immediately became apparent how difficult it is to reconcile personal and national differences of temperament and of opinion.

Detailed minutes of the early discussions of the Society of Jesus are in existence, and it is uncommonly interesting to observe by means of these documents how a number of men made the heroic attempt to overcome all their individual interests and desires, in order to submit themselves to an organized discipline. At first, the discussions only too often took the form of a disorderly debate of all with all. To avoid this evil, the companions proposed at first to retire into the wilderness, to seek there enlightenment in penances and fasting; then it was decided that each of them should endeavor to arrive at "a joyful and peaceful mood of composure" by diligent meditation.

It was not until the failure of these attempts to regulate their debates, which still smacked somewhat of romantic mediævalism, that they arrived at that method of discussion which alone seems fitted for modern assemblies: they introduced the principle of the vote and of decision by majority. It was thus finally laid down that the opposition of single members of the order to the decisions of the community were of no validity, and in this way an end was made of all individual eccentricities.

It was in the beginning by no means easy to obtain agreement on the question whether there should be a strict obligation to discipline and obedience in the order, for, at the time when the first disciples had gathered together, there had been no talk of obedience. There was a long debate on this momentous subject, and the grounds for and against the establishment of strict discipline were exhaustively discussed.

At the end of this debate, they all acknowledged that, if the other orders found obedience necessary, the new community, whose members would be scattered over the whole world, needed it still more; and it was finally decided to formulate the duty to obey in the strictest terms.

With the pope's approval of the Society of Jesus, Loyola's life-work was completed. It goes without saying that his disciples called upon him to assume the dignity of generalship of the order, but for a long time he declined to accede to their desire. Only after urgent pressing did he declare himself ready to place himself at the head of the community he had founded.

This hesitation did not arise from affected modesty; the vain, ambitious knight of yore had in the course of years overcome all vestiges of worldly vanity. He lived only for his work, which he had created "for the greater glory of God." Even as general, he strove to retire behind innumerable affairs and duties of the Society of Jesus, until at last he was called for ever from his post by death

Death and the Post for Spain

He passed peacefully away on the night of July 31, 1556. Early on the Friday morning, the brethren of the order hastened to the artist Jacopin del Conte, in order that he might make a portrait of the dead; no picture of him existed, because Ignatius, despite the entreaties of his disciples, had never allowed himself to be painted.

When, during the afternoon, the famous and busy painter was finally found, there remained only a few hours in which to do his work. On the following morning, the body was to be placed in its coffin and buried. The painter stretched his canvas on its frame, and entered the low, narrow room, where Ignatius lay on the bed as he had died. Jacopin had to work swiftly, as the oblique evening light was already entering the room through the small garret window.

He had seen Ignatius several times while he was alive. He now cast his eyes observantly over the thick-set form that stood out stark and rigid on the death-bed. Intensely, he gathered up all the shadows on the immobile face of the dead man, and sought carefully to produce an animate fire behind the lowered eyelids, to impart to the lips, so firmly closed in death, the familiar smile, placid and serene, and to conjure from those rigid limbs, so carefully placed like tools used and put neatly aside, the measured pace of the living man.

When at last the heavy bald head, which lay on the death-bed like a block of stone, slowly took on life, with that gentle nod with which Father Ignatius had so often driven home his utterances, when the stiffness of death had fallen away, and the body stood up and approached in its limping manner, it appeared to the artist for a few moments as if Ignatius lived again; and with the last stroke of the brush made, he stepped back from the canvas to view his work, and he was horrified to find that he had failed. Each detail was correct, and there were no errors to be seen either in coloring or in proportion; nevertheless, there looked down upon him from the easel a strange face, and in vain did he try to bring the forehead, the nose, the eyes, the mouth and the chin into a living and faithful representation.

Full of humble expectation, the sorrowing brothers of the order passed in succession before the painting. They came to admire, but were astonished. Gloom descended over many faces, and, disillusioned, they whispered: "No, that is not our Father."

Often after this pious disciples took their brushes and painted Ignatius, now as a heavenly knight conquering hell, now as a saint, surrounded by angels, ascending into heaven, with a face of radiant light. In increasing numbers, there came into existence pictures intended for the simple devotion of homely minds, and these showed, with numerous variations, the same round, expressionless face in the halo of a saint.

On the commission of rich houses of the order, he was painted by famous masters in ostentatious and magnificent colors, in a solemn attitude, attired in vestments embroidered in gold. Where the halo which now surrounded his head encompassed the beatific countenance of a saint, the resolute features of a knight of the faith, the austerity of a penitent, or the sanctity of a priest, it was a face arbitrarily chosen, fashioned by the artist out of his imagination or his simplicity, or according to the demands of his patron. The real face of the dead man had passed away with him forever.

Pedro Ribadeneira, one of the last of the early disciples, who, during his lifetime had been among those most closely associated with Ignatius, did not wish to depart this life before he had made yet another attempt to leave behind for the order a picture of the true face of its founder, to take the place of the numerous failures. He devoutly preserved in his cell the death-mask which had been made by someone unknown, and from this he decided that Alonso Sanchez Coello, the court painter of King Philip II of Spain, should create a faithful likeness.

Before he began his work, however, Don Alonso piously threw himself down on his knees before his easel, and, with his face raised to Heaven, cried: "Most holy Saint, help me in this work! May it deserve the praise of God and be worthy of you!" And, on each of the many days he worked on the picture, he prayed with the same fervor that he might succeed in his difficult task. Although the king's painter was not a little proud of his ability to reproduce with certainty the characteristics of any face, he felt, in this work, uncertain from the very beginning. If he had not known what a truly pious man Brother Pedro was, his religious nature would have made him feel at times that the whole enterprise was an outrage. While the painter was proceeding with his work, Ribadeneira read one holy mass after another, yet he was not able to rid himself of a feeling of uneasiness.

From morning till evening, they stood before the canvas. The brother kindled with all the burning passion of his devotion to the father, and used his eloquence to the utmost in order to convey to the artist how the face of the father had appeared; he pointed now to this and now to that part of the mask, explained eagerly what the redness of the cheeks, the light

45. IGNATIUS LOYOLA

Painting by Sanchez Coello from the death-mask.

46. THE WORK OF IGNATIUS:

THE ORDER AND ITS ESTABLISHMENTS OVER THE WHOLE WORLD.

Engraving for the Centennial Celebration of the Society of Jesus, 1640.

Death and the Post for Spain

of his eyes and effect of his smile had been like. But neither masses and prayers, nor the art of the court painter, and the tender eagerness of the living eyes. In spite of all their efforts, the portrait bore only a painfully inadequate likeness to the Ignatius whom Ribadeneira had known in life.

Brother Pedro had finally to acknowledge that Ignatius had not without purpose forbidden the disciples to have a portrait made of him, and that this prohibition was in harmony with a higher spiritual law. Now that the endeavors of the court painter had proved fruitless, Ribadeneira remembered a strange thing which had happened some years previously, when the dead man was still alive.

In those days the disciples had tried to outwit the general, and had smuggled the painter Moroni into the house of the order. When Ignatius had laid himself down to rest a little during the afternoon, Moroni, who had all his painting materials ready in the adjoining room, had come forward stealthily on tiptoe to the half-open door, had looked on the sleeper through the opening, and painted him; the portrait, however, had been a miserable failure.

Again and again Moroni had tried, a third, a fourth and a fifth time; yet all his trouble was in vain. Thereupon, he had torn the canvas to pieces and, frightened to death, he had cried out: "I have lost my art! God does not wish that this man, His servant, should be painted."

But not only to the artists did such things happen. Even to those disciples who had for a long time been associated with the father, it seemed, when they now looked back, as if they had not seen his face during later years of their association with him.

They had, of course, faced him day after day, had heard his voice, and looked into his eyes when he had discussed the affairs of the order with them, received their reports, given them their orders or had admonished them. They had met him on those frequent occasions when he limped through the corridors and rooms of the house of the order looking after everything even to the most trivial detail. It seemed to them, however, as if all this, his face, his voice and his look, had vanished some years before his death; for a long time past it had been only the affairs of the order which had bound the general to them: discussions, orders and directions, letters, reports and records, the preparation of documents and the drafting of decisions.

For in all these years he spoke only of rules and directions, and he occupied himself only with matters of administration. No longer was he swayed by passion; no longer was he to be turned aside by either vexation or joy. He was not wanting in love, but it was a temperate love, shared equally by all the brothers of the order, far removed from a profound affection for any particular brother. A higher necessity had for all time taken possession of his personal feelings, and now regulated them in accordance with the interests of the entire community.

His countenance changed from hour to hour. He laughed when it was necessary to laugh, and he let his features become cold in harsh refusal when occasion arose. He was severe or lenient, stubborn or yielding, blunt or courteous, silent or talkative, according as the business of the Society demanded. And the more the order grew, the more its many labors spread to the uttermost corners of the earth, the more did the face of the general withdraw behind the absolutely impersonal administration of these countless interests and affairs. And so finally he had departed from them, almost unobserved, peacefully and in the midst of the many pressing matters connected with the order.

The Power and Secret of the Jesuits

In the professed house at Rome, Thursday had been an especially busy day, for on the following morning the post was due to leave for Spain, and all correspondence for the branches of the order in Spain, Portugal, the East Indies and Japan was being prepared. There were statements of accounts to approve, lists of newly entered and dismissed members to be returned with comments thereon; there were questions to be answered, unintelligible statements to be amplified, new decisions to be issued, inquiries to be ordered; the brothers who were to preach and those who were to be instructors were to be clearly indicated; there were matters concerning the acceptance of converted heathens to be dealt with, and the number of missionaries who were to be sent to the new branch establishments to be determined. Especially difficult letters had to be sent to the kings of Spain and Portugal; in these the effect of each word had to be carefully considered in order that Philip II might command his Flemish bishops to admit the order into the Netherlands, and that John III might assist the mission which had only recently been sent to Abyssinia.

For some days, Ignatius had been in bad health, but he would not on that account lay down his work. In the afternoon, he was still engaged on a long letter, carefully correcting any word that was not altogether well chosen; he had studied some documents and inquired after various details of the correspondence which had not yet been dealt with.

In the middle of his labors, a bitter taste came into this mouth, and he felt that he was now to die. His secretary, Polanco, was called, and he bade him hasten to the Vatican and beg the pope for his blessing, as he was approaching his end.

Polanco was very much concerned over this inopportune commission, which threatened to disturb him in the pressing preparation of the Spanish post. "Do you really feel so bad, Father?" he asked. "Will it not be soon enough in the morning?" And he pointed out that a number of important letters had still to be finished, and that these must at all costs be dispatched on the following morning.

Ignatius understood the justifiable anxiety of his conscientious secretary, and he dismissed him, saying resignedly; "I would rather it were today than tomorrow, yet do as you deem best."

And so it happened that, while it had been possible to dispatch the Spanish mail at the proper time, the founder of the order passed silently away almost unnoticed in the night of Thursday, without the pope's blessing, indeed, without extreme unction.

PART III

THE BATTLE OVER FREE WILL

Grace and Salvation Through Good Works

Ignatius hand down to his disciples as their spiritual inheritance the doctrine of the supreme importance of the human will. By a strange concatenation of events, this theological doctrine was a hundred years after the death of the founder of the order, to lead to one of the most astonishing of political and social controversies. During the reign of *le roi Soleil*, the dispute between the Jesuits and the Jansenists agitated not only the whole Court of Versailles, the king's mistresses, his ministers and courtiers, but also politicians and professors, society ladies and simple nuns, and large sections of the population. All manner of influences became involved in the controversy: persons who had hitherto never given a thought to divine grace and its efficacy suddenly found that they had no other interest in life than to support to the utmost of their power one or other of the parties. This strange dispute even formed the subject of discussion in the salons, and eventually led to an unparalleled spiritual and social disaster: eminent thinkers such as Pascal dedicated their leisure to the controversy, and no less a personage than Voltaire exercised his wit on the vexed topic of "grace."

In the sixteenth century, just as the doctrines preached by Ignatius were beginning to spread abroad, the great Reformation movement inaugurated by Luther and Calvin extended over Europe, and it was not long before Loyola's doctrine of the saving power of the application of the will and of good works became the vital point in the fight between Catholicism and the Protestant innovations. With this in mind, Ignatius had himself, in the appendix to his *Spiritual Exercises*, impressed upon his disciples that, while retaining their reverence for divine grace, they must by no means overlook the importance of the human will, as the heretics had done: "We should not lay so much stress on the doctrine which denies the existence of free will. We should therefore, only speak of faith and grace in such a manner that our teaching may, with the help of God, redound to His greater honor, and, above all in these dangerous times, certainly not in such a way that good works and free will are thought to be of lesser importance, or are even regarded as of no value at all." For the leaders of the Reformation denied most emphatically that human merit and free will were of any moral value; they preached in the most violent terms that he who believed in the possibility of the freedom of the will and of salvation through good works was a sinner, in that he assumed to be superior to the Almighty.

Calvin sharply asserted that Catholicism cast man, "intoxicated with his imaginary power, into destruction," and inflated him "with heathen presumption against his Creator, so that he finally ascribes the credit for his righteousness as much to himself as to God."

The great Protestant divines adhered immovably to the doctrine that the human race was irrevocably doomed to destruction by reason of its original sin, and that the sinner could expect salvation only through divine grace. This view had already been decisively formulated by Luther when he made the statement that man "is not only a sinner but even sin itself"; he is unfree "like a clod, a stone, a piece of clay, or a pillar of salt."

In his famous manifest against Erasmus, *De servo arbitrio*, Luther maintains that divine grace alone accomplishes all things, and the human will nothing; "so that our judgment tells us that, neither in a man nor in an angel, nor in any other created being, can such a thing as free will exist."

On the other hand, Luther holds that salvation can come through faith alone. "Faith is by no means the same as free will . . faith is everything. . . ." As St. Paul taught, faith consists in the knowledge that Christ died to save all men. He alone is saved to whom grace is given to believe steadfastly in the divine mission of the Savior: he who does not believe this "is an infidel, and remains a sinner though he should die in the accomplishment of good works."

While Luther, in words such as the above, tried to point out another way to justification, Calvin had shut the door on even this last chance of delivery from damnation, since he denied all merit not only to good works and good will, but also to faith as such. He had thus carried the doctrine of original sin to its inexorable conclusion. While, according to Luther, all true believers are "justified," no matter who or what they may be, Calvin regards even believers as damned if God wills, "since all is in His power and subject to His will." Before time was, the Creator destined one part of the human race to eternal life, and the remainder to everlasting damnation. The entire universe is subject to the laws of predestination, "that eternal dispensation of God, which prescribes what every human being shall be."

Such a theory must necessarily deny in the most emphatic terms the freedom of man's will, and his ability to contribute to his own moral regeneration and justification. The doctrine of predestination denied to mortal man any possibility of influencing his destiny. Thus Calvin states in his *Institutes of the Christian Religion*: "Inasmuch as the human will is fettered by sin and a slave, it can achieve no manner of good; it is entirely devoid of this power of doing anything of the kind."

In his famous manifesto addressed to Emperor Charles V and the princes of the Holy Roman Empire, the Genevan reformer accuses his Catholic adversaries of being unable, by reason of their faith in the meritoriousness of good will and good works, "to understand how great are the wounds which our human nature has borne since the Fall. With us, they admit the existence of original sin, but minimize its importance by regarding the power of man as merely impaired, and not as totally destroyed.

"We, on the other hand," continues Calvin, "maintain that our nature is so corrupt that it is quite incapable of good. . . We convince man of his wretchedness and of his powerlessness, and thus bring him into a state of true humility, so that he is deprived of all confidence in his own powers and puts his trust in God alone."

In antithesis to this Reformation doctrine, the disciples of Loyola, faithful to the *Exercises* bequeathed to them by their master, upheld in the whole of their theology, philosophy and

Grace and Salvation Through Good Works

moral teachings the complete freedom of the human will and the saving grace of good works.

"The fact that Jesuitism placed free will at the summit," admits Edgar Quinet, "had the result that its doctrines harmonized with contemporary strivings after freedom. . . Luther and Calvin had denied the freedom of the will; Loyola's disciples, pressing through this breach in their opponents' defenses, won over modern men once more precisely because of this feeling for freedom."

The Jesuits, therefore, endeavored to stress, within the Catholic system, the doctrine of the freedom of the will: the liberty to choose between two opposing factors, between action and inaction, between good and evil, between Christ and Lucifer. According a man, with full freedom of choice, made his decision, so would he attain to the Kingdom of Heaven or be cast into hell.

Those men who had been educated in the scholastic spirit were, at the opening of the new era, familiar with only one method of scientific proof, that of quoting from as many as possible of the recognized authorities of the past. If they were able to support a thesis with a formidable array of such quotations, drawn wherever possible from the Bible or the writings of the fathers of the Church, their theories were at that period firmly believed to be established beyond all possibility of doubt. The idea which is so familiar to us, that an experiment or a new theory may prove the error of beliefs that have been held for centuries, was quite unknown to that age. For this reason, in the great controversy over free will, both parties endeavored to support their case by citing the largest possible number of statement by earlier authorities which were in favor of their views.

Those who championed the cause of predestination relied chiefly on the Biblical narrative of the betrayal of Peter and on the commentaries thereon of Chrysostom and Augustine. Chrysostom had declared that Peter had denied his Lord "through lack of grace" and had fallen only "because God had forsaken him." Augustine had further stated that God had deprived Peter of grace "in order to prove that man can do nothing without grace."

But many other passages in the Scriptures seem to support the doctrine of predestination. Does not the Bible contain many passages stating that we are all lost sinners, and that man has no hope save in the pardoning mercy of God?

These views were also supported by the words of the Apostle Paul, who had taught that man was not justified by his works but by his faith. "So then it is not of him that willeth, nor of him that runneth, but of God that sheweth mercy." (Romans ix, 16.)

The strongest evidence in support of this doctrine was, of course, derived from the writings of that father of the Church, Augustine, who was regarded as an authority second in importance only to the Holy Scriptures themselves. The reformers claimed that he had definitely taught the doctrine of predestination; and that, for Augustine, Adam alone had possessed liberty not to sin, while, owing to the fall of the father of the human race, all his descendants had been brought into the hopeless bondage of sin. This state of corruption could not be remedied by good works, no matter what their merit, and God Himself alone was able to restore the purity of man's original nature; for this purpose He had sent His Son, Christ, into the world, and suffered Him to die upon the cross for our redemption.

Similar support was claimed from the writing of Thomas Aquinas, the greatest of all the scholastics: it was argued that he also had admitted that grace was given by God regardless of the merits and good will of man himself. It was asserted that Aquinas held the view that it had been preordained from all time that in the Kingdom of Heaven the higher places had been set apart for the elect, and the lower for the reprobate, and that God had, before the world was created, decided the exact fate of every man.

Such arguments in favor of predestination might be regarded as overwhelming, but there was an equal wealth of arguments at the disposal of those who maintained contrary views; and, strange as it may seem, the champions of free will and of salvation through works relied upon exactly the same teachers and writings as their opponents.

They claimed that their view that man is free from any kind on inner compulsion is manifest chiefly from Holy Writ, which contained passages such as: "unto Him be everlasting glory: though tempted to sin yet sinned he not: evil might he have done, yet he did no wrong." Jeremiah had definitely proclaimed: "Behold, I set before you the way of life, and the way of death." (Jeremiah, xxi, 8.) Moreover, a close study of the New Testament revealed many passages which seemed to refer distinctly to the freedom of man's will and the meritoriousness of good works. (Romans ii, 7.)

As for the early fathers, it was again St. Chrysostom especially, whose dicta were freely quoted by the protagonists of free will. They even found support for their contention in the writings of Augustine, for he had once stated that "every man has freedom to choose either that which is good, and to be a good tree, or that which is evil, and be an evil tree." In his writings against the belief in astrology, the Bishop of Hippo had definitely stated: "God has created me with freedom of choice; if I sin, it is I who am guilty."

Like the determinists, their opponents quoted freely from the doctrines of Thomas Aquinas in support of their case. The latter had taught that the human will was not necessarily compelled to follow any specific course of action, but that man was much more free "to decide what was good according to the dictates of his reason"; if this were not so, "advice admonition, commandments, prohibitions, rewards and punishments would be futile."

Perplexities from Stagira to Trent

It may appear somewhat strange that those who upheld two diametrically opposed views were able to bring forward, in support of their respective cases, incisive quotations from the same sources. The explanation of this surprising circumstance is to be found in the fact that a problem was involved which had always been accompanied by the most profound uncertainty and perplexity.

The question at issue touches on one of the greatest difficulties of religious thought. On the one hand, man's fundamental moral feelings demand the recognition of the freedom of his will, for this would seem to be an essential premise in any attempt to evaluate the ethical significance of human actions. On the other hand, it is almost impossible to reconcile the idea of free will with the belief in an omnipotent and omniscient creator and ruler of the universe. Either man is a free agent, in which case God is not omnipotent, or else God's will governs all creation, even to the slightest emotion in the human soul, or to the falling of a withered leaf, in which case it would seem that there can be no question of any human freedom of action.

This acute antithesis in the conception of the value or lack or it of the will and of good works could not for long remain confined to the struggle between Catholicism and the Reformation movement: the Catholic Church itself soon became divided into two hostile camps, and was thus involved in a protracted and violent controversy. It was merely necessary to ascribe somewhat more importance to grace for the Calvinistic doctrine of predestination to be reached: if, on the other hand, a little too much stress was laid on the question of free will, the consequence would be that denial of divine omnipotence which was the heresy of the Pelagians. For why should it have been necessary for Christ to die for our salvation, if it were within the power of every man, of his own volition and by his own good works, to make atonement for his sins and to achieve his own salvation? Hence, according to the true Catholic faith, there was on either side a danger of falling into mortal sin, and there was great need to be careful to keep to the middle path of safety.

This insoluble question was not one that perplexed Christendom alone, for, as far back as we can trace the history of the human mind, we find a blind groping, an astounding lack of precision whenever this weighty, fundamental question arose. In the writings of the Hebrew prophets, who generally maintain in a most unambiguous manner that man is a free agent, there are passages (Jer. xxxi, 32; Is. vi, 7; Ezek. ii, 19) which cannot be reconciled with the rest, and which render obscure the otherwise definite statements concerning man's freedom.

Even the great philosophers of antiquity, acute and clear as they were in solving other spiritual problems, fail to help us in this particular matter. Neither Plato nor Aristotle was able to furnish a satisfactory reply to the question of the relationship between the human will and divine omnipotence.

Hence, down to our own time, efforts have again and again been made to claim Aristotle as a protagonist of determinism, although the sage of Stagira has always been regarded as the classical exponent of the doctrine of free will. Even in his writings may be found contradictory statements which are susceptible of varying interpretations.

Both Plato and Aristotle endeavor to make a distinction between those actions which are free and those which must be regarded as unmistakably preordained. Plato regarded freedom of will as clearly a question of reason, and thus arrived at the conclusion that the man who was guided by reason was to be regarded as free and that he who, on the contrary, was controlled by his desires, was not free. Accordingly, he considered that only by the victory of reason over desire could man free himself from his bonds.

In the third book of his *Nicomachean Ethics*, Aristotle controverts this theory of Plato's by pointing out that the yielding to a desire involves an act of free volition: he regards as involuntary actions only those done by man under compulsion or unconsciously. But he regards as voluntary all those acts of which the impulse to do then originates in ourselves and which, therefore, may be done or left undone. In the mastery over our deeds and desires, in the freedom of volition in regard to whether we do something or leave it undone, Aristotle finds the ground for praise or blame, reward or punishment: it is thus within our power to be good or bad.

The Power and Secret of the Jesuits

These considerations, however, leave unsettled the point how human freedom of action is compatible with fate and a predetermined cosmic order. The Neo-Platonic school, therefore, tried to solve this contradiction by assuming a divine "pre-knowledge," according to which the Creator had from the beginning of things the faculty of knowing the future free decisions of men, and of ordering the world in this sense.

It was, however, inevitable that compromises of this nature should result in an unedifying confusion of ideas, and should lead to the age-long, abstruse controversies of the theologians. When, therefore, the Christian theories of "original sin" and "grace" were grafted onto a problem already more than sufficiently involved in its nature, a state of absolute chaos arose.

When, in the seventeenth century, this dispute over the question of grace had reached its climax, Voltaire wrote with as much pungency and malice that the question had finally "led to the labyrinth of fatalism and freedom in which the ancients had themselves wandered aimlessly, and in which humanity has scarcely any means of guidance. But, while the ancient philosophers always carried on their controversies in a peaceful manner, the disputes of the theologians are often bloody and always noisy."

These theological disputes had begun as early as the fifth century of the Christian era, for even in those primitive times it had not been possible to arrive at agreement on the question of the extent to which salvation could be achieved by grace or by human merit. The Briton, Pelagius, was the first who, in opposition to the teachings of Augustine, had flatly denounced the theory of damnation through original sin. He argued that there was a "possibility" of will—in other words, human freedom—by which man could at any time discriminate between good and evil. Pelagius and his followers taught that all mortals were born devoid alike of virtue and of sin; God had given man only the aptitude, the ability to will or not to will; the action itself was man's very own, and it proceeded solely from his own free will.

The Pelagian doctrines caused no small stir in the contemporary Christian world, and their most violent opponent was Augustine himself. In his polemical treatise, *De gratia contra Pelagium*, he upheld the importance of divine grace as a necessary assistance, and disputed the value of human will and deed without such aid; he branded the Pelagian views as absolutely contrary to the true spirit of the Christian faith.

This great controversy was eventually brought before the Council of Ephesus, where it was decided against Pelagius; his doctrines were condemned as heretical, and he himself was excommunicated. But, immediately afterwards, arose the first Christian compromise in the form of the doctrine later known under the name of "Semi-Pelagianism." This represented an attempt to bridge over the differences between the doctrines of Pelagius and of Augustine.

Augustine offered determined opposition also to the teachings of these Semi-Pelagians, and his last theses, *De praedestinatione Sanctorum*, and *De dono perseverantiae*, were aimed particularly at Semi-Pelagianism and its chief exponent, Cassianus.

The victory of the Augustinian doctrine over Pelagianism firmly established the trend of Christian thought for more than a thousand years. Nearly all the great teachers of scholasticism, the Protestant reformers and, finally, in the seventeenth century, the Jansenists, were inspired by the teaching of Augustine.

Perplexeties from Stagira to Trent

Nevertheless, traces of the prohibited Pelagian doctrines continued to survive, and not infrequently did it occur that efforts were made by mediaeval philosophers and theologians to attribute greater merit in the doctrine of salvation to the human will and to good works. This endeavor is most clearly discernible in the writings of the great scholastic, Duma Scotus. Only once, and then it was the achievement of a great poet, was the contradiction between these two fundamental views of Christian theology bridged over—at least in appearance. By means of an artistic play on words, Dante, in the sixteenth canto of his "Purgatory," was able to establish a satisfactory relationship between grace and merit; he assumed that man's actions and divine power so react upon one another that the possession of grace presupposes that of merit and vice versa, and thus man finally achieves his salvation and eternal bliss as much by his own efforts as by divine grace.

> Ye who live now the cause of all assign
>   To heaven above as though necessity
>   Moved all with it along predestined lines;
>
> If this were so then in your deeds would lie
>   Free will destroyed and 'twere unjust to give
>   Joy for good deeds, for evil, misery.
>
> Ye from the heavens your impulse first receive—
>   I say not all—but granting that I say
>   Light too is given, or well or ill to live.
>
> And free volition, which, although it stay,
>   Faint in first flight, with those star destinies,
>   Conquers as last, if trained in wisdom's way.
>
> Ye to a better nature, Might more wise,
>   Though free, are subject; and that makes in you
>   The mind which is not subject to the skies.

After the genius of a poet had thus produced what appeared to be a satisfactory synthesis, the Christian world once more lost the unity between predestination and salvation through good works; from then onwards, grace and human endeavor were again irreconcilably opposed.

Since no other poet arose, like Dante, to declare that grace and human merit all formed part of one harmonious whole, controversies and increasingly more violent feuds broke out. When at last, in the early days of the Renaissance, the cardinals, bishops and leading theologians of the Catholic Church assembled at Trent to give a decision on this difficult question, they were unable, despite unending discussions, to arrive at a satisfactory reconciliation of the opposing schools of thought. Even though the Council of Trent, having regard to the teachings of the reformers, was forced to condemn as heretical the complete denial of free will, it was, on the other hand, by no means in a position to approve a doctrine which was in harmony with that which had long ago been anathematized as heretical when propounded by Pelagius.

The Power and Secret of the Jesuits

Accordingly, at the sixth session of the Council of Trent, an extremely cautious, complicated and ambiguously worded decision was adopted. The first part laid down, with apparent excessive clarity: "Whoever states that, since Adam's sin, the free will of man has been lost and no more exists, let him be excommunicate—*anathema sit!*"

Following upon this clause, however, it is laid down that man, despite his freedom of will, despite his good intentions and good works, can never be justified of himself alone, since original sin prevents this. Complicated theological reasons were therefore invented to reconcile these contradictory theses, it being laid down that man, through the death of Christ, had become justified and had received the gift of grace through no merit of his own: with this gift of grace he also became subject to the influence of the Holy Ghost, and, if he obeyed the Holy Ghost, he was enabled, through the aid of divine grace, to justify himself by good works.

Although this decision of the Tridentine Council was elevated to a dogma, and was endowed with infallibility, it was nevertheless a mere compromise. It is somewhat significant that, immediately after its adoption by the council, the great controversy between the advocates of both views broke out in the Catholic Church itself, a controversy which, if possible, exceeded in violence and obstinacy the earlier quarrels between Augustine and Pelagius.

The Pope's Comma

This great squabble really arose out of the excessive zeal and the exaggerated pedantry of a learned professor. Doctor Michael Baius, the leading theologian at the ancient and famous University of Louvain, had undertaken the task of refuting the Calvinistic heresies by means of a fundamentally scientific thesis. He accordingly made an exhaustive study of the early fathers, in order to strengthen in the most effective manner the Catholic view of the freedom of the will.

But good Father Baius was rather too scientific, for he studied the fathers, and more particularly Augustine, so long that, without being aware of it himself, his views gradually changed until they were Calvinistic rather than Catholic. Instead of defending free will, as he had intended at the outset, he ended by proclaiming predestination and the lack of freedom of the will.

Scarcely had the Louvain professor's book appeared when a number of learned monks of the Dominican order fell upon him and denounced him to the papal Curia. Rome at once pronounced as erroneous seventy-three of Baius's propositions which were contrary to the doctrine of free will. When the former general of the Dominican order himself became pope, he issued in 1567 a bull of condemnation in form against "heretical and dangerous principles" such as Baius had advanced.

Baius's fellow-professors at Louvain were greatly incensed by this bull of condemnation launched against one of their colleagues. The papal bull was regarded as a slur on the whole of the university, until suddenly, after making a close study of the document received from Rome, one of the professors made a saving discovery. One of the most vital clauses in the bull was, in the absence of a comma, quite ambiguous, the meaning differing according to the

47. SESSION OF THE COUNCIL OF TRENT

Copperplate engraving from the Speculum Romanae Magnificentiae of Lofreri.

48. CARDINAL BELLARMINE:

The Famous Jesuit Controversialist

49. LUIS MOLINA:

The Originator of Molinism

The Pope's Comma

position of this comma. In the first case, it could be taken as implying that the views in question were open to discussion in Baius's sense; in the second, they were to be regarded as heretical in Baius's sense. A great discussion then arose over this comma, the which, the whole university listened with bated breath.

In his spirited study, *Dogma and Compulsory Doctrine*, the psychoanalyst, Theodor Reik, has commented on the fact that all religious controversies tend to become concentrated on apparently unimportant details, but that these are debated in an all the more heated manner. This "relegation to trifles," which Reik demonstrates in detail in connection with the Arian controversy of the fourth century, became clearly evident in the case of Doctor Baius: the dispute whether man's will was free or not now turned on a comma in the papal bull.

Finally, the Louvain professors communicated with Rome, and asked with all due reverence to be informed of the position in which the Holy Father desired the comma to be inserted. The pope, however, deemed it expedient not to give a definite reply, his only answer to the professors taking the form of a copy of the bull containing not a single comma.

Since, therefore, no one knew what opinion was held by the Holy See itself, both parties were enabled to argue to their hearts' content over the question of free will. This was the moment in which the Jesuits, as professed advocates of the doctrine of free will, decided, with their disciplined spiritual organization, to enter the lists in defense of the cause. When the excitement in Louvain over the "comma-less bull" had somewhat subsided, Doctor Baius remained immune from attack until the Jesuits succeeded in obtaining for their order a theological chair of their own in Louvain. As its first occupant, they appointed Roberto Bellarmine, one of the most gifted and learned scholars among the younger members of the order.

As a Jesuit, Bellarmine had long since learned to handle external matters with caution and diplomatic skill. He therefore held his peace of a long time, and silently collected his damning evidence. Then, in the years 1570 to 1576, he delivered a series of lectures, in which he violently attacked his colleague Baius, appearing in a very skillful manner to adhere to the doctrine of grace while in reality he almost entirely eliminated it from his system. Grace, he admitted in his lectures, was certainly necessary in order that man might acquire merit through its aid, but grace in itself alone was ineffective, unless man did not resist its promptings but rather collaborated with it.

Bellarmine dealt in a particularly subtle manner with the fine distinctions between *gratia efficax* ("effective grace") and *gratia sufficiens* ("sufficient grace"), thereby rendering the problem, already a somewhat complicated one, completely involved and obscure.

In discriminating between these two kinds of grace, Bellarmine held that God by *gratia efficax* called man in such a way that he could foresee that man would obey him, whereas *gratia sufficiens* was given to mortal man in a measure which was not calculated to move him to harmony and collaboration with the divine purpose.

But despite the emphatic manner in which Bellarmine defended the cause of free will against the whole world, he was too good a diplomat ever to expose himself to criticism in regard to this delicate question. Other members of the Jesuit order were less cautious, and, impelled by their devoted zeal, became hopelessly involved in the most hazardous of controversies.

The Power and Secret of the Jesuits

The Uproar Among the Theologians

Luis Molina, the Jesuit professor at the University of Evora in Portugal, had for a long time past been engaged on the compilation of his monumental work, a commentary on certain precepts of Thomas Aquinas. Molina's voluminous tome was entitled *Concordia liberi arbitrii cum gratiae donis*, and in it the author tried to bring together all that his predecessors, Bellarmine and other theologians, had thought out on the relation between grace and free will.

Such was the difficulty of the problem that Molina's solution also could not but lack illuminating clarity. He taught that man could, through his natural powers, combined with a "general divine co-operation," attain to a knowledge of the Christian mysteries, in which case God would grant him that grace of faith which was essential for his salvation. This grace was at the free disposal of all, and whether it was effectively granted depended chiefly on the free will of the person called. Divine help was necessary to give an impulse to the act of volition; but once this impulse was given, it was a matter for man himself to decide whether or not he would accept of heavenly grace.

As though this theory were not already sufficiently complicated, Molina assumes God to possess a "middle pre-knowledge," a *scientia media*, by means of which the Creator is able at any time to foresee what will be the conduct of the man to whom grace is given. This *scientia media* embraces all objects which are neither possible alone nor actual alone, but which are both possible and actual. "They are merely possible in the sense that they may, but never will, take effect, and they are actual in the sense that they would exist if certain circumstances held good."

According to Molina, God foresees from all eternity with these "middle knowledge" how man will act in every conceivable combination of circumstances, and solely on the basis of this foreknowledge He decides how His gift of grace is to be distributed among men. Effective grace, *gratia efficax*, is that which God foresees will inevitably be accepted; sufficient grace, *gratia sufficiens*, is certainly adequate in itself to ensure salvation, but God foresees that those to whom it is granted will reject it.

The most important point in this system of "Molinism" was the assumption that man is, through his will, enabled constantly to resist grace, so that it depends on him whether it is effective or not. This had a suspiciously Pelagian flavor, for whoever postulated the human will as a decisive factor at once belittled the importance of original sin and of grace, and even expressed a doubt of the divine omnipotence. Even the Jesuit theologians, therefore, who were the most deeply convinced of the freedom of human will, were somewhat perturbed when Molina's book appeared.

All the prominent theologians in the order, Bellarmine equally with Suarez, Valentia and the rest, were of the unanimous opinion that Molina had gone a little too far, and the Evora professor encountered immediate resistance in his own order. Nevertheless, the violent attacks of the Dominicans upon Evora compelled the Jesuits for purposes of solidarity, to take the part of their own member.

Ever since the great Dominican, Thomas Aquinas, had become the unquestioned leader

The Uproar Among the Theologians

among the scholastics, the members of this order had regarded themselves as the sole authorities in all theological questions. They proudly pointed to the great number of eminent divines among their fraternity, and were by no means pleased when members of other religious brotherhoods contested their superiority in this respect.

The Spanish Dominicans, therefore, fell upon the Jesuit professor with implacable animosity. The length to which this enmity was soon carried is clearly seen from a letter addressed by Cardinal de Castro to Pope Clement VIII: "In their public speeches and lectures, the Dominicans denounce Molina's book as erroneous, and they warn people to beware of those who hold his doctrines, for the latter are heretical. . . . The two parties are fighting their case before the Inquisition tribunal and before the nuncio: the Jesuits are thus endeavoring to secure a declaration that their views are orthodox, and to have those of their opponents condemned as incompatible with the doctrine of free will. . All manner of persons are involved in this dispute, learned and unlearned men, partisans of the Jesuits as well as those of their adversaries. . . ."

The Curia saw that matters could no longer be allowed to take their course, and both parties were enjoined to suspend the debate, as the pope reserved the right to give the decision himself.

From that time onwards, Rome became the center of the most desperate intrigues for and against Molinism. The pope wavered helplessly and irresolutely between the various petitions and memoranda which were showered upon him, arrived at decisions on one day and rescinded them on the next; at one moment he ordered Molina's book to be burned, and then, on the intervention of Acquaviva, the general of the Jesuit order, he strictly prohibited the prosecution of the proceedings against Molina.

The whole matter had long become merely one of prestige, and for this reason the dispute had become embittered. The Jesuits realized that the Dominicans sought to rob them of their reputation as scholars, and defended themselves desperately against their envenomed antagonists. They exerted all the influence at their disposal, issued appeals to their patrons, and persuaded Philip III, the new king of Spain, as well as the Empress Maria of Austria and Archduke Albert to intercede with the pope on behalf of Molina's *Concordia*. The universities which were under Jesuit influence—Ingolstadt, Graz, Dillingen, Würzburg, Mainz, Treves and Vienna—had to publish learned theses in favor of Molinism; as a counterblast, their opponents issued twenty-two treatises by universities, bishops and eminent theologians condemning Molina's views as heretical.

In 1598, there was delivered in Rome a huge wooden coffer containing the whole of the documents which had been submitted to the Spanish Inquisition in the form of reports, judgments, expert opinions, and similar material. A committee specially appointed by the pope made a detailed examination of these papers, and finally issued judgment condemning Molina. This by no means satisfied the pope, who annulled the whole of the proceedings and gave orders for a fresh investigation to be held. After a further eight months, a second adverse verdict was given against the *Concordia*, and once more the pope did not dare publicly to repudiate the Jesuits.

Finally, Clement VIII was seized with such a passion for the whole case that he spent night after night in perusing the records, and, so that he might be able to decide the matter rightly, he personally made an exhaustive study of the writings of the early fathers. But when, in due course, the vast mass of expert opinions and documents which had been prepared were brought to his room, the Holy Father was considerably startled, and despairingly asked if he were really expected to read all that.

A new method was then tried: the whole dispute was to be settled by means of oral proceedings in the presence of the pope. In 1602, the celebrated *Congregationes de auxiliis* began their activities, and by the end of the following year had held sixty-eight meetings. A diligent comparison was made between the doctrines of Augustine and of Molina, and then the alleged points of resemblance between the *Concordia* and the writings of the Semi-Pelagian Cassianus were thoroughly scrutinized. The matter gave rise to endless debates; Clement VIII himself wrote a number of reports, but he died before a decision was reached by the *Congregationes de auxiliis*.

Cardinal Borghese ascended the papal throne as Paul V. The meetings of the congregations lasted for a further two years, until finally a verdict was issued condemning Molinism. The pope had had a bull of anathema prepared, and the Dominicans were jubilant over their final victory, when an unexpected political incident saved the Jesuits.

The Curia had become involved in a serious dispute with the Venetian Republic, and the Jesuits so zealously espoused the Roman cause that the pope could not bring himself to offend an order which had rendered such faithful service to him. He therefore rescinded the bull which had already been prepared for his signature, dissolved the congregations, and ordered both parties to let the whole matter rest.

Thus after a continuous controversy lasting eighteen years, this dispute over grace terminated without any definite decision. Both orders were enjoined to instruct their members strictly to abstain from any discussion of the question of Molinism, and peacefully to await a final decision by the Holy See: this final decision, however, has not been issued up to the present.

The Jesuits, however, celebrated in Spain the indecisive termination of the Molinist controversy as a great victory for the doctrine of free will. In order to enable the lower classes to appreciate the meaning of this victory, they had huge notices displayed in the streets with the inscription *Molina Victor*, and, at Villagarcia, in celebration of the official verdict in favor of free will, they held a magnificent bullfight, while other Spanish Jesuit communities, in honor of the *Concordia liberi arbitrii cum gratiae donis*, gave magnificent *bals masqués* and fireworks displays that aroused the enthusiasm of the entire population.

Grace in the Salons

With these bullfights, *bals masques* and fireworks displays, there began a new era in the controversy over free will: from this time onwards, the problem ceased to be one which concerned only the chancelleries of cardinals and ecclesiastical councils, the subject of records and reports which were as dry as they were learned: it became a topic of everyday life. The dispute over the importance of divine grace continue its mad career especially in fashionable châteaux and literary solons, and was pursued by elegant aristocrats, society beauties and cou-

50. BISHOP CORNELIUS JANSEN   51. DU VERGIER DE HAURANNE
                                  ABBOT OF SAINT-CYRAN

THE FOUNDERS OF JANSENISM

52. PORT ROYAL DES CHAMPS

53. PORT ROYAL DE PARIS

riers, and by abbés and confessors, some of them good-humored and some malicious.

Curiously enough, the second stage of this controversy, remarkable as it was for its ever-changing, variegated and mentally stimulating phases, again began with the exaggerated pedantry of a Louvain professor, who had even less reason than his predecessor, Baius, to anticipate that his exhaustive investigations would lead to so heated a controversy. Cornelius Jansen, a Louvain professor, and subsequently Bishop of Ypres, had for twenty years diligently studied the works of Augustine, and had then written a ponderous tome entitles *Augustinus*, or *The Doctrines of St. Augustine regarding the Health, Sickness and Medicine of the Soul.*

In this work, Jansen reiterated the already familiar conviction that man had, by reason of Adam's fall, lost the freedom he enjoyed in paradise, that he had in every respect become evil and corrupt, and could never through his own efforts attain salvation. He was totally unable to love God with a pure heart, and was constantly under the influence of his sinful lusts, so that all his works, inward and outward, were devoid of merit. Only divine grace could release the human will from its entanglement of carnal desires, and bring about man's conversion to that state of true purity and bliss which was acceptable to God: he to whom God granted the gift of grace was saved, and he to whom it was not given remained for ever caught in original sin.

The good Bishop of Ypres was by nature anything but a religious fanatic or even a militant reformer: during the whole of his life he performed, to the satisfaction of everyone, the duties assigned to him, and gave no cause for complaint. He died at peace with all the world, before his great work *Augustinus* was published.

That this book became the storm-center of an unprecedentedly violent religious and political controversy was due to the activities of an ecclesiastic who was a close friend of Jansen—Jean du Vergier de Hauranne, later Abbot of Saint-Cyran—and regarded it as a debt of honor to publish the great book of the late bishop and to disseminate the ideas it contained.

The abbot had influential friends in the highest social circles in Paris, and his enthusiasm quickly aroused in fashionable salons a lively interest in the problem of grace. Very soon, in addition to fashionable interest in this problem, other personal and political influences became involved, and so it was that the dispute over the learned work of the deceased Bishop Jansen suddenly developed into one of the most important matters affecting the French court and state.

"It would certainly seem," wrote Voltaire, "that there was no particular advantage in believing with Jansen that God makes impossible demands on humanity: this is neither a philosophic nor a comforting doctrine. But the secret satisfaction of belonging to some kind of party, the hatred of the Jesuits, the desire for notoriety, and the general mental unrest—all these factors soon resulted in the formation of a sect."

The principal cause of the further spread of the movement was the strange state of affairs at the celebrated Abbey of Port Royal, near Paris. Up to the beginning of the seventeenth century, life in this nunnery, as was customary at that time, and been both cheerful and secular. At carnival times, innumerable *bals masques* had been given, in which the gaily dressed nuns had taken part in a most high-spirited manner.

Things had come to such a pass at port Royal that no particular comment, much less anything in the nature of a scandal, was caused by the fact that in 1602, the leading advocate of the supreme court, Antoine Arnauld, obtained from the king the appointment of his eleven-year-old daughter, Marie Angélique, as abbess of the convent. The young abbess, like the other nuns, lived a gay and worldly life. A band of young gentlemen paid regular visits to Port Royal; there were excursions and parties, and in their leisure hours the nuns read fashionable novels instead of their breviaries.

All this came to an unexpected end when, a few years later, a Capuchin monk called Basilius visited Port Royal. He also had once been of a very worldly disposition, and had been expelled from his monastery for bad conduct; afterwards he had led a roving existence, and, when occasionally he was suddenly overcome by a fit of pious repentance, he would enter the pulpit, and, with the most convincing intimacy, describe the joys of an unworldly life.

The Abbess Angélique, who had reached the age of sixteen regarded it as her duty to invite the visitor to preach, and, as chance would have it that Basilius was just then in the throes of one of his attacks of abject penitence, his edifying sermon had an overwhelming effect on the inmates of the nunnery. Angélique resolved wholly to amend her mode of life; she immediately hastened to her cell, stripped off all her fine linen, and put on coarsely made undergarments in token of her penitence. From that time onwards, she slept on a rough straw palliasse, and caused her nuns to do the same.

So that it should be quite clear what sort of change had taken place in the inmates of Port Royal, Angélique shortly afterwards had the convent surrounded by a stout wall, which shut off all communication with the outside world. She herself refused her own family admittance to the abbey, and spoke to her relatives only through a small grille in the door.

This conversion coincided with the change in the trend of thought in Parisian society, so that the convent soon gained high esteem in fashionable circles. Many young girls, including Angélique's sister Catherine Agnès Arnauld, joined the community, and, when Angélique decided, having regard to the unhealthful and marshy surroundings of Port Royal, to transfer the community to Paris, she had no difficulty in raising the funds necessary for the building of a fine town house. This was the origin of the sister-abbey of Port Royal de Paris.

The nuns of Port Royal attracted the attention of such great French ecclesiastics as Cardinal Bérulle and Vincent de Paul, while Francis of Sales admitted that he had a "divine love" for Abbes Angélique. The removal of the community to Paris also added to the esteem in which the nuns were held in social circles, and many of the most distinguished men and women of that period became their closest adherents.

Meanwhile, however, the deserted Abbey of Port Royal des Champs had become the home of an extraordinary community of learned laymen. Famous statesmen, lawyers, theologians and philosophers, who were under the influence of the Abbot of Saint-Cyran, resolved at his instigation to relinquish their worldly careers, and, in imitation of the anchorites, to settle in the marshes which surrounded the deserted abbey. The first of these was the privy councilor and supreme-court advocate, Antoine Lemaistre, who decided to desert partisan society for the solitude of Port Royal. He was a grandson of the other great advocate, Antoine Arnauld, and hence a nephew of Abbess Angélique. At the early age of twenty, his rhetorical talents had already attracted much attention, and he had speedily become one of the most famous legal orators in Paris. At the age of thirty, however, he suddenly began to find

Grace in the Salons

his fame distasteful, and he became weary of hearing himself praised on all sides. Just at this time, he made the acquaintance of the Abbé du Vergier de Hauranne, and shortly afterwards it so happened that, during a speech which he was making in the Parlement, his gaze became fixed on a dusty crucifix which was hanging in front of him.

"M. Lemaistre is asleep instead of pleading," remarked Advocate-General Talon, causing all present to titter. This was a turning-point in the life of Lemaistre. He resolved to abandon his career, and to devote his remaining days to prayer and penitence. He therefore withdrew to the deserted valley of Port Royal, and settled down in one of the half-ruined buildings of the abbey. His brother de Sacy soon followed his example and they were joined by the brothers of abbess Angélique, Robert and Antoine Arnauld.

More and more members of the Arnauld family retired to Port Royal, until finally sixteen of them had assembled there. They were joined by other distinguished persons, including such members of the aristocracy as the Duc de Luynes, and the Baron de Pontchâteau, learned men and devout ecclesiastics such as Nicole, Tillemont, Hamon, and Singlin.

All these men had formerly occupied comfortable and highly esteemed social positions, and were members of distinguished and wealthy families. Like Lemaistre, all of them had been impelled to settle at Port Royal by a sudden feeling of revulsion against their former lives. This was in almost every case due to the instigation of the Abbot of Saint-Cyran, the fascination of whose personality was felt to the same extraordinary extent both by the nuns and by the settlers.

Their first concern was to drain the valley by digging ditches, raise the floor of the church in order to preserve it against damp, set the orchards in order, to extirpate the numerous snakes, and thereby to enable the pious nuns to return to the valley of Port Royal.

For the rest, they led a romantically severe life of penance: even during the coldest winter they scorned to warm their rooms: in front of every door there lay a heavy block of wood, and, when one of the inmates found the cold too severe, he took his block on his back and ran to the top of the nearest hill and returned comfortably warmed. They wore the coarse dress of peasants, and from early morning till late at night they carried about with them spades or scythes.

They devoted a considerable portion of their leisure to theological studies. They read and translated the Scriptures and the early fathers, and wrote learned treaties on apologetics. At a later date, these hermits founded their famous *petites écoles*, those educational establishments for boys and girls which were soon to acquire considerable importance.

This idyllic "Thebaid three miles from Versailles" was, however, to last only until the marshes were drained, and the nuns returned. Not till then did the true "Port Royal spirit" manifest itself, for then there began that great fight against the Jesuits and their doctrine of free will which has become famous in intellectual history as the "Jansenist controversy." In order to make room for the pious nuns, the "Gentlemen of Port Royal" migrated to a neighboring farmhouse and to some barns which had been built there. A lively spiritual intercourse grew up between the nuns and the members of the colony, and the fateful discussions of grace and free will began.

These "edifying conversations," however, only attained their fullest importance through the interest of the ladies belonging to the highest social circles in Paris, in whose elegant salons it suddenly became fashionable to discuss the Augustinian doctrines and original sin. From that time onwards, the Jansenist party numbered amongst its adherents the famous clique which included the Duchesse de Longueville, the Princesse de Guéménée, Madame de Pontcarré, the Marquise d'Aumont, the Marquise de Sablé, and the celebrated Madame de Sévigné: the Marquise de Sablé even had a special room fitted up for her devotional exercises at the Convent of Port Royal.

In the eyes of these ladies, the abbey, which could be reached only be coach, over bad roads which were axle-deep in mud, seemed a wilderness as terrifying as it was romantic. "It is a dreadful valley," writes Madame de Sévigné, "just the place in which to find salvation!"

The first of these converts to Jansenism was the Duchesse de Longueville, a sister of the Great Condé. "As notorious owing to the civil wars as for her love affairs," says Voltaire maliciously, "having become old and lacking occupation, she suddenly turned pious. She hated the court, felt an urgent need for intrigue, and therefore became a Jansenist convert."

Her enthusiasm for the inmates of the "Thebaid" by no means prevented the duchess from continuing to lead the life of a noble lady, and when, as Princesse de Neuchâtel, she received the Swiss ambassadors, she entertained them with the greatest pomp.

The "conversion" of the Duchesse de Liancourt, Madame de Sévigné, the Princesse de Conti, the Duchesse de Luynes and the Princess de Guéménée had the result that the Jansenist movement suddenly acquired a tremendous social influence. There was thus forced against the Jesuits a dangerous faction, consisting of intriguing society ladies who had at their disposal powerful influences at court, in the ministerial offices and among the higher clergy; with truly feminine cunning and obstinacy, they set everything in motion in order to secure the victory of the doctrine of grace over that of free will.

The "Port Royal Colony" frequently took part in these discussions in the Parisian salons, for the members often left their solitude for the capital, in order to propagate their views there. At such times, heated debates took place over the most abstruse theological problems, regarding Augustine, Thomas Aquinas and Ignatius Loyola, amidst a circle of white-wigged ladies, elegant courtiers and worldly abbés.

Regarding the strange entourage of the Duchesse de Longueville, Voltaire writes with his subtle irony: "There were assembled the Arnaulds, Nicole, Lemaistre, Hamon, Sacy, and many less well-known but none the less important people, In place of the fine wit to which the duchess had hitherto been accustomed, they displayed a profundity in their discussions and an element of impetuous and animated virility, such as their writings and their discourses reveal. They contributed not a little to the acclimatization in France of good taste and genuine eloquence, but, unfortunately, they were more concerned with the dissemination of their own views. They themselves furnished a proof of that fatalistic system which gained them so many enemies. It might well be said that, owing to their pursuit of a chimera, they were irrevocably predestined to become the victims of persecution, although they enjoyed the highest esteem and might have lived most happily had they been able to refrain from indulging in these purposeless controversies."

"Novelists and Dramatists are Poisonmongers"

"Novelists and Dramatists are Poisonmongers"

The disputes between the Jansenists and the Jesuits over grace and free will had a profound influence on the trend of French thought, and therefore on that of the whole of Europe, for in the time of Louis XIV French culture and European culture were synonymous terms. As a purely theological discussion, the controversy would nowadays hardly attract more than a specialized and historic interest, but with the history of this debate on the teaching of Augustine regarding original sin, the whole life, thoughts and actions of the greatest men of that age were closely bound up, and both Pascal's *Thoughts* and the classical plays of Corneille and Racine were conceived in the spiritual atmosphere of the Jansenist controversy.

The extraordinary theological debates between pious nuns, fanatical hermits, elegant abbés and garrulous society ladies have been immortalized in the pages of these here great writers, while it may also be mentioned that Goethe for a time entertained the idea of dealing exhaustively with the Jansenist controversy in the eleventh book of Part III of *Dichtung and Wahrheit*.

Corneille was educated at the Jesuit school at Clermont, and his dramas were, at a later date, destined to introduce to the stage the Jesuitic spirit of Molinism: his dramatis personae work out their own destinies; they know nothing of the doctrine of original sin; they believe in the freedom of their own decisions, and are able to overcome their strongest passions by the power of their own will. On the other hand, the tragedies of Racine, who was brought up under the influence of Port Royal, embody in dramatic form the Jansenist doctrine that men are the helpless victims of their passions unless they are enlightened and delivered by divine grace. While this is true even of Racine's earlier dramas, the connection with Jansenism is particularly marked in his *Phèdre*. The tragic end of Racine's characters is intended to impress upon the spectator the idea of the inevitability of the destiny which God has decreed. Since the subtlety of Racine's French is also attributable to the teaching which he received as a pupil at Port Royal, the whole of this writer's dramatic work is very closely associated with the Jansenist influence.

For a period of fifteen years, during which time he produced his best work, Racine was, indeed, on very bad terms with his former teachers; curiously enough, the quarrel was due to his dramatic talent. Even at the outset of his career, when he had written his first short sonnet, his grandmother and his aunt, both nuns at Port Royal, were greatly perturbed by so secular and impious a beginning.

When however, his *La Thébaïde* was produced, it roused a storm of indignation at port Royal: his grandmother and aunt refused to have anything more to do with him and sent him what were to all intents and purposes letters of excommunication in which they implored the youthful reprobate to "have mercy on his own soul, and think of the abyss for which he was heading."

This instance, as so many others, shows that it is hard for pious souls to understand genius, and that religious fanatics not infrequently attempt, with reproving looks and "holy hate," to discourage the development of a truly artistic spirit. So it was that the subtle gentlemen of

The Power and Secret of the Jesuits

Port Royal were not long in seconding the good nuns' disapproval. Genuinely perturbed, Nicole, Racine's former tutor, wrote regarding his pupil who had thus fallen a victim to the "poison of authorship": "Everyone knows that this gentleman has smitten novels and stage plays... In the eyes of right-minded people, such an occupation is in itself not a very honorable one; but, viewed in the light of the Christian religion and of the Gospel teaching, it becomes really a dreadful one. Novelists and dramatists are poison mongers who destroy, not men's bodies, but their souls."

Nicole's attack created a tremendous sensation among the Parisian intellectuals. Corneille and Molière at once came to the defense of their youthful colleague, and indited spirited rejoinders to the views expressed by the pious M. Nicole. Racine himself was in such a towering rage that he attacked in the coarsest of terms the colonists and nuns of Port Royal in a manifesto in which he spared neither the living nor the dead. This was the origin of the breach between the great poet and his former teachers, which was to last for fully fifteen years.

Between 1673 and 1677, Racine underwent a complete conversion, and he sought to bring about a reconciliation with his friends of former days. In the meantime, moreover, the Jansenists had come to take a less rigid view of the dramatic art, and thus Port Royal welcomed its former pupil back to the fold. It is obvious that the two plays, *Esther* and *Athalie*, which Racine wrote after his reconciliation with the "colonists" are dramatized defenses of the men of Port Royal and of their ideas. During the last years of his life, Racine tried to assist his regained friends by making use of his social influence and by writing a *History of Port Royal*.

Although, however, it was necessary for the full development of his talents that this writer should become temporarily estranged from the Jansenists, Pascal, on the other hand, owed the awakening of his mental powers to the teaching of Port Royal, where, from the first, his genius was thankfully appreciated. His mordant wit exposed the Jesuits, the opponents of the Jansenist doctrine of grace, to open ridicule, and thus destroyed their influence over the public. "All manner of means were tried," writes Voltaire, "to make the Jesuits hated, but Pascal did more because he made them ridiculous."

Even as a boy of twelve, Pascal had, in childish play, tried to prove, in chalk, on the floor of his room, one of the propositions of Euclid. His mathematical talents had at that early age aroused so much interest that he was admitted to the meetings of the French Academy. At the age of sixteen, he propounded a new theory of sound, and at about the same period he finished his fundamental work on conic sections.

Just at the time when he was engaged on the invention of a calculating machine to render easier the work of his father, then the intendant of Rouen, the latter became seriously ill. The doctors who attended him were Jansenists, as was the younger Pascal's brother-in-law, Périer. In this way, the whole family came beneath the spell of Jansenist ideas. Blaise himself, who up to then had lived the life of an honored young man of learning, was suddenly "touched by God," as had happened shortly before to his sister Jacqueline, and he immersed himself in the writings of the Abbot of Saint-Cyran and in Jansen's *Augustinus*.

Racine, in his *History of Port Royal*, writes on this conversion of the great mathematician: "Pascal already had very strong leanings toward piety, and, two or three years before, despite his predilections and his undoubted genius for mathematics, had abandoned these speculations in order to devote more of his time to the study of the Scriptures and the great truths of religion. His acquaintance with Port Royal, and the noteworthy examples of piety which he found there, made a deep impression upon him. He resolved to think in future only of his spiritual welfare, severed all his social connections, relinquished the idea of a very lucrative marriage which he had been contemplating, and from then onwards led a life of strict renunciation which he continued until the day of his death."

While living with the Port Royal community he wrote his first *Provincial Letters*, dealing with the gift of grace and the freedom of the human will. In the form of dialogues with an imaginary Jesuit, he ridiculed Molinism, and therefore the entire Jesuit doctrine of free will, which he identified with Pelagianism.

In 1656 and 1657, there appeared anonymously eighteen of these *Provincial Letters*, the authorship of which the public was at first unable to discover. "Their success was astonishing," writes Hémon. "This was perhaps due as much to the mystery surrounding the appearance of these letters as to the general interest taken in the problem and the novelty of the idea which they contained. Sought for everywhere by the officials of the chancellor, Séguier, the *Provincial Letters* seemed to defy all efforts to discover their origin. He who desired to read then found then everywhere; but he who sought to confiscate then found then nowhere."

The wit of these controversial writings was a novelty in those times, and accordingly the *Provincial Letters* were read at court, as well as in the literary solons, by the clergy and by learned professors. Enormous damage was thus done at that critical time to the Jesuits' reputation.

A contemporary report contains a graphic account of the tremendous impression created by Pascal's letters: "The chorus of praise which arose from those who first read them excited universal curiosity, and each succeeding letter was more eagerly looked forward to than its predecessor. In a short time, this interest was as keen in the provinces as in Paris. Everyone seemed to have read the letters, which, when they reached the provinces, created such a stir that the Jesuits themselves were, for the first time, greatly perturbed. Never had the post had such a profitable year; even the smallest towns in the kingdom received consignments of the pamphlets, which were forwarded to all parts of France in large parcels..."

The Fateful Five Propositions

It is a significant fact that this great dispute over a difficult theological problem had its origin in a piquant but trivial society scandal. The Princess de Guéménée had formerly lived a life devoted wholly to pleasure, but she had come under the influence of the Abbot of Saint-Cyran, who had imposed on her a strict spiritual discipline. One day, just as she had made her communion, a friend called on her, and invited her to a ball which was to take place that very evening.

The princess would gladly have attended this festivity, but Saint-Cyran forbade her on the grounds that she had just taken communion, and she reluctantly declined the invitation.

The Power and Secret of the Jesuits

There friend, however, refused to be beaten, hastened home, and returned immediately with a manuscript of the Jesuit, Sesmaisons, in which it was written that the claims of God and of the world were not necessarily opposed, and that pious behavior and innocent pleasure were by no means incompatible.

By this time, the princess really did not know whether she should or should not attend the ball, and in this pious lady's doubts originated all the subsequent virulent disputes between the Jansenists and the Jesuits.

The Abbot of Saint-Cyran at once steeped himself, full of mistrust, in the study of the writings of the Jesuit, Sesmaisons, and made the distressing discovery that they upheld the view that the more man sinned, the oftener should he obtain absolution by receiving the sacrament of the Eucharist. The young Jansenist, Antoine Arnauld, also soon heard of this Jesuit tract, and, deeply aroused, published a refutation entitled *On Frequent Communion,* in which he warned the faithful against those false counsellors, the Jesuits, who treated vice as of little account, too easily granted absolution, and profaned the sacrament of the communion by administering it to unworthy recipients.

The event aroused interest in the Parisian salons, and the question whether or not communion should be frequent immediately became the subject of animated discussion. The Jesuits were not slow in taking up Arnauld's challenge; they thundered from the pulpit against their presumptuous critic, whom they styled a "scorpion," and whom they placed in the same category as those heretics, Luther and Calvin.

Hardly had this society scandal begun when it grew to even greater dimensions. Before long, the Jesuits made determined efforts to stir up both the queen of France and the pope against Arnauld's book, but to no avail, and for the time being they had to content themselves with a campaign of insult and calumny.

The gentlemen of Port Royal jealously followed every step the Jesuit fathers took, and the latter, in turn, were overcome by jealousy whenever the literary products of the colonists eclipsed those of their own writers. The educational activities of both parties were a special cause of rivalry. Up to then, the Jesuits had had a virtual monopoly of the education of the children of the French aristocracy, but they now encountered dangerous competitors in the *petites écoles* of Port Royal. There in contrast to the practice in the Jesuit schools, elementary instruction was given in the French, and not in the Latin, language: the latter was not taught until the pupils had received a thorough grounding in French. At Port Royal, moreover, Greek was also taught by a new method, which dispensed with the use of Latin translations, while the Jansenist schools were also famous for their success in the teaching of mathematics and history. A large number of children of distinguished families now attended the Port Royal schools instead of the Jesuit college at Clermont, and the Jesuits were greatly angered by this unwelcome competition.

But this educational rivalry too was let loose by a minor scandal. A Jesuit confessor had refused the last sacraments to the Duc de Liancourt, because the latter's granddaughter was a pupil at Port Royal. Arnauld immediately took up the case, and wrote two heated attacks on the obnoxious order, thereby bringing upon himself the penalty of expulsion from the University of Paris.

54. THE NUNS OF PORT ROYAL IN THE CONVENT GARDEN

55. PROCESSION OF THE NUNS OF PORT ROYAL

56. ANGÉLIQUE ARNAULD   57. CATHERINE AGNÈS ARNAULD
THE NUNS OF PORT ROYAL

Engravings after paintings by philippe de Champaigne.

The Fateful Five Propositions

Every form of intrigue and culmination at the command of both parties was eventually resorted to in the prosecution of the dispute. The Jansenists accused their opponents of holding the heretical Pelagian doctrines, while the Jesuits declared the Port Royal confraternity to be Calvinists. Before long, each party began to accuse the other of immorality, the Jesuits publishing slanderous reports in which aspersions were cast upon the conduct of the nuns at Port Royal, while in retaliation the Jansenists accused the pious fathers of the gravest immoralities. Then both sides began to assert that their opponents were guilty of treason. The Jansenists revived all the old stories concerning the regicidal tendencies of the Jesuits, while the latter retorted by asserting that the Port Royal people were spending their money on conspiracies endangering the security of the French state.

Strenuous efforts were made to secure the support of the court and of the authorities. On the Jansenist side, the Duchesse de Longueville brought pressure to bear on a number of influential statesmen, while on the other side the Jesuit confessor at the royal court insinuated accusations against the Jansenists into the ears of the queen and of the king.

The leading spirit of the Port Royal party was the youthful but learned Doctor Antoine Arnauld, who had made it his lifelong task to defend Jansenism with passionate eloquence. "Arnauld hated the Jesuits even more than he loved effective grace," writes Voltaire, "and they hated him just as much... His own gifts, and the times in which he lived, turned him into a controversialist and party leader; but this is a form of ambition which kills all others. He fought the Jesuits until he had reached the age of eighty... A mind destined to enlighten humanity was wasted on the dissensions created by his determined obstinacy."

Hardly had Arnauld published his treatise *On Frequent Communion* when that mad controversy reached its climax. The Abbot of Saint-Cyran had meanwhile, by the use of his social influence, been able to some extent to rescue from oblivion the book of his former teacher, Cornelius Jansen. This infuriated the Jesuits, who requested the authorities in Rome to anathematize this book, as being nothing less than a revival of the old heretical teachings of Baius. They were, in fact, shortly afterwards successful in securing from the Inquisition the condemnation of Jansen's *Augustinus*.

In spite of this verdict, no one could bring himself to read this exhaustive, as well as tedious, book of Jansen's and this continued to be the case right up to the period of the most violent debate over this same *Augustinus*. It is true that hated controversies arose over the question whether Jansen's doctrines were really Christian or whether, rather, they were not heretical, but the number of those who had even glanced at this famous work continued to be exceedingly small.

At an early stage, a Jesuit had realized how few people there were who were disposed to read Jansen's own writings, and he therefore compiled for popular use a summary in the form of five "propositions." These were intended to make plain the heretical objectionableness of the Jansenist teachings, and the condensation of the three ponderous volumes into five short propositions did, in fact, bring to the notice of the world at large the theories of the long-defunct Bishop of Ypres.

After the Jesuits had for years repeatedly quoted these five propositions, the doctors at the University of Paris and the French bishops became feverishly excited by them: eighty doctors demanded that the faculty should condemn Jansen's book as heretical, while sixty others protested against this; eight-eight bishops requested the pope to intervene, while eleven bishops who held the opposite view urged the Holy Father to do nothing of the kind. The pope, finally, at the urgent instance of the eighty-eight bishops, found himself forced to brand the famous "five propositions" as heretical in his bull *Cum occasione*.

Stripped of their theological verbiage, these five propositions run somewhat as follows: (1) grace is not given to all, and those who do not possess it are totally incapable of doing good; (2) those to whom grace is given cannot escape its effect, and their actions must necessarily be guided by this gift of grace; (3) men are not free to do good or evil; (4) it is heretical to state that men are able of their own will to resist grace or to yield to it; (5) it is heretical to state that Christ died for all men.

Pope Innocent X thought fit to anathematize each individual proposition separately, but, as neither he nor his cardinals had ever read Jansen's book, the holy Father refrained from quoting in his bull the pages in the *Augustinus* in which these heretical views were expounded.

The Jansenists immediately made capital out of this fact. When the bull *Cum occasione* was published, they declared that, as good Catholics, they deferred to the verdict of the pope that the five propositions were heretical, but, at the same time, they claimed that these propositions were not to be found in Jansen's book. Doctor Arnauld, who never missed a chance of engaging in controversy, at once wrote "a fictitious letter to an imaginary duke," as was customary among literary men of the period, in which he sarcastically pointed out that, while the propositions condemned by the pope were certainly not contained in Jansen's book, they were to be found in the writings of Augustine and other fathers of the church.

The French clergy, and before all the Jesuits, were infuriated by Arnauld's statement; as none of these ecclesiastical dignitaries had read Jansen's book, each one, relying on the papal infallibility, could confidently assert that the heretical propositions were actually to be found in the book of the Bishop of Ypres.

The obvious solution was to read Jansen's book, and ascertain whether or not it contained the "five propositions," but everyone concerned shirked this task, and preferred more complicated methods. First of all, a debate arose over the question whether the pope was infallible in all circumstances. The Jansenists claimed that this infallibility applied only to matters of the faith, and not to the verification of actual facts. Hence it was within the pope's powers to determine whether or not the "five propositions" were heretical, but, on the other hand, it was not for him to decide whether these propositions had actually been written by Jansen. Peter's successor, they urged, could never by his authority convert false statements on matters of fact into truths.

Although—or perhaps even because—this Jansenist opinion was based on common sense, the French clergy who were under Jesuit influence were stirred to indignation. In the Jesuit college at Clermont, long public discussions were held upholding the theory that the pope could give an infallible decision on matters of fact. Incredible as it may now seem to us, this question at once gave rise to a violent quarrel in which the whole of France, from the poorest mendicant friar up to the *roi Soleil* himself, took part. This was the famous controversy over the distinction between infallibility *de droit* and *de fait*.

The Jesuits were finally able to persuade the majority of the French bishops to secure

58. PRINCESSE DE CONTI:

THE PROTECTRESS OF PORT ROYAL

59. MOCK PROCESSION AGAINST JANSENISM INSTITUTED BY THE STUDENTS OF THE JESUIT COLLEBE OF MÂCON

60. JEAN RACINE

61. BLAISE PASCAL

THE GREAT MINDS OF PORT ROYAL

The Fateful Five Propositions

from the papal Curia the issue of a formulary to which all the clergy were to be required to subscribe. This document was worded as follows:

"With my heart and voice I condemn the doctrines of the five propositions which are contained in the book *Augustinus* by Cornelius Jansen. . ."

In 1661 was published a royal decree ordering all French ecclesiastics to sign the papal "formulary." In order to force the Jansenists to comply with this decree, their schools were closed and their boarders and novices sent home. The Port Royal gentlemen finally deemed it expedient to yield to their enemies' superior influence, and to sign the formulary subject to a mental reservation: this, however, involved then in a quarrel with the implacable Pascal. The latter could not understand political subterfuges of this nature, and for this reason he broke with his friends, blamed them in angry words for their laxity, and went so far as to state that he regretted that he had ever collaborated with them. In vain did Arnauld and Nicole try to justify their attitude. Pascal, already at death's door, swooned away when the Jansenist leaders attempted to explain to him their motives, and afterwards declared: "When I beheld these men whom I had regarded as the most inspired representatives of divine truth, when I saw how even they were beginning to waver, I was overcome by an unbearable pain which deprived me of consciousness."

The abbey nuns, however, for a long time refused to subscribe to the formulary, and uncomplainingly endured the most brutal persecution. Jacqueline, Pascal's sister, about that time wrote to her brother: "I am well aware that it is said that it is not becoming for young women to defend the truth. But now, when the bishops have the courage of maidens, it is assuredly necessary that maidens should show the courage of bishops. Even though it is not granted to us to defend the truth, it is nevertheless our duty to die for it."

Mother Angélique, the Abbess of Port Royal, was at that time bed-ridden with dropsy: nevertheless, she continued to exhort the whole community to remain steadfast in their resistance. When she died, her place in the convent was taken by her sister Agnès, who persisted in obstinate opposition to the formulary. Eventually, the military were called out and surrounded the abbey: the unhappy aged nuns were evicted by force and transferred to various convents under the Jesuit influence.

Voltaire makes the extremely pertinent comment regarding this action of the ecclesiastical authorities and the attitude of the nuns: "One may well ask oneself which was the stranger, the assumption that by their signatures a handful of nuns could confirm the statement that five particular propositions are contained in a Latin book, or the obstinate resistance of these nuns."

A change in the occupancy of the Holy See brought with it a temporary peace. The new peace-loving pope, Clement IX, thought it desirable to put an end to the foolish dispute. But, as he did not wish to offend anyone, he had recourse to the method so often and so successfully practiced by the popes, whereby, instead of conceding that one of the two parties, both of whom were convinced of the justice of their case, was right, he restored peace by means of ambiguity. He therefore invented a compromise which might be acceptable to the Jansenists without offending the Jesuits too deeply; while maintaining the condemnation of the five propositions, he agreed to a form of submission in which it was not definitely asserted that these propositions had originated in Jansen's book. The compromise was worded in so ambiguous a manner that for a long time no one knew where he stood in the matter; even the most belligerent of the disputants were at first uncertain how they were to continue hostilities. Thus occurred that armistice in the great Jansenist controversy which is known as the "Church Peace of 1668." The government released the Jansenists who had been thrown into the Bastille, and the banished nuns were allowed to return to their abbey.

This state of affairs lasted until 1701, when a new cause for further controversy was found. In that year, a theological expert invented a problem which was calculated once more to set the parties at one another's throats. May absolution be given to a man who, although he may have subscribed to the papal formulary, nevertheless secretly believes that the pope may err in regard to facts? This doctoral question was affirmed by forty members of the theological faculty of Paris, and denied by almost as many, whereupon war begun again. Louis Antoine de Noailles, the Archbishop of Paris, decreed that infallibility *de droit* should be admitted with divine belief, and *de fait* with human belief; other eminent church authorities, including the famous bishop, Fénélon, stoutly opposed this view.

When this argument seemed likely to subside, another dispute broke out over the recently published annotated translation of the Bible by Quesnel, for, as Voltaire holds, the Jansenists desired "always to intrigue and the Jesuits sought always to be important."

The Oratory priest, Quesnel, had become the Jansenist leader after the death of Arnauld, and had thus incurred the enmity of the Jesuits. He was cast into prison as a result of their persecution, and the Jesuits eventually found no difficulty in persuading Louis XIV that Quesnel's activities were politically dangerous. "The King," Voltaire remarks scornfully, "was not sufficiently well educated to appreciate the fact that a purely speculative theory ceases to be of importance if it is left to its own unfruitfulness. To make a state matter of it is attributing far too much weight to it."

Signs and Wonders

In 1708, there appeared a papal bull in which the cloister of Port Royal was referred to as a "nest of heretics." Archbishop de Noailles, who was personally well-disposed towards the Jansenists, delegated to the Jesuit court confessor, Le Tellier, as papal commissioner, the duty of enforcing the warrant against the Port Royal confraternity.

The police cleared the convent, the nuns were transferred to other communities, and the buildings were entirely demolished. Even the bodies of the dead Jansenists in the Port Royal cemetery were disinterred and reburied in a common grave.

The spirit of Jansenism, however, survived, and manifested itself in the most insane and senseless intrigues and protests. Noailles, now a cardinal, was on terms of bitterest enmity with the court confessor, Le Tellier, whom he caused to be kept under observation, and whose correspondence he had opened: he was thus able to intercept one of the Jesuit's letters, which revealed the existence of an extensive political plot against himself. He avenged himself by making use of his archiepiscopal powers to deprive the Jesuits of the right of hearing confessions.

Le Tellier was not slow in retaliating. He was aware that at an earlier date Noailles had openly expressed his approval of the Jansenist Quesnel's book, and he now set to work to procure the papal anathema of this work, and thus indirectly to compromise the archbishop.

Clement XI hesitated for a long time and studied the question with as much zeal as had Clement VIII in regard to the Molinist problem: it was not until 1713 that he decided to issue the famous bull *Unigenitus*, which condemned as heretical one hundred and three of Quesnel's propositions.

The aged *roi Soleil* had done all in his power to expedite the publication of this bull, In order to prevent a split in the church and to allay the prevailing state of unrest, but the papal decree had precisely the opposite effect. The French clergy immediately protested most forcibly against the acceptance of the bull; many of the highest ecclesiastics pointed out that a number of Quesnel's propositions which had been anathematized by the pope were taken literally from the pages of Holy Scripture and from the works of Augustine.

This seemingly interminable dispute had now reached the period of "Appeal," so-called because a number of the most eminent churchmen, headed by Cardinal Noailles, declared that they would not comply with the bull *Unigenitus*, but that, under an ancient privilege, they would lodge an appeal against the papal authority at the next general conclave.

A great meeting in Paris of all the French bishops was called: after protracted discussions, a number of them decided to submit but a minority refused to do so. The latter party wrote to the pope direct, asking for further explanations: in the eyes of the Roman Curia so unprecedented an action was nothing less than an insult to the Holy Father. Popes Clement XI and innocent XIII for their part condemn the "Appeal" and a National Council hastily convened at Embrun hurled its anathema against the rebellious clerics.

At this period, the Ministry of the Interior found it difficult to cope with the demand of *lettres de cachet*, for the aged king had become so feeble that the Jesuits were easily able to secure the imprisonment of such of their enemies as they might desire to have incarcerated. More than twenty thousand of these *lettres de cachet* were at about that time issued against persons who held the Jansenist views.

At this stage, the Jesuits, with the pope and the king on their side, appeared to have the upper hand over the Jansenists. Nevertheless, the Jansenist duchesses and princesses continued to carry on a clever intrigue at court in favor of the gift of grace to the elect, but they could not get the better of Le Tellier who was the keeper of the king's conscience. This dispute over a difficult theological problem was, therefore, fought with very unequal weapons. The effective influence of the Jesuits was opposed only by the pens of the "gentlemen," and the malicious tongues of the "ladies of Port Royal."

In one respect only was the Jansenist spirit superior to that of Molina: it was able to work miracles! More than once during the dispute did such "miracles" occur, and, so it seemed, always at times when matters were going badly for the Jansenist cause. Not only the Jesuits, but their patrons, kings and ministers, were powerless against so embarrassing an intervention of supernatural forces.

As early as 1656, when the queen, acting under the influence of the Jesuits, was on the point of ordering the Port Royal community to be dissolved, there occurred the celebrated cure of Pascal's ten-year-old niece. The child had suffered from a chronic lachrymal fistula, which, however, immediately disappeared when it was brought into contact with the "thorn from Christ's crown" which was kept at Port Royal.

This had already made the Jesuits very uneasy. Could it be that God had suspended the laws of nature merely "to justify a dozen nuns" who asserted that Cornelius Jansen had not written this or that statement?

Father Annat, who was the court confessor at this time, immediately wrote a tract; "Short lived Joy of the Jansenists in the Matter of a Miracle which is said to have taken place at Port Royal." But Annat's refutation was of little avail. Voltaire describes how the Jesuits then bestirred themselves "to work miracles of their own, but they were unsuccessful, since at that time the Jansenist miracles only were in fashion."

The cure of little Marguerite had its effects. The event was taken as a judgment of God, and it made so deep an impression on the pious queen that she refrained for the present from all further persecutions of the Jansenists. The most important effect of the miracle, however, was that it won Pascal over completely to Jansen's teaching.

A similar case occurred a few years later. The daughter of the well-known painter, Phillipe de Champaigne, who was completely crippled, was suddenly cured while at Port Royal. This was once more regarded as divine approval of the Jansenists, and the young girl's grateful father, as a thank-offering, painted the fine picture of the nuns of Port Royal.

These miracles, however, reached their climax only at the time of the controversy over the bull *Unigenitus*, when the Jansenist cause appeared to be in danger of being finally lost. It seemed as if supernatural forces were at work to prove at all costs that the belief in free will was false and the doctrine of election by grace was true.

The first of these miracles occurred when a lady who was dangerously ill suddenly recovered at the sight of a monstrance borne by a Jansenist: similar cures followed, until finally the rapidly increasing belief of Parisian society in miracles became concentrated on the recently deceased Jansenist ascetic, François de Paris.

The latter was the son of wealthy parents; one day, however, he decided to renounce his riches, and even sold the silver table-ware he had inherited in order to share the proceeds among those who had been reduced to poverty by their opposition to the bull *Unigenitus*. François de Paris then took deacon's orders, and, finally, in abject poverty, went to live in the attic of a house on the outskirts of the city. In order to earn a living, he took lessons in stocking-knitting, and, as all day long he busily knitted hose, he mused over the project of resuscitating the convent of Port Royal.

He went about attired as a mendicant, In order to beg on behalf of others. He lived on roots and unsalted bread, and he would only take food which was nauseous to him. Finally, he went to share a small room with a madman whom he had taken under his charge, in order that the latter might trouble and torment him: he then died of hunger and weakness.

Immediately upon his death, people began to venerate him as a saint. His clothes were torn into small pieces to be preserved as holy relics. His body was buried in the paupers; cemetery of St.-Médard, which was quickly filled by sick people of all classes of society, who fell into convulsions and proclaimed themselves cured by contact with the grave. Twenty-

62. "WHILE THE SHEPHERDS QUARREL, THE WOLVES DEVOUR THE HERD"
Contemporary caricature on the clerical strife.

63. JANSENEST SATIRICAL DRAWING AGAINST THE JESUITS

four priests testified to the archbishop that they themselves had been eye-witnesses of these miraculous cures, and the general enthusiasm reached such a point that even the police officials distributed at the cemetery the Jansenist broadsheets which they had received orders to confiscate. The cemetery was eventually closed by royal decree, and thereupon an anonymous notice was affixed on the gate:

> "De par le roi, defense à Dieu,
> De faire miracle en ce lieu!"

("By order of the king, God is forbidden to work miracles here!")

This persecution by those in authority raised the popular enthusiasm for the miracle-worker to a pitch bordering upon madness. All over Paris, people were overcome by religious mania; they rolled about in convulsions; of their own free will thy lay on glowing coals; they allowed heavy weights to be dropped on their bodies, they had themselves nailed to crosses and had swords plunged into them, the while they poured forth the Jansenist doctrines and prophesied the downfall of those who supported the bull *Unigenitus*.

In the meantime, things had begun to augur badly for the Jesuits. Louis XIV had died, the last years of his life having been embittered by the interminable religious dissensions. The Duke of Orleans, who had become regent during the minority of Louis XV, was a friend of Cardinal Noailles, and his first step on assuming office was to expel from the court the father-confessor Le Tellier.

Form time out of mind the question whether the human will is free or otherwise had been debated, the only method of argument adopted by both sides being the quotation and interpretation of passages from the Bible, Aristotle, or the early fathers. Pelagianists and Augustinians, Jesuits and Jansenists, popes, cardinals, professors, nuns, courtiers and society ladies had endeavored to establish the correctness of their philosophical and theological views solely on quotations from recognized teachers of former days. Not a single one of this host of disputants had ever made an attempt to think out independently and on original grounds the problem which had been so zealously debated, or to examine it logically in the light of unprejudiced reasoning.

The same extraordinary phenomenon is to be met with in the contemporary investigations into the natural sciences. Scholastic physics was entirely based on the interpretation of Aristotle, and many centuries were to elapse before it occurred to anyone to carry out even the simplest of physical experiments.

Moreover, it should not be overlooked that the methods of the scholars had, during the course of centuries, added more and more to the number of recognized "authorities." It was no longer considered sufficient to rely solely upon the works of the classical thinkers and the church fathers and on the words of the Bible; it became necessary to quote from the writings of innumerable commentators, and, indeed, as time went on, to trust more and more to what the interpreters had said and hardly at all to refer to the original sources. Thus the dispute over the question of free will finally became a battle over the interpretation of interpreters, the commentation of the commentators.

After a struggle which resulted in the defeat of both the Jansenists and their Jesuit adversaries, the great fight between grace and free will came to a natural end: not, however, that it was in any way settled. The antagonists on both sides were the victims of a pitiless destiny, and perished in a conflict which they had themselves provoked. The time had passed when the whole world followed with bated breath, and took part in, theological controversies; henceforth the problem of the freedom of human will was destined to set at loggerheads only those philosophers who, in the era which was dawning, were to take over the leadership of European thought.

Doubt, the Source of Knowledge

Amid the opening stages of the Jansenist controversy, there was growing to maturity the man who was destined to be one of the first to make a determined effort to rescue the world from an obsolete method of thinking. During the years of endless arguments over Molina's *Concordia,* the youthful René Descartes studied at the Jesuit college of La Flèche. Father Charlet, the rector of the college, was a relative of the Descartes family, and devoted special care to the young man: he entrusted him to the supervision of Father Dinet, who subsequently became a provincial of the order, and both men were greatly pleased by the eagerness to learn and the devotion to duty of the youth.

During the eight years which he spent at la Flèche, Descartes acquired a thorough knowledge of the whole of the philosophical theories of his time. "Since philosophy is the key to the other sciences," he himself writes in his memoirs, "I regard it as most helpful to have made so thorough a study of the subject as it was taught in the Jesuit schools."

Notwithstanding his scholastic education, however, Descartes dared to discard the whole philosophical inheritance, and to think things out again from the beginning. Men like Nicholas of Cusa and Francis Bacon had, indeed, attempted something similar, but Descartes was the first to draw the logical conclusions from the failures of speculation thitherto; while philosophic thinking up till then had been founded on the judgments reached by recognized teachers, Descartes called for the Abolition of all prejudices."

Everything, he declared, can and must be doubted, even doubt itself; the capacity of men to doubt seemed to him to be the beginning of all philosophy. Recognizing that doubt, as an act of thought, postulates the existence of a thinking being, he arrived at his famous axiom, *cogito ergo sum.* "I will thus assume," he once wrote, "that the course of truth is not an all-benevolent Deity, but some kind of malicious and yet very powerful demon, who uses all his art to lead me astray. I mean that everything I perceive outside myself—heaven, air, earth, colors, forms, sounds—are but visions seen in dreams, created by that evil spirit to ensnare my credulity."

From that time onward up to our own age, doubt as the fundamental attitude of the investigator into all phenomena and hypotheses was destined to dominate the whole development of European thought. The scientific, philosophic and technological achievements of the last century have all sprung from the spirit of doubt, from the principle that experience and experiment are the starting-point of all speculation.

But as regards the question of the freedom of the will, Descartes, like his predecessors, was unable to solve the contradictions in this problem, but rather substituted newer complications for the old. It at once became evident that the truth was not necessarily revealed to a mode of thought which had freed itself from the fetters of a belief in tradition, but that it remained just as obscure as it was under the hair-splitting methods of the scholastics. Even Cartesian philosophy was unable to explain the simultaneous existence of freedom and lack of freedom, or the contradiction between the principle of causality and that of human autonomy.

In accordance with the new outlook, Descartes distinguished between one world subject to mechanical laws and another of spiritual freedom, by assuming the existence of two substances corresponding exactly the one to the other: against the physical world, which he regarded as a pure mechanism, he set the spiritual as essentially different.

In conformity with the principles of modern scientific thought, he tried to extend the region of mechanical action as far as possible. He regarded animals as mere automata, devoid alike of the power of reason and of volition, and this, he considered, was also true of the human body; on the other hand, he regarded the will alone as something not reducible to mechanism: the innate tendency of the body towards a state of mechanical inertia is influenced by the will.

It will thus be seen that this former Jesuit pupil gave free will a prominent place in his system. The will, he claimed, is in its nature infinite and free: it therefore constitutes that human faculty which approaches most nearly to absolute perfection. Only the fact that we possess free will justifies us in speaking of an analogy between man and God; there is, indeed, very little difference between our will and that of the Ruler of the universe.

Man "wills," not because he is subject to an unescapable attraction or in conformity with a law of nature, but rather by reason of his freedom; but, since the will necessarily strives after what is good and true, it endeavors in its decisions to adapt itself to the divine will, and it thus becomes all the more free the more it is in harmony with the infinite and infinitely perfect will of God.

Nevertheless, this theory was no real solution of the problem. For if, following the Cartesian hypothesis, the existence of a dual system of mechanical and spiritual substances is assumed, two alternatives at once present themselves: either the power of bringing about a causeless event must be ascribed to the will, or it must be assumed that the mechanically conditioned impulses bring about an unfree event; furthermore, these two assumptions stand insoluble contradiction one to the other.

Descartes and the Jesuits

Almost as soon as he became known, Descartes had to face bitter opposition, and it has often been stated that the persecution of his doctrines by the Catholic Church was attributable to the Jesuits. In reality, it was chiefly the theological faculties at the great universities who, out of their own learned darkness, attacked most violently the innovations of Descartes, while the Jesuits in many instance came to the support of their former pupil.

There were from the outset members of the Society of Jesus, such as the provincial Dinet, and Fathers Méland, de Vatier, Derkennis and Tacquet, who were staunch admirers of

Descartes; other Jesuits were at any rate friendly towards him, being drawn to him by his mathematical and physical theories.

On the appearance in 1641 of Descartes' first monumental work, entitled *Meditationes de prima philosophia, ubi de Dei existential et animae immortalitate,* the Jesuit Provincial Dinet, the former tutor of the philosopher, immediately gave him his wholehearted support. The leading members of the order had, with keen perspicacity, immediately realized that Descartes, so zealous a champion as he was of the doctrine of free will, was to be regarded rather as an ally than as an enemy.

The correctness of this view was speedily confirmed by the fact that Antoine Arnauld, the leader of the Jansenist party, raised pronounced objections of a theological nature to the Cartesian system. This new philosophy, which so greatly differed from the teachings of Augustine, could not but meet with hostility in Jansenist circles, and so it was that, while the men of Port Royal were deeply interested by Descartes' discoveries in the natural sciences and mathematics, they objected to his philosophy on the ground that it ought to concern itself solely with scientific natters, and should leave untouched matters of faith, human action, religion and morals.

Even though this difference of opinion between Descartes and the Jansenists met with some sympathy in the Society of Jesus, the members were under no misapprehensions over what Descartes had done in regard to breaking loose from the scholastic belief in authorities. It was not so very long, indeed, since the Jesuits themselves had been most violently attacked by the Dominicans for having departed from many of the doctrines of that teacher of the Church, Thomas. At that period, during the Molinist controversy, the Jesuits had been in a similar position to that in which they now recognized Descartes to be, and they too had had to fight against the enmity of all the rigid school dogmatists.

It is true that when Descartes became known, there were also Jesuits who opposed the new system. Thus, soon after the publication of the *Meditationes,* the Belgian Jesuit Jean Ciermans sent a number of objections to Descartes; these, however, dealt solely with problems of physics, and were couched in such flattering terms that Descartes received them in a very friendly spirit.

More dangerous seemed the attack of the Jesuit university professor Bourdin, who launched his attack on Descartes with all the weapons of scholastic polemics. Descartes was at first greatly alarmed by this attack of Bourdin's, for he feared that it was preliminary to a general attack on his system by the Jesuit order, and, so soon after the condemnation of Galileo, such a turn of affairs might indeed have caused him grave concern. It was speedily obvious, however, that Bourdin had not acted under instructions from the Society, but on his own initiative. For the provincial Dinet quickly intervened, forbade Bourdin to make any further attacks, and arranged a personal meeting between the two men which ended in a complete reconciliation.

Only after Descartes's death did there manifest itself within the order a certain anti-Cartesian trend of opinion, which, indeed, was attributable to motives of ecclesiastical policy on the part of the leaders of the order as much as to anything. From this time onward, many Jesuit writers sought vigorously to refute the doctrines of Descartes by demonstrating that they were not in harmony with the Aristotelean system.

64. FRANÇOIS DE Paris DOING PENANCE IN HIS CELL

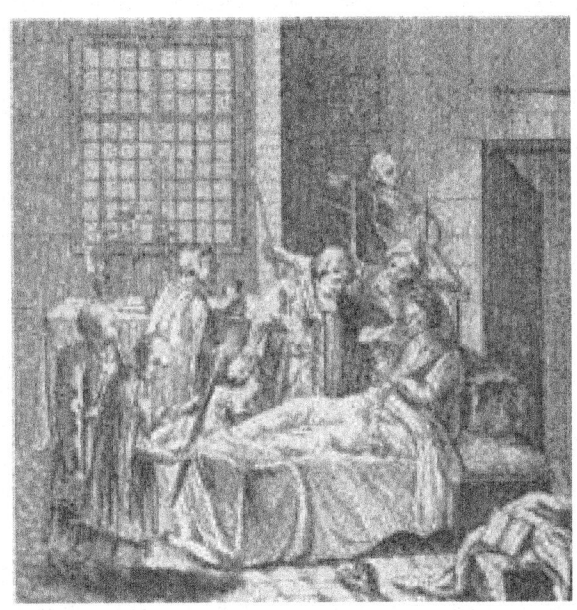

65. FRANÇOIS DE PARIS ON HIS DEATH-BED

66. LADIES OF RANK AT THE WONDER-WORKING GRAVE OF FRANÇOIS DE PARIS

It is, however, as somewhat significant fact that, notwithstanding all the orders emanating from Rome, the Cartesian philosophy has always found a number of open supporters among the Jesuits, and that, indeed, in later years, quite patent sympathies for these views again became evident. Learned Jesuits such as Honoré Fabri tried to prove that Descartes was in agreement with Aristotle, and that the physics of the Stagirite had till then been misunderstood.

This movement became so strong that it created consternation among the leaders of the order: it was deemed desirable, at the beginning of the eighteenth century, to declare that thirty propositions were not to be discussed, and these chiefly included the Cartesian doctrines. In 1732, a further ten theses were banned, which were likewise held to be in the spirit of Descartes, and which contradicted the scholastic views regarding form and matter.

It is not without interest to observe how understandingly Bernhard Jansen, a Jesuit philosopher of our day, judges the Cartesian protest against the rigid scholastic methods. Jansen, in his *Wegen der Weltweisheit*, says that Descartes, in contrast to the scholastics, who were objective and metaphysical, starts "from the subject, from the ego," and finds "by critically elaborating the facts of consciousness the way to the exterior world." This is, however, "typically non-mediaeval, entirely modern."

In matters of method, Jansen explains, "the severance from scientific and ecclesiastical authority in principle and in practice" was accomplished by Descartes. "Science was happily emancipated and secularized. Its emancipation was significantly expressed in Descartes' *cogito ergo sum*, and its secularization in Bacon's 'Knowledge is power.' The orientation of philosophy, which was predominantly metaphysical in the Middle Ages, was turned in the direction of critical, methodological and exact investigations into the natural sciences, without detriment, nevertheless, to the importance of metaphysics, the queen of all the sciences...."

Jansen then states that, at the time of Descartes's appearance, later scholasticism had already led to a greatly exaggerated belief in authority, and that accordingly the efforts which were made to break away from its unduly narrow limits were entirely justifiable. In conclusion, his judgment is that through this new movement "many individual new truths were revealed, many different individual disciplines in philosophy were cultivated for the first time or powerfully stimulated," but, above all, "through doubt the eye was opened or critically sharpened to a whole series of problems hitherto unbroached."

Leibniz, The Friend of the Jesuits

The Cartesian doctrine of the interrelation between two substances, one mechanical and the other spiritual, was destined later on to be further developed by two great thinkers. Both Spinoza and Leibniz may in this respect be regarded as the successors of Descartes.

It is true that in Spinoza's philosophy, this dualism loses much of its special character. Spinoza certainly concedes the existence of an unbroken continuity of mechanical events in the physical world, as well as a corresponding continuity in the world of thought; but, in his view, the world of ideas shows the same concatenation of causes and effects as the world of natural processes, since he regards mind and matter as identical. Both consist of the very same substances, which are different for the understanding in their phenomenal forms, their attributes. The relation between these two chains of events, therefore, consists in an exact correspondence.

A thinker who regarded the spiritual world as a subject to the laws of causality could not possibly admit the freedom of the human will; so Spinoza considered the belief in the freedom of the human will illusory. Men, so ran his doctrine, consider themselves free only because they are conscious of their will, but not of the causes which determine the will. In the same way, a falling stone, if endowed with consciousness, would believe that it was falling of its own volition, because it would be unable to perceive any external causes of its movement.

This idea of mechanical causation is formulated in an even more decisive manner in the writings of the English "philosophers of experience" of the eighteenth century. They sought to prove that the human reason and will were subject solely to mechanical laws, and to show consciousness merely as a series of physical reactions. Thus David Hume tried to prove that mental processes were governed by the same laws as were the processes of nature, and he asserted that in the human brain, just as in the physical world, the same causes produced identical effects.

Hume, entirely in the spirit of Francis Bacon, declared the will to be merely the desire to remain in a condition which has once been assumed; this was an application to the mind of Galileo's principle of inertia. He considered that there is no difference between the will and the inertia of inanimate matter; the actions of human beings appear to be completely determined by an infinite chain of causes and effects.

In contradistinction to this purely mechanical theory of the English philosophers, Leibniz postulates a sharp division between mind and matter, and, in his hypothesis of the "pre-established harmony," elaborates with remarkable beauty the dualistic idea first evolved by Descartes. He assumes the existence of two kingdoms, one of effective causes and the other of final causes; there is no relationship of dependency between them, but, according to a "pre-established harmony," there is a relationship between them of perfect correspondence.

"Souls," Leibniz tells us, "are subject to their own laws, which consist in a definite development of the ideas governing the distinction between good and evil; bodies likewise are subject to their own laws, according to which their movements are regulated. Nevertheless, these two entirely different kinds of existence meet and correspond the one to the other like two adjacent and perfectly regulated clocks of entirely different construction."

Leibniz came to the fore just at the time when the disputes between Jansenists and Molinists, Catholics, Lutherans and Calvinists over the problems of grace, original sin and human freedom had resulted in the production of an enormous amount of controversial literature. In his efforts to find a middle way between different hostile views, Leibniz sought for some kind of compromise in these questions also, and he treated of grace, original sin and free will on several occasions, both in his *System of Theology* and in the *Theodicy* and other writings.

Although he treats of original sin as the human propensity towards evil, he immediately adds: "it must be assumed that man's freedom of will was not taken from him by his fall, not even in divine things affecting his salvation; but that rather all arbitrary actions are voluntary, done of choice, and consequently free; just as no prejudice is done to the freedom of our actions in common life because we are incited to perform a certain action by the rays of light which the eyes communicate to us... Although the impulse and the help come from God, they are at all times accompanied by a certain co-operation of man himself; if not, we could not say that we had acted..."

It goes without saying that the Jesuits have always rejected all purely mechanical theories such as, for instance, those of Spinoza or Hume. As against any such physiological and mechanical determinism, the modern Jesuit philosopher, Victor Cathrein, asserts that the mechanical conditions necessary to bring about an action belong solely to the physical world, while the will is independent of them; all mental processes, including above all others the act of volition, come about "without the co-operation of any kind of physical organ" and are therefore subject to "no physiological or mechanical law."

On the other hand, it is not surprising to find that the Jesuits have always regarded with considerable favor the work and the personality of Leibniz. The order was, indeed, gratified to discover that the theories of the protestant Leibniz were in complete opposition to the doctrines of Luther and Calvin; while his theological convictions approximated closely to those of Catholicism, it was his views on the problem of free will that must have been most to the liking of the Jesuits.

The conclusions drawn by Calvin from the doctrine of predestination were expressly described as erroneous by Leibniz, when he wrote that men had "at nearly every epoch been disturbed by a fallacy which the ancients had stigmatized as being based on faulty reasoning, because it led to this, that a man should... either do nothing or at least trouble himself about nothing. For, it is said, if the future is inevitable, what is to happen will happen, no matter what I do."

Leibniz also had considerable sympathy for the system of Catholic orders; thus, he once wrote that he confessed that he had always "approved of the convents, the pious brotherhoods, and associations as well as the other laudable institutions of the same kind," for these were "a heavenly host upon earth... Whosoever ignores or despises this has but a poor and debased conception of virtue, and in stupid simplicity restricts man's duty towards God to external practices and mechanical customs which are generally performed without zeal or love."

Leibniz was on close and friendly terms and regularly corresponded with a number of Jesuits: the praise bestowed by innumerable Jesuit writers upon his works gave genuine pleasure to this great philosopher and strengthened him in his efforts "to make clear his observations regarding man's freedom and the justice of God." On several occasions, he defended the order against the charges of proselyte-hunting levelled at it in Protestant circles, while in a letter he wrote to his Jesuit patron, Father Orban, he definitely states that he wished to be regarded as a "warm friend" of the Jesuits. He had a great admiration for the works of the Jesuit Sarasa, and he himself admitted that in his *Theodicy* he had borrowed and applied several of Sarasa's propositions.

Leibniz followed with considerable interest the missionary work of the Society of Jesus, the scientific importance of which he appreciated to the full. He kept up a lively correspondence with certain missionaries in China, chiefly with Fathers Grimaldi, Verjus and Tolemei, and in 1701 he drew up a memorandum in which he expatiated on the merits of the Jesuit missionaries, and urged the Prussian Academy to establish a missionary seminary.

The attitude of the Jesuit thinkers towards the philosophic system of Leibniz is best illustrated in the book by Bernhard Jansen; this learned member of the order expresses the greatest admiration for the philosophic method evolved by Leibniz, and he is of opinion that Leibniz has earned "immortal merit" for natural philosophy by his rehabilitation of immanent teleology. Jansen makes the following enthusiastic comment: "the most remarkable feature of Leibniz's system, however, is indisputably his definition of the limits within which it is permissible to interpret events as proceeding from effective or from final causes. In its classical formulation, he surpasses all his predecessors, even an Aristotle and a Thomas Aquinas, and is surpassed by none of his successors, not even by Kant in his *Critique of Judgment*. Like an eagle, he soars in his lofty flight above the level of the contemporary mechanical theories, which knew only magnitude, number, mass, weight and motion, and attains the lofty regions of the Platonic, Aristotelean and Thomistic outlook.

"From the methodological point of view, his remarkable gift of comprehensive assimilation, combined with an extraordinary ability to collate, evolve and shape forth, his power of assembling an immense number of experiences and of working them up systematically, his harmonious balance between conservatism or tradition and critical keenness or independent progress—all these are typical of powers possessed to the same degree by only a few exceptionally gifted minds. But, of all the honored exponents of the newer philosophy, Leibniz is the nearest to the Aristotelean and scholastic system, and to the Christian mode of thought."

But in spite of all Leibniz's endeavors to bring clarity to the problem of free will, he was not successful. He himself, after explaining the difficulties presented by the question, finally writes the following resigned words: "It is better to say with St. Paul that there are certain sublime reasons of wisdom and harmony; these are unknown to mortal man, and are founded on the general order of things, the purpose of which is the utmost perfection of the universe."

Free Will in the Light of the Newer Philosophy

Immanuel Kant was as unsuccessful as his predecessors in finding a definitely satisfactory solution to the problem of free will. He was fully convinced that every real event is a link in the chain of causality, and that, therefore, in this system of reality, no such thing as free will can find a place. All human actions, as natural events, are causatively interdependent, and, if freedom is to be ascribed to our actions, this must necessarily be sought outside any casual connection in time. Kant, in regard to moral actions, accepts a similar idea of purpose outside time, and "intelligible character," in which he sees the regulative principle of ethical action. If man, therefore, is regarded as an intelligible character, he is free, while at the same time his purely natural actions, casually conditioned, seem to be completely determined.

A number of writers have already pointed out that this solution of Kant's does not really dispose of the problem, for intelligible freedom has no meaning in regard to empirical desires, with which the controversy over free will is alone concerned. But, above all, intelligible freedom, in Kant's sense, is not real indeterminateness, but is rather only a freedom in the sense of its own autonomous causality.

The manner in which Kant dealt with the problem of free will was at a later date greatly admired by Arthur Schopenhauer, who repeatedly stated that this theory of Kant's was "one of the finest and most profoundly conceived which this great mind—or, indeed, any other—ever evolved." Kant himself, however, admits, after expounding his doctrine of freedom and its relation to natural necessity: "The solution of the difficulty which is set out here, it will be said, contains many abstruse features and is hardly susceptible of a lucid explanation."

Schopenhauer was, however, not discouraged by this, and dealt with the question of moral freedom solely on the basis of the distinction made by Kant between the empirical and the intelligible character.

But when, however, Schopenhauer himself sought to remove freedom "from the sphere of individual actions, in which it is demonstrably not to be found, to a loftier region which is not so readily accessible to our cognition," he was in figurative terms expressing the view that every attempt to throw the light of philosophy on the meaning of free will is doomed to failure in the end.

Finally, in our own day, Henri Bergson has studied the problem of the will, and he too has arrived at a fundamentally negative result. According to Bergson, no attempt should be made to consider the notion of freedom from the point of view of causality, for by so doing the psychical is immediately changed into something physical, and the real "dynamic" relationship of events is converted into something static.

Every thinker since Descartes had finally to recognize the futility of his speculations on this problem, and either admitted this more or less frankly, or tried to conceal his failure by means of pseudo-solutions. If, however, since the time of the Jansenist controversy, no real progress had been made, the efforts of the new philosophers merited commendation on the ground that they were at any rate conducted in a peaceable manner. Although these quiet sages became more and more involved in contradictions, they no longer persecuted poor nuns of imprisoned zealous anchorites. Neither king nor pope interfered in the controversies of the thinkers, and he who had no interest in the various philosophic system had merely to abstain from reading the literature dealing with the matter. For this degree of progress since the times of the "often bloody, and always noisy, disputes of the theologians" humanity may well be thankful.

The Jesuits sought with more or less success to refute the arguments advanced against the theory of free will. Bearing in mind the great obscurity of all these speculative theories, and the uncertainty of all the thinkers who have grappled with the problem, the counter-theories of the Jesuits are not so untenable as to be completely disregarded. So long as the controversy over determinism or indeterminism was confined to pure philosophy, the order could remain unperturbed. Its point of view was neither better nor worse founded than was that of its opponents.

The Dispute Between the Jesuits and the Experimental Psychologists

But scarcely had the philosophers found themselves forced, towards the end of the nineteenth century, to abandon finally their attempts to solve the problem of free will, when the psychologists took up the question, asserting that it fell within their province, and that, so far as philosophy was concerned free will was only an illusory problem, while psychology, with its introspective and experimental methods, was the one means of throwing light upon the subject.

From now onwards the dispute over free will, that ominous legacy bequeathed by the scholastics, which had for two whole centuries perplexed the philosophers, was transferred to the lecture theatres, schools and laboratories of the theoretical and experimental psychologists.

Wilhelm Wundt was the first to bring the will within the range of experiment. He hoped to prove that that phenomenon which until then had been known simply as the human will might be referred back to sensations of tension, associative feelings, and their reproduction and perception. Wundt made a large number of observation in his Leipzig laboratory, and, on the basis of the various sensory and muscular reactions he noted, he came to the conclusion that the will was certainly not dependent upon mechanical causality, as the English natural philosophers had believed, but that it was determined by an inner "psychical causality."

The results obtained by Wundt with his experimental mediums appeared to lead to the conclusion that every act of the will was determined by a number of "motives." Free will was thus limited to this, that man was obviously capable "by a deliberate choice between various motives" to guide himself in his actions.

This theory of motives soon became a scientific fashion, very much like the "vogue of grace" of the seventeenth century. For it was stimulating enough to be taught that human actions were the result of some kind of occasion, but that such occasions were not to be described as "causes" but solely as "motives." But while causes necessarily brought about a definite result, this was not so with motives. The connection between the motives and the action following them was not definite and calculable beforehand like the play of mechanical forces; a "choice" had to be made, and it was this which decided the final action of the individual.

Thus this doctrine of motives made it possible to regard the will, on the one hand, as determined, thus stilling the rational doubts as to freedom, and, on the other hand, as an agent for practical purposes, and thereby restoring that illusion which man had cherished from the earliest times.

The experimental psychological method invented by Fechner and Wundt was soon to become obsolete owing to the activities of a new and apparently more modern school. The Würzburg professor, Oswald Külpe, established an experimental institution in which the higher mental processes were investigated and analyzed with greater precision. Narziss Ach, one of the leading members of the "Würzburg school," introduced an entirely new terminology for the designation of the elements of consciousness, and the most eager efforts were made to study experimentally every type of psychical action including that of volition.

For this purpose, recourse was had especially to the questionnaire method. The subject of the experiment was given a certain mental task to perform, and he was then asked what inner perceptions he had been conscious of while preforming the task. A large number of surprising results were reached in this manner, which discredited many of the former assumptions of psychology.

Quite independently of the Würzburg school, the Belgian psychologist, Michotte, was also studying the problem of the will by means of experimental methods. He endeavored to discover what really took place when a human being was called upon to make a decision. Experimental subjects were therefore required "to choose" between two given alternatives, and to make an exact note of their emotions during this process. The first result was a "sensation of activity"; the person making the choice breathed more deeply, his muscles contracted and relaxed.

From the time when skeptical psychologists had begun to conduct laboratory experiments on the will, and to record by means of measuring apparatus and memoranda the phenomena which occurred during the making of a choice, the position of the indeterminists appeared to be more in danger than ever before. So long as the study of the problem of free will had remained confined to the philosophers, the only subject of debate was that of freedom or otherwise, and doubt had never been cast on the existence of the will as an entity. But with these experiments, the will, round which was centered the whole controversy, seemed to have been resolved into reactions, sensations and reflexes, a result which cast serious doubt on the very existence of the will.

The Jesuits, however, whose theory of the will had stood the inclemencies of centuries, and whose convictions remained undisturbed whether by quotations from the fathers or by papal bulls, had now to summon all their resources in order to refute the discoveries of the professors of psychology; and once more it became evident that the free will of the learned Jesuit fathers was still able to supply proof of its obstinate vitality.

Just as at an earlier period the Society of Jesus had been able to confront the great heretical preachers with their own equally great controversialists, just as, during the period of the great astronomical discoveries which seemed likely to be dangerous to them, they were able to produce astronomers of repute to defend the old beliefs, so at this juncture the order was not at a loss. Jesuit experimental psychologists were at once set to work, in the same laboratories, with the same appliances, in order to discover data in favor of the doctrine of free will.

The Jesuit father, Johann Lindworsky, a psychologist from the Würzburg school, with no small skill, making use precisely of the most modern experimental methods was successful in reproducing proofs of the freedom of the will, and whoever studies these lucid and convincingly written works is forced to the conclusion that the entire method of experimental psychology was invented for the very purpose of affirming the correctness of the Jesuit theories of the will.

According to Lindworsky, the results of these experiments indicate an "innermost core of will-experience," which "differs from all other psychological events such as feeling, thinking, muscular sensations, and the like." Mechanistic determinations, to which other psychological events may be subject, can therefore have no influence whatever on the will. Lindworsky replied in a very emphatic manner to the question whether the modern experimental psychology admits in any way of the existence of free will by stating that he can mention no fact which disproves the effective freedom of the will."

But modern psychology demonstrates how little effect the repetition, no matter how prolonged, of energetic acts of volition has, as a general rule, on a strong will. Ignatius, as early as the sixteenth century, long before the time of Wundt, Ach and Michotte, was therefore perfectly correct in his assumption that the will must be strengthened and guided by the provision of suitable "motives." Lindworsky was surprisingly successful in twisting imperceptibly the sober experimental psychological analysis is such a manner that the reader becomes involuntarily convinced of the correctness of the Jesuit theories of free will.

But hardly had the Jesuits put themselves into the position not only to withstand the attacks of modern psychology, but also to use the new experimental methods as a mean of demonstrating the freedom of the will and the correctness of the Jesuit system, when there appeared from another direction a new and even more threatening danger for indeterminism.

Behaviorism, Plant-Lice and Pavlov's Dog

One of the finest and most noble characteristics of modern investigators, which distinguishes them so worthily from the crazy dogmatists of earlier times, is that, whenever they recognize the errors of their new theories, they resolutely abandon them.

Notwithstanding the precise measurements, the questionnaires, and all the refinements of scientific precision with which the inquiry into the will and been conducted, it had in the end to be admitted that all these experiments had no bearing whatsoever upon the act of volition and the faculty of decision. What had happened, in fact, was that, under observation, the subject had been lost, and all that remained was an extraordinarily refined method of psychological investigation.

Else Wentscher in her book on the will frankly admits this tragic result of these laboratory investigations, and she shows how, during the experiments, the experimental subject is in no way able effectively to "will" or to "choose" while his experiences are being so carefully studied. "It is obvious that an experiment having for its object the manner in which a decision is made can have no useful result, since my intention to act as a subject of experiment must be formed beforehand, and since the various reactions manifested by me during the experiment are released without any consciousness of volition in response to the order which I have received. Equally little can the experiment decide how the determining tendency proceeding from my intention would act under other stimuli and the internal or external difficulties that would then arise. For, in the case of reactions so prepared, all the factors are absent which complicate my actions in life, because they impose on me other reactions than those first planned."

Not less melancholy are the conclusions reached by William James, the founder of American "pragmatism." After many investigations, he comes to the conclusion, supported by tedious and somewhat obscure observations, that the answer to the question whether or not there is such a thing as free will depends on whether the amount of effort of which the will is capable is regarded as a fixed reaction on our part which the object that resists us necessarily calls forth, or whether, rather, it is not more closely related to what the mathematicians call an "independent variable." If the amount of our effort is not a definite function of other data, then our will may be regarded as free. If, on the other hand, the amount of effort put forth by our will is a definite and fixed function of external circumstances, then our wills are not free and all our actions are pre-determined.

Stripped of its scientific and mathematical terminology, this explanation of James's appears to be merely an empty definition which implies nothing beyond the statement that the will is not free when it is subject to causality, and that it is free when it is not subject to causality. It need hardly be pointed out that this statement can hardly be termed a discovery, and certainly not an original one.

James himself finally admits that in the end all experiments fail to produce any result when an attempt is made to explore the unfathomable complexities of the problem of the will. Whether the will is free or not, what freedom or the reverse really implies in relation to the will and, finally, what is the nature of that which is described as the will—all these things, according to the explanation given by James, are absolutely incapable of definition by psychological observations and investigations. Hence the final conclusion reached by this thinker is the truth that the question of free will is insoluble on strictly psychologic grounds."

The gifted simplicity of this statement recalls the sublime humility of the great Leibniz when, finally, after all his attempts at establishing the will philosophically, he wrote in resignation: "It is better to say with St. Paul that there are certain sublime reasons of wisdom and harmony; these are unknown to mortal men. . . ."

Psychology has thus confessed its incompetence in this matter; nevertheless it adheres to its firm conviction that in itself it is a science, and that there certainly is something which can be described as psychology. On the other hand, Bertrand Russell, that great diagnostician of the present, in his *Analysis of Mind*, points out with great perspicacity what is really wrong: the will, he holds, can certainly be observed, but in reality it does not exist. What we are accustomed to call "will," "desire" and "impulse" is fundamentally not an inner state which can be clearly described and verified as an empirically given fact. The word "will," strictly speaking, signifies nothing more than a chain of actions which reveal a definite and typical sequence. Beneath them we have to understand a causal law of our deeds and behavior, but not a something that exists in our mind as something independent and real.

It is clear, Russell holds, that we have the right to say that we wish to do this or that, and that we thus act on our intentions; in this sense the will appears as an event capable of being observed; but all theories that go beyond this, treating the will as a happening capable of isolation or as a faculty of the soul, are nothing more than a "metaphysical superstition."

Although Russell thus clearly demonstrates the futility of all psychological investigations into the will, there is in his words a respect, natural to the European, for this age-old problem in the history of the mind. The new "American science," however, with the wholly merciless ingenuousness of its youthful desire for knowledge, rejects entirely this obsolescent psychology; not only are its methods erroneous, but its very existence is based upon an error; it is a pseudo-science juggling with illusory problems.

The Power and Secret of the Jesuits

John B. Watson, one of the leaders of this new American school, in his fundamental work, *Behaviorism*, writes in these disparaging terms: "It was the boast of Wundt's students, in 1879, when the first psychological laboratory was established, that psychology had as last become a science without a soul. For fifty years we have kept this pseudo-science, exactly as Wundt laid it down. All that Wundt and his students really accomplished was to substitute for the word 'soul' the word 'consciousness.'"

But how absurd it is to speak even of "consciousness" or of any other kind of intellectual hypothesis, since the most recent physiological investigations claim to have proved that all so-called processes of consciousness are attributable to chemical and mechanical reactions!

When at the beginning of the seventeenth century, Francis Bacon heralded the dawn of a new epoch of human thought, he proclaimed that man must learn to think anew, and must for this reason, with a child's ingenuous freedom from preconceived ideas, allow himself to be taught by nature.

"Idols of every kind," Bacon states in his *Novum Organum*, "must be renounced and put away with a fixed and solemn determination, and the understanding thoroughly freed and cleansed; the entrance into the kingdom of man, founded on the sciences, being not much other than the entrance into the kingdom of heaven, whereinto none may enter except as a little child."

Although a weighty impulse to the study of the empirical sciences, as well as many influences which remain active even in our own age, is attributable to the mind of Bacon, yet, despite the endeavors which have been so fervidly made, European thought has been unable to free itself entirely from all the older traditions. It therefore remained for the new and unwearied nations, devoid of respect for the past and unfettered by piety or tradition, to give full effect to the words which Bacon had uttered three hundred years before, and to survey the world in that modern and ingenuous manner which the great seventeenth-century rebel had demanded. The Russians and Americans, these children of our culture, were alone able to encompass that "fixed and solemn determination" by which "idols of every kind" could be "renounced and put away."

With youthful absence of preconceived ideas, the Russians and Americans set to work, unhampered by any "idols," at first to study plant-lice and dogs, and on the basis of the discoveries they thus made to form an entirely modern conception of the organic world. It is especially stimulating to note the simple air of conviction with which the great American investigator, Jacques Loeb, comes to the conclusion, after studying the behavior of winged plant-lice when subjected to the influence of light, that all the processes in the human being which had until that time been termed "soul" are nothing more than exactly conditioned chemical and physical reactions.

In his work on "tropisms," Loeb describes the results of the investigations undertaken by him, according to which the plant-lice are forced to direct their movement towards a source of light, and he explains how it is possible, by the use of certain acids, to compel other species of animals to behave in a similarly heliotropic manner. According to Loeb, in all these cases, the will of the animal is in the light alone, just as the force of gravity determines the movement of a falling stone or of a planet.

Behaviorism, Plant-Lice and Pavlov's Dog

Loeb at once proceeds to elaborate the deductions to be made from these studies of plant-lice. "These experiments may be of great importance from the ethical point of view. The supreme ethical manifestation, namely, the fact that men may be willing to sacrifice their lives for an idea, is incomprehensible both from the utilitarian point of view and from that of the categorical imperative. But even in such a case it may well be that under the influence of certain ideas, chemical changes (for example, internal secretions) may be set up in the body which increase to an extraordinary degree its sensitiveness to certain impulses, so that men may be just as much the slaves of certain stimuli as the copepods are the slaves of light. That what the philosopher terms an 'idea' is an event due to the action of chemical processes on the body, does not today seem to us so unacceptable since Pavlov and his followers have been successful in producing salivary secretions in a dog by means of optical and acoustic signals."

For, while in America the plant-lice seemed to be digging a grave for free will, in St. Petersburg the dogs had produced unassailable evidence against Pelagianism. The famous Russian psychologist, I. P. Pavlov, had for many years been studying the relation between the feeling of sensual desire or the absence of such a feeling, and the salivary secretions of dogs, and had proved that it was possible to attribute merely to conditioned reflexes many events which had previously been regarded as "psychical."

This was wholly in harmony with the modern American theory of "Behaviorism," which is based on the assumption that we can know external objects only by their behavior under certain conditions: to deduce any interior happening, or a soul, from this behavior is in any case wholly unsound, and should therefore be fundamentally rejected. To treat psychology as a science seems to the behaviorists justified only so long as it limits itself to studying and noting the manner in which living creatures behave in certain external circumstances.

Pavlov's investigations speedily aroused much interest in New York where people began to make systematic experiments on dogs by burning their noses with red-hot irons, and observing the symptoms of their desires on being confronted with a ham-bone. The American records of the salivary secretions under the most varying conditions also led to the discovery that free will was a back number.

Bertrand Russell, one of whose most attractive qualities is a sense of humor, usually so uncommon among great students, describes in an amusing manner the real significance of the new American theories expounded by Watson in regard to behavior, when he writes: "The popular version of behaviorism will, I imagine, be something like this: In old days there was supposed to be a thing called the mind, which was capable of three types of activity—feeling, knowing and willing. Now, it has been ascertained that there is no such thing as the mind, but only the body. All our activities consist of bodily processes. 'Feeling' consists of visceral occurrences particularly such as are connected with the glands. 'Knowing' consists of movements of the larynx. 'Willing' consists of all other movements depending upon striped muscles."

The "Chicago school" has recently outdone all the earlier results of the St. Petersburg and new York animal experiments, and the well-known professors, Charles Child and Judson Herrick, have formulated the theory that the will belongs to the domain of the mechanical and physical "vectors"; it is a physiological "gradient" of a type which can be expressed in a very simple, brief, and mathematically demonstrable formula of "vector analysis."

These investigations by which thought becomes an activity of the larynx, sensation a function of the viscera, and the will an affair of the striped muscles seem to have finally abolished the doctrine of the freedom of the human will. But, no matter what the "behavior" of the experimental dogs in St. Petersburg and New York may be, no matter what chemical process occurs in Jacques Loeb's plant-lice, no matter what mechanical or electrodynamic "gradients" the Chicago levelling instruments may record, free will is only apparently defunct.

The Jesuits of an earlier age refused to allow their convictions to be shaken by the miracles in favor of the Jansenist doctrine of predestination, and now they are not disposed to yield to the brutal prosiness of the modern physiological, chemical and electrodynamic investigations.

They hold that with all the earlier discoveries of the empirical sciences, whether in astronomy, physics or chemistry, it had always at first appeared that the old faiths were completely destroyed by these new discoveries, as if no reasonable man could henceforth believe in the existence of God, of mind, or of free will. Nevertheless, it has ever and again been the case that from the ranks of the faithful members of the order, one member has emerged to study the stars, another has devoted himself to the logarithmic tables, a third has bent over the microscope, and a fourth has betoken himself to the chemical laboratory, in order that, equipped with the most reliable apparatus of the exact sciences, they might again prove the very contrary of that which the new investigations at first seemed to have proved.

The pious fathers made use of the same apparatus as their lay opponents, produced the same reactions on animals, and finally proved from the same dogs and plant-lice, with no less pride, that, in spite of everything, God existed, that there were such things as a soul, an intellect, and—notwithstanding the assertions of their enemies—also free will, and that these were from all time to all eternity.

To the haughty "finis" of secular science the Jesuits, at the conclusion of their studies, in Christian humility, retorted with a not less firm and resolute "amen." Thus, Father Erich Wasmann, the great Jesuit zoologist, has succeeded, by means of his well-known studies of ants, bees and other insects, in proving the existence of God, and, by means of the "behavior" of the insects, revealed the existence of an omniscient and benevolent Creator and Ruler of the universe. By the aid of palæontological entomology, Wasmann is even endeavoring to establish the Biblical story of the Creation more firmly and more unshakably than even the most enlightened priests and the most learned scholastics were ever able to do.

In opposition to the Monistic doctrine of existence which denies that there is a God or mind, the Jesuits have produced a regular "insect-theology," and they will be fully capable of defending free will with some measure of success against the new Russo-American attacks. It may be anticipated that once again the Society of Jesus will make use of the same weapons as its opponents, and we may shortly look for a "Behavior-Molinism" as the latest Jesuit theory. Pavlov's dog may bark never so loudly, the army of Loyola's disciples, which has been journeying for so many centuries, will nevertheless move steadily and unperturbedly onwards.

PART IV

THE MORAL PHILOSOPHY OF THE JESUITS

Free Will and Responsibility

Not infrequently, examinations into the fundamental problems of human existence have ultimately led to the conclusion that, notwithstanding the utmost efforts to arrive at definite solutions, nothing else remains but to accept resignedly the fact that the much-discussed problems are incapable of solution. With the exception of professional thinkers, philosophers, theologians and psychologists, humanity has, in general, without demur, and, indeed, without any appreciable regret, accommodated itself to a situation that cannot be altered and has definitely abandoned all hope of exact information. Further discussions and investigations have been readily left to institutions maintained for this purpose, universities, seminaries, laboratories and monasteries; in these institutions those persons who desired to probe further into insoluble problems were discreetly secluded from the outside world, thus humanity has succeeded in maintaining through centuries and ages its continued existence under tolerably favorable conditions, unmoved by the obscure problems of existence.

Controversy over the freedom of the will has alone broken down the unwritten pact between humanity and its thinkers, has disturbed this agreement, by virtue of which the philosophers, in order to relieve an otherwise over-harassed world of supererogatory troubles, were to confine themselves within their sleepy academies and wearisome congresses.

With a persistence and a violence totally unfitted to a problem of such depth and importance, the doctrines about the freedom or otherwise of the will have penetrated into all classes of society, and, like an evil pestilence, have demanded their victims. The strongest as well as the weakest heads have fallen victim to the epidemic, ardent theological controversialists and literary men of intellectual standing, no less than barren pamphleteers and nuns of gently nature and pious minds.

The explanation of the devastating consequences of this brooding over the question of free will is to be found in the vague, perhaps false, but nevertheless quite indisseverable, relationship which the human mind from the earliest times has established between the will and the ethical and juridical judgment of human actions. For this reason, the problem whether our wills are in fact free seems to have acquired enormous practical significance in the whole field of civil and ecclesiastical law in the western world.

The Power and Secret of the Jesuits

This fateful association of ethics with the problem of the will can be traced back to certain doctrines of Aristotle, and it may well be said that this Greek philosopher bequeathed to mankind not only a fund of valuable knowledge, but also a number of really momentous errors. It is to the views propounded by this Greek thinker that we owe the whole subsequent lack of certainty, prevailing even today, in the determination of moral and juridical problems; and whoever attempts to study, with all due impartiality, even the most modern moral teachings or works on the philosophy of law, will, quite early, feel himself enshrouded in a dense obscurity arising out of the mass of age-old false conceptions.

Democritus had, indeed, handed down two pronouncement to the effect that, not man's actions, but the intention behind the actions, should form the criterion of moral judgment: "Virtue does not consist in refraining from doing evil, but in willing no evil. . . an evil person is not he who does evil, but he who designs to do evil." Plato also declared in his ninth book of *Laws* that the man who performs an action unconsciously and without definite intention cannot be held to have done wrong. The fundamental thing is not the act performed but the thought behind it.

But it was Aristotle, in his *Nicomachean Ethics,* who was the first to work up into a system this relationship between the will and ethics; and his conclusions accordingly became the basis of most later conceptions in morality and law. Aristotle sets out by assuming that virtue is a form of activity of the will; the will can, however, be regarded as the underlying basis of morality only if it be recognized as having full consciousness. He considers that our will is at all times able to form conscious decisions, and, accordingly, it is always within the power of man to decide whether to do right or wrong.

Later jurisprudence in the states of ancient Hellas conformed entirely to the views formulated by Aristotle: for example, under Greek law, deliberate murder was regarded as a serious crime meriting death, whereas the killing of a person unintentionally and without premeditated malice was visited with a much less severe punishment. The Roman Stoics also adopted this view, and similarly upheld the doctrine that virtuous and reprehensible actions were distinguished one from the other only by the good or evil intention of the doer.

The celebrated conception of the *dolus*, or evil intention, evolved with such care by the Roman jurists, is based entirely on the acceptance of the principle that the conscious will is the bearer of moral and legal responsibility; a *dolus* exists only when the will to act in a manner forbidden by the law is there. Whereas originally, in assessing the punishment that should be inflicted, considerable weight had been given to the consequences arising out of an action, under the later conception, influenced by the Greek philosophy, practically equal importance was attached to both the action and the wrongful intention.

In this, as in many other matters, the Christian world, during the Middle Ages, adhered closely to the Græco-Roman traditions. In the writings of the fathers of the Church, Chrysostom and Ambrose, as well as of the patriarch Germanus and later Abelard and his great opponent Bernard of Clairvaux, there are numerous passages which clearly indicate agreement with the legal conception of the freedom of the will. St. Chrysostom writes: "God punishes or rewards not the deed as such but the intention." Abelard too, expressly says: "God does not judge actions but intentions."

As scholasticism fell more and more under the influence of the writings of Aristotle, so in Christian mediaeval thought did the views of the Stagirite get more clearly the upper hand. Thomas Aquinas evolved a complete system out of the principle that no action as such had any moral content, except in so far as it sprang from an act of the free will. But in due course temporal jurisprudence as well fell more and more under the domination of the principle that not the deed, but the intention of the doer, should form the basis of adjudication.

The Jesuits and Absolution

All the numerous text-books on morals written by Jesuit authors are filled with instructions to the father-confessors to practice, wherever possible, the utmost leniency in the exercise of the office they have received from God as judges of morals, so as not to render it unduly difficult for believers to partake of the penitential sacrament and not to bar their road to salvation. The father-confessor is, therefore, urged to act towards the penitent in such a way "that from the moment he leaves the confessional, he is disposed to return to it quickly," "Send no one away dejected," wrote Ignatius to his disciple, Simon Rodriguez, at Lisbon.

According to the unanimous view of all Catholic theologians, man stores up for himself, during his life here on earth, rewards or punishments, which are meted out to him in the life after death; upon his behavior on earth his future fate depends, and he who departs this life unreconciled with God has no further opportunity for reconciliation with the Creator or for securing the remission of the condemnation he has incurred.

The Jesuits, however, knew that, although man's conscience urged him to adhere to virtue, he was constantly impelled to commit sin by evil desires. The task of ensuring eternal bliss for all men of good will appeared, therefore, to be continually brought to naught by the imperfections and sinfulness of man: how could the poor mortal, conscious of his weakness and his many failings hope for salvation? Daily and hourly be found himself in conflict with God's ordinances.

Thus then, the chief aim of the Jesuits was to draw as many as possible, by the exercise of lenience, to the confessional, so that, by the dispensation of absolution, they might be saved from eternal damnation. For absolution granted by the priest, according to the Catholic creed, was held to have the effect of restoring the sinner to a state of complete innocence. Or at least of commuting the eternal punishment of hell for a punishment of limited duration. As, however, the Jesuits were fully conscious that humanity in general is inclined to take alarm at too much strictness, and that people were seldom prepared to endure severe penances in this life in the hope of salvation in the next, a completely new system of indulgence in the judging of all sinful failings had to be thought out.

Catholic teaching distinguished between two forms of repentance for sins committed: the so-called "natural remorse," or *attritio*, arising from fear of God's punishment, and the "full penitence," or *contritio*, arising from the consciousness of the sinful nature of an action and from love towards God. According to the doctrines of the moral theologians, "attrition" sufficed for the remission of an offence and for the admission of the sinner to the sacrament, provided that the intention existed to refrain from the commission of further sin. Certain among the Jesuits have gone very far in this respect. Thus, for example, the causist Fillucius writes that the slightest degree of repentance is quite sufficient to secure absolution, even if the penitent merely acknowledges that he would willingly feel repentance.

In their endeavor to bring as many human sins as possible within the compass of absolution, the Jesuits were very effectively aided by Aristotle's doctrine of the freedom of the will, which had already hitherto exercised such a strong influence on the ethical and juridical judgment of human actions. For the Jesuits, whose whole energies were devoted to ensuring for even the weakest of mortals the attainment of bliss and admission into the kingdom of heaven this system was bound to assume the utmost importance.

If, for example, man were credited with a will of which alone it depended whether good was good and evil evil, it was possible, by a thoroughly plausible argument, to reach the conclusion that humanity did not contravene God's moral decrees quite so frequently as might originally have appeared to be the case. To be sure, everyone was constantly committing what, to all outward appearances, were wrongful actions; but in how many cases could it not be said that the freedom of the will and, therefore, the responsibility of the wrong-doer were restricted or entirely eliminated by a variety of circumstances!

The pupils of Loyola, therefore, endeavored, systematically and with all that logical accuracy which was a feature of the scholastic mind, to judge every conceivable case of human transgression according to whether the ultimate underlying intention was good or bad; and in this way indeterminism found in Jesuit moral casuistry its most practical application.

It is this, however, which gives to Jesuitism its exceptional significance. The question how far the conscious will enters into the performance of an action, and what relationship exists between intention and guilt, is still even today widely disputed. Jesuit morality has made it possible, because it has drawn the most extreme conclusions from an indeterminist code of morals, to observe the results to which such a system, based entirely on the thesis of the freedom of the will, must ultimately lead.

According to the Jesuit conception, morality consists in establishing harmony between the human will and that of God; consequently, human acts are capable of a moral evaluation only in so far as they are accomplished by "election," by a voluntary choice between good and evil. It thus follows that generally only those actions which are the result of such a "free elective decision" can be regarded as moral or immoral; the action in and for itself acquires its ethical character only through conscious intention.

"As the law was given to man and not to beasts, and, accordingly, must be fulfilled in human fashion," writes the celebrated moral theologian Busembaum, "the fulfilment of every moral prescription, whether it be human or divine, must constitute a human act, and, consequently, must be accomplished in freedom and with the will of the actor."

It follows from this, however, according to Busembaum, that an act can be regarded as sinful only if, in the performance of the act, the intention exists to violate the moral order of the world. For just as a good action is nothing else than a voluntary compliance with moral law, so a sinful action is a "voluntary departure" from moral standards, "an action or an omission which is not merely intentional, but also is free, and contains some evil intention."

This principle, the Jesuits maintain, still holds good even in the case of a person attacked by reprehensible desires. So long as he does not "give way to them of his own volition," he is either entirely blameless or at least his responsibility is very much minimized. Accordingly,

The Jesuits and Absolution

one cannot be held to account for sinful thoughts, heretical impulses, sensual imaginings and carnal cravings, unless they are "brought about intentionally" or are "wilfully assented to."

As an example of a sin which loses its reprehensible character by reason of lack of acquiescence of the will, Gury quotes the case of a woman to whom violence has been offered: "A woman who has offered every possible resistance to violation commits no sin, even if her chastity is defiled; for none sins in that which happens against his will."

Even in the earliest instructions and letters of the founder of the order, this conception of the sinlessness of involuntary desires is evident; in the year 1536, for instance, Ignatius wrote to his friend, Theresa Rejadella, who, as a nun, in her convent at Barcelona was tortured by sinful temptations: "Do not distress yourself regarding wicked or sensual cravings, or on account of the sense of your imperfections or weakness, so long as they are in no degree attributable to your conscious vice. For not even St. Peter of St. Paul has gone so far as to contend that humanity is entirely proof against such things. . . What alone is of importance is that I should govern my spirit according to God's will. . . ."

The Jesuit writings on moral casuistry all emphasize in the introductory chapters that the father-confessor must examine closely into the intentions of the penitent before pronouncing judgment. Thus, while it is recognized that unchastity is essentially a grave sin, yet it should be regarded as such only "when the yielding to cravings of the flesh is conscious and deliberate."

Gury, in his moral teachings, cites a large number of cases where apparently grave offences against the law of chastity should go unpunished. Not only is it no sin to read improper books, provided the reader does not deliberately seek sensual excitement, but also "*pollution nocturna culpa vacat*," if it is not "intentionally brought about" and "acquiesced in." A variety of actions may indeed involve the danger of sensual excitement, but are, nevertheless, not sinful, provided the intention prevails not to give way deliberately to the sensual excitement which may be expected to arise.

"If," writes Busembaum, "a person, without constraint or necessity, performs an action which he knows will normally bring about stimulation of the flesh—as, for example, when, from curiosity, he reads or listens to something evil—he is guilty only of a minor sin, if no direct intention and no risk of assent exists. If he has any justifiable reason for his action, he commits no sin at all."

Even in the case of offences against the principles of the faith, Gury applies the principle of exculpation in the absence of conscious acquiescence of the will. He certainly emphasizes this, that to doubt God's revelation is a grave sin against the authority of the revealing Deity, but this is at the same time qualified as follows: "He who, though outwardly professing a heresy, is not inwardly heretical, is not a true heretic." Only he who, of his own will and with the consent of his mind, doubts the truths of the faith is to be regarded as a heretic.

The apparently simple assumption that an action was wrongful only when a wrongful intention definitely existed enabled the Jesuits in many instances to absolve sinners who had outwardly contravened the laws of the Church. This absolution attained a much wider latitude when it became the practice to examine logically, quite in accordance with the doctrines of Aristotle, into the precise circumstances governing the extent to which the will was free or restricted. According to Aristotle, the will can be regarded as being free only in cases where comprehension and reasoned judgment are preliminary to the exercise of the will; a free decision of the will is possible only on the basis of a clear appreciation of the circumstances prevailing within and without. This led the Jesuits, quite logically, to the moral principle that man's actions are capable of judgment from a moral standpoint only if, in their performance, the will and reason have functioned freely. The object of the will, therefore, can only be that which has first of all been understood by the mind; without understanding, no true act of will can take place.

Consistently with this theory, the most modern Jesuit moral theologian, Victor Cathrein, regards morality as "merely a certain manner in which an action proceeds from the reason and the will." If something is performed in such a way "that the reason is mindful of the relationship of the action to the established standards of human conduct and the decision of the will is freely reached," then the action is moral; in cases where these conditions are not satisfied, then the actions "are no longer susceptible of moral judgment, and are neither praiseworthy nor blameworthy."

Thus, according to the Jesuit notion, two conditions have to be satisfied before an action can be judged from a moral point of view. The reason must be in a position to judge the relationship of the contemplated action to the moral law, and the will must "decide freely on action in the light of this understanding." "If my reason tells me," says Cathrein, "that an action conforms to moral law, and I decide freely on the action, then the action is morally good; if my reason tells me that the action is opposed to moral standards, and I, nevertheless, decide on the action, then it is morally bad." If, however, in this way, every action which is susceptible of moral judgment presupposes the exercise of the reason, then only those persons who are fully able to exercise their reasoning powers can properly be judged strictly according to the laws.

This basing of responsibility on reasoned judgment, on consciousness and on "due reflection" creates manifold possibilities of limiting the number of man's sins. According to this doctrine, man must in no wise be held accountable for actions performed in ignorance, even though they may have been intentional and in themselves sinful; ignorance annuls the necessary freedom of choice of the will and, therefore, all responsibility.

The degree of guilt is furthermore minimized by every other factor which might influence clear judgment and conscious thought while the will is reaching its decision. Chief among these factors are forgetfulness and inattention. Whoever omits to perform a good action on account of lack of thought is to be held accountable only in a very limited degree for any sinfulness involved in the omission. "The light of knowledge which is essential for the free exercise of the will" is also absent in this case.

A careful distinction is made in the Jesuit moral theology between *ignorantia juris* and *ignorantia facti*, between *ignorantia vincibilis* and *ignorantia invincibilis*, according to the effort made to acquire the necessary knowledge. Believers are, however, comforted by a reference to the fact that "there is no law which requires that any very strong effort should be made."

The same blameless ignorance can be invoked in the case of actions prompted by inordinate desire, for in these cases too we are, to some extent at least, deprived of our powers of clear reasoning: "An action which is the outcome of an inordinate desire is certainly an act of the will." Says Gury, "but it is by no means formally voluntary and free; for, as the attention of the mind is completely annulled. So too must freedom and self-determination be completely lacking."

Similarly, fear sets aside clear judgment and free decision, and, consequently, responsibility; like inordinate desire, therefore, it acquits of grave sin. But fear also ensures exoneration even when a moral law has been violated by someone because otherwise a material prejudice was to be feared. "Moreover, it often happens," writes Busembaum, "that certain prescriptions are not binding when their observance would bring about a grave injury. Whoever, therefore, from fear of such injury, fails to observe a prescription does not commit sin, since, in this case, the prescription is not valid."

Therefore, according to Gury, an adulteress is not compelled to confess her fault to her husband, as, by so doing, she would expose herself to the danger of incurring his hatred and thus place her life in peril, or at least otherwise prejudice herself seriously. Further, a servant is permitted to aid and abet his master in wrong-doing, when a refusal would cost him his place.

Thus, with the premise that actions could acquire a moral character only when they were prompted by the clearly conscious will, and when the will, in turn, was governed by the mind, it came about that there was a whole series of sins for which man should not be made fully responsible. Naturally, the sinner could not in every case be straightway acquitted of his offence, but in most cases it was possible to find means of at least minimizing his guilt. In those cases where it did not appear possible to grant complete absolution forthwith, the system enabled the offence to be regarded as a "venial sin" instead of a "mortal sin."

For the Catholic Church distinguishes between those grave offences against God's laws which are severely punishable, and which are designated as "mortal sins," and those minor offences which are nothing more than a "falling short of God's demands." Whilst "mortal sin" excludes man from the Kingdom of Heaven, and brings down the wrath of the Creator on the offending mortal, the punishment for venial sin is not nearly so severe: even the most righteous are not free from such sins, and God is appeased by a light earthly penance.

The Jesuits, who were concerned first and last with securing for weak mortals absolution from their sins, found, with the help of the ancient conclusions of Aristotle, an easy means of transforming a large number of mortal sins into venial sins. Their moral theologians, while adhering closely to the definitions of the Church, taught that the "objectively grave sin" was also "subjectively" grave, involving eternal damnation, only when the sinner offended against the law of God "consciously and deliberately, and, therefore, with full appreciation and with complete freedom of the will." The punishment for deadly sin, they declared, is so severe solely for the reason that such sin must be regarded as a conscious and deliberate defiance of God; if, however, a clear consciousness of the sinful nature of the action is absent, or if the freedom of the will is lacking, then the subjective guilt is only of a venial nature, however grave the sin may appear objectively.

Ignatius himself draws this particular distinction, based on the acquiescence of the will, between mortal and venial sins; he once wrote, for instance, that man commits a grave sin "if he acquiesces in an evil thought," whilst only venial sin is committed "if the thought of committing a mortal sin enters into a man's mind," and he "entertains the thought for a very short time or derives some sensual satisfaction from it," but finally denies his assent to it.

This view is to be found throughout almost the whole field of Jesuit moral casuistry. Juan de Castillo, for example, holds that even theft is a venial sin, if it is committed without due reflection. With correct understanding and anticipating our modern conception of "kleptomania," he recognizes "that there are people who appropriate a thing before they become fully conscious of what they are doing."

"The End Justifies the Means"

The Jesuits were, however, clever enough not only to develop the negative side of the theory of the freedom of the will into an organized system of absolution by demonstrating in numerous cases that the offender had no intention of committing evil, but also, on the other hand, to indicate, from the positive character of the will, a number of grounds for the exoneration of wrong-doing. If an attempt is made to determine, as regards a particular act, what the real intention of the "will" was in the matter, it is frequently observed that, although objectively the act may have been inadmissible, yet subjectively the intention may have been good.

These considerations soon led, indeed, to very difficult and thorny ground. Everything was clear enough so long as it was a question of the simple relationship between the intention and the intended act; whoever strove with good will to do good could not possibly thereby transgress the moral laws. What, however, was the position when the good intention was directed towards a remote end, the attainment of which was possible only through the employment of some intermediate means, which is and for itself was not willed? Would this means, in every case, become good because it was to serve a good end?

The Jesuits now hold the view that, in many instances a good intention can justify even the choice of less good means. They contend that, in the abstract, man's moral consciousness is certainly primarily disposed to regard the application of immoral means to a moral end as essentially to be condemned; in practical life, however, innumerable instances have over and over again, tended to lead to the opposite conclusion. How often does it not happen that we are compelled to tell a lie to avoid injuring someone, and it is easy to conceive of a case in which a lie might be the means of saving a person's life.

Thus it can often enough happen that man's moral consciousness may place the ultimate purpose of an act on a higher plane than the means by which it is attained; it is by no means an unusual thing to feel that the person responsible for an act had no intention of committing an offence, that the purpose in view was, on the contrary, good, and that the employment of reprehensible means was a necessity.

The ancient Jewish moral code had of old permitted a wide use of means, in themselves forbidden, when these were to serve a praiseworthy end. Thus the Talmud expressly says that, where necessary, even unchastity and idolatry are permissible in order to preserve God's holy name from profanation (Qiddushin, 40a; Sanhedrin, 107a; and Yebamoth, 79a). Martin Luther, too, frequently defended wrongful actions performed in the cause of the true faith, as, for example, when, on the occasion of a meeting with the councilors of the

"The End Justifies the Means"

Landgrave of Hesse, he made the remark: "What wrong can there be in telling a downright good lie for a good cause and for the advancement of the Christian Church?"

Similarly, many of the fathers and scholars of the mediaeval church acknowledged the permissibility of immoral acts for a moral end. Chrysostom himself says: "Seest thou not how not only God but man too accepts the principle that regard should be had not to the nature of an action, but to its purpose?" The patriarch Germanus expressed himself still more plainly: "Everywhere the aim of the actor is taken into consideration, and this aim either acquits him of guilt or condemns him."

Similar maxims can be found in Augustine: "The intention justifies the deed, but faith prompts the intention. Pay no great heed to what a man does, but rather to what he has in mind in doing... One and the same matter, measured by the varying purpose behind it, becomes a subject for approbation or abhorrence, merit or condemnation."

"I venture to say," writes Bernard of Clairvaux, "That only the good intention is worthy of praise; good will is not shorn of its merit even when the action itself is not good." Similar views are expressed by Abelard, Albertus Magnus, Bonaventura and Thomas Aquinas; the last asks the question "whether human actions are, in general, good or bad, according to the end in view," and answers it very decidedly in the affirmative.

The question of the relationship between the end and means was, in the hey-day of scholasticism, the subject of a heated dispute between Thomas Aquinas and his Nominalist opponent, the *doctor sublimis,* Duns Scotus. The latter had contended that there are considerable number of actions, in themselves indifferent, which cannot be brought into any moral relationship with the causing will. Thomas Aquinas, on the other hand, denied the possibility of any such indifferent acts, and maintained that in every action man has some purpose in view, which is necessarily either in conformity with or opposed to his judgment, and thus must be either morally good or bad; morally indifferent actions are, therefore, quite inconceivable.

According to this conception of Thomas Aquinas, which later became solely predominant, the morality of every action is apparently determined entirely by the end in view. An act of volition which had for its object the fulfilment of the divine law rendered all actions necessary to its accomplishment morally praiseworthy and imparted to these actions "its specific goodness."

The victory of the Thomist view over that of Scotus must later have been uncommonly welcome to the Jesuits, since they saw in it the possibility of extending the "remission of sins" much further than would otherwise have been feasible; so that, on this point too, they made of Thomas's system one of the main pillars of moral philosophy.

Nevertheless, it is erroneous to assert that the Society of Jesus, out of the moral significance of the ultimate end, coined the maxim that the end justifies the means. In point of fact, this celebrated maxim was originated, not by the Jesuits, but by Machiavelli, who in his treatise of *The Prince* declared that immoral means may be chosen, if the end to be achieved by them outweighs the evil. The Society of Jesus, on the contrary, has never expressly advanced such a thesis, and, even though many Jesuit casuists hold that to whomsoever the end is permitted must also the necessary means be allowed, yet the qualification is always added that wrongful means are always to be deprecated. In this sense, the Jesuit moral theologian, Laymann, expressly declares: "The presence of a good purpose lends no goodness to an action in essence bad, but leaves to this action its badness in every way." Gury also says that it is never permissible to do the slightest wrong as a means of doing good.

Cathrein, the most recent Jesuit moralist, writes on this question very clearly: "The will, if directed towards a morally wrongful object, cannot be make good by virtue of any outward purpose. Whoever, therefore, acknowledges the wrongful nature of theft cannot decide to steal for however good a purpose, without imparting to his will the quality of wrongfulness. If the principle that 'the end justifies the means' is to be wrong or sinful, then it is to be absolutely repudiated... The Jesuits merely hold, as do all reasonable persons, with St. Paul (I Cor., x, 31) that morally indifferent or good actions may and should be justified by good intentions."

Nevertheless, the opponents of Jesuitism have from the first onwards transformed the doctrine of the judgment of the will into the maxim, that a good end justifies even wrongful means, and have asserted that the order expressly upholds this reprehensible maxim. It was, in especial, Protestant and Old-Catholic theologians who, in later times, repeatedly revived this thesis; finally, the same accusation was in 1873 brought before the Judiciary Committee of the German Bundesrat.

The books in which this principle has been attributed to the Jesuits fill whole libraries, and this fact is not least due to Pascal's attack on the Society of Jesus.

In the *Provincial Letters*, Pascal introduces a Jesuit with whom he carries on a long dialogue on the spirit, the moral principles and the activity of the Society of Jesus. The Jesuit advances with an amiable smile the most reprehensible moral principles, and supports then in every case from the writings of Jesuit moral casuists. Shocked by the maxims he has just heard, the author of the letters hastens to a Jansenist friend, who demonstrates to him by means of ancient authors that the Jesuit moral philosophy constitutes a perversion of all the principles of the Catholic Church.

Pascal attacks with exceptional severity the Jesuit doctrine that the morality or immorality of human actions is determined by the will. "We at least purify the intention," Pascal makes his Jesuit say, "when we cannot prevent the action itself, and in this way, we better by a good purpose the evil of the means."

This doctrine, Pascal thinks, separates the intention from the deed, pleases the world, because it sanctions every action, and at the same time satisfies the Gospel, because it purifies the intention.

But this statement of the matter could have meant only that the Jesuits used the relationship between the end and the means in order to lend a semblance of goodness to something that is bad; the accusation, which later became so notorious, that the order propounded the doctrine that the end justifies the means does not appear in the *Provincial Letters*. But the whole manner in which Pascal expounded Jesuit moral philosophy must necessarily have suggested this reproach to later critics, and, accordingly, it is to some extent due to the *Provincial Letters* that the Jesuits, in later writings, have repeatedly been accused of so cynical a doctrine.

To this polemical work of Pascal's is also to be traced back the charge that the Jesuits had devised an artifice whereby it was made possible for a person to speak untruthfully without being guilty of telling a formal lie; that, by means of an astute method which the Jesuits had evolved, it was possible to swear false oaths and to practice every form of deception and fraud on one's neighbor just as readily and easily as was formerly possible only by committing the two sins of perjury and lying which the Church forbade with the utmost vehemence.

"I will just explain to you," the Jesuit declares in the *Provincial Letters*, "those facilities which our teachers have provided for avoiding the commission of certain sins in our relations with our fellow-men. The commonest and greatest difficulty in this connection is to avoid lying; but it is here that our principle of the use of ambiguous words is of very considerable value; according to this principle, it is permissible to use vague terms and to employ them, when speaking to another person, in a sense other than that which is in the mind... Do you know what is done in those cases when it is not possible to think of such ambiguous expressions? It is a new discovery: it is the doctrine of the secret mental reservation."

In actual fact, the Jesuit casuists deal with two forms of permissible deception: that of "amphibology" and that of *reservatio mentalis*. "Amphibology" is nothing else than the employment of ambiguous terms calculated to mislead the questioner; "mental reservation" consists in answering a question, not with a direct lie, but in such a way that the truth is partly suppressed, certain words being formulated mentally but not expressed orally. In both cases, nothing openly inconsistent with the truth is formally brought forward, and to this extent, therefore, the Jesuits consider that both amphibology and the mental reservation can be excepted from the general interdiction of lying.

The numerous Jesuit works devoted to the defense of the order against the charges levelled against it on account of this doctrine are mostly concerned with demonstrating that we are not compelled to render account of intimate matters to every uninvited questioner. How often does it not happen that a full disclosure of the actual truth might result in grave prejudice to the person making the disclosure, or to others; furthermore, it frequently happens that a statement of the actual truth is not possible without a violation of the principle of professional secrecy or at least a serious breach of confidence.

Moreover, the Jesuits assert that their casuistry admits of amphibology and the *reservatio mentalis* only in cases where a very strong ground exists for the preservation of secrecy; such an expedient must, on the other hand, never be employed when it is definitely incumbent upon a person to speak the truth, as, for example, when giving evidence in a court of law or when concluding a contract.

The Jesuits have, indeed, provided for the case where a person is called upon to give evidence before an unauthorized judge or under an irregular procedure; in such a case, the witness is certainly permitted to answer ambiguously or with reservations: "To swear equivocally is permissible," writes Busembaum, "if the oath is wrongfully demanded or if the taking of the oath is required by an unauthorized person, as, for example, an unqualified judge. The same applies if the oath is not in accordance with the established procedure of the court or if the swearing of the oath is enforced either by violence, injustice or fear...."

As regards the mental reservation in particular, this is permissible, according to the Jesuit apologetic writings, only in those cases in which the person addressed "is able to ascertain the truth, if not from the words alone, at least from all the circumstances surrounding the person, the time and the environment." A person's remarks should always be considered in relation to the conditions at the time, and the questioner has only himself to blame if he fails to interpret correctly what is said by the other person. The Jesuits hold that neither intentional ambiguity nor the fact of making a mental reservation can be regarded as lying, since, in both cases, all that happens is that "one's neighbor is not actually deceived, but rather his deception is permitted only for a justifiable cause."

The Jesuits draw attention to the fact that the Bible itself contains instances of equivocal remarks and of the *reservatio mentalis*: according the Gospel of St. John, for example, Jesus said that he would not go to Judea to the Feast of the Tabernacles (John, vii, 8 et seq.), but, nevertheless, he went "not openly, but as it were in secret." The Jesuit explanation of this passage is that Christ, while declaring that he would not go to Judea, manifestly made a mental reservation.

Of St. Paul, too, it is stated in the Acts of the Apostles (xxiii,5) that he said: "I wist not, brethren, that he was the high priest"; since, however, Paul knew the high priest perfectly well, this passage must be interpreted as meaning that the apostle meant to convey: "I know only one high priest and that is Jesus Christ."

Reference is also made to passages from the writings of the fathers of the Church, which would seem to sanction such expedients in order to avoid a direct lie; Augustine, for example, in his twenty-second letter denouncing the schismatic, Faustus, declares that, in certain circumstances, the use of equivocal forms of speech is permissible, and supports his contention by references to Genesis, xx, 2.

In spite of all these arguments, numerous instances of equivocal speech and mental reservation, which are held by the earlier Jesuit casuists to be excusable, appear nevertheless to be essentially of a very doubtful nature. It is possible to arrive at a clearer understanding of this original method of permitted deception only if we bear in mind the exceptional severity with which the Christian moral laws condemn lying as the most heinous of all sins.

According to the precepts of the Catholic Church, the confessor had always to impute a mortal sin to a penitent who confessed to a lie, and the many grounds for remission which were available to the confessor in the case of other sins could not be applied in the case of this particular sin. The categorical nature of this prohibition of lying had always, however, stood in sharp contradiction to the realities of life, since, time and again, it seemed practically an impossibility to speak the absolute truth at all times and in all circumstances. Recognizing the existence of this conflict between religious law and the practical things of human existence, the Jesuits favored those interpretations of the law which appeared to offer the only means in many cases of absolving the penitent instead of severely condemning him.

Aristotle, the Progenitor of Jesuit Moral Philosophy

In the fourth of Pascal's *Provincial Letters*, there is an imaginary conversation between the author and his Jesuit authority, in which the reprehensible moral principles propounded by the casuist Baunius are discussed. Pressed hard by the arguments adduced by Pascal, the Jesuit is compelled to concede point after point until, after reflecting for a while, he suddenly recovers and triumphantly continues: "See, here are the weapons with which I shall bring you low.... Just read the passage quoted by Baunius from Aristotle, and you will have to admit either that the works of this great philosopher should be burned or that our doctrine is the true doctrine."

Pascal's fictive Jesuit had every reason to fall back on Aristotle, for, in point of fact, throughout the whole of the Jesuit moral theology there is scarcely a view which is not adumbrated in the *Nicomachean Ethics* of the Stagirite.

Just as Ignatius taught that man can attain perfection by his own will and his own powers, so too the Greek philosopher had long before asserted that man can attain to happiness only through his own efforts: while the extent to which virtue may be developed depends on a person's natural qualities, both judgment and conscious effort are also necessary. It is true that one person's natural qualities, both judgment and conscious effort are also necessary. It is true that one person's natural qualities may not be so good as another's but, in the long run, everybody can develop the necessary qualities predisposing to virtue if only he wishes to do so.

Even the conclusion which the Jesuits draw from this supremacy of the will, that the rightful or wrongful character of human actions depends upon the direction of the will, is also to be found in the *Nicomachean Ethics*.

According to Aristotle's moral doctrines, an act is right or wrong only if it is performed voluntarily; an act which is not performed voluntarily can be neither good nor bad. A righteous person is one who intentionally and deliberately practices right actions; the essential thing is that the actions shall be voluntary.

Aristotle also discusses the question of the restriction of free will, and, therefore, of the limitations of responsibility, owing to external circumstances and influences, such as, for example, fear: "if an action is performed out of fear of greater evils, the question is open to discussion whether such an action is involuntary of voluntary." Similarly, he deals with the difficulties associated with the problem of the relationship between the end and the means, and expressly lays down to what extent importance should be attached to the intention when judging an action. The source of action is the intention; the source of the intention is the will or the purpose. Accordingly, therefore, intention presupposes the capacity to think and the power to reason "as permanent moral attributes."

Of "ingenuity," Aristotle gives, in his *Nicomachean Ethics*, a definition which immediately calls to mind the principle that the end justifies the means: ingenuity, he says towards the end of the sixth book, is the ability to devise and apply the appropriate means towards a given end. "If, therefore, the aim be good, the ingenuity is praiseworthy, but, if it be bad, it becomes craft."

Similarly, all the basic principles of the entire Jesuit moral philosophy can be traced back to the *Nicomachean Ethics*. It was, therefore, by no means the work of chance that, from the moment they ceased to be a band of religious zealots and applied themselves to scientific thinking, the Jesuits evolved an intellectual system based on Aristotle's theories.

The Jesuits have, from the outset, striven by all available means to secure a predominant influence for Aristotle's teachings in the moral philosophy of their age. In the first rules

The Power and Secret of the Jesuits

which the order laid own for the training in their schools, it was provided that philosophy and physical science were to be taught "not only in accordance with truth, but also in accordance with the teaching and the spirit of Aristotle." When, then the *Ratio Studiorum,* or detailed regulations governing instruction in all Jesuit schools and colleges, was compiled, the authors of this work expressly emphasized that the instructions were "never to deviate from Aristotle in matters of any importance."

These regulations were drawn up precisely at a time when it might have seemed that the authority of Aristotle had come to an end: in the newly arisen experimental sciences, especially mechanics, astronomy and medicine, quite new discoveries had, in fact, been made, and one after another of Aristotle's propositions had been found to be false. Thus, at the turn of the sixteenth and seventeenth centuries, the peripatetic system, which, during the whole of the scholastic Middle Ages, had maintained its eminence, was driven from the circle of the sciences. Even the views of the Stagirite on ethics and logic were no longer unopposed, for the newly rediscovered Platonism had entered the field against them.

From all sides the attack on the Aristotelean school of thought was made, and, with the new scholars of the Renaissance, it became a point of honor to disparage Aristotle in favor of Plato. The Jesuits alone, in spite of all the newer conceptions, remained faithful to the author of the *Nicomachean Ethics,* and held fast to the view that had been universally accepted in the Middle Ages, that the Greek philosopher, whom Dante referred to as *"il maestro di color chi sanno,"* was something akin to a prophet whose teachings were second only in dogmatic value to the revealed doctrines of the Christian faith.

This stubborn adherence to a system already, in appearance, obsolete, regardless of the recent scientific discoveries of the Cartesian criticism, as well as of the enthusiasm for Plato's philosophy of the courts and salons of the Renaissance period, may at first seem all the more remarkable as the Jesuits had always hitherto striven "to be all things to all men" and to keep pace with the progress of the world as far as was at all possible. This apparent obtuseness is seen on closer examination, to have its origin in a correct instinctive feeling that Aristotle's system, in face of all the assaults made on it by the new principles of astronomy, mechanics, physics, medicine and philosophy, possessed an unassailable quality; that convincing formal logic, armed with which the opinions of the Jesuits might successfully resist the centuries.

For the arguments of the Stagirite continues to exercise an unfailing influence on men. By his method of strict deduction, things which were obscure, incapable of explanation or even erroneous could be made as clear as truth itself. Starting from a well-established first principle, one proceeded from state to stage, in accordance with all the rules of the syllogism, until the required conclusion was reached. Such a chain of uninterrupted demonstration was always irresistible, and was effective in convincing the intellect, even if sentiment was not disposed to accept the ultimate conclusion.

In the case of Ignatius, the belief that it was possible to attain perfection by means of the human will certainly sprang from his personal experiences. While on his sick-bed in Loyola, he told himself that he could, of his own free will, decide for the kingdom of heaven, and this arbitrary decision governed his whole subsequent career. Nevertheless, this theory of the freedom of the will advanced by the Spanish knight could never have gained such general acceptance without the support afforded it by the logical deductions of Aristotle. It was only through the system of the Stagirite that the Jesuit doctrine of the freedom of the will was able to acquire its terminology, its lucidly arranged structure, and the seductive skill of argument; Aristotle furnished the Jesuits with the weapons which enabled them to emerge with honor from the bitterest struggles with theologians and philosophers. And it cannot be denied that the Society of Jesus, while adhering to the Peripatetic system, has maintained itself successfully for centuries. The stanchness with which the order has clung to Aristotle's philosophy has ensured the continued existence of its system of instruction in the midst of the most stormy upheavals of thought.

"Does that satisfy you?" triumphantly asks the Jesuit in the *Provincial Letters*, after he has demonstrated that the Jesuit doctrine of the direction of the intention found support in Aristotle; and Pascal is forced to admit somewhat ruefully: "It certainly seems as if Aristotle is of Baunius's opinion, but it surprises me very much. . . Is it possible that Aristotle could have spoken thus? He is generally held to be very wise and learned!"

Somewhat perplexed, Pascal hastens to his Jansenist friend, and inquires how it came about that Aristotle should have propounded such questionable maxims. After searching for a while, the Jansenist finds another passage in Aristotle which appears to refute the arguments of the Jesuits, and points with childish delight to a passage in the third book of the *Nicomachean Ethics*, which states: "Not every evil person knows what he ought to do or from what he ought to abstain, and it is through such lack of knowledge that men become unjust and depraved. Ignorance in the choice between good and evil had not for effect that an act becomes involuntary, but only that it is bad."

To Pascal, a quotation from Aristotle gainsaying the Jesuits appeared to settle the matter once and for all in the sense of his convictions, and at the time of the Jansenist dispute, when proof and refutation were sought in a series of quotations from the "authorities," this might well have appeared to constitute a satisfactory triumph over the Jesuit moral philosophy.

Whoever, though, today studies closely the *Nicomachean Ethics* as a comprehensive whole, will experience some difficulty in resisting the conclusion that the Jesuit in the *Provincial Letters* was more justified in his argument than the Jansenist, and that the somewhat free interpretation by the Jesuits of Aristotle's theory of the freedom of the will approached more closely to what was actually in the mind of the Greek thinker than that of the rigorists.

The thinker of Stagira expressly broke away from the rigid doctrine of Plato, under which everything ethical was of divine origin, and which demanded a ceaseless striving on the part of man after an unattainable ideal lying outside human existence. Out of this Platonic doctrine of an ideal goal, forever unrealizable, Aristotle had evolved a theory of virtue attainable in man's earthly life.

Plato had seen the ultimate meaning of morality as an imperative, in the "Idea of the Good," in which alone lay the truth, and which, therefore, constitute the sole aim of moral endeavor. He taught men "to love truth" and to relate all their conduct to it, and not to relate truth to the final aim of their own narrow purposes. It is precisely on this point however, that Aristotle took leave of his master, and in the first book of his *Nicomachean Ethics* strongly opposed this Platonic notion of an "Idea of Good" which could never be realized. For, so runs a celebrated passage of his, "if both are my friends, Plato and truth, then it is m bounden duty to put truth first." Aristotle interprets "the uniform and universal conception of the

Good" as nothing more than "that which may be accomplished or attained by man. . . ." It certainly sounds "very plausible that the Idea establishes the standard by which man may recognize the good wherever he meets with it," but, unfortunately this does not find "confirmation in the sciences (namely, the practical sciences). . . Of what use, in fact, is the knowledge of the Idea of Good to the weaver or carpenter in his handiwork, or how will he who had contemplated it become, therefore, a more skilful physician or officer? The physician does not inquire after health in general, but after that of man, or rather that of the individual, for he is concerned with the cure of the individual."

In clear words, any transcendentalism in the aims of morality is here denied, and, altogether in the Aristotelean sense, morality for the Jesuits means no "ideal aim lying outside of existence," but the regulation and ordering of "the virtue attainable by man."

The Jesuit moral philosophy likewise lays down no generally applicable ethical principles; it rather decomposes morality into as many individual "cases of conscience" as possible, into "aporias," in Aristotle's sense, which are adapted to the requirements of practical life. It does not stipulate anything extra-human, any abstract, ideal requirement, for it is less concerned with the objective "Idea of Good" than with the individual man; in Aristotle's sense, it is a real "science of healing, which is not concerned with health in general, but with the care of the individual."

For this reason, in Jesuit moral philosophy, as in Aristotle's, there can be no clinging to the severity of an ideal demand, and the latter must yield to a far-reaching insight into the peculiarities of man. It follows, therefore, that the measure of morality is not the "demand" but "attainability." Not divine norms but the human footrule is the measure; not divine commands but the paragraphs of a law govern actions and judgment.

"In order to determine what is a reasonable demand on the individual person in concrete circumstances," writes Aristotle in the *Nicomachean Ethics*, "there is not objective measure, equal for all, but this measure is the nature of the person himself according to his individual needs." Accordingly, Aristotle defines the idea of morality as the maintenance of the "golden mean," in all things, as determined by a "healthy intelligence."

"Virtue is a habit, accompanied with deliberate preference, in the relative mean, defined by reason and as the prudent man would define it. It is a mean state between two vices, one in excess, the other in defect; and it is so, moreover, because of the vices, one falls short of, and the other exceeds what is right, both in passions and actions, whilst virtue discovers the mean and chooses it."

Two thousand years later, Ignatius endeavored, with almost identical words, to explain in one of his letters his conception of that which "found favor in the sight of God." After declaring that anything in excess could neither please God nor be lasting, he continues: "If you wouldst lead an ordered life, then must thou keep to the mean between two extremes, so that thou mayst not attempt presumptuously that which is beyond thy powers. God does not demand of thee the destruction of the body, but victory over sin; he asks nothing impossible, but only that which promotes salvation. He dispenses good counsel, and provides for the needs of life to the end that thou mayst employ thy body for the betterment of the soul, but requires that due moderation shall be exercised in all things."

67. FRANSICSO SAUREZ   68. ANTONIO ESCOBAR Y NENDOZA

THE MOST FAMOUS OF THE JESUIT MORAL THEOLOGIANS

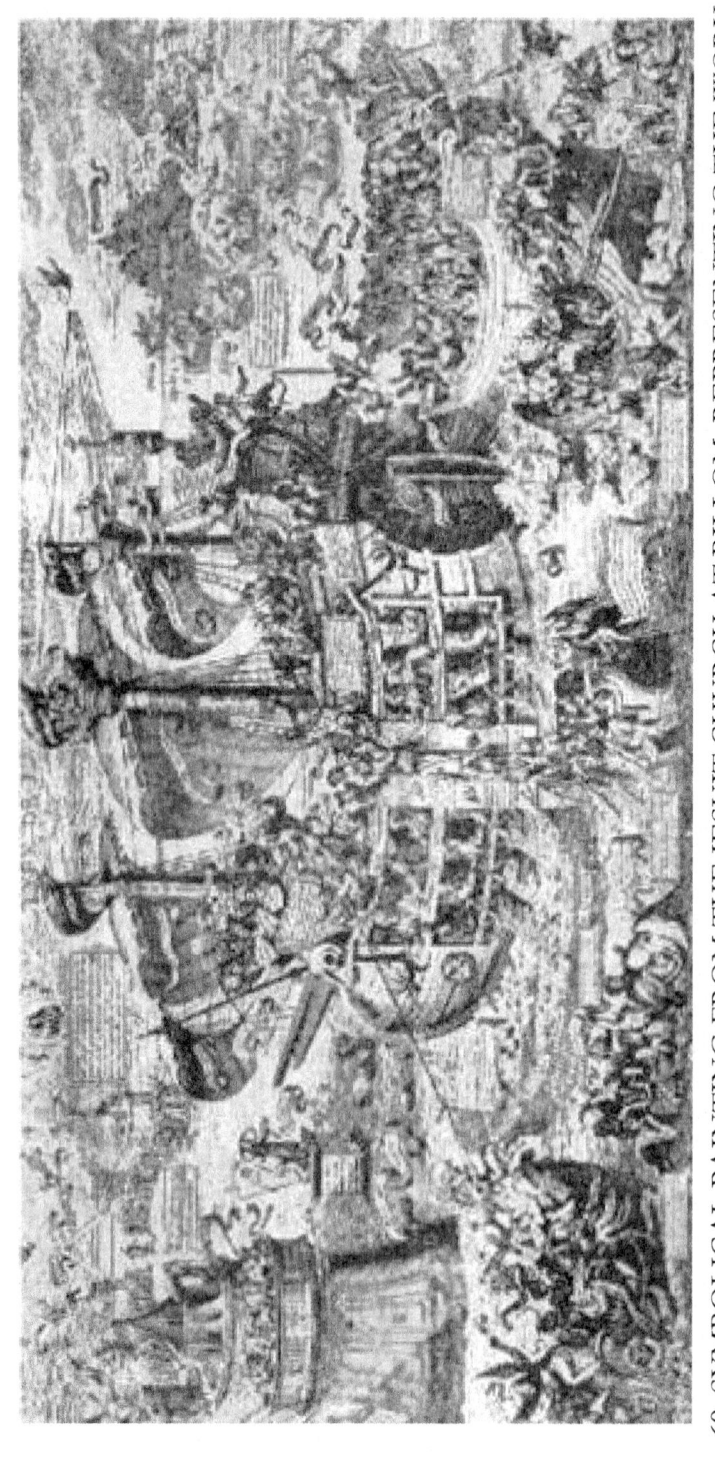

69. SYMBOLICAL PAINTING FROM THE JESUIT CHURCH AT BILLOM, REPRESENTING THE WORK OF SALVATION OF THE ORDER

The Atomization of Morality

According to Cathrein's moral philosophy, it is "an excessive and altogether impossible demand on weak humanity" to require the exercise of all the virtues prescribed by the natural moral code. Aristotle, however, who, long before, had argued against the "excessive" demands of Platonic morality, and had, in his own moral doctrine, adopted the "attainable mean" as the standard of virtue towards which man should aspire, supplied his Jesuit posterity also with the means by which it was possible for them to make due allowances for human weakness and to provide for the exercise of a general tolerance.

Thus, the Jesuit moral philosophy, that "perverted doctrine of Satan," which for centuries has been subjected to the most violent attacks by infuriated but somewhat superficial opponents, had, in reality, for its spiritual founder no less a personage than the celebrated Greek sage who, even today, is held in great honor. To attack Jesuitism signifies, therefore, an attack on those ancient doctrines which have influenced our intellectual thought for thousands of years. If fatal defects show themselves in the Jesuit philosophy, then it must be stated that the responsibility for these faults lies with no other than the great philosopher of Stagira whom they chose as their master.

The Atomization of Morality

In limiting himself to specifying by name the various human virtues, instead of setting up ideal moral demands, Aristotle had necessarily to substitute for unified ethical Idea a series of prescriptions, laws and rules of conduct. The conception of the moral Idea, he considered, might perhaps have the merit "of serving as a spur and in incentive to the young of noble nature," yet such a conception was "not fitted to lead the mass to a high moral development." Accordingly, it was necessary to ensure that "the life and general conduct of the citizens should proceed in an ordered manner" by the laying down of fixed and intelligible laws which could be fulfilled. He therefore accomplished the transfer from the transcendental ethics of Plato to a schematic code of "moral laws."

For Plato it is an ethically regulative imperative that alone gives moral law, an imperative that by no means represents a rigid, absolute datum, but rather an ever-living and eternal task, an eternal aim. Plato's Idea of the Good is, therefore, "difficult to comprehend," and is never more than a "paradigm" which we must regard in the same way "as the mathematicians regard their proofs"; the mathematician does not treat of the figures which he draws, but of the purely mathematical images themselves, to which the figures drawn stand in a paradigmatical relationship.

Aristotle, on the other hand, considers that a distinction should be made between the manner in which a geometrician and a carpenter draw a straight line. The former is concerned with truth itself, while the latter is only concerned with the nature of a straight line in so far as may be necessary for the purposes of his practical work. Aristotle, as Werner Jaeger pointed out, treated of the science of political ethics "from the point of view of the carpenter and not from that of the geometrician." For Plato's "doctrine of ideas" he substitutes a descriptive account of all possible forms of the virtuous and the good, and, in this sense, the *Nicomachean Ethics* represents the earliest comprehensive and detailed exposition of moral conduct in everyday life. And hence sprang that form of literature which in much later times was to become known as "moral casuistry."

This method of describing the various virtues and vices individually was continued by the Stoics. Originally, the Stoics had held closely to the conception of the unity of ideal virtue, and had taught that moral judgment was absolute and could take no account of practical considerations. An action must be either moral or immoral; between good and bad there could be no intermediate stages. A virtuous person must be wholly virtuous, and he who fails of it must be entirely void of it: "He who is a yard under water is drowned just as effectually as he who is five hundred fathoms down."

Later, however, the Stoa was forced to take account of the fact that these rigid exhortations to virtue were in no wise compatible with the realities of life, and eventually it could not resist a certain adaptation to the customary notions of good and evil. Its teachers were forced to make material concessions to the practical considerations influencing man's actions, and in so doing evolved a graduated moral code. Cicero himself had expressly declared that the "sages" of the Stoic philosophy did not exist in reality, and that their rigid moral code could not be applied in daily life.

Seneca, too, expressed the same view, that the adaptation of moral laws to the realities of life was more important than the setting up of abstract ideals of virtue; that which does not affect man's actual moral state could serve no useful purpose from a moral point of view. Seneca, therefore, considered that, in addition to the laying down of general principles, exhaustive inquiries into conduct in specific cases were also necessary, and himself devoted a large part of his writings to such considerations.

In this way, the doctrine of the Stoa on the duties of man, originally so rigorous, turned into a systematic casuistry of practical conduct, that is, into a literature that stood in sharp contradiction to the actual convictions of this school.

A similar lapse from the unity of the ethical imperative into a multiplicity of moral rules also took place in Judaism; it is the self-same spiritual tragedy which apparently plays itself out whenever humanity strives to force within the narrow limits of practical utility the limitless perspectives opened up by a doctrine of abstract morality.

The prophets, the classical representatives of Jewish antiquity, had, it is true, expressly emphasized that the moral act alone led to God, and thus had shown themselves to be clearly opposed to the mystical belief in the possibility of salvation through indulgence in profound meditation. The way to God, they taught, lies not in abandonment to spiritual contemplation, nor through faith, but solely and simply through humanly moral conduct. Nevertheless, as Auerbach shows in his beautiful work, *Die Prophetie*, in classical Judaism men's actions appear to be constantly referred to an infinite end, determined by an ideal imperative and never confined within humanly finite limits.

Later Judaism shows clearly a departure from this idealistic conception, a replacement of the Idea by "attainable virtues," by precepts which should and can be followed in this life; and nowhere else, perhaps, has the attempt been made in so crude a fashion to break up an ethic into innumerable single precepts as in the later Jewish moral code.

In Christendom, to, a similar turning to casuistry is quite early evident. Thus Tertullian deals exhaustively with the question of the pagan ceremonies in which the Christian soldier in

The Atomization of Morality

the Roman military service may participate without offending against his faith. Subsequently, many of the Church fathers, in particular Basil, Chrysostom, Gregory of Nyssa and Ambrose, endeavored to discriminate between inadmissible actions, on the one hand, and, on the other hand, acts dictated by and consonant with the Faith.

The great scholastics, too, included in their "summae" collections of cases of conscience as examples for their general moral doctrines. The *Summa de poenitentia at matrimonio,* which the Dominican monk, Raymund de Pennaforte, wrote towards the middle of the thirteenth century, represents the first systematically arranged work on moral casuistry; it sets out in order and judges all the various sins of matrimonial life. The object of this work, Pennaforte stated, was to assist father-confessors in judging the offences of their penitents, and to enable them, in the confessional, to determine difficult and complicated cases.

That, in the later Middle Ages, moral casuistry should have followed such a line of development, is closely attributable to the increasing significance of confession, The fourth Lateran Council, in the year 1215, definitely laid down that every believer must go to confession at least once a year, and the effect of this was that the father-confessor, from an occasional counsellor, became a regular spiritual and moral judge.

As early as the fourteenth century, therefore, numerous comprehensive and exhaustive works on moral theology had appeared; the *Pupilla oculi* of the chancellor, Juan de Burgo, examines, in ten volumes, the application of the divine laws, the sacrament, and all other Christian moral prescriptions; in the *Summa Silvestrina* of the Dominican monk, Sylvester de Priero, 715 cases draw from theological practice are dealt with and decided. In addition, there were numerous smaller manuals for father-confessors, such as the *Confessionale* of the Franciscan monk, Bartolomeo de Chaymin, and the *Summula confessorum* of St. Antoninus.

Thus there already existed a wealth of casuistic literature when the Jesuit order was founded, and the writers of the Society of Jesus were able to link up with a long-established tradition in applying themselves to this branch of theological literature. They were, however, far from being alone in concerning themselves with moral casuistry; at the same time, secular priests and monks of all orders and even the Protestant clergy were producing studies on "cases of conscience." Among the Protestant authors may perhaps be mentioned the Cambridge University professor, William Perkins, who wrote a work entitled *Decisions of Cases of Conscience.*

It is to the Jesuits, however, that the casuistic method owes its particular significance and its highest development.

In this Catholic "Counter-Reformation," the Jesuits were certainly the most able fighters. They strove everywhere, as missionaries in the most remote lands and as upholders of the faith in protestant areas, to influence the masses in the direction of the Catholic church through the medium of confession, and it is therefore only natural that they should have developed moral casuistry with exceptional thoroughness.

Soon there was no other religious fraternity which could show so many authors on the subject of morality as the Jesuit order, and the most celebrated theologians of the Society of Jesus penned great works on moral casuistry.

That the Jesuit moral theology was able to take a really predominating position in the

The Power and Secret of the Jesuits

Catholic Church is, however, primarily due to the casuist Alfonso dei Liguori, who was not himself a member of the Society of Jesus, but became the founder of the Redemptorist order. Liguori's *Moral Theology* is a work incorporating almost all the earlier conceptions in moral theology and, of the 815 authors whom Liguori uses as his authorities, the Jesuits, in especial, provided the principles he adopted. The popes have particularly approved of and recommended his work, and ultimately gave it their full sanction by canonizing the author. Since then, the moral views of the Jesuits, through Liguori, have been spread in every place where Catholic priests minister to spiritual needs and exercise the office of confessor.

Problems of Confessional Practice

According as the hearing of confessions increased in extent, so did it become more and more difficult for the priest, whose duty it was "to bind and to loose," to form a right and just decision on the scruples of conscience put to him. As the conception of "attainable virtues" had by this time replaced that of an unattainable ideal, of a general moral imperative, the rules and prescriptions in which these virtues were formulated were more and more adapted to what was passible and attainable. At the same time, every individual case demanded particular treatment, an extremely specialized application of the moral principles.

In Aristotle's time, it might well have appeared to be a simple matter to arrange in specific categories the world with all its circumstances and man with all his virtues and vices. In the days when the Master of Stagira, had, but his descriptive enumeration of good and bad qualities, provided the first example of a systematic moral casuistry, the "world" was not much greater, in comparison with the known world of today, than a small province. To Aristotle, culture was the totality of those easily surveyable conditions which ruled beneath the clear Hellenic sky; his interest was, in fact, even within this narrow field, confined to the still narrower circle of Greek aristocrats and scholars to which he himself belonged. To him, this handful of select men represented "humanity" purely and simply; what went on below this stratum among the slaves, the peasants and the craftsmen, did not fall within the scope of discussions on morality.

And how limited was the knowledge possessed at that time! The primitive conception, accepted without question, held man to be constituted of a few clearly comprehensible components, of body, of three souls: vegetative, animal and rational, of mind, will, desire, virtue and vice; a correct mixture of these components appeared to ensure complete harmony and therewith the felicity of the sage, and accordingly Aristotle drew the conclusion that evil arises only from a disturbance of this equilibrium. An exact knowledge and description of these components is sufficient, he considered, to obtain forthwith an accurate conception of all disturbances of the moral order.

On the basis of the observations which he had been able to make in his native country, in his associations with his aristocratic friends and enemies, Aristotle wrote his *Nicomachean Ethics*, in which he described in sequence all vices and virtues, voluntary and involuntary actions, within his knowledge, which were either wise of foolish, noble or base, courageous or cowardly. After having completed this comprehensive classification of humanity, he could be content in the belief that there was really nothing more to be said, and that the means had

Problems of Confessional Practice

been found for enabling a just judgment to be pronounced on men and their conduct.

Many centuries after Aristotle, the Jesuits, likewise, made a similar attempt to classify comprehensively every know action and delinquency and to this task they devoted much honest endeavor and the utmost diligence. They examined systematically every "particular case," so that It might be possible to characterize human conduct at all times as praiseworthy or blameworthy, having regard to the circumstances.

In the meantime, however, two thousand years had gone by, and in this space of time humanity had, like the world around it, suffered a fundamental change. The narrow Greek skies which had arched over Stagira had expanded to a limitless firmament, and on the enormous expanse of the earth, which was spanned over by these skies, most exceptional and inexplicable things were happening. With the passing of a long epoch of human history, all earthly relationships had become infinitely involved; multiplied a thousandfold were the ideas which now influenced man, and many and varied were his aims, interests and activities.

The passions, the noble and the base sentiments, were no longer to be classed in a few hard-and-fast categories; on the contrary, all man's various perceptions appeared rather to merge rainbow-like one into the other, so that it was no longer possible to draw any clear dividing line between good and evil, wisdom and unwisdom, courage and cowardice. Where Aristotle had postulated three or four "dianoetic" and eleven "ethical" virtues, Chrysippus and his successors had arrived at a whole "swarm of virtues"; the number of good and bad qualities had mounted into the immeasurable, and the niceties and subtleties of distinction were scarcely comprehensible.

Furthermore, the simplicity of thought with which man had been wont to record and schematize his perceptions had ceased to be so simple as in the days of the Greek thinker; Christianity had replaced the simple intelligible criteria by a highly technical and complicated system of morality. So long as the judgment of good and evil had remained within the powers of the understanding, it had been possible to discriminate between two main categories, the virtues and the vices. Virtue was everything of which a healthy mind approved, and vice, anything that was inconsistent with all due reason.

Under the Christian world of later times, this simple judgment of reason was, however, transformed into a much more complicated process of thought. Good and evil were no longer distinguishable with their original clearness, but were determined in accordance with a whole scale of moral evaluations, with "sanctity" at one end of the scale and "mortal sin" at the other. In addition to the commands of "natural laws" which had prevailed from the earliest times, and with which Aristotle was fully acquainted, there now appeared commands and prohibitions which were regarded as revealed by God, and which went far beyond the comprehension of the reasoning powers.

It and not, indeed, always been an easy matter for the later Greek philosophers to determine what was consistent with reason and therefore good, and they had themselves compelled manuals of casuistry; but now any moral judgment had become a thousand times more thorny, since the rule of conduct was no longer formed by mere reason alone, but also by the revealed law of the Faith.

According to Catholic theology, there were two forms of revelation, one "natural" and the other "supernatural," and, corresponding to these, there were two forms of laws, a "natural" moral law and a "positive" law. The natural moral law was defined as "the light of reason by nature existing within man," which enabled him to determine what he should do and what he should avoid.

Even under this "natural law," several forms of ordinance were distinguished: prescriptions of a general nature and dealing with no particular object, and those rules of moral conduct which automatically arose out of the first group when the general prescriptions were applied to the relationship of man to God, to his fellow-men and to himself. A third type consisted of those further rules which necessarily follow "as an obvious logical consequence" from the first two types.

As may be imagined, the "natural law" was complicated enough; but the difficulties increased considerably when the "positive law" was examined more closely. They could be either divine or human, according to whether it was decreed directly by God or by a human authority by virtue of divine mandate. This positive law, as the final authority, determined numerous questions which were not fully and unequivocally settled by natural law. Natural law, in many points, contained only general principles, the application of which to concrete cases was governed by the positive laws.

In accordance with these two main categories of moral laws, the theologians distinguished duties as being "natural" and "positive." In addition, further distinctions were made between "affirmative" and "negative" obligations, between duties towards God, towards one's neighbor and towards oneself.

The conscience itself even, no longer appeared as an entity, but was analyzed into categories. The "anterior conscience" had for its object future actions and the "posterior" conscience, those already accomplished; the former was also described as "guiding" or "binding," and the latter as "judging" or "denouncing."

How often did it happen in practical life that command and prescriptions conflicted one with another, and how difficult a matter it then became to decide which rule was to take precedence! Theologians may, indeed, have held the view that such a conflict of duties existed only in outward seeming, since every duty eventually originated from the will of God and God could not stand in contradiction with Himself; but for the poor mortal it was often a difficult enough matter to find the way out of these difficulties, even if they were only apparent.

As if all these difficulties confronting the father-confessor in forming a right judgment of human actions were not sufficient of themselves, he had always to bear in mind that human sins, according to the faith of the Church, were to be classified in varying degrees of seriousness. It was the firm conviction of all Catholics that every mistake made by the father-confessor in judging the sins committed by his penitents must have the most dire consequences; upon the absolution granted by the priest depended the eternal salvation of the person making confession. Whereas the venial offence was expunged by an earthly punishment of limited duration or in purgatory, the punishment awaiting the sinner who had gravely offended against God was eternal damnation, unless the Church, with its power to bind or to loose, came to his aid.

Problems of Confessional Practice

In the profusion and fullness of the natural and positive laws, with their studied arrangement in numerous sub-sections, it was, indeed, laid down how the Christian might attain true perfection, and what his duties towards God and the world were. Upon the priests, however, who sat in the confessional and whose function it was to adjudicate on the sins of weak, erring mortals, devolved the difficult task of applying these standards to the many weaknesses and imperfections of man as he really is The problem facing them was to deduce from the general law the special applications to individual cases, and this further involved the reconciliation of God's requirements of man with the manifold difficulties and complications of practical life.

For of what avail was it to the father-confessors to be thoroughly conversant with the laws and to know what was prescribed, permitted or forbidden, if penitents came to them who felt and thought quite differently, who lived under the most various conditions, and were influenced by an infinite variety of personal factors, temptations, desires and passions, and were entangled in pursuits, cares and labors of very nature?

All the inexhaustible types of living life pressed to the priest in the confessional, compelling him to pronounce judgment on murder, theft, lying, deception, unchastity and fraud, as well as on surgical operations, the bottle-feeding of children, the rights and duties of officials, the most intimate details of sexual life, buying and selling prices, the grade of paper used for printing books, the degree of *décolletage* that might be permitted in a young girl's dance frock, whether it was wrong for an heir to rejoice over his rich uncle's death, and how far it was sinful for a churchman to read an unchaste book.

The cases in which the father-confessor was called upon to adjudicate became a thousandfold greater when the attempt was made to examine more closely into the particular circumstances of the sin committed. Immediately were revealed within the individual categories of offences a thousand new variations, distinguished one from the other by the utmost diversity of motives and causes. Yet a proper judgment could be pronounced only after all these special circumstances, essentially different conscientiously into account.

Those priests who accepted the philosophy of the old heathen of Stagira, and, like him, saw in morality the adaptation of the "Idea" to the "particular case," thus found themselves in actual practice faced with an exceptionally difficult task. For whoever lent his ear to the many voices of men and women, old and young, princes and beggars, pouring out their confessions, learnt so much of the realities and facts of life that he was eventually constrained to recognize that, although the moral law was equally binding on all, yet it was often necessary for its field of application to be modified, restricted or extended, if right was to remain right and not to become a frightful hardship.

The Jesuit moral casuists, therefore, came to the assistance of the father-confessors by placing at their disposal "manuals" as works of reference, comprehensive folios in which leaned and experienced men had set down systematically all possible "cases and conscience," had arranged them according to their nature, and had decided upon them to the best of their knowledge, in accordance with the divine laws.

The Power and Secret of the Jesuits

The Judge in the Confessional

Many of these text-books of morals occupy as many as ten folio volumes, and are arranged in hundreds of paragraphs with the various sections numbered in roman and innumerable sub-sections numbered in Arabic figures. All the problems and events of life, from the harmless dance of youth to the crime of murder, were intended to be included within them and examined from the moral standpoint. Their wide experience gained in the confessional made the priests acquainted with very many "cases of conscience" which arose in actual practice, and they were therefore able to supplement this collection of empirically assembled material with combinations of their own devising. All the innumerable *casus conscientiae* were handled in full detail and with bureaucratic orderliness and system, so that the father-confessor could look up, as the occasion required, the correct judgment to be pronounced on the offences of his penitents.

The summary terms of the fifth commandment of the Decalogue, for example, were, as became immediately apparent on closer examination, by no means adequate to meet the case of the killing of a man. According to the special circumstances of the particular case, the moral theologians distinguished between "permissible," "conditionally permissible" and "prohibited" killings; to which of these three categories the case under consideration belonged was a matter which could be determined only after *all* motives and other circumstances had been examined.

Account was to be taken of the fact that it often happened that a man was compelled to defend his own skin and to kill his assailant to save his own life. This case, simple enough in itself, immediately became complicated by other eventualities; what was the position when, in self-defense, a son killed his father, a monk his abbot, or a citizen his sovereign? Moreover, was a wife allowed to kill her husband who was threatening her life? Was it permissible to do away with a false witness in order to save oneself from being wrongfully condemned to death? Might a nobleman who had received a box on the ear, and was accordingly discredited in the sight of his compeers, slay the person who thus insulted him? Was a soldier entitled in war-time to kill innocent people, if ordered to do so by his superior officers? Might a military leader burn down a tower in which were non-combatants as well as hostile troops? All these questions were carefully examined in the various Jesuit works on moral casuistry and, according to the particular circumstances of the case, answered with a definite affirmative, a conditional affirmative or, either definitely or conditionally, in the negative.

Theft was dealt with in the same manner; external or inherent circumstances such as poverty, hunger, error or *force majeure* could similarly influence to a considerable degree the moral evaluation of the offence. Theft was regarded differently according to whether the case was one of a poor person stealing from a rich person, a poor person from another poor person, a rich person from a rich person, a rich person from a poor person, a wife from her husband, a servant from his master, or an official from his superior.

In the first place, it was necessary to take into account the various circumstances constituting "extreme necessity," by reason of which a theft could be excused, and the enumeration of which occupied a number of paragraphs; in addition, the circumstances constituting

The Judge in the Confessional

"almost extreme necessity" in all their possible combinations had to be examined, as, for instance, when a person had committed a theft in order to escape the precise amount over and above which it could be asserted that the sin of theft began had to be stated, and this was only possible in relation to the material circumstances of the thief and the victim. How was a theft by a son from his father to be regarded? The case might be one of a son's stealing twenty gold pieces from a father who earned fifteen hundred gold pieces; the case was different if the income of the father were greater and the amount stolen by the son were less. Thus, the single case of "The son steals from his father" gave rise to a series of variants, which had to be dealt with on scientific lines in appropriate paragraphs, sections and sub-sections until all possible combinations of the varying amount stolen and the varying amount of the income were exhausted.

Special complications also arose when considering the "obligation to make restitution" in accordance with which the father-confessor requires the thief to make compensation for the wrong he has done. The Jesuit casuists, therefore, indicated the precise cases in which this obligation should be enforced unconditionally, when it may be relaxed or when it may be entirely waived. For instance, the obligation may be waived "if restitution could not be made without serious prejudice to the person on whom the obligation falls, as, for example, if, by making restitution, he would be unable to maintain himself in his station, or would himself be reduced to penury. . . When, therefore, a nobleman would be unable to make restitution without depriving himself of his servants, his horses, or his estate, or a prominent citizen would be thereby compelled to carry on an unaccustomed trade, or a workman would be forced to sell his tools, restitution may in these cases be deferred. . ."

How difficult must it have been for the spiritual pastor to approve or to condemn certain commercial practices! Valuable help was to be derived in these cases from the manuals of casuistry, for they laid down that a merchant who quoted an excessively high price with the intention of selling the particular commodity at that price was guilty of a grave sin; it was a different matter, however, if the merchant merely quoted the high price in order to induce the buyer to make an offer, and thus, after some bargaining, to arrive at the suitable price.

These reference books also determined the question whether European merchants commit a sin by selling in India cheap knives and mirrors at relatively high prices. Through his manuals of casuistry the father-confessor was taught that the usual price of a commodity is determined by its value to the buyer; since, then, mirrors and knives are scarce in India, there could be no wrong done if merchants sold such objects at high prices there.

The works of Lessius and Escobar also deal with the obligations of a bankrupt merchant, and allow him to reserve for himself so much of his material effects as may be necessary to enable him to maintain a reasonable existence; the fact that his debts may have been unjustly contracted does not affect the case at all. Whoever wrongs his fellow-man owes him satisfaction, and the father-confessor must exhort the offender to make amends. What, however, is the position when the victim and the offender belong to widely different social classes? Is it sufficient if the person of higher social position greets the inferior whom he has wronged, or must he formally ask pardon? Or, if the two persons are of equal standing, is it sufficient to pay a personal visit to the wronged person? What is to be the attitude of a person towards his superior to whom he owes satisfaction?

The Power and Secret of the Jesuits

As cases may well occur in which a citizen, troubled by scruples of conscience at not having paid the proper amount of taxes due, comes to make confession, the Jesuit moral theologians also deal with this type of problem. Their decision in these cases is frequently to the effect that no one is compelled to pay a tax the justice of which is doubtful. As the payment of taxes is, in the opinion of many of them, a "hateful thing," *res odiosa*, the citizen may confine himself to paying only such taxes as are beyond doubt just. Consistently with this view, public finance officers who have been remiss in their duties through being too indulgent towards the tax-payers are themselves judged indulgently, "especially if they exercise lenience in minor matters, particularly towards poor persons and those who normally pay promptly."

It frequently happened that pious persons were troubled by scruples about the binding nature of the laws of the Faith, and in these cases, too, it was by no means always easy for the priest to make a correct decision. Accordingly, the casuists dealt with such questions at very considerable length; whether it was permissible to remove furniture on Sundays; whether a tradesman was permitted to sell meat on fast-days; whether, when visiting heathen countries, it was permissible to put on the dress of the unbelievers; whether a Jewish nurse might be engaged, and whether it was permissible to visit Protestant churches out of mere curiosity. These matters were similarly complicated by considerations of class distinction. Was it permissible for a cook to prepare meat dishes for her employers on fast-days?

In any attempt to deal exhaustively with all the cases of conscience met with in confessional practice, all the many and varied sexual problems had necessarily to be considered. The moral theologians accordingly endeavored to register carefully the sexual relationships and to determine when and how they were sinful. The duties and failings of husband and wife escaped the attention of the casuists as little as did the sins of professional prostitutes, the wildest excesses of libertines, the half-repressed desires of right-living young men and women, and the slightest offences against strict propriety.

How was a priest living in celibacy and lacking all experience of such matters to adjudicate rightly upon these sins? Men and women who had offended against the law of chastity or else entertained a variety of reprehensible desires or thoughts constantly came to him. The one might confess to having been guilty of the utmost excesses, while another might complain that he was unable to rid himself of an ardent desire the gratification of which was forbidden. A wife might have sold herself in order to obtain money which she badly needed either for herself or for her family. Was she to be required to return the money obtained through forbidden means? Was a house-owner who had let his house to prostitutes to be granted absolution?

The father-confessor to whom his penitents had confided such offences needed only to consult his manual on casuistry to obtain straightway the fullest information regarding all these things, and thereby be enabled to pronounce competent judgment upon them.

The casuists did not fail also to determine carefully the obligations arising out of the seduction of a young girl; their works give directions on when an offer of monetary compensation was proper or required *pro amissa virginitate*, in what cases the seducer was to be required to marry the girl he had seduced, what action was to be taken if the girl had in the meantime offended with another man, or if the man and the girl were of widely different social sta-

70. CONFESSION
French engraving

71. THE JESUIT GIRARD AND HIS CONFESSANT, "LA BELLE CADIÈRE"

Anti-Jesuit carricture of the period.

tions.

To the consideration of the question whether the procuring of an abortion, which was so rigorously forbidden by the Church, was excusable in individual cases, many paragraphs were devoted. The case might perhaps be one of a midwife who, in order to save her from committing suicide, assisted a girl who had been seduced; or a doctor may have interrupted pregnancy in a woman solely for the reason that her life would be gravely endangered by motherhood.

With that most admirable gravity, to which the Latin language lends itself, the casuists dealt with those difficult problems of marital life of which the confessor know so little: *"Non peccat negans, quando alter immoderate petit, v. gr. Post tertiam vel quartam vicem eadem nocte. . . "* *"Culpa vacant oscula quaelibet honesta aut tactus in partes tum honestas, tum minus honestas (si leviter fiant), inter conjuges ratione affectus conjugavis demonstrandi aut amoris confovendi itiamsi aliquando per accidens sequeretur involuntaria pollution . . ."* *"Non pecat graviter, imo juxta communiorem et probabiliorem sentientiam nec leviter uxor, quae seipsam tactibus excitat ad seminationem statim post copulam in qua vir solus seminavit."*

It often happened that poor and rich women had avoided the main object of marriage, the *procreation prolis*; the father-confessor was now able to determine whether such an act was always to be regarded as reprehensible and sinful. How fortunate it was or them that the casuists had dealt fully with such a matter!

To the conscientious moral theologian, the most trivial offence was of no less importance than the most serious, and accordingly, the worthy fathers had not failed to seek out the minutest infringements against the moral law, and to surround them with a host of mitigating circumstances, so as to ensure that a venial sin should not wrongly be judged too harshly.

If, for example, a woman came to confess that she was guilty of an excessive love of finery, the priest had only to consult Escobar's work in seven volumes, *Universae theologiae moralis problemata*, to find the ruling; "If a woman affects finery without any wrongful purpose, but only from natural vanity, she is guilty either of a mere venial sin or of no sin at all."

Again, by consulting Gury, the father-confessor was enabled to ascertain whether it was a grave sin for a woman to appear publicly *en décolleté*; this author held that it constituted a grave sin for a woman to expose her bosom "for the greater part of half-way"; "if, however, the exposure is not excessive, custom may easily absolve her of grave sin."

There was, apparently, nothing with which these reference books on moral casuistry did not deal; there were detailed examinations into the question whether a servant might saddle the horse of his master who was setting out on some affair of gallantry, as well as regulations for booksellers on the sale of immoral books. Such works Gury, for example, considers might in certain circumstances be sold to wise and educated men "whose only object in reading them is to condemn them or to warn others against them."

Even the various forms of dancing were subjected to a close moral study, since the father-confessor might well be called upon to give guidance to young girls and boys upon what forms of entertainment were allowed or forbidden. The Jesuit casuists, concerned to deal with everything, saw to it that the priest should not experience any difficulty in dealing with this matter either, and accordingly they gave a full survey of all the legitimate pleasures associated with dancing. "To dance with all due propriety or to attend well-conducted dances, when there is a certain obligation to do so, does not constitute a sin, if there is no reason to anticipate that the senses will be excited." Quite a different view was, however, to be taken in the case of a young man who "takes or presses a woman's hand for the physical pleasure it affords him"; in such cases "the guilt is the greater or the less according to the degree of danger it involves."

The priests are instructed also on the restricted rights of the socially outcast criminals, vagrants and beggars. If a criminal is illegally examined by a judge, he may commit falsehood; a prisoner convicted wrongfully may not only escape from prison, but may delude his warders or make them drunk in order to achieve his end; similarly, he may assist his fellow-sufferers in escaping. In precisely the same manner, the particular cases of conscience of high and mighty persons are dealt with, in that the casuists prescribe in detail the circumstances in which princes and commanders may embark on wars, suppress rebellions and exact indemnities.

While, therefore, there was scarcely any point of doubt left undetermined regarding any wrongful action, these works on moral theology laid down, on the other hand, precise directions for the observance and fulfilment of the Christian duties and virtues in everyday life. In the same way as the vices, the virtues too were systematically arranged under innumerable paragraphs and sections, and just as the casuists had not been content with the general nature of the commandments such as "Thou shalt not steal," so they had not been content with the excessive simplicity of the laws of virtue.

The ideal exhortation: "Thou shalt love thy neighbor as thyself" could not satisfy them, for the reason that, in practical life, it was rarely, if ever, possible to carry out this precept to its full extent. The Jesuit moralist, who never omitted to deal with the special case within the general law, proceeded on the lines of the principle formulated by Molina: "The duty of love does not require that we should deny ourselves advantage in order to preserve our neighbor from suffering prejudice in an equal degree."

A carefully graduated system was, therefore, drawn up, according to which the requirements of the divine commandment in question were held to be duly fulfilled: "In the matter of the love our neighbors," writes Gury, "we must also bring a certain order. For, on the one hand, we must love persons who are more or less perfect, or who stand to us in a nearer or farther relationship, and, on the other hand, the good which we wish them, or to which we must help them, is more or less useful."

Gury accordingly recommends that, "all other things being equal," our love for our neighbor should be greatest in the case of those persons "who are nearest to us either though kinship or friendship or by virtue of our office, of their creed or their origin." Thus, a man should place "(1) his parents before all others, (2) his wife before his children, his children before his brothers and sisters, his brothers and sisters before his other relatives, (3) his friends, benefactors and superiors, and those persons who perform the greater service for the common good, before all others."

Naturally, too, the extent to which a man is called upon to assist his "neighbor" is not left undetermined; this is graduated carefully on the basis of the degree of need in the individual case. In this connection, two main categories are to be distinguished: the "bodily" and the "spiritual" need, each of which categories is again split up into three sub-divisions.

The virtue of the giving of alms also is not left unregulated: "in cases of great or extreme need, sufficient should be given to the poor person to relieve this need. . . Nobody is, however, called upon to lay out a considerable sum of money in order that a poor person may be saved from the risk of dying, or that he may obtain very costly medicaments. . . . . In a normal case of need, it would appear to suffice if one gives alms to the extent of a tenth or a twentieth part of one's yearly income, after deducting expenditure on the wages of employees and other such items."

Specific regulations were also laid down governing the duties of the master towards his sick servant. Was the father-confessor to require a rich man, out of pure charity, to continue to pay his sick employee wages during the period of the illness, or even to reimburse him for his expenses for medical treatment? The majority of the casuists answered this question in the negative; the master was not obliged to pay the wages or the living costs, or even the costs of treatment of the sick servant, "excepting perhaps in isolated cases, out of pure Christian charity, if the sick person is in considerable need."

The learned authors of these treatises on moral theology were not unfamiliar even with the innermost workings of the human soul, and in almost every case they have a word of excuse even for what outwardly are very wrongful wishes and thoughts. The question whether it is inconsistent with love for one's neighbor to wish him some harm for his own ultimate good is answered by Gury in the negative, "if the true order of love is preserved." Such evil wishes, he considers, are excusable "(1) in consideration of the spiritual profit to the fellow-being himself, (2) in consideration of the common good, whether spiritual or temporal, (3) in consideration also of the advantage accruing to a number of persons, if of much greater significance." Gury, however, qualifies this with the remark: "nevertheless, such wishes are entirely superfluous and other and much better should be entertained."

The Jesuit casuist Hurtado holds that a son may rejoice at his father's death in view of the inheritance he acquires, "not however from personal hatred, but only on account of the advantage he derives." Other Jesuit moralists explain that the intention of the person formulating the wish in such cases is directed, not to the death of the father, but to the fortune inherited, and accordingly the father-confessor should not condemn the son point-blank on account of an emotion so easily explained psychologically and so humanly understandable.

Earnestly concerned as were the learned authors of these works on moral theology to furnish the priest with the necessary exact knowledge for the exercise of his difficult office, yet in many cases their views were widely divergent. Whereas, for example, in Escobar's works the father-confessor was informed that the petty thefts of a servant amounted, under certain circumstances, only to a venial sin, yet Sanchez, under identical circumstances, held them to constitute a mortal sin, while Molina didn't regard them as a sin at all.

Busembaum had written: "A son who steals a large sum of money from his parents commit's a grave sin," and Lessius had expressed the view that, if the father were rich, this "large sum" began at two gold pieces. Sanchez, however, wanted to fix the minimum at six gold pieces. Banez, on the other hand, held an entirely different view, and wanted to fix the amount at not less than fifty gold pieces; Lugo and Lacroix rejected this, except in the case of the son of a prince, and Liguori wanted exemption up to twenty gold pieces.

Similar differences of opinion had arisen also on the question of the amount of meat that might be eaten on fast-days. Whilst one moralist fixed the amount for the purposes of constituting a grave sin at upwards of sixty grammes (one-eighth of a pound), another allowed of a hundred and twenty, and a third even a hundred and forty grammes. Similarly, disagreement existed on how many pages of a book banned by the Church a person might read, and how many days he might have the book in his house. Some authors allowed three pages and one day, while others more indulgent, extended this limit to six pages and three days.

The Moral Philosophy of the Talmud and of the Stoics

As early as the seventeenth century, the Jesuits were accused of having "corrupted" Catholic Christianity "with the pharisaical-rabbinical spirit," and with having perverted the clear moral laws of the Gospel into "subtle Talmudic formulas." Even today, there appear from time to time pamphlets which, by reason of such points of similarity, endeavor to show that the Jesuits and the Jews are alike in spirit.

It is, in fact, remarkable how far the similarity between the Jesuit moral theology and the prescriptions of the Jewish *Mishnah* extends, and it is often a difficult matter to say off-hand, whether a quotation is taken from the one or the other of the two schools of doctrine.

For instance, the Jesuit Gury (viii, 672/1) deals with the case of "the servant Didacus," who, overnight, puts a very valuable piece of crystal glass belonging to his master in a corner of the room where nobody is likely to pass, with the intention of putting it in its proper place early on the following day. "But the same evening Basilius comes home, and, in the darkness, knocks against the glass and breaks it. What is just in this case?"

The *Mishnah* (Chap. III, Example 5) provides as follows: "If two persons, the one carrying a vessel and the other a beam, collide, and, in the collision, the vessel is broken by the beam, the latter person is exempt from all liability since the former could have made way for the latter. If the person carrying the beam is in front and the person with the vessel is behind, the former is similarly not liable. If, however, without adequate reason and only for the purpose of resting, he stops, then he is liable for the smashing of the vessel; he is, on the other hand, exempt from liability if he had previously told the person carrying the vessel to stop also. If the one carrying the vessel is in front and is followed by the one carrying the beam, then the latter is liable. . . Likewise must be judged the case where, of two persons, the one is carrying a light and the other a load of flax, and the flax is set alight."

The *Mishnah* further prescribes (Chap. II, Example 3) as follows: "If a dog or a goat jumps off a roof and breaks something, then the damage must be made good since it is in the nature of these animals to jump. If, however, a dog steals a cake baked on the coals and runs off with it to a heap of corn, eats the cake and sets fire to the heap of corn through a live cinder adhering to the cake, then the owner of the dog must make full compensation for the cake but only to the extent of half for the corn."

The Moral Philosophy of the Talmud and the Stoics

An entirely similar passage is contained in Gury's moral theology (VII, 672/2), as follows: "Quirinus decides to steal a length of cloth; he breaks at night time into a factory, kindles a light, but is careful to avoid all danger of a fire. Through some unforeseen circumstance, as, for example, a cat's jumping, he drops his torch onto the litter lying around, and in a short while the whole factory is ablaze and it is only with difficulty that he succeeds in saving his own life. What is the position of Quirinus?

"The answer is: he is not responsible, since he had not been able to anticipate this particular risk. . . That he was in the act of taking the cloth was not the cause of the fire nor did the fact that he was carrying a torch, provided sufficient care were taken, constitute an immediate risk of fire. If, however, the thief was not merely about to take the cloth, but had actually completed the theft. . . and if, subsequently, through some mischance, as in the lighting of a torch, a fire breaks out, he is bound to make restitution. . ."

Gury describes a further case as follows (VIII, 672/3): "From motives of revenge, Pomponius, unseen by anyone, shoots at Maurus's goat as it is browsing quietly in its master's field; instead of the goat, which is unhurt, he hits and kills Maurus's cow, as, unbeknown to him, it lay beneath the hedge. What is Pomponius's liability?

"The answer is: none. For he has incurred no liability in respect of the goat which he intended to hit but which was unhurt, nor in respect of the cow, since the loss inflicted on Maurus could not have been foreseen. . . ."

The *Mishnah* (Chap. VI, Example 3) treats of similar cases concerning animals: "If a person hires an ass in order to ride up into the mountains and instead rides it down into the valleys, or conversely, and the ass dies, then he is liable for compensation. If the ass goes blind or is seized for statute-labor, the hirer can say to the owner of the ass: Your property is returned to you. If, however, the ass dies or breaks a leg, then the hirer must make good its loss. If the hirer hires the animal for the purpose of riding up into the mountains, and instead rides it down into the valleys, and the ass slips and injures itself, then the hirer is not liable (since this was more likely to happen in the mountains); if, however, the animal dies from exhaustion, then the hirer must make good its loss. If, on the other hand, the animal is hired for the valleys and is ridden up into the mountains, the hirer is liable for compensation if it sustains injury from slipping down, but not if it suffers harm through exhaustion, since this might equally well have happened in descending into the valley."

Just as in the case of the Jesuits, the Jewish casuists fall into stricter or more tolerant schools. Whereas, for instance, the believer, according to one moral theologian, is allowed to eat a certain quantity of meat on fast-days, another moral theologian allows only a much smaller quantity. Similarly, one rabbi decides that a cripple with a wooden leg may go out on the Sabbath, another prescribes that he must not.

The Talmud says: "The House of Shammai declare that a man becomes unclean from sitting on the seat of a bride even though the covering has been removed; the House of Hillel, however, holds that he does not become unclean, since the seat no longer serves for a bride but is to be regarded as broken. . . ."

It is accordingly a simple matter, in view of such points of agreement between the Jewish and the Jesuit moralists, to arrive at the conclusion that the Jesuits were merely concerned with perverting the Christian faith. Whoever, though, rejects the ready facility with which trivial pamphleteers arrive at conclusions is forced to ask himself what is really at the basis of these remarkable instances of similarity of thought. He will then immediately see that the very obscure and subtle conclusions at which Jesuit casuistry often arrives by no means represent an "insinuation of the spirit of the Talmud into the Christian faith," but that, in Judaism as well as in Jesuitism, the same inevitable process has operated that invariably comes into play whenever man attempts to apply moral precepts of a general nature normatively to the individual case arising in practical life.

Such attempts can produce nothing more than a collection of pedantic decisions based partly on experience and partly on logical deduction. If the analysis of the ethical laws into concrete rules of conduct is carried sufficiently far, then it must necessarily result in such abstruse decisions as are to be found in abundance in the Talmud and the casuistic works of the Jesuits, and, indeed, in the earlier writings of the Greek and Roman philosophers. In principle, it amounts to the same thing if, like the Talmud and the Jesuit moral theology, Aristotle examines into the question how man should act if he cannot be both courageous and just or whether a virtuous man may be the friend of an evil man or conversely.

The Academic and particularly the later Stoic schools adduced and discussed, in the course of their further examinations into the interrelationship of the various virtues, a number of "cases" which bear a striking correspondence to the Talmudic and Jesuit moral problems.

A much-discussed case of this nature was as follows: "A righteous man brings from Alexandria to Rhodes a large shipload of corn at a time when corn is exceptionally dear in this town on account of famine. He is, at the same time, aware that a number of other merchants from Alexandria are immediately following him, and that, accordingly, in a very short while, the shortage will no longer exist. Ought he then to announce the good tidings to the people of Rhodes, or ought he to keep silence and sell his corn, which in the meantime is exceptionally valuable, at the highest possible price?"

This and other similar problems of casuistry had been discussed at length by the Stoics, Diogenes the Babylonian and Antipater of Tarsus. Hecato's work, *Of Duty*, was also concerned with such inquiries and contained, among others, the question; "Is it proper that a righteous man in times of acute famine should fail to provide his slaves with subsistence?" After going at length into all arguments for and against, Hecato is inclined to the view that the master, with due regard of course to his own interests, is not called upon to keep his slaves in time of need. The conflict between morality and material interest is most clearly expressed by the further question of Hecato; "If, at sea, it is necessary to throw anything overboard, which should be sacrificed first, a valuable horse or a cheap slave?"

Carneades of Cyrene similarly treats in his writings of a series of cases of conflict between material advantage and morality, in connection with which we find the view already advanced that to kill a fellow-man is permissible in order to save one's own life.

Nowhere, however, does the examination into the individual case with all its attendant circumstances so clearly bear the stamp of casuistic treatment as in the works of Cicero, who in his *De officiis*, to some extent follows the doctrine of his predecessor Panætius regarding man's duties, and to some extent supplements it. This is all the more significant, since it was Cicero who in later times exercised a very pronounced influence on Catholic Christianity, and, along with Aristotle, ranked as the highest among the early authorities. The Jesuits, in particular, paid great homage to this roman eclectic, and accorded him a prominent position in their educational system.

In his treatise on the duties of man, Cicero lays down in the same manner as did the Jesuits in later time, how the moral laws should be applied in practical life. The third book on this subject is devoted exclusively to those cases of conflict, the investigation of which Panætius had indeed contemplated, but had not carried out—and in this book are to be found very numerous instances of analogy with the moral theology of the Jesuits.

Even at this early stage, Cicero gives clear expression to the maxim for which the Jesuits have so often been held responsible: that, under certain circumstances, it is permissible to omit to fulfil an obligation that has been incurred, such as an obligation arising from an oath or a promise: "Justice may sometimes require," writes Cicero, "that a man may violate and fail to observe an obligation to restore property entrusted to him, to fulfil a promise he has made, or other duties imposed upon him by integrity and justice...

"It may be that a man, while of sound mind, entrusted thee with his sword, and then while no longer possessed of his reason, asks that the sword be delivered again to him; in such a case it would be wrongful to restore it to him, though a duty to restore it.

"If one who has entrusted money to thy keeping is about to engage thy country in war, must thou restore to him that which was entrusted to thee? I think not; else wouldst thou offend against the state, which by thee would be held most dear.

"Thus, there are many matters of conduct which, in themselves, appear to be morally good, but which become morally bad in certain circumstances. To keep one's pledge, to abide by one's contracts, to restore property entrusted to one, all these things cease to be morally good with a change of interest... Who is there that would not hold that it is not necessary to fulfil a promise extracted by fear or secured by cunning?"

Furthermore, there are clear evidences in Cicero's works of that remarkable differentiation in the matter of love for one's fellow-man which the Jesuits made on the basis of the relationship existing between the individual and his fellow-man: "Were a classified and comparative list drawn up of all those to whom our obligations are greatest, then our country and our parents would occupy the first place... next would come our children and all those within the circle of our family... then would follow those of our relatives living in concord with us and with whom we share in common the external circumstances of life. Accordingly, therefore, it is our duty to provide the necessary means of life for these persons before all others."

Similarly, too, as was later the case with the Jesuits, differences of opinion existed even among the casuists of antiquity regarding the most trivial problems. To the question whether the wise man who had received bad money in exchange of good might give this money in settlement of a debt, Diogenes of Selucia replied in the affirmative, Antipater of Tarsus in the negative, and Cicero, who quoted this discussion, upheld, for his part, the view of Antipater.

Probabilism

If, therefore, the learned casuists, even as far back as classic antiquity, were not always in agreement; if Diogenes and Antipater, and, later, Escobar and Sanchez, differed over the right decision in cases of conscience, how could the simple Catholic father-confessor know how to deal with all the infinite variety of cases of conscience he met with? It thus necessarily happened that the priests who, although for the most part their education was not of the best, nevertheless strove honorably after justice, often experienced the utmost perplexity.

The casuists had, to be sure, furnished the father-confessors with valuable assistance through their reference books, by means of which a decision in many difficult cases could be facilitated; nevertheless, it repeatedly happened that a helpless woman, a girl tortured by an uneasy conscience, or a man involved in worldly practices, turned to the priest for counsel, and that the priest was unable to trace the particular case in question in his manual.

The casuistic works did, indeed, contain examples of similar cases and the correct determination of the conflict of conscience in these cases was always clearly and plainly set out. It was not, however, always possible to apply the given decision directly to the particular problem confronting the father-confessor. The closer they were studied, the greater became the divergence between the "example" of the casuists and the actual case of the penitent.

The confessor was, therefore, often enough left to his own resources, either by reason of the fact that the matter in question was not dealt with at all in the books, or because the rulings of the various theologians conflicted with one another. Occasionally, it was a matter of grave doubt whether, under given circumstances, a specific rule was still applicable, or whether, having regard to the special considerations attaching to the case, it should not be relaxed in the particular instance in question.

This difficulty arose from the nature of the law itself; the laws and regulations were for the most part simple and clear as the light of day, so long as their general nature only was concerned; they immediately, however, became obscure as soon as an attempt was made to apply them in actual practice to the particular case; the process of judgment then suddenly became exceptionally difficult and uncertain.

The moral theologians had, however, also provided for such eventualities, and had laid own principles for dealing with doubtful cases of conscience. In this connection, two fundamental possibilities were distinguished which, in the Latin of the theologians, were described as *opinion pro lege* and *opinion pro libertate*. For, in cases of doubt, the view could be adopted that the law must always be followed, even though its validity in the given case appeared to be only probable, or else that individual freedom of decision could be reserved, and not be bound by the law.

According to the greater or less rigidity of their convictions, the various moral casuists had upheld the one or the other of these views, or adopted a middle course, and ultimately a number of different schools had arisen, each of which counted its zealous supporters. The "Absolute Tutiorists" contended that the law must be adhered to in all circumstances, even if only the shadow of a probability of its applicability to the case in question existed; the "Moderate Tutiorists," on the other hand, held the view that it was obligatory to observe a doubtful law only so long as its inapplicability was not beyond question or was at least extremely probable. The "Probabiliorists" considered the non-observance of the law was permissible if the probabilities against were greater than those in favor of its applicability; the "Equiprobablists" favored non-observance of the law in every case in which the arguments against its applicability were as strong as those in favor.

Finally, the "Probabilists" held that only those laws need be observed which were unquestionably applicable to the case in point, since man was a free agent by nature, and this freedom could be restricted by definite obligations alone. An ambiguous law, they contended, was without binding force: *Lex dubia non obligat*.

If, therefore, reasonable arguments existed both for and against the legitimacy of an action, the action, according to this view, was permissible; the fact that the arguments against may prevail over those for does not affect the case. So long as it is possible for two opposing views to be entertained, the law is ambiguous and accordingly not binding. If, therefore, there is a probability that an action is permissible, then it may be performed with a clear conscience, even though there exists a greater probability that it is contrary to the law.

The Jesuits, then, adopted this theory of "Probabilism," and made it one of the most prominent ideas of their moral system. Not that they were the originators of this doctrine; similar views had already been propounded by the ancients. Proceeding from the fundamental hypotheses of Aristotle, Carneades of Cyrene had developed the thesis that no truth could be assumed for any of our ideas, but only "probability." This probability he held, could be classified in varying degrees.

In close conformity with Aristotle's logical system, Carneades had also carefully examined the considerations which it was necessary to take into account in determining the greater or lesser degree of probability, and he had laid down the principle that, while the possibility of error was always present, this fact could not rob us of certainty in action. For, since nothing in life is absolutely certain, and we can, indeed, assent to no idea in the sense that we declare it to be "true," nevertheless, we can always find a way out on the grounds of "strong probability." Carneades expressly drew attention to the fact that this "theory of probability" applies particularly to ethical convictions and moral principles.

Many of the scholastics afterwards expressed similar views, until eventually, in the year 1577, its final theologico-philosophical formulation was given to the probabilistic system by the Dominican monk, Bartholomeus de Medina. In his commentary on Thomas Aquinas's *"Prima Secundae,"* Medina wrote that, although, logically, the more probable view was always the more certain, yet man was not always bund to take the more certain course; man might also follow that decision which has been acknowledged as merely "good and certain."

But even in later times, Probabilism was not the exclusive property of the Jesuits; for a considerable period, in fact, it was accepted by almost all the teachers of moral theology. Exponents of the Probabilist system were to be found not only among Catholic theologians, but also among Protestant writers; thus, for example, the Lutheran theologian, George Calixtus, wrote, in almost the identical words of Medina: "If, of two opinions, the one is more probable, it is not necessary to choose the more probable; the less probable may be adopted, if it is supported by strong arguments or has authority."

It was the casuist Vasquez who, towards the close of the sixteenth century, was the first among the Jesuits to take over Probabilism from the Dominicans. From then onwards, this doctrine spread ever more quickly throughout the Society of Jesus, whilst, on the other hand, the monks of Bartholomeus of Medina's order turned towards the more rigid doctrine of Probabiliorism," with its principle of the "more probable opinion." Thus, it ultimately came about that the Dominicans became violent opponents of the principle they had originated, while the Jesuits, on the other hand, became its most ardent defenders.

As is plainly evident from the works of Carneades, Probabilism, with all its premises, rests upon the doctrines of Aristotle, and therefore was eminently fitted to the Jesuit system, since, according to the *Nicomachean Ethics*, moral actions are nothing else than the outcome of mental deliberation, of a reasoned choice between two contradictory possibilities, between good and evil. The will, which has to decide in favor of one or other of these two alternatives, is, however, guided and determined in this process by the reason.

To attribute to the reason and to the will, which is governed by the reason, the function of determining the moral value of an action necessarily presupposes a strong doubt whether the moral principles laid down are categorically and unconditionally binding in all circumstances. Only he who is not inwardly already certain how he should act in all cases can find himself in a position in which he has to choose, by reasoned deliberation, between two alternatives.

As a logical consequence, therefore, Jesuit moral theology recognized that the moral laws and precepts cannot be regarded as having an absolute and binding force. If, for instance, the Jesuits conclude, the natural laws inspired by God in the human heart and the revealed standards laid down by positive law had absolute and binding force and were to be observed whatever the circumstances, then this would constitute a negation of the principle of the freedom of the will, since the binding nature of a particular moral law and the resulting obligation would directly preclude the free exercise of judgment by the reason and, therefore, actions of a voluntary nature.

Since, however, under the fundamental principle of the Jesuit philosophy, the freedom of the human will cannot be disputed, the individual moral laws cannot be regarded as binding in all circumstances. It is understandable, therefore, that Cathrein should have said that the moral law imposes on us merely a "conditional or oral compulsion," and that it "consists only of a conditional obligation" arising out of the exercise of reasoned judgment

This shifting of morality to the plane of choice governed by reason became the basic idea of the whole Jesuit moral system, and through it the Jesuits arrived directly at that intellectualist conception of the conscience which is such a distinctive feature of their philosophy.

The question of the nature of the conscience has, however, for centuries divided not only Jesuitism from the non-Jesuit world, but also, in general, Aristoteleans from Platonists. The fundamental difference in the conception of the nature of the conscience was not the least of the factors which caused the secession of the Reformers from the Catholic Church,

The "Certain" and the "Uncertain" Conscience

Even in the early days of Christianity, a remarkable blending of early Greek thought with the images of the Old Testament had taken place; in this connection the doctrine of *synteresis* is especially significant. The conception of *synteresis*, of the "preservation" or "safeguarding" of the paradisiacal state, is first expressed by the early church fathers, as, for instance, Gregory of Nazianzus, and it represents a *methexis*, a "participation" of the human soul in the world of eternal Ideas.

St. Jerome, one of the fathers of the Latin church, writes very beautifully on this subject in his commentary on the prophet Ezekiel: he declared that what the Greeks had described as *synteresis* was "a spark of the conscience," which had remained alive in the breast of Adam even after his expulsion from Paradise, and which guides man at all times amid the difficulties and perplexities of earthly life, and makes him conscious of his sins.

The German mystics, in particular master Eckhart, never tired of glorifying this divine "spark," and under the Reformation, it was regarded as comforting proof of the fact that every individual being was in direct communication with God, Out of the conscience, they derived the "certainty" that everyone is called upon to justify himself by faith before the Creator, let him but pay heed to the voice of God within his heart.

Against this line of thought influenced by Plato has, however, always stood opposed a conception of Aristotelean origin, which has been formulated most sharply in the Jesuit system of moral theology. Aristotle had entirely rejected Plato's doctrine of ideas and held that the Idea of Good was not applicable "to the practical sciences"; for, he pointed out, ethics was comparable to rhetoric rather than to mathematics.

A "low" conception of ethics such as this later on formed the basis of the majority of the moral theories of the Stoics, the scholastics and, finally, the Jesuits. From it arose the problems of casuistry and ultimately, too, those of Probabilism, under which the good appears repeatedly as the result of a reasoned examination of a particular case. According, therefore, to Aristotle's Jesuit disciples, too, the conscience could not signify anything else than the process of rational deliberation supposedly preceding every action. In accordance with this interpretation, the Jesuit Gury defines the conscience and a "practical expression of the reason, or a practical judgment whereby we decide that something shall be done because to is good, or shall be left undone because it is evil." Gury expressly adds that it is precisely this functioning in every practical case which distinguished the conscience "from *synteresis*, which merely lays down general principles."

The complete intellectualization of the conscience is perhaps still more clearly illustrated by a passage from the Jesuit moral philosopher, Cathrein, which is very reminiscent of Aristotle: "The conscience is virtually, at least, the conclusion of a syllogism. It is, therefore, possible to examine both the general principle of this syllogism (the major premise) and the concrete fact to which it is applied (the minor premise) and thus perhaps arrive at a certain conclusion."

Whoever, like Plato, believes in "the world of eternal Ideas," in an imperative which represents the governing principle of every human action, must regard it as an absolute obligation to act morally; in this conception there is, however, no place for a reasoned and syllogistic examination into the arguments for and against, for a free decision between two possibilities. Whoever, on the other hand, considers, like Aristotle, that it is not incumbent upon him to recognize the absolute nature of the imperative, for him exist no absolute principles governing human actions; rather does he consider that his reason is able to achieve the "attainable good" by wise judgment and a proper exercise of the will.

Whilst, however the manifestations of a conscience based on the platonic "imperative" can be conceived of only in the form of complete certainty, Aristotle's conception of "the good" demands the closest examination by the reason and a subsequent "choice." Such a conscience is not absolute, and accordingly admits of deliberation, doubt and hesitation; in place of certainty, we then have "opinion." An opinion can, however, never have behind it anything but a more or less great probability; very appositely, therefore, Gury defines "opinion" as "an uncertain judgment, resting on an uncertain basis, accompanied by the fear of being wrong, or the acceptance of a judgment accompanied by the fear that another may also be right."

Thus then, by the substitution of opinion for the certain knowledge of what is morally right, all the premises of Probabilism were found: where the "conscience" has been changed into something "uncertain," then opinions may exist which are "probable," "more probable" and "less probable," and the need for system becomes felt to guide the seeker through the wilderness of conflicting "opinions." In this matter, he will, as Carneades had indicated in his doctrine, always have to content himself with probabilities, and relinquish all hopes of absolute certainty.

"The necessary certainty for action," writes Cathrein therefore, "need not be absolute. It is sufficient if that moral certainty in the wider sense exists which is commonly sufficient for reasonable people in practical life. On the average, this agrees with truth, although, exceptionally, an error may arise."

Immanuel Kant, in whose philosophy the principles of Plato and also those of the German Reformation received their fullest expression, had necessarily to reject any attempt of this kind to substitute reasoned deliberation for the conscience. Thus, in his *Religion within the Bounds of Reason Only*, he writes that reason may indeed determine whether an action is definitely right or wrong; "but regarding that which I am about to do, I must not only form a judgment or an opinion, but I must also be certain that it is not wrong, and this exigency is a postulate of the conscience, to which Probabilism, i.e., the principle that the mere opinion that an action may be rightful is sufficient to justify its performance, is opposed. . . The conscience does not judge actions as cases falling under the law; that is done by the reasons insofar as it is subjective-practical (hence the *casus conscientiae* and casuistry as a kind of dialectic of the conscience); in this connection, however, the reason of itself judges whether all due care had been exercised in judging of actins (whether they are right or wrong), and makes man bear witness, either for or against himself, that this care has or has not been exercised."

For Kant, as for Plato, Master Eckhart and the Reformers, the conscience is the direct "participation" of man in the idea of the Good, and accordingly a guarantee of his moral autonomy. Consequently, Kant writes in the above-mentioned work, at the beginning of the paragraph, "Of the direction of the conscience in matters of faith"; "The question here is not how the conscience should be directed. The conscience needs no directing influence; it is sufficient that it exists. . . The conscience is a consciousness that imposes its own obligation. . . The consciousness that an action which I contemplate is right is therefore an unqualified obligation in itself."

Thus, in Kant's ethics, the conception of the direct autonomous certainty of men in all moral questions is most emphatically expressed, and, in this connection, Kant also upholds the doctrine of the unconditional nature of all obligations recognized by the conscience.

Whilst, however, the Platonic conception of the ideal significance of morality and the binding nature of the conscience necessarily leads to autonomy, the Aristotelean intellectualization of the conscience must logically lead to a heteronomous morality. If, for instance, the good is really the mere outcome of a decision of the reason, and if the conscience cannot afford absolute certainty, but merely a certain degree of probability, then the case will repeatedly arise in which man, owing to the imperfection of his mind, will be unable to arrive at a clear judgment regarding his duties. He will fall into "doubts of conscience" and immediately be tempted to ask a fellow-being for his judgment and to conform to this judgment. Cicero had already expressed the view that it is not inexpedient, "in cases in which doubt exists, to seek the counsel of learned and experienced men, and to ascertain their judgment on what duty demands in individual cases. . . ."

Since the theory of Probabilism spoke originally of "valid grounds" for the probability of an opinion, the "authority" of a teacher must soon follow from such grounds. This transition from what the moral theologians describe as "inner Probabilism" to "outer Probabilism," based solely upon the opinion of others, is clearly expressed in Escobar's writings in which it is stated, in this connection, that an opinion is probable if it "is based on grounds of some importance." From this, it is evident "that at times a single authority, if he commands respect, can render an opinion probable; a man who is entirely devoted to the pursuit of knowledge will not identify himself with an opinion unless it rests on good and adequate grounds." In the same sense, Sanchez says on this point that a probable opinion is one "which does not rest on superficial grounds; the view of a wise and learned man is, however, not a superficial but, rather, a material ground."

Ignatius himself had expressly sanctioned the principle of subordinating one's own judgment to the authority of an acknowledged teacher, when he declared, on the question how soldiers should conduct themselves in a war of doubtful justice: "If a man knows the war to be just or has become convinced of its justice after consulting trustworthy persons or in some other probable manner, then he commits no sin in taking part in the war." In the *Directorium* dictated by Ignatius for Jesuit father-confessors, it is further stated that absolution should not be denied to a penitent whom on the authority of an eminent teacher, had believed a particular action not to be a mortal sin.

To the Jesuits, in their efforts to minimize the number and gravity of all sins, the Probabilist system must naturally have been uncommonly useful. For, with this "doctrine of moral probability," it was possible in many instances to regard actions as guiltless, even when there were serious doubts of their permissibility; the existence of a single probable ground in favor of the permissibility of an action sufficed to outweigh all other opposing grounds. In this way, the possibility now always existed of appealing to the less severe opinion, which permitted something otherwise prohibited.

"For, although the opinion supported by stronger grounds is more perfect and certain," declares Escobar, "no one is required to follow what is more perfect and certain, for the reason that, as it is impossible to arrive at absolute certainty, God does not demand it. God demands of us only that we should act with such moral certainty as is to be found in the probable opinion. It would be an intolerable burden and would cause endless scruples if we were, in fact, to be bound always to follow the more probable opinion." Busembaum, too, justifies the right to adopt the most tolerant view, when he says that it would represent "an intolerable burden" for man "if he were to endeavor to ascertain in every case what was more probable and more certain."

With the aid of Probabilism it now became possible, in accordance with the numerous rules which are to be met with in this connection too in the Jesuit works, to deal leniently and indulgently with penitents. Probabilism gave the father-confessor authority to exercise leniency in a large number of cases, and to judge sins as venial or completely innocent.

For both Vasquez and Escobar had taught that the father-confessor might, in certain circumstances, advise the penitent to adopt a line of conduct which was opposed to his own conviction, in so far as the latter had only probable grounds in its favor; the casuist Baunius, too, in his treatise on penances, had declared that the penitent whose action was supported by a probable opinion must be absolved, even though the priest may hold a contrary opinion. To the same effect, Busembaum says: "The father-confessor or any other leaned man may advise a person, who comes to him for counsel, in accordance with the probable view of others, if this view is more favorable to the person concerned; in such a case, the father-confessor must disregard his own more probable and certain opinion."

The worthy casuists who labored with the utmost pains and care in the perfection of their system of exculpation had, moreover, not over looked the possibility that even after prolonged searching it might not be easy to find a probable opinion in favor of the penitent; in this case, they held that the person might be permitted to continue his efforts to find a more lenient judgment until such time as he eventually succeeded: "Condemnation should not be pronounced on those who go from one authority to another, until they fine one whose opinion is favorable to them, provided that the authority seems learned, pious and not entirely alone in his opinion."

"Austere and Morbid Pascal"

With biting sarcasm, Pascal causes his Jesuit to declare with satisfaction that it rarely happens that all the Jesuit casuists agree among themselves: "they disagree in many cases, but that is no matter. Each of himself makes his opinion probable and certain. They often contradict one another—so much the better! Scarcely ever do they agree, and only rarely can a question be found which is not answered in the affirmative by the one, and in the negative by the other. In all these cases, both the one and the other opinion are probable."

"Austere and Morbid Pascal"

Thus, Pascal argues, Probabilism had made it possible always to choose an authority who gave his assent to the particular act intended; this, however, inevitably led to the abandonment of all established standards of morality, and morality in this way became entirely void of meaning. As an instance of the disastrous consequences of this doctrine, Pascal quotes Escobar's dictum that a judge, in deciding a lawsuit, should relinquish his own conviction of right in favor of a probable opinion.

In actual fact, Probabilism led, particularly towards the end of the sixteenth and beginning of the seventeenth century, to a surprising laxity in the moral ideas of the clergy, and, in the result, Probabilism degenerated more and more into that "Laxism" which has been so much condemned. The fact that, even within the Church itself, a strong reaction against this development set in is attributable, for the most part, to Pascal's attacks; this is openly admitted even today by Jesuit authors. The *Provincial Letters*, with their malicious and provocative selection of quotations from Laxist moral treatises, did not fail to make an impression even in Church circles, and in Rome itself attention began to be paid to Probabilism and its dangerous developments.

In the years 1665 and 1666, not long, therefore, after the appearance of the *Provincial Letters*, Pope Alexander VII condemned a number of the ultra-lax principles of the Probabilist moral theology. And Innocent XI is said to have seriously contemplated for some time the condemnation of Probabilism altogether, but finally confined himself to the issue of a disapproving edict which Alexander VIII subsequently supplemented with still further orders for the revision of scandalous works on morality. In particular, the Dominicans exerted all their influence at Rome in order to win a victory for their more severe Probabiliorist system over the Probabilism of the Jesuits.

The political powers of Europe, too, began at that time to pay some attention to these moral doctrines since the influence of the Jesuits in affairs of state had in many cases become extremely important. The Probabilists had, indeed, put up propositions that, from the standpoint of the state, seemed somewhat dubious; for instance, Escobar had taught that it is morally permissible for the subject to refuse to pay a tax which, according to a probable opinion, is unjust.

But not only the irate Pascal, the jealous Dominican, and the state authorities, concerned about their national revenues, ranged themselves against Probabilism; seen within the Society of Jesus itself this philosophy had had, for a long time, its convinced opponents. As early as the year 1609, half a century before the appearance of the *Provincial Letters*, the Jesuit Comitolus had written his *Responsa moralia* as a direct challenge to the Probabilist system; similarly, the Italian Jesuit Bianchi, in 1642, attacked this doctrine in a treatise entitled *Opinionum praxi*. In 1670, de Elizalde published a treatise attacking Probabilism, and this wave of hostility reached its peak with the publication in 1694 of the *Fundamentum theologiae moralis* by Tirso Gonzalez, the general of the order, which contained a vigorous criticism of the Probabilist system.

Later on, stimulated by Pascal's *Provincial Letters*, the Idealistic school of philosophy sought to track down the errors of Probabilism; not only Kant but Hegel especially, in his *Philosophy of Right*, dealt exhaustively with this subject. "go then thyself to the Jesuits!" Pascal's Jansenist is made to say, "Thou wilt there find such ignorance regarding the Christian virtues, such detachment from love, which is the spirit and the life, thou wilt find so many vices palliated and so many excesses condoned, that thou wilt no longer be surprised that they assume that sufficient grace is extended at all times to all men for them to be able to live in the pious state they depict."

Pascal's condemnation of the Jesuit moral philosophy was destined to exercise a predominating influence on public opinion generally for a long time. Fanatical preachers and pamphleteers, governments jealous of their power, ambitious universities, and royal mistresses whose vanity had been wounded took care that the bad opinion in which the Jesuits were held should never be revised. Even in our own age there are men who pride themselves on their modern open-mindedness, but who cannot rid themselves of their belief in the "criminal doctrines and practices" of the Society of Jesus There had been scarcely a single case of regicide, or *coup d'état*, or political intrigue in the last three centuries in which it has not been suggested that the Jesuits were at the bottom of it all, and there is scarcely a conceivable form of fraud, infamy and sexual licentiousness which the Jesuits have not been declared to have encouraged or even practiced.

The majority of such statements and accusations have, indeed, since been refuted and shown to be fabrications, commencing with the celebrated book of secret criminal instructions, *Monita secreta*, which served for a long period as incontrovertible evidence against the Jesuits. Nevertheless, there are still to be found men of standing who, like the Jansenist of the *Provincial Letters*, meet every attempt to defend the Jesuits with the reply: "Go then thyself to the Jesuits!" Do not the books of the Jesuit moral theologians afford proof that the sole purpose of this Society is "to palliate every vice"?

It has been frequently alleged that the material for Pascal's attacks on the Jesuit moral system, which subsequently gave rise to a flood of literature directed against the Jesuits, was furnished to him by friends, and that he himself did not verify its accuracy. In his *Thoughts* he denied this, however, and, therefore, it must be accepted as a fact that he did actually look out the passages in the Jesuit works on casuistry. Nevertheless, certain inaccuracies have slipped into the quotations, and the Jesuits have since never tired of referring to these inaccurate quotations in the *Provincial Letters*.

More regrettable, however, than this lack of strict accuracy is the fact that he makes no attempt whatsoever to examine the philosophic principle of Jesuit morality. Only in very few places does Pascal attempt to adduce arguments of a purely moral-philosophic nature, whilst, on the other hand, he invariably seeks to refute the quotations from the Jesuit works by other quotations and by purely theological arguments.

Blaise Pascal, like Descartes, had indeed rightly realized that the study of philosophy and the natural sciences could progress only if the methods of scholasticism were abandoned. "The respect paid to antiquity," writes Pascal in his *Thoughts*, "is so great today, in those matters in which it is least due, that all its ideas are turned into oracles and even its obscurities are made into mysteries, so that it is no longer safe to advance new views, and the text of an author is sufficient to invalidate the strongest arguments of reason."

But when it came to matters of theology, Pascal had not the courage to cut adrift from the accepted faith in authorities. In theology, he writes, authority is absolutely essential, "since the authority is inseparable from the truth and we can perceive the latter only through the former; so that, in order to establish complete certainty regarding matters which are not comprehensible by the reason, it is sufficient to turn to the holy books; similarly, to establish the lack of certainty in the most probable matters, it is only necessary to show that they are not contained therein."

It was a fatal error of Pascal's to regard the investigation into the Jesuit moral philosophy purely as a theological problem that could be disposed of merely by quoting from "authorities." A man of his exceptional intellect was undoubtedly qualified to bring light into the obscurity and confusion existing from time immemorial in conceptions of morality, and would thereby have earned our utmost gratitude. But in this direction Pascal has done little more than the meaner intellects of this time could have done: the *Provincial Letters*, in which he endeavored to crush the Jesuits, did indeed, by their literary skill and wit, excite universal admiration, but beyond that they have contributed little towards a clearer understanding.

The Jesuits had been accustomed, from the time of the Molinist controversy, to defend their views at great length in learned volumes, but they had no experience whatever of literary pamphleteering. For a long time, therefore, they chose to make no public defense at all, and thus strengthened the opinion of the public that Pascal's attacks were unanswerable. When eventually they realized the necessity for action, and issued their various "Replies" to the *Provincial Letters*, the effect was practically negligible.

All things considered, victory appeared to lie completely with Pascal, and even the burning of the Provincial Letters by the public executioner did not affect the position in the slightest. Pascal had the laughers on his side, and this to the public, was of much greater importance than the question whether the author was entirely in the right.

Scarcely had the laughter subsided when some doubts arose even among Pascal's friends regarding the methods employed by him; many a reproach was levelled against the philosopher, who, indeed, persisted in his attitude, and in his *Thoughts* declared: "I have been asked whether I do not regret having written the *Provincial Letters*, To which I reply: so far from experiencing regret, were I at present engaged on the letters, I should be even more severe in them."

Scarcely a lifetime later, however, we find Voltaire already endeavoring to demonstrate the untenability of Pascal's attacks. The *Provincial Letters*, Voltaire declared, rested on false bases. "The extravagant opinions of particular Spanish and Flemish Jesuits were skilfully attributed to the whole Society of Jesus. Similar material could have been unearthed from the works of the Dominican and Franciscan casuists, but it was sought only in the case of the Jesuits. These Letters endeavored to prove that the object of the Jesuits was to pervert the morals of humanity—an object which has never dominated any sect or organization, nor can ever do so. . . ."

PART V

BEHIND A THOUSAND MASKS

Merchant Among Merchants and Soldier Among Soldiers

On a morning early in the year 1515, once again the spectacle-loving Romans were given an occasion to throng the streets: a fantastic procession wound over the Bridge of Saint' Angelo, along the "royal way" of the Borgo Nuovo, towards the Vatican: mules with brocade trappings, swaying dromedaries, elephants with panthers hissing and spitting on their backs, and a cavalcade of magnificent horses, in gorgeous apparel brought up the end of the procession, and, in their midst, with head held high and feet in stirrups of pure gold, rode the ambassador of the king of Portugal. It was his duty to present to the Holy Father, in his sovereign's name, these treasures and curiosities of the newly conquered Indian kingdom, as a proof of the Christian sentiments of the court of Lisbon.

Many years later, when Protestantism had already caused the apostasy of countless souls from the Catholic Church, when sadder and sadder news was received from Germany, England and Sweden of the loss of whole lands with their princes and priests, the people of Rome still thought often and pleasurably of this procession. However many lost souls the Lutheran heretics might send to hell, there was growing up in place of them, in distant India, a new realm of the Catholic Church, much larger than all Europe together.

For, since the day when Vasco da Gama's fleet, with great red crosses on the sails, reached the Indian coast, every foot of soil conquered by the Portuguese navigators had become a piece of new, Catholic country; priests appeared everywhere at the same time as the soldiers, to baptize the conquered, and the ground which the conquerors had taken from the natives was immediately hallowed by the erection of churches.

In the third decade of the sixteenth century, it was determined to carry on the work of the evangelization of India with redoubled efforts. Hitherto Dominicans, Franciscans and secular clergy had spread the Gospel in the new colonial territory, but King John III decided to ask the pope to permit the sending of some of the members of the newly founded Society of Jesus. The king had heard high praise of the activities of these priests, and hoped that they would labor for the spread of Christianity among the heathen with even greater zeal than the other missionaries.

Actually, this decision of the king's introduced an entirely new epoch, not only for

The Power and Secret of the Jesuits

Catholic missionary activity, but also for the Society of Jesus; the achievements of the Jesuits as apostolic preachers completely eclipsed all the successes of the other missionary orders, and it was through its activity in the mission field that the Society of Jesus first won its real world renown.

The very first Jesuit who made his way to India proved himself the most gifted and successful missionary ever produced by the Catholic church, which was the more remarkable since it was an accident that brought about Francis Xavier's call to this task. Ignatius had originally appointed his disciple Bobadilla for the journey to India, but he fell ill at the last moment; another brother had to take his place, and, as Francis Xavier was just then in Rome, Ignatius decided to send him.

Xavier employed the last night left to him in patching up his tattered cassock. The clothes he stood up in, his breviary and a few provisions constituted his sole possessions when he set out on his journey early next morning in company with the Portuguese ambassador on the overland route to Lisbon. After a year's sojourn there, Xavier set foot on the sailing ship which was to take him to India by the Cape of Good Hope; many more weary months elapsed before he set eyes on that marvelous land from which a new world was to be won "to the greater glory of God."

The ship glided upstream, between the banks of the broad river Mandavi, with their dark coconut groves, until Goa, the capital of the Portuguese territory in India, was visible on the right bank. European embattlements, dockyards and arsenals, the buildings of the Franciscan convent and the high towers of the cathedral and of the other churches showed at first glance that here Christianity had gained a great victory over the heathen.

On landing, Xavier surveyed with astonishment the motley crowds which surged through the streets, crying and singing, between elephants and sacred cows; white, brown and black forms in long garments and caftans; peasants and traders; Arabs, Persians and Hindus from Gujarat and Ormuz; between them, walking about under huge parasols, the conquerors, the Portuguese hildagos in gorgeous garments of taffeta, silk, and costly stuffs; they were followed by countless pages and troops of Kafir slaves. Everywhere on the walls great notices proclaimed where and when indulgences could be gained, and at what time the various festivals of the church took place.

Xavier's way led first in front of the cathedral, and here the magnitude of the triumph of Catholicism in these distant lands was made manifest to him. He saw the rich and distinguished personages of the city passing by in their palanquins; splendid sedan chairs made their way through the crowd, and out of them stepped dark-skinned ladies, loaded with precious stones, with painted faces, and feet in high-heeled shoes. Pages hurried quickly into the cathedral, and, while they spread out the rugs they had brought with them and placed the gilded seats and the prayer books in readiness, the ladies, followed by their children and maidservants, moved proudly to their places.

But there were also crowds of those peculiar people whose clothes and color proclaimed that they were natives. They too wore heavy rosaries round their necks, and bowed the head piously when they passed through the portals of the church.

Pride and joy filled the missionary's heart, at the thought that, after so long a journey of many thousand miles, he had found in the land of the heathen a second capital of Christendom. Xavier wrote joyfully of his first impressions gained by a tour of the city: "Goa is entirely populated by Christians. . . . We must be very thankful to the Lord God that the name of Christ flourishes so splendidly on this distant soil and among these hordes of unbelievers!"

This delight, however, was to last but a short time, for, when Xavier became better acquainted with the land and with its Christian rulers and the natives, he was forced to recognize that he had been deceived by the high European embattlements, the cathedrals and the throng of worshippers at the church doors.

When Pope Alexander VI laid down the lines of demarcation in the Far East which were to bound the Portuguese colonial territory, he commanded the king "to bring worthy, God-fearing men into the newly discovered continents and isles," who might "instruct the inhabitants of these regions in the Catholic faith and in good morals." But, actually, the Europeans who made their way to India were almost without exception adventurers and speculators, eager for spoils, who thought of nothing but winning wealth quickly and unscrupulously.

It was true that every day there was word of the many conversions among the heathen, but closer inquiry led to doubt whether all was well, for the Portuguese priests might baptize whole hordes of natives, but, as these did not understand their language, they had to dispense with any preliminary religious instruction. The people, for their part, went passively through the ritual of baptism, and then proceeded peacefully to their accustomed temples to do reverence to their elephant gods, lion gods, ape gods and the like.

The worst feature, however, was the behavior of the Portuguese colonial officials, who favored on the rich heathen, and, for suitable compensation, reserved for them the most influential places in the administration, and allowed them to oppress the newly baptized natives.

On all hands, wherever Xavier journeyed in Christian India, the same picture confronted him: everywhere great churches, governors' palaces and custom houses were rising above the reed huts and wooden houses of the native towns, and crowds of Europeans and natives could always be seen in the cathedral. Yet everywhere the natives sought their idols in the ape and elephant temples, and everywhere the colonial officials were corrupt.

When Xavier had learnt to know the behavior of these Portuguese officials to whom the evangelization of India was entrusted, he wrote to the king at Lisbon: "Unless you threaten your officials with chains, prison, and confiscation of goods and actually carry out the threat, all your commands for the furtherance of Christianity in India will be in vain. It is torture to look on patiently at the way your captains and other officials ill-treat the new converts!"

Thus the Jesuit missionary soon saw that a large part of his task would be to convert to Christianity, in the first place, the Christians who were living in India, and he had already learnt in Europe how hard it was to win Christians for Christ.

He had, however, learnt at the same time how often, in order to attain a pious end, it was necessary to proceed with "holy cunning"; accordingly, after his arrival, he conducted himself towards the resident clergy with that wise submission which his master Ignatius had usually employed in such cases. Although he carried with him a papal brief, which gave him the rank of legate, and thus placed him above all the clergy in India, he waited humbly on the bishop, fell on his knees before him, and entreated him to regard him as the humblest fellow-laborer in the work of Christian evangelization, and to dispose of him entirely at his good pleasure.

And, while the other priests of Goa lived in splendid houses, he, the papal legate, took up his dwelling in a modest little room at the hospital. He could, however, have scarcely found a more suitable quarter for his work, for here from the very first day he came into touch with all classes of men, and learned to know them in the condition in which they were readiest for spiritual exhortation. All of them—brutal soldiers, greedy officials, superstitious idolaters, proud lords of commerce and poor slaves—in the hospital showed themselves quite ready to talk with the worthy priest, and to let him console them in their affliction. Even when they returned cured to their homes, there nearly always remained in their hearts a memory of Xavier's edifying words.

The spiritual conversations of the missionary, with the oppressed and ill-treated slaves especially, were for the most part entirely concerned with their future life. The Christianity of which the foreign priest spoke sounded to them like a promise of future bliss, which should be the best compensation for all their sufferings on earth. Xavier, who had come to them in his simple dress, spoken to them with gentle, homely words, and sympathized fully with their smallest troubles, soon seemed to them like one of themselves.

Accordingly, they helped him in his labors as best they could, and informed him secretly of the conduct, deeds, vices and misdemeanors of their masters. In this way, Xavier had opportunity to obtain accurate information on the life, character, interests and peculiarities of the people whom he wanted to convert. He knew, before he visited a house, whether he had to do with men who were living polygamously with native women, or whether with those who practiced usury, committed deeds of violence, used their offices for shameless extortion, or ill-treated their slaves. When one or other entertained him, Xavier always appeared to have the same interests as his host. If the host was a merchant, he discussed eagerly with him the state of business and the possibilities of acquiring more wealth; in the usurer's home, he showed an astonishingly expert knowledge of all forms of credit undertakings, and knew how to perform the most complicated calculations of interest; on the other hand, if his host was a mariner, he conversed with him on nautical and astronomical questions, so that the host had immediate confidence in him. Officers, again, were astounded to find how much at home this simple priest was with military problems, and what professional questions he could put. Everyone listened to him with interest and attention, and he was invited again and again.

Neither did he forget the members of the domestic staff: he praised the maid who brought in the food, and, after the meal, asked to be allowed to speak to the cook and talked to her about cooking, and, when the servant showed him to the door at his departure, he questioned him sympathetically on his personal circumstances, aspirations and troubles. Only after a long time, when masters and men had already taken him to their hearts, did he come to speak, with caution and in a casual, light-hearted manner, of his own ends. Then he sought to convince the usurer that there were other less questionable and equally profitable methods of business; he made the harsh exploiter realize that slaves would work far more willingly and better if they were not so inhumanly treated; he spoke cautiously of the disadvantages of polygamy, and drew an attractive picture of the pleasures of the well-ordered, proper marriage state. So he carried on his missionary work, and, true to the teaching of his spiritual father, Ignatius, became all things to all men that he might gain all.

Nor did he hesitate to enter the most notorious sailor's taverns Sometimes it happened that the roisterers made as if to stop their game out of respect for the priest, and he would tell them kindly not to disturb themselves on his account, as soldiers and sailors were not required to live as monks; he would sit down beside the gamesters and tipplers and follow their amusements with interest.

What a stern zealot could never have accomplished with these rough folk, the boon-companion achieved with no difficulty; they became so accustomed to telling him their hopes and fears, that soon they were willing to confess to him as well.

Once, on a sea voyage from Goa to the south of India, he heard a sailor who had just lost his all at play cursing horribly. Xavier went up to him, offered him some money, and told him to try his luck again. This time the sailor won, and Xavier did not lose the opportunity of making the player's cheerful mood the occasion for an edifying discourse, just as Ignatius had once made a game of billiards the occasion for directing a student's attention to the exercises.

In the instructions which Xavier left later to his helper and successor, Barzæus, he himself describes the methods which he followed in India. He exhorts Barzæus to deal with everyone adroitly and with presence of mind, and so to win the necessary respect of all sorts and conditions of men: Let the moneyed people see that you are just as well versed in everyday affairs as they are; then they will feel admiration and confidence; otherwise the priest's admonitions will merely be derided.

"Take pains from the very first to find out," Xavier continues, "what kinds of business are carried on at each place, and what are the manners and customs of the land and the neighborhood. . . Find out, too, to what sins the people are prone, to what end sermons and the confessional should be directed. . . Make yourself informed also on the more common legal cases, frauds, perjuries and briberies. . . .

"Talk privately to the sinners about their faults, speaking always with a smile, without solemnity and in an amicable and friendly tone. According to the personality concerned, embrace the one and behave deferentially to the other. . . If you wish to bring forth good fruits in your own soul and your neighbor's consort constantly with sinners so that they may gain confidence and open their hearts to you. Hearts are the living books, which are more eloquent than any dead book, and which you must study. . . ."

With the Pearl-Fishers and Rajahs

In the far south of India there lived the Paravas, a race of about twenty thousand souls who gained a scanty livelihood from the pearl-fisheries. In 1530, these Paravas were attacked by a wild Mohammedan tribe, and, in their desperate state, they decided to appeal to the Portuguese for help.

A deputation of pearl-fishers made its way to Goa, and announced that, if the Portuguese would rid them of the Mohammedans, they were ready in a body to embrace the faith of the Europeans. The viceroy was satisfied with this arrangement, and merely stipulated for an annual tribute of two boat-loads of pearls.

Immediately, a Portuguese flotilla appeared of Cape Comorin, and drove off the marauding Mohammedans; thereupon, the Catholic priests, under the leadership of the vicar-general of the country, landed from the flotilla to baptize the tribe. The Paravas assembled from far and near, and arrayed themselves in readiness, then the priests said something in Latin which the pearl-fishers did not understand, and every one of the Paravas answered something in Tamil which the priests did not understand. The necessary ceremonies were quickly performed, pieces of paper bearing Portuguese baptismal names were distributed among the people, and the flotilla with the vicar-general and the other ecclesiastics on board returned to Goa. But the Portuguese colonial officials could report to their king with pride that they had succeeded in saving a further twenty thousand souls from eternal damnation and had brought them into the Holy Church.

From this date, the Paravas paid their tribute every year, and the white men, for their part, saw to it that the Mohammedan raiders kept far from the pearl coast. But beyond this, the Paravas could continue peacefully to follow their ancient customs; never again did a Christian priest appear in these regions, and the only memento which bound the Paravas to their change of faith was the piece of paper on which an incomprehensible name was written in incomprehensible characters.

When Francis Xavier arrived in Goa, eight years had already passed since this conversion of the pearl-fishers; it was eight years, too, since a priest had last been among the newly born community in the south.

The poor, palm-roofed huts of this people lay directly behind Cape Comorin on a bare, barren stretch of coast, whose burning sand dunes were but sparsely covered with thickets of thorn and with fan-palms. Here, in little villages, lived the Paravas, lean, sinewy people with dark skins. Day after day, they set forth at sunrise in their tiny boats with sails shaped like swallows' tails, to return at sunset to their reed huts, with their booty of pearls.

At Tuticorin, the chief town of the district, there were still the old, heathen temples with colored idols, bright red-and-white painted clay heaps, clay horses, stone altars with sacred snakes, bulls, cows, and apes; and, in the little villages too, there were on all hands countless grotesque and obscene symbols of the ancient faith to which the pearl-fishers had for centuries belonged.

The baptized Paravas visited these shrines, and, when they went in fear of the fire-spirits which danced over the sea at evening-time, foreboding ill, they hurried to make offerings of fishes to their gods or to build new temples of clay and reeds.

One day Xavier appeared among them, barefooted, wearing a garment patched a hundred times and with a shabby cowl of black wool on his head. He carried a little bell in his hand, rang it incessantly, and called to them in Tamil, with a strange accent; it sounded like "Come here, come here, I have good news for you!"

While he was still in Goa, Xavier had had some sermons and prayers translated into Tamil by interpreters, and had with great pains learned them by heart. Now, travelling through the villages of the Paravas, he attracted the native children to him with his little bell, taught

72. THE DEATH OF FRANCIS XAVIER

Painting by Maratta

73. STREET LIFE IN GOA

From the travel work by Linschaten, 1599

them the catechism, showed them how to pray and to sing an Ave; and the children did what they were told as readily as if it had been a new game.

It was the children, too, who helped him the most in his campaign against the heathen idols. They were happy and gleeful to find that, under the guidance of the white priest, they could destroy the statues of the old gods to their hearts' desire. Xavier wrote joyfully to his brothers at home: "When cases of idol-worship are reported to me, I collect all the children of the place and go with them to the place where the idols are. The calumnies which the devil receives from the children outweigh the honor shown him by the adult heathen. For the children take the images beat them to dust, finer than ashes, spit on them, tread them underfoot, and insult them yet more grossly."

Soon the whole purpose of the children was to inspire their parents too with enthusiasm for the strange man, and what had happened in the city with the Portuguese lords and their slaves happened now with the pearl-fishers: they grew to love Xavier, trusted him implicitly, and saw in him at the same time a higher being; for, since his bell rang at evening-time and his strange words of an invisible God, of the kingdom of the blessed in heaven, and of the place of the damned deep under the earth, resounded over the land, the fishers no longer saw the dreaded fire-spirits deporting themselves over the waves. It seemed to them that his bell had exorcized the eerie apparition.

After the mission to the fisheries had been begun with such success, Xavier visited in turn all the territory of the Portuguese colonies in India. Soon he was journeying along the coasts through deserts where the hot sand scorched the feet, and then again through impenetrable, primeval forests. His wonderful gift for language had made it possible for him to become tolerably acquainted, in a short time, with the Malay language which was commonly understood in Further India. Wherever his path led him, he sought to preach, and, for the purpose, he utilized every case in point which might bring clearly before his hearers the power of God and the danger of eternal damnation. Thus, on the island of Homoro, which was covered with volcanoes, he said that these were the chimneys of hell, and that down below, in the place from which the poisonous smoke arose, the idol-worshippers were burning forever.

In those days, mass conversions to Christianity in exchange for Portuguese military protection, begun with the Paravas, had become popular throughout India. Thus, when the prince of Kandy in Ceylon was threatened by neighboring peoples, he asked for Portuguese troops, and promised in return the conversion of his whole people. He made fairly high demands for military assistance, for he could appeal to the fact that in his principality was the celebrated rock on which Buddha's footprint could still be plainly seen, and that in a pagoda in the capital was cherished a tooth of the Sublime One. This being so, the prince was willing to renounce the faith of his fathers only at the price of a strong contingent of troops.

As was customary, there arrived in Kandy with the white soldiers monks who immediately baptized the prince and the people. But, when the hostile Mohammedan tribes had been beaten off and the Portuguese expeditionary force had left Ceylon again, the prince immediately returned to the old faith and had the temple containing Buddha's tooth reopened.

A year later, however, at the time when Xavier was in South India, the ruler was one more involved in a military conflict, and again urgently needed Portuguese support. Xavier's fame had already reached Ceylon, and the prince besought him to intercede with the governor of Goa. Xavier readily agreed to do this, and he himself accompanied the Portuguese forces to Kandy, and endeavored to reconvert the people.

Here again he made use of the children to put an end once and for all to idol worship. At his bidding, they broke into the famous temple and purloined Buddha's tooth, and they also worked eagerly rubbing down the sacred rock until the footprint of the saint could hardly be seen any longer.

Other rulers too invited to their courts the missionary who knew so well how to deal with the Portuguese authorities, for again and again it became necessary to put down local unrest with the help of the Europeans. Where this was the case, Xavier appeared also, so that, in exchange for the military assistance, he might call together with his bell the inhabitants of the principality concerned for instruction in the catechism.

After six years of activity in India, Xavier had made for himself a large sphere of work. At the beginning of the year 1549, he wrote to Ignatius: "At this moment, members of our Society are living in all parts of India where there are Christians. There are four on the Moluccas, two in Malacca, six at Cape Comorin, two in Cochin, two in Bassein, and four on the island of Sokotra. Each group is directed by a superior."

His letters took a year, by the long sea-route, to reach home. When such a letter reached Europe, it meant a festival for Catholic Christendom, so straightly pressed by heresy.

King John of Portugal was enraptured by the success of the mission which he had himself inaugurated and commanded. He sent Xavier's letters to Spain, where, by order of the Archbishop of Toledo, they were read from all the pulpits.

"We are now known throughout Spain," wrote Peter Faber to Ignatius. "Where formerly no one had heard of us, or where we had been slanderously criticized, there is now, thanks be to God, no longer any place, no palace, no prison and no hospital where anyone, rich or poor, noble or commoner, learned or ignorant, woman or child does not know how we live and what is the object of our order."

The Dream of Chinquinquo

Since the time when Marco Polo brought to Europe the first news of an island empire to the east of China, this distant country had occupied the mind of many a merchant and priest. At a later date, a Portuguese trading ship was driven by a storm on to the Japanese coast, and thenceforward a tentative trade between India and Japan was carried on. But, as neither party understood the other's speech, goods were always exchanged by dumb show, and the mystery surrounding this land was still unrevealed.

One day there appeared at Malacca, the most easterly port of Portuguese India, a Japanese by name Anjiro. This man had committed a murder in his native land, and had fled from the Japanese authorities on a Portuguese ship which lay at anchor in his home town of Kagoshima. For a large monetary consideration, the captain brought him to Malacca, and, on the way, Anjiro heard much from the sailors about the Christian faith, about heaven and hell, repentance, the forgiveness of sins and eternal salvation. The Japanese youth, with a murder on

The Dream of Chinquinquo

his conscience, was soon filled with a burning desire to embrace Christianity, and to obtain pardon for his sin in this new religion.

When, on one of his journeys, Xavier revisited Malacca, Anjiro sought him out and implored him for absolution of his sins in the name of the Christian God. The missionary saw before him a man who had committed a murder and was threatened by hell; only through the power of the one Church which held the keys of heaven could this poor heathen be saved. He baptized Anjiro without delay, and gave him the name of "Paul of the Holy Faith."

His acquaintance with Anjiro opened up to Xavier new wide vistas. The Japanese told him much about the religion of his countrymen, and said that this was the faith of the whole heathen world in Eastern Asia. "According to the information which Paul has given me," Xavier wrote at the time to the brothers in Europe, "China, Japan and Tatary follow a common religious system which is taught in a city called Chinquinquo. Paul himself does not understand the language in which this religious system is set down; it is, he says, a language which, like Latin with us, is used only for religious books. He can give us no information concerning the contents of these books."

This religious system of which Anjiro had spoken was the law of Buddha, and the sacred books were the writings of northern Buddhism. The language which, like Latin, was understood only by the initiated, was Sanskrit. With regard to the mysterious Chinquinquo, Xavier thought that it was a collection of high schools, a kind of "Asiatic Rome," and as such the center of the whole religious life of Eastern Asia.

Xavier proposed to make his way to this center to destroy, with the weapons of the true faith, the false doctrine under whose shadow lay Japan, China and Tatary. "We shall have there to oppose ourselves to learned men," he wrote, "but the truth of Christ will lead us to victory." Where this mysterious city Chinquinquo really was, Anjiro himself could not clearly say.

"When I asked Anjiro whether the Japanese would embrace Christianity after I arrived," Xavier continued, "he replied that this would not happen immediately. His countrymen would begin by asking me questions, and would then reflect on my answers, and would carefully prove whether my life corresponded to my teaching. But, if I satisfied them on both these points, by giving them convincing answers and endeavoring to live a blameless life, then within six months the king, the nobles, and all enlightened people would be willing to be baptized."

Xavier had now learned sufficient about the mentality of the Japanese to know that it would be necessary to demonstrate the superiority of the Christian faith over the heathen "law" with the whole art of dialectic, for Anjiro had always said that the Japanese could be convinced and won over only by reason.

The first thing to do was to secure an audience with this "king" of Japan, to convince him by the art of dialectic of the unique truth of Christianity, and thereby to win with one blow the whole island realm for the Catholic faith. From Japan, a way into the rigidly closed country of China might be opened, for the "kings" of Japan and of China, Anjiro assured him, were firm friends; an introduction from the Japanese ruler might therefore, secure his entry into that "Middle Kingdom," surrounded by its great, impenetrable wall, from which foreigners were usually excluded on pain of death.

What especially strengthened Xavier's hopes, however, were the peculiar points of resemblance which, according to what Anjiro told him, existed between the faith of the Japanese and the Christian religion. Anjiro told him of monks who lived, celibate, in monasteries with common refectories, kept strict fasts and performed nocturnal devotions. They spoke their own language, which was not understood by the people, preached often, believed in one God, were under obedience to an abbot, and led a virtuous life. Moreover, they taught that there was a hell, a purgatory, and a heaven, and in honoring their countless saints, they were not worshipping idols, for, like the Catholics, they only besought the saints to intercede for them with the one almighty God.

When Xavier head all this, he immediately wondered whether the Gospel had not already been preached in those lands in time out of mind, and whether the religion of the Japanese was not a kind of Christianity, debased by heathen additions. In any case, he thought that, with such considerable similarities between the two religions, it would not be difficult to win the Japanese over to the one true doctrine.

With Anjiro's help, he eagerly set about learning the Japanese language. He had the most important articles of the Christian faith translated into Japanese, and learnt them by heart. He took with him three members of his order who had in the meantime arrived in Asia, and with them and Anjiro he crossed over in a Chinese junk

After a long voyage fraught with adventures and dangers, the Japanese coast came at last in sight. On Ascension Day in the year 1549, Francis Xavier landed at Kagoshima, Anjiro's native town, and immediately wrote to Europe in triumph: "God has brought us to the land of our heart's desire."

Never before had a native of Kagoshima crossed the sea, and, accordingly, Anjiro was received by his countrymen with admiring envy. Nobody mentioned the murder which had caused his flight; the general impatience to know what was to be seen and heard in the distant "Land of the Southern Barbarians" was too great.

The arrival of Xavier and his white companions naturally aroused even greater astonishment. Xavier had hardly settled down in the house of Anjiro's parents, before there arrived crowds of Japanese men and women, in long, gaily colored garments, put on one on top of the other, and with colored paper sunshades, and with them came close-cropped Japanese priests in white robes.

From morning until evening, the house was filled with visitors, and everyone had so much to ask that no one would let his neighbor speak. Soon, too, the prince, the powerful Daimyo Shimatsu Takahisa, sent one of his court officials, and had the strangers invited to the castle.

Thanks to certain Portuguese merchants who had once visited Kagoshima, the daimyo knew of the existence of cannon, and, in the troublous times through which Japan was passing, cannon seemed to him of no little importance for the safety of this throne. But many other valuable products were sold by the Portuguese, who, moreover, provided a ready and lucrative market for many goods produced by Japan. When, therefore, the daimyo heard that the foreign priest was held in high honor by the Portuguese, he surmised that his residence in Kagoshima would have a favorable effect on trade. He received the missionary, therefore, with all

The Dream of Chinquinquo

those ceremonies which are customary in giving audience to an important and powerful personage.

Xavier was led to the state-room of the castle, where the daimyo, surrounded by his household, sat on a raised dais, while the lower officials reclined round about on the floor and awaited his commands. Shimatsu Takahisa politely invited the guest to seat himself on a mat at his feet, and then for three hours without ceasing he asked him questions: what were the customs of the Europeans, and in particular whether they had many ships, goods, cannon and soldiers. At each of Xavier's answers, which Anjiro translated into Japanese, the prince was overcome by respectful astonishment.

When, in conclusion, Xavier produced a beautifully bound prayer-book and presented it to the daimyo, the latter announced solemnly that he would cherish with great care the book containing the Christian law and would have its contents explained to him; if this law was really good, he would accept it.

On being commanded to ask for a present in return, Xavier astonished the whole court by refusing, with thanks, to accept any gift, and asking instead to be allowed the favor of freedom to preach, a favor which the daimyo immediately granted. Only when Xavier made the further request that the daimyo would make it possible for him shortly to journey on to the "king" of Japan did Shimatsu Takahisa find himself to some extent in a dilemma. He was unwilling to part so soon with this holy man whose presence might attract Portuguese trading vessels to Kagoshima, so he made an evasive answer, and put Xavier off to a more favorable opportunity.

When the rich and distinguished inhabitants of Kagoshima saw with what respect their ruler had received the stranger, they immediately invited him, one after another, to their houses, and, before long, an earnest court official actually embraced Christianity; his subordinates, with their families, followed his example, and soon it was the fashion in good society in Kagoshima to converse with Xavier on religious matters and to be converted by him.

But, with the common people as well, the missionary gained much success. He had, in the meantime, materially improved his knowledge of the Japanese language, and was now able to read out from a notebook a number of sermons in Japanese. Twice a day, he sought out the most popular streets, sat down on the edge of a well, brought out his notebook, and began to preach. On returning to his house, he was usually followed by a crowd of inquirers, who carried on eager discussions with him until late at night.

"These Japanese are so curious," wrote Father Torres, one of Xavier's companions at the time, "that since our arrival not a day has passed without priests and laymen coming from morning till night to ask us all sorts of questions."

For the first time, the Japanese learned of a God who created the world in seven days, of a Son of God who became man and died on the Cross, of a Last Judgment, of heaven and eternal damnation. But the Japanese marveled yet more at the explanations which Xavier was able to give of the universal forces of nature. The Japanese were not quite clear how the world had really come into being; according to one tradition, the world consisted of an egg which was broken to pieces in a storm--the white of the egg became the sky, the yolk became the sea and the shell the dry land. The writings of other sages, again, described the creation of the world in quite a different way, and so the people did not to know exactly what to think.

Xavier, however, could explain to his astonished listeners the course of the sun, the appearance of comets, the phases of the moon, solar eclipses, and the various meteorological phenomena in a completely new and illuminating way. "Our answers," he wrote to Europe, "were much to their liking; they accepted us as good sages, and this helped us in our work of conversion."

However highly he appreciated the Japanese thirst for knowledge, however, he sometimes became thoroughly weary of this eternal, tireless curiosity. What did the Christian God really look like, they inquired, was he red, gilded, black or green like the Buddhist idols, had he a long nose, was he tall of stature and of a terrible countenance, or was he, on the other hand, beautiful like Shaka and Amida, and seated on a lotus leaf? Xavier had to explain that God had neither form nor color, but was a pure Substance, and, as such, was different from all the elements which He Himself had created.

But from what material had God made the human soul? What was the appearance, the form and the color of this soul? Why had God endowed man with a propensity for evil? Why was it so difficult to reach heaven? Why had God only revealed His law to man at such a late date? What happened to those people who were not intelligent enough to apprehend God?

Many of these questions put even Xavier, the accomplished student of dialectic of the University of Paris, in a painful predicament. The connection of God with the problem of evil was a particularly delicate question. How was it to be explained that the good Creator had also created evil spirits? When Xavier answered that the devils had originally been good, and had become evil through their own fault, and were accordingly punished by God through all eternity, the Japanese at once objected that a good God would surely not leave mankind in the power of evil spirits. Xavier's statement that the pains of hell were eternal, and that from them there was no redemption, likewise always produced great objections. Many of the Japanese argued that the God of the Christians could not be merciful if He delivered to eternal damnation all those people who had learnt nothing of Him. "To answer them to their satisfaction," Wrote Torres regarding these discussions, "you must be clever and cautious. . . these Japanese are very sharp-witted."

Here, therefore, Xavier saw before him a much more difficult task than had confronted him in India; a few only could be reached by means of the homely little bell, and the demonstration of the volcanoes, which had so deeply impressed the Malays, could not be applied to Japan, where it was necessary to vanquish the understanding of men eager for knowledge, to give explanations on the subtlest questions, and to bring into play all the weapons of a mind practiced in scholastic dialectic.

But the man who in Goa had in a few weeks' time penetrated all the tricks of the pepper trade, who had made himself conversant with strategy and seamanship, so as to win over merchant or officer or sailor for Christ, soon discovered with what rejoinders he should meet the objections and difficulties of the disputatious Japanese. His former fellow-students from the college of Saint Barbara would have been speechless with admiration, could they have heard him arguing with the greatest possible dexterity with his Japanese opponents.

Now were his efforts without success, for, as Xavier reported to Europe, "if you can explain reasonably the compatibility of the existence of evil with God's omnipotence and the necessity for the incarnation of God, the battle here is half won."

When a Japanese was once converted, however, he immediately became an eager professor of the new faith. Instead of constantly pronouncing the name of the god Amida, as heretofore, the neophytes baptized by Xavier were just as constant in the repetition of the names of Jesus and Mary. In place of the holy water in which the emperor had bathed his feet, they honored the water blessed by Xavier; instead of the Buddhist rosary, they used the Catholic. Whereas formerly they had been wont to receive from their priests, for money given in alms, pieces of paper on which they were assured that in another life the expended amount would be doubly and trebly repaid, they were now just as eager to obtain Roman indulgences.

It looked, indeed, as if the high hopes with which Xavier had set out on his missionary journey to Japan would not be disappointed. Every day produced new Japanese who declared themselves ready to accept the Christian faith.

The sovereign, however, as time went on, began to be a little doubtful about Xavier. Had he not somewhat overestimated the significance of this stranger from the land of the "Southern Barbarians"? Month after month went by, without the arrival of the desired Portuguese trading vessels at Kagoshima. The daimyo therefore had it proclaimed one day to the people that from henceforth further conversions to Christianity would be punishable by death.

During the course of his later experiences in japan, Xavier had, therefore, already learnt to appreciate the value of Portuguese trading vessels to missionary enterprise, and he took particular care to make the arrival of such vessels serve his evangelistic work. As often as he heard that a Portuguese ship had arrived at any Japanese port, he hurried there forthwith and took care that the captain and seamen prepared a ceremonial reception for him with a display of flags and a salute of cannon.

Moreover, he knew how to draw the right conclusions from his observations, and in many respects to alter his appearance according to the customs of the land. In India, where his main task was to win the poor and humble lower castes, he always wore his torn cassock and a shabby woolen cowl. In Japan, however, this made no impression, for here people admired splendid silken robes and pomp and ceremony. So Xavier put on the most magnificent apparel he could have made for him, and went about with an imposing following of servants.

There is hardly another Christian priest who has given such proof of genuine humility as the very Francis Xavier, but in Japan humility was of no account; here the missionary had to show pride and arrogance if he wished to make an impression on princes and people. These were not people, he reported, who regarded modesty as praiseworthy; on the contrary, they valued only him who knew how to conduct himself as proudly and nobly as they themselves did. So, in this land, where humility called forth nothing but contempt, he put on the "mask of pride."

Once in Yamaguchi it happened that, after his reception by the daimyo, Xavier was surrounded in front of the palace by a threatening mob and overwhelmed with abuse. The nobleman of Navarre found no difficulty in confronting the howling mob with the greatest arrogance and provocative contempt. He briskly called to account a samurai who had shouted an insult at him, and poured forth on him such invective that the man, finding himself shouted down, fell silent. It was immediately proclaimed in the crowds that the stranger really seemed to be a distinguished man, and perhaps his teaching was not after all so bad as had been at first believed.

At the Court of the Great Voo

For the whole of the time he was preaching Christianity at the courts of the daimyos and in the streets and market-places, Xavier never for an instant lost sight of his real object—that he had come to convert the ruler of all Japan.

Everything that the people in the south could tell him of the imperial residence, Miyako, only increased his desire to reach it, for it was said that the capital also contained a great university "very similar to the University of Paris." Here was obviously one of the most important seats of paganism in East Asia. Xavier, therefore, constantly urged that he should be allowed to continue his journey as quickly as possible, and longed for the great, decisive minute when he should as last appear before the "king."

He had landed at the extreme south of the island realm of Japan, and, to reach the residence of Miyako from there, five hundred miles had to be traversed, partly by ship, partly by neglected roads over high mountain chains and through dangerous districts, infested with robbers and marauding troops. The time of year was as unfavorable as possible, for the winter was unusually severe, so that the traveler was often compelled to wade through show up to the knees. Xavier overcame all obstacles, and was, moreover, always in good spirits: he jumped for joy like a little child when Miyako came at last in sight. The imperial city, the Kyoto of the present day, appeared to the stranger like a sea of black roofs, overtopped by high temples and towers, surrounded by snow-covered mountains.

Xavier believed that he had at last reached the goal of his hopes, whereas, in reality, a surfeit of the bitterest disillusion awaited him. As soon as he entered the city, he noticed that houses and streets showed unmistakable signs of the disturbances of war, and gave a comfortless impression of decay and poverty. For the year-long, embittered strife between rival noble houses had laid waste the whole city; the dwelling-houses of the nobles and even the pagodas had been changed into fortifications and surrounded with barricades and trenches; in between them, deserted, smoke-blackened ruins bore witness to rapine and plundering.

The mysterious high school, where Xavier had purposed to teach the Christian doctrine, proved to be deserted; the convents of the priests were empty, for even the monks were eager partisans. After wandering about all day in the death-like city, Xavier at last succeeded in discovering the palace of Gosho, where dwelt the sublime Emperor, Go-Nara.

The Great Voo was venerated as the descendant of the sun-goddess, Amaterasu; living in retirement in his harem, he showed himself but seldom to his court, who, when he did appear, greeted him in silence prostrate on the ground. The spotless purity of the emperor was held to be sullied if an ordinary man so much as looked at him. He never left his palace, for he could not set foot on the ground without defiling himself. Every day, his women brought him new garments; his food was brought to him in porcelain vessels, fresh each day from the

At the Court of the Great Voo

furnace and broken after being once used.

Xavier requested one of the court officials to secure him an audience with the Voo; he was commissioned to convey to the ruler a message from the pope, the mighty lord of Christendom; he had brought from his native land marvelous gifts in token of respect. The court official said that he would do his best, but that, in any case, the decision would take some time; in the meantime, the stranger was welcome to his hospitality.

When Xavier inquired about the correct ceremonial to be observed at an audience, the official, who found the guest to his liking, began to tell him exactly how things were at court, and how the emperor lied. Xavier learnt, to his amazement, that the Voo, the sublime Son of God on the Japanese throne, was venerated as if he were himself a god, but that, since the feudal lords had deprived him of all power, he was no more than an idol, without any influence or the smallest political significance.

Go-Nara, the descendant of the sun-goddess, Amaterasu, was actually short of money, because, owing to the civil war, taxes were no longer regularly paid. He had not even means enough to repair the broken-down walls of the palace, and the people could, therefore, peer through the great cracks and rents; as, however, the ceremonial commanded that the emperor should always be protected from rude glances, there was nothing for it but for the court officials to surround him with paper screens.

As heretofore, his meals were brought to the Voo in porcelain dished, which were broken after being used, but the food on these dishes was poor and scanty. The Voo was even compelled to earn money by the work of his own hands, copying music for rich connoisseurs.

As his clients might not see the emperor face to face, they placed the sum to be paid behind a curtain of the audience chamber, and returned some time later to fetch the emperor's manuscript. If it ever became necessary for his customer to speak personally with the emperor concerning the price of the copy, he had to take great care that throughout the audience he never looked on the sublime Son of God.

The loquacious court official also told the missionary of the hard case of the hungry princesses and court ladies, who were often compelled to beg sweet potatoes of the street-traders through the breaches in the palace wall.

Xavier heard these sad tidings with genuine emotion and felt a lively sympathy for the ruler's straitened circumstances. He had, however, a higher task before him, and was obliged to draw the proper practical conclusions from this surprising news.

His firm intention was to win the whole of Japan and China for the Catholic Church, and, for this purpose, an emperor was of no use to him who albeit so sublime that no one might look upon him, had to support himself by writing, whose court begged potatoes for food, and from whom the ground, on which he was not permitted to set foot, had long since been reft away by powerful insurgents.

So the missionary sked the court official who really exercised authority over japan, if not the emperor. He leaned that it was the shogun, the general-in-chief, who ruled the land. When he sought to discover more about the shogun, however, it appeared that the present general-in-chief, Ashinaka Tashiteru, was a fifteen-year-old boy, who was of no account and who was at the moment fleeing from his enemies. The official at last admitted sorrowfully that, to tell the truth, the only people who had real power in Japan at present were the upstart daimyos.

"Deus" Against "Dainichi"

On his way to the capital, Xavier had passed through a great and prosperous city called Yamaguchi; as, however, at that time he was still inpatient to reach Miyako, he had taken no more account of the daimyo of Yamaguchi, Uchi Yoshitaka, than of all the other princes whom he had come across on his travels. Now, however, that he knew that the daimyos represented the sole authorities in the land, he remembered the prince of Yamaguchi and his magnificent court. Indeed, since Miyako had been laid waste by ceaseless civil war, a large number of the imperial nobles had fled to Yamaguchi, and thus this city had become the real capital of Japan.

In great haste, Xavier journeyed back to Yamaguchi. He put on for the audience with Uchi Yoshitaka the costly vestments which he had originally intended to wear at his audience with the emperor, and to the daimyo he tendered too the message from the pope of Rome, the credential from the governor of Goa, and the presents intended for the Voo.

When the daimyo learnt what high honor the stranger was showing him, when he heard this Christian priest, clad in his glittering vestments, addressing him with all the titles and homage due to the emperor, very little persuasion was needed to convince him to the usefulness and truth of Christianity.

But, after Xavier's speech was at an end and the parchment rolls with the greetings of the pope and the Portuguese governor had been handed to the daimyo, the supreme moment came when the stranger brought out of his bag one splendid present after another.

Immediately a court official was called and ordered to record for all future time with what words the ambassador from the Land of the southern Barbarians had addressed the daimyo, and with what marvelous gifts he had presented him as a sign of homage.

"A clock," inscribed the chronicler, "which strikes exactly twelve times by day and twelve times by night; a musical instrument which gives out wonderful sounds quite by itself and without being touched; glasses for the eyes, with the help of which an old man can see as well as a young man."

With a loud voice, the daimyo ordered it to be proclaimed in the city on the very same day that the stranger had permission freely to preach his faith, and that all subjects were allowed to embrace Christianity.

The news of the arrival of a marvelous man from the Land of the Southern Barbarians was soon spread abroad throughout japan by merchants, vagrants and sea-captains, and so it came about that Otomo Yoshishige too, the daimyo of Bungo, heard of Xavier and his amazing treasures, Immediately, this prince commanded his samurais that by all means they must bring the holy man to his court. "I have a great desire to see you," he wrote himself to the missionary, "and to speak with you privately. I am filled with emotion by the hope of your early arrival."

"Deus" Against "Dainichi"

It seemed as though heaven itself had a mind to make Xavier's journey to Bungo especially successful, for, just as the missionary arrived there, a Portuguese ship came into the harbor. At Xavier's wish, the Portuguese immediately did everything to provide the priest whom they held in such high honor with a correspondingly splendid appearance. They bore him to Funai, the residence of the daimyo, in a gaily decorated shallop, accompanied by many slaves in costly raiment, and, when Xavier was received by Otomo Yoshishige, the Portuguese ship's officers spread their rich cloaks on the ground so that Xavier might sit upon them.

All this did not fail to make an impression upon the prince. Immediately, complete liberty of conscience was proclaimed for all Bungo; the daimyo himself expressed a wish to keep the priest from the Land of the Southern Barbarians constantly in his company, a request which Xavier declined.

The success which the missionary had achieved during his short activity in Japan was great; already there were five towns with Christian communities, and the number of baptized Japanese exceeded a thousand; moreover, these were not, as in India, merely members of the lowest classes, but in great part were nobles and court officials.

Nevertheless, Xavier could not forget that up till now the most important part of his task remained undone; the bonzes, the priests of the false belief, were not only not yet conquered, but proved themselves bitter and dangerous enemies.

On Anjiro's advice, Xavier had at first referred to the Christian God by the name current in Japan of *Dainichi,* "Creator of All Things"; the bonzes had thereupon explained with satisfaction that this God was none other than their own god and that Christianity was a kind of Buddhism. "Between you and us," they said to Xavier, "there is only the difference of language; our belief is the same." At first, they received the "foreign brother" in the friendliest fashion, invited him to their monastery, and prepared a festive reception for him there. It happened, too, that certain priests embraced Christianity and suffered Xavier to baptize them.

But, when Xavier had himself investigated the teachings of Buddhism and Shintoism, he found to his horror that Anjiro's information had led him astray. The good fellow had certainly proved to be a veritable Paul, preaching Christianity with fiery tongues, but, at bottom, he was, as now appeared, quite uneducated, and most of his information was inaccurate.

Xavier now saw that the resemblance with, Anjiro maintained, existed between these heathen creeds and Christianity rested only on unimportant externals. Actually, Buddhism knew nothing of a Saviour whose sufferings redeemed mankind, nor of the struggle to obtain eternal blessedness; the goal of the Buddhist was not heaven but nirvana, complete extinction in non-existence. The adherents of Shintoism prayed to sun and moon, legendary heroes of war and brute beasts, and this the Catholic missionary could not but regard with aversion and contempt

Xavier, therefore, became more cautious, and, to avoid any misunderstanding, referred to God only by the Latin mane Deus. In order to make good his original error, he was quick to explain everywhere that the *Dainichi* of the bonzes was no God, but the offspring of Satan.

This, however, brought to an end his good understanding with the Japanese priests; these became his bitterest opponents and made every effort to oppose him and to defeat his doctrine.

The Power and Secret of the Jesuits

Before the Gates of China

In the verbal battles which now took place everywhere, the Buddhist priests often adduced an argument which perplexed Xavier. It was impossible, they declared, that the doctrine of the Christian "Deus" could be the right one, as the Chinese knew nothing of it; this seldom failed in its effect on the Japanese audience. Xavier realized how much the Japanese were influenced in all their opinions and judgments by the example of china; Japan had, indeed, taken over its religion, its writing and almost all its spiritual culture from China.

Gradually, influenced by these discussions, Xavier came to the idea of attempting the conquest of Japan by way of China. If he succeeded in converting the Chinese, Japan, which imitated China in everything, would follow automatically. He tried, therefore, with increasing earnestness to collect information about the state of things in the Middle Kingdom, and what the Portuguese merchants whom he interrogated told him sounded attractive enough.

China, he heard, was the prototype of a land of righteousness, and surpassed the whole of Christendom in this respect. The religion of the Chinese was really a venerable moral system, while very little regard was had for the heathen gods. In China, unlike Japan, there was an emperor who really exercised authority over the whole realm; the people were peace-loving and unusually devoted to the sciences particularly to law and astronomy.

"I think," Xavier wrote home, "that I shall set out for the residence of the King of China this very year. This is a land where the Faith of Jesus Christ can be widely disseminated. When the Chinese have one received Christianity, it will be of great assistance in the destruction of the Japanese sects... China must be won as was once the Roman Empire: with the conversion of the king, the people will follow."

On the return journey from Japan to India, Xavier fell in with a Portuguese merchant, by name Pereira, and told him how earnestly he desired to enter China. The Portuguese listened to him with the greatest attention, and thereupon unfolded the plan of organizing an official embassy from Portugal to the Chinese emperor, and penetrating in this way into the kingdom which was so formerly barred against all foreigners. Pereira wanted to see himself in the role of Portuguese ambassador, and was therefore prepared to meet from his own pocket all the cost involved in this embassy. He pointed out that Xavier was on very good terms with the viceroy in Goa, and would certainly be able to arrange with him the drawing up of the necessary credentials for Pereira. When this was carried out, Xavier himself might accompany Pereira to Peking, and there preach the Gospel to the emperor of China.

Xavier entered eagerly into this project. As soon as her returned to Goa, he sought out the viceroy and obtained his approval of the enterprise; then he journeyed again to Malacca, where Pereira was already awaiting him, to proceed with him to China.

In Malacca, however, an unexpected difficulty presented itself. The port commander there had his own plans for opening up a profitable trade with China, and was, therefore, determined to take every means to prevent the departure of a competitor. Xavier appealed in vain to his position as a papal nuncio, a thing that he had never done before, and threatened excommunication. The port commander was more avaricious than pious; he would not be

74. PORTUGUESE GALLEY MANNED BY NATIVES OF MALABAR

75. THE KING OF COCHIN AND HIS RETINUE

From the travel work by Linschaten, 1599

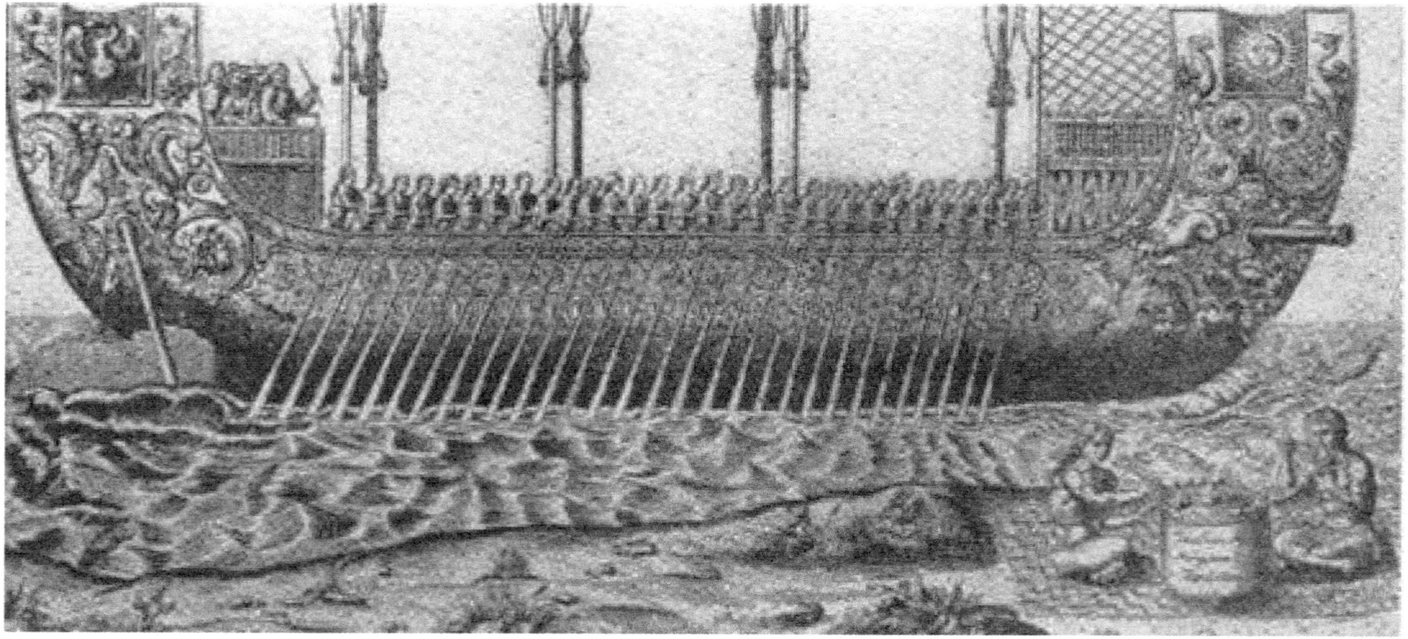

76. STATE GALLEY OF THE KING OF TONKING
From the work on missions by P. Marini, Rome, 1663

intimidated, and declared roundly that he did not care a fig for the papal commission; as long as he had authority in Malacca, Pereira should not set sail.

Xavier was by no means disposed to let his great project of winning China for Christianity founder because of the petty jealousies of a port commandant and a merchant. If he could not go to China with Pereira, then he must go without him. So he set sail on a Portuguese trading vessel to the island of Chang-chuen-shan (St. John Island), which lay on the route to Canton, where for some time a secret exchange of goods between Portuguese and Chinese merchants had been carried on.

Immediately after his arrival there, he entered into negotiations with the Chinese shipowners to find out whether it was possible to get himself transported to Canton; the Chinese merchants, however, refused, for they would risk their heads if they dared, despite the stern prohibition, to smuggle a foreigner into the middle Kingdom.

At the very gates of China, therefore, Xavier waited from day to day, in a miserable reed hut, for an opportunity to set foot in the land of promise. At that time, he wrote to Pereira, who still hoped that he might be able to put his thwarted plan into practice the following year; "When you reach China, you will find me either in prison at Canton or at the imperial court at Peking." At last, he succeeded in securing a Chinese smuggler, at the price of twenty hundred weights of pepper. The Chinese declared himself ready to bring him by night secretly in a little boat to Canton, and to hide him there in his hut for the first few days. On an appointed day, he would come and fetch the missionary away.

But the smuggler did not appear again; a month of anxious waiting went by, and then a second. It was already October, the Portuguese merchants had discharged their business on the island, and one ship after another set sail, to vanish southwards. At last, only Xavier, with one faithful servant, remained on the deserted island. Every day he went to the shore, and sat there for hours in silence, looking sorrowfully towards the west, where lay the great heathen kingdom which was to be won for Christ.

The weather became cold and inclement, and one day Xavier fell ill. A prey to ague and sickness, he was soon unable to take any nourishment, and from day to day his condition grew worse. Lying on his straw pallet, in a fit of ague, he still awaited the Chinese vessel which was to fetch him and take him over the sea, whipped along by autumn storms, to Canton.

One morning, he became delirious; with his eyes raised to heaven and with a joyful countenance, he began to preach in several languages at once-perhaps Tamil, Malay, Japanese and Basque.

On the eighth day of his illness, he lost the power of speech, and no longer recognized his servant. Early in the morning of December 1, 1552, he died.

Jesuits as Brahmins and Yogis

The death of Xavier had prevented the realization of his great plan, but the work begun by him was, nevertheless, destined to be carried on with astonishing success. Immediately, the dead man's place was filled by a host of successors. Dozens and even hundreds of Jesuit missionaries applied themselves to the task of achieving what Xavier himself had been prevented from doing; each and all were inspired by the same enthusiasm and zeal, and all possessed in the same degree the facility of so adapting themselves that to the merchant they were fellow-merchants, to the soldier they were companions-in-arms, to the prince they were counsellors, to the slave they were friends and confidants; to the proud-spirited Japanese they were able to oppose an equal pride of spirit, and, to the learned bonzes superior powers of debate.

Everywhere, whether to Portuguese who had fallen into a vicious mode of life, to Indians, Malayans and Japanese who were pursuing the cult of their false gods, the Jesuit missionaries appeared preaching the Christian faith. Each and all were untiring, self-sacrificing, tactful and skillful; if, for any reason, one of them was prevented from carrying on his work, either on account of age and physical weakness or because he had been called upon by Rome to accomplish other work, or even for the reason that he had been thrown into prison or tortured to death by fanatical heathens, his place was immediately taken by another, who was as courageous, clever and resourceful as his predecessor.

For centuries, Jesuit missionaries have succeeded one another in this way in all quarters of the globe, and yet, right from the time of Xavier up to the present day, the same face appears to be hidden behind the many and varied masks assumed by them according to the different countries and prevailing usages.

In Ormuz, on the Indo-Persian border, Father Barzæus with his little bell came and went through the streets. In this town, famed for its wealth, merchants of all races and creeds met together: Persians, Jews Brahmins, Jainas, Parsees, Turks, Arabs, Armenian Christians, Greeks, Italians and Portuguese. Barzæus knew how to win them all over. The merchants sought his advice in their complicated affairs of business; among the Jews he was, in effect, himself a Jew, so that the rabbis were amazed at the profound knowledge of the Talmud displayed by this Christian priest, and eventually invited him to expound their holy scriptures to them in their synagogues before the whole community.

It was not long, too, before the Mohammedans came to regard Barzæus as a new prophet, and, on one occasion, when he appeared in their mosque, they hoisted him aloft on their shoulders, and acclaimed him as a newly risen John the Baptist. Barzæus was successful in gaining the confidence of the Brahmins even, so that he visited their temple, and debated with the most learned among them the analogies between the Christian and the Indian doctrines of the Trinity. Finally, Barzæus found himself compelled to lay down a regular weekly program: on Thursdays he preached to the Mohammedans, on Saturdays to the Jews, on Mondays to the Brahmins, and to the Christians on other days of the week.

Xavier himself had been taught much about the Brahmins by a learned Indian. "He disclosed to me under the seal of silence," wrote Xavier at that time, "that the true doctrine was always to be kept a close secret... There exists a secret language which is employed for the purposes of education in the same way as Latin is used with us. He disclosed to me the precepts of this doctrine, giving me a good explanation of them all..."

This information did not, however, create any appreciable impression on Xavier; he considered his most important task in India was to devote himself primarily to the slaves and pearl-fishers, who appeared to him to be particularly suitable soil in which to sow the seed of the gospel of salvation. He had no appreciation whatsoever of the significance of Brahminism:

Jesuits as Brahmins and Yogis

"There exists here a race of men who call themselves Brahmins... It is the most depraved race in the world." Thus he once wrote to his fellow-priests.

His successors, however, who worked in India after his death soon recognized clearly of what little practical value were the greatest successes in the conversion of fishermen, slaves and even princes, so long as the Brahmin castes refused to accept Christianity. These Jesuits already gauged the profound importance of caste in India, a point which Xavier had entirely overlooked; so long as they were unsuccessful in converting the highest caste and successes in converting the lower castes would be of an isolated nature and would not be lasting.

The Brahmins however, maintained an exceptionally mistrustful attitude towards Christianity; the Portuguese colonists and soldiers who confessed to this faith could, according to Indian ideas, be regarded only as outcasts since they ate meat, drank wine and carried on everyday intercourse with all castes without discrimination, whilst the Brahmin regarded himself as defiled if even the shadow of a pariah fell upon him. Accordingly, then, the Brahmins necessarily regarded the Christian priests too as pariahs, and to adopt Christianity seemed to them to involve automatically loss of caste.

The Jesuit missionary, Robert de Nobili, the nephew of Cardinal Bellarmine and scion of an old branch of the Italian nobility, was the first to take in hand the task of converting the Brahmins, and, for this purpose, he approached them as a Brahmin himself. When, after a long period of preparation, he appeared in the town of Madura in southern India, he did not present the slightest resemblance to his fellow-Jesuit missionaries, who travelled from place to place wearing torn and dilapidated cowls, received the confessions of the poor and the slaves in the hospitals, and with their little bells hastened through the fishing villages. Like the Hindus of high caste, he wore a long gown of a yellowish linen, a turban on his head and wooden sandals on his feet.

If he were asked by the Brahmins whether, by any chance, he were a Portuguese, he repudiated the suggestion with injured pride, and declared that he was a Roman prince and a Brahmin by faith; he had come to India solely from motives of admiration for his brother-Brahmins in India, reports of whose profound wisdom had reached him in his own country.

The Brahmins soon came to recognize that not only the dress and general conduct of the stranger were in accordance with their caste, but that he also strictly observed all the laws of the Hindu faith. Like themselves, he never ate meat, never touched a drop of wine, and lived exclusively on rice, milk, vegetables and water. He established himself in the quarter in which the highest-class Brahmins resided, and surrounded himself with a staff of servants consisting entirely of Brahmins. He never spoke with a member of any of the lower castes, and even strictly abstained from any intercourse with those white priests with tattered cowls who were striving to secure the spiritual salvation of the pariahs.

What most astonished the Brahmins, however, was his extraordinary knowledge of their faith. Nobili could speak their language fluently, and with scarcely any foreign accent, could read the most difficult Sanskrit texts, and excelled the most learned priests in his ability to intersperse every religious and philosophical discussion with a profusion of quotations from the greatest works of the national poetic art. With the greatest reverence, they listened to the missionary, when, with the voice of a wise philosopher who has renounced the world he recited passages out of the Vedas, and *Apastambra-Sutras* and the *Puranas*; moreover, he himself composed religious works in Sanskrit, and wrote them on palm leaves. On occasion, too, he delighted his hearers by rendering Indian ballads, for he knew the most ancient "ragas," and possessed in an exceptional degree the faculty of being able, for hours on end, to vary them while duly observing all the rules of the art.

He had given such conclusive proofs of exceptional learning and enlightenment that the Brahmins did not venture for a moment to question the truth of his words when, as the opportunity presented itself, he proceeded to speak about the points of agreement between the sacred writings of India and the Christian teachings. In principle, he explained in both cases the ideas were the same, the only difference being that, in Christianity, the Brahmin faith was developed and perfected. In a short while there was scarcely a Brahmin in Madura who would not have accepted Nobili as his fellow and equal, and many already were of the opinion that this stranger was, in fact, better than any among them.

Those who thought in this way were readily disposed to follow the example of such a pious and learned man and even to become "Christian Brahmins." Thus Nobili succeeded where all other missionaries before him had failed. A number of prominent Indians of the highest caste were baptized, and henceforeward no one could any longer contend that Christianity was fitted only for pariahs.

At first, however, it seemed that the achievement of this great success was made possible only through the sacrifice of missionary work among the lower castes, for Nobili had strictly avoided all intercourse with the lower castes. He himself soon, however, found a way out of this difficult dilemma: he knew that there was in India a class which was free to associate with all castes without becoming defiled; these were the Yogis, the Penitents. He accordingly proposed to his fellow-missionaries that they should be split up into two distinct groups, the one group representing themselves to be Brahmins and the other Yogis.

Whilst, then, Nobili himself continued to associate only with his Brahmin friends, there appeared one day the Jesuit da Costa in the disguise of a Yogi, and, soon after, other Jesuit Yogis whose object it was to make converts among the lower castes. As a result, the mission in Madura soon achieved very considerable success. When Nobili withdrew from the scene of his labors, there were already over 40,000 converted natives, including a large number of Brahmins. O the nine missionaries who continued to work in Madura, seven represented themselves as Yogis and two as Brahmins.

The majority of then had a thorough knowledge of Sanskrit, and, like Nobili, were so well versed in the Indian sacred writings that they were accepted everywhere as authorities. The missionary Father Calmette could well, at that time, report triumphantly to Rome: "Since we have been able to obtain possession of the Veda, we have extracted from it passages by means of which we are able to convince the heathens of those fundamental truths which cannot fail to overthrow their idolatry; the unity of God, the attributes of the true God and the states of blessedness and damnation, all these conceptions are to be found in the Veda."

At the Court of the Great Mogul

Whereas, in southern India, Christianity had to be introduced surreptitiously and only in a prudent and unobtrusive manner as a form of perfected Brahminism, in the north of India, at the court of the Grand Mogul Akbar, it had to fight its way through open debate with the exponents of the most varied creeds.

The Emperor Akbar, the great-grandson of the terrible Timur Lenk, had, from the age of thirteen years, persistently sought after the true faith, which he wished to adopt himself and introduce into his empire, so that his people might become the most perfect of all peoples. Brought up in the faith of Islam, he had never found true satisfaction in it; he was equally averse to accepting the faith of the repressed Indians, wince he was inclined to regard both the one and the other as nothing but the mere products of the human mind. For many years, he meditated in his magnificent palace of Fatehpur Sikri on the question how he could attain the true religion, a faith which, unassailable by all external influences, should stand radiant in its simple purity.

At one time, he imagined that the true and original faith could be found only through the medium of children who had been allowed to grow up uninfluenced by any form of training, and, as the result of these ideas, he tried a strange experiment. At his order, thirty children who had not yet learnt to speak were brought to a spot entirely isolated from the outside world, and allowed to grow up there in the charge of nurses, who were forbidden but utter a single word to them. In vain did Akbar wait to see what language and what religion these children would produce of themselves. Naturally, the experiment failed, since not one of the children ever uttered any form of articulate speech, still less manifest any religious faith.

The emperor made up his mind to try another experiment. He invited exponents of all the religions known to him to come and debate before him at his court. By means of this debating contest between the various priests, he hoped to be able to determine which was the true faith. Thus a remarkable religious debate took place in Fatehpur Sikri: Brahmins, Mohammedans and Parsees congregated there with the object of demonstrating before the emperor all the advantages of their own faith and all the defects of the other creeds.

When, one day, Akbar learnt that on the Indian coast there was a new faith with very clever priests, he immediately sent a messenger to Goa, and formally invited the Jesuits to come and take part in the religious discussions. The Jesuit fathers were not slow to appreciate the exceptional significance of this event. If only they were successful in convincing Akbar of the superiority of the Christian faith then the whole of the mighty empire of the Mogul would be won at a single stroke for Catholicism. The Jesuits already had visions of finding in Akbar a second Emperor Constantine, and, accordingly, they dispatched to Akbar their most skilled dialecticians and theologians Rudolfo Acquaviva, Jerome Xavier, a nephew of the great apostle, Emanual Pinheiro and Benedict Goes.

Right from the outset of the discussions, the Jesuits demonstrated their superiority over the Brahmins, the Buddhists, the Mohammedans and the Parsees, since they were thoroughly conversant, not only with the Vedas but also with the Buddhist doctrines, with the Koran and with the traditional utterances of Zoroaster. They always proceeded in such a way that, if, for instance, they were debating with the Parsees, the latter at first nodded approvingly; everything which the Christian missionaries said appeared to support the Parsee faith. If the debate was being conducted with the Mohammedans, then the arguments advanced by the Jesuits appeared to accord in the fullest degree with the teachings of the Prophet, and the mullahs broke into smiles of satisfaction. Even the Brahmins were made to feel that never had their sacred scriptures been so beautifully and clearly interpreted as by these white priests.

Finally, however, the Jesuits concluded by contending that the doctrines of the Catholic Church embodied the same truths as were contained in the creeds of the Mohammedans the Hindus and the Parsees, but that these truths received their fullest and clearest expression in the Christian faith. At this, however, the Parsees, Brahmins and Mohammedans shook their heads, for they were not prepared to acquiesce in such a conclusion.

The Emperor Akbar was, however, on the verge of deciding in favor of Christianity. He accorded to the missionaries the unrestricted right to preach and baptize, permitted his subjects to go over to Catholicism, and sanctioned the establishment of a church and a Jesuit college in Agra. What alone prevented him from personally adopting the Christian faith were the doctrines of the trinity in unity of God and the incarnation of the Creator in the person of Christ; furthermore, the doctrine of humility preached by Jesus seemed to the ruler to be unworthy of a son of God, and excited his displeasure. For many days and nights on end, Akbar discussed these problems with the Jesuits, and urged them earnestly to rid him of his scruples by satisfactory explanations.

The outbreak of war called the emperor into the field. So great was his eagerness, however, to elucidate those points of the Christian doctrine which were still not quite clear to him that he took the Jesuit fathers with him on his campaign. They rode beside him through the steppes of Hindustan, and at night, under star-lit skies, sitting around the campfire, he plied them incessantly with innumerable questions.

Never yet had God placed such a heavy responsibility upon the shoulders of his faithful missionaries. Here was the possibility of winning over to the only true faith a powerful and noble ruler, and a single word, perhaps, was all that was lacking to reveal to the emperor the meaning of the principles of the faith. To find this word might mean that, in Akbar the Great, a second Constantine the Great would arise! With the utmost earnestness and with all the resources of their learning and eloquence, the Jesuits answered the ceaseless questionings of the emperor; nevertheless, they failed to find this single word which might have dissipated the doubts of the Great Mogul. The Emperor Akbar died unconverted, and, with his death, was extinguished one of the greatest hopes of the Jesuit mission to India.

From Agra, the Jesuit missionaries were the first Europeans to penetrate into Central Asia and Tibet. Whilst at the court of the Great Mogul, they had heard of a wonderful empire called Cathay, the religion of which was said to be closely akin to Christianity. Setting out in search of this kingdom of Cathay, Father Goes joined one of the caravans travelling north, and, passing through Kabul, over the Pamir Plateau, through Turkestan and the desert of Gobi, reached the western boundary of China. This first expedition was followed, in 1624, by a second exploratory expedition, undertaken by Father Antonio Andrada. Traveling up the valley of the Upper Ganges, Andrada crossed the Himalayas via the Mana Pass at a height of over 15,000 feet above sea-level, and eventually reached the town of Chaprang in Western Tibet, where he remained for the following nine years.

Two other Jesuits later left Bengal, and, travelling through Nepal, reached the eastern part of Tibet. Their reports, and those of Andrada, provided the first, and for a long time the last, reliable information known in Europe concerning those parts of the world.

77. A JAPANESE PREACHER
French engraving

78. THE JESUITS IN JAPAN

Japanese representation from the sixteenth century

79. DAIMYO NORUNAGA:

THE FRIEND OF THE CHRISTIANS

80. DAIMYO HIDEYOSHI:

THE ENEMY OF THE CHRISTIANS

From the Tea Ceremonial to Martyrdom

From the Tea Ceremonial to Martyrdom

"Nine foot in stature, his head small in relation to his body, his face red, his eyes brown and a long nose. Looked at from the side, his shoulders were seen to droop; his mouth extended to his ears, and his pure white teeth resembled those of a horse. His finger-nails reminded one of the claws of a bear. His expression was one of profound humility, and his voice sounded like the cooing of a dove. When he raised his arms aloft, one could almost imagine one was faced by a bat with outspread wings. He presented a hideous sight."

It is with these words that a Japanese chronicler of the year 1552 describes the Jesuit Father Organtino; at that time these new-comers from the land of the "Southern Barbarians" still appeared to the Japanese as strange and in many respects sinister human phenomena.

Not long after, however, the self-same missionary, Organtino, was able to report optimistically to Rome: "In ten years' time, the whole of Japan will be Christian." For the sons of the most distinguished Japanese families now sought acceptance into the newly founded Jesuit school of novitiates, and daughters, wives and sisters flocked to join a union of Japanese Christian women which, under the leadership of the Jesuit fathers, worked to secure the conversion of the whole country.

In the meantime, the missionaries had already thoroughly learnt how to adapt themselves to Japanese manners and customs, so that in their general conduct, their courtesy, and even in their pronunciation of the Japanese language, they resembled distinguished Japanese. They comported themselves, bowed, and seated themselves entirely in accordance with the rules of Japanese etiquette; they were familiar with all the niceties of the tea ceremonial, and they knew, like natives, just want polite forms of speech the occasion demanded, and the manner in which substantives and verbs required to be inflected according to the rank of the person addressed.

As they knew that the Japanese were very fond of anything spectacular, they did everything possible to organize elaborate ceremonials on the Christian feast-days. On good Fridays, they posted Japanese soldiers in gorgeous uniform before the Holy Sepulcher in their churches; then a procession of children in ceremonial dress carried the emblems of the Savior's passion around the body of the church, whilst young women converts chanted chorus in the Japanese tongue the story of Christ's passion.

Whenever one of the fathers died, his colleagues arranged a ceremonial burial, such as might have aroused envy in the hearts of many a shogun, for the Jesuits were also by now aware to what extent the importance of a person was judged in Japan by the degree of pomp attending his funeral obsequies.

The varied and extensive knowledge of the missionaries was the instrument by which the educated classes in the country were won over. The Jesuits established schools, instituted courses of debates, and had a printing press sent out from Europe with which they produced books in Japanese: grammars, dictionaries, literary works, theological treatises, Æsops Fables translated into Japanese, as well as extracts from the Chinese classics, particularly from the works of Confucius. Produced in many thousands of copies, these cheap books found their way throughout the whole of Japan.

With the same resourcefulness the Jesuits found the means of winning over the uncultured classes; they scorned no means of influencing the masses, and knew how to exploit the wildest superstitions of the people for their own purposes. When, on one occasion, certain bonzes expressed their desire to bewitch Father Almeda, he immediately declared his readiness to submit and, for his part, maintained that he would prevail over the demons by virtue of the Cross. The bonzes smeared the missionary with unguents, placed idols on him, wound snakes around his neck and uttered various magic formulas, but Almeda continued to wave his cross, and declared that with its help he had driven off the evil spirits. The result was that a number of the onlookers immediately offered themselves for baptism.

Wherever a new daimyo succeeded to power in this or that principality, a Jesuit soon appeared, and recounted the enormous advantages that the country would derive from trade with Portugal. Instances occurred with ever-increasing frequency of rulers who not only adopted Christianity themselves, but even destroyed the Buddhist temples and expelled the bonzes.

When on one occasion, a certain daimyo threatened to obstruct the cause of Christianity, a Jesuit father arrived at his court, and observed quite casually that, through commercial intercourse with Portugal, it was possible to procure supplies of firearms; the Christian princes in the neighboring provinces and, in fact, already availed themselves freely of this possibility. The hint sufficed to impel the daimyo to lose no time in asking to be baptized.

Eventually, the time arrived when the Jesuits were able to exercise their influence even at the court of Miyako; a daimyo of the name of Oda Nobunaga had attained to the position of undisputed ruler over the whole of Japan, and, under his rule, the town of Miyako, which had fallen into semi-decay, became once again a place of splendor as the seat of the court.

This was the dream of Xavier realized: there now existed in Japan a single mighty monarch, and the possibility presented itself of Christianizing the whole empire by winning him over.

At the time when Nobunaga was still fighting for power, the Buddhist priests had been particularly hostile to him; in order to destroy their power, he sought to promote the cause of Christianity. He accorded the missionaries full freedom to preach, exempted them from all taxation, urged them to build a church and a mission house at Azuchi, the new seat of the court, and to this end he presented to them a fine plot of land. So that none should doubt his benevolence towards Christianity, he burned down everywhere the monasteries of the hated Buddhist priests, destroyed with his own hand the idols of his house, and mercilessly imprisoned every bonze he could lay his hands on.

It was not long before the Jesuits played, at the court of Nobunaga, the role of trusted counsellors; they had free access to him at all times, he invited them to join him at meals, and discussed his most ambitious plans with them. These had for their object nothing less than the conquest of China, and the Jesuit fathers cherished the hope of gaining before long entry into Peking in the train of the Japanese ruler. For this expedition, a fleet was necessary. On the recommendations of the Jesuits, Nobunaga decided to have this built in Portugal, the missionaries holding out to him the prospect of securing, through their agency, especially

81. THE MARTYRS OF THE JESUIT MISSION TO Japan
Painting, Rome, Gesù

82. THE MARTYRS OF THE JESUIT MISSION TO Japan

Painting, Rome, Gesù

From the Tea Ceremonial to Martyrdom

favorable prices.

But Nobunaga was murdered before he found the opportunity of embarking upon his campaign against China. His successor, Toyotomi Hideyoshi, was certainly at first equally kindly disposed towards the Christians, but very soon changed his attitude. What first displeased him was the fact that certain young Christian girls, towards whom his fancy was attracted, declined to surrender themselves to him, on the grounds that it would be contrary to the laws of their new faith. On top of this, however, came another and graver occurrence.

A Spanish merchantman had been stranded on the Japanese coast, and the authorities had confiscated the valuable cargo. In order to secure its surrender, the crew had endeavored to intimidate the Japanese by pointing out on a map of the world the enormous expanse of territory under the rule of the Spanish monarchy. In reply to an inquiry by one of the Japanese officials how it came about that the king of Spain was able to subjugate so many countries, they said: "Our rulers begin by sending priests to those countries they intend conquering. When the priests have converted a part of the people, troops are sent who join forces with the new Christians, and then the whole country is brought under the domination of the Spanish crown."

The party supporting the bonzes at the court of Hideyoshi did not fail to inform the sovereign of this inflammable utterance, and to add suitable comments, and Hideyoshi, who already could no longer tolerate the missionaries on account of the obstinate coldness of the young Christian girls, thereupon decided to exterminate complete this "treasonable" doctrine.

From then onwards, the position of the Jesuit fathers became exceptionally difficult. By strict edicts, the priests were prohibited, under penalty of death, from carrying on any proselytizing activities, and the population from adopting Christianity; those who had already been baptized were compelled to revert to their original faith forthwith.

Under Iyeyasu, the successor of Hideyoshi, the persecution of the Christians became still more rigorous, following upon the arrival in Japan of the first Dutch merchantmen. The clever Dutchmen had, in the meantime, likewise discovered the ocean-route to the Far East, and it was not long before an official Dutch ambassador appeared and proposed to the Japanese government the conclusion of a formal trade agreement. This removed the last considerations which had prevented the Japanese ruler from proceeding to extreme measures against the Jesuits. After trade relations had been established with Holland, the Portuguese could quite readily be dispensed with, and there was no longer any need to make religious concessions to them. Accordingly, an edict was issued ordering the destruction by fire of all Catholic churches, and providing for strict penalties against all missionaries who remained in the country. The Christians, so the decree alleged, were striving "to spread abroad a pernicious code, to exterminate the true faith, to overthrow the government, and to make themselves masters of the whole empire."

When the Jesuit fathers had definitely realized that everything had conspired against their work, they came to the conclusion that a God who hitherto had demanded of them skill, adaptability, zeal and ingenuity now required them to sacrifice their lives in order that the truth of the Christian faith might be clearly manifested before the eyes of the heathen Japanese. And, with the same ready spirit with which, earlier, they had applied themselves to the study of the most difficult Sanskrit tenets, had disguised themselves as Brahmins, and learnt the rules of Japanese etiquette, and thereby had won souls for the Kingdom of Christ, the Jesuits now accepted martyrdom also in furtherance of the honor of God.

With calm resignation, they allowed themselves to be imprisoned, tortured and crucified, for the Japanese had learnt of this form of execution, which was hitherto unknown in Japan, from the sermons of the Jesuits on the crucifixion of Christ, and it now afforded them derisive satisfaction to nail to the cross the priests of the crucified Saviour. Others of the fathers were suspended by their feet, until they died a lingering and agonizing death, whilst still others were beheaded and their bodies thrown into the sea.

Whilst, however, they were hanging on the cross, or, head downwards, were awaiting their end, or were being led to the executioner's block, they continued to preach, up to their last breath, that the Christian faith was the true faith. After all the many victories which they had gained in Japan by their skill and ingenuity, the manner in which they met death for the honor of God could not fail to have lasting effects. Indeed, when, many years later, Catholic missionaries were once again permitted to enter Japan, they discovered large communities who secretly confessed Christianity; they were the descendants of those Japanese who had once witnessed the martyrdom of the Jesuits.

After the missionaries had been excluded from Japan, towards the year 1600, the Jesuits turned towards Cochin China and Tonking, where Father Alexander de Rhodes achieved great success. The number of natives who were baptized there amounted in a short while to close upon 400,000.

Father Ricci—Doctor Li

The early beginnings of the mission to Japan had been closely bound up with the question of trade with Portugal, since the daimyos had always counted on the fact that the arrival of the missionaries would promote intercourse with the Portuguese colonial empire. In China, however, the Portuguese had always been hated from the earliest times, and every effort was made to keep them out of the country.

This fundamental hostility to foreigners arose primarily from the unfavorable impression which the Portuguese had made on their first appearance in Chinese waters. Thus, in the year 1516, the viceroy of Canton had written to the Emperor of China to the effect that the foreigners, under the pretext of trading, had no other purpose than to plunder the coast and to establish strongholds. Furthermore, at the time when the Jesuits began their activities in the Far East, the ruling dynasty was that of the royal house of Ming, which was strongly nationalist in spirit and aimed at keeping the "Middle Kingdom" immune from all foreign influences.

The Jesuits had always found a way of turning every situation to account, and, just as, in Japan, they had exploited the anxiety of the authorities to trade with Portugal, so they now found the means of applying the hostility of the Chinese to foreigners towards their own ends. When, therefore, three Portuguese merchants, who had made their way into Canton, were arrested, the Jesuit Fathers Barreto and Goes undertook to conduct the negotiations with the Chinese authorities over the amount of ransom that was to be paid. In their capacity, then, as negotiators, it was possible for them to reach Canton without molestation.

Father Ricci—Doctor Li

Barreto presented the Chinese governor with a watch which the latter noticed the missionary wearing, and which he eagerly coveted, and this soon paved the way to such a close friendship that the governor permitted the two priests to remain on in Canton after the question of the ransom had been settled. He even raised no difficulties when a number of other missionaries came in the wake of their two brother-priests, for both he and his fellow-officials were already strongly attracted by these strangers who seemed so pleasant, tactful and learned.

Barreto and Goes had only an imperfect command of the Chinese language, but the Jesuits who arrived later had already learnt to speak Chinese fluently, and were able to discuss the most learned matters with the officials, for Father Valignani, who was responsible for the general organization of the East Asiatic mission, had organized a regular "siege" of China, and taken comprehensive steps to ensure that the missionaries should, on their arrival in China, possess all the necessary knowledge. In the college of Macao, they now learned all the niceties of speech among the better-class Chinese as well as the dialect of the simple people: they studied the difficult hieroglyphic writings and acquired from a variety of books an extensive knowledge of the history, the customs the laws and the literature of China.

Before embarking on their mission, they carefully collected together suitable gifts by which they hoped to gain the goodwill of the high officials, and, if the opportunity offered, of the emperor himself. It was already known that the natural sciences were held in especially high esteem in this country, and, accordingly, the Jesuit missionaries had provided themselves with every available scientific instrument of European origin which, it might be anticipated, would afford pleasure to the Chinese.

Their intimate knowledge of the mentality and character of the Chinese saved the Jesuits, from the outset, from adopting a line of action which would inevitably have ended in a complete failure. The Chinese were inordinately proud of their advanced culture and intellectual development, and firmly convinced of their superiority over all other nations of the world. On their maps, the "Middle Kingdom" was shown as covering by far the largest part of the earth; beyond the borders were shown just a few small countries designated as "Barbarian Countries." With such a people, who regarded all nations lying outside the bounds of the Chinese Wall as negligible quantities, it would have been entirely impolite to start off by preaching, since the Chinese were convinced that they had nothing to learn from any other race of people.

With a full appreciation of this fact, the Jesuits proceeded, at the outset, with the utmost caution and, for a long time, kept their true purpose a close secret. With the Chinese, so wrote one of their missionaries to Rome at this time, it is necessary to walk with guile, and carefully guard against any indiscreet over-zealousness; it might otherwise easily happen "that the gates, which the Lord God has opened into China, will be closed again." If they were asked what was the real reason that had brought them to China, they replied that the fame of the Chinese institutions had reached them in their own country, and that they had been irresistibly attracted by the wisdom and high moral development of the Chinese.

They affected the dress of the Chinese and assumed Chinese names; furthermore, since they knew that the Chinese looked with particular scorn on the Portuguese, they persistently denied having anything whatsoever in common with the barbarian sea-robbers.

Among those men who had followed the first two missionaries to Canton was Father

The Power and Secret of the Jesuits

Matteo Ricci, whose subsequent work laid the real foundations for the astonishing success the Society of Jesus was later to achieve in China. Ricci appeared in Canton wearing the simple cowl of a Buddhist priest and under the assumed name of Li Ma-teu. At first, he adapted his mode of life strictly in accordance with that of the bonzes, begged alms like them before the temples, discussed eagerly with them the doctrines of Buddha, and in this manner sought to gain their confidence.

On one occasion, however, he had the opportunity of discussing astronomy with an educated mandarin; in this, Ricci was in his own element, for he had spent many years in Rome studying astronomy and mathematics under the celebrated Jesuit authority, Christoph Clavius. Thus, he was able to impress the mandarin with his knowledge to such an extent that the mandarin eventually gave him an important piece of advice. "Your knowledge," he said, "has profoundly astonished me, and for this reason I advise you to give up your present mode of life. In the condition of poverty in which you have elected to live, you can bring your knowledge before only a limited public. Live like our men of learning and you will be everywhere received with honor."

Ricci straightway decided to follow this advice. He exchanged the cowl of the Buddhist priests for the distinguished silken robe of the Chinese "literates," and, with the change of apparel, the pious bonze he had hitherto represented himself to be disappeared for ever.

With the help of the articles he had brought with him for distribution as presents, he transformed the living-room of his small house, in which he had been installed by the governor of Canton, into a regular laboratory; distributed all over the room were a variety of instruments used in the study of mathematics, physics and astronomy, glass prisms through which all the colors of the spectrum could be seen, horological instruments of all kinds, gauges, compasses, musical instruments, books, pictures and maps.

Very soon, the news spread in Canton that a very learned man had arrived from abroad, and had brought with him a large collection of strange articles; his name was Li, he could speak the language of the mandarins, and wore the dress of a literary man. It was not long before the little house of the "Holy Doctor Li," as Ricci was now generally called, was besieged by high-class Chinese.

"Doctor Li" naturally observed in every detail all the courtesies due to his visitors, but beyond this he maintained the silence of a man who is wholly engrossed in his scientific studies. Only when he was asked to explain this or that piece of apparatus, book or picture, did he go into detailed explanations. In so doing he never adopted a patronizing or pedantic tone, but rather showed the greatest respect for the extensive knowledge of his guests, and humbly apologized for his own lack of knowledge. The mandarins and scholars took pleasure in the discussions with this "Doctor "Li," who was so skilled in enlightening them in matters beyond their knowledge, while at the same time never making them feel that they were being instructed.

The very first thing each of them wanted to know was what all the various instruments and appliances were for. Ricci explained to them the purpose of the instruments and their method of use, and he had to repeat his explanations time and again. One after another, he explained the horological instruments, glass prisms and compasses until his visitors eventually were led to examine more closely the charts hung on the walls.

83. THE JESUIT MISSIONARY ROBERT DE NOBILI

84. THE JESUIT MISSIONARY RICCI AND A CHINESE CONVERTED BY HIM

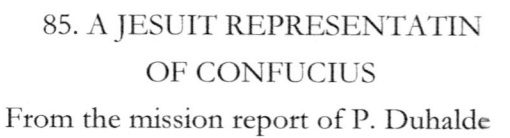

85. A JESUIT REPRESENTATIN OF CONFUCIUS

From the mission report of P. Duhalde

Father Ricci—Doctor Li

In the most conspicuous position in the room, Ricci had placed a map of the world and when the Chinese asked him to explain the map, he told them in a matter-of-fact tone of voice that it was a map of the world drawn true to scale.

On it, however, China was by no means represented as the "Middle Kingdom" but merely as a relatively small country surrounded by great empires and peoples constituting the larger part of the earth. By means of this map and the explanations which the astute Li furnished to his visitors, they were made acquainted with the scarcely credible act that there existed other great countries and nations besides China. On the day when the first Chinese gazed on the map in Doctor Li's room, a belief which had prevailed for three thousand years was shaken; on that day, a new epoch began in the history of Chinese civilization.

At first, Doctor Li's sensational statements met with many a challenge. Had not every classic authority hitherto taught that China was the center of the universe, and that all surrounding countries were small and insignificant? Were not the ancients endued with the most profound knowledge, and who could presume to uphold anything that was not in accordance with their teachings?

Doctor Li expressed the utmost esteem and admiration for the wisdom of the Chinese authorities, while at the same time conducting his guests around the room so that they could not fail to observe the other maps, engravings and paintings hanging on the walls; these depicted all that Europe boasted of in the way of large towns, architectural wonders, and artistic beauty. All these tended to show that the people of these countries were not uncultured barbarians, as had previously been thought in China, but were at least the equals of the Chinese in technical knowledge and general culture. By the time his guests had completed their tour round Li's room, they had begun in some degree to doubt whether the classical authorities were altogether right in alleging the pre-eminence of China over all other countries.

The more the mandarins and scholars discussed with Ricci, the greater became their esteem for those foreign peoples. If, in the countries outside China, all the people were like Doctor Li, then much of considerable value to the Chinese Empire might be learnt from the Europeans.

Among the first to apply the recognition of this fact to practical advantage was the governor of Canton. It seemed to him to be highly desirable that Doctor Li should acquaint the Chinese fully with all the developments and discoveries of value in those countries; China might equally well apply them to her own advantage. He also begged Ricci to give him a copy of his map of the world in which the names of all the countries, peoples and towns lying outside China should be in Chinese characters. He had copies of the map printed and sent to all his friends. The missionary wrote at that time to Rome saying that his map had brought it about "that by degrees the Chinese have been led to form quite a different conception of our countries, our peoples and above all our men of learning from that which they formerly entertained." The displaying to the Chinese of the map of the world "was more effective than anything else that might have been done in China in those early days."

It was not until much later, when the Chinese had become fully convinced of the fact that the Europeans were the equals of themselves, that Ricci proceeded step by step and with the utmost circumspection to speak of matters of faith. When one of his Chinese friends was visiting him for the tenth or twentieth time, he unobtrusively placed among his many books and drawings a picture of the Virgin Mary and other emblems of a religious character, and, when his guest asked what they represented, he answered quite curtly that they were emblems of the religion of Europe. He followed this up by making a casual remark about the good practices observed by the Christians, which in many respects reminded him of Chinese customs, and varied his theme in this connection until the Chinese, filled with curiosity, pressed him to tell them more about the religion and customs of the Europeans.

When, shortly after, the viceroy of the province of Kwang-si invited the Jesuit father to visit his capital, Ricci was received on his arrival with all the homage becoming a learned and celebrated man, for already his map of the world was known everywhere. An exceptionally difficult task awaited him here, however: in Canton it had sufficed for him to convince the Chinese of the existence of a civilized humanity outside China, whereas here, where were assembled a number of the most prominent men of learning, the task that confronted him was that of demonstrating the superiority of European learning over that of the Chinese.

The scholars of Kiang-si were primarily mathematicians, and they possessed no small fund of knowledge in this science; the ancient textbooks of T'ung—chih-kang-mu had indeed set out not only the more elementary methods of calculation and the measurement of superficial areas of all kinds, but also the method of extracting the square and cube roots as well as the rules of alligation, the bases of trigonometry and various by no means simple equations.

But Ricci had not sat under Father Clavius at the college of Rome for nothing; the Chinese mathematicians could not confound him. Day and night, he studied the works of the Chinese authors, until he had discovered errors and omissions. He compiled in the Chinese language a textbook on geometry based on Euclid, in which was set out fully and in systematic order everything of which the Chinese had previously only a fragmentary and imperfect knowledge. Ricci followed this by showing difficult astronomical calculations. Furthermore, since they were interested in the study of the nature of sound, he explained to them the elementary principles of acoustics, and, as the result of all this, excited their highest admiration.

When then, later, he composed his first writings on morality and religion, the Chinese already regarded him as "one of the most learned and greatest of teachers" and accepted his every word as a scientific revelation. He was fully familiar with the teachings of Confucius on the reconciliation of the divine law with the natural reason, and, if he now proceeded cautiously to announce Christianity in his tracts, he was careful to support his remarks with those passages in the classical Chinese literature which presented undoubted points of similarity with the teachings of Christianity.

He transformed the catechism, so as to conform to Chinese ideas, into a learned dialogue between a Chinese philosopher and a Christian priest; this work met with the best of receptions, and the highest mandarins considered it an honor to be presented by Ricci with a copy. A considerable time later the books of this missionary were included in the classical collection of the best Chinese literary works, and, in this way, as a Jesuit father wrote at the time, "the fragrance of our faith began to spread over the whole of China."

It must be admitted that the number of men whom Ricci definitely converted to Christianity and baptized was uncommonly small; they were, however, in every instance, persons moving in the highest circles, mandarins and professors held in high esteem, and their conversion therefore represented an exceptionally valuable commendation of the doctrines of Christianity.

Conversion through Clock and Calendar

Surrounded by a double ring of mighty walls stood the imperial palace of Sin-ching in the Tatar town of Peking. These walls were more than thirty miles long and thirty feet high; twelve horsemen could gallop abreast on them. At regular intervals along the walls stood strongly constructed watch-towers, through the embrasures in which stared the lances and guns of the troops stationed there at all times for the defense of the palace.

The emperor bore the title of "Son of Heaven," for the gods had entrusted him with the duty of guiding and governing the world in accordance with their desires. The emperor's name was held in such awe and veneration that it was never uttered aloud, and the good Chinese subject even avoided the use of those written characters which occurred in the imperial monogram. No one outside the court officials had access to the palace, and among these only very few had ever seen the emperor in person.

Matteo Ricci had, however, long decided to win over the emperor himself to the Christian faith, since only by so doing could he complete his work in the Middle Kingdom. He established himself outside the capital, and, after making the acquaintance of a high official, he requested the latter to take into the palace a present for the emperor; this present was an ingenious and beautifully embellished European clock.

The Chinese official took the missionary's gift to one of the gates of the palace, and handed it to the court official on duty there. At first, the official hesitated for a long time whether he should pass the gift on, but, when he had examined the clock more closely, it filled him with such wonderment that he called his superior officer up and showed him the strange marvel. Ricci's clock thereupon passed through the whole hierarchy of officials in the palace up to the highest minister, and ultimately reached the emperor himself.

Even the "Son of Heaven" had never before seen a spring clock, and was filled with rapture by it. Of course, it was far beneath his exalted dignity to make even the suggestion of an inquiry about the mortal who had sent him this present. On the following morning, however, the clock suddenly stopped ticking. The emperor summoned one of his officials to set it going again, but all the efforts of the mandarin were vain. The whole of the royal household in turn tried their skill, but not one among them could set the clock going again.

Thus it came about that, escorted by two mandarins of the court, the astute Doctor Li passed through the mighty portals of the imperial palace, mounted a marble staircase guarded by two copper lions, and proceeded along the bank of the stream that wound its way right through the whole palace. Filled with astonishment, he observed the innumerable artificially constructed lakes and hills, the many buildings roofed with golden-yellow glazed tiles, the dragon bridges made of black jasper and the numberless vases of marble and porcelain.

After they had been walking for some considerable time, his escort conducted him through a second gigantic enceinte into a courtyard which seemed even more extensive and magnificent than the first. On a terrace rose a large building of white marble where were assembled a number of the highest mandarins clad in bright silken robes.

These dignitaries surrounded the stranger, and one of them held out to him the clock and commanded him to set it going again. Doctor Li bowed with all due veneration took the clock, opened it, and by a few quick movements did something to the works. He then returned the clock to the mandarin, and lo! It was ticking away again just as it had done before. The mandarins gave polite expression to their wonderment, and thanked Doctor Li, after which he was conducted out of the palace again.

On the following morning, much to the chagrin of the emperor, the clock stopped again, and the court officials were compelled once more to summon Doctor Li to the palace. This occurred a third time, and this time Li brought with him two religious paintings and a reliquary set with valuable stones. He asked to be allowed to present these as a humble tribute to the Son of Heaven, along with an illuminated petition in the most elegant Chinese characters, which ran as follows:

"Your humble subject is an authority on astronomy, geography, geometry and arithmetic. By means of instruments, he studies the stars and has a knowledge of gnomonics. His methods are precisely the same as those of the Chinese professors. Should the emperor deem fit not to spurn an ignorant and unworthy man, but rather permit him to turn to account his limited talents, then he could entertain no grater desire than to devote himself entirely to the service of so illustrious a sovereign."

The offering and the petition were, in accordance with the prevailing ritual, submitted first of all to Li Pu, the Minister of Ceremonies; the latter passed it on with a by no means favorable report to the Grand Council of the court mandarins.

"Europe," wrote Li Pu "has nothing to do with us and does not accept our laws. The pictures which Li Ma-teu brings as tribute, depict a 'Lord of the Heavens' and a Virgin and are of no particular value. The stranger is also offering a casket which, so he claims, contains the bones of immortals, as if immortals when they go to heaven did not take their bones with them! In a similar case, the learned Rann Yu decided that much new and unfamiliar objects should not be introduced into the palace, since they brought ill luck. Accordingly, we are of the opinion that the gifts should not be accepted, and that Li Ma-teu should not be permitted to stay at the court. He should be sent back to his own country."

The emperor, however, preferred to decide otherwise. Then he dismissed the Jesuit father after the first audience, the Son of heaven already knew how the clock could be made to go again after it had run down; nevertheless, he commanded Doctor Li to return on the following day, and the same happened on the succeeding day.

The reason for this was that Ricci, on the first morning, told the emperor of a new astronomical instrument that was in use in Europe, and gave better results than the old measuring instruments. The emperor accordingly wanted further information how this European gnomon was constructed. After Ricci had given a full explanation of the following day, the interest of the emperor was aroused in a further branch of astronomy by an apparently casual remark of Doctor Li's.

In this way, Ricci skilfully contrived at each audience to let fall a remark which excited

Conversion through Clock and Calendar

the curiosity of the ruler, and caused him to order the missionary to return again. It was not long before the stranger who possessed such an amazing fund of knowledge became indispensable to the emperor. Sometime later, he instructed the missionary to bring his brother-priests, of whom Ricci persistently spoke, to the court; these other Christian priests, Doctor Li asserted, were even better versed in astronomy than himself.

Soon the Jesuits had established their residence within the "rose colored wall," in the quarter where only the highest officials were permitted to reside, and a monthly allowance was made to them by the emperor in the form of rice and silver. The pious painting on which the minister of ceremonies had once expressed himself so disparagingly now hung on the finest wall of the reception hall, and in front of them, stood the reliquary on a magnificent, richly carved socle; in the large bronze receptacles incense was kept continually burning in front of these gifts of the foreign doctor, and, in sconces fashioned like gaily colored birds, wax candles, on which were painted animals and flowers, burned now held.

Eventually, Ricci was entrusted with the task of instructing the emperor's favorite son in the mathematical Sciences and in ethics. As an inevitable sequel, the ministers also invited Doctor Li to visit them, and likewise wrought his regular instruction in the mathematical sciences and ethics. In a short time, many baptisms took place at the court of Peking.

When Ricci died, there were already over three hundred Christian bells to be heard in the Chinese Empire; the emperor announced his readiness to provide for Ricci's burial, and, for this purpose, he presented to the missionaries a large plot of land. The new fathers who succeeded Doctor Li were likewise held in the highest respect at the court and their advice was sought in all matters of state.

When, in the northern part of the empire, certain mandarins expressed their disapproval of the ever-increasing power of the foreign priests, the prime minister issued a decree in which the virtues of the Jesuits were extolled in fulsome terms: "Professor Li was the first to come to China from the Far West in order to teach Christianity. The emperor received him as a guest. Accorded him a pension, and provided for his burial. Since that time, the learned men from the West have continued to arrive in the capital. . . Princes and ministers, viceroys, governors and district chiefs all respect and love the strangers and look up to them. . .

"You people who dwell on the land, do you then deem yourselves more enlightened than the heaven-inspired emperor, or the ministers who are the scholars of the learned Confucius? Be persuaded that in the hearts of these learned men from the Far West there is neither lust for fame nor lust for worldly gain! Nine times ten thousand miles have they travelled in their journey to our country, defying monsters and cannibals merely that they might save us from eternal damnation. Was there ever such nobleness of spirit!. . . .

"I say to you then, men of learning and common people, cast aside your prejudices, overcome you hostility, take up the books of the wise men from the West, and study them profoundly. From them you will receive enlightenment, and thereafter tremble with dismay at your former errors!"

The highest law of China was the Tao, the law of the universe, according to which the stars followed their courses, the moon moved across the heavens, the sun was veiled in darkness, plants sprouted from the soil, trees assumed their canopy of foliage, streams rippled on their ways and the seas ebbed and flowed. Man's aim must be to adapt his life and actions in accordance with the operation of the Tao; only by so doing could he hope, in harmony with the divine harmony with the divine ordering, to attain happiness and prosperity.

To the emperor, the gods had delegated the task of directing the people by laws and regulations, so that man's Tao should harmonize with that of the Deity; to this end, the primary duty of the ruler was to provide his subjects from year to year with an accurate calendar.

Long ago, the Emperor Yao had arranged for the issue of a *Book of Indications for Seasons*, and not a single year had gone by since without the preparation of the imperial "Tribunal of Mathematics," with the help of the instruments installed on the southern wall of the palace, of careful astronomical calculations.

It had been known for a long time that the duration of the year was 365 days and 6 hours; it was also known that 19 revolutions of the sun coincided with 325 revolutions of the moon, and by means of clepsydras the culminating periods of the principal constellations and the periods of the moon as well as those of the planets had been calculated with a considerable degree of accuracy. The Chinese astronomers thus possessed sufficient data to enable them to forecast fairly accurately each year the astronomical events which might be anticipated during the year. The new calendar was issued to the accompaniment of a special ceremonial. The officials of the mathematical tribunal proceeded in ceremonial apparel to the "Dragon Pavilion," and there deposited the copies of the calendar destined for the use of the emperor and his consorts; then those for the royal princes and the highest dignitaries were placed on red tables in other pavilions, and, finally, as a token of homage to the new law of the year, followed a solemn procession throughout the whole of the palace. The calendar determined, on the basis of a close study of macrocosmic events, when certain actions should or should not be performed. It indicated in red and black letters what days and hours were favorable for cultivation of the soil, marriage, changes of residence, the repairing of ships, hunting, pasturing of cattle, burials and executions. Whoever observed correctly the promptings of the calendar could always be certain of the success of his undertakings.

To the emperor the calendar was of primary importance as the instrument by which he was enabled to maintain order in his empire. The absolute obedience which every Chinese was ready to show to the divine Tao expressed itself in complete submission to the ruler, for had he not provided them with the most important of all books?

If the commencement of the new year, the "Cheng," had been correctly fixed by the mathematical tribunal, and the calendar was therefore accurate, peace and order throughout the empire were assured. Then the emperor ruled in accordance with the laws of heaven, the officials exercised their office faithfully, and the tiller of the soil could rejoice over a good harvest. If, however, the "Cheng" had been wrongly fixed, or if then, instead of directing the people unerringly in accordance with the Tao, the calendar on the contrary led the people away from the true system of the universe; those terrible calamities would happen against which the wise Yue'-ling had uttered such urgent warning.

Now for many years past it had happened that the harvests had become poorer and poorer, executions had grown more and more numerous, the ministers had become self-seeking in their administration and stole like ravens. The Emperor Wan-li of the Ming dynasty could scarcely any longer enforce his order, for the whole empire was in a ferment. It was

Conversion through Clock and Calendar

more and more frequently stated at the imperial court, in the palaces of the mandarins and in the simple huts of the coolies that the Middle Kingdom was falling into chaos, because the government was no longer possessed of the true divine Tao.

In great concern, the emperor discussed day and night with his ministers how to avert this increasing evil, and, in his perplexity, he turned at last to the Jesuits. The fathers pondered for a long time, made measurements, covered sheets of paper with calculations, and finally established the fact that the mathematical tribunal had made grave errors in the framing of the calendar; for a long time past, they asserted, the astronomical calculations of the tribunal had been faulty, and the celestial kingdom had accordingly for decades past been governed by false calendars.

This allegation caused great consternation in the imperial palace. As was only natural, certain worthy mandarins arose in defense of the old tradition, and voiced their strong indignation that foreign priests should make so bold as to criticize their ancient institutions; it was not long, however, before the heavens themselves bore witness in favor of the Jesuits. In China, eclipses of the sun were regarded as exceptionally important phenomena; the emperor had to be informed of the impending occurrence at least a month in advance, and all the exalted mandarins were required to assemble at the prescribed time, bearing the insignia of their rank, in the courtyard of the astronomical tribunal. It happened that the Jesuits had predicted an eclipse of the sun for a certain day, and had, in fact, announced the exact hour at which it would take place, although in the official calendar there appeared no indication of any such occurrence.

When it actually happened that the sun began to grow dark, that all the dignitaries assembled together threw themselves down and beat the ground with their foreheads in accordance with the prescribed ritual, when throughout the town the beating of drums and cymbals was heard, then, indeed, the Jesuits had won a lasting victory, for it had been clearly shown that the methods of calculation used by the Chinese astronomers were of no value, and that the calendar in accordance with which the empire was governed was, in fact, inaccurate.

The emperor immediately issued an order that, in future, the mathematical tribunal should no longer, as hitherto, follow the Mohammedan system, but should adopt the European system of calculation; the Jesuit Father Adam von Schall was also commissioned to carry out the reform of the calendar. Henceforward, he was regarded as a second Confucius, as a man of exceptional learning whom heaven itself had sent to restore the disturbed ordering of the universe. As a result of his efforts, it was confidently anticipated that henceforward the harvests would be more fruitful, that the administrative officials would no longer steal, and that the unrest in the country would come to an end.

Before, however, the improved system of calculation of the calendar initiated by Father Schall could be fully developed, there came upon the dynasty of the Ming emperors those disasters which could only be the inevitable consequence of government in accordance with false calendars. Internal disturbances were rife, and the Tatars in the north and west of the empire profited by this fact to break through the Chinese wall.

Once again, the Jesuits proved true friends to the emperor, in that they now showed themselves to be quite as well versed in military affairs as they were in astronomy. Just when the ministers and generals were at their wits' end how to withstand the attack of the Tatars, Father Schall offered to initiate the Chinese into the art of casting guns, and to establish an arsenal on European lines without delay.

Under the direction of the fathers, the manufacture of guns was eagerly pushed forward, and it was to the missionaries that the task of training their crews was entrusted. As the result, it soon became possible to confront the Tatars with a Chinese army equipped with superior artillery, and, finally, the invaders were compelled to retire again beyond the Great Wall.

Nevertheless, the Jesuit fathers had come too late to China to be able to bring the rule of the Ming emperors into complete harmony with the law of the Tao. Some little time later, disorder broke out again; an army of rebels advanced to the capital, and even took the imperial palace. The Son of Heaven saw no possibility of evading capture, and committed suicide. In the midst of the general confusion, one of the Chinese generals called in the Tatar Manchus to help in repressing the rebels. They came and suppressed the rising, but advanced immediately upon Peking to seize the empire for themselves. The last prince of the house of Ming died in exile in the south of the country, after he and his mother had adopted Christianity and submitted to baptism, at which he took the name of Constantine.

The Jesuits, however, continued to serve the Manchu emperors with the same fidelity with which they had served the Ming emperors, since to them it was all the same in the end who governed China, provided that the possibility still remained open to them of winning the Middle Kingdom for Christianity by slow and methodical work. The new rulers, in spite of their Tatar origin, also regarded themselves as "Sons of Heaven," on whom devolved the duty of ruling the world in accordance with the laws of the Tao; they therefore needed a reliable calendar, and, as a consequence, the help of the Jesuit astronomers.

In the early decades of the Manchu rule, it was also evident that things were by no means proceeding smoothly for the new dynasty. The young Emperor Shun-chi lost his favorite wife and their only child, and this bereavement so upset him that he abdicated and retired into a Buddhist monastery. If further misfortunes of this nature were to be averted, it was of supreme importance to devote the utmost attention to the preparation of the calendar; accordingly, Father Schall was appointed director of the mathematical tribunal, and given the rank of "Mandarin of the First Class."

At that time, the emperor issued an edict, in which not only European science, but also "the law of the divine Ruler," that is, Christianity, was extolled. Ten eunuchs of the court, including the favorite servant of the emperor, accepted baptism, and, even if the Son of Heaven himself could not be induced to take the same step, he nevertheless afforded the missionaries his protection and allowed them full freedom to preach, even acquiescing in the establishment of a Christian church in Peking.

Father Schall further acquired very considerable distinction as a military adviser, and continued to conduct his course of instruction in artillery. His authority grew to such an extent that soon the usual jealous rivals, enemies and intriguers began to make their appearance. The moment for their appearance was propitious, in that the Council of Regents, who at that time were governing on behalf of the Emperor K'ang-hi, a minor, were little disposed to regard innovations with favor.

Conversion through Clock and Calendar

The Mohammedan mathematician Yam-kam-seim, who himself aspired to become president of the mathematical tribunal, proceeded to accuse Father Schall of treason against the state, alleging that his presence in China was hostile in purpose, and therefore constituted a grave danger to the government.

The Regency council were not quite sure of their authority and scented conspiracies everywhere; Schall was arrested, tried and finally condemned to death. It was ordered that the improvements introduced by the Jesuits in their methods of calculation of the calendar should be abandoned, and their books burnt. Yam-kam-siem was appointed chief of the mathematical tribunal.

Nevertheless, Schall was not to terminate his career under the executioner's blade, nor was Yam-kam-siem to occupy the seat of president of the tribunal. It came to pass that, after the calendar had again been calculated on the old methods, the mandarins assembled one day in the courtyard of the mathematical tribunal, and awaited in vain an eclipse of the sun which Yam-kam-siem had predicted; the sun did not show the slightest inclination to accommodate itself to the calculations of the chief astronomer.

The Jesuit Father Verbiest had, however, declared some weeks earlier that this eclipse of the sun would occur on a different day and at a different hour; as, however, no one had paid heed to the words of the missionary, the authorities neglected to greet with the prescribed ceremonial this momentous phenomenon when it did in fact occur in accordance with Verbiest's predictions.

Thus a further striking proof was furnished of the incompetence of Yam-kam-siem and of the accuracy of the Jesuit calculations. If the empire was not to collapse there was no alternative but to entrust the Jesuits once again with the fixing of the calendar. Father Verbiest was accordingly summoned before the emperor, to whom he straightway declared that not only were the calculations of the Chinese astronomers inaccurate, but that, furthermore, the ancient instruments of the Peking astronomers, which dated back to the time of Kublai Khan, no longer functioned correctly. He expressed his readiness, however, to construct new and thoroughly reliable apparatus, such as was used by the great European astronomer, Tycho Brahe.

Before scarce a year had passed, the new Jesuit observatory had been erected on the summit of a hill, equipped with the necessary instruments, an armillary sphere for determining the position of the stars, an astrolabe for calculating the length and breadth of the celestial bodies, instruments for determining altitudes and azimuths and a telescope. Verbiest had had all these instruments made exactly in accordance with Tycho Brahe's calculations, and at the same time he did not forget to ornament then in the Chinese style with a variety of dragons' heads and Chinese characters.

Henceforeward, the eclipses of the sun occurred as predicted in the calendar, for Yam-kam-sien had been dismissed in ignominy and Verbiest had succeeded him. The ministry of ceremonies, which, at the time of Schall's trial, had expressed open hostility to Christianity, now equally openly expressed the view that the religion of the strangers was in no respect inimical to the interests of the state, but that, on the contrary, the Christian moral code could only be described as "altogether admirable." All orders and dispositions issued against the missionaries were cancelled and those Jesuits who had been arrested were awarded compensation by the government.

When Father Verbiest died, the emperor arranged for an elaborate burial ceremony, such as accompanied the funeral of only the highest dignitaries. Distinguished mandarins, including the emperor's brother-in-law, the officer in charge of the emperor's bodyguard and the commandant of the palace, were required to accompany the bier on horseback. The Christians from the capital and neighboring districts, bearing candles and banners, led the procession, being followed by the missionaries in white robes, whilst fifty horsemen of the Imperial Guard closed the procession.

When, some time later, the viceroy of a certain province was inclined to persecute the missionaries and their Chinese converts, the Emperor K'ang-hi issued a decree in terms which secured them full toleration. "The men from the West," declared the ruler, "have ensured the accurate calculation of the calendar; during the war, they repaired the old guns and manufactured new ones. They have, therefore, served will the interests of the empire, and have always spared no efforts in this direction. Although full liberty is granted to attend the Lamaist, Buddhist and other temples, there to burn incense, you would deny similar liberty to the Europeans, who are guilty of no unlawful conduct. This discrimination appears to us to be illogical, and we are of the opinion that henceforward none shall be prevented from burning incense in the temples of the Lord of Heaven. By virtue of this edict, the freedom of the Christian faith was henceforward formally recognized in China.

Teachers and Diplomats at the Peking Court

"They may all come to my court, and those who understand mathematics may remain with me in my service." Thus the Emperor K'ang-hi decided when the Jesuit father sought his consent to a proposal to bring additional members of the order from France.

Father Schall, to whom the education of the young emperor had been entrusted, had managed to instil into the boy a lively thirst for knowledge; it was on account of Schall's teaching that K'ang-hi, during the whole of his life, was governed by the desire for further knowledge and that it was his constant endeavor to obtain precise information on all subjects between heaven and earth.

Who other than the learned Jesuit fathers could have satisfied and at the same time stimulated K'ang-hi's curiosity? When Father Schall closed his eyes, he could commend his soul in peace to the mercy of the Lord, for he knew that his pupil would all his life ask questions, and that, so long as K'ang-hi did this, the Jesuits would enjoy power and respect at his court.

Every morning, the emperor called the fathers to him, in order that they might explain to him some physical law, mathematical equation, or geometrical construction, the solution of which he had wrestled with in vain during the night. Even during the day, the ruler often left the most important matters of state, and hastened to the Jesuits because an astronomical calculation had come into his mind which he was himself not able to master. In the evening, fresh questions still occurred to him, and only with difficulty could he tear himself away from his European teachers in order to take a short rest.

Soon, he became so that a mere theoretical knowledge no longer sufficed him, and,

86. THE ASTRONOMICAL OBSERVATORY ERECTED IN PEKING BY THE JESUITS

From the mission report of P. Duhalde

87. THE JESUIT COURT ASTRONOMERS OF THE EMPEROR OF CHINA, TWO CHINESE CONVERTED BY THEM, AD THE CHINESE CROSS THEY USED. —From the mission report of P. Duhalde

when the missionaries had explained a geometrical construction to him, he wanted to prove by a practical test that the calculations made were correct. For this purpose, he had made, from various materials, cubes, pyramids, cylinders and cones, and he found their area, height and volume. With the fathers, he computed the weight of different spheres of given diameter, or their diameters from given weights, and he gave his instructors no rest until they had performed with him the levelling of a river. With the aid of his newly acquired trigonometrical knowledge, he determined the width of streams and ponds, or the height of buildings, and he was immensely pleased when the result arrived at was confirmed by measurement.

One day, Father Benoit presented him with a chart of the heavens and an explanation in Chinese which contained an outline of the system of Copernicus. From this, K'ang-hi learned for the first time of the turning of the earth round the sun, and these ideas put him into such a state of excitement that for days he received not a single official of his court; the most pressing affairs of state he left unattended, while he endeavored to master the new and wonderful view of the world which had been disclosed to him.

After this, there came in turn chemical and medical problems, followed by the puzzles of optics and acoustics and, finally, the endless field of philosophical speculation opened before the emperor.

K'ang-hi soon found that he could not live without his Jesuits. In order that he might have them near him, he set aside all rules of court etiquette. He permitted them to be seated in his presence, while those in the highest offices and even the imperial princes had to remain kneeling in the presence of the Son of Heaven. Occasionally he so far forgot his dignity as to pay visits to the missionaries to converse with then for hours at time.

The missionaries had to rise at four in the morning, so that they might attend their impatient master at the right moment; only at nightfall were they dismissed, and they had then to prepare the imperial lesson for the following day. Left alone, the emperor sedulously repeated the lesson he had just learnt, read over the notes of the fathers and explained to his sons what he had himself learnt only a short time before.

As K'ang-hi would not let a day pass without receiving some instruction, Father Gerbillon had to accompany him even on a journey to Tatary. The missionary reported the pompous meeting of the emperor with the Tatar nobles, described the splendid ceremony of the "Great Kotow," and the banquet at which some eight hundred Tatar princes were present. Even then, K'ang-hi dismissed all the guests as quickly as possible in order to talk with Gerbillon on the subject of the ecliptic and the earth's orbit.

Finally, with great circumspection, the Jesuits turned their talk to the subject of Christianity, and so won the emperor over to this religion and K'ang-hi presented them with land on which to build a church, and contributed ten thousand taels towards the cost of its erection. When the church was completed. K'ang-hi gave the Jesuits an inscription, which he had himself composed, to be placed over the door. It contained a regular form of worship of the Christian God, who was described as the "true Creator of all things without beginning and without end."

Further, the fathers told him so much about the dignity and power of the pope that K'ang-hi proposed a marriage relationship with the Prince of Christendom, and wrote a letter to the pope in which he sought the hand of the latter's niece.

The original of this strange document, which is preserved in the archives of the French Ministry of Foreign Affairs, begins with this allocution: "To you, Clement, most blessed of all popes, blessed and great Emperor of all Popes and Christian Churches, lord of the Kings of Europe and Friend of God!

"The most powerful of all powers on earth," it continues, "who is greater than all who are great under the sun and the moon; who sits on the emerald throne of the Chinese Empire, raised upon a hundred golden steps, in order to expound the word of God to all faithful subjects; who exercises the power of life and death over a hundred and fifteen kingdoms and a hundred and seventy isles, writes this epistle with the virgin feather of an ostrich.

"All hail and long life!

The time has come when the bloom of Our Imperial Youth shall bring to maturity the fruit of our age, so that at the same time the desire of our true subjects may be fulfilled and a successor to the Throne given to them for their protection. We have resolved, therefore, to unite ourselves in marriage with a beautiful and distinguished maiden, who had been nurtured on the milk of a courageous lioness and of a tender roe. Since the Roman people have always had the reputation of progenitors of brave, chaste and unsurpassable women, we would stretch forth our powerful hand, and take one of them to wife. We hope that it may be your niece or that of another great priest on whom God looks with favor. . . .

"We wish her to have the eyes of a dove contemplating heaven and earth, and the lips of a mussel feeding upon the dawn; her age shall not exceed two hundred moons; she shall not have grown taller than a bade of green wheat, and her girth shall be as a handful of dried corn. . . .

"In gratifying our desire, Father and Friend, you will create an alliance and eternal friendship between your kingdom and our powerful land. Our laws will be combined as a creeper clings to a tree. We shall ourselves disseminate our royal blood through many provinces, and shall warm the beds of your princes with our daughters, whose portraits the mandarins as our ambassadors will bring to you. . . .

"In the meantime we rise from our throne to embrace you. We declare to you that this letter is sealed with the Seal of our Empire, in our Capital of the World, on the third day of the eighth moon in the fourth year of our reign."

The marriage project was, however, never realized; nevertheless, Christianity made rapid progress in the family of the emperor; some of the thirty-five sons and twenty daughters of K'ang-hi were baptized. The result of the extraordinary partiality of the emperor was that the missionaries enjoyed the greatest respect among the people, and that they were able to make many converts; Christian communities and churches sprang up in all parts of China.

Soon, a further opportunity offered itself to the fathers for the extension of their missionary activities. K'ang-hi charged them with the task of preparing a new map of the whole empire, and, in carrying out this command, the fathers had to travel far. Since they appeared as commissaries of the emperor, and were accompanied by large escorts, their arrival everywhere made a deep impression, and gave moral support to an extraordinary degree to Christianity in the provinces. On these geographical expeditions, the missionaries at the same time visited the Christian communities, regulated their affairs, and made arrangements for the erection of new churches.

A political conflict soon made it possible for them to render useful service to the emperor in another direction. Owing to incessant disputes in the Sino-Russian border provinces, there was a danger of war, and, since some of the more dangerous Tatar races threatened to take sides with Russia against China, efforts were made in Peking to avoid open conflict. But in this the Manchus lacked experience in diplomatic negotiations, and they failed to find a reasonable basis for agreement. The Jesuits arranged a peace conference, and even took part in the discussion as interpreters and mediators.

Father Gerbillon went immediately to the camp of the Russians, and explained to them how advantageous it would be for them to obtain from the Chinese, in exchange for certain territorial concessions, a profitable commercial treaty. The Russians were sufficiently good traders to perceive the reason in Gerbillon's statements, and declared themselves ready to withdraw from the disputed territory in China, if they could have, in return, permission to send a trade delegation each year to Peking. In the late evening, when Gerbillon returned to the Chinese camp, he brought with him a complete commercial treaty, the terms of which were in every way acceptable to the Chinese. Two days later, the agreement was signed; it was the first treaty the Chinese had concluded with a European power.

Great importance was attached in China to the part played by the Jesuits in this diplomatic success; the most distinguished mandarins congratulated them, and Prince Sosan, the official leader of the peace delegation, thanked them most courteously for the valuable services they had rendered.

The missionaries who and stood faithfully by the side of the emperor in all phases of his government also showed themselves to be valued helpers when K'ang-hi, aged, weary, sick and tormented by pain, began to pine away.

The Fathers Gerbillon and Bouvet appeared at once in the ruler's sickroom, and brought with them a box of little balls of dough; these had, they assured him, cured the mighty Dauphin of France of a serious illness. And, in fact, scarcely had K'ang-hi taken a number of these pills when he felt himself quite restored to health again, and with renewed strength he could apply himself to the government of the empire and the theorems of Euclid.

Some months later, he again fell sick with a malignant fever, which set in with greater intensity at the same hour each day. The missionaries were again called to him, and they saw at once that K'ang-hi was suffering from intermittent fever. They recommended the use of a curative bark which the brothers of the order had discovered in India; it was the "Jesuit's bark" which later was to be known all over the world as "china bark."

But in this the fathers met for the first time with some opposition from the imperial family. The crown prince protested that his father was asked to take a medicine which was unknown in China, and he said that it was not known whether it would not do the emperor harm. As the condition of K'ang-hi was becoming steadily worse, it was finally decided that the effects of the medicine should at first be tried on four princes. After this test had been successfully carried out, it was resolved to give the bark to the emperor. The next day the expected fever attack did not appear, and the same thing happened on the following day.

Soon after his recovery, K'ang-hi went out from the palace into the town with a great following, and he permitted the people, who were generally driven away when the emperor was riding in the town, to remain in the streets, a thing which had never happened before. Among those accompanying him were the four fathers, Gerbillon, Bouvet, Fonteney and Visdelon; they were allowed to stand while even the highest officials went down on their knees and touched the ground with their foreheads.

In a loud voice, the emperor then said, turning towards the missionaries: "You Europeans have always served me with zeal and affection, and I have not the least thing for which to reproach you. Many Chinese mistrust you, but I, who have carefully watched all your movements, am so convinced of your honesty and probity that I openly and publicly say: You shall be believed and trusted!" K'ang-hi then proceeded to tell the people how ill he had been, and how the foreigners had restored him to health again.

Twice had the Jesuits saved the ruler; a third time, when he returned from hunting with severe inflammation of the lungs, they were able to do no more for him than to ease his passing. They calmed his wildly beating heart with an electuary, and then gave him some of their mass wine to drink which they obtained every year from Manila; it is the blood of Christ, they told the emperor, and the wine from the Christian altar did in effect renew the sick man's strength for a short time, K'ang-hi died with reverence for the Christian God who had helped him pass the last hour of his life without pain and in a peaceful spirit.

Meanwhile, rumors of the wonderful remedies of the Europeans had spread throughout China. Hundreds of sick persons rushed to the fathers, and all received medical treatment. In this, the missionaries had abundant opportunities to speak of their beliefs and to move the grateful patients they had cured to become baptized. Thus many souls were gained for the Kingdom of Christ with the aid of French pills, Indian powders and Spanish wine.

The Order of Gardeners and "Lightning Artists"

The accession of the new emperor, Yung-chêng, to the throne ushered in a period of trouble and persecution for the Christians in China. While he was a crown prince, K'ang-hi's son had not concealed his dislike of the Europeans and their beliefs; after his accession, he appeared to pay still more attention to the insinuations of his anti-Christian counsellors.

The imperial censor Fan now declared in a memoir: "The Europeans teach a false and dangerous religion. They maintain that the God of Heaven was born at the time when Han-gai-ti reigned in China, in a district named Yu-ye-a. He had taken the blood of a holy and virgin maid named Ma-li-ya, and from it formed his human body. Under the name of Ye-su, he lived thirty-three years, and then he atoned for the sins of the people on a cross.

"We have not this belief, and it has not been handed down to us from antiquity. Those who accept this law receive the so-called baptism; older Christians are instructed in secret mysteries, and drink the holy substance. I do not know what magic this is.

88. CHINESE FESTIVAL
From the mission report of P. Duhalde

89. A JESUIT REPRESENTATION OF THE GODS OF CHINA

The Order of Gardeners and "Lightning Artists"

"They do not observe the customs of the empire, but have their own rites and books. Is this not acting in opposition to the ruling powers? Is it that our old doctrines are insufficient? There is already a large number of Christians in the precincts of the court, and, if something is not soon done to check their activity, they will eventually overrun the empire."

An inquiry into Christianity was instituted by the Tribunal of Rites in Peking, and, as the emperor was ill-disposed towards the missionaries, this judicial inquiry found against the Europeans and their religion. Soon afterwards. Yung-chêng issued an edict, under which numerous Christian churches and communities were destroyed, and three hundred thousand Chinese converts were arrested and forced to abjure.

This difficult situation, however, gave the Jesuits at the court a further opportunity of showing what they were able to do for the glory of God; the disfavor of the new ruler served only to urge them to increase their activities to the utmost, and in this way save the results of long and painstaking labor from destruction.

A short time after the accession of Yung-chêng, when a Russian mission came to Peking to conclude an important commercial treaty with the Chinese government, it again happened that the Jesuit fathers were the only people who knew how to negotiate with the Russian delegates. Again, when the first Chinese ambassador was being sent to Russia, the fathers alone knew what instructions he must take with him, and how his credentials should be worded if he were to be favorably received by the tsar in St. Petersburg.

In the end, the Jesuits carried on the negotiations with the Russian plenipotentiaries almost unaided, and reached a settlement which was more favorable to China than had been expected. The result of this success of the missionaries led the emperor to have a better opinion of them, and Father Parrenin made use of this opportunity to obtain a considerable alleviation of the measures directed against the Christians.

Yung-chêng had not inherited his father's interest in scientific matters, and had little understanding of mathematics and astronomy; he recognized, however, that the Jesuits were better acquainted with public administration than his own ministers; henceforth, therefore, he treated the missionaries in a friendly manner, and even allowed them to fetch two brothers of the order to the court from Europe.

Thus the Jesuits had once again risen to an influential position, and the imperial favor which they now enjoyed also protected in a considerable degree the Christian communities in the whole of China; the mandarins in the provinces dared not proceed harshly against a religion the priests of which enjoyed such great respect in Peking.

During the reign of K'ien-lung, the next ruler of the Manchu dynasty, the missionaries and the Chinese Christians once more suffered a serious setback. K'ien-lung had only hate and mistrust for foreign beliefs, which he regarded as dangerous to the state, and, consequently, he soon issued decrees which aimed at the total extermination of Christianity.

This time, the situation appeared hopeless, for no person below a minister or lord dared make representation to the emperor and move him to moderate his edicts. Whatever K'ien-lung commanded had immediately to be done and his word had to be regarded as the word of greatest wisdom and as a direct command from heaven.

The Power and Secret of the Jesuits

This fourth ruler of the Manchu dynasty was prouder than even the proudest of the Mings had been. He lived in close seclusion in his palace, the rooms of which contained the most magnificent works of art and jewels procured in China, Japan and India. Surrounded only by his wives and eunuchs, K'ien-lung was like a god devoted to his own adoration. When ministers and princes reported to him, they had to lie on the floor with their faces to the ground, silently await the emperor's commands, and immediately carry them out to the very letter, as though they were divine instructions.

If K'ien-lung left the palace in order to pass through the streets of the capital, mounted soldiers would, the day before, gallop through the streets along which the emperor intended to pass to ensure that all shops were closed, and that all doors and windows were covered with thick cloth, so that no mortal might gaze on the august ruler.

So for a long time the Jesuits found no opportunity of speaking to a potentate so wrapped up in his own godliness, and of inducing him to adopt a more lenient attitude towards the Christian doctrines Of course, the fathers still held the presidency of the mathematical tribunal, because there was nobody besides themselves who knew exactly how to compute the annual calendar. And so the Jesuit president of the tribunal had from time to time to submit his reports to the emperor along with the other dignitaries; this, however, had to be done while extended on the ground, and the emperor honored him as little as he did the other mandarins.

It made no impression on the emperor, when, as was often the case, the other fathers whom the former emperor had permitted to come to Peking, and who were living there, showed themselves to be skilful in mathematics and diplomacy. With the indifference of a true and exalted son of God, he took the services rendered to him without a word, and he did not for a moment consider it necessary to show himself grateful by being especially gracious.

At the time, however, when it seemed as if all further efforts of the Jesuits in China were to be hopeless, K'ien-lung's assumption of divinity came to their aid and made it possible for them to approach him. K'ien-lung had always felt that his palace and his garden, in spite of their sumptuousness, were not sufficiently magnificent to serve as the residence of the most illustrious son of God. Unceasingly, he pondered how he could improve the luxury of his earthly abode.

He had the walls of his rooms covered with pure gold and precious stones, and the best painters in the empire were required to cover the golden background with birds and flowers. He applied himself eagerly to the development of his summer residence, Yoen-ming-yoen. The gardens by which the many pavilions and temples were linked up surpassed everything that had ever been done in any part of the world; since nature alone could not satisfy the tastes of the emperor, artificial mountains, valleys, forests and rivers had been made; large and small brooks wound their way through pleasant valleys round artificial bends, the banks now narrowing between artificial hills and rocks, now widening again to become lakes on which floated luxurious boats.

On a rocky island in the middle of one of these lakes stood the great palace with more than a hundred apartments; from here could best be seen the other buildings, which numbered more than two hundred. Galleries, avenues, terraces, amphitheaters, forests of flowers were all united in a picture of incomparable charm.

The Order of Gardeners and "Lightning Artists"

But still the emperor was not satisfied; he constantly sought out painters, gardeners and technicians, who might make the walls of his pavilions still more beautiful and the artificial landscape of his gardens still more pleasant.

These painters, gardeners and mechanics were at the same time the only persons who had free entry to all parts of the imperial palace. And, further, as K'ien-lung personally supervised the various works it was the workers and artists alone who were in a position to see the ruler at close quarters.

When the Jesuits heard of the emperor's passion the Society suddenly appeared to be a guild of painters and architects, Christianity assumed the semblance of a doctrine designed for gardeners. If the emperor became dissatisfied with the manner in which his gardens were laid out, his ministers combed Peking for the best horticulturists they could find. The Jesuits would apply, declaring that there was nothing connected with this art with which they were not thoroughly conversant. If K'ien-lung sought for somebody to beautify his ponds and brooks, the Jesuits informed him that nobody knew better than they how to do such work. They were portrait-painters when the emperor desire portraitists, and, if he wished to decorate his walls with birds and flowers, a father was immediately found who was highly skilled in this work. Within a short time, a group of Jesuit missionaries were occupying the small house set aside for the various handicraftsmen and technical workers at the entrance to the gardens of the summer palace, and the fathers themselves belonged to that small band of favorites who dwelt in close proximity to the exalted son of God.

As at times they worked in the innermost rooms of the private residence of the emperor, and at other times in the gardens or in the pavilions of the imperial family, they went everywhere and saw everything in the palace and nothing remained unrevealed to them. They saw also the strange private town which K'ien-lung had had built, and which had no equal in the whole world. In order to compensate himself for the close seclusion which his exalted position imposed upon him, K'ien-lung had hit upon the original idea of building within his palace an artificial town for his own pleasure.

There were walls, towers, streets, squares, temples, halls, markets, shops and palaces, all built in the ordinary way; there was even a harbor. If the emperor desired to see how his subjects actually lived, he went into his private town, and had his eunuchs stage a Chinese working day for him. The eunuchs dressed themselves as merchants, workers or soldiers; one pushed a wheelbarrow, another carried a basket; ships entered the harbor, the shops were opened, dealers landed their wares, the people crowded into tea-houses and wine-shops, hawkers and tradesmen strolled about, they quarreled, shrieked and clamored, and there were even pickpockets who were arrested, dragged before the judge and punished with the bastinado.

When the emperor came across his new painters, builders and mechanics at their work, he sometimes condescended to speak to them; he gave them orders himself, said how he wished this or that to be ornamented, or he let fall a few words expressing himself satisfied with their work. It was a distinction for which a Chinese would have sacrificed all he possessed, and this immense good fortune was now being enjoyed by the Jesuits, the preachers of a religion which at the same time was being persecuted with unrelenting severity throughout the empire.

The Power and Secret of the Jesuits

Since the emperor visited the rooms and places where the Jesuits were working, the fathers were afforded an opportunity of entreating his mercy on behalf of the persecuted Chinese Christians. On one occasion, Father Castiglione was busily engaged on a fresco in one of the imperial chambers, when K'ien-lung received it in a kindly manner and said; "I will read your petition; be calm and continue your painting!"

To be sure he decided not to repeal the former orders, but, as he was pleased with Castiglione's fresco, he ordered his ministers to cease persecuting the Christians.

Indefatigably, Fathers Sickelpart, Panzi, Sallusti and Poirot painted portraits, landscapes, fruits, birds and fishes, in oil on glass and in watercolors on silk; Sickelpart's art pleased the emperor so much that the was made a mandarin of the first class. Father Brossard was also successful in gaining the favor of the emperor with his glass-work, which was of the most exquisite delicacy. Soon K'ien-lung entrusted the Jesuits with the management of a regular academy, accommodation for which was found in a building near the palace, and there Chinese pupils were instructed in this European art.

It was often difficult to satisfy the whims of the emperor, and conform to his varying desires without opposing him. Woefully one of the fathers reported to his native land: "All our work is superintended by the emperor. First we submit plans, which he often amends as it pleases him; whether the alteration is good or bad, it must be accepted without question, for the emperor is the best judge of all things."

When once a number of rebel Tatar princes announced their submission, Father Attiret suddenly received a command to depart for the hunting-seat at Ge-hol in Tatary, as the emperor wished to have a pictorial record of the submission ceremony. Having entered Ge-hol, the poor father was so confused by the many faces, pursuits and festivities that he did not know for a long time how he was going to depict it all on canvas. Scarcely had the ceremony of the submission of the Tatar princes ended, however, when a minister conveyed an order to the missionary to begin painting his picture on the spot, as the emperor which to see the finished work on the evening of the same day.

Attiret painted in desperation; he placed the emperor, clad in gorgeous raiment, in the center of the picture, and around him he sketched in, with all possible speed, some hundreds of figures. Very soon the minister appeared again, and reported that the emperor already wished to see the picture. Attiret's sketch pleased K'ien-lung so much that he exclaimed repeatedly: "Hen-hao!" ("Very good!").

Exhausted, the father had retired to rest, but, early the next morning, he was called to the palace, where the emperor had just appointed eleven of the recently subdued Tatar princes to the rank of mandarin, and he was ordered to paint their portraits with all possible speed. What could the unfortunate missionary do but carry out this new command for the glory of God?

He went into the room where the eleven Tatars were already awaiting him, and set to work painting the first. While he worked, the other princes crowded round him, and plied him with all sorts of questions; he had to answer them, and, at the same time, continue with his painting, and he might not even with a glance allow his irritation to be observed. This went on for six days until the portraits were completed. The Tatars were much astonished at the likeness of the portraits; they looked at each other, and, on comparing their features with the painting, they burst into shouts of laughter.

On his return to Peking, K'ien-lung wanted a number of engravings made to commemorate the capture of Turkestan, and on these the important events of the campaign were to be portrayed. None of the fathers had ever been engaged on work of his nature before, and consequently they were at first at their wit's end how to deal with this unexpected order. Then, however, Father Benoit decided to read up the art of making copper plates, and, at last, he actually succeeded in producing one hundred and four large plates which were printed in France, and which pleased the emperor very much.

They were always receiving new commands which had to be carried out immediately; it was necessary even for the aged Attiret, who was then very ill, to be constantly painting the emperor in new poses, now on horseback, now seated, now standing. "To be chained up day by day," wrote the harassed Father Attiret to his colleagues in Rome, "with only Sundays and holidays free for prayer, and to be unable to paint anything my heart might dictate, all this would urge me, the sooner the better, to return to Europe; but I think that religion is profiting by my brush, and that my painting favorably impresses the emperor towards the missionaries. This and the hope of seeing heaven when my troubles and trials are ended are the only things which encourage me and the other brothers to remain here."

The Triumph of the Fountain and the Mechanical Lion

One day, a drawing of a fountain came into the hands of the son of God, and immediately he commanded the missionaries to make one for the gardens of his pleasure palace. The fathers painted picture after picture in vain; in vain did the gardeners invent new schemes; K'ien-lung was not interested; he wanted a *shui-fa*, a fountain.

The Jesuits had no idea at all how such things were made; they counted skilled watchmakers and expert mechanics among their numbers, but not one of them understood anything about hydraulics or the casting of pump-barrels and water-pipes, But, as K'ien-lung insisted on his *shui-fa*, Father Benoit studied an endless number of books, and puzzled over them night and day, until, finally, he had penetrated the basic principles of hydraulics.

Six months later, the first column of water rose in the emperor's gardens. K'ien-lung was enraptured, and he at once ordered other fountains to be made which were to be still more artistic than the first.

When these were finished, the emperor, sitting on his throne in his summer palace at Yoen-ming-yoen, could admire, on his right and left, two great fountains, and, before him, an artistic group of fishes, birds, and other animals from which water spurted. In Peking, the Jesuits built in one of the courtyards of the imperial palace a large basin with twelve mythical figures of animals, which served as a clock; every two hours a stream of water spurted from the mouth of one of these figures.

It then occurred to the emperor that these fathers, who seemed to be able to do anything, might be able to make artificial animals. Before he had expressed his desire, Father Thibault had set to work on an automatic lion, which in size and appearance exactly resembled a living beast.

That such an automaton was being built was not disclosed to the emperor, and one day, while he was walking in the garden, the missionaries set the clockwork in motion. The lion ran up to the emperor on the garden path, and at first he fell back terrified, until he realized that the fathers had divined and fulfilled his most secret desire.

"It is truly astonishing," wrote Father Amyot from Peking to his fellow-Jesuit Latour in Paris, "how our beloved brother Thibault, with the simplest principles of watch-making, succeeded in making an automaton which is a great mechanical achievement. I speak as an eye-witness, because I have myself seen the artificial animal run."

The lion was followed by a tiger, and, when the emperor began to tire of automatic animals, Father Sigmund set about making a mechanical man. While he was engaged on this clockwork, the emperor sat from early morning until the evening in the father's workshop, and asked in great detail about each part of the mechanism.

"If the father succeeds in this work," wrote Amyot in one of his letters, "soon afterwards you may be sure the emperor will say to him: 'You have done it, now make it so that it talks!' I myself have received from him an order to make two men carrying a vase and moving along with it. I have already been working seven months on it, and it will be quite another year before the work is completed. I have, however, often the opportunity of coming into close contact with the emperor."

Nevertheless, it was on the occasion of the celebration with great pomp of the sixtieth birthday of the Dowager Empress that the best work of the fathers was performed. All the painters, sculptors, builders and joiners from Peking were engaged for months on the preparations for this festival; they were busy decorating the whole road from Yoen-ming-yoen up to the capital with stately buildings. Temples and summer-houses were erected everywhere to accommodate choirs and troupes of players and to serve as refreshment-houses. In Peking itself the streets from the gates of the city to the entrance to the palace were decorated with wooden colonnades, pavilions and garlands of flowers and other ornaments in silk, gold and mirror-glass. At intervals along the route, there were artificial hills on which deer were tethered; in other places were children dressed as monkeys, and children clothed in feathers stood on columns draped in silk, and imitated the movements of flying birds.

On this occasion, the fathers had determined to surpass everything they had hitherto done, and ultimately they succeeded by their joint efforts in creating a marvelous mechanical work of art. At a place which the procession had to pass, they placed a stage which one of the missionaries describes in his report.

"It had on each side," he says, "three scenes draws in perspective; at the back there was a figure clothed in Chinese fashion holding a written greeting to the emperor. In front of each scene, there were little Chinese statues, each holding a copper cymbal in the right hand and a small hammer in the left. In front of the stage, there was a simulated water-basin made of mirror-glass, on the edge of which a dial with European and Chinese characters was to be seen. An artificial goose was moving about in the water. All this was set in motion by hidden springs, and a magnet which ran round the dial attracted the goose so that it showed the time.

When it was the hour, the statue holding the inscription stepped forward from the rear of the stage and bowed; thereupon the six other statues played together a little tune, striking the cymbals with the hammers. When the music ceased, the figure with the inscription returned ceremoniously to its place."

The emperor was so enraptured with this present from the fathers that he immediately ordered it to be taken into one of his private chambers, there he preserved this piece of work with the greatest care for the rest of his days.

"Also," says the missionary's letter in conclusion, "we endeavor, for the sake of our religion, to earn the goodwill of the emperor by means of useful and necessary services. If we cannot move him so that he is favorably disposed towards the Christians, we can at least influence him so that he no longer persecutes them, and so that he allows the servants of the Lord the liberty to preach the Gospel."

The emperor knew quite well that the fathers would remain at his court only so long as they saw before them some hope for their missionary work. Thus, the Christian churches in Peking were kept open and the Chinese Christians, some nine thousand in number, were in no way molested. One of the fathers reported as follows: "There are a large number of Christians in Peking who are allowed full liberty to visit the church. . . In the provinces also our fathers are not so carefully hidden that they cannot be found when required. But the mandarins close their eyes to our activities, for they know how we stand here with the emperor."

Profanation or Toleration?

When the triumphs of the Jesuit missionaries in China became known in Europe, they immediately excited the jealousy of the Dominicans, who were already angry with the Jesuits on account of the Molinist controversy. The Franciscans, who had themselves been engaged in missionary work for a long time, also grudged the Society of Jesus its surprising success, and the Jansenists, as a matter of principle, hated everything the Jesuits did and neglected to do.

Opposition was made all the keener on account of the unfortunate end of the mission undertaken by the Dominicans and Franciscans. Priests of these two orders had just made an attempt to get a firm footing in China, but, unlike the Jesuits, they had refused to make any compromise with the national customs of the Chinese, and from the very beginning had remained strong in their principles.

And so Dominican and Franciscan monks alike preached that all the emperors of China, as well as the wise Confucius, were, as heathens, damned to the everlasting fires of hell. Of course, such a doctrine in a country where the greatest reverence was shown towards former rulers and statesmen could only arouse general indignation. Therefore, the new missionaries were soon taken by the authorities, cast into prison and deported.

The Jesuits, on the other hand, had begun their missionary work with maps, clocks, mirrors, reading-glasses and paintings, and, with these, had been successful. On this account the Dominicans and Franciscans accused them of spreading the teachings of Christ in an undignified manner, and, therefore, of having profaned the word of God.

The Power and Secret of the Jesuits

The fathers of the Society of Jesus answered their opponents smartly, and declared that Christianity in China had been placed in the greatest danger by the imprudent behavior of the mendicant monks; indeed, the clumsiness of these missionaries had aroused the anger of the authorities, and, as a consequence, had to some extent been the cause of sending numerous Chinese Christians needlessly to their martyrdom.

The conflict between the religious fraternities was extended by the no less malicious intrigues of international politics. The sending of a Jesuit mission to China by Louis XIV aroused the jealous anger of the Portuguese government, which claimed, on the ground of papal privilege, the sole right of conducting the work of converting the peoples of the Far East to Christianity. Portugal at once opened a strong diplomatic attack on France at the Papal See, and immediately gave chase to the French Jesuit missionaries who had left for China; one of them was captured by the Portuguese and was imprisoned at Goa until his death.

Further disputes arose in connection with the filling of the bishopric established in Peking. The French maintained that the bishop should be a Jesuit of French nationality, while the Portuguese demanded a Portuguese bishop from the Order of Christ. Thus the Chinese mission was the source of continual and complicated political intrigues in Paris, Lisbon and Rome.

The Inquisition of the Holy See was inundated with accusations against the Jesuits. The fathers working at the court of Peking were accused of having, in their capacity as members of the mathematical tribunal, occupied themselves in the determination of days of good and ill fortune; this implied the encouragement of objectionable superstition and was quite inadmissible.

Against all precepts of the Church, they wore a head-covering similar to the old Chinese scholar's cap when reading mass; they did not read the liturgy, the missals and the breviary, as prescribed, in Latin, but in Chinese; in the baptism of women, they neglected to anoint the nostrils, shoulders and breast, on the rather feeble ground that the Chinese would not tolerate the touching of their women by foreigners.

All the enemies of the Jesuits were greatly perturbed by the fact that the missionaries permitted their converts in China to participate in the customary rites in honor of the dead. These funeral ceremonies, at which strips of paper were burnt, and meat and wine placed on the tables for the souls of the deceased, were, in the opinion of the Dominicans and the Franciscans, altogether heathen ceremonies, the practice of which must be a sin. Nevertheless, the Jesuits had not only permitted these customs, but had also practiced them.

The most serious accusation made against the Jesuits, however, was that the fathers in China had systematically kept secret the death of Christ on the cross, and that they baptized the Chinese without telling them a word about the crucifixion of the Lord. In their churches in China, the Jesuits had no crucifix, but only representations of the Saviour in his glory and the Mother of God enthroned in heaven.

On the other hand, the Jesuits laid detailed statements before the inquisition tribunal. In these, they said they had never denied the crucifixion, but, in the interests of the Faith, it had been necessary to impart the Gospel to the heathens with care and with tact. Crucifixion in China was a great disgrace, and the Chinese could only with great difficulty be made to believe

90. THE FIRST MAP OF THE MISSISSIPPI

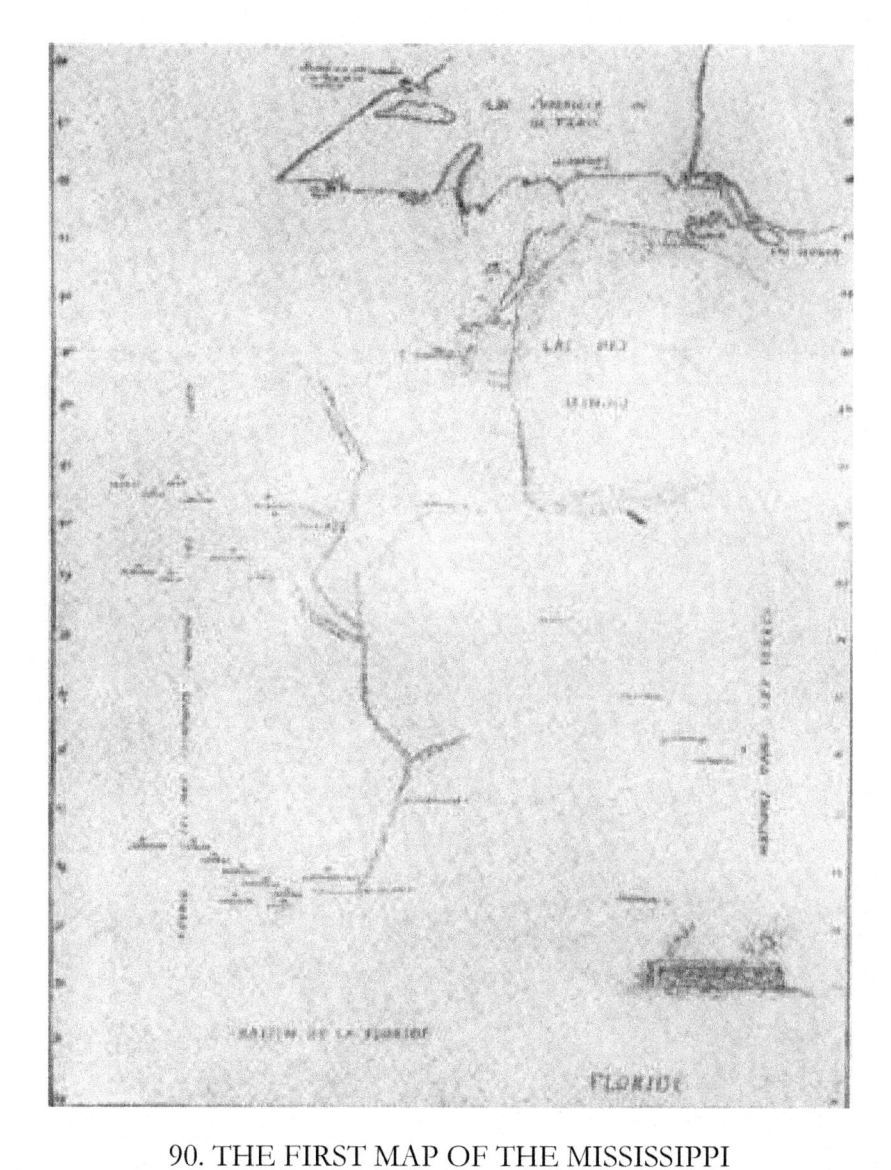

Drawn by the first explorer of the river, the Jesuit missionary Father Marquette

91. THE TORTURE OF THE JESUITS BRÉBEUF AND
LALEMANT BY THE CANADIAN INDIANS

Profanation or Toleration?

in a God who had been executed in so shameful a manner. For this reason, the Jesuits had refrained from relating the crucifixion of Christ until such time as the converts had been sufficiently prepared. So far as concerned the rites, the toleration of which they were reproached with, it was not a case of religious ceremonies, but of a certain form of piety, against which there could not be the least objection from the Christin point of view. The funeral celebrations of the Chinese meant nothing more than the expression of a childish reference for their forbears. Further, these customs were absolutely binding on all Chinese, and to forbid them would render abortive any attempt at conversion to Christianity.

Much more serious was the struggle in which the whole Catholic priesthood were soon involved. The Dominicans Moralez and Navarette, wrote one large volume after another in which they accused the Jesuits in China of open treason; the indefatigable Antoine Arnauld came out with similar polemical writings. The popes hesitated for a long time between the Jesuits and their opponents, for nobody in Europe had a clear idea of the actual importance of the Chinese rites which were, in the main, concerned. It had to be ascertained whether the souls of the dead were worshipped as deities; it had to be made clear how far the tables on which the forbears were offered food were regarded as altars. The contending orders advanced statements about all this which were in substance diametrically opposed.

As the popes could not, in such circumstances, judge objectively, they gave their decision according to their own connections with the Dominicans or the Jesuits. Paul V said, in 1616, that he was, in principle, ready to approve the conduct of the Jesuits, but he neglected to issue a formal decision to that effect. In 1635, the Dominicans addressed a denunciation to Pope Urban VIII, but a settlement of this question was not reached until the College of Cardinals under his successor, Innocent X, decided that the funeral celebrations should be prohibited. Under Alexander VII, the Jesuits, however, again attained great influence at the Curia, and thus the Roman Inquisition of 1656 stated that the Chinese rites were "merely a civil and political cult," and could, therefore, be tolerated.

Clement IX, who became pope in 1667, was an expressed enemy of the Society of Jesus; it is, therefore, not surprising that a decree against the cult of ancestors was immediately issued. This unfavorable development for the Jesuits reached its climax in 1715, when the constitution issued by Clement XI imposed a formal oath against the cult of ancestors on all missionaries working in China. A papal legate went to China to supervise the carrying into effect of this order, and principally to inquire into the question in dispute on the spot.

The Chinese themselves now learned of the bitter struggle they had unwittingly caused during many years past, and they were anything but edified by it. When the papal legate informed the Emperor K'ang-hi that the Holy Father had damned the cult of the ancestor as heathen idolatry, the emperor remarked angrily: "How can the pope judge of things which he has never seen, and with which he is not acquainted? So far as I am concerned, I would never presume to pass judgment on customs in Europe of which I know nothing.

A Chinese judge having to pass sentence on a Dominican monk who had been taken prisoner declared at the time: "I know the Jesuits well; they are true preachers and brave men who have brought us books, clocks, telescopes and similar useful objects. You others, however, are false preachers, for you neither know the high science of mathematics or astronomy, nor have you brought us clocks or books."

The Power and Secret of the Jesuits

The Fish-Hook Mission

In the early decades of the seventeenth century, a movement began in England which for some time past had been proceeding in Spain and Portugal; hosts of adventurous people embarked for the new world in order to exchange the unsatisfactory conditions of their native land for the attractions of a virgin country.

First, there were the Puritan emigrants who, fleeing the hardships of religious persecution, flocked to North America; their example was soon followed by "Papist" nobles for the same reason. Sir George Calvert, who later became Lord Baltimore, organized the first of these Catholic expeditions, and from the very beginning he found zealous assistants in the Jesuits Parsons and Blount. When the small band of Catholic colonists actually set out for America in the year 1634, they had a few Jesuit fathers with them.

They landed to the north of Virginia, and named their new colony Maryland. They worked hard building houses, and making the land productive, clearing forest land and providing food and sustenance by hunting and fishing. The Jesuits assisted in all these labors, and in all things they did as the others did.

"Near the mouth of the Potomac," wrote Father White, one of the members of this expedition, "we came to a small river in the north as large as the Thames. On one bank, we have laid out our plantations, and built the town of St. Mary; on the other bank lives King Chitomachon."

This native prince, who had pitched his tents to the south of the present city of Washington, was a kind of Indian emperor, and was revered by his subjects as "Tayac," the "chief of all chiefs." He and his people distrusted the white immigrants who had taken possession of their forests and prairies, and for a long time, the Indians regarded as a hostile demon the God of whom the white people spoke. For this reason, the redskins had mercilessly massacred the first missionaries, who, in 1570, had attempted to preach the Gospel in this neighborhood.

In order to protect themselves from the attacks of the Indians, the English settlers on American soil had relied on the law of retaliation, and any Indian who fell into their hands was made to pay the penalty for the crimes of other members of his race. The governor of the new colonies issued orders under which the settlers were authorized to shoot all Indians at sight.

Such cruel measures, naturally, did not moderate the hostility of the redskins towards the Europeans, and the Jesuits devised other methods of making peace with them. First, they worked eagerly for months learning the language of the Indians, and, when at last they set out to go to the Indians, the only weapons they took with them were a quantity of fish-hooks, needles and confectionery. With such baggage, they crossed the river, and one day stood before the tent of the terrible Chitomachon.

When he saw the fine fishing-hooks and needles, the use of which the fathers explained in perfect Indian, and when he had tasted the confectionery, he quickly made friends with the new-comers. Soon he permitted them to explain the elements of the Christian faith, and, sometime afterwards, he expressed a wish to embrace Christianity. On the advice of the fathers, he even separated from all but one of his numerous wives, and, with this wife and his

The Fish-Hook Mission

little son, accompanied by a stately following, he went to the Maryland settlement to be baptized.

"On July 3, 1640," the report of the missionaries stated, "after a sufficient instruction in the secrets of the Faith, he took the sacrament. At the same time, his wife and their child, as well as one of his chief councilors and his son, were born again at the baptismal spring. Then, in the afternoon, the emperor and his wife were married according to the Christian rite, and, after this, an enormous cross was set up; the emperor, the governor, his secretary and all others present helped to carry it to the most suitable spot, whilst two of us sang the litany of the Holy Virgin."

The Jesuits spread the Christian faith among the neighboring Indian races in a similar manner, and still other chiefs came forward to receive their confectionery, fish-hooks and needles. Although this must have seemed inconceivable to the Christian colonists, who, brought up in the faith of their fathers, had relied hitherto on fire-arms, they had reluctantly to acknowledge the success of the new Jesuits' methods. Hence, soon afterwards, a report of the colonial authorities stated "that the native, when treated in a friendly and just manner, show themselves to be quite peaceful. Every wise man will from now on regard it as his duty to treat the Indians well, to instruct them in the use of tools, and thereby keep them loyal and engaged in useful work."

The harmony which, in these early days, existed between the settlers and the priests did not last long. As new immigrants continued to arrive, land became scarce, and covetous eyes were turned on those properties which the grateful Indians had presented to the missionaries. The authorities in Maryland drafted a law under which the land belonging to the Catholic clergy was to be sequestrated. The clever fathers showed, however, that they were a match not only for wild Indians, but also for the civilized colonists, for, when the necessary legislative formalities had been completed, it came to light that the land had for a long time ceased to be the property of the fathers, and that, on the contrary, it had already been placed in the faithful hands of a very respectable farmer, and had thereby been made safe against all seizure.

From now onwards, the missionaries had frequently to defend themselves against the attacks of their enemies, for, in the colony which had originally been Catholic, the protestants were now in the majority, and the latter persecuted the "Papist" priests in every possible way. Exiled from Maryland, the fathers disappeared without leaving any trace behind them, and soon afterwards reappeared in the guise of farmers under common names; some of them actually left Maryland, and sought to continue their work in other parts of the English colonies.

Towards the end of the seventeenth century, an opportunity offered itself for successful work in New York as the owner of this colony at the time, the Duke of York, openly sympathized with the Catholics. Full of hope, the provincial Warner wrote to the general of the order: "In this colony there is an important town where it may be possible to establish a college to which those of our colleagues who are scattered over Maryland may retire until a further opportunity offers itself for them to advance into Maryland."

Soon after this, when the Duke of York ascended the English throne as James II, the Jesuits of his time acquired power and influence at the court of Whitehall; in those days the mission in New York flourished, and the newly established Jesuit college in that city was much resorted to. But the "glorious revolution" suddenly put an end to the reign of the last of the Stuarts. Under his successor, William of Orange, the position of the Jesuits in New York became untenable; whereupon the fathers immediately appeared again in full force in Maryland, and there discharged the duties of their office among the Catholic population.

A simple means made it possible for them to hold their ground amid the difficulties of changing political conditions, a means which even their enemies could not but appreciate; wherever it seemed at all desirable, they established schools for both white people and Indians. An American senator has declared that the Jesuit missionaries, during the early colonization of America, took in hand the task of educating the people, and thereby "performed a task which neither the government nor anybody else had been able to accomplish."

In Georgetown, now a suburb of the city of Washington, the federal capital, they established a seminary, the first Catholic educational institution in United States territory; from there, they extended their activities to Virginia, Delaware, New Jersey and Pennsylvania. Indeed, it is to a certain degree due to their activities that the newly formed United States included in its Constitution the principle of religious freedom.

In those days, one of Benjamin Franklin's friends was a Jesuit; this was John Carroll, who had been brought up in Maryland, and who later, on Franklin's special recommendation, was appointed a prefect apostolic and afterwards became the first Catholic bishop of the United States.

Father Marquette, The Explorer of the Mississippi

In the seventeenth century, almost simultaneously with the English, the French landed on the coast of North America, and there, on the territory we now know as Canada, they founded a "New France," Some Jesuit fathers landed with the first officials or the French trading company, and one of the first buildings of the new settlement of Quebec was the Jesuit college.

Bancroft, in his *History of the United States*, writes: "the origin of all towns in French America is closely associated with the work of missionaries; not a cape was rounded, not a river discovered without a Jesuit's having shown the way."

In their simple black coats, their packs on their backs, they marched through virgin forests in order to reach remote Indian races.

It was on such travels that Father Marquette and Louis Joliet became the first Europeans after DeSoto to reach that legendary stream of which the Indians had so often spoken to them, and in their boats they followed its course as far as New Orleans. Two statues in the Capitol at Washington proclaim today the fame of these tow explorers of the Mississippi.

Other missionaries pressed on up the Missouri, through that impassable tract west of Lake Superior, as far as the Yellowstone River; the Jesuit Dolbeau explored the mountainous districts north of the St. Lawrence River and Father Albanel was the first white man to reach Hudson's Bay.

Father Marquette

The brothers of the order won over the Indians of the primeval forests of Canada by the same means as they had employed in the south: the priests spoke to them in their own language, and lavished presents upon them. The results achieved by this policy can best be seen in an extract from a report of the Marquis of Denonville to the government in Paris: "The Indians can be kept in order only by these missionaries; the fathers alone are able to win them over to our interest, and keep them from the rebellion which might otherwise breakout at any moment. According to my own observations, I am firmly convinced that the Jesuits are the most suitable people to make the Indians peaceably disposed towards us."

Father Brébeuf had no sooner reached the Huron Indians, who numbered some 25,000 souls, than the redskins built for him a cabin of honor on the finest clearing, and they would not allow him to depart. The missionaries found here that the work of conversion was much more difficult than in the case of Chitomachon, who had been won over by a few fish-hooks and some confectionery The Hurons were a good-natured people, but, at the same time, they were sensual, and, when the missionaries had explained to them without any great difficulty the elements of the Catholic doctrines, the Indians could never understand why God should demand that they should give up all but one of their wives.

"I fell no little fear," wrote the clever Father Brébeuf, "when I reflect that it is now time to speak another language to the Indians, that we must preach the obligation to curb the desires of the flesh, and to regard matrimony as holy. When we tell then all this, and describe to them the judgment of God on sinners, they will, I fear, resist this rigid religion."

Only with "sweet cunning" could this difficult problem be solved, and so Brébeuf and his fellow-workers endeavored to move the Indians to accept the strange and unusual Christian moral customs by lavishing beautiful wedding presents on each Indian who married a wife in accordance with the Catholic faith. They gave the young couple the restive clothes, an ox-hide to serve as a couch, and the meat for the preparation of a great feast. The marriage was celebrated with great ceremony, and, on such occasions, the Jesuits decorated their forest chapels with glittering metal candlesticks and life-size images of the Virgin Mary.

This splendor, which was such as the Indians had never before seen, actually had the effect of making Christian monogamy seem much more tolerable to the Indians than hitherto.

In 1639, the Jesuits founded the mission station of St. Mary of the Hurons in the center of the district inhabited by the Huron Indians, and from this station they imparted the Christian teachings to more than 15,000 Indians; at the same time a number of Huron lads were sent to Quebec, to study at the Jesuit college. The number of converts constantly increased, so that the Jesuits hoped that in time they would convert the whole Huron tribe.

But the English were not disposed to remain inactive while the French continued to extend the territory under their rule in North America; the rivalry between England and France soon developed into a bloody conflict, in which the Indians were the first to be engaged. The English colonists took the Iroquois Indians living in their territory into their service, and these immediately attacked the Hurons, who were fighting for the supremacy of France.

The Iroquois were far superior in numbers and better armed, and, in the end, the Hurons were almost completely wiped out. Now, at that time when it was a matter of life and death, the Jesuits did not desert the Hurons. They advised them in their plans of campaign, and were beside them in the fiercest hand-to-hand encounters. On more than one occasion, there were Jesuits among the prisoners taken by the Iroquois; one of them, Father Jogues, had, as a slave of the Iroquois, to do forced labor of the hardest kind for them, while Fathers Brébeuf, Lalemant, Bressani and Daniel were scalped, burned at the stake, seethed in boiling water, and tortured to death.

No sooner had the Jesuits been compelled in this way to give up all hope of converting the Huron Indians into a Christian race than they boldly determined to win over to Christianity the Iroquois who had emerged victorious from the fight. That a number of the best brothers of the order had been sacrificed to the fury of this tribe seemed to them to be merely a further inducement for them to lead these wild redskins to the Church.

One of the first to obtain influence with the Iroquois was Father Milet. He had been captured by them, and the day on which he was to be scalped with all due ceremony had been fixed. The missionary, however, succeeded in so amazing his guards by the tricks he performed with his girdle, that they entered into conversation with him, and finally decided to receive him as a son. After the father had performed his tricks with the girdle to the best of his ability before the assembled war council of the Iroquois, he was ceremoniously received into the tribe, and soon succeeded in persuading them to take his advice and obey his orders without question.

This strange career of a French priest among the Iroquois must have caused the governor of New York some serious misgivings; he saw here a political danger, and he did everything which could possibly be done in such a case; his efforts, however, were in vain. "The Iroquois will not deliver him up," he wrote to the Board of trade, "although I have offered a sum of money and an Indian boy in exchange."

Soon other fathers also gained the confidence of the Iroquois in the same way as they had done with the Hurons. Father Simon Le Moyne simply walked one day into the camp of the Iroquois Onondagas, and made then an offer of peace on behalf of the French authorities. "I talked for fully two hours," says the father. "I spoke just like an Indian chief, and walked to and fro like an actor on the stage, as is usual with these people."

After a long consultation among the Indians, the missionary was placed on a seat of honor decorated with leaves, whereupon the chief of the Onondagas said to him: "Tell the white men that we are ready to acknowledge the God of whom you have spoken. You yourself may settle here. Care for us like a father, and we will obey you like children."

Another missionary made successful use of his painting ability in the conversion of the redskins. With paint-box and palette, he appeared at the wigwams of the Indians, and, surrounded by astonished spectators, he sketched pictures of hell, of heaven, of angels, and of the Devil. Afterwards, he explained their meaning, and, by means of this object lesson, he actually converted a number of the Iroquois.

Lord Bellomont, the governor of New England, saw no other means of destroying the Jesuit influence among the redskins than placing a price on their heads. In 1699, he reported to the higher authorities: "By means of money or special gifts, I might induce the Mohawks and the Onondagas to deliver up all Jesuits living with them. If I can do this, the Jesuits will never again dare to go among these people; moreover, a lasting and unquenchable hatred will spring up between the Indians and the Jesuits."

Indeed, the governor even went himself to the Iroquois, and said to them in an impressive speech: "For every Papist priest or Jesuit, you shall receive as your reward one hundred pieces-of-eight ($113) in cash, for we have in this province a law which entitles us to arrest such disturbers of the peace."

Friends of the Red Men

Wherever the Spanish or Portuguese conquistadores occupied fresh territories in the New World, they were followed by Jesuit fathers. If unknown regions were to be explored, it was the Jesuits who volunteered to undertake the task; when peace treaties or alliances were to be concluded with the Indians, the authorities made use of the services of the fathers, for they alone were acquainted with the native dialects, and, on account of their constant friendliness, enjoyed the full confidence of the chieftains.

In Mexico, the Jesuits were the first to venture among the still unconquered northern tribes; they penetrated as far as the mountain races on the upper reaches of the Rio Yaqui, and traversed the pathless mountain vastnesses of the Tarahumares. When the fathers first appeared in the mountains and valleys in which these tribes dwelt, the Indians fled to the shelter of their caves; nowhere were the white races more distrusted than in Mexico, where, a century earlier, the "White Saviour" had massacred tens of thousands of the natives. But even here the glittering presents and kindly words of the missionaries did not fail to produce the desired effect. Father Glandorff, who, with remarkable zeal, traversed the country seeking everywhere to make converts, speedily succeeded in persuading the natives to leave their homes in the mountains, and to assemble at prearranged places on the plains to take part in the meetings which he arranged for prayer and religious instructions.

With Mexico as their base of operations, the Jesuits pushed forward into New Mexico, Arizona, California and Texas; the German missionary, Kühn, explored the regions to the north of the Colorado River, while we also owe to the zeal of the Jesuits the first accurate descriptions and maps of Lower California.

A century later, Robert Louis Stevenson referred in glowing terms to the good work performed by the order in California, contrasting it with the subsequent misdoings of the "greedy land thieves and sacrilegious gunmen" in the same region. "So ugly a thing," he says, "may our Anglo-Saxon Protestantism appear beside the doings of the Society of Jesus!"

In Peru and Bolivia, moreover, the Jesuit fathers succeeded in discovering more than a hundred Indian tribes hitherto unknown, whom they concentrated in fixed settlements, in which they carried on agricultural work, cattle-raising and various industries, teaching the savages how to make all kinds of implements and how to build huts, and supplying the sick and injured with European medicines. In Lima, Cuzco and other Peruvian cities, they founded special schools for the Indians, in which the sons of the *caciques* could in future be educated under their supervision. They were also zealous in the preservation of the historical traditions of the vanished ancient Inca civilization, a task in which Father Blas Valera, himself a descendant of the Incas, especially distinguished himself. In Lima, they set up a printing press within the precincts of their school, in which were produced books and grammars of the Quichuan language compiled by the fathers.

In Brazil, Father Anchieta, with untiring zeal, made long journeys among the scattered Indian settlements, during which he converted many of the natives to the Christian religion. He lived the same nomadic life of the natives as they, travelling from place to place in the forests, studying the different dialects, and endeavoring to reduce them to a system. While so doing, he conceived the bold idea of setting systematically to work to abolish the local variations in the South American Indian dialects, and to establish a standard language, which could be used in all parts of the continent as a means of intercourse. He compiled grammars and dictionaries on which were based the linguistic researches of all the later missionaries, and from that time onwards the whole order collaborated in the scheme initiated by Anchieta.

Alexander von Humboldt writes, in reference to these efforts of the Jesuits, that they seem to him to be "very sensible:" "They were only doing what the Incas or priestly kings of Peru succeeded in doing centuries earlier in order to retain under their influence and to civilize the barbarian tribes on the Upper Amazon."

The missionaries in South America also rendered valuable service as intermediaries between the white race and the Indians; thus Father Anchieta once entered the camp of an insurgent native tribe to offer himself as a hostage for the peaceful intentions of the Europeans.

The Archbishop of La Plata, writing to the king of Spain in 1690, said that "the Jesuits, with no help other than their own zeal, accomplished in a short space of time a task which it had been found impossible to carry out by means of large armies and the expenditure of vast sums of money. They turned enemies into friends, and converted the wildest and most intractable of nations into your majesty's obedient subjects."

In course of time, the missionaries of the Society of Jesus thus opened up vast tracts of territory for the white colonists; as a French traveler wrote during the nineteenth century, they had conquered more land for their nations than had the greatest military leaders, and at the same time that, with their mild methods, they were bringing the wildest of tribes into subjection, they were doing much towards laying the foundations of a prosperous colonial empire in America.

For this reason, the earlier official reports never omitted to refer in grateful terms to the services rendered by the fathers; nevertheless, it was not for long possible to suppress the fact that, in their zeal for religion, these priests went rather too far, and to an ever-increasing extent exceeded their proper functions.

The colonists were certainly alive to the fact that the propagation of the Christian doctrines among the heathen was of material assistance in the acquisition of considerable wealth, for once the suspicious and timid aborigines had been won over to the Church, they became useful and dependable slaves for the Europeans. But, in the eyes of the colonists, here the task of the missionaries ended.

But the fathers, as they converted the natives, began to manifest a most disconcerting form of activity. The whole of their method of dealing with the baptized savages, humoring their idiosyncrasies and treating them on an equal footing with themselves, must, the colonists considered, give these barbarians quite a wrong impression of the meaning of their conversion; in fact, it would even seem that the Jesuits wished to give their converts almost the same rights as human beings!

The Spanish and Portuguese clergy had up to that time made a protest against slavery only in exceptional cases; had not St. Paul written (I Cor., vii, 21): "Art thou called being a servant? Care not for it"? And had not Thomas Aquinas and St. Anthony of Florence also recognized the validity of slavery? The Jesuits, however, quoted the words of St. Augustine: "Man should not have dominion over man, but only over the animal world."

The attitude of the missionaries towards the black slaves soon became such as to cause great vexation to the white settlers. Like all the other colonists, the fathers owned their own negro slaves, whom, in accordance with the general custom, they branded in token of their bondage. But they did not refer to their blacks as "slaves," as they ought to have done, but called them "servants" or merely "negroes," and granted them rights and privileges to an unheard-of extent. The priests allowed their slaves to possess land of their own, and required them only to work for a certain number of hours, allowing them, under the pretext of religious instruction, to spend the remainder of their time in idleness. This was bound to have an adverse influence on the discipline of the other slaves.

But the Jesuits did an even more unheard-of thing. With the cunning for which they were famous, they induced the authorities to issue an order requiring the other settlers to allow their slaves a certain amount of occasional leisure for the purpose of receiving instruction in the Christian doctrines, which meant that their masters would lose some of their slaves' labor and would thus suffer pecuniary loss.

A Jesuit father called Petrus Claver made himself very unpopular in Cartagena, the principal entrepôt of the South American slave trade. The great slave-ships regularly discharged their cargoes of newly captured African negroes at this port, where they were impatiently awaited by the dealers, who at once dispatched them to the mines and plantations. It was already the practice to baptize the slaves as soon as they were landed at Cartagena, for the slave-dealers were mindful of their duties as Christians; but the ceremony was carried out with the utmost expedition, and there was practically no delay in handling the traffic.

But Petrus Claver, by his cunning speeches, persuaded the local authorities to issue an order to the effect that no newly arrived negro might be baptized until he had received "adequate instruction in the Christian religion." Claver arranged for this instruction to be given in such a manner that it lasted several days; inasmuch as thousands of slaves were involved, this new regulation was very inconvenient to the dealers, causing as it did an appreciable loss of interest on the capital which they had invested in black ivory.

Almost as soon as a new slaver was signaled of Cartagena, Claver hastened to board the vessel, taking with him biscuits, fruit and sweet-stuffs as presents for the fettered passengers. He even went so far as to go between decks, where the slaves lay huddled in filth, surrounded by the corpses of those who had perished during the voyage. He there attended to their wants, bandaged their wounds and comforted them. After they were landed, he had them quartered in clean huts, where, under the pretext that their instruction in the Christian doctrines required some time, he retained them until they had regained their strength, and had recovered from the effects of their wounds.

The Power and Secret of the Jesuits

Moreover, the manner in which Claver baptized the slaves almost verged on the blasphemous; in the chapel which he used for this purpose, he and set up an altar-piece depicting a number of baptized negroes as the happy children of God. This was calculated to give the negroes the impression that they were something more than unclean animals and that the all-powerful Christian God was really interested in their conversion.

In his altruistic zeal, Claver did not remain content with baptizing the slaves, but afterwards took a great interest in their welfare. When no slave-ship was expected, he travelled through the length and breadth of the country, visiting all his former converts, and, by his attentions, gave them quite an erroneous impression of their earthly purpose.

The attitude of the Jesuits to the Indians was even worse; it seemed indeed that, in their zeal, they had entirely overlooked the rightful interests of the white settlers. Although at first, in recognition of the services they had rendered, efforts were made to turn a blind eye to the excesses of the fathers, this state of affairs could not last for long Now that the primeval forests were opened up, and the savage Indian tribes were brought under the white yoke, it became necessary to put a stop to the fathers' exaggerated concern over the matter of brotherly love.

Trouble first broke out in Canada. The Jesuit missionaries there had ample opportunity to die as martyrs for the honor or Christian New France, to be scalped by the redskins, burnt at the stake, or tortured by immersion in boiling water. But the ambitions of the members of this order seemed insatiable, and they were by no means content with the martyr's crown which the secular authorities did not begrudge then. They demanded to be allowed to interfere in matters of government which were really no concern of theirs!

Hitherto, the sale of brandy to the Indians had constituted one of the most lucrative trades of the French merchants in Quebec. But these fathers came on the scene, and demanded in the name of Christian charity that the government should prohibit the sale of alcohol to the Indians. In support of this extraordinary request, they pointed out that brandy caused dreadful ravages among the redskins, and impelled these otherwise good-humored savages to commit the most horrible excesses.

At first, the authorities endeavored to comply with the demands of the fathers and of the bishop who had associated himself with them, but in such a manner as not to inflict unnecessary harm on the brandy trade. The Supreme Council of Quebec therefore issued a decree which strictly prohibited the Indians from drinking alcohol. The Jesuits, however, demanded that, instead of this, the whites should be forbidden under severe penalties to sell brandy to the Indians, a request, which was quite unacceptable to the government. Rebuffed by the whites, the missionaries then addressed themselves to the Indians, and tried to convince them that the "fire-water" would lead them into hell, and that the white people let them drink it only in order to sell them to the Devil. By such talk they caused trouble between the redskins and the brandy-sellers, which brought upon them the deadly enmity not only of the latter, but of the governor, Frontenac, who himself had an interest in the trade.

Such a course was akin to high treason in the eyes of the governor, who therefore sent a report to the authorities in Paris. His efforts were, however, fruitless, for at that period Père La Chaise was the king's confessor, and he did not fail to use his influence with the king on behalf of the Jesuits. The judicial investigation accordingly resulted in a verdict in favor of the

Friends of the Red Men

Canadian missionaries.

Some of the more far-seeing members of the government did not, it is true, fail to appreciate the danger of acceding to the Jesuits' demands for the prohibition of the sale of alcohol. This, considered the Minister of Marine, Hugues de Lyonne, was doubtless very Christian and sound in principle; but it was fatal from the commercial point of view, "since the Indians, who like drinking, will in future no longer sell of their beaver pelts, but will barter then for brandy to the Dutchman at Albany."

The dissensions between the colonists and the fathers regarding the treatment of the Indians in the Spanish and Portuguese South American colonies assumed an even more violent form. In those days the traffic in Indian slaves was regarded as the best and most lucrative kind of business, and the inhabitants of the various settlements regularly held slave-hunts, carrying their victims to the great slave-mart at Rio de Janeiro. A favorite method of securing Indian slaves was to incite the various tribes to make war upon one another. The whites then bought the captives from the victors in exchange for needles, pocket-knives and tobacco, and disposed of them at a substantial profit.

The Jesuits publicly denounced this traditional practice of holding Indian hunts and slave-markets, and went so far as to take the part of the savages against the white people. For instance, Father Anchieta, after arranging a peace treaty with the Tamuyo tribe, on one occasion stated in a sermon delivered in the public square of Rio that the Tamuyos had been in the right in their fight with the Portuguese. "you attacked them, despite the treaty," he thundered at the astounded Portuguese, "and you have enslaved them contrary to all the laws of nature!"

Anchieta also wrote a play in verse, mercilessly ridiculing the vices of the whites and denouncing the slave traffic; he had this play performed by natives, and invited all the Indians in the district to witness its production. Literary misdemeanors of this type could not but weaken the respect of the savages for their white masters, so that the annoyance of the Portuguese can easily be understood.

Unfortunately, it was difficult to take any effective action against the machinations of the Jesuits to prevent the Indian hunts, for the practice was one which was tacitly tolerated, but was not quite sanctioned by law. The missionaries even began to interfere in the old-established custom of *encomiendas,* and did their best to make mischief. For a long time past, the government had granted to every well-to-do Spaniard who had rendered any kind of service to the colonies a number of Indians as *encomendados;* the possessors of these *encomiendas* were required to give their "protégés" instruction in the Christian faith, in return for which they had to perform a certain amount of forced labor. Hitherto, this system had worked to the entire satisfaction of the colonists; but it was the basis of the whole of the Indian slave-system.

It had been hoped that the missionaries, by their conversions, would provide new *encomendados,* and would thus substantially increase the number of available slaves, but these anticipations were balked by the fathers. A sentimental governor allowed himself to be persuaded by the Jesuits to issue a decree ordering that in future the Indian proselytes were not to be treated as private property, and, at a later date, by dint of their ceaseless agitations at the court of Madrid, the Jesuits even secured the issue of a royal order to the effect that the Indians were henceforth to be compelled to work "solely by the sword of the Divine word." In these circumstances, it was feared that the South American colonial possessions would be completely ruined.

Soon after this, the Jesuits were accused of making common cause with the Indians against the whites, of weakening the subservience of the savages to the royal officials by animadverting against the vices of the Europeans; the Jesuits, so their opponents asserted, were striving for nothing less than the establishment of an independent Indian kingdom under their own influence.

The Jesuits' Musical Kingdom

This suspicion of the slave-hunters and the owners of *encomendados* was to a certain extent well founded. The Jesuits, who had become familiar with the customs and inclinations of the colonists in the South American cities, had indeed come to the conclusion that the so-called "savages" of the primeval forests were much better fitted for the establishment of a religious state than were the white people. "For not only," wrote the fathers in their reports, "do the Spaniards make slaves of the Indians, but they also destroy them, inasmuch as they are addicted to many vices of which our simple children of nature know nothing."

The missionaries therefore began to cherish the idea of entirely segregating the Indians from the whites, thereby not only protecting them from tyranny, but also guarding them against the corruption of bad example; it frequently happened that the intercourse of the Indians with the Spaniards undid in a few short weeks what the missionaries had been successful in accomplishing after years of hard work.

Eventually, the Jesuits submitted their project to the king of Spain. They thought that, if the king would grant them the right of setting up an Indian state completely independent of the Spanish colonial officials, they on their part would promise complete recognition of the Spanish sovereignty together with the payment of an annual poll-tax to the court of Madrid.

For some time past, King Philip III had been in constant need of funds, so that the financial inducement offered by the wily fathers favorably influenced his decision. He therefore granted a patent conferring the desire powers on the Jesuits, and, at their express request, ordering that in future no white man with the exception of the governor should enter the Indian settlements administered by the missionaries, without the permission of the latter. This patent was confirmed by Philip IV, who, when he ascended the throne, inherited the financial embarrassments of his predecessor.

The Jesuits were not in a position to set to work in the forests and pampas of eastern South America, mainly on both banks of the river Uruguay, to establish that ideal state in which pure gospel principles should alone hold sway. From the outset, they rightly appreciated the fact that a real "Kingdom of Christ upon earth" could be founded only among savage Indians in the densest virgin forest, and subject to the complete exclusion of the European Christians.

The geographical conditions favored the scheme of the fathers. The Spanish settlers, who had at first been attracted by the search for silver to the south-eastern regions of South America, had settled at the mouths of the great rivers; the interior, except where accessible along the banks of the rivers, not having been opened up by them. But, as the Jesuits found on their explorations, the River Uruguay formed at one point of its course a huge cataract with dangerous rocks and rapids which prevented its navigation by European craft; above this impassable barrier, there stretched the territories inhabited by the Chiquito and Guarani tribes.

"Our missionaries," wrote the Tyrolese Father Sepp, who later visited the country after the establishment of the Jesuit state, "are all of the opinion that God made this waterfall and these rapids for the benefit of our poor Indians, for the Spaniards, impelled by their insatiable greed for wealth, have come thus far in their great ships, but no farther. Up to the present, they have not set foot in our dominions and have been unable to open relations or do business with our Indians."

The cautious fathers, however, relied neither upon nature nor upon the royal patent which had been granted to them; but in addition they did all in their power to prevent the intrusion of European civilization into the territory entrusted to their guardianship. Not only did they most strictly prohibit the natives from holding intercourse with the whites, but they also took the precaution of ensuring that the former learned neither the Spanish nor the Portuguese language. They even went so far as to urge their protégés to use force against any stranger who might venture to enter their territory without express permission.

When the first Jesuits explored the virgin forests of Paraguay along the river banks, any kind of missionary work seemed well-high impossible, for the Indians persisted in timidly fleeing from them. But the fathers noticed that, when they sang religious melodies in their canoes, the natives peered out of the bushes here and there to listen to them, and gave signs of extraordinary pleasure. This discovery supplied the missionaries with a method of enticing the Indians from their forest haunts. They took musical instruments on their voyages, and played and sang to the best of their ability.

"The Indians fell into the pleasant trap," writes Chateaubriand in his *Spirit of Christianity*. "They descended from their hills to the river banks in order the better to hear the enchanting notes, while many cast themselves into the water and swam after the boats. Bows and arrows fell unheeded from the hands of the savages, and their souls received the first impressions of a higher kind of existence and of the primitive delights of humanity."

The missionaries were now able to expound to the astonished Indians in the native tongue the meaning of what they had sung; the Jesuits aroused such interest that the savages invited then home to their forests and plains, there to sing to the old people and explain the meaning of what they sang.

The fathers thus penetrated into regions hitherto unexplored by any European, in which the Guaranis and Chiquitos dwelt in a state of unspoiled nature. There they found human beings who, according to the accounts given by the missionaries, were clad in deerskins. The girls and boys went naked, their long, uncombed hair hanging like manes to their shoulders. Their noses were pierced, and from them, by threads, hung bones or colored feathers, while their throats were similarly adorned. The women were ugly; their jet-black hair fell in coils over their sunburnt, wrinkled faces and down their backs.

These savages were of a childish, friendly nature, and the first missionaries who discovered them reported that they had seen "two hundred thousand Indians" who were "in every way fitted for the Kingdom of God."

The fathers, aware of the wonderful effect of music on the Indians, overcame any opposition they met with by striking up a solemn chant. But, more remarkable still, the Indians themselves tried to imitate the musical performances of the missionaries, and, under the guidance of the fathers, set to work with enthusiasm to learn to sing difficult chorales in several parts. The growth of the state that was about to be born owed its original impetus to this closer association through music; for the Indians, who had hitherto lived in scattered forest settlements developed an ever-increasing common consciousness due to their community singing.

The first families to concentrate in one locality were certain of the Guarani tribe to whose settlement the Jesuits gave the name of Loreto; shortly afterwards were founded the Christian Indian communities of San Ignacio, Itapua and Santa Ana, all situated on the middle reaches of the River Parana. From this nucleus of Indian villages arose the "reductions" of Paraguay, which soon comprised considerable portions of the present states of Argentina, Paraguay, Uruguay, Chili, Brazil and Bolivia. During the most prosperous period of this strange state, there were in all thirty-one such reductions, each of which had a population of between three and six thousand souls. The total population of the whole country amounted at that time to about 140,000.

Almost every function of everyday life was performed to the strains of music. As early as 5 A.M., the people were summoned by a fanfare of trumpets to church, where mass was celebrated with much singing, intoning of responses and instrumental music, for the missionaries held that "nothing was so conducive to inculcating in the Indians a reverence for God and love of his worship, or to make the Christian doctrines more easily understood by them, as their accompaniment by music."

By nature, the Indians were very much averse to manual labor, but here again music came to the aid of the fathers in overcoming their laziness. As the men marched forth to work in the morning, they were headed by a band of instruments; they tilled the soil to a musical accompaniment, and in the same manner they felled trees and erected buildings; they ate their midday meal to music, and in the evenings they returned to their villages headed by a band.

The German protestant, M. Bach, who was employed by the Bolivian government in the forties of the last century, during which period he made a thorough study of what vestiges survived of the Jesuit republic, relates that even the Indian children had to visit the music school for a certain number of hours daily; constant practice, combined with a considerable amount of innate talent, had the result that "even in a chorus of thousands of voices a false note was never heard." Among these natives, it was regarded as the first duty of a citizen to be able to sing properly.

All the missionaries expressed the greatest admiration for the extraordinary musical talents of these people; they could not adequately express their surprise at the quickness with which mere boys among the Indians learned not only to sing, but also to acquit themselves in a most skillful manner in the handling of difficult European wind and string instruments it was chiefly the German fathers who gave instruction in music; they regularly conducted church

92. INDIANS OF THE JESUIT REPUBLIC OF PARAGUAY

Engraving of the period

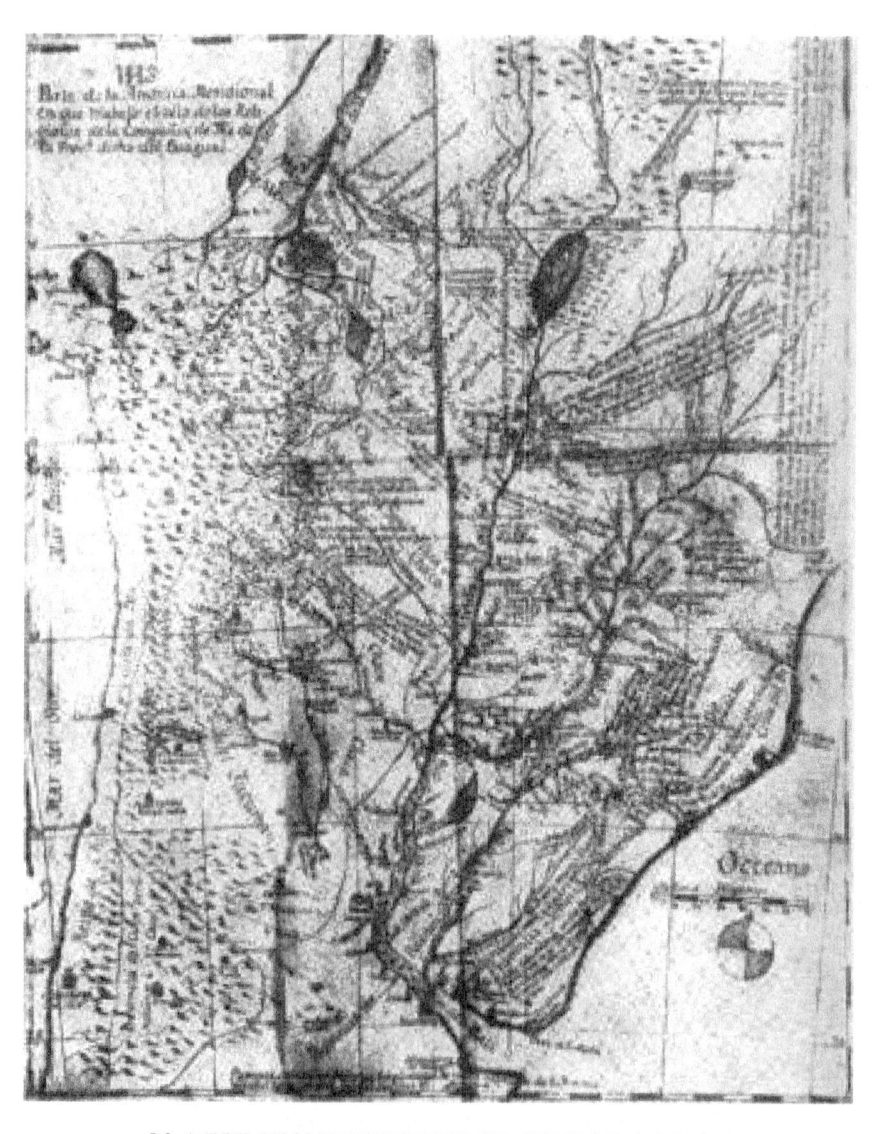

93. THE JESUIT REPUBLIC OF PARAGUAY

Map of the period

The Jesuits' Musical Kingdom

choirs and even full orchestras, which included "violins, contrabasses, clarinets, flutes, harps, trumpets, horns and tympani." Every village had, so the fathers recorded, at least "four trumpeters, three good lutanists, four organists, as well as reed-pipe players, bassoonists and singers." Their repertoire included, in addition to church music, marches and dances imported from Europe, and even selections from Italian operas.

"Among the simple Indians in the virgin forests of America," the missionary Francis of Zephyris commented on one occasion, "the fathers were unable to claim any success in the teaching of mathematics, because no one there understood or wished to possess such knowledge, but they acquitted themselves well with music. . . ."

Besides the musical instruction, the missionaries took great pains to provide all kinds of amusements for the recreation of the inhabitants of their Indian state, for they held that a joyous life was not detrimental to virtue, but rather tended "to make the latter better liked, and to encourage it." They therefore frequently arranged popular festivals with games, athletic contests and sham fights. Father Charlevoix records how the Jesuits had introduced into the settlements "the laudable custom of the Spaniards" of celebrating with dances the festivals of the Church, so that the Indians might find greater joy in Christianity.

"Sometimes they performed complicated dances," related the father; "sometimes they played the games of chivalry, either mounted or on foot; sometimes they gamboled on stilts six yard high; and sometimes they walked the tight-rope, or tilted at the ring with lances. On another occasion, I made them act short comedies, in which, after I had taken much trouble to get their parts into their dense heads, they gave a most excellent performance." These primitive theatricals pleased the Indians so greatly that, many decades after the expulsion of the Jesuits, they still performed the plays which they had been taught by the fathers.

The Tyrolese missionary Sepp gives a graphic description of a great festival which was held on his arrival in Paraguay. "We landed at sunrise, and were greeted from the bank by the Indians with the joyous cry of "Yopean! Yopean!" They all hastened from their huts, some half naked, some clad in garments of skin; one mounted his black horse, another his grey; one seized his bow and arrows, another his sling and stones, and one and all ran, as only they could, to the river bank. . . .

"There now appeared in the middle of the stream two splendid craft, like armed galleys, filled with drummers, reed-pipe players, trumpeters and musketeers. The bands played, the trumpets sounded and the guns were fired, and a sham fight took place between the two vessels. The Indians leapt into the river and fought, partly below and partly above water, a pleasant sight to behold. Finally, they all swam round our boat, greeting us joyfully.

"On the bank stood the father superior with two troops of cavalry and courted with Spanish equipment. They were armed with sabres, muskets, bows and arrows, slings and cudgels; they staged a very fine sham fight. While this was in progress, four standard-bearers waved their flags, four trumpeters rallied the people, the cornets, bassoons and reed-pipes sounded the alarm, while we gradually appeared from our verdant leaf-covered huts, embraced and, to the sound of joyous pealing of bells, entered the church under green triumphal arches, accompanied by some thousands of Indians. . . ."

Particularly impressive was the way in which Corpus Christi Day was celebrated, many of the inventions of the missionaries recalling the festivities of the Chinese imperial court. Living birds of all hues were tied to triumphal arches of flowers and branches. Here and there were placed "chained lions and tigers," as well as basins of water containing wonderful fishes. These arrangements were intended to convey the impression that all nature's creatures were taking part in the homage rendered to the Blessed Sacrament.

During the Easter procession were carried life-size figures, manufactured by the Indians, portraying various episodes of the Passion. In order further to intensify the impression made on the natives, the fathers also made use of statues of the saints with movable limbs and eyes, and strewed the ground with herbs and flowers, which were then sprinkled with perfumed water.

A Benevolent Dictatorship

As time went on, the fathers discovered that their protégés possessed a surprising aptitude for making exact copies of European models. If a crucifix, a candlestick or some similar object were shown to an Indian with the request that he should reproduce it, he immediately made a copy which was hardly distinguishable from the original. The women could reproduce very closely the most costly Brabant lace, while a number of Indian workpeople even constructed a remarkable organ based upon a European model. They engraved metal figures and made copies of missals in such a way that no one could tell which was the printed and which the written copy. The trumpets made by the Indians were fully equal to the products of the Nuremberg instrument-makers, and their watches were in no way inferior to those made in the most famous Augsburg workshops.

Work of this nature gave great pleasure to the Indians, who set to work willingly and with the greatest zeal when articles were required for their festivals and the adornment of their churches, or in connection with their musical instruction. By the skilful and unobtrusive manner in which they encouraged such occupations under the guise of recreations, the fathers overcame the innate inertia of the Indians; there thus arose among the virgin forests of Paraguay a regular industrial system.

Eventually, there were to be found in all parts of the country joiners, smiths, weavers, tailors, shoemakers, tanners, turners, pewterers, watchmakers, sculptors, painters, bell-founders and instrument-makers; the workshops were generally situated close to the mission house. "in the courtyard stood the sugar-mill," writes M. Bach, "while in the rooms surrounding the courtyard were to be found those who were employed in sugar-boiling, the blacksmiths, the silversmiths, the carpenters, the joiners, the turners, the wax-bleachers, the dyers, and the weavers with between forty and fifty looms. . ."

In addition, each reduction specialized in one particular trade; thus statues and carving were made in Loreto, the best instrument-makers were to be found in San Juan Bautista, while other settlements made a speciality of leather work.

At a certain age, the children were sent by the fathers into the workshops, where they were allowed to choose the trade for which they had a special preference. The missionaries thus sought to ensure that "the vocation was determined by natural aptitude."

With the same skill and mildness with which the Jesuits made use of the good qualities of the savages in the service of civilization did they strive to overcome their weaknesses and deficiencies. They soon recognized that, while the Indians possessed great aptitude for music and for work requiring manual dexterity, and learned to read and write fairly readily, they could by no possible means be taught to reckon; the majority of them had no head for figures. With much effort, and by making use of their fingers and toes, they were able to count up to twenty, but any number above that they could only describe as "many."

This defect also rendered them totally incapable of any kind of "domestic economy" or of "taking thought for the future," and as, moreover, they were possessed of an insatiable appetite, it was all the more difficult to persuade them to make a reasonable distribution of their foodstuffs. In the early days, if the fathers gave the head of a household a cow which would provide three days' food for himself and his family, the Indian would usually devour the animal in a single meal, and would then come back the next day complaining to the missionaries that he was tortured by hunger. More than once it even happened that the natives slaughtered and devoured in the open fields the oxen which had been given to them for their ploughing.

In these circumstances, it was quite out of the question to persuade them of the necessity of reserving from their harvest sufficient grain for the following year's sowing or of providing reserves against unforeseen calamities. The Jesuits were, therefore, forced to set up their own granaries, in which the crops were stored under lock and key, and from which each Indian daily received his exact ration.

Part of the land belonged to individual Indians, but most of it was the property of the community. On his own land, the so-called *abamba* or "man's field," each native could plant what he wished, but the cultivation of the communal "God's field" was carried out under the supervision of the fathers, and the crops were stored in the granaries. Privately owned land could not be sold, nor could the houses change hands. No form of property was hereditary, but all the children were brought up at the expense of the community, and, on attaining their majority, they were given *abambas*.

The crops produced on "God's fields" provided resources for the maintenance of the sick, aged and infirm, as well as the cost of building houses, churches and farm buildings and the amount of the taxes remitted annually to the Spanish crown. The missionaries themselves did not share in the distribution, and lived on a small stipend granted by the king.

The fathers not only saw that the foodstuffs stored in the granaries were systematically distributed, but also arranged for the clothing of the Indians. Widows and their daughters, who lived in special "widows' homes," regularly received quantities of cotton, which they were required to spin into yarn, and this was then converted into clothing material in the weaving shops. All the men and women received new garments once and the children twice a year, and thus the Indians in the Jesuit settlements were better, though more simply, dressed than the majority of the Spaniards in the adjacent territories.

This scrupulous apportionment of the products of the soil was accompanied by an equally careful distribution of the tasks required to be performed by the Indians. Every citizen of this state was alike required to perform some kind of work, but the fathers saw to it that no one was called upon to exert himself unduly, and that ample leisure was allowed to the Indians for recreation and education. By skilful management it was found possible to ensure the economic tillage of the soil with a general working day of eight hours. Three days in the week the Indians had to work on "God's fields," and they could spend the other days in tilling their own land, but he who neglected his private property was called upon to devote a greater part of his time to working on the communal lands.

Money was unnecessary in this country which depended solely on its natural resources. All business was carried on by barter. He who wished to buy an ox or a cow paid for it with so many yards of cloth; a knife purchased a horse, and a fish-hook a calf.

Even the foreign trade of the republic was not conducted by means of money. The natural products and home-manufactured wares of the country, such as sugar, wax, honey, tobacco, hides, tamarinds, cotton goods, leather, turnery-wares, and the like, were exchanged for European products. The fathers were particularly successful in growing in a cultivated form the native plant *ilex paragwayensis*, which they raised as a kind of tea plant; the so-called "Paraguay tea," or *yerba mate*, for a long time constituted one of the most important exports of the settlements.

All goods intended for export were transported to Santa Fe or Buenos Ayres, where the Jesuits themselves supervised their exchange. Any surplus moneys which were realized were devoted to the carrying out of improvements or the erection of new industrial or agricultural plants.

At times, it was found necessary to invite Spanish merchants to the settlements, in order that they might inspect articles which were for sale or might show the goods which they themselves had for disposal. The Jesuits, however, took care that the Indians did not come into contact with these itinerant merchants.

"In certain villages, such as San Xavier, San Jose and Santo Corazon," writes M. Bach, "were built, away from the other houses, so-called *ramadas*, which were equipped with all the necessary furniture and in which the foreign merchants had to stay. Here they were given plenty to eat and drink and a good bed, with every possible comfort, everything being provided free of charge, but they were kept under supervision like prisoners. As soon as they arrived, armed guards were posted at all the approaches to the *ramada*, with strict orders not to speak to the visitors... the foreign merchant was allowed to stay three days at the *ramada*."

Not only were the Indians protected against monetary temptations by the fact that natural products constituted the only form of wealth, but those in charge of this unique state were also never in a position to accumulate riches. They had themselves persuaded the Spanish crown to issue a decree that the fathers should not have a share in the produce of the settlement, but that on the contrary, the Indians should receive the entire profit which accrued. The heads of each reduction were therefore required to submit periodically to their provincial detailed accounts of their income and expenditure.

Each reduction constituted a self-contained unit. Two fathers took charge of the settlement, serving as priests, doctors, teachers and overseers of the work to be carried out. The civil administration was delegated to a *Corregidor* elected by the community, several *regidores* and *alcaldes*, together with a communal council; all these officials were Indians, the Jesuits endeav-

A Benevolent Dictatorship

oring to encourage the greatest possible degree of autonomy. Under the guidance of the fathers, the natives administered justice, managed the food-stores and supervised the normal progress of work. In addition to these political organizations, there were regular trade guilds with native officials; thus the weavers, the smiths, the carpenters and other trades had their own *alcaldes*, the women elected a female overseer and in addition there was for the young people an *alcalde*, who looked after the children until they reached the age of seventeen.

Father Peramas gives the following account of the external appearance of one of these settlements: "The church always formed the center of the regular reductions; it was spacious, built of solid materials and usually extremely handsome. On one side of the church was the cemetery and on the other the collegiate buildings, including the school. Near the latter stood the village hall together with the granaries in which the goods of the community were stored, and the artisans' workshops. Near the cemetery was the widows' home, a part of which served as a hospital. In front of the church there was always a spacious square containing a statue, and around this square stood, usually arranged at right angles to one another, the one-storied dwellings of the Indians with their projecting roofs or galleries.

"An Indian parish police force was responsible for the preservation of law and order, performing its functions with the greatest possible leniency and indulgence. Should it be necessary to bring a transgressor to justice, he was first interrogated by the *Corregidor* in the absence of witnesses; should this course be fruitless, he became liable to penalties which might include whipping and imprisonment. In every settlement, the death penalty was totally abolished, and incorrigible malefactors could be punished only by banishment to distant reductions. Women could be punished by enforced confinement in the widows' home.

"From the constitutional point of view, Paraguay might best be described as a confederation, for the reductions were completely autonomous in regard to their domestic affairs, only such matters as foreign trade and military service being dealt with by the settlements as a corporate state. The relations with the kingdom of Spain were analogous to those of a modern dominion; Paraguay owed allegiance direct to the ruling monarch, and under the royal patent possessed complete autonomy, having its own courts of law and its own military organization. The settlements were only required to pay an annual tax, and, in case of war, to render military assistance only within the bounds of South America; in other respects, the Madrid government had no voice in the administration of affairs."

In this way the Jesuits, basing their scheme on an accurate study of the capabilities and weaknesses of their Indians, had been able to set up in Paraguay that communist state which, two centuries later, humanity still regards approvingly as an ideal to be aimed at. Everything that could ever be hoped for by a Utopian under a communist regime was here to be found translated into reality: the state ownership of natural products and of foodstuffs, the abolition of the monetary system which was the cause of so much unhappiness, the equality of all citizens of the state, the abolition of every form of material distress, provision for the need of the aged, infirm, widows and orphans, the liability of all citizens to perform some kind of work subject to an eight-hour day, the education of children at the expense of the state, and freedom on the part of all to choose their own vocation.

From the administrative point of view, moreover, the Indian state harmonized with the most modern democratic demands, for its citizens were not subject to the repressive measures of autocratic officials their freedom being restricted only where necessary in the public interest; the officials of this republic, elected as they were by popular suffrage, were merely selfless agents for the welfare of all.

Nevertheless, private ownership of property was not entirely abolished, and, side by side with communal property, there existed a system of individual ownership, although such wealth could not be acquired by the exploitation of others, nor could its growth constitute a danger to the community. This state of affairs had been brought about without any resort to force, indeed its introduction had been acclaimed by those concerned, and the national organization under which such a model mode of life existed continued to function for a century and a half.

In that it actually existed, and that without ever costing the lives of those who held differing ideas, the communist state of the Jesuits in Paraguay differed materially from the similar experiment of the present day, an experiment which, despite the sacrifice of innumerable lives, has so far remained a Utopia chiefly on paper.

The Armed Forces of the Jesuit Republic

Such a state, founded as it was on the theory that the Indians possessed rights as human beings, and established as it was amidst a colonial territory the chief industry of which was the slave trade, could not but be regarded as a bold challenge to its neighbors. Had not this independent state of Paraguay recently robbed the man-hunters of their valuable prey? To tolerate this would be tantamount to endangering the whole of European civilization in South America.

At first, efforts were made to negotiate with the Jesuits with a view to dividing certain of the settlements situated on the frontiers into *encomiendas*, but the master of Paraguay quoted the royal patents and talked of Gospel brotherhood, an argument which the colonial officials regarded as most irrelevant. Nevertheless, the royal patents could not be questioned, and therefore the whites had at first to leave the matter to the so-called "Mamelukes."

This word was used to designate a horde of *mestizos*, descendants of European bandits and convicts, who had intermarried with Indian women. In well-armed troops, the Mamelukes traversed the country around their settlements, robbing and plundering on all sides.

The colonial authorities now thought fit to draw the attention of the Mamelukes to the existence of the Indian settlements, and to suggest that they should make these the object of their future forays. The Mameluke troops therefore invaded Paraguay in rapidly increasing numbers, captured all the natives whom they could seize, and sold then in the ports. At the beginning of the eighteenth century, some 60,000 reduction Indians were thus dragged into slavery.

After exhausting every possible means of inducing the Governor of La Plata to intervene, the Jesuits decided to evacuate the regions exposed to the incursions of the Mamelukes, and they removed 12,000 of their Indians down the Parana through the thick forests, into a more remote and less exposed district.

But the Mamelukes soon began their incursions into this latter district, receiving a good

The Armed Forces of the Jesuit Republic

deal of encouragement from the Portuguese authorities. True, the Jesuits were able to secure the issue of a special papal brief, in which the Governor of Brazil was required, under penalty of excommunication, to put a stop to this state of affairs, but as the Mamelukes were acting in the interests of all the man-hunters and slave-dealers, the pope's words went, of course, unheeded.

In these circumstances, Father Montoya, who was at that time in charge of the threatened settlements, was forced to the conclusion that in this world even the Kingdom of Christ could not dispense with firearms, he therefore petitioned the king of Spain for authority to supply the Indians with European weapons. As he was able to convince the king that such a native army might be able to render useful service to the crown, his request was granted.

Only now did this extraordinary Republic of Paraguay, which had its beginnings in a kind of "Indian Choral Society," become a real state. The fathers immediately set up an efficient military system, armed the Indians throughout the country, and established cannon-foundries and small-arms factories. From this time onwards, each reduction had to maintain two companies of soldiers under the command of Indian *caciques*: officers and men wore uniforms of a Spanish pattern, and regularly held drills and maneuvers under the supervision of the fathers.

"Every Monday," a missionary wrote home at that period, "the local Corregidor holds a parade on the square and has the troops drilled. They are then divided into two sides which attack each other, sometimes with so much ardor that it becomes necessary to sound the retreat lest an accident should occur. . . A troop of cavalry constantly patrols the neighborhood and reports on everything which it observes. The narrow passes giving access to the country are closely guarded. . .In case of emergency, we could at once raise a force of 30,000 mounted Indians who are well acquainted with the use of sabre and musket, who can form squadrons and carry out their maneuvers correctly. They are all paraded and drilled by the fathers."

This armed force soon had an opportunity of proving its military skill. When the fortress of San Sacramento was beleaguered during a quarrel with the Portuguese, the Republic of Paraguay, within eleven days, sent to the aid of the Spanish commander a corps of 3,300 cavalry and 200 sharpshooters with the necessary baggage train. During this campaign 600 Indians and a German father were killed by the enemy. King Philip V had therefore every justification for describing the Paraguay army as the "military bulwark of Spain."

Moreover, the Spaniards were soon afterwards to be afforded ample evidence of the excellence of the Indian army, when they themselves had to take the field against them and suffered reverse after reverse. This occurred on 1750, when the courts of Madrid and Lisbon decided to settle their continual disputes regarding their respective frontiers at the expense of the Paraguay settlements, Spain agreeing under a treaty to hand over to Portugal seven districts in the Indian territories.

The Portuguese authorities then demanded that these settlements should be evacuated by their Indian inhabitants, a proposal which met with great opposition from the latter. The Jesuits had recourse to diplomatic pressure, enabling them to secure a postponement of the official surrender of these territories to Portugal, during which period they were able to organize an armed resistance, and the Spanish and Portuguese officers who were appointed to settle the new boundary line had to retire on encountering considerable bodies of Indian troops, leaving their task unaccomplished.

The Portuguese General Gomez Freire d'Andrade, in a letter addressed at this juncture to the Spanish commander, the Marquis of Valdelirios, said: "Your Excellency will have satisfied himself from the letters and reports which you have received that the fathers of the Society are virtual rebels. If we do not remove these "holy fathers' from the villages, we shall meet with nothing but mutiny, sedition and contempt... All these facts, the mere report of which horrified us, can no longer be doubted now that we have had an opportunity of investigating the circumstances."

During the following year, Spanish and Portuguese forces proceeded to attack the Jesuit Republic. The Spaniards, however, had to withdraw to the banks of the La Plata, on encountering bodies of Indian troops of considerably greater numerical strength than themselves, while the Portuguese, who had advanced westwards from São Pedro do Rio Grande, were equally unsuccessful; the Indians, under the leadership of the fathers, continually harassed them and enticed then into ambushes, thereby compelling them to conclude an armistice.

It having become evident that separate action was impracticable, the Spanish joined forces with the Portuguese in a combined attack. They immediately found themselves faced by a regular system of fortified works defended by guns, from which the Indians could be evicted only after a desperate struggle costing many lives, after which the Indians withdrew to a new line of defense in the mountains, the capture of which so exhausted the troops that a further advance had to be deferred for some weeks. It was not until six months after the commencement of hostilities that the European troops entered the first Indian settlement, which had been abandoned by its inhabitants and put to flames. One after the other, the seven districts to be surrendered to Portugal had to be conquered, during which process an entire Spanish cavalry brigade was attacked and captured by the Indians.

Only by bringing up a fresh army as reinforcements was the Portuguese general finally able to cope with the situation; the Jesuits withdrew their troops to the eastern bank of the Uruguay, where the expeditionary force now found itself confronted by an Indian army 14,000 strong.

In the meantime, the Republic had also had to fight for its life in the north, for in that direction also a Spanish-Portuguese frontier agreement had been concluded at its expense. As the Jesuits did not possess sufficient troops to offer armed resistance simultaneously on two fronts, they organized a complete strike and an extensive boycott movement in the north.

The Boundary Commission wishing to leave the Rio Negro, the Indian workpeople in Para, the capital of the province, went on strike in order to prevent the departure of the commissioners. Boatmen could not be found to row their crafts, and when eventually they were forcibly recruited, it was learned that, under the orders of the Jesuits, the Indians had deserted their villages in all parts of the province, taking all their foodstuffs with them.

In a letter from the Bishop of Para to the court of Lisbon, it is stated that "the missionaries went so far in disobedience as explicitly to forbid the natives in all the villages on the banks of the Tapajos to plant breadfruit trees. Acting under their instructions, the Indians refused to sell anything to the white people..."

In the meantime, the fathers also endeavored to make the Portuguese troops harmless by undermining their discipline. The governor general reported at the time that "Father Aleixo Antonio tried to get on friendly terms with certain officers, and, under the virtuous pretext of instructing then in the *Exercises* of Saint Ignatius, persuaded them to remain in the college. . . he and his fellow-fathers did their best to convince the officers that I had left the city without orders from his Majesty, and that I had of my own initiative led the army into these forests where they were doomed to perish of starvation. All this, they stated, I had done to gratify my own whim."

It soon afterwards happened that Portuguese troops deserted to the Jesuits, taking with them their ammunition and rations. But the fury of the higher command reached its climax when, during a further advance, the troops found themselves confronted by a Jesuit defensive work armed with guns and held by the Indians under the leadership of two fathers. This fortress was so skilfully constructed that the Portuguese suspected that the two fathers were really not priests at all, but disguised engineer officers.

A Forest Utopia

But soon after this period, better times were to dawn for the South American slave-dealers, for now, after the unexpected difficulties over the boundary settlement, their complaints against the accursed fathers who for a century and a half had ruined their business were to find willing listeners. Even the authorities in Madrid and Lisbon allowed themselves to be convinced that the "human rights of the Indians" constituted a grave danger to the whole colonial policy.

The most serious accusations were made against the Jesuits; it was alleged that the taxes levied by the Jesuits bore no proportion to the enormous trade income of the country. It was further stated that the fathers had arbitrarily concluded formal treaties with the neighboring Indian tribes, that they had gone so far as to order their subjects to refuse obedience to the Spanish and Portuguese authorities. And even that in Paraguay there was a Jesuit king called Nicholas, who had issued golden coins bearing his own image.

If all this was not sufficient to induce the authorities in Europe to adopt energetic measures, the enemies of the Jesuits were able to bring forward another argument which could not fail to produce the desired effect. It was now alleged that the fathers had discovered gold mines in Paraguay, whose existence they had kept strictly secret.

An Indian even came to the Governor of Buenos Ayres with a map of the country showing these gold mines, on which the fortifications constructed by the Jesuits for the defense of this treasure were also clearly marked. The governor immediately set out to investigate the natter on the spot, but, though he failed to discover the least trace of the gold mines, no one from that time onwards had any doubt regarding the existence there of untold wealth. This firm conviction had an effect which would not have been produced so rapidly in any other way; all concerned with the Spanish colonial possessions, from the prime minister down to the least junior official, were inspired by the one passionate idea of obtaining possession of this gold.

The general enmity which had meanwhile grown up against the Society of Jesus in the

The Power and Secret of the Jesuits

European courts, in the convents, boudoirs and professors' studies, naturally strengthened the decision to overthrow the Jesuit Republic. In 1759, the order was banished from Portugal, and in 1767 the same thing happened in Spain, and the Spanish premier, Aranda, took the necessary steps to put an end to Jesuit rule in Paraguay.

A number of commissioners were dispatched to the settlements, and these officials ransacked every college and every drawer, in search of the mythical wealth of the Jesuits, but in this they were bitterly disappointed.

"Their first concern," Father Florian Baucke reports regarding his experiences at the hands of these commissioners, "was to take possession of my few belongings. Even the most unimportant item of furniture was recorded, the length and width of the table, and the wood of which it was made. After searching every coffer and box, they asked where the money was. I told them that we had none, since we always obtained everything we needed by barter. . ."

"When the Jesuits in Santa Fe were thrown into prison," also writes Alexander von Humboldt, "no trace was found on them of the piles of piasters, the emeralds of Muzo, the gold ingots of Choco, which the enemies of the Society had alleged they possessed. The erroneous conclusion was arrived at that these treasures had really existed, but had been entrusted to faithful Indians, and concealed in the cataracts of the Orinoco until the order should be restored at some future date." Disappointed of their booty, the Spaniards and Portuguese treated the imprisoned fathers with every brutality, at first keeping them in close confinement like malefactors, and then transporting them to Europe between decks in their men-of-war.

The churches, schools and workshops of the Jesuits were either demolished or allowed to fall into ruins. As to the fate of the library established by the Jesuits in Paraguay, a Protestant author writes as follows: "this magnificent collection suffered the same fate as the famous Alexandrian library. It was not an Omar, nor the savages of the Gran Chaco who destroyed them, but Christians, spiritual descendants of that Theodosius who ordered the destruction of the Alexandrian library. They used most of the Jesuits' books for making cartridges, for baking biscuits, or for lantern lights, and I had a similar experience to that of the historian Orosius, who found in Alexandria only the empty bookcases of the library which was formerly there."

Secular officials were appointed to take charge of the settlements which had been deprived of their masters, and they made it their first business to seize for their own benefit the church ornaments, the foodstuffs in the granaries, and the cattle. But, as they could no longer sing and make music in the settlements, many of the Indians escaped from their new rulers by fleeing to and wandering aimlessly in the dense forests which the fathers had formerly induced them to leave.

In theory, the system of common ownership of property remained in force in the depopulated settlements, and it was not until 1848, that the Paraguayan dictator, Lopez, issued a decree finally abolishing the communist form of government among the Indians. As from that date, the inhabitants of the former Jesuit state became citizens of the Paraguayan Republic, and their storehouses and property were sequestrated by the state.

"When we consider," writes Joseph de Maistre, "that this order, inspired by the doctrines of the Christian church, founded its rulership in Paraguay solely on the influence of its virtues and of its talents, that the Jesuits taught the savages of South America to appreciate the magic

94. THE CASTLE OF SAN AUGUSTINDE ARECUTAGUA IN PARAGUA

From a contemporary report

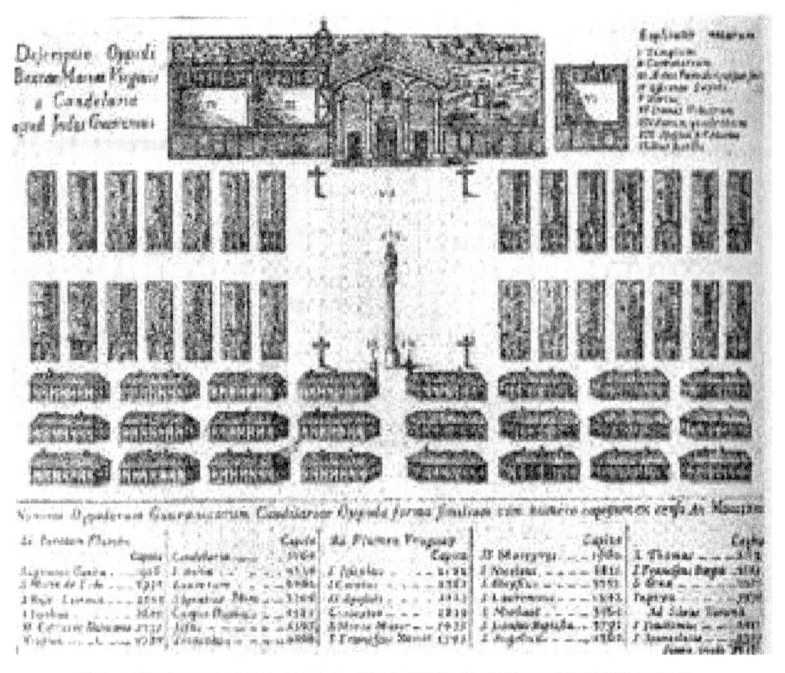

95. THE PLAN OF A JESUIT REDUCTION IN PARAGUAY

96. RUINS OF THE MISSION CHURCH OF SAN MIGUEL

influence of music, when finally we remember that it was only through the co-operation of corrupt ministries and of courts of justice which had been seized by madness that it became possible to overthrow this magnificent Society, then only can we visualize in our imagination that madman who rejoicingly tramples a clock beneath his feet, crying the while; 'I will stop your noise!'"

Again, Montesquieu remarks in his *esprit des lois*: "The Society of Jesus may pride itself on the fact that it was the first to prove to the world that religion and humanity are compatible." Even the "Encyclopædists," those bitter enemies of the Jesuit order, were forced to admit that, in that unique state in the primeval forests of Brazil, a high moral project had almost been carried into effect. "By means of religion," remarks d'Alembert, "the Jesuits established a monarchical authority in Paraguay, founded solely on their powers of persuasion and on their lenient methods of government. Masters of the country, they rendered happy the people under their sway; they succeeded in subduing them without ever having recourse to force." Finally, Voltaire describes the Jesuits' missions as "a triumph of humanity."

It is true that, from the early days of the eighteenth century up to our own time, there have been those who have sought to depreciate the value of what was done in Paraguay, and to cast doubt on the fathers' integrity. They simply could not admit that such an ideal state really existed, still less that it should have been the work of the hated Jesuits.

Those critics who, as the result of investigations, were compelled to admit the reality of the Indian state of Paraguay and of its institutions denied that the Jesuits possessed any originality, and sought to prove that what they had established was founded on certain political novels written in the sixteenth century. It is true that, if we compare the Jesuit Republic with the Island of Utopia which was invented by the English Lord Chancellor, More, we find remarkable coincidences: like Paraguay, Utopia consists of a number of cities planned on the same lines, each of them forming the center of an agricultural district of a prescribed size. The inhabitants are not the owners but the tenants of the land, which belongs to the community. Each citizen had to perform a certain amount of agricultural work and is further allocated a trade to follow. The men carry on weaving, mason's and potter's work, woodwork and metalwork, while the women are chiefly engaged in spinning.

We find equally surprising resemblances between the institutions in the Jesuit settlements and those in the "City of the Sun" which was imaginatively described by the Dominican monk, Campenella. This "City of the Sun" is a republic ruled by a priest, its whole social life being based on pure communism and on the administration of productive wealth by the state. All property is held in common, and every citizen is required to work, the lighter forms of labor being allotted to the women. Among the arts, music is specially cultivated, and when the "Solarians" make thank-offerings to their God, these take the form of music.

It would, however, be equally easy to find similar parallels in every other communist Utopia, but it has ever been the case that all these visions of ideal state with no class distinctions have sprung from the world-old day-dream, common to the whole of civilized humanity, of Paradise Lost.

This reflection brings us nearer to an understanding of how it came to pass that the Jesuits were able to set up their Utopia in Paraguay. Far from having modelled their state on any preconceived theories, the fathers rather made the primitive innocence of their Indians the basis of the whole of the economic and political organization of their settlements.

When a group of learned dreamers attempted to bring about the establishment of Communism in the twentieth century, they were at once faced by an infinitely difficult task. For, no matter how backward the Russians may be, compared with the remainder of Europe, they are nevertheless Europeans in this, that they differ from one another in innumerable ways according to the nature of their talents and vices, of their desires and passions; they had long since lost that holy simplicity, that absence of individuality, that lack of material needs, which in Paraguay facilitated the establishment of a classless and ideal state.

For this reason, despite immeasurable bloodshed, Bolshevism has so far fallen far short of its aims, but the Jesuits in Paraguay had merely to adapt their rules to the desires and needs of their uncivilized forest Indians, and, under their guidance, the "ideal Communist state" came into being entirely of its own motion.

PART VI

THE END AND THE MEANS

The Struggle with the English Police Agents

For weeks past Queen Elizabeth's spies had examined, from deck to hold, every boat that put into Dover, in search of the dangerous Jesuit priests of whose arrival confidential reports had been received. Commissioned by the pope, these paid emissaries of Rome were to create unrest among the English people, and to stir up conspiracies against the queen and the established Church.

Ship followed ship into Dover, however, without the slightest trace of the expected Jesuits, until eventually a captain who had crossed from Calais was able to give what seemed to be reliable information concerning them. Two Jesuits of the names of Robert Parsons and Edmund Campion, so he alleged, were making their final preparations to cross to England on the next boat. The captain described in full detail the appearance of the dress of both priests and for hour on end kept the police agents on tiptoes listening to his account of the treasonable aims of these Papist emissaries.

Before the captain left them in order to proceed to London, he mentioned that in a few days' time an Irish merchant of the name of Patrick would arrive in Dover; he requested the harbor-master to endorse the papers of this man Patrick with as little delay as possible, as he had important business to transact with him in London.

When, shortly after, the Irish merchant in question did, in fact, arrive, accompanied by a servant, and reported to the authorities, the harbor-master was only too ready to pass in the friend of the worthy captain who had supplied such valuable information regarding the infamous Jesuits.

Some few days later, however, the master received a sharp reprimand from his superior officer: how did he account for the fact that the two Jesuits, Parsons and Campion, had arrived in England in spite of all the precautionary measures that had been taken? Their presence in London had been established beyond all doubt. It was only then that the unhappy police at Dover realized that the distinguished ship's captain who had instructed them at such length concerning the Jesuits was none other than Father Parsons, whilst the second Jesuit, Campion, had slipped in in the guise of the Irish merchant Patrick.

A feverish search for the Papist priests was started throughout London, especially as secret advices had reached the authorities that the fathers had held a meeting of Catholics, and exhorted those present to remain stanch to the Roman church and to resist the commands of the queen.

A clever spy ascertained that the traitors for whom search was being made were staying at the house of the Catholic, Gilbert. They were living there in a small, isolated attic at the top of the house, and opened their window cautiously only at nighttime. If they went out in order to visit their fellow-conspirators, they did so between the hours of two and four in the morning, when no one else in the neighborhood was awake.

Gilbert's house was surrounded and thoroughly searched, and the whole household closely interrogated, but no trace of the fathers was found. They had changed their quarters. By the time the whereabouts of their new retreat had been betrayed, it was at once apparent that the fugitives had changed their quarters again. In the end, it almost seemed as if the Jesuits spent every night under a different roof.

Finally, the authorities compiled a list of all the houses in London that were occupied by Catholics and might serve as places of concealment for the Jesuits. Hardly had the list been completed, however, when the news was received that the fathers had left London some considerable time previously, that they had appeared in Oxford, and had distributed among the students there an inflammatory libel against the established Church.

After prolonged investigations, the police agents succeeded in ascertaining that this pamphlet had been printed by the Jesuits on a secret printing press at Stonors Park near Henley; when arrangements had been made to confiscate it, it had already disappeared, and the pamphlets were now being distributed from an outlying county. When search was made for the Jesuits in that particular county, the residents declared that they had indeed been there, had preached and heard confession, but had already disappeared on their way to another county, leaving no clues behind them. On only one occasion did the government agents fall aright on a Catholic country house, merely to see in the distance Father Campion galloping off on horseback.

"We shall not long be able to escape the hands of the heretics," wrote Campion at that time from his hiding-place to Rome; "so many eyes are centered on us, so many enemies beset us. I am constantly disguised, and am continually changing both my dress and my name."

Finally, the police did actually succeed in seizing Father Campion at the moment when he was in the act of celebrating mass before a small Catholic community. With his hands tied behind his back, his feet bound by a rope passing under the belly of his horse, on his hat a notice which read "Edmund Campion, the rebellious Jesuit," he was brought to London, and conducted through an avenue of gaping onlookers to the Tower. After vain efforts had been made to induce him by torture on the rack to disclose the names of his accomplices, he was condemned to death for high treason, hanged and quartered.

Thus, at least, was the "Irish merchant," who had for so long fooled the queen's officers, prevented for all time from doing any further mischief; but of what avail was this, when reports were now coming in from all parts of England of new activities of the Jesuits? On all sides, papist priests appeared in every conceivable disguise, and incited the people against the government, declaring the established Church to be the offspring of Satan; they then administered the sacrament to the Catholics, after which they disappeared completely again.

The Struggle with the English Police Agents

Such news was received from many parts, and it seemed as if the whole of England were suddenly overrun by Jesuits. It was some time before the government agents discovered that they had to deal, not with many hundreds, but with a handful of opponents. Although long lists had been prepared of all the known names and personal descriptions of the Jesuits active in England, it became apparent that ten or twenty of such named belonged to one and the same priest, that ten or twenty of such descriptions represented merely the various disguises of a single priest.

One among this evil group at last fell into the hands of the law, one for some years. His real name was Thomas Holland, but even among his closest associates he was known under the name of Saunderson, and this Father Holland-Saunderson assumed various identities, appearing now as a clean-shaven young man, now as an old man with a flowing beard, now as a servant, now as a wealthy merchant, and now as a haughty nobleman. It was not without justification that the police agent into whose hands he at last fell boasted that, in the person of this one man, he had arrested at a single stroke a dozen treasonable conspirators.

An Englishman by birth, Holland-Saunderson was clever enough to be able at will to invest his native tongue with a French, Flemish or Spanish accent, and in addition to speak French, Flemish and Spanish so perfectly that everybody took him to be a foreigner. He had often appeared disguised among his friends, who had time and again believed themselves to be in the presence of a foreigner. After his arrest, quite a collection of false beards, wigs and apparel appropriate to every station and walk of life was discovered among his effects.

After every arrest, the police could indeed strike out a number of names from the list of agitators for whom they were searching; but they immediately had to add a like number of others. However many false beards, wigs and disguises they succeeded in confiscating, there were always more than enough beards, wigs and disguises available to the Jesuits to enable them to continue their activities.

Where, however, was the center of all these treasonable practices? The English police authorities diligently sought out these secret headquarters of the Jesuits, and the informer who could assist them in the discovery was sure of a rich reward.

Such an informer appeared, and directed the attention of the police agents to Hindlip Hall near Worcester, the seat of the Abingtons, a distinguished Catholic family. The castle, which the police proceeded to raid, was a strong building. Square in shape and surrounded by a solid wall. Its gates were burst open, but those who broke in were immediately lost in a maze of winding passages and staircases which had obviously been designed to make it difficult for strangers to find their way about. When, therefore, the police agents, after very considerable trouble, had searched all the apartments of the castle, they had to confess that the extensive building was unoccupied and deserted. Finally, they departed discomfited.

Not long afterwards, a stanch Anglican nobleman rode in from the neighborhood of Hindlip, and reported to the authorities that, shortly after the withdrawal of the police agents, the castle had again been occupied, and that not only the Abington family but a number of strange papists had been seen passing in and out.

It was not until a considerable time later that, under the inducement of a large reward, a servant employed at the castle was found who was prepared to afford the police the solution of the mystery. To their amazement, the queen's agents learned that the paneled walls of the large hall of the castle concealed any number of spacious hiding-places, that all the rooms were connected by secret staircases and trap-doors with the cellars, and that even the fireplaces contained, alongside the flues, small chambers into which a person could crawl.

In the meantime, however, the Jesuits had scattered to houses of the most varied types; whenever the authorities learnt of this or that address, the most exhaustive search of the building produced no results. It was as if each of these houses had become another Hindlip Hall, in which the hard-pressed conspirators could, on the approach of the police, disappear into the strangest of hiding-places. They contained sliding panels, revolving pictures, trap-doors and false ceilings so ingenious in their construction and arrangement that the police agents, in spite of all they had already learnt regarding such things, were continually deceived.

It became of the utmost importance that the demon who devised these hiding-places should be traced and his activities cut short. As the result of denunciations made by numerous informers, the authorities were at fist led to the assumption that a number of such trap-door constructors were at work; one, they believed, was called Oven, another Draper, a third Andrews, a fourth Walton, and a fifth "Little John"; later, however, it became evident that, in actual fact, there was only one, Father Oven, who proceeded from one place to another under five different names. Of him it was said by his fellow-priest, Gerard, that none other among the Jesuits had rendered such valuable service to the Catholic cause in England, "since, through his skill and ingenuity in devising places of concealment, he had saved the lives of hundreds of people."

The police agents had by this time been sufficiently taught by experience to take builders' craftsmen with them when raiding suspected dwellings. Father Aylworth gives the following account of his experiences during such a raid: "they began by assailing the walls with hammer and pickaxe, probed into every corner and left no stone unturned. Not only were the walls demolished, but also the floors and even the outhouses and stables were not spared; they thrust their swords into the stacks of corn and other heaps of grain and dug into the unpaved parts of the garden and yard with iron staves.

"I had, however, in the meantime crept under a table standing in the middle of the room, the cloth on which hung evenly, and thus diminished if it did not entirely divert any suspicion that there could be anyone hidden under it. There I crouched as well as I was able, my feet drawn up, my head bowed down, and my whole body huddled up. In this painful position, I had to remain for a full seven hours, until, by the grace of God, the police agents left the house, and I was able to creep out from under the table."

Father Aylworth showed no less presence of mind when later he left London in a coach, in order to escape from the increasingly imminent danger of capture. Among his fellow-travelers was an Anglican priest, who kept on staring at the Jesuit father with suspicion. "Then, by God's special providence, it happened that four Jews, who were to travel with us in the same vehicle, entered the inn in which we were stopping at the moment. The moment I noticed them, I thrust myself into their company, addressed them in Spanish, greeted them and embraced them as if we had been the oldest and best of friends. Our worthy preacher called me to him, and said in a scornful voice: 'All along I had thought you were one of them!' Under other circumstances, I should have given the man a plain answer, but I confirmed his

97. KING JAMES I OF ENGLAND

98. THE JESUIT THEOLOGIAN EDUCATOR OF PHILIP III OF SPAIN

| 18 | *An Apologie for* |

on the iust, yet moderate punishment of a part of these hainous Offenders; shall easily see that ~~gracious Prince~~ as free from persecution, as they shall free these hellish Instruments from the Honor of Martyrdome.

5. But now hauing sacrificed (if I may so say) to the *Manes* of ~~my defunct Soueraigne, as well for the discharge of my particular duetie, as for loue of Veritie, I must next performe my duetie to his Maiestie present, in testifying likewise the truth of his Actions in this matter. Wherein I must for the loue of Veritie confesse~~, That whatsoeuer was her iust and mercifull Gouernement ouer the Papists in her Time, ~~his Maiesties~~ Gouernement ouer them since hath so farre exceeded hers, in Mercie and Clemencie, as not onely the Papists themselues grewe to that height of Pride, in confidence of ~~his~~ mildenesse, as they did directly expect, and assuredly promise to themselues libertie of Conscience & Equalitie with vs in all things; But euen ~~we~~, I must truely confesse, ~~his Maiesties~~ best and faithfullest Subiects, were cast in great feare and amazement of ~~his Maie--~~

99. THE CONTROVERSIAL WORK OF JAMES I AGAINST THE POPE —Page with corrections in the king's own hand.

conjecture, and pledge him in a glass of wine."

The most important and difficult task had been assumed by the Jesuit Prescott: in spite of the most rigid regulations and counter-measures, he continually devised new ways of smuggling the sons of English Catholics out of the country to the Continent, where they were trained as priests in the colleges especially established for this purpose at Rome, Madrid, Seville, Lisbon, Douai, Rheims and St. Omer. In this way, the Jesuits ensured that there would be an uninterrupted succession of English clerics who returned to their native country and kept alive the opposition of the Catholic populace to the Anglican regime. In sheer despair, an English police chief declared at that time: "You may hang Jesuits until you are tired; there are always others to take their places!"

The Theologian on the Royal Throne

For almost half a century, this bitter struggle had been proceeding between the agents of the English government and the Jesuits, since, even as early as the forties of the sixteenth century, when Henry VIII had just broken away from Rome, and established an English national church, the Jesuit fathers had actively striven to influence political affairs in England. At that time, the two disciples of Ignatius, Brouet and Salmeron, had, as agents of the pope, appeared in Ireland, and had endeavored, although without success, to stir up the Catholics there to revolt against the king. Since then, the Jesuits had never abandoned their attempts to keep alive and to foster enthusiasm for the Catholic cause in England.

This dour struggle between the English police agents and their Jesuit opponents was, however, the reflection of a much more momentous conflict affecting the history of the world. In spite of all that Rome did to prevent it, what Dante had once prophetically anticipated was now proceeding towards fulfilment: humanity was divided against itself, the "seamless mantle of God was rent asunder"; in place of the undivided Catholic faith which had prevailed until that time, embracing all the peoples of Europe, a national consciousness had appeared which rebelled against submission to the hegemony of the papacy, and more and more imparted to the religious consciousness of the several peoples its national character.

To all outward appearances, it might certainly have seemed as if England's break with Rome was attributable merely to the whim of an amorous sovereign; not the least among the considerations which had prompted Henry VIII, to whom the pope had refused to grant a divorce, to establish a Church of his own was the fact that he would then be able to marry Anne Boleyn without papal sanction.

That this step met with such strong approval in wide circles in the country and that parliament immediately gave the king its unanimous support was, however, made possible by the fact that the breakaway from Rome satisfied a strong desire in the English national spirit for release from every form of foreign tutelage.

Thus it came about that the English Church lived on even after the death of Henry VIII, and, in fact, did not become fully established until then. The period of the Counter-Reformation under Queen Mary, Henry VIII's daughter by his wife Catherine of Aragon, to whom he had been married in accordance with the laws of the Catholic Church, represented only a temporary interruption of this development. Queen Elizabeth, the daughter of Henry's irregular marriage with Anne Boleyn, who, according to Catholic views, could never be regarded as a lawful heiress to the throne, soon displayed considerable energy in establishing on secure foundations the national Church founded by her father. Indulgence in Catholic worship was henceforward subject to severe penalties, and every priest and servant of the state had to swear an "oath of supremacy," in which he acknowledged the queen as the highest authority in spiritual and temporal matters.

In Rome, however, all hope of a restoration of the mediæval unity of the Christian peoples under the supreme authority of the pope had not yet been abandoned; the opinion prevailed that all that was necessary to induce England to abandon forever her efforts to secure independence was to overthrow the Tudors, and replace them by a Catholic dynasty.

Accordingly the Papal See directed its energies primarily against the Tudors, and upon the Jesuits devolved the task of inciting the English people against them, so as to pave the way for the accession of the Catholic Stuarts to the throne. When, however, after the death of Elizabeth, the Stuarts did in fact, ascend the English throne, it became plain that the papal See had formed a wrong conception of the real causes of England's breakaway. Even Rome was forced to realize that an historic evolution was taking place that was far too powerful too be influenced at all permanently by the will of this or that sovereign. The Stuarts, too, were forced to yield to the increasingly intense movement for independence among the English people, and, as the result, their religious policy soon showed little variation from that of their predecessors.

James I, the son of Mary Stuart, had promised, before ascending the throne, to show favor to the Catholics; his successor, Charles I, had definitely pledged himself to support the Catholic cause, and Charles II had even secured the material assistance of France by declaring his intention of bringing England back to Catholicism. One after another, James I, Charles I and Charles II found themselves compelled, almost as soon as they had ascended the throne, under pressure from the Anglicans and Puritans, to take energetic measures against Rome and to persecute the Catholics with the utmost rigor.

The Jesuits again, who, under Elizabeth, had been most active in support of the Stuarts, were compelled, once the Stuarts were on the throne, to renew their struggle against the sovereign and his police agents. They forbade the Catholics to take the oath of allegiance to the king; they forbade them to participate in Anglican forms of worship; they declined to allow them to conform in any way with the demands of their sovereign upon his subjects. In the year 1605, the discovery was made of a plot laid by certain distinguished Catholics, who had hidden casks of gunpowder in the cellars of the Houses of Parliament with the object of blowing up the king and the government. It immediately became known that the Jesuits Greenway and Garnet had been associated with the conspirators, and that Catesby, the ringleader, had confessed his plan to them.

Only on a single occasion during this struggle did an English sovereign depart from the practice, observed since the reign of Henry VIII, of asserting his supremacy in matters of faith by legislative repression and the executioner's axe; only once did the Jesuits depart from their conspiratorial method, involving as it did the use of false beards and trap-doors, which they

The Theologian on the Royal Throne

had employed since Henry VIII's time in the cause of the spiritual ascendancy of the pope.

King James I, "Europe's most learned fool," as the duke of Sully had called him, was impelled to take the somewhat unusual course for a sovereign of asserting his supreme authority not only by police decrees but also by argument; in a learned work, he sought to demonstrate that the highest authority in spiritual as well as in temporal matters had been delegated by God to the reigning sovereign.

Scarcely had James published his work when the Jesuits picked up their pens and composed works intended to refute the arguments of the philosopher-king. The latter had sent a copy of his treatise to all European sovereigns, and the Holy Father feared that the arguments of James, to the effect that the power of the sovereign was, by divine dispensation, subject to no limitation, might impress many a Catholic ruler.

Accordingly, the pope instructed his "light cavalry" to attack and confound the heretic king with all the available weapons of theological controversy. It was, then, with the same ingenuity with such they had resorted to every form of political machination against the English crown that, meeting the need of the moment, they succeeded in evolving a convincing system of theological philosophy.

The works of the Jesuit controversialists Suarez and Bellarmine directed against the English king, James, were intended to be read by the same crowned heads as the king had honored with his book. This circumstance, therefore, necessitated the adoption of a tactful and discreet tone, so that the insistence on the papal supremacy over temporal princes should not be unduly distasteful to the latter. For this reason, then, the argument, once advanced by Pope Gregory VII, that worldly power had its origin in robbery, murder and tyranny, could no longer be used; the supremacy of the papal over imperial authority had rather to be established and demonstrated by more subtle and less direct reasoning.

Accordingly, the investigations of Suarez and Bellarmine were primarily concerned with a strictly theoretical consideration of the origin of bodies politic. After Suarez had endeavored to show that a natural impulse to combine into communities is innate in man, he led up from this, in the manner of the mediæval authorities, to the conception of an authority vested only in the public as a whole, a *potestas publica*. This authority rests with the people as a whole; it cannot be exercised by an individual alone. Wherever, then, an individual is possessed of this public power, he can have acquired it only by reason of the fact that it has been voluntarily delegated to him by the whole people.

On the other hand, Suarez advanced the argument, based on the Bible, of the purely divine origin of the Church; Christ himself, he contended, founded the true, perfect community of the Church, and designated the pope as the successor of St. Peter. From this fact, that the authority of pope proceeded directly from God, whilst worldly rulers exercised their power only as instruments of the people, it followed that the pope was supreme over all who held political power.

This brought the question to the stage at which earlier theologians would have straightway applied the "two swords theory" which the mediæval Church defended so stubbornly. The Jesuits, however, appreciated to the full the altered times and circumstances; they accordingly carefully refrained from advancing any longer the extreme theory that God has bestowed on the pope the "two swords," the highest authority in temporal as well as spiritual matters, and that the pope had passed on the sword of temporal power to the crowned heads entirely of his own free will. The principle of the subjection of all worldly princes to the pope that was the logical outcome of such a theory could, as the Jesuits knew full well, no longer be insisted upon at the beginning of the seventeenth century, even where "the most Christian kings" were concerned.

But Thomas Aquinas had already propounded a theory which was much less likely to give offence, and of which the Jesuits could now avail themselves. Temporal power, the "angelic doctor" had held, was subordinated to spiritual power only in those matters affecting the welfare of the soul, whilst in matters of material welfare obedience was due to temporal authority rather than to spiritual authority.

In accordance with this view, Bellarmine now declared, in his reply to King James, that spiritual authority was directed towards the welfare of the soul, whilst temporal power was concerned only with the welfare of the body. As long as temporal power was not used to imperil the spiritual welfare of others, but was confined to the regulation of secular matters, the pope could not claim to influence the rule of the sovereign; on the other hand, the Church was entitled, and, in fact, bound, to intervene in temporal administration, if spiritual interests, which were of much greater importance, were at stake.

Thus Suarez and Bellarmine had devised a formula in the age-old struggle between Crown and Church which was more adapted to the changed circumstances of the times in the matter of material power, and which, nevertheless, reserved to the popes all those prerogatives which alone could enable him to sustain a struggle with heretical monarchs.

All this philosophizing, however, proved itself eventually to be nothing more than a futile pastime. The Jesuits could the more readily afford to indulge in it since they possessed the necessary organization and each had his allotted task; whilst some were engaged at Coimbra and Rome in composing polemical works, others in England were continuing to elude the snares of the police agents. King James was soon, however, forced to the conclusion that it was more useful to sign death-warrants and arrest-warrants than to busy himself with theoretical treatises. To execute his opponents was, without question, a more effective demonstration of the power of the temporal ruler than any argument of theological philosophy, however conclusive it might be. Accordingly, James I henceforward adopted the same policy as his predecessors had done, and as his successors maintained until the close of the seventeenth century. The Jesuits were persecuted, hunted down, arrested, sentenced and hanged.

The "Sovereignty of the People" and Tyrannicide

In France, the struggle with the Jesuits, which, in England, was waged through police agents and informers, was carried on by supreme court advocates and university professors. This arose from the fact that, as far back as the fourteenth century, King Philip IV of France had achieved what the English sovereigns were only now, in the sixteenth century, trying to do. Under Philip, Pope Clement V had been compelled to recognize the full independence of

The "Sovereignty of the People" and Tyrannicide

the French national Church and to exclude France expressly from the scope of his bull *Unam sanctam*, by which he proclaimed the subordination of worldly power to spiritual power. In the year 1407, the national synod in Paris had asserted the independence of the "Gallican Church," and, without definitely breaking with Rome, deprived the pope of all direct authority over the disposing of ecclesiastical offices and revenues in France. From that time onwards, whole generations of learned men had elaborated in all details the constitutions of the Gallican church, and secured them by judicial decisions in the Parlements and by professorial declarations.

The defense of these liberties was the responsibility of the Parlements, the highest legal courts of the realm; they had the right of scrutinizing all papal decrees from the point of view of ensuring that they were not inconsistent with the privileges of the Gallican Church, and, if they were, of refusing to recognize them. It was the function of the university to furnish the Parlements with the requisite expert theological advice in all matters of dispute.

The learned advocates and professors of Paris soon, however, showed themselves to be the fiercest opponents of the Jesuits, and, in repressing them, displayed more bitterness, tireless energy and persistence than all the spies and informers in England put together. No matter what the Jesuits were minded to do in France, the defenders of Gallicanism immediately opposed it. Every word, every action of the Jesuit fathers immediately evoked, as in ancient tragedy, a threatening chorus of hostile advocates and professors, pronouncing, as with one voice, the tragic fate that would one day befall the Jesuit order in France.

King Henry II had, with his characteristic unconcern about the consequences of his actions, in the year 1551 granted the Jesuits permission to settle in France. When the order set about securing the necessary registration of the royal patent by the Parlement of Paris, in accordance with constitutional law, the chorus of members made itself heard again, declaring that the Society, "which, by some strange fancy, presumes to adopt the name of Jesus," was robbing the temporal and spiritual authorities of their rights, was promoting "unrest, discontent, dissensions, disunion, and a host of other evils." "All things considered," declared the Parlement of that day, "the society appears to be calculated to jeopardize the Faith, to disturb the peace of the Church, and to destroy far more than it will ever build up.

When the Jesuits then endeavored to secure for their schools certain academic liberties and privileges, Étienne Pasquier, the leading spirit of the university professors, rose up and declared that, in his view, the system of order constituted "a grave danger to the peace and security of the state"; the Jesuits, he declared, were designing "to sow the seeds of disorder in France," and Ignatius Loyola was no better than Luther, since he also aimed at "undermining respect for established authority, at weakening the discipline of the Church, and bringing about general confusion in the affairs of God and man.

That it was primarily considerations of a national character that promoted the hostility to the Jesuits on the part of the responsible bodies in France is clearly shown by the remark of the advocate-general, du Mesnil, when, in the year 1565, he declared that the Jesuits were bound by solemn oath to carry out the orders of a general living in Rome; they were accordingly subject at all times to the authority of a foreigner, and this constituted a serious danger to law and order in the state.

The Jesuit fathers did not, of course, experience any difficulty in showing that this unfavorable attitude of the Parlement and the Sorbonne was prompted by petty motives of envy, covetousness and wounded pride. The very considerable privileges which the pope had granted to the Jesuits excited the ill-will of other ecclesiastics, and the achievements of the Society in pedagogic matters aroused the envy and hostility of the university professors. Nevertheless, the Jesuits made the same mistake as they did in England, in imagining that the hostility against which they had to fight was nothing more than the ebullition of personal bigotry; in reality, beneath the self-conceit of the French advocates, professors and priests, just as behind the desire for power of the English monarchs, there lay the historic power of a growing national consciousness. It was, in effect, the national consciousness of the French people which prompted the parliamentary advocates, the professors of the Sorbonne and the Gallican clergy to be so violent in their condemnation of the "Romanists."

The Jesuits certainly had an easier task with the rulers of France than with those of England. The woman on the French throne with whom, after the death of Henry II, the Jesuits had to deal was, at the bottom of her heart, a good Catholic, and, moreover, as a true representative of her sex, was easily influenced and readily disposed to allow herself to be won over by astute tactics on the part of the Jesuits.

Catherine de' Medici, who governed in the name of the new king, a minor, might well have vacillated between the Huguenot and Catholic parties; but an earnest and forceful discourse by the Jesuit general, Laynez, at the ecclesiastical colloquy at Poissy, so far influenced the queen-regent as to cause her to lean more and more towards the Catholics.

"Make no concessions to heresy," Laynez had declared, addressing himself to the queen-regent, "but rather uphold the Catholic faith with all your authority! Then will God, mindful of your piety, preserve to you your earthly kingdom and admit you to the kingdom of Heaven. If, God, then tremble lest, together with the heavenly kingdom, you lose also your earthly kingdom."

At the Council of Trent, Laynez expressed himself still more clearly regarding the fate that awaited an heretical ruler. Sovereign power, he declared in one of his celebrated discourses, was originally vested in the people, and had been voluntarily delegated by them to the monarch; if the sovereign failed to govern in accordance with the wished of his subjects, then they were free to reassert their prerogatives and depose the sovereign. This applies, he declared, more particularly in the case where the ruler of a Catholic country falls away from the faith which alone can procure salvation, and so brings about the eternal damnation of all his subjects.

Though a theoretical discussion of the doctrine of the sovereignty of the people had sufficed to induce the impressionable Catherine de' Medici to turn away from the heretics, such bald theories and unctuous exhortations had little effect on Henry III; it needed an actual revolution to bring home to this monarch the rights of the people.

Henry III was a man of strange passions. He wore large gold earrings, surrounded himself with a group of effeminately bedizened young people whom he called his *mignons*, and entrusted to them the greater part of the most important affairs of state. Indifferent to religious matters, he did not scruple to resist the increasing influence of the Catholic nobility by allying himself with the Huguenot party. It was then, however, that the warning which Laynez had once uttered to the king's mother was fulfilled. The Catholic nation rose up against its

100. THE "LEAGUE": PRCESSION OF ARMED CROWDS UNDER THE LEADERSHIP OF PRIESTS

101. THE ASSASSINATIN OF HENRY III BY THE MONK CLÉMENT

102. EXECUTION OF THE JESUIT GUIGNARD FOR GLORIFYING THE REGICIDE CLÉMENT

The "Sovereignty of the People" and Tyrannicide

heretically inclined ruler, and united to form the revolutionary *Ligue*, while from every pulpit the people were exhorted to armed rebellion the agitators using as their principal argument the doctrine once propounded by Laynez, of the "sovereignty of the people."

Thus the Jesuits had furnished the ideological justification for the French revolution of the sixteenth century; they were not found lacking either when it came to securing recognition of the demands of the Catholic people by force of arms. In order to overthrow the *Ligue*, King Henry had by now openly allied himself with his cousin, Henry of Navarre, the leader of the Huguenots, and now the Jesuits placed themselves at the head of the remaining clergy and of the Catholic population; they demanded the deposition of the traitorous king, and did not rest until he had been driven from Paris by an armed uprising. When Henry thereupon joined forces with his Huguenot cousin and besieged the capital, which was in open rebellion, it was the Jesuit fathers who were most active in keeping up the spirits of the hungry Parisians, in urging them to hold out, and in everywhere organizing the military defense of the town.

The act of an assassin gave a new turn to the embittered struggle: Jacques Clément, a young Dominican monk who was carried away by the revolutionary fanaticism of the "leaguers," and had decided to rid the country of the "heretic king," stole into his camp and stabbed Henry III to death.

Even after Henry of Navarre, the murdered king's cousin, had mounted the throne of France, the Jesuits by no means ceased their attacks on the Crown. Notwithstanding that the new king had deemed "Paris worth a mass," and had gone over to Catholicism, and notwithstanding that the Parlement, the university and the Gallican priesthood had sworn allegiance to him, the Jesuits persisted in their refusal to acknowledge Henry IV, since he had been excommunicated by the pope as a heretic, and, accordingly, in their view, had forfeited his title to the throne.

Two attempts on the life of Henry IV occurred in quick succession. A soldier of the name of Barrière was arrested before he was able to strike his blow, while a nineteen-year-old youth of the name of Castel succeeded in approaching the king and wounding him with a dagger.

The Parlement and the University of Paris had by no means a clear conscience so far as these plots were concerned, for, before Henry of Navarre's victory was definitely assured, these two bodies, in alliance with the League, had called down death and destruction on the head of the "heretic." The newly published work of Jesuit Mariana, however, afforded the Parlement the opportunity of clearing itself, and throwing upon the hated Jesuit fathers the sole responsibility for the attempts on Henry's life.

Mariana, who had been active at the court of Madrid as tutor to the future King Philip III, had written for the edification of his pupil a tract entitles *De rege et regis institutione*, upholding the theory Laynez had expounded, to the effect that the power of the sovereign was delegated to him by the people, and that the sovereign was accordingly responsible to the people of ensuring a just rule. He went still further, however, by advancing the view that if, instead of ruling justly, the sovereign rules despotically and abuses his power by oppressing his subjects, then the people are justified in ridding themselves of their despotic ruler, even by violence if need be. The proper procedure in such cases was for the people assembled in solemn conclave to deprive the ruler of the prerogatives vested in him, and to pronounce formal judgment of death on the tyrant; if, however, by reason of external circumstances, it was not possible to adopt this procedure, then, in certain circumstances, every individual citizen was justified in giving effect to the will of the people as a whole, and in removing the tyrant by violence.

In this connection, Mariana had referred to Clément, the murderer of Henry III, and, regarding his crime, had written that it would perhaps have the salutary effect "of bringing home to the minds of rulers that it is not only a just but a praiseworthy and meritorious action to slay them, if they oppress the community, and, by reason of their vices and malpractices, become intolerable." Regarding Clément himself, Mariana declared: "The majority of people look upon him as having done honor to France. . ."

This book furnished the advocates and professors of Paris with the desired pretext for representing the Jesuits as being primarily responsible for the murder of Henry III and for the two attempts on Henry IV. Furthermore, there was the fact that the would-be regicide, Castel, had studied for a considerable period in a Jesuit college. This was sufficient for the Parlement to order the arrest of the two Jesuit fathers, Guéret and Guignard, who had been Chastels' former teachers. In the possession of Guignard were found a few early pamphlets of the time of the League, and forthwith the father was pronounced guilty of high treason, sentenced to death and hanged.

The loyal zeal of the Parlement, which had so suddenly become a stanch supporter of the sovereign, was carried so far that it was not content merely with the cruel execution of Chastel, but even ordered his house to be razed to the ground. On the spot where it had stood, a pillory was erected, on the base of which was inscribed the judgment pronounced on Chastel, and a number of aspersions on the Jesuits. Mariana's book was publicly burnt by the hangman, and the Parlement was at last able to realize its long-cherished desire, and order the expulsion of the Jesuits from Paris.

Expelled as heretics, rebels, and inciters to murder, the Jesuit fathers found themselves forced to depart from the French capital amid scorn and ignominy.

Comedy of the Disguises

Wherever in Europe the interests of Rome required that the populace should be stirred up against the king or that any measures of a temporal ruler which might be inconvenient to the Church had to be countered by intrigue, propaganda and, if the occasions called for it, open rebellion, the Papal See knew full well that, for carrying out such work, there were none more reliable, more resourceful and more courageous than the fathers of the Society of Jesus. Furthermore, when the aims of the pope had to be furthered by discreet and tactful discussions with vacillating sovereigns, and force of eloquence was needed to prevail upon a Catholic ruler to suppress heresy, the Jesuits again proved themselves the cleverest and most successful workers for the cause of Rome. Notwithstanding the fact that the Papal See had at its disposal an army of learned legates and cardinals, there were one among them so competent as the Jesuits to convince a Catholic people of its rights with regard to an heretical ruler, or, con-

Comedy of the Disguises

versely, a Catholic ruler of his rights over an heretical people.

The kingdom of Sweden seemed, up to the middle of the sixteenth century, to be lost to Catholicism, the people having almost unanimously adopted Lutheranism. It was then that a faithful daughter of the Roman Church set herself out to accomplish what all the papal legates had hitherto failed to achieve. The Polish Princess Catherine Jagiellonika had wedded the Swedish King John III, and soon contrived to shake the faith of her husband in Protestantism, so that he lent a ready ear when Catherine told him of the mysteries of the only true Church.

In the year 1574, King John, under the influence of his wife, declared his readiness to enter into negotiations with the Papal See with a view to the re-entry of Sweden into the Catholic Church. As, however, the people were strongly inclined to Protestantism at heart, and at that time would have resisted with the utmost energy every open attempt to introduce Catholicism, King John suggested that the pope should send agents who should in no circumstances disclose the fact that they were Catholics.

Thereupon, the clever Polish Jesuit, Stanislaus Warsewicz, set out for Stockholm in the guise of an elegant courier. So well did he give the appearance of being just an ordinary man of the world that no one suspected him of being an emissary of the pope, with the result that he was able to initiate his discussions with the king without exciting the slightest suspicion. Two months later, John III had been so far won over that he declared his readiness to introduce the Catholic liturgy into the Swedish Church.

Then, one day, there suddenly appeared in Stockholm a Protestant professor of theology of the name of Lorenz Nicholai, who began to deliver himself of the most striking sermons and lectures on the teachings of Luther. The king made the learned theologian a professor at the newly founded seminary in Stockholm, and strongly urged all Protestant priests and prospective priests to attend his course of lectures. He himself, together with his whole household, attended the professor's lectures, and followed his remarks with the closest attention.

After Nicolai had dealt, one after another, with all the principles of the Lutheran doctrine in such a way as to excite general admiration for his skill, he suddenly adopted a critical tone, and began to state the objections that might be levelled against this or that protestant conception. As lecture succeeded lecture, more and more attention was devoted to these criticisms, which became more and more convincing. So that many among the audience no longer knew what to think; eventually it almost seemed as if Protestantism was a thoroughly misguided faith, whilst the true faith was only to be found in the teachings of the Catholic Church.

Finally, this remarkable professor of theology quoted a number of extracts from Luther's works which he used as the basis of a powerful attack on the whole structure of the Protestant faith. Thereupon, King John himself jumped up from his seat in annoyance and began an argument with Nicolai, during the course of which he fervidly defended Protestantism and attacked the pope violently. The counter-arguments of the professor, however, sounded much more authoritative, unimpeachable and convincing, so that the king was at last forced to admit himself beaten.

The public acclaimed Nicolai, and entirely failed to appreciate the fact that the doctrines which the king had endeavored to defend were those of the Protestant faith of Sweden, whilst the professor had propounded none other than the infamous principles of "Popery."

This Stockholm argument was throughout a masterpiece of Jesuit stage management, for the ostensible Protestant Nicolai was in reality a Jesuit, and his argument with the king a carefully prearranged deception. John III and Nicolai had previously discussed with one another every point and every turn of the discussion, and they had in common accord taken care to ensure that the arguments to be used by the king in support of the Protestant cause should be ineffective and crude, whilst Nicolai's attack on Protestantism was to be off such a nature as to convince every hearer. By means of this theatrical staging of a theological discussion, the belief of the congregation that Protestantism was the only true faith was to be shaken, and the way prepared for the reintroduction of the Catholic religion.

It did, in fact, happen that the students of theology flocked to the celebrated Professor Nicolai who had defeated their king in open debate, and it was not long before he was able to send a number of newly converted students to the German College of the Society of Jesus at Rome. This completed the task of Nicolai, for the conversion of Sweden had entered on a new stage, and required to be carried on by another worker.

The man selected for this purpose by the papal See was the Jesuit Father Antonio Possevino, the greatest diplomatist of the order, and, in fact, one of the cleverest negotiators of the seventeenth century. Clad as a nobleman, with his dagger at his waist and his two-cornered hat under his arm, Possevino made his appearance in Stockholm. At the court and to all the authorities, he gave himself out to be an ambassador of the German emperor, and no one but the king knew that he was a member of the Society of Jesus.

His task was, with all due tact, to remove the last obstacles that stood in the way of securing Sweden's conversion to the Roman Church. King John had already advised the pope of his readiness, in principle to adopt the Catholic faith, but had laid down certain conditions of a liturgical nature; unless the rule regarding celibacy were relaxed, unless the administration of the sacrament in both forms were sanctioned, and unless divine worship were allowed to be celebrated in the national tongue, Sweden could not, in the view of the king, be won over to Catholicism. The task now delegated by the pope to Possevino was so to arrange it that King John should be won over to the Catholic Church without the Papal See's being compelled to comply with this conditions, for in no circumstances would Rome have been prepared to grant such wide concessions.

The Jesuit diplomat did not fail to utilize every available means of influencing John. On one occasion, he handed to him a letter from Philip II of Spain, in which the latter congratulated the Swedish king in the most fulsome terms on his adoption of the Catholic faith, and, to assist him in the financial expenses arising out of the country's change of faith, offered him a sum of 200,000 sequins from the national exchequer; on another occasion, Possevino delivered himself of a flaming discourse on the tortures of eternal damnation which awaited every heretic.

Notwithstanding, John was slow in deciding in favor of the official introduction into Sweden of the Roman Church, as he was afraid that such a step would cost him his crown. Possevino did his utmost to convince the king that, by divine right, he was entitled to exercise a free determination of the religion of his subjects; under the promptings of the Jesuit, King

Comedy of the Disguises

John had a Catholic chapel constructed in his palace, in which he regularly heard mass, confessed, and took communion; furthermore, John frequently declared to the Jesuit emissary that the regarded himself as a faithful servant of the Catholic Church.

Possevino would certainly have succeeded eventually in overcoming the last scruples of the king, and so have deprived Protestantism in Europe of its strongest pillar, if this mighty undertaking, originally initiated by a women, had not been wrecked by another woman.

Catherine Jagiellonika, the worthy spouse of King John III, had brought her husband into the Roman Church, had paved the way for the conversion of Sweden to Catholicism and finally had given birth to an heir, who had straightway been placed under the charge of Jesuit tutors; having accomplished all this, she faced the call to heaven with an easy conscience. After her death, however, the Protestant Gunnila Bilke became the wife of the widowed king, and, as a good follower of Luther, did not even wait until the honeymoon was over before proceeding to discharge her religious duties. For at that time, in view of the fact that zealous Catholic princesses secured for their religion great political successes, the Protestant princesses were likewise organized and called upon to take an active part in furthering the interests of their faith.

King John III, like many other sovereigns of both earlier and later times, was easily influenced when in the intimacy of the royal bedchamber, and so it happened that within a short while Gunnila Bilke had undone all that Catherine Jagiellonika had done for the cause of Rome. The clever, worldly-wise Father Warsewicz found himself compelled to retire hastily from Sweden closely pressed by the agents of the new queen, and even the great Professor Nicolai was forced to seek another country in which to continue his Lutheran exegesis, for true and stanch Protestants had by now resumed their teachings at the theological seminary at Stockholm. The "imperial ambassador," Father Possevino, however, whom further important tasks awaited at other courts, adjusted his dagger, placed his two-cornered hat under his arm, and disappeared as suddenly as he had once appeared.

Only in one respect did the former Catholic queen, Catherine, appear to prevail from beyond the grave over her successor; she had given an heir to the country, and had ensured that he, the heir to both the Swedish and Polish thrones, later brought up by the Jesuits and in time married to an Austrian princess, should never forsake the Roman Church.

But the Protestants could afford to be equally satisfied with the work of Gunnila Bilke, for, even if the present queen could do nothing to alter the succession, she took care to ensure that the Lutheran spirit should predominate in Sweden, and that, as the result, her stepson should come up against insuperable difficulties if ever he attempted to convert the country to Catholicism.

Immediately after the death of King John, a meeting of the Riksdag was convoked, at which the nobles, the knights, the clergy, the provincial governors and the burgomasters drew up an anti-Papist declaration which the new king Sigismund was to be called upon to sign before his coronation.

Sigismund, who had in the meantime become King of Poland, refused to comply with this demand, and, at the head of a Polish army and accompanied by numerous Jesuits and a papal legate, arrived in Sweden with the intention of introducing the Catholic religion into the country by force of arms. The Swedes, however, offered resistance, defeated Sigismund's army, and crowned Duke Charles of Södermanland king. The federal states, at an assembly at Upsala, upheld the Augsburg Confession as the only national faith, abolished all "Papist" ritual which had been introduced into the Church during the time of Possevino, and removed from their office a number of the clergy who were suspected of leanings towards Catholicism.

In this way, all the Catholic hopes centered on Sweden were destroyed for a long period; indeed, this country was destined some few decades later to become, under Gustavus Adolphus, the strongest bulwark of Protestantism in its struggle with Rome. It was not until Gustavus Adolphus's daughter Christina came to the throne that the Jesuits once again found the opportunity of returning toe Stockholm and successfully carrying on their activities.

The Mediator of War and Peace

Before, during and after the negotiations with John III, Possevino had occasion to carry out a variety of diplomatic missions in other parts of the world on behalf of Rome. He enjoyed the confidence of the pope as well as of the Habsburg monarch, of the Archdukes of Graz and Vienna as well as of the Great Council of Venice. He was acquainted with the innermost aspirations of all the chancelleries of Europe; he was fully informed of the financial situation of every government; he knew the military strength of every country, and, accordingly, was able to pursue diplomacy in the grand style, and to excel his lay colleagues in such matters.

In the year 1580, he was entrusted with a political mission of supreme importance. A Russian emissary had arrived in Rome, bringing the pope a letter from Ivan the Terrible, in which the tsar, who was being hard pressed by the victorious troops of the Polish king, Stephen Báthory, entreated the pope to initiate peace negotiations, and, in return, offered to take part in a combined campaign of all Christian princes against the Sultan.

This appeared to offer Rome an opportunity of bringing nearer to realization a long-cherished plan, since, for centuries past, the papal See had persistently striven to deal a crushing blow to the Mohammedans, its traditional enemies, and to promote a new crusade against Islam. This great project had hitherto always failed to come to a head, because the Christian princes, instead of combining for a united attack on the Sultan, were constantly engaged in wars among themselves; the never-ending troubles between Russia and Poland, in particular, had always prevented the Russian Empire from being drawn into the great anti-Turkish coalition.

At last, Ivan the Terrible's request offered the Holy See the opportunity of bringing about peace between these two countries, and, at the same time, encouraged the pope of reuniting the Byzantine Church with that of Rome, since, if the pope succeeded in securing for the tsar a favorable peace, the Russian ruler might, out of gratitude, be prepared to grant religious concessions.

In view of the exceptional importance of this matter, Pope Gregory XIII decided to entrust the necessary negotiations at Vilna and Moscow to his most skilful and astute agent, the Jesuit Father Possevino. His journey to Russia was also to be utilized for the conclusion of other negotiations in connection with the projected campaign.

The Mediator of War and Peace

A war against the Turks could have no prospect of a successful issue unless the cooperation of the Republic of Venice, the greatest maritime power in the Mediterranean, were secured; for several years past, however, the Republic had been swept by remarkable waves of pacifism, which by no means pleased the diplomats in Rome. All the papal briefs calling upon the Venetians to fulfil their Christian duties and to share in the fight against the Moslems met with no response; the Republic for San Marco took the greatest pains to avoid any conflict with the Sultan, and refused to be inveigled into any form of alliance against the Turks.

When, then, Possevino made his appearance in Venice with the object of securing the participation of the Council of Ten in the projected grand coalition against Constantinople, he talked of practically nothing else but the potential commercial advantages which the Signoria would derive from an alliance with Russia. He contrived to paint a picture of the advantages that would result from the establishment of permanent business relations with Moscow, with so great a command of his subject and with such glowing colors, that the doge and the Council were filled with enthusiasm. The proposals of the Papal See suddenly appeared to them in quite a different light.

Having so far succeeded, Possevino proceeded to Graz, where he had a number of other commissions of lesser importance to execute. It was essential that the Archduke Charles of Styria should be spurred on to energetic measures against the Protestants of his land, and, with this object in view, Possevino presented a consecrated rose of gold to the archduke's wife, Maria, and promised the archduke the financial assistance of the pope. This was more than enough to revive the religious zeal of the archduchess and her husband. Then again, there was a matrimonial plan to be discussed in Graz: the Crown Prince Sigismund of Sweden was to wed a bride who should be a stanch Catholic, and to this end Rome had designated one of the daughters of the Archduke Charles. Both Charles and Maria readily allowed themselves to be convinced by Possevino of the advantages of this alliance, and gave their consent.

Having thus raised another pillar in the structure that was to support the Catholic world hegemony, Possevino proceeded to Vienna, where he was welcomed most heartily by the Archduke Ernest of Austria. The latter had been the candidate of Ivan the Terrible in the last election for the Polish throne, and accordingly was on the best of terms with Moscow. From him, Possevino obtained a letter of recommendation to the tsar.

Possevino was less fortunate in Prague, for the Emperor Rudolph II had, some little time before, again applied himself to the study of alchemy, and was accessible to no one, not even the highest princes of the realm or foreign ambassadors. But Possevino found a means of paving the way for future negotiations by forming a friendship with the emperor's equerry, to whom he communicated his proposals; it need only be added that, under Rudolph II, grooms of the chamber, furnace-feeders and equerries were the most influential personalities of the Hradčany. Possevino therefore left Prague with the calm assurance that his cause was in the best hands, and that the emperor, prompted by the equerry, would be sure to grant him an audience on the next occasion.

On arrival at Vilna, the headquarters of the king of Poland, he found Stephen Báthory and his general staff actively engaged in preparations for a new campaign against Russia. King Stephen's intention was to press the advance that had already begun against Polotsk and

The Power and Secret of the Jesuits

Smolensk, to invest these fortresses, and so to open up the way to Moscow. His eventual object was to dictate to the humiliated Ivan a peace under the terms of which Russia was to be definitely thrown back into Asia.

The moment was, therefore, by no means favorable tor Possevino's task of inducing the Polish king to conclude peace, and even to form an alliance with the Muscovites. Very little comfort was to be derived from the fact that the warlike Stephen Báthory was a true son of the Catholic Church, and, both in earlier times, when he was prince of Transylvania, and now, as King of Poland, had always shown considerable favor to the Society of Jesus. While, therefore, he might certainly be disposed to lend a respectful ear to the papal counsels and exhortations which Possevino had to deliver to him, there were, however, very serious obstacles standing in the way of the fulfilment of the plans cherished by the Papal See.

In the first place, the Voivode of Transylvania had had, on his election as King of Poland, to swear to the national Diet that he would recover from the Russians all those provinces which had been taken by violence from the Polish Empire; in an empire where the sovereign was elected by public vote, the elected ruler could not so easily ignore his sworn duties as elsewhere, and, accordingly, Báthory was bound to pursue the war against Russia until it was crowned with complete victory.

Furthermore, he was not in a position to enter so readily into a combination directed against the Turks, for not only did he, as Voivode of Transylvania, owe allegiance to the Sultan, but he also urgently needed the support of Turkey in his operations against Russia; it was for this reason that the Polish ambassador in Constantinople had already entered into tentative negotiations with the Sublime Porte for an alliance between the two counties.

Right at the outset of his conversations with Stephen Báthory, Possevino realized that the ruler was devoid of any feelings of an emotional character; it seemed, in fact, that he was susceptible to no romantic emotions whatsoever, and was influenced solely and simply by considerations of a material nature. When Possevino informed him that his Holiness had contemplated appointing him commander in-chief of the whole of the forces to be led against the infidels, the king did not show any sign of gratified pride at the honor, but quite unconcernedly proceeded to inquire about the strength of the forces to be sent against the Sultan, the number of galleys and transports that were available., and the extent to which the allied armies were equipped with artillery. Until he had exact particulars regarding all these matters, it would be impossible for him, he declared, to form any reliable conception of the prospects of the whole undertaking.

That the Polish king lacked any sense of the romantic was probably due to the fact that, among the other obligations he had taken on himself when ascending the throne, was that of marrying the fifty-four-year-old Princess Anne Jagiellonika, the last representative of the former royal house. It was this marriage that turned the king into a completely unemotional soldier, for thenceforward he devoted the whole of his energies, his self-sacrificing spirit and his skill only to politics, whereas other ruling princes were wont to apply some part at least of these personal qualities to their relations with the fair sex. King Stephen was, therefore, an exception to the general run of contemporary princes, and had developed into a ruler with a firm will and ideas of his own.

So far as Possevino was concerned, there was no personality, however strong, which he could not have succeeded in influencing in the direction he desired; there was no personal view which he could not contrive so to adapt that it was in harmony with those of Rome. This student of Loyola had a sufficiently profound knowledge of humanity to know intentions to be so firmly rooted that it is not possible to influence them in an entirely opposite direction. Like his fellow-priests in China, Possevino recognized immediately the weak points through which he could exert his influence on the headstrong and warlike king.

Along with this devotion to the art of war, Báthory still loved to indulge his penchant for intellectual speculation, a trait which had survived from the time when he was a student in Vienna. He was very fond of philosophizing regarding God and the world, of burying himself in the works of Aristotle, of meditating on the various doctrines of Catholic asceticism, and, above all, of discoursing in high-sounding Latin phraseology. But who among all the statesmen and generals in the camp to Vilna could have been more in this element with such discourses regarding God, Aristotle and Catholic asceticism than the learned Jesuit father?

In his external mode of living, too, Stephen Báthory showed his individuality. He hated everything in the nature of pomp and ceremony, wore simple and sometimes even patched clothing, ate, as his favorite dish, beef with cabbage, and preferred that those around him should dispense with all forms of court ceremonial; among his officers he liked those who were bold enough, when conversing with him, to take his arm and to stroll off with him.

No one at court, however, during the long years of war, had dressed himself of simply as Possevino; no one knew as well as he how to appreciate the virtues of beef and cabbage; no one could take the king's arm and stroll off with him with such a natural spontaneity as the pope's agent. It was not long before Stephen Báthory was on the best of terms with Possevino, whose sentiments and views harmonized so well with his own. Whenever the king and the Jesuit discussed with one another, using subtle Latin phraseology, it immediately became evident that they were of one and the same mind, and that Possevino merely gave exact expression to what was on the tip of the king's tongue.

In the furtherance of his tasks, the Jesuit father was greatly assisted by the fact that, at the outset, he had informed himself fully of the exact state of affairs in the Polish state, and also as regards the army and the national exchequer. However eloquently Báthory at first led forth regarding the certain prospects of victory for his army, the supreme qualities of the celebrated Polish cavalry, the bravery of the Hungarian infantry and his other military units, Possevino countered with the argument that the troops were thoroughly wearied by the long war, that they were inadequately equipped to sustain the forthcoming severe winter, and that the national finances were also exhausted.

All these things he commended with the upmost tact to the king's consideration, and, by very sound arguments, gradually succeeded in shaking the king's confidence in the ultimate victory of his army.

The outcome was that Báthory himself expressed the wish that peace negotiations should be instituted, and was extremely pleased when Possevino offered to proceed to Russian and to institute preliminary discussions of a non-binding nature.

Out of tactical considerations, and in order to preserve external appearances, Poland was to proceed for the time being with her military preparations for the new campaign; Possevino himself advised that this course, which both the king and the chancellor were about to propose, should be adopted. Whilst, then, the military preparations were being eagerly pressed forward, the papal legate was furnished with a guard of honor consisting of Polish cavalrymen, and set out accompanied by numerous interpreters and officials on his journey to the tsar.

A Jesuit at the Court of Ivan the Terrible

The ruler of all the Russians had his residence in a small fortress town named Staritsa on the Volga, and had already made the necessary arrangements for receiving the pope's emissary with impressive pomp.

Possevino was met outside the gates of the town by numerous gorgeously arrayed dignitaries, who presented him with a magnificent black horse as a gift from the tsar to his guest. Mounted on this horse, the Jesuit father rode into the fortress accompanied by the Russian court officials and escorted by a *sotnia* of troops in picturesque uniforms.

He had not long to wait before the master of ceremonies informed him that he would immediately "be permitted to gaze into the clear eye of the tsar." He was thereupon conducted to the palace, on the threshold of which he bowed his head to the ground as a token of respect. He now found himself before the all-powerful ruler of Russia, who, seated on his glistening throne of gold, arrayed in costly brocade ornamented with precious stones, his crown on his head and his scepter in his hand, resembled a rigid, awe-inspiring idol.

Whilst, however, the whole royal household stood with bowed heads humbly and anxiously waiting for the tsar to speak, Possevino, who had already met many powerful princes fact to face, was by no means disposed to allow himself to be overawed by Ivan the Terrible. He too, if the occasion required, knew how to command respect by the adoption of an impressive and proud bearing; accordingly, after making a profound ceremonial obeisance, he straightened himself up proudly, and said in a solemn voice: "Our most Holy Father, pope Gregory the Thirteenth, Lord Bishop of the All-Embracing church, the Vicar of Jesus Christ on earth, the successor of Saint Peter, ruler of many states and provinces, servant of servants of God, greets your majesty and extends to you his blessing!" This dignified pronouncement did not fail in its effect, for, at the first words uttered by Possevino, the tsar stood up and heard the remainder standing.

At a great feast which followed, the tsar, his foreign guests and the distinguished boyars of the empire were all assembled; during the two hours the feast lasted, Ivan showed the utmost cordiality towards the papal emissary and his companions. One after another, he called upon the various boyars by name, and ordered them to drink a toast to the guests; the dignitary who happened to be summoned had thereupon to take his place in the middle of the room, to bow down to the ground before the guests, and to empty a huge goblet of wine, a ceremony which was repeated some sixty times during the course of the meal. Ivan himself then rose, toasted Possevino, and delivered a very flattering speech regarding the pope and his legate.

This very promising welcome was followed by difficult days for Possevino, when it came to active negotiations with the tsar's officials concerning the terms upon which peace was to be concluded with Poland. At first, the slow and unsystematic methods of the Russian diplomats were intolerable to the Jesuit's, mentally disciplined, clear-minded and swift-thinking, and accustomed to independent action as they were. Whenever the discussions took an unforeseen turn, the Russians immediately arose and declared that they would have to obtain further instructions from the tsar. The proceedings were, thereupon, suspended for a number of hours, and, when the negotiating officials did at last return with yard-long and closely-written sheets of paper in their hands, they recommenced the proceedings by invoking the Holy Trinity and mechanically reciting all the titles of the tsar, only to conclude, after the most circumstantial discussions, by an inconclusive and evasive statement.

At first, Possevino was often on the verge of despair, until he came to realize that this method of long-drawn-out discussions was not only adapted to the Muscovite temperament, but also served a tactical purpose: the Russians clearly desired to gain time so as to obtain a fuller appreciation of their opponent, to familiarize themselves better with his personal characteristics, and, moreover, to weary him to such an extent that, in order to bring matters to a conclusion, he would at last be disposed to make wide concessions. As soon as Possevino realized this, he proceeded to adopt the same tactics; thenceforward he was the most patient of negotiators, and gave the appearance of being even less in a hurry than the Russians. He met their long-winded explanations with replies equally abounding in trivial detail, and, if the tsars diplomats recited on every occasion all the various titles of their master, the pope could likewise be qualified by a sufficiently lengthy series of distinguished titles, the enumeration of which provided an admirable means of wasting time.

Thus it came about that, after a month spent in fruitless negotiations regarding all sorts of trivial matters, the Russians themselves grew impatient and pressed for a speedy settlement. Within the space of a day, Possevino saw the greater part of his demands conceded, the tsar invested him with all the necessary powers, hastily ordered a sledge to be prepared for him, provided him with warm furs, stores of provisions and a cask of wine, and, in the presence of all the boyars, bade the heartiest of farewells to the papal emissary.

"Go to King Stephen," he said cordially, "give him our greetings and then, when peace had been concluded, come back to us. Your presence, out of regard for him who sent you and in consideration of your loyalty to us, will always be welcome."

It was not long before Possevino succeeded also in overcoming the last obstacles on the Polish side. The pious King Stephen could not do otherwise than agree with this Jesuit friend, when the latter pointed out to him that God had already sufficiently helped the Polish army on to victory, and, accordingly, it would be presumptuous on the part of the king not to be content with the successes already won. A certain degree of forbearance by no means implied weakness, but rather a laudable subservience to the will of God.

How wise this sounded at a time when the Polish troops had, in fact, suffered a number of reverses! Who could say whether God was not in the act of withdrawing his hand from Stephen's army? The chancellor Zamoyski, who had just been appointed commander-in-chief, nevertheless raised objections, fearing to be deprived of his laurels by a premature peace. Until the whole of Livonia had been secured, declared the chancellor, no thought of peace should be entertained, and, under the influence of Zamoyski, the king again wavered.

Possevino, who had learnt patience in his dealings with Ivan, waited calmly, and spent evening after evening with Báthory, discussing Aristotle with the keenest interest until the Polish troops were again defeated at Pechersk. "God has spoken!" he cried bluntly but impressively on hearing the news. "Since victory has deserted the Polish colors, the moment has come for the conclusion of an honorable peace!"

This time he won the day, and even Zamoyski had to give way. Ivan was advised that Poland was ready to negotiate, and forthwith the small village of Jam Zapolski on the road to Novgorod was chosen as the meeting-place of the peace delegates. Both parties immediately agreed that Possevino should take part in the peace conference as president and neutral arbitrator.

Thus was achieved one of the greatest triumphs of Jesuit diplomacy. Two powerful monarch had placed their fates confidently in the hands of a Jesuit priest, and looked to him, as the authorized agent of the pope, for a just decision; this constituted for the Papal See, which thus for the first time was called upon to exercise the role of arbitrator between two Slavic empires, a very considerable accretion of moral power.

Jam Zapolski, hitherto an unknown and miserable hamlet lying amid the snowy wastes of Russia, became in a moment a center of the highest political significance, and its general appearance underwent a corresponding transformation. The tents of the two sets of negotiators sprang up rapidly, and, as the Russian delegates also carried on all forms of commerce, the place soon assumed the animated appearance of an annual fair. Possevino had been accommodated in a peasant's hut, and had installed in its single room a portable alter. In this room there met together under his chairmanship the representatives of both parties, and, after the Russians had once again severely tried his patience, he was at last able to secure the conclusion, in the name of the pope, of the agreement by which the Russo-Polish war was terminated.

Gratification at the extent of the success that had been achieved did not, however, occasion any lapse on the part of the Jesuit priest into self-satisfied inactivity. Having accomplished one part of his mission, it now remained for him to proceed towards the realization of his further aims; there was still work to be done in securing the conclusion of a commercial agreement between Venice and Russia, and the participation of the tsar in the anti-Turkish coalition. Furthermore, the papal legate still cherished the ambitious aim of reuniting the Russian and the Catholic Church, and of thus paving the way to the mending of the great schism that had rent the Christian world for so long.

All these things appeared to indicate the necessity of exercising strong pressure on Ivan. Accordingly, Possevino set out straightway for Moscow in a sledge drawn by a team of fast horses. What he saw and what his experiences were while there are described in great detail in the accounts which he prepared for the pope, and these reports, better than anything else perhaps, reveal the keen powers of perception possessed by this religious diplomat.

Possevino succeeded in penetrating in an amazingly short time into the secrets of the Russian administrative system, and in applying his observations and knowledge to the framing of valuable advice to serve the purposes of all subsequent political interventions by the pope in the affairs of Moscow. The descriptions, too, which he gives of the external appearance of the Russian capital are also distinguished by their colorfulness and animation.

To him, Moscow appears as a huge village in the middle of which rises the Kremlin like a

A Jesuit at the Court of Ivan the Terrible

small town reserved for the "elect." Beside the palace constructed of hewn stone, in which the tsar was wont to receive the foreign emissaries, towers up the magnificent Cathedral of St. Michael; in the Red Square, the fantastic Church of Vasili Blazhennyi, upon which the rays of the sun strike with iridescent effect, excites the admiration of the stranger; in the trading quarter of the town he is amazed at the animation and activity amid the mean shops, which were filled, however with the finest of wares.

In this country, asserts Possevino, where the tsar himself appoints the highest priests, where the people vegetate in complete ignorance, the sovereign is regarded as the fount of all knowledge and justice; no one could be more enlightened than he, his every action is good, and there is no law other than his will. All this, notwithstanding the fact that Ivan, during his attacks of mad cruelty, laid waste whole towns and slew many of his closest friends and even his own son.

The Jesuit does not, however, fail to notice the signs of mental derangement and bodily decay in Ivan. The tsar's eye seems to have lost its brightness, his hands tremble and his cheeks are sunken. At times, tortured by his conscience, he flees into the church, and, wearing a monk's cowl, chants and rings the bells, or else stands, clad in a chasuble, a tiara on his head and the cross in his hand, for hours on end., like a demented high priest, before the scintillating ikons, making the sign of the cross unceasingly over the heads of the trembling boyars.

His frequent association with monks had enabled him to acquire a certain amount of knowledge regarding matters of religion and church history, for which he took very considerable credit to himself, as a set-off against his horrible excesses; at times when he was mentally normal, he showed considerable pleasure in displaying his theological knowledge, and in quoting numerous passages from the Bible "with a greater degree of assurance than of knowledge of the actual text."

Possevino hoped to be able to exploit this weakness of the tsar for theological discussions, in the furtherance of his object of bringing about an understanding between Rome and Moscow in matters of church politics. Whenever an opportunity presented itself during the course of the negotiations regarding the anti-Turkish alliance, the Jesuit endeavored unobtrusively to lead the discussion into the religious sphere.

Ivan recognized full well towards what end these allusion, which, at first, were veiled, but, as time went on, became more and more open, were directed; for a long time, he avoided being drawn into a theological debate, as he had no intention whatsoever of entering into serious negotiations regarding a fusion between the Orthodox and the Catholic Churches; the Papal See had helped him to bring an end to the troublesome war with Poland, and beyond that he had no further interest in Rome.

But the Jesuit adhered persistently to his purpose, and, relying on "the wonder-working power of repetition," again and again spoke of the superiority of the Roman over the Byzantine Church, until finally Ivan could no longer restrain his passion for debate and declared his willingness to hold a public discussion with Possevino on the subject. The tsar anticipated overwhelming the Jesuit with his theological arguments before the whole court, for had he not already carried off signal honors in a debate with the emissaries of the Bohemian Brethren? Possevino, for his part, hoped, as the result of this discussion, to shake the faith with which the Russians held their Church to be the only true Church.

The Power and Secret of the Jesuits

The great audience chamber of the palace was elaborately decorated, and all the boyars were commanded to attend in full force. The tsar and the Jesuit, flanked on both sides by interpreters, were seated opposite one another, and in front of each was a mass of folios, manuscripts and notebooks.

At a polite invitation from Ivan, Possevino arose, and brought to the attack the arguments by which he hoped to establish the fact that the Catholic faith was the only true faith. The Greek church of the patriarchs Athanasius, Chrysostom and Basil, he asserted in conclusion, was bound by indissoluble ties to the Catholic Church, and the pope himself even did not in any sense desire to break with the time-honored traditions of the first councils; all that was required of the Russians was that they should decide to abandon those errors which had been introduced in later times by men such as Photius and Michael Cerularius. Points of divergence in external ritual such as did in fact exist between the two churches would be no obstacle to a union in the faith, when once Russia had acknowledged the authority in theological matters of the pope, as the representative of God on earth.

Ivan replied that in earlier times the popes had been acknowledged by the Orthodox Church and revered as saints; in later times, however, the papacy had fallen away from its original single-mindedness, and the bishops of the roman church had begun to arrogate to themselves divine honors, and the corruption of many of the popes had completely discredited the whole institution.

This thrust, which produced a powerful effect on the boyars, could not remain unparried if the prestige of the Holy Father was to be upheld. Accordingly, to the horror of all present, Possevino replied with an engaging smile that in this respect the same applied with regard to the tsars as to the popes; the fact that certain individual wearers of the crown may have shown themselves to be immoral was not a ground for belittling the Russian rulers as a whole.

The eyes of the boyars were fixed in the greatest horror on the throne; with lowering expression and awe-inspiring bearing, Ivan had half-raised himself from his seat, and scornfully retorted to the papal envoy that the Roman pontifex was no shepherd, as he chose to describe himself, but a wolf. Possevino, however, smiled more engagingly than ever, and, with unmistakable irony, asked why, if such were the case, the tsar had asked a "wolf" to negotiate peace with Poland.

There was only one reply to be made at the court of Ivan the Terrible to such brazen audacity; the boyars were in no doubt over what was about to happen when the tsar sprang up and seized the celebrated cudgel with which he had already smashed in the skulls of many who had ventured to oppose him. After a moment's hesitation, however, he let the stick drop, sat down again, and remained for some moments in silent meditation. At last, he said in a reproachful tone of voice: "It must have been from the peasants in who knows what disreputable places that you learned to speak to me in this manner, as if I were a peasant myself!"

Possevino had suitably repelled the attack on the papacy; he was not called upon to do more than defend the authority of his master at the court of Moscow. He could, accordingly, adopt a conciliatory attitude, and, in the most courteous manner, offer satisfaction to the tsar. He hastened up to him, and assured him that it had been far from his intention to offend him; eventually, he begged the favor of being allowed to kiss the tsar's hand, and thereby touched the feelings of the tsar so much that he embraced Possevino, and, for his part also, apologized for his attacks on the pope.

At the conclusion of the proceedings, the tsar asked to be furnished with a written copy of a passage from the Book of Isaiah which Possevino had quoted during the course of the debate, and the Jesuit profited by this opportunity to present to the tsar a copy of a treatise by the Patriarch Gennadius on the primacy of the pope. After further emphatic assurances of friendship had been exchanged on both sides on the following day, Possevino left the Kremlin loaded with honors and gifts, in order to accompany to Venice and Rome the Russian envoy who was to carry on the further political negotiations. Thus the strange spectacle was presented of a Russian diplomatic mission proceeding to Western Europe under the leadership if a Jesuit.

Scarcely had Possevino arrived in Poland when he found himself faced immediately with a further important task. This was to prevent the outbreak of a threatened war between Stephen Báthory and the Emperor Rudolph, a conflict which would once again have cut right across the pope's policy of an alliance against the Sultan, and accordingly had to be obviated by every possible means.

The object of the quarrel was the country around Szatmár Németi, which had been wrested some decades earlier from the Voivode of Transylvania by the Emperor Maximilian II. As these lands formed the hereditary territory of the house of Báthory, King Stephen demanded that they should be returned to him, and threatened to support his demand, if necessary, by force of arms; on the other hand, Rudolph II stubbornly declined to surrender an inch of any territory to which he imagined he had a title.

Possevino already knew how to deal with Báthory; accordingly he began by spending every evening discoursing in Latin with the king, until he had induced him to accept the offer of papal mediation. Then Possevino endeavored to find a basis for negotiations with the emperor. Rudolph II was at that time in Augsburg, where he was presiding over the imperial Diet, and Possevino immediately proceeded there. With his customary resourcefulness, he first of all informed himself fully of the emperor's finances, and, when he and learnt that Rudolph was in a particularly straitened financial situation, he based his representations at the court on the heavy expenses that the fortification and defense of the contested lands would involve.

In the course of the negotiations, this argument had the hoped-for effect. The emperor announced his readiness to surrender the hereditary territory claimed by Báthory in return for other territorial concessions; a joint commission was appointed, which was to proceed to Kassa, and there, under the chairmanship of Possevino, was to determine the extent of the compensations to be granted to Rudolph. Thus the Jesuit had once again so arranged matters that, as the pope's legate, he was called upon to exercise the office of international arbitrator, and, as the result, the authority of the Holy See could not fail to be enhanced.

Whilst Possevino, as the intermediary between tsars, kings and emperors, was concerned in high politics, he did not neglect, as became a far-seeing diplomat, those minor affairs which, under certain circumstances, might assume considerable importance. At the time when he was engaged in the first negotiations with Báthory, he had shown a lively interest in the situation in Transylvania as regards religious matters, and had spurred the king on to take energetic measures to combat the growing Calvinistic leanings of the inhabitants. At his prompting, Báthory undertook to make a considerable grant towards the setting up and maintenance of Jesuit colleges in Transylvania, and the pope also, as the result of his representations, agreed to make an annual grant.

In the year 1583, Possevino himself set out for Transylvania, and, on the way, visited the ten-year-old prince Sigismund Báthory, whose confidence he immediately won, after which he proceeded to convert to Catholicism a number of distinguished Protestant families in the prince's entourage. Among these was the house of Pázmány, from which Peter Pázmány, the organizer of the Counter-Reformation in Hungary, was later to spring.

Even in Poland too, Possevino, in company with his fellow-Jesuit, Peter Skarga, worked energetically towards the strengthening of the Catholic faith, and not only concerned himself with the establishment of further Jesuit colleges, with the appointment of bishops and the training of the future priests, but also with the setting up of printing-presses and the publication of the Catholic catechism in both Polish and Lithuanian. He attached particular importance to the winning over to Rome of the Ruthenians. Since they were under Polish domination, the Catholic church was free to develop among them without hindrance under the protection of King Stephen; after the Ruthenians had been converted, Possevino's object was to take advantage of their national kinship with the Russians by using them as Catholic agitators in Russia. Similarly, Possevino saw in the Baltic provinces, which were again under the dominion of Poland, a further bridge across which Catholicism might penetrate into Russia, and accordingly he vigorously promoted the Catholic cause in those lands.

Thus Possevino shows himself in all his actions to be a truly far-sighted statesman, about to bring to a successful conclusion the most complicated diplomatic matters, and thereby to prepare the ground, through his unfailing attention to detail, for the prosperity of the Roman cause in later decades and centuries. The value of his personality and of his work for Catholicism cannot therefore, in any sense, be gauged merely by those of his great achievements which are immediately apparent; it reveals itself rather, on more than one occasion, in the developments of much later times.

The "False Demetrius"

Even after Possevino's death, the active furtherance of the Catholic cause in Poland, with the object of making it a center from which Russia might be won over to the Roman Church, remained one of the most important tasks for Jesuit diplomacy. The fathers who now applied themselves to this task were animated by the same spirit of zealous energy and resolute courage as their predecessor had been, and it was their lot to achieve in Warsaw and Moscow successes the like of which Possevino could scarcely have dreamt of achieving.

Nevertheless, this particular period, in which Jesuit diplomacy in Eastern Europe had apparently been crowned with complete success, was subsequently to reveal itself as the least successful and least glorious epoch in the political history of the Society of Jesus. Those upon whom Possevino's mantle had fallen were certainly, like him not lacking in courage, devotion and imagination; but their energetic zeal was not tempered by that far-sightedness and art of moderation which alone can lead to lasting results. Consequently, their courage was carried to the point of romantic temerity; their imagination led them on to venturesomeness and their

The "False Demetrius"

zeal involved them in intrigue; as the result, bitter disillusionment followed upon every success they achieved.

With Sigismund III, the son of the Swedish king John, who acceded to the throne of Poland on the death of Stephen Báthory, a pupil of the Jesuits for the first time ascended the Polish throne; but this ruler, whose every decision was guided by the advice of his instructors, soon forfeited the crown of Sweden, while his rule in Poland was constantly threatened by risings and upheavals. Indeed, his readiness to obey the Jesuits in everything soon precipitated both him and his advisers into a fantastic adventure which ended in catastrophe.

Ivan the Terrible had died, after appointing a regency council of five boyars for his son Dimitri, who was a minor. One of the members of the council, the forceful Boris Godunov, soon usurped all the power to himself, and had the heir to the throne, Dimitri, abducted and murdered. After a short time, during which the weak-minded Feodor, Ivan's second son, had been nominally tsar, Boris Godunov possessed himself of the throne.

Before long, his oppressive rule gave rise to a popular legend that the young Tsarevich Dimitri had not really been murdered, but had been rescued by faithful servants, and was living somewhere in concealment until the hour when he should come forth and possess himself of his inheritance. The Russian people longingly awaited deliverance at the hands of this legendary figure of the tsar's son, Dimitri, from the despotism of Godunov.

Then one day, in 1603, there appeared at Kiev, a young Orthodox monk, who had come to visit the shrines there. The Lithuanian prince Adam Wisniwiecki got to know the pilgrim by chance, was attracted to him, and took him home with him, whereupon the young man suddenly complained of unbearable pains, and called for a priest.

"I feel my end approaching," said the sick man to the Igumen Arsenin whom Prince Adam had called to his protégé's couch, "and I have only one thing more to ask: bury me with all the honors befitting a prince. I carry my secret with me to the grave; but after my death you will find a confession in this bed!" With these enigmatic words, the unknown man sank back among the pillows, as if he were about to give up the ghost.

The affair seemed to the igumen too significant politically to justify silence on religious grounds, so he overcame his conscientious scruples concerning the seal of the confessional, and told Prince Adam what the dying man had confided to him. An examination of the pillows and mattresses on which the pilgrim was still lying motionless brought to light a document which proclaimed that the unknown monk was no less a person than Dimitri, the son of Ivan the Terrible. This seemed to be confirmed by a gold cross, set with diamonds and other precious stones, which lay on the sick man's breast, and, as moreover certain distinguishing features agreed, Prince Adam was soon fully convinced that here before him lay the rightful heir to the imperial throne. In consequence, the prince and the igumen hailed it as a most significant miracle, when the man whom they believed dead suddenly opened his eyes again, and within a few hours was wholly restored to health.

The newfound tsarevich was immediately seated in the prince's travelling coach, brought to Poland, and there presented first to the near relatives, then to the other nobility of the neighborhood, and finally publicly exhibited. The Russian emigrants who had incurred Boris Godunov's displeasure and had fled to Poland hastened to confirm the pilgrim's identity with the tsarevich; protocol was heaped on protocol, and a host of men, who all hoped of speedy advancement for the appearance of this claimant to the Russian throne, rallied to the young Demetrius.

The greatest enthusiasm was shown by George Mniszek, the Palatine of Sandomir. This man had already married one of his daughters to a rich and powerful prince, and now conceived the idea of making her younger sister Marina the wife of the Tsarevich Dimitri, and thus the future Empress of Russia. The palatine's plan pleased Prince Adam; Demetrius was taken at once to Sandomir and left alone with Marina sufficiently often, until at last the girl's father was able to bestow his blessing upon the young couple.

The Palatine of Sandomir immediately proved himself a worthy father-in-law to a future sovereign. He spared no expense to help Demetrius to victory, and brought him at once, in a state coach drawn by six black horses, to Cracow, where a great feast was immediately held for the principal personages of the city. Even the papal nuncio consented to appear at it, and gained a not unfavorable impression of Demetrius on the occasion, "His long white hands," he reported to the pope, "betoken a noble ancestry; he is at ease in conversation, and his manner and bearing may be called truly dignified."

But, in order that the great plan might be put into effect, it was vital to secure the favor and support of the Jesuits, without which at that time in Poland no great political enterprise could hope for success. The palatine's house chaplain undertook the office of interesting the Jesuits in Demetrius, and set forth the case in the professed house of the Jesuits at Cracow.

The fathers at once realized that they were being offered the possibility of consummating the great work of Possevino; if they succeeded in gaining Demetrius for the Church of Rome and assisted him to ascend the tsar's throne, it would be an easy task through him to unite all Russia for ever to the papacy.

In a personal interview with Fathers Sawickii, Barshch and Skarga, Demetrius avowed his readiness to accept the Catholic faith himself and to introduce it into Russia, if the Jesuits would only help him to depose the usurper Boris. Later, Demetrius made a solemn abjuration of the Orthodox faith to Father Sawicki, and made his confession to him. Afterwards, another meeting between Demetrius and the papal nuncio took place, which resulted in a formal pact between the Vatican and the future tsar. Demetrius announced proudly that he intended "to unite Russia with the Catholic Church, and thus to introduce a new era for the whole of Christendom." Thereupon, it was unanimously agreed to support the claimant's enterprise by all possible means.

King Sigismund was easily persuade to lead a campaign against Boris Godunov; he relied herein entirely on the good fathers, who decided day and night in his stead what the king should do and leave undone. He wrote at once to the chancellor and field-marshal, Zamoyski; "Demetrius will be a powerful aid to us against the Turks; Livonia will be pacified; Sweden will be regained by us; and over and above all this there will open for us an immense field of trade, stretching to Persia and the Far East."

The rich Palatine of Sandomir was responsible for all the necessary expense; the troops were paid and armed from his coffers; and a few months later Demetrius crossed the Russian frontier at the head of a considerable army, and drove before him the feeble forces of Boris

The "False Demetrius"

Godunov.

With Demetrius the Jesuits too re-entered Russia. On the march over the endless steppes, Fathers Czyrzowski and Sawicki rode beside the tsarevich, prepared with him the strategic plans, and inspired the troops to press forward without wavering. Soon Demetrius, at Krasnoie Selo, near Moscow, was receiving countless deputations of Russians who were dissatisfied with the rule of Boris Godunov, and accepting their assurances of devotion. Already there had spread throughout Russia the belief that God was angry with the usurper Boris, and had therefore raised up his victim Dimitri out of the grave. So, when Godunov, during an audience, suddenly had a hemorrhage and died within a few minutes, nobody doubted that this was a judgment of God, and Demetrius was able unhindered to enter the holy city of Moscow. Just as Boris Godunov had celebrated his accession to power by having the widow and the son of Ivan the Terrible taken prisoners and killed, so now Demetrius, risen from the grave, had Godunov's widow and her offspring taken and strangled. Thus were the scales of justice once more brought level over Russia.

The solemn address of welcome at the entry of the new tsar into the Kremlin was spoken by Father Sawicki, the address at the coronation by Father Czyrzowski. One of the first of Demetrius's enactments concerned the establishment of Jesuit colleges, seminaries and churches throughout the realm. When Marina, the palatine's daughter, had to be fetched from Sandomir to Moscow, this honorable mission was entrusted to Father Sawicki, and, when the new tsar wished to open up diplomatic relations with the Holy See, he appointed the same father as Russian ambassador to the Vatican.

Demetrius would undertake nothing without previously obtaining the advice of his faithful fathers; but care had to be exercised to prevent the Orthodox Russian people from discovering too soon the Catholic intentions of their tsar. To this end, Demetrius suddenly expressed an unappeasable desire for knowledge, and during an official audience he addressed the fathers in these term: "Two things are particularly necessary to a monarch: a knowledge of the art of war, and a thorough grounding in the sciences. In order to acquire the latter knowledge, which I require as sovereign, I have decided to claim your help."

For reasons which were not very apparent, familiarity with the writings of the Roman rhetorician Quintilian appeared to the young ruler especially necessary to the right exercise of his authority, so Fathers Czyrzowski and Sawicki spent several hours each day with Demetrius, studying with him all the subtleties of Quintilian's *institutio oratoria*.

In order that no one should be suspicious of the frequent intercourse of the tsar with the Jesuits, several boyars were present, as witnesses, from the very beginning. But, while the tsar's interest in Quintilian increased from day to day, the attention of the Russian listeners—who moreover understood not a work of the Latin text which was being expounded—flagged, and the boyars came to regard these hours of instruction as a time for slumber.

The demon of suspicion at court did not sleep, however, and so it came about that an ill-wisher asserted that the fathers were utilizing their ostensible educational office to counsel the tsar concerning the destruction of the venerable Orthodox Church. The alleged writings of Quintilian were actually a secret language by means of which the Jesuits, while the boyars slept, conversed with the tsar on the most important affairs of state.

The old hatred of the Roman Church flared up again in many Orthodox hearts, and was directed too against Demetrius, the protégé and devoted servant of the Catholic clergy. One morning, the whole city was in an uproar, the life-guards, as usual, went over to the side of the insurgents, and Demetrius, who had run from room to room in a vain effort to escape, was taken prisoner, insulted and shot down, his corpse pierced through and through with sword-thrusts.

Thereafter, the "tsar's son," once accepted with such enthusiasm, was called nothing but "the false Demetrius"; people said that he had really been an escaped monk, Grishka Otrepiev by name, and had let himself be used as a tool for the devilish machinations of the pope, the Jesuits, and the king of Poland. It was a mercy that true Russians had brought this shame and infamy to an end in good time!

The Success and the End of the "Jesuit Kings"

Thus the power of the Jesuits in the Kremlin was once more at an end; but in Poland, even after this unhappy enterprise, their political influence not only continued, but actually only now reached its real zenith.

It is true that King Wladislaus IV, Sigismund's successor, did not show himself very well disposed to the fathers, and even tried to restrict their power; soon, however, he gave up the vain struggle, and, when his younger brother John Casimir ascended the throne, the Jesuits had every reason for jubilation.

For John Casimir had been brought up in Rome, and from his earliest youth been completely under Jesuit influence, and had finally himself entered the Society of Jesus. Although, by first accepting cardinal's rank, then ascending the throne of Poland and finally marrying his brother's widow, he had officially forfeited his membership to the order, he remained a true Jesuit at heart, and strove to promote in everything the interests of the Society.

Yet the rule of the "Jesuit king," John Casimir, ultimately meant a sharp decline in the power of the Jesuits in Eastern Europe. For, from the very beginning, this ruler followed a most unwise policy both in home and foreign affairs; he alienated his own people by various foolish measures, and involved himself in military undertakings against Sweden and Russia, which ended in heavy losses and in the cession of valuable provinces. These failures finally forced him to abdicate in 1668, and therewith ended the rule of that Vasa dynasty which, during the eighty years of its government in Poland, had nearly always been faithful to the Jesuits.

In England, the short ascendancy of the Jesuits was as adventurous as in Russia and Poland. After they had striven there as conspirators and rebels for a century and a half, first under the Tudors and then under the Stuarts, they found, in the eighties of the seventeenth century, a willing instrument for their schemes in James II.

It is true that his predecessor, Charles II, who, in his lifetime, had persecuted and condemned the Jesuits, had been converted on his deathbed to the Roman faith. James II, however, had always been a convinced Catholic, and had a particular leaning towards the Jesuit order. Father Ruga could now proclaim with joy that the new king had proudly declared to him, "I am the son of the Society of Jesus," and that the queen had immediately added, "And I am

103. KING JAMES II OF ENGLAND

104. THE JESUIT SCHOOL, HEYTHORPE COLLEGE, IN OXFORDSHIRE, ENGLAND

The Success and the End of the Jesuit Kings

their daughter!" The fathers of the college at Liège could hopefully and joyfully report to their brothers at Freiburg that King James had affiliated himself with the Society of Jesus, and had promised with the help of the Jesuits to recover his country for Catholicism.

Until then the fathers working in England had had to evade police investigations by means of a thousand disguises; but now they sat at court in the greenish black habit of their order, and directed the destiny of the kingdom to their ends. The Jesuit Father Petre became the all-powerful adviser of James II, who made him a member of the Privy Council. "'Of all the evil counsellors who had access to the royal ear," says Macaulay, "the Jesuit Petre bore perhaps the largest part in the ruin of the House of Stuart."

The king attended the Catholic mass in full state, received the papal nuncio with honor at the court, released countless Catholics from prison, filled every office that became vacant with men of Catholic sympathies, and even conceived the intention of catholicizing the Universities of Oxford and Cambridge, the strongest bulwarks of the Anglican Church; in Savoy Buildings in St. James's, the Jesuits with all ceremony opened a college; and England seemed well on the way to become a powerful support of Catholic world-politics.

Only one circumstance deeply troubled the Catholic party: the king had no son, and both his daughters were Protestants—born of James's first wife, who was a Protestant—and had married Protestant princes. "If the king," wrote Father Ruga at that time, "has no legitimate male successor, nobody can tell what will happen after his death, and how the Catholics will continue to exist in the midst of so large a number of heretics; there are, indeed, about twenty heretics to one Catholic. Oh, how necessary it is to beseech Our Lord to provide what is needful!"

Soon the anxious fathers at the court of Whitehall were considering whether James should not place the decision concerning the succession in the hands of Louis XIV, "for it would be better for English Catholics to be vassals of the king of France, than slaves of the Devil." Then, at last, a son was born to the king by his second wife, who was a Catholic.

This happy event seemed to secure the continuance of Catholic power in England; but, in reality, there happened here what had happened in Russia and in Poland: the apparent triumph led directly to the downfall of the Jesuit hopes.

For the fact that the king now possessed an heir to the throne destroyed the last hopes of the Anglicans, and goaded them to the bitterest opposition to James and his pro-Catholic policy.

Very soon, however, court gossip provided the opponents of the Jesuits with a dangerous weapon, against which even the influential councilor of state, Petre, and the papal nuncio were powerless. This gossip asserted nothing less than that at the queen's delivery a child had been substituted by the Jesuits. It was whispered that the king was already too old to beget heirs; people pointed to the suspicious circumstances that during her supposed pregnancy the queen had not allowed a single Protestant woman to touch her, and, finally, they took exception to the remarkable size of the child, who, immediately after the "birth," looked as if he were already several weeks old. In the end, it was reported throughout London that the Jesuits had got a nun with child, and so had procured the existence of the infant who was now given out to be the heir to the English crown. Pamphlets asserting this were circulated throughout the land, and were even brought into the royal palace of Whitehall.

Owing, not least, to this gossip, the people of England fell away from King James, and turned to the Prince of Orange, the husband of the king's daughter Mary, who, as an ardent Calvinist, seemed the right man to put an end to the "papistical nuisance."

So there came about the "glorious revolution" which cost King James, and ultimately the Stuart dynasty, the crown of England. William of Orange landed in England with an army, James's troops for the most part deserted to his side, and the king had to flee to France in a small boat. The English Parliament, however, passed a solemn resolution that the king, who had endeavored to subvert the constitution and who "by the advice of Jesuits and other persons" had violated the fundamental laws, had thereby forfeited the throne. William of Orange was proclaimed king, and the Jesuit power in England miserably overthrown.

In comparison with these severe disillusionments, the success which the Jesuits had achieved several decades previously, by the conversion of Queen Christina of Sweden, counted for little. The daughter of Gustavus Adolphus, who had early manifested a burning interest in science and religion, and at whose court philosophers of the standing of Descartes foregathered, had been converted to the Catholic faith through her friendship with the Portuguese Jesuit, Antonio Macedo, and had obtained through the general of the order certain learned fathers with whom she could go thoroughly into the dogmas of the Roman Church. In the year 1655, she went over publicly to Catholicism.

It was, indeed, a great moral victory for the Jesuits that the daughter of Gustavus Adolphus had returned to the bosom of that Church which alone had power to save; but, as Christina, before her conversion, had had to renounce the throne of Sweden, the event had no further political consequences.

The Struggle Against the German Reformation

"The Jesuits know how to insinuate themselves everywhere," lamented a Protestant pamphlet of the sixteenth century. "As from the pulpit they lead the people astray to idolatry, in the schools offer up unfortunate youth to Moloch, so they creep into the houses, attach themselves to persons of distinguished or humble position, seduce the poor with gifts of bread and other food, in short, where anything is to be obtained by stealth, there at every opportunity and in every guise you find the Jesuits."

When the first members of the Society of Jesus appeared in Germany, it seemed as if the Reformation was about to be completely victorious; indeed, nine-tenths of the population had already gone over to Protestantism. The Catholic Church, with her disordered organization and her demoralized priesthood, could obviously no longer offer serious opposition to the further spread of the new doctrine, and even in Rome the complete secession of Germany from the Catholic Church, in the immediate future, was expected.

At the beginning, hardly anyone would have seen in the Jesuits, who seemed so modest and quiet and appeared satisfied with quite subordinate kinds of work, the power whose supe-

The Struggle Against the German Reformation

rior organization was to check the further advance of Protestantism. Peter Faber, who in 1540 had gone to the religious conference at Worms as the companion of the imperial orator, Ortiz, confined himself to preaching here and there to students, priests and cathedral clergy and giving them the *Exercises*, to giving alms to the poor and caring for the sick in the hospitals; and Fathers Le Jay and Bobadilla and the Jesuits who succeeded them did the same. But, through their very unobtrusive ardor and their noiseless activity, they were soon able to make a number of wavering clergy and laity into convinced Catholics once more. "To the exercises, which were undertaken by many of the Germans," Peter Faber could report to Rome, "nearly all the good which has happened since in Germany is due." Again, their care for the sick, the prisoners and the poor won for them the sympathy of the people, who had for long been unaccustomed to see Catholic priests concerned with works of love for their neighbors.

The Jesuits had realized from the beginning that a successful campaign against the Reformation could be waged only if the conditions within the Catholic priesthood were first improved. "it is not the case," wrote Peter Faber at the time, "that the Lutherans have brought about the secession of so many people from the Roman Church through the apparent righteousness of their teaching; the greatest blame for this development lies rather on our own clergy. Pray God that in this city of Worms there are even two or three priests who have not formed illicit liaisons or are not living in other known sins!" Thus the Jesuits appeared in Germany not at first as opponents of Protestantism, but as reformers of the Catholic priesthood.

When later they transferred their energies to direct opposition to Protestant doctrine, they refrained for some time from provocative polemics. "We must begin with what brings hearts nearer to one another, not with the things that lead to strife!" these were the words with which the Jesuits began their campaign. Ignatius himself had insisted when the first disciples went to Germany that they must "meet heresy with gentleness and discretion."

"Your defense of the Apostolic See, and your efforts to maintain the people in submission to this See," so ran Loyola's instructions, "should never go so far that you lose control of yourselves and get decried as Papists; thereby you will merely bring about general suspicion. . . Try to make friends with the leaders of the opposition and with those who have most influence among the heretics and wavering Catholics, and loose them from their error through wisdom and love..."

The letters of the first Jesuit missionaries also bear witness to the realization that German Protestantism must be combated first with friendliness: "He who wished to be of use to the heretics of the present day must be conspicuous first of all for his great love for them and must banish from his mind all thoughts which could in any way lessen his opinion of these men. Then we must try so to gain their hearts and wills, that they love us too and have a good opinion of us. We shall easily attain this if we have friendly intercourse with them, and without any strife touch only on that on which we are at one."

In another respect too, the Jesuits proved their political wisdom in their dealings with German Protestantism. While they mistook the actual situation in the Anglican Church for the mere malicious spite of the sovereigns and saw in Gallicanism only the ambitious petty jealousies of a few parliamentary advocates and university professors, they realized at once in Germany how close was the connection between the secession of the people from the Roman Church and the awakening of German national consciousness.

The Power and Secret of the Jesuits

They understood from the first that the German language represented the most powerful stronghold of Protestantism: the people, who heard German sermons, read the German Bible and sang German hymns, soon lost through this alone their intimate union with Rome, and the national literature which was flourishing at that time in consequence of the Reformation completely severed the connection of Germany with the Latin culture of the Roman church.

Peter Canisius, whom Peter Faber had gained for the order, and who was to become the founder of the Jesuit colleges at Vienna, Ingolstadt, Prague and Freiburg, first took account of this fact, and for this very reason became the most successful champion of the Catholic cause in Germany. He realized that Catholicism's struggle with Protestantism was not least a fight of the printing-press, and that the victory would fall to that party which could create an effective literature of propaganda. For in Germany, as Canisius once wrote, a writer was accounted of more worth than ten professors. He therefore recommended the establishment of a special Jesuit college for writers, which should apply itself to the production of the requisite polemic literature in the German language.

He himself became an extraordinarily prolific writer, compiling catechisms of Catholic doctrine for every age and for every degree of education. He worked away at perfecting and improving these books until his death in order to "make the matter not only shorter but plainer, in accordance with the requirements of the time."

The most important factor in the recatholicizing of Germany was, however, the educational activity of the Jesuits. In all the more important towns of the land colleges were opened in rapid succession, the remarkable success of whose teaching even the Protestants had to recognize.

Religious instruction if the *Spiritual Exercises*, exhortations to the worldly clergy, mildness and friendliness to the Protestants, instruction in the catechism and the erection of numerous schools—these were the means by which the Jesuits set about the Counter-Reformation in Germany.

When the Protestants at last realized the great success attained by the Society of Jesus through these quiet, inconspicuous activities, they believed that the *Exercises* by which so many laymen and clergy had been regained for the Catholic Church must be a "very work of the Devil" intended to intoxicate the "unhappy victim," to lead him to forswear God and "to deliver him right into the claws of Satan!" the zeal of the Jesuits to improve the conduct of the clergy was designated as "hypocrisy," and the friendliness of the fathers appeared to the Protestants as "low, devilish cunning." In the writings of the Jesuits they saw the dangerous weapons of "soul-murderers."

"The Turk hews off heads with his scimitar," cried the Lutheran theologian, Wiegand, at that time, concerning Canisius, "and everyone is horrified at it. . . But this murderer of souls has with his book whetted and drawn his sword, for he hews down souls to destroy them forever and to deliver them as a prey to Satan, in the eternal flames of hell. . ."

At the beginning, Jesuit controversial literature was also carefully designed to maintain the "friendly tone." When the general of the order, Acquaviva, learnt that one of the fathers was disseminating a spiteful tract against Luther, he forbade him, with the assertion that a too bitter and biting pamphlet would only do harm to the Society itself. "Neither is this fitting for us, as we should fight with discretion and solid learning and not with calumnies and insults."

Soon, however, it became apparent that the particular characteristics of religious controversy in Germany made a sharper note in polemics desirable, since it became more and more customary in Germany for men to express the strength of their religious convictions by filthy insults directed against their opponents.

True to their constant principle of adaptation to the given circumstance, the hitherto peace-loving fathers immediately turned over a new leaf. After the "weapons of courtliness" had served them for a century, they brought out the "weapons of abuse," and employed them freely.

When the Lutherans wrote that the Jesuits were "the most arch and arrant betrayers and persecutors of Christ, the very spawn of hell which the dragon of hell spews out, Papist asses, wolves and miserable devils," the Jesuits answered back that the protestants were "at once cats and wolves, tearing each other to pieces like cats and wolves, and must be loaded with every ignominy, coming as they do from hell."

It was not always easy to attain the degree of spiritual plain-speaking reached, at that time, by protestant polemics, since the Lutherans actually declared that the Jesuits at Munich had abused boys, and had murdered a number of girls in their church; it was said of Cardinal Bellarmine, whose controversial writings had drawn down upon him the wrath of Protestant theologians, that he "always had in the stable four goats which he used for his pleasure, and had them brought to him adorned with the most costly jewels, precious stones, silver and gold."

But the "courtly" fathers knew admirably how to make their voices loudly heard in the general exchange of recriminations; their abuse was no less coarse than that of Protestants.

The main objective of the Jesuit attack was naturally the person of Luther; Fathers Keller, Vetter, Forer and Gretser, the "specialists in the foul insults" that the Jesuits had now perfected, could not say enough in condemnation of Luther's immoral way of life. Henry Dionysius and Francis Costa, again, dared in their *Censor* to demand the death penalty for stiff-necked heretics, saying that Luther and his adherents ought to have been executed forty years ago. The Ingolstadt Jesuit Mayrhofer, too, taught in his *Mirror for Preachers* that the putting to death of Protestants was "no more unreasonable than to say that thieves, counterfeiters, murderers and rebels can and should be punished with death."

The Jesuits in the Thirty Years' War

While the fathers in this wise, with exercises, catechisms and colleges, with courtliness and coarseness, endeavored to check the rapid decay of Catholic belief in Germany, they were also pursuing at the courts of princes that Counter-Reformation which was so powerfully to influence the destiny of Europe for so long a time.

Here the task presented to the Jesuits was most delicate, for the progressive development of the states of Europe since the Middle Ages and of their varying interests had made of the politics of the temporal powers a chaotic confusion and apparently conflicting transactions, leagues and oppositions. It was, therefore, increasingly difficult, in the face of this uncontrollable, unregulated medley of forces striving for predominance, to carry through the stern, unbending policy of the Roman church, which still aimed at the realization of the universal monarchy of the pope, and recognized only one purpose, to spur on all the Catholic countries of the world to a concerted advance against the foes of the papacy—the Turks, and the Protestants.

But, while the Curia strove in every imaginable situation for this union of the whole Catholic world, and utterly abominated any alliance with "heathen" and "heretic," kings and emperors were often enough induced, by the hope of immediate advantage, to ally themselves, regardless of religious considerations, with those powers with whom they had common interests; sometimes too it seemed to them advisable, for the purpose of defense against external foes, to come to an agreement with the Protestants of their own lands, even when this necessitated religious concessions. Thus even the policy of good Catholic princes came into conflict more than once with the principles of the Holy See.

This was seen with particular clearness in Germany, for there the emperor and the few princes who had remained true to the Roman Church were scarcely ever in a position to bring their pursuit of their own advantage entirely into line with the principles laid down by the Curia. Although the Emperor Charles V, in the early days of the Reformation, tried, in accordance with the wishes of Rome, to suppress the teaching of Luther, he desisted immediately he stood in need of the financial and military help of the German Protestant princes in the war against France.

The Catholic rulers were in the same position as the emperor: whenever they required the constitutional assent of the Protestant Diet, they were forced to purchase it by religious concessions.

This was the situation with which the Jesuits had to grapple. It was their task, in foreign politics, as far as possible, to prevent conflicts between Catholic powers, but, in home politics, on the one hand, to restrain the emperor from giving way to the Protestant German princes, and, on the other hand, to encourage the few Catholic rulers to be firm in their attitude towards their Diets.

In the choice of means employed by the Jesuits to this end can be seen the same adaptation to the requirements of the moment and the same prudent wisdom which is evident in almost all their actions in Germany. Only one Jesuit offended against this fundamental principle of the order, namely Bobadilla, one of the first of Loyola's disciples. When, in 1555, Charles V, in the "peace of Augsburg," allowed the Protestants equal rights with Catholics, Bobadilla, who was still swayed by that spirit of romantic fanaticism which the other members of the order had long laid aside, rose up in open opposition, proclaiming that the emperor was not justified in making such far-reaching concessions to the heretics.

This emotional noisy protest was completely unsuccessful: the emperor had Bobadilla imprisoned out of hand and banished. Ignatius, however, was extremely incensed at the out-of-date and unpractical behavior of his disciple, which he feared would endanger the further activities of the Jesuits in Germany, and, when Bobadilla came to Rome, would not receive him.

This first blunder, however, was to the last; thereafter the Jesuits always managed to win

105. VIENNA

Engraving of the eixteenth century

106. PETER CANISIUS 107. PETER FABER

THE FIRST JESUITS IN GERMANY

for themselves the friendship and trust of Catholic princes. They had succeeded in this with Ferdinand, the "king of the Romans," the brother of the emperor Charles. Ferdinand had received first Bobadilla, then Le Jay, with great amiability, and had finally become particularly friendly with Canisius. The Curia made excellent use of this relationship, when, after the abdication of Charles V, the danger arose that Ferdinand would purchase his election as emperor with great concessions to the protestant Electors. Canisius was immediately sent to Ferdinand, and he admonished him in such a way that Ferdinand gave him his solemn oath that he would be obedient to the pope in all things and would not surrender to the heretics.

When, with Maximilian II, an emperor came to power who sympathized openly with the Protestants, the anxious Curia decided to send the Jesuit Francis Rodriguez to Vienna to appeal to the emperor's conscience. Rodriguez was soon convinced that hardly anything could be done with Maximilian, and thereupon turned his attentions to his wife, whom he inspired with ardent zeal for the Catholic faith, so that the emperor was restrained, at least indirectly, from a policy too favorable to the Reformation.

Under Rudolph II, again, it was Fathers Maggio and Scherer who had the task of inducing the lethargic and weak-willed monarch to take a firm stand against the Protestants. The two Jesuits produced a memorandum setting forth the emperor's duty to stay the future progress of the Reformation, and, indeed, shortly after the presentation of the memorandum, the emperor issued an order forbidding the practice of the Protestant religion in Vienna.

The Jesuits were equally successful at the courts of the Catholic princes. Archduke a Charles of Styria had been compelled by his need for money to make such considerable concessions to the Protestant Diet that the Catholic religion had been almost entirely ousted from Graz. In order, therefore, to make the Archduke independent of the good will of his Diet, the Jesuits procured him ample funds from Rome; whereupon Charles immediately forbade the Protestant education of the young, gave over the University of Graz to the Jesuits, and banished a great number of Protestant preachers from the country.

In Bavaria, too, the Catholic Church had to thank the Jesuits first all for Duke Albert IV's firm stand against Lutheranism and for making his country the greatest stronghold of Catholicism. Soon the fathers could say with satisfaction that Munich was well on the way to becoming "a German Rome."

In spite of their many successful interventions, the Jesuits would hardly have been able to attain their real aim had they limited their activities to more sporadic diplomatic transactions; the whole character of their appointed task demanded, rather, a persevering, continuous exertion of influence over rulers. For the slow, vicissitudinous, historical process which was at that time developing in Germany created new situations continually, and necessitated ever fresh decisions on the part of the sovereigns. Although a Jesuit father may have for the moment restrained a prince from yielding to the Protestants, yet, at the next opportunity, when the Jesuit had departed, a new situation might arise inducing the ruler once more to take a step which was not in accordance with the policy of Rome. Only when the fathers were in a position to influence and to guide the princes at all times and in all situations could the Catholic cause hope for true success.

The institution of the confessional provided a continuous and truly effective means of securing the success of the diplomatic activities of the Jesuits. Hitherto the confessional, even with crowned heads, had had nothing to do with affairs of state; on the contrary, it had merely served to offer to princes, as sinful men, an opportunity of spiritual cleansing; the task of the spiritual director had been to restrain his penitent, by counsel and advice, from moral faults, and to show him how to live in such a way as to please God.

In these days of great religious schisms, however, there automatically arose a close connection between the confessional and politics, for, in the eyes of a Catholic priest, secession from the Church necessarily appeared the most heinous of all sins, and salvation from "heresy," salvation from the eternal fires of hell. Thus the confessor regarded it as his highest religious duty to restrain a ruler from such political actions as might advance heresy.

Owing, however, to the fact that the Jesuit confessors at the courts of princes now made politics an affair of conscience and identified every agreement with the Protestants with mortal sin, they took control to a considerable extent of the business of state at the same time as they undertook the direction of the prince's conscience.

Thus it came about that, although Ignatius and his first successors in the office of general had originally entertained considerable doubt concerning the acceptance by members of the order of the position of court confessor, the Society of Jesus was unwilling to dispense permanently with this important means of influence. Dared they refuse a position from which the sorely endangered Church, the kingdom of Christ on earth, could be the most effectively defended? It was made easier for the Jesuits to decide to accept the office of court confessor by the fact that there was no need whatsoever for then to sue for the position; on the contrary, the Catholic priests of Germany kept entreating the order to send them spiritual directors.

As confessors at the courts of Germany, the Jesuits defended most earnestly the theory that a prince was entitled to legislate, at his discretion, concerning the religious beliefs of his subjects, and they were able, with their customary scientific profundity, to support their arguments with numerous excerpts from the early fathers and from the old jurists. Bellarmine, Suarez and Mariana had demonstrated, with the greatest spirit, the inalienable sovereignty of the people, and now the Munich Jesuit Contzen demonstrated the opposite just as convincingly, in a learned work in ten volumes.

Here, indeed, the Jesuits could also appeal to an array of legal acts which laid down the principle *Cujus region, ejus religio*, and expressly accorded sovereigns the right to compel their subjects by force to accept the religion agreeable to the ruler; they could also point out that the Protestant princes made abundant use of this right to suppress Catholicism in their countries.

The Jesuits first attained political influence in Munich, for Duke William V of Bavaria, as early as the second half of the sixteenth century, took care always to discuss all his more important political affairs with his spiritual director, Mengin. Moreover, the duke had his son and heir, Maximilian, educated at the Jesuit college of Ingolstadt, and he always remained an obedient pupil of the Jesuits.

Archduke Ferdinand of Styria, too, the future emperor, had been brought up at Ingolstadt under the care of the Jesuits, and, after leaving the college, he immediately went on a pilgrimage to Rome, accompanied by one of his teachers, in order to obtain the pope's blessing. On the way, he visited the famous shrine of Loretto, and made there a vow to do his ut-

The Jesuits in the Thirty Years' War

most to banish Protestantism from his ancestral lands of Styria, Carinthia and Carniola.

Scarcely had he assumed his sovereignty in Graz when he subordinated himself entirely to the counsels of his Jesuit confessor, Stephen Rimel. The rector of the college at Vienna was able to report to the general of the order: "Our Father Stephan has the full confidence of the archduke, who asks and receives his advice in the most important concerns. . . The prince is very well-disposed to us. Whatever Father Stephen proposes to him, he carries out with the greatest pleasure."

The enactments of the young archduke soon showed in what direction his confessor was influencing him. Ferdinand declared that all the rights which his father had conceded to the Protestants were abolished, and banished the evangelical preachers and teachers from the land. He actually succeeded in so cowing the Styrian Diet that it no longer offered opposition to the energetic Counter-Reformation which was beginning.

As Rimel's successor at the archducal court of Graz, Father Heinrich Blyssem was appointed, and, after his departure, the office of confessor passed to the rector of Graz, Bartholomæus Viller. His political significance became considerable when, in 1617, the Emperor Matthias had the Archduke Ferdinand crowned King of Bohemia. On Viller's advice, Ferdinand at once proceeded vigorously to oppose Protestantism in his new dominion also.

This enterprise led, within a short time to the outbreak of the bloody religious war which was to convulse all Europe for the next thirty years. After the "Defenestration of Prague" in 1618 had proclaimed the outbreak of open rebellion, the old Emperor Matthias immediately wished to withdraw. However, he no longer possessed the energy to oppose his opinion to the will of King Ferdinand, whom his Jesuit confessor controlled, and the last hope of a peaceable settlement of the conflict was wrecked.

Meanwhile, the Bohemian Diet, by a special decree, had solemnly banished the Jesuits, whom they regarded as the originators of the civil war, from the country. "We, lords, knights, deputies of Prague, Kuttenberg and other estates," so runs this interesting document, "together recognize in what great danger this kingdom of Bohemia has stood ever since the introduction of the hypocritical sect of Jesuits. He have, moreover, found in truth that the originators of all this mischief are the above-mentioned Jesuits, who occupy themselves in contriving how they may strengthen the Roman See, and bring all kingdoms and lands under their power and might, who to this end employ the most illicit means, inflame rulers against one another cause rebellion, and unrest among superiors against subordinates, subordinates against superiors. . . Now, therefore, as they are in these ways the cause of the evil state which has befallen the kingdom, they have justly merited to be no longer tolerated in the said kingdom. . ."

Silesia and Moravia soon followed the example of Bohemia, and at the same time the Hungarian Protestants, provoked by the energetic Counter-Reformation work of the Jesuit Peter Pázmány, joined the Bohemian revolt.

In the middle of the ever-increasing confusion of wars, Emperor Matthias died, and Ferdinand was elected as his successor; his old confessor, Viller, accompanying the new emperor on the journey to his coronation. When, shortly after, Viller died, Ferdinand, on the recommendation of the general of the order, chose the Viennese professor of theology, Father Becan, as his confessor. The confidence which the emperor placed henceforth in Becan is shown in his own letters, in which he frequently remarked that he would undertake no important decision without having first taken the advice of his confessor.

As it became increasingly plain that Ferdinand, in his struggle with the Protestants of Bohemia, could expect active support only from the Bavarian Duke Maximilian, it became the most important task of the Jesuit confessors in Vienna and Munich to effect a union between Ferdinand and Maximilian. In exchange for his military assistance, the duke demanded the rank of Elector and a part of the Palatinate, and finally Becan actually succeeded in inducing the emperor to accept these conditions. In addition, appeals to Rome and to the Spanish court secured considerable financial assistance from the pope and an expeditionary force from the king of Spain.

The battle of the White Hill near Prague decided the first stage of the Thirty Years' War in favor of the emperor, whereupon Father Becan immediately found himself obliged to intervene to prevent another threatening conflict. For it soon proved to be impossible to carry out the cession of the Palatinate provinces of the overthrown "Winter King," Frederick, to Maximilian of Bavaria, as King James of England, the father-in-law of Frederick of the Palatinate, raised objections to this. Becan thereupon came to an understanding with Contzen, the spiritual director of Maximilian, and the two fathers formulated a compromise which provided that the Palatinate should be given back to Frederick, the original ruler, if Frederick's son were brought up as a true Catholic. Father Contzen had now to ensure that Maximilian agreed to this solution, which he soon succeeded in doing.

Even within the house of Habsburg there were in these days many conflicts to settle, for a disagreement had broken out between the emperor and his brothers, the Archdukes Ernest, Leopold and Charles, which threatened to become serious. The general of the order, Vitelleschi, wrote to Becan at the time, telling him to do everything to restore peace between the brothers, and, as Father Scherer was confessor to Archduke Ernest, Father Balbach to Archduke Leopold, and Father Scheiner to Charles, it was inevitable that the united efforts of these Jesuit confessors should soon lead to a settlement of the differences.

After Becan's departure, Father William Lamormaini took over the office of confessor to the Emperor Ferdinand, and as early as 1626 the papal nuncio at Vienna was able to report to Cardinal Barberini: "it is certain that the Jesuits, through the favor of the emperor, which cannot be overestimated, have attained to overwhelming power. . . they have the upper hand over everything, even over the most prominent ministers of state, and domineer over them, if they do not carry out their will. . . . Their influence has always been considerable, but it has reached its zenith since Father Lamormaini has been confessor to the emperor."

All the ambassadors' reports and diplomatic writings of the time speak again and again of the mighty power of this priest, who in his personal way of living observed the greatest simplicity, and who refused to take part in festivities, to live at court, or even to partake of the food which the emperor sometimes had sent to him.

The influence of Lamormaini acquired particular importance from the period of its exercise—for he held office for almost the whole duration of the thirty Years' War. The decisive political events of this period, indeed, made the greatest demands on Lamormaini, and to be equal to them he required extraordinary political capacity.

The Jesuits in the Thirty Years' War

For the relations between the two Catholic allies, the emperor and the Duke of Bavaria, were not always of the friendliest. The general of the order could not sufficiently often impress on Lamormaini how much it was to the interest of the whole of Christendom to prevent conflict between Vienna and Munich. On Ferdinand and Maximilian rested, "as on two pillars," Rome's hope of bringing victory once more to the Catholic cause in Germany.

But how difficult it was already to reconcile ecclesiastical and temporal interests is shown with especial plainness by the conduct of the Jesuit court confessors at Vienna and Munich. Lamormaini had become so much of a politician that he was identified more and more with the Habsburg state, whereas, on the other hand, Maximilian's confessor, Contzen, who regularly took part in the meetings of the Privy Council, and who had, moreover, prepared programmes for the financial administration and the fiscal system of Bavaria, could not avoid taking the side of his prince and his prince's advantage. Thus it came about that Lamormaini and Contzen were soon at daggers drawn, instead of working together under the terms of their instructions. Only when the general of the order had strongly intervened was it possible to induce the two fathers to work in agreement again, in the spirit of Rome.

Meanwhile, the campaign in Lower Saxony and Denmark, the second main division of the Thirty Years' War, had also ended with uncommon success for the Catholic cause, and the emperor, on Lamormaini's advice, decided to utilize his victory to make an energetic advance against Protestantism in the empire. In the year 1629, he issued an "Edict of Restitution," by which all institutions and ecclesiastical property that had been seized by the Protestants were taken away from them again.

The edict roused the Protestants to the utmost opposition, and this, together with the invasion of the Swedes under Gustavus Adolphus, gave a highly unfavorable turn to the emperor's situation. During the succeeding period of the Swedish war, Lamormaini found himself, moreover, in a delicate position with regard to the imperial general, Wallenstein. At the beginning, there had been firm friendship between the Jesuit and Wallenstein, and even in 1629 the general wrote most affectionate letters to the confessor. But later, when it became known that Wallenstein was opposed to war to the utmost and was trying, over the emperor's head, to reach a friendly settlement with Sweden, Lamormaini accounted it his chief task to oppose the general's policy. Thus the murder of Wallenstein in 1633 relieved the Jesuit father of that heavy care.

Just before the end of his political career, Lamormaini had at Rome's behest to exert his influence on the emperor when, in 1635, he decided to make peace with the German Protestants, and, united with them to wage war on external foes, Sweden and France. The papal nuncio charged the confessor to appeal to the conscience of the emperor, and the general of the order, too, Vitelleschi, wrote many anxious letters to Lamormaini, lest the peace should be too favorable to the Protestants. The general would have preferred to see the emperor allied with Catholic France, in order that they might together suppress Protestantism in the empire. This time, however, the temporal interests of the emperor triumphed over the religious and political aspirations of the Curia and even Lamormaini could not move the emperor from his determination to make peace at home and war abroad.

Lamormaini's continuous efforts to bring about a reconciliation between the principal Catholic powers, the emperor and France, often brought him into open conflict with the policy of Spain, which aimed at uniting all the strength of the house of Habsburg in an annihilating campaign against the French. Again and again Lamormaini's counsel and advice were directed against this anti-French policy of the Spanish court, so that, finally, the Spanish government complained to Rome about the imperial confessor.

Since the accession of Ferdinand II, it was known throughout the empire that the Jesuits were the persons who possessed most influence at court, and even aged Father Viller had been overwhelmed with requests from all quarters. After Lamormaini took over the office of confessor, and there was scarcely any important matter on which the emperor did not consult him, Lamormaini's modest little dwelling became a state chancellery. His workroom was filled from floor to ceiling with cabinets, in which, neatly labelled, all the political correspondence of the priest was kept; there was one with the superscription "Internal Affairs," another for documents connected with the conduct of the war another bore the title "Spanish," a fourth, "Italian."

It was inevitable that these records of the Jesuit father should attract unfavorable attention; many persons considered it their duty to warn the emperor against the excessive activity of his confessor, and even to inform the general of the order of their opinion.

Finally, indeed, Vitelleschi found himself compelled to issue a serious warning to Father Lamormaini, "people complain of your prolific correspondence," he wrote to the confessor, "and, although I can see nothing blameworthy in this of itself, it seems to me desirable either to remove this record of correspondence altogether, or at least to hide it from the eyes of visitors by a curtain."

The Conscience of Kings

If the rise of the Jesuits in Germany from homely, scarce-regarded preachers and catechists to the most powerful personalities in the realm seems astonishing enough, the brilliant career of the order in France is yet more remarkable. At the end of the sixteenth century, the accession of Henry IV marked the nadir of the Jesuit's power; suspected of complicity in the murder of Henry III, they had been banished from the land, and a pillory in the middle of Paris still bore witness to their misdeeds. Nevertheless, under the same ruler who had exiled them, they were to return in triumph, and to attain the greatest political influence as confessors to the king.

The history of this sudden rise from ignominious exile to the royal confessional shows better than any other phase of the order's existence those peculiar Jesuit tactics, which consisted primarily in always adapting their behavior to the requirements of the time, and not shrinking even from a complete change of standpoint when this seemed to them necessary for the attainment of their end.

This readiness at one time to support the sovereignty of the people and at another to stand, with Byzantine zeal, for the rights of the ruler, may appear as nothing but "lack of principle," unless the behavior of the Jesuits is considered in relation to the universal policy of Rome, when it nearly always appears direct and purposeful.

The Conscience of Kings

When the Jesuits in France, at the time of the League, inflamed the people against the king and proclaimed civil war, this was quite consistent with their point of view, since their object was to defend the Church against a "pro-heretic" ruler. But, the situation having fundamentally changed, and Henry IV having gone over to Catholicism and the Huguenot danger being past, the Jesuits had every reason to support the king to the utmost of their strength.

Henry IV found himself involved in a wary and dangerous war with Spain, which he could not bring to a victorious end until the pope had removed the ban of excommunication which had been pronounced on him, and had thus robbed Henry's enemies of moral support. On the other hand, it seemed desirable that the Curia, should ally itself with the French king, so that he should not fall in with the Gallican tendencies of his realm, and, after the English example, effect a complete separation from Rome.

When the Jesuits realized this situation, with all its implications, it was they, the very people whom King Henry had originally banished from France, who, with the greatest zeal, were the first to attempt to bring about the conclusion of peace between the king and the Curia. They exerted all their influence with the pope to obtain the lifting of henry's excommunication, employing for this purpose their best diplomatists, Bellarmine and Possevino, whose united efforts actually succeeded in persuading the pope to take this important step.

After this, it was not difficult for them to approach anew the king to whom they had rendered so great a service, and to obtain from him the restoration of the order in France. Henry was wise enough to assess the power of the Jesuits at its right value, and decided in 1603 to recall the Society of Jesus officially to France.

Still, however, he could not entirely overcome that distrust which the anti-Jesuit campaign of the Parlement and the university had awakened; accordingly, he demanded of the fathers a solemn oath in which they promised never to undertake anything against the king or against the peace and quiet of the realm; further, a member of the order, as security for the good behavior of the whole society, was to remain permanently at court at the king's disposal. These conditions were unquestionably humiliating for the Jesuits, so that even the general of the order said at the time that their recall under these conditions might be called a punishment rather than a favor.

The enemies of the Jesuits were not long in discovering, however, that Father Coton, living at court as a "security," had, by his pleasant, polished ways, won Henry's good-will, and was seen more and more often in confidential conversation with him. One day, the king asked Father Coton to take the office of his spiritual director, whereupon the "security" suddenly became an influential adviser.

Soon after the king had received absolution from Father Coton for the first time he gave the order to have the pillory demolished. Such a clear mark of favor for the Jesuits naturally produced the greatest uneasiness in those circles where hatred of the "Romanists" was still lively, and some members of the Royal Council of State even expressed themselves against this step. When the Duke of Sully suggested that the monument might at least be pulled down by night, Father Coton, replied smartly that Henry was no prince of darkness, but a king of light, and his measures had no need to shun the light of day. This argument so pleased the king that he immediately gave orders for the pillory to be pulled own at noon.

The Power and Secret of the Jesuits

Naturally, the fathers at the French court did not find it always easy to influence the ruler's decisions so that they might be in accordance with the policy of Rome. It is true that the reconciliation between Henry IV and the pope was accomplished, and the war between the Catholic powers, France and Spain, which had been for so long a thorn in the side of the Curia, seemed at least for the moment to be done with; but, in order to pacify the Huguenots, the king had had to issue the famous Edict of Toleration of Nantes, and this action had caused great displeasure at Rome. The Jesuits, therefore, were all the more pleased at Henry's decision to have his marriage with marguerite de Valois dissolved, and to marry the zealous Catholic, Marie de' Medici. This union seemed to offer a guarantee that France would remain true to the cause of Rome.

The intention of a king to rid himself of his wife and to contract a new marriage which, in the case of Henry VIII of England, had led the indignant Apostolic See to pronounce a ban of excommunication, this time roused feelings of delight in all Catholic hearts, for here the king was to be provided with a true daughter of the Church. Far from forbidding the dissolution of his marriage, the Curia hastened to bless Henry's new union with Marie de' Medici, and once more the Jesuits did their part in bringing Rome to this decision.

Great anxiety was caused to the fathers by the differences between France and Spain, which, in the meantime, had come more emerged; for scarcely had peace been made when Henry provoked the danger of another Spanish war by the support he gave to the rebellious Netherlands. The Jesuits hurriedly intervened as conciliators, and, as the king declared that he must insist on the separation of the Netherlands from Spain, they proposed that he should marry his daughter to the second son of the Spanish king, so that the Netherlands should fall to the descendants of this marriage. Clever as this project was, it was immediately shattered by the overbearing behavior of the Spaniards.

Thereafter, the political aspirations of France were again uppermost in Henry's mind, and, to Father Coton's great alarm, his penitent began active preparations for a great war against the Spanish and German Habsburgs, in alliance with the German Protestants.

But, just before he set out to join the army, Henry was stabbed to death by Ravaillac, a hedge-lawyer from Angoulême, who was impelled by the irresistible belief that he had to remove by force a king who meant, in alliance with heretics, to make war on Catholic powers.

What was more likely than that people should immediately accuse the Jesuits, who had already instigated so many royal murders, of being the spiritual authors of this deed also, which was so much to the advantage of their political views? It actually came out that Ravaillac, not long before, had made his confession to the Jesuit Father d'Aubigny, who, when the judge examined him, merely answered that God had granted him the gift of immediately forgetting what he heard in the confessional.

The Parlement and the Sorbonne once more rose up in violent opposition to the Society of Jesus; but it was now too powerful at court for such attacks to be able to shake it. Marie de' Medici, acting as regent for her son, the future Louis XIII, who was still a minor, was completely convinced of the good faith of the Jesuits, and paid not the slightest attention to the attacks of the Parlement and the Sorbonne.

The widow of Henry IV had entrusted herself blindly to the guidance of the Jesuits, and

The Conscience of Kings

this manifested itself in a complete change in the policy of France. There was now no talk of France's supporting the Protestants against the Spanish and German Habsburgs; on the contrary, the queen, under the influence of Coton and the papal nuncio, sought an alliance with Spain for the concerted advance against the Reformation.

The Jesuits immediately made use of their power at the regent's court to bring their old struggle with the Parlement and the university to a successful conclusion. They obtained a decree from the queen, which accorded them the right to give public instruction in all the faculties, thus breaking the teaching monopoly of the Sorbonne and laying the foundations for the future development of the Jesuit College of Clermont.

The hopes which the fathers had set on their pupil, the young king Louis XIII, soon proved deceptive. Louis was, no doubt, of a Catholic turn of mind, but his morbid hatred of his mother immediately created the greatest difficulties for the Jesuits. Hardly had the king taken up the reins of government, before he treated his mother as a prisoner and recalled all the advisers to Henry IV. Mainly from opposition to the policy of his hated mother, Louis XIII now pursued all those designs which his father had been prevented, through death, from accomplishing: he prepared for a war against Spain, and allied himself with the German Protestants, which naturally filled the Jesuits with the greatest uneasiness.

Father Coton was confessor to the new king also, and tried with gentleness no less than with energy to combat Louis's crazy enmity towards his mother. This inevitably brought Coton into conflict with the influential favorites of the king, among whom the Duc de Luynes was sufficiently powerful to have Coton removed from his office.

Fathers Arnoux, de Seguiran and Suffren then acted successively as confessors to Louis XIII, and they, finally, so far succeeded in undermining the power of the Duc de Luynes that he found it desirable to abandon an openly anti-Roman policy. In the year 1629, Father Suffren attempted to prevent the threatened entry of France into the thirty Years' War, by getting into touch with Lamormaini, and asking him to advise the emperor to ally himself with France. Lamormaini was delighted to do this, and immediately reported to Suffren that he had spoken with the emperor and advised him to consider favorably the peace proposals of France.

The fathers believed that they had once again achieved a great victory through their perseverance and tenacity; but they did not reckon with the will of that man who, with iron hand, had now seized upon the control of the policy of France.

Cardinal Richelieu harbored designs which were quite at variance with those of the Jesuits: he encouraged the weak king to pursue, with great determination, the anti-Spanish policy of Henry IV, and without scruple to send Marie de' Medici, who opposed his plans into exile. The confessor Suffren, who hitherto had always tried to mediate between mother and son, now allied himself entirely with the queen and went with her, whereupon Richelieu appointed Father Caussin as confessor to the king.

Caussin himself writes concerning the reasons which had led to his appointment: "the Minister of State, Richelieu, who appoints the king's confessor without leaving him any choice, looks for men who not only have the reputation of leading a good life, but at the same time are completely devoted to him... He now thinks that I shall be weak enough to tolerate an evil deed...."

This assumption of Ruchelieu's soon proved to be incorrect, for Caussin made the upmost use of his position to restrain the king from any step which was contrary to the policy of Rome. He wrote to his brethren in the order; "I will have no other care than to be as much use as possible to the church and the public weal." At the same time, he recorded in this letter his conception of the duties of a court confessor, saying that it was his task "to combat the sins which the royal purple brings forth . . . he who thinks that the sins of the great are serious only if they are of a human nature, while what they do as rulers is of little importance, sets himself in opposition to the opinion of all wise men . . . Is not the harm done by the sins of monarchs, and the infection of their bad example, the greater in proportion as their position is an exalted one?"

These "sins which the royal purple brings forth", which Caussin had made it his task to combat, naturally consisted in the following of Richelieu's counsels, which amounted to concluding alliances with Protestants and even with Turks, in order to make war on the Catholic empire of the Habsburgs. In fiery indignation, Caussin, in the year 1637, made an address to the king, and declared that the plans of the French government were absolutely detestable, and that the king's unscrupulous treatment of his mother was a gross offence against the fourth commandment.

This speech, however, merely resulted in the dismissal of Caussin, for Richelieu without more ado had the inconvenient confessor removed from the court and interned, as a political offender, at Rennes. So the Jesuits had to recognize that all their efforts to gain influence over the king were unavailing, since Louis XIII was himself much too weak to undertake anything contrary to the will of his powerful adviser Richelieu.

In Cardinal Richelieu, who now directed the destinies of France, the idea of the modern, absolutist state, which Roman policy combated with every means, seemed to have taken bodily form in a powerful, all-dominating personality. Richelieu himself had often said that his personal interests were identical with those of France, and even his enemies saw in his person the state itself. On his deathbed, Richelieu could declare that he had never had an enemy who was not also the enemy of France.

Everything that he did was subordinated to the interests of the state, and he rid himself without scruple of those who seemed in any way dangerous to the state, even if they were personally associated with him. More than once, he received one of his acquaintances with affection, and ate with him at noon, only to have him imprisoned an hour later.

Richelieu in his later years, crippled in all his limbs and racked with pain, had himself carried from place to place in an enormous sedan chair like a little room, necessitating the pulling down of town walls and the filling in of ditches on the way, to make the journey of the important invalid more comfortable. And throughout the country, wherever the cardinal appeared in his portable room, the people fell on their knees, and sought to kiss his raiment, for all France saw, in this crippled old man, the incorporation of the state.

Richelieu was, indeed, a pious Catholic and bore the cardinal's purple; he had set up in his palace in Paris a golden chapel with the most costly vessels for the celebration of mass; but, before everything else, he was a Frenchman, and, where the interests of France diverged from those of the Church, he did not hesitate an instant to give the former the first place.

Nothing seemed more necessary for the greatness of the French nation than release from the ever-threatening Spanish danger: the Habsburg world-power must be overthrown, Spain must be driven from the Netherlands, if France was to develop freely in the future. Therefore, Richelieu prepared in every way for war against the house of Habsburg, and for this purpose welcomed any ally, from the king of Sweden to the Sultan.

This man was no weak king, whom his confessor could deter from his plans by threats of eternal damnation; all the methods which the Jesuit order had hitherto found effective in their political activity were useless as applied to him. For here, for the first time, the fathers found themselves opposed to a really great statesman, great in the very qualities which had heretofore established the superiority of the Society of Jesus over its allies and opponents. Richelieu was just as clever and logical in his plans, just as determined and unscrupulous in carrying them out, as the Jesuits themselves.

Against such an opponent, only one policy would serve, that of compliance. The leaders of the order early recognized this, and, accordingly, Vitelleschi did not praise the confessor Caussin for his obstinate behavior; but, on the contrary, severely censured him. The succeeding Jesuit confessors at the French court carefully avoided anything which might annoy the powerful minister of state, and the general himself assured Richelieu of his complete devotion.

The cardinal desired no more: he accepted amiably the Jesuits' offer to lend him a helping hand, and thereafter encouraged particularly the educational activity of the order. For just as the interests of the state had caused him to repress the fathers so long as they showed opposition to him, so, now that they were conducting themselves discreetly, it seemed to the advantage of France to desire their advancement.

For Richelieu had always been of the opinion, recorded in his will, that the welfare of the realm demanded, unceasingly, "the opposition of two mutually antagonistic tendencies." Against the undesirable power of the university, therefore, it seemed to him opportune to encourage the educational activity of the Jesuits, and to let the two institutions exist side by side, equally powerful, "whereby, through their mutual rivalry, they will render one another harmless." This attitude of the government remained unchanged when Richelieu was succeeded by his docile pupil Mazarin, who now ruled in place of the minor, Louis XIV.

The Confessors of Louis XIV

Richelieu and Mazarin had provided kings with an impressive example of what authority the holder, for the time being, of the supreme power can amass in his own hands if he is sufficiently determined, and Louis XIV, with his pronouncement, *L'état, c'est moi*, was merely repeating what the two great cardinals had not only said, but actually effected, before him.

With Louis XIV, however, it was for the most part nothing but a pathetic gesture: he liked to be called the "Sun King" and, in order to invest his person with the nimbus of divine sublimity, he surrounded himself with an etiquette which resembled religious ceremonial. It became the greatest privilege of courtiers and ministers of state to be allowed to present the king with the washing water at his morning toilet, and, when mass was celebrated in the court chapel, the people present turned their faces not to the altar but to the king.

Naturally, the relation of this convinced autocrat to the Church and to the Papal See was in the beginning ruled by the spirit of complete independence: Louis not only denied the pope any influence in the government of his kingdom, but also he sought to interfere arbitrarily in the administration of the French Church.

It looked as if once more a Catholic ruler was about to sever himself for ever from the policy of Rome, and anxious minds saw in Louis XIV a new Henry VIII of England. Only the Jesuits remained quiet and optimistic, for, while in the mouth of Richelieu—a ruler not indeed by birth, but in spirit and will a truly powerful one—identification with the state had had actual meaning, the wise fathers knew well enough what to make of the claims of conceited monarchs. They had had to deal with "fearful tyrants" sufficiently often in Sweden, Poland, Germany, Japan and China, to know how to handle a royal character of this kind.

So they left their "Sun King" happy in the belief that he was "the State," and, when the courtiers officiously handed the washing water to the exalted lord, and during the mass turned their backs on the altar, the fathers knew well enough that all this was harmless child's play. Neither was a monarch's fancy that he was divine anything new for the Jesuits, and they foresaw from the beginning that the "Sun King" would sooner or later become an instrument of the Society of Jesus, like many another autocrat before him.

They had not long to wait: even Father Annat, the first confessor of Louis XIV, succeeded at last, through his perseverance, in gaining considerable influence, and his successor, Ferrier, in 1670 obtained the right to recommend to the king suitable candidates for all vacant benefices.

But though the king, once so inflexible, was beginning to give way a little in affairs of state, thereby filling the Jesuits with hope, the private life of Louis XIV was in no way conformable to the demands of the Church. The placid, blonde and virtuous Spaniard, Marie Thérèse, Louis's lawful wife, had from the very first so wearied her husband that he, had sought, first with Mazarins' two nieces, then with the beautiful Mademoiselle de la Vallière, and finally with the witty and amusing Marquise de Montespan, that consolation without which his whole "Sun Kingdom" would have been a weariness to the flesh.

Concerning the curious situations which arose from Louis's amours, the Duc de Saint-Simon writes that the spectacle of a married king who "had two mistresses at the same time, and travelled about with both of them," created great scandal: "The ladies sat in the queen's carriage, and the people streamed by in crowds to see the 'three queens.'"

The confessors were again and again in the painful position of having to refuse the Easter communion to the ruler, for in those days Louis preferred the danger of eternal damnation to a breach with his mistresses. It was in vain that the celebrated Jesuit preacher, Bourdaloue, made bold to appeal to the monarch's conscience, in front of the whole court, and to order him to break with Madame de Montespan. "Let the mass of the people," cried Bourdaloue to the king in his Easter sermon in the year 1675, "clearly recognize that you are no longer the man whose example had been so pernicious... Flee from those pleasant places whose air is

108. EXPULSION OF THE JESUITS FROM PARIS UNDER HENRY IV

109. HENRY IV'S HEART BEING TRANSFERRED TO THE JESUIT COLLEGE OF LA FLÈCHE

110. LOUIS XIV AND HIS COURT RIDE IN STATE TO THE JESUIT CHURCH

dangerous to you, from those meetings which are so apt to inflame your passion anew!"

Although these admonitions had no results, Father la Chaise, who had taken over the office of confessor to the king, did not give up hope of improvement. With his own trust in God, he waited politely smiling until the sensual emotions of the king had quieted; he knew that, when Louis was older, he would prove more ready for spiritual counsel. Without insisting on immoderate, stern measures, therefore, La Chaise let gentleness and forbearance rule for the time being, thereby bringing down on himself later the reproaches of many historians.

He who sees in the behavior of this priest merely an example of the infamous "Jesuit laxity," overlooks the fact that la Chaise held it to be more in the interests of his task to play the role of a gentle mediator and to leave strong action to Father Bourdaloue; by this means, he could always intervene with conciliatory words, if the rigor of Father Bourdaloue threatened to put the king out of humor and thus to endanger the whole work. This work, the attainment of the end desired by the Church, was the only thing that mattered. In expectation of this, La Chaise waited patiently, avoided as much as possible speaking with the king on the delicate subject of "carnal sins," and discoursed willingly with him on numismatics.

Later events were to prove him right: entirely through his gentle and inoffensive behavior, he succeeded gradually in achieving a result concerning which the Jansenist Abbé Dorat reported to a bishop with whom he was on friendly terms: "It is true that the king has changed his manner of life in a quite astonishing way. Father La Chaise has led him imperceptibly where he wished to have him. The man in the black habit has clothed his penitent in a white garment, so that now the whole court must exercise the greatest restraint." Louis had, in fact, changed his mistresses so often that he finally chanced on a religious devotee, and as, in the meantime , he had become older and fatter, and was beginning to suffer from gout and fistula, he now devoted himself with his whole heart to those moral interests which his confessor and his new mistress placed before him.

With true feminine instinct, Madame de Maintenon, herself no longer in her first youth, had realized at once that the ageing king must be captivated by other than merely sensual means, so in her relations with Louis she brought to the front the homespun in her character, and, imbuing the king with the fear of death and eternal damnation, incited him to piety, and, to a certain extent, showed him the way to heaven.

The success which Madame de Maintenon achieved by these means exceeded all expectations. Soon the king's greatest pleasure was to sit for hours, arm-chair to arm-chair, discoursing on religious things with his new friend. He practiced secret penances, prayed fervently, and gave alms wherever he could. The ladies of the court had suddenly to appear in modest garments, and the equivocal speech and blasphemies which had been so popular before were now taboo.

In order that the claims of morality should be satisfied, Louis, after the death of his queen, was secretly married to Madame de Maintenon, so that Father La Chaise had really no longer any grounds for refusing the king absolution. Henceforward, even the Council of Ministers was held in Madame de Maintenon's room, while she worked at the spinning-wheel like a modest housewife, and only occasionally threw in remarks and advice.

As regards politics, too the king had completely changed his opinions, and, though formerly he had energetically combated the claims of the papacy, now he submitted himself in every respect to the wishes of Rome. The only task that remained to good Father La Chaise, who was now reaping the reward of his patience, was really to rationalize the king's wild urge for submission to ecclesiastical authority, and to direct it into politically useful channels. Often, indeed, he had to exercise a moderating influence, and to restrain Louis from measures which, in their exaggerated "Popishness," could only lead to harm. For Madame de Maintenon, now that she had surrendered herself completely to piety, recognized no limits, and she led the elderly king farther and farther on the road of religious intolerance. But La Chaise, with all his religious faith, was no zealous fanatic; he was a statesman, and felt himself to be the ambassador of a great world-power, with the task, no doubt, of bringing France under the domination of Rome, but of avoiding any unnecessary complications in so doing.

Accordingly, the bigoted way in which Madame de Maintenon wished to give effect to her religious zeal was painful an unsympathetic to him, while she on her side could not tolerate the conciliatory, pliable Jesuit. Again, and again, there were disagreements concerning the degree of piety desirable at court. Madame de Maintenon wanted all theatrical performances forbidden, as they "nourished the evil passions, "while La Chaise defended the theatre, and said that, if youth were deprived of innocent and educative pleasures, it would merely devote itself to other sins.

But the opinions of the confessor and of Madame de Maintenon differed too on the question of the persecution of Protestants in France. La Chaise was certainly of the opinion that Louis XIV could best expiate the sins of his youth by combating Protestantism; but he raised objections to the violent methods which Madame de Maintenon was constantly advocating.

Owing to pressure from her, the Protestants were excluded from all dignities and offices, and at last even from civil occupations, seven-year-old children were forcibly compelled to come over to Rome, and the Huguenots harassed by "dragonnades" until they renounced their faith. When the king finally, in the year 1685, completely repealed the Edict of Nantes, and ordained the full suppression of the Protestant church, pious Madame de Maintenon was quite convinced that everything had been done to secure that she might one day enter unhindered into the kingdom of Heaven on the arm of the most Christian king.

Although La Chaise also took part with zeal in the "conversion" of the Huguenots, and for this purpose organized Jesuit missions in the protestant provinces of France, all this in his opinion had to be done slowly and inconspicuously, with "hopefulness and kindness." This is quite in accordance with the Duc de Saint-Simon's description of the confessor as a peace-loving and moderate character, and the praise that even Voltaire gives to his gentleness, "which always left open the way of conciliation." Even a contemporary protestant, Pastor Jurieu, defends the court confessor against the popular accusation that he had caused the revocation of the edict of Nantes: "La Chaise is no more to blame for this than anyone else; true, he belongs to a Society which from its very nature is our deadly enemy; but no one has ever observed that he is one of those hot-heads whose pride it is to provoke unrest by false zeal, and to pour out blood... It would be a great mistake to think that it was he who induced the king to destroy us."

The Society of Jesus—which had managed to supply trained hydraulic engineers to the Chinese emperor who wanted fountains—found no difficulty, after the death of Father La

111. KING LOUIS XIV OF FRANCE

112. MARQUISE DE MONTESPAN

113. MADAME DE MAINTERON

114. MADEMOISELLE DE LA VALLIÈRE

LOUIS XV OF FRANCE

116. MARQUISE DE POMPADOUR

117. THE FATHER-CONFESSOR PERUSSEAU

Chaise, in supplying the *roi Soleil*, who had now become a gloomy fanatic and an unrelenting persecutor of the protestants, with a confessor after his present taste.

The sour Father Le Tellier, who took over this office, had neither friends nor relations; he had risen from the lowest ranks of the people, and, like the king and his friend, had no liking for worldly pleasures.

The period during, which he held office at Versailles does not by any means belong to the glorious epochs of the order's history. Under him occurred the undignified quarrel concerning the bull *Unigenitus*, and the unscrupulous persecution of the Jansenists, in which Le Tellier labored unceasingly, merely made new enemies for the Society of Jesus.

Thus it came about that the first thing that Philip, Duke of Orleans, who became regent after the death of the *roi Soleil*, did was to banish the hated Le Tellier from the court. The Jansenists and Gallicans who had been imprisoned at Le Tellier's instigation were released from prison, and Cardinal de Noailles, the implacable enemy of the Jesuit order, was now made, in Le Tellier's place, the chairman of that "Council of Conscience" which exercised ecclesiastic patronage in France. The University of Paris immediately availed itself of the opportunity to declare that it would not in future grant degrees to students of the Jesuit College of Clermont.

The Jesuits found themselves in a particularly difficult position with Philip of Orleans; indeed, their situation was almost as desperate as in the days of Richelieu. For while, at that time, they had been unable to make headway against the invincible energy and the firm will of the great cardinal, they now found that all their efforts and arts were wrecked on the complete cynicism which the Regent displayed in regard to all problems of faith and politics. Philip of Orleans was a skeptic, a mocker, who took neither the Church nor the Crown seriously, who despised the Jesuits just as much as he did the Protestants and the Jansenists. He regarded all men without distinction as rogues, some of whom possessed intelligence and wit, the others not.

Wearied with the affairs of state, the regent escaped as often as possible to a circle of boon companions and questionable ladies, and he spent his nights in the worst quarters of the city; it was commonly reported of him that he maintained an incestuous relation with his daughter, the Duchesse de Berry, and he himself did not even consider it worth the trouble to contradict these rumors.

When the Jesuits realized that nothing useful could be gained from this man, they applied themselves to the regent's favorite, the Abbé Dubois, and declared themselves ready to obtain for him the coveted cardinal's hat. Dubois showed his gratitude to them, when he was made prime minister, by opposing the Gallicans and Jansenists with all his energies.

The Tribulations of Madame de Pompadour

"At last we have a king again!" cried the people in the streets, when Louis XV, the great-grandson of the *roi Soleil*, drove through Paris on the day of his official accession to government. But the Jesuits hailed the end of the regency with particularly bright hopes, for the new ruler had been brought up by them, and promised, by his whole character, to remain their true disciple.

Actually, in political matters Louis XV followed exactly the directions of his confessors; but in his private life he gave the Jesuits no less trouble than his pious great-grandfather. Like him, he was lacking in that Christian submission which would have enabled him to suffer with decorum a tedious, legitimate marriage, and he soon found in the pretty Duchesse de Châteauroux the diversion he sought. As he once declared to his Minister Choiseul, it was his conviction that, as "the Lord's anointed," he could very well indulge in such intercourse without going to hell for it.

However prudent and conciliatory the Jesuits might be in other respects, they had no indulgence for sexual irregularities. Again and again, they impressed on the king that divine "anointing" would not of itself avail to bring to heaven, and that, if he wished to avoid eternal damnation, he must renounce all unlawful sensual pleasures.

The sternness with which the Jesuits combated adultery constituted the only departure from the principle of gentleness and compliance which was otherwise a fundamental rule of the order, and had been the cause of its success, and it was not least this inconsistency which was to wreck the Society of Jesus, and this under the rulership of that very king who had been from the beginning so devoted to them. By refusing to tolerate Louis XV's mistresses, the Jesuits kept placing the king in the dilemma of having to choose between the heavenly reward held out to him if he renounced his amours, and the much more accessible earthly pleasure of intercourse with beautiful women. Usually Louis decided for his mistress; but often enough some external circumstance impelled him to a temporary change of mind. Once when he was with the Duchesse de Châteauroux at Metz, and was there attacked by high fever, the confessor who had been hurriedly summoned refused to give him extreme unction so long as the duchess remained within the city walls. The monarch, in terror of his life and of his soul's salvation, immediately had the lady sent back to Paris in a coach with curtained windows. But hardly had he recovered before he told the confessor not to trouble any more, and sent for his lady-love again.

When the Marquise de pompadour had succeeded the Duchesse de Châteauroux, she managed so well to banish the eternal boredom of the king by ever new festivities and amusements, that it became more and more difficult for the monarch to meet the demands of his confessor even approximately. But on this point Father Perusseau displayed an invincible obstinacy. While the highest personages outvied each other in their eagerness to be received by the marquise, Perusseau flatly refused to have anything to do with her, and, when Easter approached, he always insisted firmly that she must leave the court before he could give the king communion.

"Much is said in society about the king's wish to keep Easter," wrote the Minister d'Argenson in the year 1749. "People most positively assert that his majesty has had an interview lasting two hours with Father Perusseau. The marquise weeps continuously, and her adherents show the greatest uneasiness... It is certain that the king in the last two weeks has conversed often with Father Perusseau, and it is no less certain that he has said to the marquise: I command you to spend a month at Crécy!"

In the jubilee year 1751, Madame de pompadour was in a particularly nervous state, so that everyone said she was suffering from "jubilee fever"; the truth was that this feast would

The Tribulations of Madame de Pompadour

in all probability once more bring up the question of the king's communion. On this account, the Minister Machault, an ally of the marquise, sought on every imaginable pretext to restrain the king from taking part in the festival and so to prevent the recurrence of the painful question of communion.

Madame de Pompadour, who had boldly defied all intrigues, lampoons and revolts of the people, lived in ceaseless fear of the Jesuits and humbly courted their favor. In order to dispose the fathers more favorably, she suddenly became pious: she was continually to be seen deep in the perusal of pious books, and, when she attended mass in the queen's suite, she remained longer than any of the other ladies on her knees with folded hands and bowed head. In spite of everything, Perusseau remained obstinately unshakable in his demand that the marquise should leave the court of Versailles, and would not budge even though she declared that her relation with the king was now of a friendly nature only, and the king adduced the pronouncements of many theological authorities in support of the permissibility of his friendship with Madame de Pompadour.

The death of Perusseau brought no relief from these difficulties; indeed, the minister of state, Chioseul, declared of the new confessor, Desmarets, that he was "even narrower than his predecessor, and like him surrounded by persons who wished to remove Madame de Pompadour from court."

As, in these circumstances, Father Desmarets could be reckoned on as little as his predecessor, Madame de Pompadour turned to another Jesuit, Father de Sacy, who, she thought, would give her the sacrament, and thus legalize her position, as it were, from the point of view of the Church. De Sacy, however, proved just as obdurate, and demanded, in the first place, that Madame de Pompadour should be reconciled to her lawful husband, d'Étioles, and should ask him to live with her again.

The proud woman actually consented to take this humiliating step; to her great relief d'Étioles immediately replied that he would have nothing more to do with her, and she thought that she was now adequately covered by her husband's refusal. "My return to my husband," she wrote at the time, "is no more in question, as he has refused this for ever. So my conscience is quite at ease on this point. Nothing else will raise any difficulties."

Nevertheless, Father de Sacy raised difficulties, of which Madame de Pompadour herself writes: "He commanded me, on grounds of decorum, to have the stairs leading to my apartment rebuilt, so that the king could in future only come to see me by way of the salon. This, and other rules of conduct which he prescribed for me and which I faithfully followed, created a great sensation in court and in the whole town."

But, as the rebuilding of the castle stairs did not satisfy the Jesuits, who in questions of morals were almost insatiable, and, as they actually demanded that the marquise should absent herself entirely from the court until further notice, she finally gave up the idea of a reconciliation with the Jesuits, and applied to a secular priest who had been recommended to her by the lieutenant-general of police, and who took it upon himself to give her communion without further conditions.

Fathers Perusseau, Desmarets and de Sacy had neglected a really unique opportunity of securing for the order the protection of the all-powerful favorite, and they were to pay dearly for the stern morality which was so mistaken politically. Not without some truth could Cardinal de Bernis declare, some years later, that the suppression of the Society of Jesus in France was due mainly to the refusal of Father de Sacy to grant absolution to Madame de Pompadour.

"Enlightened Despotism"

The hatred of ministers, favorites, mistresses, and intriguers against the Jesuits had by this time grown powerful in all Catholic courts, for the holders of these positions, in which, before the days of Jesuit court confessors, it had been possible to exercise unlimited control over the sovereigns, saw their positions more and more seriously endangered by the influence of the fathers. It was inevitable that people in every country who were being adversely affected by the Jesuits should stretch out their hands to one another, over the frontiers, and should unite in a firm league against the order.

The first to take decisive steps was the Portuguese prime minister, the marquise of Pombal, for in his country, since the Braganza dynasty had provided the realm with a number of unusually weak-minded rulers, the Jesuits had attained to considerable influence, and were standing in the minister's way.

Pombal was fully determined to become a second Richelieu, and indeed the weakness and incapacity of the king provided a splendid opportunity. Just as Richelieu had built up his power on the weak will of Louis XIII, so Pombal with even greater confidence could rely on Joseph I of Portugal, who in this respect presented the ideal for an ambitious prime minister. This monarch really troubled about nothing; he was lazy, sickly, eternally bored, and on principle left the business of state to others; his favorite occupation was to go for walks along the Tagus, surrounded by beautiful women and musicians.

While it should not, therefore, have been difficult, with such a ruler, to become an all-powerful dictator, there were two obstacles in the Marquis of Pombal's way: the power of the proud, high aristocracy and the influence of their close allies, the Jesuits. In vain had Pombal sought, for a long time, to penetrate into the aristocratic party and to win its support for his plans; the haughty nobles saw in Pombal nothing but an upstart from the burgher class, and treated him accordingly with the greatest contempt. The Jesuits again, though they had supported the minister at the beginning of his career, had given him clearly to understand that they were not willing to surrender their influential position at court.

Only the personal cowardice of the king could help the marquis to gain the victory: if it was possible to imbue him with fear of the high nobility and to convince him that the Jesuits were seeking his life, then King Joseph, as Pombal very well knew, would not rest until every member of the Society of Jesus was safely imprisoned or expelled by force from the land.

An attempt against the king served Pombal's turn excellently. Joseph entertained tender feelings for the young Marchioness of Tavora, and used to visit her in the evening. The husband of the lady disapproved, however, and lay in wait for the king on one of his journeys to the rendezvous, in order to curb his desire for further nocturnal adventures with a few shots from a pistol. Joseph was slightly wounded in the arm, and returned in a panic to the castle.

"Enlightened Despotism"

The violent action of the young nobleman, who had dared to protest in so decisive a manner against his cuckoldry, was such an astonishing and unusual thing that no one believed that the marquis had come to it on his own initiative. Who had ever heard of the husband of a king's mistress making difficulties or resorting to force? Malignant seditionaries must have been at work, inciting the marquis to such behavior, which exceeded all the bounds of etiquette! But who could have contrived such atrocious wickedness, if not the Jesuits—crafty, audacious and capable of any baseness?

Pombal immediately had the whole Tavora family, and the old Duke of Aveiro, imprisoned: the latter had had nothing whatever to do with the affair, but had been imprudent enough to let the prime minister feel, more than once, his bourgeois origin. At the same time, Pombal gave orders to have the Jesuits' houses surrounded by soldiers, and the three Fathers Malagrida, Mattos and Alexandre taken prisoner as accomplices in the plot against the king. This indictment was based solely on the circumstances that the Jesuits had been the friends and confessors of the Tavora and Aveiro families, but Pombal hoped that the court of inquiry, with the help of torture and other approved methods, would soon be able to produce further evidence against the fathers.

Contrary to expectation, however, all efforts to discover any tolerably useful material in confirmation of the charge against the Jesuits failed, until at last Pombal hit upon the expedient of having Malagrida, imprisoned for high treason, tried of heresy. The old, reputedly fanatical father had produced a number of mystical writings and exercises which offered a good handle for a trial by the Inquisition, and, as this tribunal was well-skilled in discovering heresy, the desired result was soon obtained; Malagrida was pronounced guilty and burnt at a solemn auto-de-fé.

To this, and all other decisions of Pombal, King Joseph eagerly assented, so great was his indignation that the Jesuits, according to Pombal's assertion, should have so treasonably counselled the husband of the beautiful marchioness to interfere with the pleasures of an anointed ruler. Moreover, the indignant king hastened to sign a decree by which the Jesuits were denounced as "traitors, rebels and enemies to the realm,' and banished for ever from Portugal; this entailed the not inconsiderable advantage that the crown could confiscate all the goods, revenues and lands of the order. The prime minister saw to it that this edict was carried out at once, with the greatest determination and brutality, not only in Portugal itself, but also in Portuguese colonies of South America.

In order to justify the measures, Pombal deluged the whole of Europe with a flood of anti-Jesuit manifestoes and publications; it was perhaps the first time in European history that a government had made use of the printing-press to rehabilitate itself in the eyes of other states. The minister confidently hoped that the intellectually emancipated circles in France, who were ill-disposed to the Church, would welcome the expulsion of the Jesuit order from Portugal. But herein he was mistake, for the philosophers were as much repelled by the foolishness of Pombal's quite incredible assertions, as by the inquisitorial methods by which the Portuguese government had taken action against the Jesuits. Voltaire, who at once saw the true intention of Pombal's "despotic enlightenment," said, on the other hand, that here there were found together "a superfluity of the laughable with a superfluity of the horrible."

The European chancelleries, however, for the most part allowed themselves to be convinced by Pombal's pamphlets without any closer investigation, and accepted as pure gospel everything asserted therein about the politically dangerous doings of the Jesuits.

In France particularly, the action of the Portuguese government made a great impression, and the French opponents of the Society of Jesus took courage for energetic action; for what had been possible in little Portugal must surely be capable of achievement in France as well.

Just at the right moment there occurred that open scandal which is almost indispensable for the success of decisive political measures: the sensational law-suit of the Jesuit Father Lavalette.

This man, the leader of the Jesuit settlement on the island of Martinique, in an endeavor to place his mission on a secure financial footing, had undertaken extensive trading enterprises, utilizing all means of commercial credit. One day, some of his cargoes were captured by the English, and Lavalette found himself unable to meet his bills of exchange.

A trading firm in Marseilles, which had suffered to the extent of two and a half million francs, applied to the order and requested that the loss should be made good. This the Jesuit general refused, with the explanation that Lavalette, through his commercial undertakings, had broken the rules of the order, and that the Society of Jesus was not liable for his debts. There was a law-suit before the court of justice at Marseilles, and judgment was given for the complainant firm.

Instead of meeting the bills and thus avoiding any further unwelcome attention, the order, in the absurd belief that the Paris Parlement would be more likely to accord them justice, appealed to the Parlement. Nothing could have been more welcome to the lawyers of the Paris Parlement than this foolish step of the Jesuits, by which the order was delivered into the hands of its sworn foes.

As the question under dispute was whether Lavalette, by his trading concerns, had violated the rules of the order, the Parlement demanded the production of the hitherto secret *Constitutions*. Not satisfied with dismissing the Jesuits' appeal against the Marseilles judgment, the Parlement finally pronounced that it had found that a number of the rules of the Jesuit order were immoral and a danger to the state, a decision which immediately filled the whole of Paris once more with the spirit of the Jansenists. In the elegant houses of the fashionable world, as in the back rooms of the small shopkeepers, people eagerly disputed anew over the half-forgotten questions of the doctrine of Probabilism, the *reservation mentalis* and laxist Jesuit morality. The old scandal of the Jesuit Father Girard was brought up again—the father who three decades before had been tried for having led his penitent, "la belle Cadière," into all kinds of immoral behavior. It was true that, at the time, Girard was released by the court of justice, but this did not prevent anyone, thirty years later, from regarding his guilt as proven, and bringing it up as evidence of the viciousness of the whole order.

On August 6, 1762, the Parlement decided that the Society of Jesus, being incompatible with the welfare of the state, should be at once suppressed, and its members expelled from the country. The provincial Parlements confirmed this decision of the Paris courts.

True, the consent of the king without which the decisions of the Parlements could have no legal force, was still outstanding. This consent was not easy to obtain, as it was difficult to convince Louis XV that the Jesuits were the most immoral men in the world; he above all peo-

118. THE EXPULSION OF THE JESUITS FROM PORTUGAL

119. THE EXPULSION OF THE JESUITS FROM SPAIN

120. THE PROFESSED HOUSE OF THE JESUITS IN VIENNA

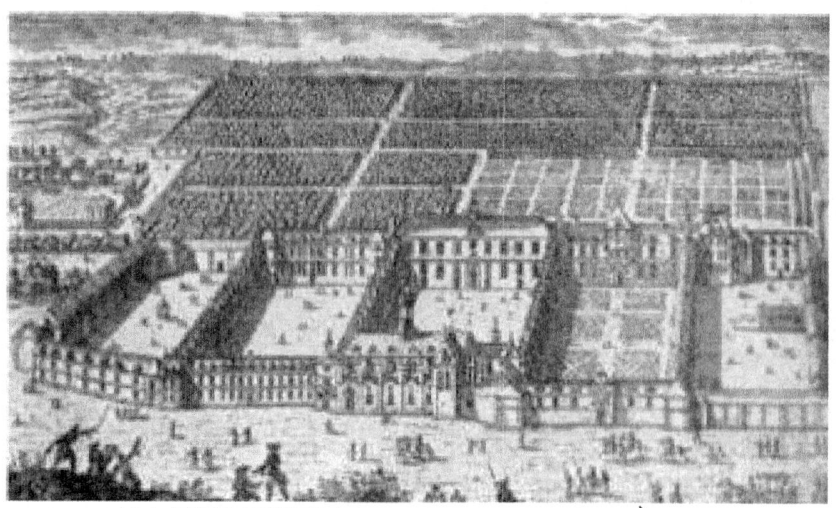

121. THE JESUIT COLLEGE OF LA FLÈCHE

ple, for whom the fathers had so often made difficulties with regard to the Easter confession had painfully experienced the opposite.

Choiseul, however, the favorite of Madame de Pompadour, explained to the king that the whole people and the Parlement were utterly embittered against the Jesuits, and that there was danger of a general revolt if he did not yield to the pressure of the nation.

Madame de Pompadour spoke the decisive word. When the king discussed the question with her, she said one thing only: "I believe well enough that the Jesuits are honorable people; but it will not do for the king to sacrifice to them his Parlement at the moment when this is so necessary to him." Just at that time Louis was in urgent need of money, and could obtain the required taxes only with the Parlement's approval; thus with her brief observation Madame de Pompadour achieved the desired result, and the king, "exhausted rather than convinced," gave his assent. "It will be charming," he said regretfully, "to see Father Perusseau once more as abbé in the next world."

The Jesuits had now, in France also, to close their schools, professed houses and churches, and either to remain in the country as simple secular priests, or to leave the land. The beautiful Madame de Pompadour had at last won the victory over the obdurate confessors.

The "Mutiny of the Hats"

At the court of Madrid, the Jesuits, since the time of the all-powerful Father Neidhart, who as minister of state had from 1665 to 1676 ruled Spain as he pleased, had always been very influential personalities; here too, therefore, all other aspirants for political power desired their suppression. But, whereas in Portugal and France long and tiresome intrigues had been necessary in order to induce the rulers to expel the order, in Spain it was the king himself who decided on this measure on his own account. For Charles III of Spain would let no one else govern, and, although he had little more aptitude for his calling than the kings of France and Portugal, it was at least his ambition always to decide everything for himself.

He who wished to obtain the king's support for a measure, therefore, had merely to indicate to him that this or that circumstance would endanger the absolute sovereignty of the monarch. The courtiers early recognized this, and soon made the king aware that the Jesuit order was the main obstacle in the way of a truly absolute monarchy, since the Jesuits owed greater obedience to their general than to the sovereign of the country. In this connection the courtiers kept instancing the misuse which the order had made of its independent position in Paraguay.

Charles III, however, found particular confirmation of the assertion that the Jesuits laid plans which were dangerous to the state, in the circumstance that the fathers, as the police reported, held a remarkable active intercourse with the common people. It was said that they regularly gave the populace spiritual exercises, and even conversed with coachmen, lackeys and other menials; they also appeared frequently in the galleys and prisons to talk with the convicts over their needs and troubles, and to console them.

In the eyes of an autocrat like King Charles, such occupations could only appear as "suspicious actions," prejudicial to the required submission of the people to the ordinance of the government, for, in the opinion of the king, the people had neither to consider nor to complain, but simply to obey.

Soon the police agents brought to their superiors the disquieting report that people wearing hats with unusually wide turned-up brims and full cloaks were more and more frequently to be seen in Madrid. Only a negligent government would have dared to regard this phenomenon as harmless; an autocratic regime, intent on order and security, had perforce to see in this new hat-and-cloak fashion a sign of the alarming increase of the spirit of rebellion.

So Charles III decided to publish a stern decree, in which the wearing of wide hats and cloaks was for all time most strictly forbidden. But the people of Madrid were not prepared to give up their broad, turned-up hats at any price, and held to this fashion with the holy defiance and the heroic determination of a deeply injured nation deprived of its rights.

A dark mass, composed of thousands of wide, turned-up hats, swept through the streets one day like a disastrous tempest, and swarmed round the royal palace. In vain were the Walloon guards called out; tearing down every obstacle, the stream poured into the broad square before the king's palace.

Charles III was mortally afraid, when, staring down from his balcony, he saw before him this "mutiny of the hats." He made a speech, expressed his willingness to repeal the order he had issued, and even to dismiss the generally hated finance minister; but, in spite of this, the crowd would not give way. Only when the Jesuit fathers hurried up, mingled with the demonstrators and spoke to them did they scatter just as suddenly as they had appeared, and quiet one more reigned in Madrid.

The speed with which the Jesuits had succeeded in pacifying the malcontent aroused strong suspicion in the king and his ministers. Charles III, who regarded his people merely as a rabble to be kept down by force, had seen with his own eyes how the Jesuits had quieted the insurgents simply by reasonable speech; he could account for this only by assuming that the Jesuits had plotted the whole uproar in order to pacify it again, and to prove the king thereby how indispensable they were. Immediately, it was decided at court forcibly to expel from Spain the order that had perpetrated such a thing. That this measure was carried through with suitable brutality and despotism was ensured by the prime minister, Aranda, an enthusiastic adherent of the French philosophers of enlightenment and progress.

Aranda immediately made it his ambition to carry out a master-stroke of autocratic, mysterious conduct: all governors throughout the Spanish possessions received by special messengers sealed packets containing an order written in the prime minister's own hand, and a further, similarly sealed packet. In Aranda's order, they were instructed, on pain of the severest penalty, not to open the inner packet until April 2nd, and then to follow exactly the instructions contained in it.

Thus it came about that on the night of the second of April and the early morning of the third, of the year 1767, troops appeared throughout the Spanish dominions, at about the same time, in front of the Jesuits' colleges and houses, seized upon the fathers and led them away in safe custody. At the same time there was published everywhere a royal edict, in which the Jesuits were collectively denounced as criminals. "Moved by just causes, which I retain in my royal mind," ordained Charles in this document, so truly worthy of an autocratic ruler, "I command by virtue of my supreme authority, which the Almighty has placed in my hands, that all members of the Society of Jesus shall leave my land, and that their goods shall be confiscated." Every demonstration and every attempt to discuss the edict in any way was designated lèse-majesté, for it was "not for subjects to criticize and explain the decisions of the ruler."

As a Catholic ruler, however, Charles III thought himself obliged to explain his procedure to the pope, but as it was known that Clement XIII was entirely on the side of the Jesuits, and had energetically defended them two years earlier in the constitution *Apostolicum pascendi*, the king thought it desirable to tell the Holy Father of the expulsion of the order from Spain after the event.

"Your Holiness knows as well as anyone else," Charles wrote to the pope, "that the first duty of a sovereign ruler consists in watching over the quiet of his lands and the peace of his subjects. In the fulfilment of this task, I have found it necessary to expel all the Jesuits that were in my kingdom and to have them transported to the Papal States under the direct, wise rulership of your Holiness, who are the most noble Father and Lord of all believers... I pray your Holiness to regard this my decision as unavoidable, and as having been taken with all deliberation after the most mature consideration..."

Hereupon, the king gave the order that all Jesuits imprisoned in Spain and the Spanish colonies, about six thousand in number, should be packed like herrings in the holds of Spanish men-of-war, and deported to the Papal States. The example of Spain was soon followed by the Bourbon states of Naples and Parma. The Neapolitan government justified this step even more simply that the Spanish, by declaring in the decree that the king was answerable to God alone concerning the reasons for his behavior.

Still, however, the ambition of Charles III was not completely satisfied, for he now desired to prove that his power was great enough to annihilate the Society of Jesus, even beyond the Spanish frontiers. At his instance, the free courts of Paris, Madrid and Naples presented to the pope the categorical request that he should suppress the Jesuit order throughout the world.

Clement XIII died immediately after receiving this note, and so was spared the difficult decision of suppressing an order which had been regarded by most of his predecessors as the strongest support of the Catholic Church. This painful task remained to his successor.

Dominus ac Redemptor

In the hey-day of "enlightened despotism," the power of the Holy See had already so far declined that the Bourbons could declare that they would recognize as pope only someone who would guarantee to suppress the Society of Jesus. Cardinal Ganganelli, who promised in scarcely veiled terms to do this, was sufficiently acceptable to the Jesuits' enemies, and he was able, as Clement XIV, to mount the throne of Peter.

Even Pombal, who ten years previously had broken off diplomatic relations with Rome, was appeased: as the new pope had promised to make an end of the Jesuits, the Portuguese dictator was graciously pleased to make peace with him. Von Lebzeltern, the Austrian ambassador at Lisbon, reported to Vienna at the time: "the government here is now showing itself particularly satisfied with the behavior of the Roman court, and is beginning to have no more doubt that the complete suppression of the Society will shortly follow."

But Clement XIV tried repeatedly to postpone the fulfilment of his promise, and, when the king of Spain kept sending him, through his ambassador, new urgent notes, Clement appealed to the fact that the Empress Maria Theresa had not yet signified her consent to the suppression of the order, and the pope declared that without the agreement of all Catholic powers he could not carry out the proposed measure.

Maria Theresa had herself been a pupil of the Jesuits, and was still attached to her former teachers. As late as the year 1768, she had declared to Father Koffler: "My dear father, be without any care! As long as I live, you have nothing to fear!" Accordingly, Mahony, the Spanish ambassador at Vienna, had at first to report to his government that his empress refused "to proceed against members of an order who in her lands had done nothing worthy of punishment."

Later still, when the order had already been disbanded, Maria Theresa frequently expressed her good feeling for the Jesuits,. "I have just learnt, through a courier, of the suppression of the Jesuits," she wrote on August 30, 1773, to her son, the Archduke Ferdinand. "I confess that I am painfully moved thereby, as I have seen nothing that is not edifying in them." And on October 16th of the same year, she complained to the Countess Enzenberg: "I am inconsolable and in despair on account of the Jesuits. I have loved and honored them throughout my life. . ."

Nevertheless, Maria Theresa, under recurrent pressure from the court of Madrid, at last agreed to the suppression of the order. "I am glad to be able to comply with your wishes in a thing which lies so close to your heart," she wrote on April 4, 1773, to the Spanish king. "I hope that your Majesty will be satisfied, as there now remains nothing for you to wish for. I ask in confident trust of the continuance of your friendship, in particular for our beloved children in Naples and Tuscany and in good time in Parma."

What would not Maria Theresa have done for these "beloved children"! For before everything else this empress was a simple mother, whose greatest care was the happy marriage of her numerous daughters. If her various sons-in-law of the house of Bourbon and their ministers intended the downfall of the Jesuits, then the good fathers must be sacrificed to dynastic considerations. And if it seemed necessary to keep the courts of Madrid, Naples and Tuscany in good humor so that the "beloved children" should experience no difficulties at home, it was by so much the more necessary to stand well with du Tillot, the minister of the Grand Duchy of Parma, for it would largely depend on this whether yet another little daughter could "in good time" be married.

It seemed, however, particularly important to the empress to take account of the wishes of the court of Versailles, now that she had at last succeeded in marrying the Archduchess Marie Antoinette to the Dauphin, the future king of France! This "best match in Europe" must in no circumstances be disturbed and the good Father Koffler would be sure to understand that the empress could not now quite keep to the promise she had once given.

But even in Vienna many wise men advised that the Society of Jesus should no longer be afforded protection. The chancellor, Kaunitz, was opposed to the Jesuits, as was the royal

Dominus ac Redemptor

physician, van Swieten, but the fathers were particularly hated by Joseph, whose opinions, now that he was "King of the Romans" and co-regent, had always to be considered. "I know these people as well as anyone," wrote Joseph to Choiseul in the year 1770, "I know of the projects they have carried out and I know the pains they have taken to spread darkness over the surface of the earth and to dominate and confuse Europe from Cape Finisterre to the North Sea."

The remaining Catholic princes of the empire also supported the suppression of the order on every possible ground; the Electors of Mainz and Bavaria were particularly indignant because the Jesuits had republished Bellarmine's work on the power of the papacy, a book in which as the Elector of Mainz declared in an ordinance, the power of temporal princes was completely undermined, the authority of the bishops limited, the general peace disturbed and sedition bred everywhere.

At last, the pope had to take serious steps. His immediate action was to close the order's seminary at Rome in October, 1772; soon afterwards the remaining Jesuit seminaries in the territory of the Papal States were closed. Finally, on July 21, 1773, Clement published the *breve Dominus ac Redemptor*, which pronounced the complete suppression of the Society of Jesus.

"We have recognized," read the concluding paragraph of this voluminous document, "that the Society of Jesus was no longer in the position to produce those rich fruits and remarkable advantages for the sake of which it was instituted, approved by so many popes, and accorded so many splendid privileges; it appears, moreover, quite impossible to maintain a true and lasting peace within the church as long as this order exists. Guided by these weighty considerations, and impelled on other grounds which the wisdom and the wise administration of the whole church have laid before Us and which We preserve in the depths of Our heart. . . after mature consideration with Our unerring judgment and from the fullness of Our apostolic power, We hereby suppress the Society of Jesus. We declare void all its offices, functions and administrations, houses, schools, colleges, hospices and all other places in its possession, in whatsoever province, kingdom or state they may be. . ."

The Power and Secret of the Jesuits

PART VII

THE STRUGGLE WITH PROGRESS

The Resurrection of the Order

Even though, towards the end of the eighteenth century, the Catholic powers, whose trustiest agents the Jesuits had once been, had joined forces against the order, and although the pope himself had decreed that his "light cavalry" should be disbanded, the Society of Jesus notwithstanding all the royal edicts and papal briefs, did not for one moment cease to exist. Fortunately for the Jesuits, there still remained, in spite of their tireless activities, countries that had not been brought under the Roman yoke, and the Society of Jesus was now destined to find refuge with "heretical" and "schismatic" princes.

Immediately after the publication of the brief *Dominus ac Redemptor*, Frederick the Great informed the pope that, at the annexation of the Silesian provinces he had conquered during the Seven Years' War, he had promised to maintain the existing religious orders, and was, therefore, unable to agree to the dissolution of the Jesuit order. "Since I am regarded as a heretic," Frederick wrote with Voltairean malice, "the Holy Father can absolve me neither from keeping my promise nor from behaving as an honorable man and king." The king's real reason, however, for maintaining the Jesuit schools in Silesia was that, if he had closed them, he would have had to engage paid teachers to replace the fathers, whose educational activities were carried on without payment.

Catherine II adopted a similar attitude. Under the first partition of Poland in 1722, White Russia, and with it quite a number of Jesuit colleges, had been assigned to Russia; when the papal nuncio endeavored to persuade the tsaritsa to give effect to the *breve Dominus ac Redemptor*, Catherine replied that she had promised to recognize the Jesuits; that, moreover, she regarded it as her most important duty to promote national education; and that she was, therefore, unable to despoil an order which devoted itself so zealously to educational work.

The Society of Jesus was thus enabled to weather, in Russian territory, the most stormy periods of persecution; in 1801, its *de facto* survival was, indeed, recognized by Pope Pius VII, who authorized the Jesuits domiciled in Russia again to style themselves the "Society of Jesus," while at the same date Father Kareu was appointed general for Russia, "duly charged and entrusted with the requisite and necessary authority to follow and maintain the rule of St. Ignatius Loyola."

But, even in Catholic countries, the order had not entirely ceased to exist; on the contrary, various attempts had been made after its dissolution to reconstitute it under different but similarly sounding titles. Thus, a Jesuit professor called Paccanari founded in Rome a "Society of the Faith of Jesus," the members of which lived strictly in accordance with Loyola's *Constitutions*. These "Brothers of the Faith of Jesus" speedily extended their activities beyond the Italian frontiers into Austria, Switzerland, and even England and Holland.

A similar scheme was adopted by the French priests who had fled into Austria before the victorious revolutionary armies and had settled at Hagenbrunn, near Vienna; they called themselves the "Society of the Heart of Jesus," and from an affiliated sisterhood of pious women arose the famous congregation of the "Dames du Sacré Cœur.

The Society of the Faith of Jesus speedily became suspect in the eyes of the French government, hostile as the latter was to the Jesuits. The revolutionaries, Robespierre in particular, had tried from the outset to repress by force all religious congregations, and, during the Reign of Terror, a number of the then Jesuit fathers had been guillotined. But Napoleon was also bitterly hostile to the Jesuits, for he was in temperament no less Gallican than the Parlement advocates had been in their day. He wrote, in most categorical terms, to the minister of police, Fouché, that in no circumstances would he allow the Jesuits to settle in France again. "No matter what guise they may assume, I will tolerate neither a 'Heart of Jesus' nor a 'Confraternity of the Holy Sacrament' nor any other body resembling a militant religious organization."

"Notify the editors of the *Mercure* and the *Journal des Débats*," Napoleon instructed the minister of police on October 9, 1804, "that under no circumstances do I wish to see the Jesuits referred to as such. Anything likely to call attention to this society must be avoided by the newspapers. I will never allow the Jesuits to be readmitted into France. . . . Instruct the various prefects to guard against the possibility of an agitation in favor of the return of the Jesuits being even initiated."

But the omnipotence of the great emperor was soon destined to be overthrown. Even before Moscow was put to the flames under Napoleon's eyes, the Jesuit general was directing from St. Petersburg an attempt to restore the order in Spain, which was then struggling against the French occupation. In August, 1814, a few months after Napoleon's abdication, pope Pius VII, in a bull *Sollicitudo omnium Ecclesiarum*, sanctioned the reinstatement of the Society of Jesus in all its former rights and privileges.

At the restoration of the order, there was only one survivor, the eighty-year-old Father de Clorivière, of those who were members of the French province at the time of its dissolution. He had lived in Paris, concealed in a cellar most of the time, during the whole period of the Revolution, but was imprisoned when Napoleon came into power and incarcerated in the Temple for five whole years. He was now entrusted by the general of the order with the reestablishment in France of the Society of Jesus, a task to which he devoted himself with the utmost zeal. With the aid of the "Fathers of the Faith of Jesus," he enrolled a large number of novices, and, during the few years that elapsed before his death, Clorivière succeeded in establishing a new province of the order in France.

This second stage in the history of the order is as full of vicissitudes as were the sixteenth, seventeenth and eighteenth centuries. Once again, it frequently occurred that the Jesuits were expelled from a country as dangerous to the state, and found refuge in another, and that they were later on driven out of the latter and at once found shelter elsewhere.

The Resurrection of the Order

First of all, they were banished from Russia, the very country in which they had found an asylum during the period in which they had been generally persecuted. Here they had acquired considerable influence, inasmuch as they had extended their schools as far as Astrakhan, Irkutsk and Omsk; their schools in St. Petersburg and Moscow, in particular, were attended by the sons of the most aristocratic and distinguished families.

Unfortunately for them, however, they had not restricted themselves to the imparting of purely secular education or to the giving of religious instruction to Catholics, but had devoted themselves with rather greater zeal to the conversion to the Roman Catholic faith of the children of Orthodox parents. Finally, when a member of one of the most noble families, young Prince Galitsin, became a Catholic under their influence and, in his exalted enthusiasm, clad himself in a penitential robe and covered himself with holy images, Tsar Alexander was so infuriated that he expelled the Jesuits.

Simultaneously, however, with their withdrawal from Russia, they were allowed to re-enter Spain. Shortly afterwards, they were also able to resume their public activities in England, where, during the whole of the seventeenth century, they had had to endure the repression of exceptional laws, for the Emancipation Act of 1829 had at last conceded complete religious liberty to Catholics. Even then, however, as Cardinal Newman says, the word "Catholic" still sounded unpleasantly like superstition, and, for this reason, the Jesuits built their first church in London in a half-derelict district behind a mews, and not in a main thoroughfare.

While the order was beginning to flourish in England, it was being expelled from other countries. The attempt of the Swiss Catholic Cantons, in 1845, to form the Sonderbund, a separatist league, with the aid of Metternich, and to offer armed resistance to the endeavor of the Radicals to exclude the Jesuits, was unsuccessful owing to the determined attitude of the federal government, and in 1847 the fathers had to leave Switzerland. In the following year, the Austrian revolution resulted in the temporary banishment of the order, and shortly afterwards the anti-Roman policy of Cavour brought the same fate upon the Jesuit communities in Sardinia; and, when Garibaldi had become master of Sicily and Naples, he too decreed that the Jesuits should be expelled from these states. The Society of Jesus also experienced many vicissitudes owing to the unsettled condition of Spain in the nineteenth century. Driven out by the civil war of 1836, it returned in 1852, only to be dissolved once more in 1854; its subsequent re-establishment was speedily followed by a third ejection as the result of the revolution in 1868.

But the most determined opposition to the Jesuits came from Prussia, the very state which, under Frederick the Great, like Russia under the Tsaritsa Catherine, had afforded a refuge to the Society of Jesus at the time of the papal edict decreeing its dissolution. While Frederick, like Catherine, had praised the educational activities of the father, the nationalistic spirit of the seventies gave rise to a *Kulturkampf* against the "unpatriotic international spirit" inculcated in the youth of Germany by Jesuit training.

Bismarck himself declared, in one of his Reichstag speeches, that the Jesuits were dangerous not so much by reason of their Catholicism as on account of "their whole international organization, their abjuration of and absolution from all national bonds, and their disintegration and destruction of all national bonds and national movements wherever they are to

The Power and Secret of the Jesuits

be found. . ."

Influenced by views similar to these, the Reichstag passed a special act in 1872 providing for the suppression of the Jesuit communities in Germany, and subjecting their members to various exceptional measures of police supervision. This act remained in force after the end of the *Kulturkampf*, and it was not definitely repealed until 1917.

The fate of the re-established order in France was particularly eventful: soon after the publication of the bull *Sollicitudo omnium Ecclesiarum*, Jansenism lifted its head once more, and joined forces with the Liberals against the Jesuits, and the weak government of Charles X was finally compelled to re-expel the Society; two years later the July Revolution brought the reign of the Bourbons to an end.

Much the same thing happened under the "Citizen King," Louis Philippe. This time it was for the most part the professors and writers, including such men as Jules Michelet, Edgar Quinet and Eugène Sue, who in violent language demanded the ejection of the readmitted Jesuits, and one more the government tried to allay the increasing unrest in the country by expelling the order. But this time too the banishment of the Society of Jesus was almost immediately followed by a political upheaval, which brought Louis Napoleon to the helm of state.

The period of the Second Empire, which drew its support entirely from the Clerical party, was, it is true, one of peace and progress for the Jesuits; but a number of fathers perished as victims of the popular wrath during the stormy days of the Commune. Chiefly owing to its policy of secularizing education, the liberal Republic once more came into conflict with the Jesuits. As far back as 1880, all the religious organizations were threatened by dissolution, and, in 1902, the Society of Jesus, together with fifty-three other congregations, was suppressed by law.

In Portugal, the Jesuits were ejected by the revolution of 1910, in company with the Braganza dynasty. On the other hand, in Spain the order has, during the twentieth century, once more acquired a large measure of power and influence, especially so far as education is concerned. The Jesuit college at Deusto, near Bilbao, is regarded as one of the leading educational institutions in the country, and receives all the assistance the government can give it.

Of late years, Catholicism has made considerable progress in England, a fact which is largely due to the activities of the Jesuits. A devotional guild with a large number of members, at the head of which is the Jesuit Provincial Bodkin, has been founded, and issues its own paper, *The Cohort*. "We are not a dwindling organization," Cardinal Bourne recently announced at a Catholic congress; "rather do we see indications of progress in every direction."

Finally, the order has for a long time past carried out much systematic and successful work in the United States, where it has not been hampered by legislative restrictions. After the order was dissolved in 1773, the fathers reconstituted themselves as a legal corporation, and, as such, administered and preserved their by no means inconsiderable property until the order was re-established. During the nineteenth century, the colleges in Maryland, New York, Missouri and Louisiana were instrumental in winning many new converts to the Roman doctrines.

"I do not like the reappearance of the Jesuits," wrote ex-President John Adams, as early as 1816, to his successor, Thomas Jefferson. "Shall we not have regular swarms of them here, in as many disguises as only a king of the gipsies can assume, dressed as printers, publishers,

The Resurrection of the Order

writers and schoolmasters? If ever there was a body of men who merited eternal damnation on earth and in hell, it is this Society of Loyola's. Nevertheless, we are compelled by our system of religious toleration to offer them an asylum...." Jefferson replied to his predecessor: "like you, I disapprove of the restoration of the Jesuits, for it means a step backwards from light into darkness..."

The Jesuits speedily sought to reoccupy their former spheres of activity in the missionary field. In North America, they were successful in re-establishing themselves in the Indian reservations, and there are now some eighty thousand Roman Catholics among the Indians.

In Mexico, just before the great dispute between the Curia and the Calles government, they made considerable number of converts among the Indian tribes, particularly in the Tarahumare region, formerly the scene of Father Glandorff's labors, while, in South America also, Jesuit mission stations were once more established in almost every state on the continent during the nineteenth century. In the territory of the erstwhile "Jesuit Republic," however, they made but little headway, for, in the interim, the Spanish and Portuguese colonists had inspired the Indians with a profound distrust of their former protectors. Following an invitation which the Jesuits received from King Leopold of Belgium to settle in the Congo, they also established themselves in Africa, where they founded new missions in Rhodesia and Madagascar.

On their return to India, they at once found that, during their absence, the religion of Islam had made great advances, and that the earlier work of Xavier and his successors had been all but destroyed. Only on the Pearl Coast did the Jesuits find traces of the survival of a Christian tradition, on which they were able to graft their teachings; at the present time, as in the days of Xavier, there is a large Catholic community under the charge of a native-born Parava, a member of the Jesuit order. In Madura, the former scene of the missionary work of the "Christian Brahmin," Robert de Nobili, the French Jesuits have founded a college, the chief purpose of which is to convert Brahmins and prepare them for admission to the order.

The Jesuits returned to Japan in 1913. They have set up a high school in Tokyo, and when the German Jesuits who were working in India had to leave British territory in consequence of the World War, they settled in Yamaguchi, the town in which Xavier had so successfully won over the daimyo.

After the suppression of the order, its missionary work in China was carried on by the Lazarists, until the Jesuits were able to return, under the protection of the French government, in the forties of the last century, to the scene of their former triumphs.

In china, the remarkable manner in which the order has endeavored to adapt itself to the changed conditions of modern times is particularly noticeable. While formerly every effort was made to acquire influence at court, and thus to carry on missionary work "from above," these tactics had to be abandoned as the enfeebled empire slowly dwindled in importance. Ever since Emperor Kia-k'ing was killed by lightning in 1820, the reigning dynasty had completely lost its authority in the eyes of the superstitious masses, and the real balance of power had slowly but surely passed into the hands of the people and of the educated classes.

Accordingly, on their return, the Jesuits entirely ignored the now insignificant imperial court, and pursued a popular policy, founding schools in order to gain influence over the masses and the educated classes. They endeavored, by training able students, to win to themselves the future leaders of the country.

The Catholicization of Thought

It will thus be seen that, by their tenacity and adaptability, the Jesuits have succeeded, right up to the present day, in maintaining themselves against all the changes and fluctuations of fortune, which have overtaken them as the result of political developments. It is true that, despite all their efforts, despite all their utilization of ever-changing means, they have been unable to achieve their great aim, that of founding a universal Roman kingdom; for the increasing divergencies in the developments of European policies arising out of various national, economic and social factors could not be arrested, much less turned back, by even the most skilful of tactics.

Nevertheless, the fact that, even in the twentieth century, the Catholic Church has been able to assert itself as a political power is not least the work of the Jesuits; it is they who have, with all their skill, all their zeal and all their worldly wisdom, upheld the secular power of the papacy against every hostile influence.

But if this struggle for the "Catholicization of European Policy" has demanded mighty efforts of the members of the Society of Jesus, the "Catholicization of European Thought," that not less important task which the Jesuits took upon themselves, has proved to be infinitely more difficult. For only in the Middle Ages was the conception of the political unity of the Christian world under the papal rule accompanied by a similarly Catholic outlook in which all irreconcilable elements were harmonized; but in modern times the decay of the secular supremacy of Rome has gone hand-in-hand with the dissolution of this spiritual universality.

When European man had won through confusion and disorder to a higher spiritual life, the new Romano-Germanic mentality was founded on the Augustinian school of Christianity. St. Augustine had succeeded in establishing, not only in his own personality but also in his works, a harmony of the ancient culture based upon reason with the Christian conception of religion.

While demanding the obedient *assensio* of the spirit, he always tried to permeate the content of faith with reason, in which process faith was to pave the way for rational perception. With the aphorism, *Credimus ut cognoscamus*, Augustine was convinced that he had found the perfectly satisfying formula, by which faith could at all times be brought into harmony with reason.

The rediscovery of Aristotle, for which the eleventh century has to thank Arabian and Jewish philosophers, did not at first sight confute this harmonious theory of the universe. In the beginning, the mediæval philosophers regarded the Aristotelean theory of knowledge merely as a new method by means of which the content of the Catholic dogmas could be explained rationally. It never occurred to them that reason and revelation could ever disagree; neither did anyone suspect how little reconcilable in the long run was the rational, logical investigation of the cosmos demanded by Aristotle with the irrationality of a religion that was in opposition to the discoveries of the human mind.

Nearly all the early scholastics had contented themselves with applying the results of ra-

122. POPE CLEMENT XIV (GANGANELLI),
WHO ABOLISHED THE JESUIT ORDER

GALILEO GALILEI

The Catholicization of Thought

tional perception reached by the philosopher of Stagira, as a means of strengthening and explaining the Christian beliefs. The works of Peter Lombard, the "Master of the Sentences," as well as of the *Doctor universalis*, Albertus Magnus, were written for this express purpose. Even to an Abelard, the terms "Christian" and "logician" seemed synonymous, although, unlike Bernard de Clairvaux, he held the rather unorthodox opinion that faith should be founded on rational perception, if it were to be certain of its truth.

This conflict, the existence of which had scarcely become apparent, seemed at first sight finally disposed of when Thomas Aquinas in his *Summa* succeeded in condensing into a uniform system the whole of the tenets of contemporary Catholicism. He taught that reason and dogma were but two differing forms of perception, since faith itself was a cognition directed towards the transcendental, and hence was a continuation and deepening of intellectual perception: *Actus fidei essentialiter consistit in cognitione et ibi est ejus perfectio*. Reason, Thomas maintained, was the auxiliary of revelation, and the *lumen naturalis rationis* emanating from God could never be contrary to the *lumen divinae revelationis*.

He accordingly made use of whatever he knew of the Aristotelean theory of knowledge, metaphysics and ethics, solely to interpret the sense and content of the Catholic dogma, at the same time to translate religion into the language of philosophy, and thus to prove the existence of God by reason. Faith to him was the perception of God; revelation, a system of intelligible ideas; and even the eternal bliss of the life to come he, deriving from Aristotle, regarded as nothing else than a perfect knowledge of the divine principle, *perfecta Dei cognitio*. Since faith was thus posited as a high form of perception, it seemed that a perfect harmony between reason and faith had been reached, which contemporary philosophers believed was a *philosophia perennis*, destined to last for all time.

But this achievement of the great scholastic was an artificial creation, too closely dependent upon the outstanding personality of its inventor to remain unquestioned for long after his death. Sooner or later, the two contradictory elements which Thomas had welded together in his system were bound to clash once more. Once the Middle Ages, through Aristotle, had been awakened to the importance of deductive reasoning, and had at the same time learned his logical methods, it was inevitable that reasoned reflections should begin to go their own way, and thereby come more and more frequently into conflict with faith.

For the impulse to acquire a rational knowledge of the world and of its phenomena was bound to lead to dissatisfaction with the principles of Aristotelean physics handed down by the scholastics, and men, taking as their starting-point the ascertainable data furnished by observation of and experiment with the outside world itself, could not but arrive at conclusions concerning the universe independent of religion and the authority of Aristotle, or even opposed to them.

The Franciscan, Roger Bacon, was one of the pioneers along the way. As early as the thirteenth century, he advance the view that the universe should be studied not merely in its relation to God and revelation, but also in and for itself, by means of nature studies and experiment.

The great "dispute of over universals," the weightiest scientific controversy of the Middle Ages, clearly reflected the division of scholasticism into its two basic elements. While the exponents of "realism" ascribed actual existence to general ideas, and hence in the world of concrete phenomena saw only subordinate particular cases of the universal ideas, the "nominalists" regarded ideas merely as *nomina* devoid of metaphysical reality. In this way they carried on the empiricist system of thought which starts from the particular case, admits this alone as real, and therefore gives to rational knowledge based upon experiment the preference over purely conceptual speculation.

The rapid decay of scholasticism could not be arrested by the endeavors of a Nicholas of Cusa, who once again tried, with his theory of the *docta ignorantia* and of the *coincidentia oppositorum*, to reestablish the lost harmony. His efforts were rendered all the more vain in that humanism was soon to bring about the complete collapse of the scholastic methods.

The coming into favor of empiricism now led to the inevitable consequence that theology, the erstwhile universal science, to which all other branches of knowledge were but humble "handmaids," now became gradually deposed from its proud pre-eminence. It is true that, even in the sixteenth century, the Christian world was yet far from desiring to assail the truth of the doctrines of faith; but, none the less, the demand that theology should cease to hamper scientific investigation, by prescribing its aims *ab initio*, became louder and louder.

Hence, while on the one hand the secular sciences were striving to achieve their emancipation from the fetters placed upon them by dogma, the leaders of the Reformation movement, on the other hand, were seeking to purge Christianity of every trace of knowledge based upon reason, and to rebuild the Christian faith solely upon the divine Word. Luther, although fully aware of the widening breach between religion and reason, made no attempt to bridge the gap by a new syntheses, but rather sought to eliminate the "prostitute, reason," from the sphere of faith.

Just as the Catholic Church had striven to maintain the universal sovereignty of the pope in a world of political differentiation, so too it now also endeavored to reassert the spiritual supremacy of Catholicism against all these movements tending toward the dissolution of the mediæval unity of thought and faith. But as, during the sixteenth century, no outstanding personality arose who, like St. Augustine or St. Thomas, could, in one powerful synthesis, weld all the opposing elements into a new unity, no other course remained open than, by means of collective consideration, to proceed with a codification of all those principles which might prevent a final and definite collapse.

Bishops, cardinals and theologians assembled at Trent, and, point by point, discussed all the problems which had troubled the spiritual life of the church during the preceding century; a definite and authoritative answer was given to every question, with which, from that time onwards, every good Catholic had to be satisfied.

The task of securing general compliance with the decisions of the Council of Trent fell for the most part to the Jesuit order; this applied not only to the theological and political findings of the Council, but also to its decrees concerning the sole permissible *Weltanschauung*. From then on, the Jesuits had to see to it that the human mind, in its desire for enlightenment, should never overstep the boundaries marked out for it by the Church, and that thus the mediæval Catholicization of thought should be maintained even into modern times.

The skill with which the disciples of Loyola acquitted themselves of this undertaking was in no way inferior to, in no way less astounding than, that which they displayed during their struggle to uphold the political hegemony of Rome. The men of this order, who had proved themselves to be such excellent statesmen, handled with equal distinction the intellectual weapons of the exact sciences, research, mathematics and the classics, wherever these could avail them in their battle with the spirit of "progress."

Their tactics also were the same; wherever possible they avoided any semblance of harsh intolerance; they made concessions and tried to accomplish their object by mildness, worldly wisdom and prudence; but, these methods proving of no avail, they did not hesitate, in the intellectual struggle as in the political, to resort to those violent means which here the power of an absolute monarch and there the censorship of the papal Index offered.

The Jesuits and Galileo

When the Council of Trent assembled in 1545, in order to restore the unity of the Catholic *Weltanschauung*, just two years had elapsed since Copernicus, in his *De revolutionibus orbium coelestium*, had in fact destroyed for ever the harmony between science and faith.

On the basis of his astronomical researches, Copernicus had in his book expressed the conviction that not the earth but the sun formed the immutable center about which the universe circled. Thereby the foundation of the Aristotelean and Christian doctrines was overthrown, for to deny that the earth was the center of the universe was equivalent to admitting that man was not the Lord of Creation. The hypotheses on which the religion, philosophy and ethics of the Meddle Ages were founded were seriously imperiled by the substitution of the heliocentric system for the geocentric.

Nevertheless, this most revolutionary of books remained unchallenged for eighty years. The few learned men who were aware of its existence regarded it merely as a clever, mathematical *tour de force*, which need not be taken very seriously. But, a year after the Council of Trent had concluded its deliberations, a man was born who was destined to arouse the world to the real significance of the work of Copernicus, and who was thus bound to come into conflict with the Church and its most zealous champions, the Jesuits.

Galileo was well aware of the difficulty of convincing his contemporaries that Aristotle's theories of the structure of the universe, hitherto regarded as beyond doubt, were wrong, and for this reason he refrained for a long time from openly upholding the views of Copernicus. He once expressed the opinion that, if the stars themselves descended to earth to offer their own testimony, the great majority of learned men would refuse to accept their evidence; for had not a number of eminent astronomers of the day obstinately refused even to look through Galileo's telescope? As Prince Cesi wrote to Cardinal Bellarmine, they "would by observation and reason, depart by one jot or tittle from them, and add to or alter their rules and decrees."

Regarding the mentality of these narrow-minded philosophers who adhered so religiously to the Aristotelean physics, and with whom he would have to contend, Galileo himself wrote to Kepler in 1610: "these men believe that truth is not to be found in the world or in nature, but, to use their own words, in the comparison of texts..."

At first, the Jesuits took a considerable interest in Galileo's ideas; even though they foresaw the dangers with which his astronomical discoveries threatened the Catholic outlook, they were nevertheless determined as long as possible to be "scholars with the scholars," and to counter the perils of scientific investigation with their own studies. The celebrated Jesuit astronomer, Christoph Clavius, verified Galileo's observations, and did not hesitate to admit that he could confirm them as the result of his observations.

When Galileo visited Rome in 1611, the Jesuits entertained him most hospitably at their Roman college. "I stayed with the Jesuit fathers," he wrote at the time to a friend, "and had a long discussion with Father Clavius, two other fathers who had a thorough knowledge of our subject, and their pupils. . . I discovered that they had verified the actual existence of the new planets, and had been constantly observing them for two months; we compared notes and found that their observations agreed exactly with my own."

Cardinal Bellarmine, the most influential person in the Jesuit order, also took a close interest in Galileo, and asked the specialists at the Collegium Romanum whether they were able to confirm his discoveries; with minor reservations, the reply of the Jesuit astronomers was in the affirmative. In the following year, one of the fathers gave a lecture at the Collegium Romanum, in which he lauded Galileo as one of the most famous astronomers of the age.

Shortly after this, Galileo published a thesis in which he tried to refute, in emphatic terms, the Aristotelean theory that the buoyancy of floating objects depends essentially on their shape. On this occasion, it was the Jesuit Father Grienberger, a pupil of Christoph Clavius, who, in his lectures, upheld Galileo's views.

However, the friendly relations between Galileo and the Jesuits were to be of brief duration. The first ostensible cause of dissension was a personal squabble between Galileo and the Jesuit professor, Christoph Scheiner, over the discovery of the spots on the sun. Scheiner, one of the leading scientific investigators of the order, who had been the first to point out that the retina was the essential organ of vision and to demonstrate the accommodation of the eye, and who was widely known by reason of his discovery of the pantograph, had in 1612 observed dark spots on the sun, and had published a report of his discoveries. Galileo, however, claimed to have been the first to make this discovery, and accused Scheiner of improper conduct.

But, although such private differences appeared on the surface, the real reason of the Jesuits' break with Galileo lay deeper. As the great investigator declared himself more and more definitely in favor of the Copernican system, the more inevitable became the hostility of the Jesuits. The fathers were, indeed, prepared to admit, up to a certain point, the truth of new ideas; but the Copernican doctrine which declared that the sun, and not the earth, was the immutable center of the universe, could not but be unacceptable to them; for did it not stand in flat contradiction not only to the physics of Aristotle, but also to the teachings of Holy Writ and the early fathers? When Father Scheiner had advanced this argument in refutation of Galileo's views, the latter, in a letter to his disciple, Castelli, made certain remarks which illustrate in a marked manner the spirit of modern times. "Inasmuch as the Bible," he said, "in many places calls for an interpretation differing from the immediate sense of the words, it seems to me that, as an authority in mathematical controversy, it has very little standing. . . . I believe that natural processes which we either perceive by careful observation or deduce by cogent demonstration cannot be refuted by references to passages in the Bible, even though the latter appear literally to assert something different; for not every statement in the Bible is subject to such strict laws as are the phenomena of nature. . ."

But, despite the widening breach between them, Father Scheiner sent to Galileo a copy of his book attacking the Copernican theories, accompanied by a courteous letter which made his conciliatory attitude quite clear. "if you wish to advance counter-arguments," he wrote, "we shall in no way be offended by them, but will, on the contrary, gladly examine your arguments, in the hope that all this will assist in the elucidation of the truth."

Cardinal Bellarmine also tried up to the very last to avert the impending quarrel by friendly admonishments to Galileo, in which he advanced argumenta reflecting no small credit on his keen scientific outlook. Stripped of their theological dress, the views which Bellarmine put forward in regard to the relative value of the Copernican doctrines are closely related to the most modern theories that the geocentric system is just as deserving of credence as the heliocentric.

"It seems to me," the cardinal wrote to Galileo's disciple, Foscarini, "that you and Galileo would be well advised to speak not in absolute terms, but *ex suppositione,* as I am convinced that Copernicus himself did. . . If there were real proof that the sun in the center of the universe, and that the earth revolved round the sun, and not the sun round earth, it would be necessary to exercise the utmost caution in discussing those passages in the Bible in which the contrary seems to be stated. . . But I shall not willingly believe that such a proof exists until it is produced to me. Even if the hypothesis that the sun is the center of the universe, and that the earth is in the sky, explains many phenomena, this does not effectively prove that the sun *is* the central point and the earth *is* in the sky. The first assumption may possibly be susceptible of proof, but the second one seems very dubious to me. . ."

The Inquisition soon had its first opportunity of dealing with Galileo as the result of denunciations, with which, however, the Jesuits had nothing to do. But even this dreaded authority, in this matter, set to work in a very cautious manner: Galileo himself was not summoned to appear, the only action taken being to secure a theological report on the question whether the Copernican theories were inadmissible from the ecclesiastical point of view. An affirmative reply being given by the experts, the Index Congregation, without specifically mentioning Galileo, issued a ban on all writings in which the heliocentric system had been or was in future to be discussed in any but a purely hypothetical manner. Cardinal Bellarmine undertook the task of inducing Galileo, in a friendly manner, to comply with this decision.

The real controversy, which has become so famous as the "Galileo Process," was not, however, to break out until 1632. The scientific convictions of the great astronomer impelled him to continue to defend the Copernican theories: as he himself had given his word to Cardinal Bellarmine to comply with the orders of the Index Congregation, he could do this only in a very cautious and seemingly hypothetical manner.

Written in the form of a dialogue, his book, *Of the Two Chief World Systems,* contained an exposition of both the heliocentric and the geocentric systems, with all the arguments which had been advanced for and against both points of view. Although Galileo refrained from drawing any definite conclusion, he put the weightiest arguments into the mouth of the champion of the Copernican doctrines, while the fact that in this dialogue he gave the defender of the Ptolemaic system the undignified name of "Somplicio" significantly illustrates the secret intentions of the author.

Nevertheless, Galileo was convinced that the cautious and indecisive form of his dialogue would reassure the inquisition, especially as he had introduced the book by a clever preface in which he pretended that the whole work was a justification of the ban on the heliocentric theory. His intentions were, however, perfectly obvious to the authorities in Rome, and now it was the Jesuits in particular who urged those in power to place a ban on the dialogue. "I am told on very good authority," Galileo wrote at this period to a friend, "that the Jesuit fathers have persuaded those concerned that my book is more reprehensible and more calculated to harm the Church than were the writings of Luther and Calvin."

In the trial itself (which, as will be remembered, ended in the condemnation of, and enforced abjuration by, Galileo), the Jesuits took no active part beyond the submittal by Father Inchhofer, one of Scheiner's pupils, of a damning report on Galileo's dialogue. Inchhofer tried to establish that, in his book, Galileo had, "in definite and assertive words," taught the Copernican doctrines, and that scarcely any doubt existed that it was his intention to uphold this theory in defiance of the earlier decision of the Inquisition. This report, together with the opinions formulated by two other expert witnesses, formed the basis of Galileo's condemnation, a verdict which was, in later times, not only to do the Catholic Church no good, but to cause it infinite harm.

Scholars Among Scholars

Galileo's famous contemporary, Johan Kepler, was, even more so than Galileo himself at the time of his first visit to Rome, closely associated with the Jesuits, both as a scientist and as a friend of the order, the members of which, for several years, looked forward to the "conversion" of this great Protestant scholar. Eventually, however, these hopes were disappointed, and the friendship between Kepler and the Society of Jesus ended in a resounding quarrel.

Kepler kept up a regular and close correspondence with Scheiner, Grienberger and numerous other Jesuit scholars; the missionaries of the order in China occasionally asked his advice in difficult mathematical problems; and Father Zucchi, the inventor of the reflecting telescope, presented his with the first telescope which Kepler could call his own. When at first he was unable to get his *Almanac* printed, the Jesuit college at Ingolstadt at once assumed responsibility for the publication of this book. Moreover, the fathers came to his assistance in material difficulties. When in 1600 Kepler was banished from Graz, Father Decker interceded on his behalf, Father Lang obtained permission for him to take up residence in Munich, and Father Guldin provided him with financial assistance and secured him introductions to influential people.

Kepler was on particularly friendly terms with Father Guldin, who earned lasting fame with his "barycentric rule" which enabled the cubic contents of rotating bodies to be ascertained, and it was Guldin who undertook the task of winning over the great astronomer to the Catholic Church.

Scholars Among Scholars

To begin with, the Jesuit father hinted to his friend that, by his conversion to Catholicism, Kepler would considerably improve his prospects in Austria; but this argument completely failed of effect. Kepler at once declared that he would dispense with the emperor's favor, and even give up astronomy altogether, rather than confess a faith which he regarded as "tares among the real wheat of the Apostolic doctrines." Since it was thus evident that Kepler must be genuinely convinced, Guldin immediately set to work with great zeal to bring this about. From then onwards, there began between them a correspondence on theological matters in which the Jesuit endeavored to convince the scholar that the Reformation was a mistake, and that the Catholic faith was the only true one. How presumptuous, said Guldin, was it to assume that a handful of novelty-seekers should suddenly claim to know better than all the early fathers, martyrs, bishops, monks, universities, and synods of the Church!

"Forgive the frankness," wrote Guldin in conclusion, "with which I tell you all this; I have painstakingly tried not to use a single word which might in the least offend you. . . Add to your immortal fame the glory of having attained the lofty heights of the true faith by the use of the eagle wings of your exalted mind!"

Even after the failure of Guldin's efforts, the Jesuits did not abandon all hope of converting Kepler. At a later day, the astronomer, Father Curtius, who resided at Ingolstadt, made a determined effort, by "friendly warfare," to convert Kepler to the Catholic faith.

Kepler's firm belief in the truth of the Copernican system, and his conviction that no quotation from Holy Writ could override the proofs furnished by scientific observation, eventually resulted in the alienation of his Jesuit friends. After his death, they made no secret of their hostility to his teachings, and, in a letter to Galileo, Kepler's son complained of the animosity of Christoph Scheiner, who desired to suppress "all doctrines and hypotheses which were displeasing to the Church," and who was seeking to prevent the posthumous publication of Kepler's works.

Nevertheless, measured in the spirit of theological intolerance which was generally prevalent at the beginning of the seventeenth century, the attitude of the Jesuits towards Galileo, and even more so towards Kepler, may be regarded as extremely conciliatory. For the other contemporaries of these two scholars were, in the great majority, essentially hostile to any innovation; the members of the religious orders, and more particularly the Dominicans, sternly opposed with truly mediæval bigotry any attempt to change the existing philosophy, and endeavored to persecute, by means of the Inquisition every exponent of modern ideas, while, on the other hand, the Protestants showed themselves equally narrow-minded and intolerant. Luther had expressed his view of the work of Copernicus in the scornful words: "the fool wants to turn the whole science of astronomy upside down!" and Melanchthon opposed the heliocentric theory with as much violence as the most bigoted Catholic theologian. The Protestants, moreover, had marshalled against Kepler the same Biblical argument as those which were, only a few years later, used by the Roman Inquisition when presenting their case against Galileo.

But the tolerant and progressive attitude of the Jesuits had its limitations, so, while they rightly appreciated the fact that in scientific just as in political matters, obstinate adherence to obsolete views was of little avail, and that, on the contrary, modern discoveries must in a large measure be taken into consideration, yet the only real link between the Jesuits and science was, and continued to be, their endeavor to subordinate every new discovery to the theocentric view of the world.

Thus, despite all their good-will and understanding, they were unable, for any length of time, to collaborate on friendly terms with a Galileo or a Kepler. Sooner or later, they were certain to come up against the divergencies of purpose separating the investigations of these great scientists from those of the Jesuits. For, no matter how good a Catholic Galileo might be, or how good a Protestant Kepler, neither one of them, in his experiments, observations and theories, concerned himself at all with the question whether his conclusion accorded with the theological convictions of his Church. In the eyes of the Jesuits, on the other hand, ecclesiastical authority constituted an insurmountable limit which, at a certain point, repeatedly brought their studies to a standstill.

For instance, when the Jesuit astronomer, Adam Tanner, had concluded a series of observations which offered a flat contradiction to the Aristotelean theory of the immutability of the heavens, he felt himself compelled to adhere to the beliefs which his own studies had refuted, because such beliefs were supported by the authority of Holy Writ. Again, when Christoph Scheiner publicly announced that, because of certain astronomical phenomena, he had doubts about the permanence of the stellar universe, this fact was immediately reported by Father Tanner to Acquaviva, the general of the order. The latter at once wrote to Scheiner, enjoining him to desist from any future deviations from the doctrines of recognized authorities: "One thing I would urge upon your Reverence, namely, that you should, relying upon the sound doctrines of the ancients, avoid the opinions of certain writers of the present day. You may rest assured that such views are highly displeasing to us, and that we will not permit them to be published by members of our order. . . . "

The case of Father Giovanni Battista Riccioli was particularly strange. He had been especially charged by the order with the task of scientifically refuting the Copernican theories; but, in the coarse of his studies, he had become such an enthusiastic admirer of them that, although, for the sake of appearances, he attacked them with all the arguments at his command, he nevertheless described them as the "finest, simplest and best." It was, therefore, inevitable that such unbecoming language should bring upon him sever censure from the authorities of the order.

This restriction of scientific inquiry be an exaggerated faith in authority is distinctly noticeable in the methods of argument and literary style of contemporary Jesuit writers. They are continually dragging the Bible and the pronouncements of the early fathers into discussions of a purely scientific nature. Thus, in his book, *Rosa Ursina*, Scheiner relies on the Scriptures, Tertullian, Ambrose and Bonaventura in the same way as on Mersenne, Kepler and Galileo.

Although the works of the Jesuit scholars were characterized by no small amount of perspicacity, sincere work, earnest study and scientific ability, they were constantly handicapped by having to keep theological considerations in the foreground, so that, for this reason alone, they were unable to meet their secular opponents on equal terms.

This state of affairs changed little as time passed. Even later, the Jesuit order produced a large number of eminent scholars who made it their task to pursue their scientific inquiries to the highest attainable point, in order, if this were at all possible, to guide them back to the theocentric point of view prescribed by the Church.

Foremost among the Jesuit scholars who rendered valuable services to the progress of science should be mentioned the Belgian, Grégoire de Saint-Vincent, who, with Descartes and Fermat, laid the foundations of analytical geometry. Of no less importance is Francesco Grimaldi, on whose fundamental discovery of the diffraction of light much of Newton's work was based. A few years ago, the astronomical discoveries of Father Maximilian Hell formed the subject of a special study by the great American astronomer, Newcomb.

Another member of the order who gained fame as a far-seeing scientist of genius was Father Roger Joseph Boscovich, whose theory of "repelling forces" seems to be a forerunner of Maxwell's electrodynamic discoveries. Gustav Theodor Fechner describes him as "the real discoverer of the physically simple atomic theory with spatially discrete atoms." According to Fechner, Boscovich "did not confine himself to enunciating in general terms the principles of the simple atomic theory, but endeavored to develop from this basis the main doctrines of physics." Friedrich Albert Lange, in his *History of Materialism*, also attributes great importance to Boscovich's discoveries.

Always desirous as they were of keeping abreast of the latest discoveries, the Jesuits were indefatigable in going over again the experiments of others, checking the results obtained, and, in this way, often adding discoveries of their own. At the same time, the order, in the service of the Church, constantly sought to suppress with all the weapons at its disposal any important result of scientific inquiry which threatened to imperil the unity of the structure of their philosophic and theological beliefs.

The Educational Work of the Fathers

Their attempt to incorporate the results of scientific inquiry into the Catholic-Scholastic system of thought constituted but one aspect of the Jesuits' campaign against progress. Going beyond this theoretical endeavor, they sought to model the whole of human life in this sense, and here too to bring about a compromise between the inheritance of the Middle Ages and the spirit of modernity. They set themselves no less a task than the attainment of a human type which, while it would be modern, should nevertheless not be at variance with the demands of the Church, in which dogmatic faith should exist simultaneously with the urge for knowledge founded upon reason, the morality prescribed by the Church with the secularism of the modern spirit, the imagery of the Christian doctrines with the æsthetic sense of beauty awakened by humanism and the Renaissance.

The Jesuits regarded the education of the young as the most important means of achieving this aim, for thus could the mind, reason and imagination of innumerable young people, from their first inclination towards independent thought and emotion up to full maturity, be permanently and systematically influenced in the best and most effective manner.

The attention of the order had originally been drawn to the importance of the educational problem by the fact that the Protestants were, to an ever-increasing extent, making use of humanistic teachings to attack the Catholic religion in matters of Biblical criticism and ecclesiastical history, and had in many places founded schools in which young people could be brought up in a humanistic and Protestant spirit.

Protestant universities had arisen in Jena, Marburg and Heidelberg, and existing colleges had been reorganized by the Protestants, while the intermediate school system had also received a considerable impulse after the Reformation. Because of his pedagogical works, Melanchthon had become the *Praeceptor Germaniae,* and Johann Sturm had won considerable merit by reason of his Protestant grammar schools.

If the Society of Jesus were to be successful in combating this intellectual superiority of Protestantism, its own members must first of all be in a position to make use of the identical weapons of humanistic education, while at the same time it was essential to break through the educational monopoly of the evangelical schools in Germany by setting up new Catholic institutions. Ignatius himself had, in a letter to the Duke of Monteleone, expressed the opinion that the chief service which the Jesuit order could render to the Roman cause would "depend much less upon preachers than on teachers."

Hence, wherever the Jesuits were able to effect a permanent settlement, they made it their chief concern to establish schools, to secure benefits and privileges, for which they brought into play their political influence with the rulers of the land. In the German Empire they succeeded in founding colleges, first in Cologne, and soon afterwards in Vienna, Prague, Ingolstadt, Dillingen, Mainz, Speyer, Würzburg, Fulda, Münster, Graz, Innsbruck, Augsburg and Munich.

Between 1690 and 1700, they had so far succeeded in their project that many protestant parents were entrusting their children to the Jesuits. "how many of us," asked a contemporary protestant preacher, "are so learned and well educated as the Jesuits? How many of us are so zealous and skilled in teaching as these emissaries of the Roman Antichrist?"

The establishment by Ignatius of the Collegium Germanicum in Rome had marked influence on the revival of Catholicism in Germany. In it, especially gifted German youths, selected by the Jesuits, were trained as priests, receiving a thorough grounding in Catholic theology, and being inspired with an enthusiasm for the Roman cause which the majority of the German clergy of the period entirely lacked. About 1600, the Bishops of Salzburg, Breslau, Olmütz, Augsburg, Trieste, Würzburg and Passau were all former students of the Collegium Germanicum, and the nuncio at the court of Vienna was able to inform the pope that "our success is chiefly due to the work of the young men who were educated in Rome." The Jesuits speedily extended their educational activities from Germany into the neighboring cantons of Switzerland, where, in 1574, they were entrusted by the municipal authorities of the Catholic city of Lucerne with the task of establishing a school. A college was founded in Freiburg by Peter Canisius, who, after successfully accomplishing this task, died there.

While the Jesuits very quickly succeeded in establishing a firm footing for their schools in protestant Germany, their efforts in Spain, the most Catholic of countries were much slower in coming to a head. They were unable to obtain any real influence until the seventeenth century, when Philip IV founded the school of San Isidro for the nobility, and handed it over to the Jesuits. Since almost all the heirs of the leading noble families were educated at this institution, this decision of the king's gave the Jesuits for many years the undisputed mastery over the Spanish educational system.

The Educational Work of the Fathers

In France, the Society of Jesus at once found itself faced with difficulties and the hostility of the Parlement and university, and it was a considerable time before the small band of novices whom Ignatius had sent to Paris under the leadership of Father d'Eguia were able to secure for themselves the right to set up a college for their own. It was chiefly due to the energetic help of Guillaume du Prat, Bishop of Clermont that the Jesuits were allowed to establish themselves at Billom, in the Auvergne, and later to set up their Clermont school in Paris.

As early as 1550, thanks to the instigation of Francisco Borgia, the Collegium Romanum had been founded in Rome as the center of the Jesuit education scheme. Here, as Ignatius explained in a letter to Borgia, the most suitable educational methods were to be tested, from here all the curricula and most of the textbooks to be used were dispatched to all the other colleges, and thither were all the best students from every country sent to complete their studies.

While the Collegium Romanum was the center of the educational activities of the order in Europe, the college at Coimbra performed the same function for the Jesuit schools in the mission fields; for by means of education, even in the most remote countries, it was intended that men should be imbued with the Catholic outlook on life. Missionaries and teachers, after being educated at Coimbra, were sent to all the regions beyond the seas, in order that they might found further schools there.

In India, the Jesuits were soon in possession of St. Paul's College at Goa, as well as seminaries in Bassein, Cochin, Quilon, St. Thomé, Tuticorin, Delhi and Agra; in Japan, Jesuit schools were set up in Arima and Miyako in which young Japanese received instruction in Latin and in Christian theology. In China, the college of Macao formed the center of all missionary work, and, as the Jesuits secured a foot-hold in North and South America, they founded numerous schools for the colonists and Indians.

In order that the educational work in all the Jesuit schools should be put on a uniform basis, the leaders of the order issued in 1599 a *Ratio atque Institutio Studiorum Societatis Jesu*, laying down the rules to be followed in the conduct of colleges, seminaries and high schools.

The chief object of the *Ratio Studiorum* was the harmonizing of the mediæval forms of thought of the scholastics with the new humanistic aims of the day, on the one hand asserting the authority of the Church in an unobtrusive manner, while on the other giving free scope, up to a certain point, to the intellectual activities of the new generation.

Ignatius himself, during his own education, had been subjected to both scholastic and humanistic influences for while, during his stay at Alcalá and Salamanca, he had buried himself in the study of the works of the mediæval scholars, he had also acquired, while at the Collège de Sainte-Barbe in Paris, a profound knowledge of the spirit of humanism; and, although in the appendix to his *Exercises* he stresses the admonition that his followers must devote "considerable attention to positive and scholastic theology," since it is "the duty of the scholastic theologians to discover, oppose and refute the errors, faulty conclusions and misleading opinions of the present time," he also demanded of his disciples a thorough education in the humanities, the absence of which, as he clearly recognized, rendered it impossible successfully to combat the "misleading views of the time." He therefore insisted that every novice in the order should have acquired a knowledge of those branches of the humanities which were usually taught, before being admitted to the study of theology.

The Power and Secret of the Jesuits

From the very outset, the rules of the studies reflected the spirit of compromise which characterized the order in so marked a degree, for, while it was laid down in the *Constitutions* that scholastic theology should be taught "in accordance with St. Thomas," Ignatius was of opinion that this rule should hold good only until in the fullness of time, another author should be found whose writings might be of greater value for educational purposes. Philosophy, again, was to be taught strictly in accordance with the theories of Aristotle, quotations from non-Christian commentators being used only with considerable reserve; if, however, the *Ratio Studiorum* added with true Jesuit caution, it was not found possible to avoid such references, care must be taken, in mentioning such authors, "at least to avoid praising them in any way."

Fundamentally, the teaching at the Jesuit educational establishment was arranged in three main stages, which were designed to train the minds of the students in the spirit of that compromise between modern thought and the creeds of the Church aimed at by the Jesuits. The lowest of "Grammar" class, in which Latin was taught, was intended merely for the thorough exercise of the memory; the following classes in the "Humanities" and "Rhetoric" were to develop the formulation and expression of ideas. The chief authors used in these were Cicero and Virgil, together with selections from the works of other Latin authors. The final stage, that of "dialectics," was intended to enable students correctly to assess the importance of contradictory arguments, and to accustom them not merely to solve contradictions by an affirmative or a negative, but, in accordance with the methods of mediæval scholasticism, to raise them to a higher unity.

As, moreover, in this course of training, every care was taken to avoid any too close contact with the empirical sciences, there seemed to be no danger of exposing students to unduly disturbing influences likely to imperil the unity of the religious view of life, and the fathers felt justified in the hope that their pupils would be permanently satisfied with this harmonious reconciliation between the rationalized knowledge which they had acquired and the revelations of faith, the result which was reached, or at any rate was intended, by this dialectical synthesis.

That the Jesuit educational system produced, in many cases, excellent results is evident from the opinion expressed by Voltaire, who, in his *Age of Louis XIV*, testifies concerning his own experiences while at the College of Clermont: "What did I observe during the seven years which I spent under the Jesuit roof? A life full of moderation, diligence and order. They devoted every hour of the day to our education or to the fulfilment of their strict vows. As evidence of this, I appeal to the testimony of the thousands who, like myself, were educated by them."

Lamartine, again, writes in the most touching terms of his boyhood years which he spent at the Jesuit college at Balley. "I was a bitter and obstinate boy," he writes, "and I was softened and won over, so that I willingly subjected myself to a yoke which skilful teachers made light and pleasant for me. The whole art was to arouse in us the love of God, and to guide us by their own will and through our own efforts.

"Our souls had found their wings and together soared upwards towards the good and beautiful. . . I there learned what can be made of human beings, not by compulsion, but by encouragement. . . they made religion and duty attractive, and inspired us with the love of

God... With a level such as this, which had its fulcrum in our own hearts, they could do anything... they began by making me happy—they would soon have made me good..."

The Jesuit Theatre

The imaginative powers needed just as much care as the guidance of the understanding, in order that, within the limits imposed by the Church, they might receive satisfaction. How important it was to assist the training of the mind by bringing a parallel influence to bear on the imagination, Ignatius had himself realized, and his exercises were based as a system on this knowledge. In the *Spiritual Exercises*, every proposition, once it has been grasped by the mind, is immediately presented in a figurative form, and thus indelibly stamped on the consciousness. The Jesuits incorporated this principle into their educational methods. As in the *Exercises*, they sought first of all to instil into their scholars' minds a knowledge of the truths of religion by means of rational observation, and then to fix in their imaginations the convictions reached by the rational processes.

The tendencies, plots, theatrical methods and modes of presentation of the Jesuit theatre correspond in an unmistakable manner to the hell and passion drama prescribed by Ignatius in the *Exercises*. It might almost seem that the dramatists and stage managers of this theatre, mindful of all those things that Ignatius had tried to awaken in the imagination of his followers, had now brought them on to a real state, assisted by striking settings, costumes and properties.

The utilization of the theatre for the purpose of religious propaganda appeared to the Jesuits all the more necessary inasmuch as, just about this period, the stage was manifesting an ever-increasing tendency to emancipate itself from the yoke of the Church and to stride forward along new paths. For some time past, the impulse towards new dramatic subjects had tried to break through the barriers imposed by the religious mystery plays of the Middle Ages; since humanism had brought with it a breath of the spirit of antiquity, a general interest in man, his activities, his virtues and his vices, had been awakened, so that the theatre of the sixteenth century could no longer be restricted to hieratically severe plays dealing with the Transfiguration of the Redemption, or the soul's descent into hell and ascension to heaven, but rather extended its scope to deal realistically with all the human passions.

It was at this period that English players began to appear on the continent, and afforded their audiences a glimpse of the wealth of characters contained in Shakespeare. Moreover, the performances of the German strolling players, primitive and coarse though they were, were a further step in the direction towards which the present-day theatre, freed from all religious fetters, was tending.

But in another respect still the theatre now presented a danger to the Roman Church, for, ever since Luther had recognized the importance of the stage for the propagation of the evangelical doctrines, a humanistic and Protestant drama school had been developing in Germany, which, by its violent polemic tendencies, was doing considerable harm to the Catholic cause.

The Power and Secret of the Jesuits

For this reason, unless the Jesuits were to allow the imagination of the masses to be entirely secularized or to fall under the influence of their Protestant adversaries, they found themselves forced to organize a "theatrical Counter-Reformation." Accordingly, almost simultaneously with the beginning of their educational work, they started a systematic theatrical activity in order that the human love of spectacular effects, which showed signs of breaking away from the Church, might be gratified and at the same time maintained in the spirit of the Catholic religion. Within a brief period, the world-wide network of Jesuit scholastic establishments was supplemented by a similar system of Jesuit theatres.

In most cases, the stage consisted of a platform in the hall, although the larger colleges had their own theaters. The pupils provided the entire cast, the students in the rhetoric class being chiefly called upon to play the principal parts. Usually, the performances lasted from two up to seven hours, although occasionally festivals were arranged at which cycles of plays were performed on three successive days.

The audiences consisted of distinguished members of the court and of the municipal authorities, ecclesiastical dignitaries, and the parents and members of the pupil's families. During his childhood, Louis XIV was on more than one occasion a member of the audience at Clermont College, and in 1653, he attended a performance, accompanied by Cardinal Mazarin and the exiled king of England. In Vienna also, the court and nobility were in the habit of attending the Jesuit performances; during the peace negotiations at Münster, the plenipotentiaries in a body paid a state visit to the theatre of the local college.

Everywhere, large audiences attended the Jesuits' performances. In Vienna, the number of spectators amounted to as many as three thousand, while, in 1737, at Hildesheim, the city police had to be called in to keep back the public. The effect of the plays which were staged was sometimes remarkable. In Munich once, fourteen important members of the Bavarian court withdrew from public life in order to practice devotional exercises, so strongly were they impressed by the Jesuit play, *Cenodoxus*.

As in Europe, the Society of Jesus also made use of the theatre in the missionary field, in order to work on the feelings of the people, and to make them more accessible to Catholicism. Sometimes, indeed, the theatre appeared the sole effective means of bringing peoples of foreign culture over to Christianity.

Simultaneously, therefore, with the setting up of Jesuit theatres in all parts of Europe, similar institutions sprang up in India, Japan, Brazil, Mexico, Peru and Paraguay. Everywhere, the heads of missions regarded it as one of their most important duties to become competent theatre managers, producers and dramatists, and the pupils at the mission schools were zealously trained to become not only good Christians, but also good actors.

In many cases, the Jesuits were able to base their repertory on traditional religious plays of native origin, on to the structure of which they grafted a Christian motive; in this respect, as in all their other missionary work, they tried wherever possible to adapt their plays to the racial characteristics of the heathen nations.

The mission theatres attained their greatest degree of perfection in India, where there already existed a highly developed dramatic art, and where, in consequence, the natives willingly attended the dramatic performances arranged by the foreign priests, and took part in them to the best of their ability. "Nothing has attracted the poetry-loving Indians more effectively than our plays," reported the Jesuit missionaries in these regions. In Goa, in particular, a stage was set up in front of the church, on which the Jesuits' pupils enacted scenes from the life and work of St. Francis Xavier.

In Japan, the theatrical activities of the Jesuits met with a no less sympathetic reception, for in that country also there had existed since time immemorial a national stage of high cultural standard, on which stories of the gods and national heroes were produced, including dances, rhymed dialogues and musical settings. Here also the Jesuits retained the traditional forms almost in their entirety, merely replacing the Japanese mythical subjects by stories taken from the Bible. In Bungo, the Jesuits produced religious play cycles representing an intermediate stage between the Japanese pantomimes and the Spanish *autos*. In the colleges and seminaries at Nagasaki, Arima, Osaka and Miyako there were permanent school theatres.

The Society of Jesus found similar points of contact in Mexico and Peru, where the Aztecs and Incas had been in the habit of holding regular performances in the market-places and temples which included symbolical dances and dramatized legends. One of the favorite plays which the Jesuits now introduced was that of the rich man and the poor beggar, Lazarus—a theme which the Jesuits treated in a manner that gratified the Indians, being aimed against the colonists, as it was.

In Paraguay, the Jesuit mission theatres naturally reached a high stage of perfection. The plays which were performed in this country were written solely in the Indian dialect, and could therefore be fully understood by the natives.

It cannot, of course, be denied that the Jesuit missionary theatre was not destined to produce any vital development. On their arrival in a strange land, the fathers immediately sought to discover the form of dramatic art most suited to the people concerned, and there they stopped. The tastes of the peoples with whom they had to deal permitted them mostly to adhere to a style which they had once found to be suitable; for the peoples of Asia and America, with their deep-rooted ritualistic observances, were lacking in any need for variety, and were as much impressed on seeing a play for the hundredth time as at its first performance, even though the piece had not suffered the slightest change.

It was quite different in Europe. Here adaptation to the tastes of the people meant as well adaptation to a progressive development, and, if the Jesuit theatre was to continue to influence the imagination of the European peoples, it was necessary to make ever new concessions to worldliness.

In the beginning, the matter of the Jesuit drama was in the main taken from the Bible or the sacred legends. Even when some topical event was to be presented, a suitable Biblical story, which permitted of clearly intelligible allusion, was as a rule chosen for the purpose. Thus, in 1645, the Jesuits produced in Vienna a play in honor of the Emperor Ferdinand, and, which bore the title *Arma Austriaca, or the Victory of David over Goliath*. Again, in Lucerne, they celebrated the conclusion of an alliance among the Catholic cantons of Switzerland by a festive play entitled *The Battle of the Maccabees*.

Use was also made of the material furnished by the mediæval mysteries, and, in especial, the theme of the "dance of death" and the "Everyman" motive had every possible change rung upon them. In an endeavor to improve the manners of the people, they produced dramas written with a moral purpose, especially attacks on drunkenness and swearing.

For a long time, the fathers made it their endeavor that nothing "should happen on the stage that was not serious and worthy of a Christian poet"; in particular, all mention of sexual love was scrupulously avoided. Since the early Jesuit dramas were devoted entirely to religious themes, it was a matter of course that Latin alone, the language of the Church, should be used for the dialogue. All this was expressly laid down in the *Ratio Studiorum*. "The subject of all tragedies and comedies," it is there stated, "which are to be in Latin and are only seldom to be performed shall be sacred and pious; a woman or a woman's gown must never appear on the stage."

In the course of time, however, the Jesuits showed themselves to be, in this respect also, as little harsh and unyielding as in other things. As the attainment of their object made this necessary, the prescriptions of the *Ratio Studiorum* concerning the Jesuit theatre were, in the end, broken in almost every respect.

The Jesuit plays did, indeed, as a rule retain their didactic and moralizing purpose; but female characters, although represented by male actors, soon began to appear on the stage. How otherwise could plays like *Esther* or *Saint Mary Magdalene* have been performed on the stage? So too, the supremacy of Latin was challenged, short plays in the national tongue being interposed between the Latin tragedies, and, in course of time, more and more place being given to them.

Furthermore, the desire to entertain the public led to the introduction of comic scenes into serious dramas. The action was enlivened by the comedy of mistaken identity and disguise; clumsy servants, ridiculous magicians' apprentices and cheating tradesmen brought out the comic element still more clearly.

In 1700, the German Jesuit, Father Johann Baptista Adolph, wrote a large number of comedies for the school of theatre, the action of which turned entirely on low comedy, such as humorous peasant and beggar scenes. In a report of that period from the Munich college to the headquarters of the order at Rome it is stated that there is "no better means of winning over the Germans, of making friends of heretics and other enemies of the church, and of filling the schools" than farces.

In France, a similar turning from tragedy to comedy was early observable. The three most important Jesuit authors or that period, Fathers Porée, Le Jay and Ducerceau, always, indeed, called their works "dramas" or "fables"; but the character of these pieces distinguished them clearly as comedies. This is evident from their titles, and, in fact, these are reminiscent of Molière: *Damocles, or the Philosopher Ruler, the Inconveniences of Greatness, Philochrysus, or the Miser.*

In his *Ratio docendi it discendi*, Father Jouvancy taught in vain that comedy should "only seldom and in moderation" be used in Christian and religious schools, "as this form of art easily leads to all kinds of buffoonery, which is not compatible with the religious training of the young." The secular-comic element soon gained the upper hand, to such an extent that for a time the original aim of the Jesuit theatre was completely lost. The continually expanding "interludes" offered opportunities for *risqué* jokes and extempores; the introduction of the

124. SCENERY FROM THE JESUIT THEATRE AT CLERMONT

125. GRAND FESTIVAL IN THE COLLEGE OF CLERMONT IN CELEBRATION OF THE BIRTH OF LOUIS XIII

national tongue gave the actors a chance to bring the house down with coarse allusions.

In the endeavor to compete with the wandering troupes of actors, the Jesuits began more and more frequently to introduce into their pieces secular matters and love tangles; finally, the stereotyped character of the nurse was taken over from the English drama to the Jesuit theatre, and here, as in Shakespeare, she plays unmistakably the part of a shameless matchmaker.

The subjects of the Jesuit theatre and their treatment had travelled so far from the early prescriptions that the leaders of the order had more and more frequently to issue warnings and prohibitions. As early as 1591, the South German Province of the order was exhorted from Rome to exclude devils, beggars, drunkards and cursers; and, nearly a hundred years later, the general of the order issued a circular to the provincials, drawing attention to the numerous complaints which had been received in regard to objectionable love scenes and vulgar jesting, and calling upon them to put an end to this state of things.

Jesuit Opera and Jesuit Ballet

Just as, thanks to its adaptability, the Jesuit theatre had gradually found its way from the religious miracle play to modern comedy, so too did it contribute considerably to the development of the opera. For more and more frequently the Jesuit pieces had included lyrics, and choruses of joy, sorrow and consolation; and from the systematic arrangement of these in strophe and antistrophe the operatic treatment of the chorale was gradually evolved. It was the Munich Jesuits who led in this, with choruses composed for the drama, *Samson*, by Orlando di Lasso, Soon, the dramas of the Jesuit theatre became regular oratorio, into which, later on, the elements of the pastorale, then coming into vogue, were introduced.

In 1617, a *Musical comedy of the Liberation of Ignatius Loyola, founder of the Society of Jesus* was produced in Würzburg, and thirty years later, in Munich, the Jesuits played a religious musical drama, under the title, *Philothea, or the Wonderful Love of God for the Soul of man, Drawn from Holy Scriptures and Set to Delightful Melody*. Christ, Philothea, Justice, Charity and similar allegorical characters appeared in this strange opera as actors and singers. Sung by seventeen artists and accompanied by fifteen instruments, this work was so well received that it had to be played ten times. A similar opera, *Theophilus*, followed in Munich in the same year.

The composers were, for the most part, directors of the cathedral choirs in the various cities and the music teachers of the Jesuit schools. Other musicians were at times called upon, and among these latter was no less than Wolfgang Amadeus Mozart. In the year 1767, at the age of eleven, Mozart was commissioned to compose an opera in Latin as an interlude for the tragedy, *Clementia Croesi*, which was to be produced at the Jesuit college in Salzburg. The title of this small musical composition was *Apollo et hyacinthus seu Hyacinthi Metamorphosis*; and, on the play-bills, the author was described as follows: *Auctor operis musici nobilis dominus Wolfgangus Mozart, undecennis, filius nobilis ac streuni domini Leopoldi Mozart, Capellae Majistri*. After his performance, Mozart gave the audience a recital which lasted far into the night.

With the increasing refinement of the forms of social intercourse at the courts, dancing had won for itself much greater respect in high circles. Louis XIV, in 1661, established in

Paris an academy of dancing, and, in the patent founding this institution, he stated that skill in dancing should be regarded as "one of the most excellent and important disciplines for the training of the human body"; therefore, "the art of dancing is very important for our nobles and for all those who have the honor of approaching us."

It was only natural that the Jesuits, to whom, in all Catholic countries, had been entrusted the education of the young, could not ignore the cultivation of dancing; otherwise, there might have been a danger that this important branch of the training of the man of the world might have led young people outside the limits drawn by the Church. In order that dancing, too, might be included in the Jesuits' syllabus for the systematic training of youth, they admitted it to their theatre. Father Jouvancy wrote: "Place should certainly be found for dancing; it is a worthy entertainment for well-bred men, and a useful exercise for young people."

Suffered at first only in the interludes, dancing soon won a large place in the Jesuit theatre; it was on the Jesuit stage that the ballet assumed that character of magnificent mounting which it has maintained from then on to the present day.

The most celebrated dancing-masters of the time were called upon to superintend the rehearsals of the Jesuit ballets and even took part in them. Since at that time skillful dancers enjoyed an extraordinary popularity, their brilliant performances formed an added attraction for the Jesuit institutions. Much more than is the case today, the ballet, in the seventeenth and eighteenth centuries, depended mainly on allegory, and this entirely corresponded to the tendency of the Jesuit school theatre. Thus there appeared on the stage at Clermont a *Ballet of Night*, a *Ballet of Proverbs*, a *Ballet of Gratification*, a *Ballet of the Seasons*, a *Ballet of Dreams* and a *Ballet the Arts*. Other French Jesuit ballets served to celebrate festival occasions, such as the weddings of the king, the birth of the dauphin, or the peace treaty of Nymwegen.

Entirely abstract philosophic problems were even put on the stage in the form of allegorical dance scenes. Especially characteristic in this respect is the pantomime *Fate*, which was performed at Clermont College in the year 1669, i.e., the time of the Jansenist controversy, and which was nothing more than a representation of the triumph of the free will over predestination.

The ballet shows, first of all, how "Ignorance," "Falsehood," "Stupidity" and "Error" draw forth "Fate" from hell, and set it on the throne; gods and people are immediately fettered, and must show reverence to the new tyrant. For a long time, the world endeavors in vain to free itself from the reign of terror of Fate, until at last the gods revolt against the yoke imposed upon them and force Fate to abdicate the throne it has usurped, and to return with the Furies to hell.

On German soil, the ballet was mostly used only to fill up lengthy plays; but in these they assumed considerable prominence. In the six-act drama, *Godfrey de Bouillon*, performed in Munich, one scene was laid in the churchyard, where the graves opened, and a great round-dance of death struck up.

The Stage Management of the Jesuits

The Jesuit stage played an important part in the evolution of the theatre, owing especial-

The Stage Management of the Jesuits

ly to the great prominence given to stage management and production. From the very beginning, the Jesuits sought to fascinate the public with brilliant settings, scenic effects and complicated technical apparatus, and by these means to entice them from the wandering troupes of actors and the Protestant school theatres, whose only means of attraction were the spoken word and the subjects of their pieces.

The Jesuits were soon, however, forced into ever-increasing magnificence of stage effects by the severe competition of the Italian opera. This was particularly the case in Vienna, where the court maintained at great expense an Italian opera company. If the fathers were to maintain the position of their theatre as second court theatre, they had to compete with the Italians on every count, and to surpass them, not only in music, but also in scenic and technical production.

By means of clever arrangements of large curtains, the Jesuits managed to divide their stages into middle, side and back stages, and thus, as well as by a horizontal division of the space, make simultaneous action possible. The decorations were by no means limited to a mere suggestion of scenery; these, on the contrary, copied reality with even too great exactitude. Actual bushes were often used for scenery; for the furnishing of interiors, they sought, as far as possible, to procure genuine pieces of splendid furniture, and, when a scene included a banquet, the fathers borrowed the table-ware from the court. The expenditure of luxurious colored costumes was very great.

The stages of the great colleges were equipped with all the latest inventions of the Italian theatre. By means of decorations and scenes arranged in strict perspective, as well as by means of "ditches," effects were attained which at that time must have surprised every member of the audience. In Vienna, the wings were arranged in triangular revolving prisms, so that a treble change of scene could be effected by simply moving a lever.

In many Jesuit theatres, there were trap-doors for ghost apparitions and vanishing acts, flying machines and cloud apparatus. On every conceivable occasion, the Jesuit producers made divinities appear in the clouds, ghosts rise up and eagles fly over the heavens, and the effect of these stage tricks was further enhanced by machines producing thunder and the noise of the winds. They even found ways and means of reproducing with a high degree of technical perfection the crossing of the Red Sea by the Israelites, storms at sea, and similar difficult scenes.

F. X. Zimmermann has found among the archives of the town of Görz a record of a festal play produced in the Jesuit theatre of that town, in which it is stated: "First the crafty Odysseus crossed the stage in a ship... then the astonished crowd saw and heard Orpheus, the gentle conqueror of wild beasts and stones, who sang so sweetly beyond expectation to the lyre that beasts, rocks and pillars moved and followed his melody. This was so cunningly contrived that many stupid people thought that the animals, rocks and pillars had actually become living things; many spectators, indeed, came on to the stage after the performance, in order to see in what manner these things had been given life..."

For certain effects, the fathers even made use of the magic lantern, the Jesuit savant, Athanasius Kircher, having been one of the first to draw attention to this possibility. With the help of such projection apparatus, they made visions and dreams especially appear on the stage.

The Power and Secret of the Jesuits

Many other Jesuit inventions surprise us by their similarity to quite modern stage tricks. Thus, in the performance of the drama, *Godfrey de Bouillon*, in Munich, actors mingled with the audience, and, suddenly taking part in the action of the play, joined in the dialogue with the actors on the stage.

In the same way as many of our modern managers, the Jesuits also strove to thrill the public by means of crowd scenes. Battle scenes, hunting expeditions, triumphal marches and coronation processions as well as national gatherings offered an opportunity of setting in motion great hordes of supernumeraries, whose number at times exceeded a thousand. In Munich, in 1575, a drama, *Constantine*, was performed, in which there appeared, *inter alia*, four hundred horse men in Roman equipment.

On the occasion of the celebration of the centenary of the foundation of the order, in 1640, a great play, *The Vocation of Francis Xavier*, was performed in the hall of the college at Vienna, and the public was moved to enthusiasm by imposing choirs of angels, hordes of riders and numerous magnificent group pictures. In the middle of the hall stood a pyramid swathed in green, and, on four platforms, in the corners, there appeared an allegorical representation of the "four quarters of the globe," bound together by chains of lanterns.

At the same time, however, the fathers did not omit to devote great care to the diction, the gestures and the mimicry of the various actors; in the treatises of the Jesuit critics and, above all, in Father Franz Lang's *Dissertatio de actione scenica*, such matters as deportment, modulation of voice, an the play of the features are dealt with in great detail. Thus Father Lang tells the actors how to express all shades of emotion by means of varying glances, the position of the lips and the head and the tension of the forehead and the eyebrows.

It was inevitable that great hostility should manifest itself towards the whole style of the Jesuit theatre, particularly towards its magnificence. It has often been asserted that the concessions which the Jesuits made to the people's love of show had the result of completely banishing all elements of true dramatic art in favor of an empty spectacle.

Against this, however, stands the testimony of Goethe, who at Regensburg was present at a theatrical performance in the Jesuit college there, and who wrote regarding this in his *Italian Journey*: "This public performance has again convinced me of the cleverness of the Jesuits. They despised nothing which could in any way be effective, and treated the matter with love and attention. This is not cleverness as one thinks of it *in abstracto*; it is a delight in the thing, a participation in the enjoyment that is given, as in the ordinary ways of life. Just as this great religious society counts among its numbers organ-builders, sculptors and gilders, so are there some also who devote themselves with knowledge and inclination to the theatre, and in the same manner in which they distinguish their churches by a pleasing magnificence, these intelligent men here have made themselves masters of the worldly senses by means of a theatre worthy of respect."

The Jesuit theatre was not without influence on the development of the dramatic art; several of the most famous European dramatists received their education in the colleges of the Jesuits, and obtained their first artistic stimulus in the Jesuit theatres. This is true of Molière as of Corneille, both of whom were Jesuit pupils. Father Porée again was Voltaire's tutor and in later years his friend; similarly, Diderot made his first acquaintance with dramatic art in one of the Jesuit colleges.

The Society of Jesus and the Arts

In Spain, Lope de Vega, Tirso de Molino and Calderon grew up under the direct influence of the Jesuit theatre and, later on, Calderon, in his *autos sacramentales*, worked up to powerful poetic purpose all those elements of the allegory, religious passion and scenic effects which are so characteristic of the Jesuit drama. Personally, too, this greatest of Spanish dramatists was, during his lifetime, an enthusiastic supporter of the Society of Jesus and particularly of the founder of the order. In one of his later pieces, *The Great Prince of Fez*, he makes his hero enter the order with a hymn to Ignatius.

That the ranks of the order itself produced relatively few poets of importance may, in a large measure, be attributed to the preponderating use of Latin; in those days, the beginning of modern times, Latin had become too stiff a vehicle and was too far removed from active life for any artistic literary work of value to be possible in it.

As typical representatives of the Jesuit school drama in Germany, we find foremost Fathers Bidermann and Avancini; Bidermann wrote a number of historico-legendary plays of an edifying character, while Avancini was especially distinguished for his cleverness in obtaining scenic effects. He it was who created that *ludus caesareus*, which found its clearest expression in the great festal play, *Pietas victrix sive Flavius Constantinus Magnus de Maxentio tyranno victor*, produced in Vienna. A true poetic perception, on the other hand, among the Neo-Latin writers of the order, is perhaps only to be found in the works of Johann Jacob Balde, a number of whose odes were translated into German by Herder.

Of the Jesuit playwrights of France, actually only Father Porée, Le jay and Ducerceau can be named as having also partly written in the national tongue, and as having not without success, adapted themselves to the new style of French character comedy.

Incomparably more important than all Jesuit drama are the lyric creations of two German members of the order, who both wrote in their mother tongue, and whose works deserve to be counted among the most outstanding of their time.

Johann Scheffler, who has immortalized himself, under the name of Angelus Silesius, as the author of a collection of aphorisms, *Der Cherubinische Wandersmann*, was the son of Protestant parents; he became friendly with the Jesuit father, Athanasius Kircher, and later, influenced mainly by the mystic writings of the Jesuit, Maximilian Sandäus, was converted to Catholicism, finally joining the Society of Jesus. Friedrich von Spee again, who, in his *Trutz-Nachtigall* songs, expressed in beautiful language a natural sincerity and a passionate religious sentiment, became an enthusiastic member of the order, and yearned always to be sent to India, there to work in the spirit of Francis Xavier.

The Society of Jesus and the Arts

The age of humanism rediscovered antiquity and the human body at the same time, and, in the measure that artists and public gave themselves up to delight in purely sensuous beauty of form, the religious content of new works of art became less and less important. The subjects of Renaissance paintings were, it is true, almost invariably taken from the Gospels and the sacred legends; the treatment of these themselves, however, betrayed much less a sincere religious sentiment than a pure aesthetic joy in artistic composition. As the papal court had itself become the center of the humanist movement, it seemed as if any opposition on the part of the Church to this progressive aestheticism of art was not to be expected.

The Counter-Reformation which began in the middle of the sixteenth century created, however, in this respect too a change which was distinctly noticeable. Those men who seriously endeavored not only to struggle against "heresy," but also to reform the Catholic Church from within and obtain the recognition of more rigorous principles, soon demanded from sculptors and painters that they should in their works aim less at sensuous beauty than at the expression of severe religiousness, and, in particular, that they should abstain from all leaning towards "paganism," which was unworthy of the true faith. It is this mood which explains how it was that a prince of the church condemned Michelangelo's *Last Judgment* as "not Christian enough," and that, soon after, the far too shocking "nudities" of this masterpiece were painted over. Often in those days the establishment of a regular censorship of works of art was demanded, analogous to the Index of prohibited books which was introduced at that time.

Against such fanatical efforts, the Jesuits contended that it would not be wise to have art forced back again to an earlier stage of its development. Only by prudent adaptation did they consider it practicable to hold art to the further service of the Church, and, therefore, here too they sought to find a compromise which, on the one hand, would be compatible with the demands of the faith, and, on the other, would meet the tastes of the time.

For delight in the beauty of form and color seemed to the Jesuits to be objectionable only when it threatened to result in emancipation from the whole field of religious sentiment; from the moment, however, when painters and sculptors again appeared who represented sensuous beauty in an inner relationship to the faith, the fathers of the Society of Jesus were the first to receive such artists with open arms.

In opposition to the strict reform party, the Jesuits strengthened their view that no real antithesis could exist between the Church and art, by pointing out, in particular, that "iconoclasm," the fanatical hostility to all beauty, was characteristic of the "heretical" spirit of Calvinism and Anabaptism. Could Catholicism, indeed, find more effective weapons than the plastic and graphic arts in the struggle against the Reformation? These were, in fact, more suited than anything else in the world to appeal to the feelings of the masses and to enlist supporters for the Catholic cause even in the Protestant camp.

Therefore, the order of Jesuits, the strongest exponent of militant Counter-Reformation, even in its beginnings paid great attention to art and to artists. Ignatius himself had made a close friend of the greatest genius of his time; in 1554, Michelangelo, an old man nearly eighty years of age, declared himself ready, without fee, "for the love of God," to draw up plans for the Jesuit church which it was proposed to build in Rome; but certain difficulties in acquiring the building site they had in view and the death of the master soon afterwards disappointed the Jesuits' hopes of a house of God planned by Michelangelo.

At the beginning of the seventeenth century, the order also won Peter Paul Rubens to itself. As a pious Catholic, he was very susceptible to the ideas of the Jesuits; he had performed the exercises, and was a zealous member, and for a time even a prefect, of the Marian Congregation founded by the Jesuits. Rubens, at the order of the Society of Jesus, painted a large number of important works, including especially the pictures which were later destroyed by fire in the Jesuit church at Antwerp. The great altar-piece, *Ignatius Cures One Possessed*, shows clearly how Rubens regarded the founder of the order as a powerful high priest of the Catholic faith. The great painting, *The Last Judgment*, over the high altar in the church of the order at Nieburg is characteristic of the artistic freedom which permitted Rubens, in the service of the Jesuits, to paint even "shocking things.

In the decoration of the Jesuit Church at Antwerp, Van Dyck also collaborated as the assistant of his teacher Rubens; from his hand came the great ceiling piece for this building, of which we have now only the cartoon. In addition, Van Dyck was later commissioned by the Jesuits to make numerous engravings for the devotional books published by the Jesuits.

Lorenzo Bernini, the greatest sculptor of the baroque period was a close friend of the Jesuits and especially of the contemporary general of the order, Oliva, and had, under the latter's direction, absolved the exercises. The first biographers of Bernini, Baldinucci and the Chevalier de Chantelou, are unanimous in regard to the conspicuous piety of the master. Baldinucci writes: "With so ungovernable a longing did he strive for eternal salvation that, in order to attain it, he attended the devotional exercises of the fathers of the Society of Jesus at Rome throughout forty years, and took the holy sacrament of the communion twice a week." The sepulchral monument of Cardinal Bellarmine in the Jesuit church at Rome was the work of Bernini, as was also the series of energetic illustrations to the sermons of his friend, Oliva, from which the whole of Bernini's artistic peculiarities may clearly be seen.

But even those monumental creations which stand in no external relation to the Jesuit order betray how Bernini's whole artistic nature was penetrated by Jesuit ideas. For, while Rubens and Van Dyck, in spite of their close relations with the Jesuits, show no definite trace of this association in their work, the art of Lorenzo Bernini is so much influenced by it that that most eminent of historians of Italian art, Venturi, describes the master as the "most powerful advocate of the Society of Jesus."

None knew better than he how to impart to the human body an expression that seemed to link it with the supernatural. Bernini never strove after beauty for itself, but appeared to seek it merely as a means of directing the beholder to a world beyond. His characteristic inclination for propagandist effect, often, indeed, by artistically doubtful means, may be said to be Jesuitical. He it was, too, who, especially in the "Cattedra" of St. Peter's blended architecture, painting, sculpture and chiaroscuro in such a way as to give a general effect that is downright theatrical.

Still another branch of baroque art shows an unmistakable kinship with the spirit of the Jesuits; this is the Spanish naturalistic sculpture of the seventeenth century, particularly with works of Montañes and Mena. With that sharpness and clarity which Ignatius endeavored to attain in his *Exercises* the sufferings of the Saviour and the martyrs are depicted in the works of these masters; just as, in Loyola's *Spiritual Exercises*, it is prescribed that the disciple should strive to imagine the torments of Christ on the Cross as if he himself were actually suffering them, so the naturalism of these Spanish artists, as in a sort of panopticon, produced upon the beholder the most terrifying impressions. It is, therefore, certainly more than pure chance that Montañes and Mena made plastic portraits of Ignatius and Francisco Borgia, the great generals of the order.

Even though the influence exerted by the Jesuits on the plastic and graphic arts was very great, the order itself, as in literature, produced only a few men of any talent from among its ranks. Although there were numerous Jesuit painters, these were mostly without originality, and followed the example set by Rubens or Pietro da Cortona. Of the artists of the order's Italian school, Pietro Latria, Ottaviano Dandini and Giuseppe Valeriani may be mentioned; more important is the painter of battle scenes Jacques Courtois or Jacopo Cortese, as he was called, who was a friend of Guido Reni, and, in the somewhat restricted field of flower-painting, Danial Zeeghers, a pupil of J. Breughel, made a name.

One Jesuit artist alone has exerted any considerable influence on the development of painting; Andrea del Pozzo was not only the creator of numerous spirited paintings, especially in the Church of Jesus in Rome, as well as in important buildings such as the cathedral at Laibach, the Church of St. Martin in Bamberg and Church of the University of Vienna; his greatest merit, however, is that, in his writings, he was the inventor of a system of graphic perspective. He drew up those exact manuals for the construction of simili-architecture, ceiling-pieces and prospects having a plastic effect, with the aid of which numerous great and lesser artists over the whole of Europe and even in distant China later carried on that "illusionism" which is so characteristic of the baroque period.

Here again we notice the typical endeavor of the Jesuits to make accessible, by means of practical manuals, those qualifications which up to that time had been regarded as the privilege of specially favored persons. As formerly Ignatius had sought to indicate in his *Exercises* a path to perfection which might be trodden by all, so Father Pozzo, in his own sphere, was now at great pains to make accessible to diligent pupils an art which until then could have been learnt only in the workshops of the great and talented masters.

It is so quite characteristic that Pozzo chose perspective as the subject of his studies; in other words, a technique with the help of which painters were able to make the greatest impression on the beholder. In one shrewd sentence, Pozzo pointed out the ultimate purpose which this means of illusion was to serve. He writes, in the introduction to his manual: "May the reader be pleased to take up the work with joy and with the intention to draw the lines of his subjects always to the true point of vision that is, to the glory of God."

The Society of Jesus, through its numerous building and painting commissions, as well as by its friendly relations with many great masters, has closely allied itself to the baroque and used this on every possible occasion in the service of the Counter-Reformation Its intention was that people all over the world should, by magnificent churches, altars flooded with light, gilded sacred pictures, statues, confessionals and ceiling paintings with their perspectives reaching up towards heaven, be torn again from the sphere of everyday interests and directed towards things divine.

The church of the order in Rome which was designed by the great architect Vignola and completed by his pupil, Jacomo della Porta, makes it abundantly clear how much the baroque style was in keeping with the desires of the Jesuits. Whilst the façade shows a not too great deviation from the customary compositions of the late Renaissance style, and can be distinguished from the latter only by a livelier movement of the heavily crowded masses, the interior exercises a great psychological effect. The theatrical lighting, with its sharp contrasts between the dim half-light of the side chapels and the full light which pours down from the cupola on to the high altar, draws all those who enter almost bodily towards the sanctuary, and seems immediately to throw the mind into a rapture of faith.

The Jesuit church in Rome has innumerable times served as the model for churches of the order in other cities and countries, and this constantly observed connection between the arrival of the Jesuits and the erection of places of worship of a particular kind has often led people to refer to a "Jesuit style."

The art historians of the Society of Jesus, among them Father Joseph Braun in particular, have, however, pointed out that such a Jesuit style did not in fact exist, and that, on the contrary, the order, in the building of their churches, always made use of those forms of art which appeared to them, in each case to be most adapted to their purposes.

Father Braun writes: "Although the Jesuits, in all questions affecting the doctrines, ritual and rights of the Church, took the Roman, that is to say, the Catholic, point of view... in purely secular matters—and, therefore, with art—they everywhere paid due regard to the sentiments and views of the people among whom they were living, and from whom, indeed, they themselves sprang."

Indeed, in places where the Gothic style was still indigenous, especially on the Lower Rhine and in Belgium, the Society of Jesus, on their first appearance, adopted this style. They adhered longest to the Gothic style for their churches in Switzerland, where the Collegiate Church at Freiburg was built in this style as late as the beginning of the seventeenth century.

The non-Gothic German Jesuit churches were, up to the second half of the seventeenth century, mostly erected in the Renaissance style, until the baroque had penetrated generally into Germany. Then, of course, the order erected numerous churches in the baroque style, such as the Church of St. Michael in Munich, and the Collegiate Churches of Regensburg, Dillingen, Constance, Innsbruck, Halle and Eichstätt.

As in Germany, the buildings of the order in Belgium were at first in the Gothic style until, first as regards decoration, and later as regards general composition, Renaissance and baroque gradually became predominant. In the churches at Tournai, Mons, Ghent, St. Omer and many others, the transition from the Gothic to a more and more marked Renaissance and baroque character may clearly be followed. The Collegiate Churches at Brussels, Bruges, Namur and Louvain, on the other hand, are in their construction unmistakable imitations of the Roman types. Finally the church at Antwerp, with its fine baroque façade and its unusually charming spire, may be regarded as the most valuable example artistically of Jesuit architecture in Belgium.

In Spain, also, the Society of Jesus, in the early days of its activities, built some gothic churches, but the Renaissance and baroque styles swiftly predominated. In addition to the baroque churches of San Isidro in Madrid, San Juan Bautista in Toledo, the Collegiate church at Alcalá and the church of the Collegium Regium at Salamanca, the great Colegio Imperial at Loyola should be mentioned as especially typical; it is an enormous school building with a church in Italian late baroque, which has been built round the birthplace of the founder of the order.

Although, therefore, in an artistic and historical sense, the existence of a peculiar "Jesuit style" can scarcely be affirmed, nearly all the buildings of the Jesuits, and especially the manner in which these churches have been decorated, express a quite distinctive and uniform sentiment and intention. Goethe clearly felt this, when in the *Italian Journey* he wrote that the Jesuit churches had "something great and complete about them," which secretly inspired all people with reverence.

"As decoration," he adds, "gold, silver, metal and polished stone are heaped up in such splendor and profusion that it must dazzle the devout of all classes. In places, there are even things in bad taste, which might be calculated to propitiate and attract humanity. This is, indeed, characteristic of the Catholic genius in the external service of God; I have, however, never seen it developed with so much understanding, skill and consistency as the Jesuits have done. Everything they do is so conceived that, unlike the members of other spiritual orders, who persist in an old, outworn devotion, they reinvigorate all things with pomp and splendor in the spirit of the times."

The Revolt of the Scholars

Bur for all the deliberation displayed by the fathers in sending their most able astronomers, physicists and mathematicians into the field, establishing schools in all towns, and giving the best possible education to their pupils; for all the performances in their theatres of stirring plays, amusing farces, melodious operas and brilliant ballets, with simultaneous scenes, trap-doors and flying machines; for all their churches in the gothic and baroque styles, painted by the greatest masters of the time and decorated with statues—their efforts were powerless against the spirit of modern times, a spirit daily increasing in power and opposed to their purpose.

The good fathers had in vain made concessions to the thirst of modern humanity for knowledge, allowing it to turn its telescopes to this or that harmless star, and to doubt many things which were unimportant in relation to the Faith; they could not halt the progress of the human mind towards that stage in history which is usually described as the "age of enlightenment."

For, once Francis Bacon, Descartes, Galileo and Newton had directed philosophical and scientific thought towards new knowledge and discoveries, the moment had to come when doubts of the dogmas of the Church surged up, together with notions of man and his relation to creation as well as to the Creator which were unconnected with the teachings of Christianity. Bacon having already pointed out that the extension of human power through knowledge was the only aim of natural science. English philosophy, after Newton, applied itself with increasing cogency to the question how the observed laws of nature were to be explained; the answer to this question, however, by no means satisfied the demands of the church, which would have the regulation of the world traced back to the action of a personal God.

It was now more and more frequently announced that for science there was nothing supernatural or incomprehensible; on the contrary, all phenomena could be explained, the mind needing for their complete understanding the aid of no revelation.

What must have seemed particularly serious to the Jesuits in this revolt against the faith

126. SCENE FROM THE JESUIT FESTIVAL PLAY "PIETAS VICTRIX" IN VIENNA

127. SKETCH OF A SCENE FOR THE JESUIT THEATER IN VIENNA BY LUDOVICO BURNACINI

128. JESUIT FESTIVAL IN VIENNA TO CELEBRATE THE AVERTING OF THE PLAGUE

129. CARNIVAL PROCESSION OF THE JESUITS IN MEXICO, 1647

The Revolt of the Scholars

was the strange circumstance that "Enlightenment" opposed them with just those principles which they themselves for two hundred years had always upheld against the protestant and Jansenists. Ignatius himself had often pointed out that religion needed intelligent understanding for its support; in all the great struggles of the order against the protagonists of the "doctrine of grace," within and without the Catholic church, the defense of intelligence as a "valuable aid to faith" and always been in the forefront.

Now intelligence, so eagerly protected by the Jesuits, was turned against the church, instead of serving it like a "handmaid" in the sense of mediæval theology; no longer content to support and substantiate revelation with a thousand rational arguments and "divine proofs," the intellect had emancipated itself from all religious guardianship, and claimed, in its "presumption," to displace faith.

At the beginning of the eighteenth century, the Englishmen, Collins and Lyons, flatly denied the necessity for revelation, and claimed complete "infallibility" for intelligence. Only a little later, the young Voltaire entered upon the scene with the first of his writings directed against the Church, and intended to prove that the revealed doctrines of the Bible contained numerous contradictions which could not hold in the forum of reason, and must therefore be rejected.

Voltaire, indeed, like his intellectual predecessor, Locke, remained a "Deist" in all his attacks on dogmatic Christianity, and adhered to the conviction that nature without God was unthinkable. It was the later supporters of "enlightenment" who went one step further, and substituted Atheism for Deism. Starting from Newton's theory of gravitation, these moderns—very much in contradiction to the convictions cherished by Newton himself—said that the motion of matter was not attributable to a "divine mover," but, on the contrary, was a property of matter itself. Thus they reached a purely mechanical interpretation of the workings of the world. Within which there was no room for a God.

Lamettrie was the first "enlightener" to make the attempt to reduce the so-called spirit to purely material causes; but it was Diderot who gave to this materialistic conception of the universe its most comprehensive formulation; in his *Explanation of Nature*, he announced that matter alone exists; there is no spirit, nor can the belief in a Creator enthroned above the universe subsist before the tribunal of reason.

The great *Encyclopedia*, edited by d'Alenbert and Diderot, gave the "Enlightenment" an opportunity to set up a lasting memorial to their new teachings. Unavailingly did the Jesuits make use of every resource of polemical agitation against this *encyclopædia*. Father Berthier in his *Journal des Trévoux* sharply condemned it; Father Chapelain preached against it before the king. d'Alembert did, indeed, become discouraged, and resigned from the editorship; but the only consequence was that Diderot thenceforward was able to urge his materialistic convictions still more bluntly. The *Encyclopædia* was justly regarded everywhere as the codification of a philosophy of life which had decisively cut loose from all ecclesiastical traditions, and for that very reason the work was greeted with enthusiasm.

For "unbelief" had, in the meantime, become the latest fashion in society circles. It found a nursery in the salons of Madame de Tencin, Mademoiselle de Lespinasse, Baron d'Holback and *le philosophe*, Helvétius, where the Encyclopædists associated with the most eminent statesmen, writers, artists and foreign visitors.

The Power and Secret of the Jesuits

One of its strongest arguments in favor of the "religion of intelligence" and against the doctrine of revelation, the enlightenment found in the exemplary philosophy of China and, in particular, the moral philosophy of Confucius. But who, if not the Jesuits, had brought the knowledge of these Chinese ideas to Europe?

More progressive than all other Catholic clerics, the Jesuit missionaries, with their receptive and submissive minds, had immediately recognized what great moral worth lay in Chinese culture. Towards the end of the seventeenth century, Father Couplet, on his return from China, spoke everywhere with enthusiasm of the sayings of Confucius; Father da Costa had even described the Chinese thinker as the "wisest teacher" of moral and political philosophy, and soon afterwards the Jesuits had published the first translation of Confucius, which was quickly succeeded by popular editions and anthologies. In the eighteenth century, the work of Father Duhalde, *Description de l'empire chinois*, spread the knowledge of Chinese customs and institutions so widely that, at that time, it could safely be said that Europeans knew more about China than they did about many provinces of their own countries.

Of course, the Jesuits had not foreseen the extent to which the Enlightenment would make use of Chinese examples as a basis for their quite unecclesiastical doctrines of state and society. Adolf Reichwein writes, in his spirited study, *China and Europe in the Eighteenth Century*, that the Jesuits became the intermediaries between the enlightenment of ancient China and that of the eighteenth century in Europe; they had themselves "brought to Voltaire and the Encyclopædists the weapons which one day were to be turned against themselves."

For, if the cultural ideal of the enlightenment lay in the foundation of all human relationships on reason and on a "bourgeois virtue" springing from rational considerations, this corresponded exactly with the political science of Confucius, "with astonishment," Reichwein remarks, "it was discovered that, more than two thousand years ago, Confucius had thought out the same idea and had fought the same battles in the same way; thus Confucius became the patron saint of the enlightenment."

While a student at the Jesuit college at Clermont, Voltaire had heard much of China from the fathers, and, when he wrote his *Essai sur les mœurs*, he began with a long chapter on Chinese institutions. With witty malice he suggested that, instead of sending Christian missionaries to the Far East, the Chinese should have been begged for missionaries to spread the light of Chinese culture in Europe. Diderot, in whom the Jesuits had implanted an admiration for Confucius, also wrote in similar vein, saying that in, intellect, wisdom and philosophy, China could compete with the "most enlightened countries of Europe."

Extremely unwelcome as it was to the fathers to have the enthusiasm for China which they themselves had evoked turned to the setting up of the "religion of intelligence" of heathen Asia as superior to the Christian religion, it must have touched them still more painfully when the Enlightenment started to recast another of the pet theories of the Jesuit order in an anti-religious sense. The time, it was the doctrine of the "sovereignty of the people" which had been laid down by the scholastics, and had been elaborated by the Jesuits, Laynez, Mariane, Suarez and Bellarmine, and which now in Rousseau's treatise on the *Social Contract* underwent an unexpected resurrection.

In their defense of the sovereignty of the people and of the contract theory, the intention of the Jesuit teachers had been, of course, merely to demonstrate the superiority of the papal over secular authority; to this end, they had sought to show, in a Thomist sense, that the secular ruler could have received his power only from the people as a transfer of the *potestas publica*. But, in the struggle with the rapidly spreading absolutism, the Jesuits arrived at propositions, which, in their wording, were of a very democratic character. "surely," Bellarmine for example, writes, "everybody prefers a form of government in which each man has part, and such a form is also the only one which we can propose; for not birth, but the capacities of a man, should count."

Led by the desire to lay down the rights of a Catholic people in face of a heretic monarch, some Jesuits had gone so far as to concede to the people, in certain circumstances, the right of disobedience, and even of "tyrannicide"; only the authority of the Catholic Church, "established by God," and of the pope, its head, being regarded as immutable and inviolable.

The Enlightenment, however, developed these theories in quite a different sense; Rousseau held, as did the scholastics, that the state springs from a contract between the people and their ruler; but from this he draws the conclusion, opposed to the claims of the Church to power, that all authority on earth is a purely human creation, established upon agreement, and that there can be no "divine authority," such as the pope ascribes to himself.

The Enlightenment had thus made use of many of the ideas of the Jesuits in order to build up on them a revolutionary philosophy inimical to all the beliefs of the Church; but, furthermore, many of the most eminent leaders of this movement had grown up in the Jesuit schools, and had there received their first intellectual training.

Descartes, whose doctrine of doubt as the foundation of all knowledge led to the Enlightenment, had been a pupil—a model pupil in fact—at the Jesuit college at La Flèche. And what love and care had Fathers Olivet, Porée and Tournemine lavished on the young Voltaire, who, when ten years old, entered the college at Clermont, and for seven years enjoyed the instruction of the Jesuits! What further could be hoped from all pedagogic zeal, if that Voltaire, who, on his own confession, had "experienced only good and beautiful things" at the hands of the fathers, should demand with the words, *écrasez l'infâme*, the destruction of the Church, as the bearer of superstition and of fanaticism?

Voltaire, indeed, in spite of his many mischievous and malicious attacks on the Church, never took the step from scorn to blasphemy. What he scourged in the Christian religion of all creeds was intolerance alone, and, as often as the Church had sought to persecute the Encyclopædists, so often did Voltaire oppose it with his *écrasez l'infâme*. But, when the enlightenment itself became intolerant, Voltaire did not hesitate to refuse to follow his "free-thinking" friends.

The consistency with which Voltaire fought for tolerance explains his oft-misconstrued attitude towards the Jesuits. In their incessant endeavors to adapt themselves to the people and to the times, and to find a compromise between the stern demands of the Church and the capacities of weak humanity, Voltaire discovered a spirit towards which he was not unsympathetic; whilst in the rigid faith of the Jansenists he saw nothing more than an abominable and dismal fanaticism. His whole life through, he maintained friendly relations with his former teachers, especially with Father Porée, and once, when staying as a guest at the castle of ex-King Stanislaus of Poland, he associated in the most unaffected and cordial manner with the Jesuits in the king's entourage. One of them, Father Adam, he took with him to

The Power and Secret of the Jesuits

Ferney, and kept him there for thirteen years, because Father Adam was an adaptable person and a good chess-player.

Yet, shortly before his death, Voltaire became a Freemason, being introduced into the fraternity by Benjamin Franklin; when, however, he felt that he was nearing the end, and, just at the right moment, the Jesuit Gaultier appeared, he received him immediately. "A great duffer," he remarked, "but I can now make use of him."

On his death-bed, he sent for Gaultier again, and declared politely: "If you like, we'll get the little affair over at once." He made confession to the surprised and delighted Jesuit, and wrote a last testament; in it he said that he wished to die in the Catholic faith in which he had been born trusting that God in His mercy would forgive him his sins.

The fathers had considerably more difficulty with their other former pupils who were now at the head of the Enlightenment, especially with Denis Diderot, who, as an eight-year-old boy, had entered the college at Langres and had even received the tonsure. For Diderot had become an unrelenting and fanatical atheist, and had even turned vehemently against all Christian conceptions of virtue, which he described as meaningless, and against which he pitted the sole virtue of "humanity." He taught that everything depends on this, and that everything must be done "to the greater honor of humanity," and, in its service, the end justifies the means; whatever is of use to the earthly well-being of men is good, whatever hurts it is bad.

The article, "Jesuits," which he himself wrote for the *Encyclopedia*, is characteristic of the antagonism which Diderot cherished for his former teachers. Without any critical examination whatever, Diderot repeats all the accusations which till then had been made against the fathers of the Society of Jesus, and he charges them again with having corrupt morals, with the assassination of princes, and with the hatching of political unrest.

"I write this neither from hate nor for revenge against the Jesuits," he remarks in concluding the article; "my purpose is merely to vindicate the government that repressed the order, and the authorities who condemned it. . ."

But not only had the philosophic and scientific thought of the new generation by this time completely passed beyond the guidance of the Jesuits; but also the endeavors of the fathers to restrain the dramatic impulses of their scholars by means of their school theatre were in vain.

Poets like Calderon and Corneille had, indeed, proved themselves to be dutiful pupils of the Jesuits and, in their words, had sought to render service "to the greater glory of God." Molière, who, in the middle of the seventeenth century, had attended Clermont College, and had there made the acquaintance of the comedies of Plautus and Terence, became later on that poet who never tired in his comedies of poking fun at the scholasticism so highly esteemed by the Jesuits. And although Molière, even after the appearance of his *Tartuffe*, maintained friendly personal relationships with Jesuits like Fathers Rapin, and Vavasseur, the effect of his work was highly prejudicial to the dignity of the church.

To no less an extent must the Jesuits have felt disappointment in the dramatic creations of their former pupils, Voltaire and Diderot, and, last of all, there came an ex-Jesuit who wrote frivolous society comedies. This was Louis Gresset, whose *Le méchant* brought upon

130-133. SKETCHES FOR FESTIVALS AND GAMES BY THE JESUIT MENESTRIER

134. SKETCH FOR A CHURCH FESTIVAL BY POZZO

the stage for the first time, in masterly and lively fashion, the witty, cynical and scoffing people of modern society.

It was also a natural consequence of the Enlightenment that the direction of education was taken away from them; thus was brought to an end a dispute which had begun in the seventeenth century with the efforts of the Moravian school reformer, Johann Amos Comenius, In his *Janua linguarum reserata*, which he had compiled on the lines of a Jesuit education manual, Comenius had, in the thirties of the seventeenth century, for the first time endeavored to combine instruction in languages with object lessons, for, simultaneously with the teaching of the words, he taught the children to understand the meaning of the elements, starts, animals, parts of the body, arts and trades. Comenius demanded that instruction should be based on the perceptions and independent thinking of the pupils, and not on the witless memorizing of facts and phrases; the scholars should above all be enabled to find out for themselves the causes and relationships of things. Comenius spread his ideas with still greater success in the *Orbis pictus*, which appeared in 1658 and immediately attained great popularity.

From then on, the demand for the greater consideration of reality in education could not be silenced, until, at the end of the seventeenth century, as second great champion of this new tendency was found in the person of the great English philosopher, Locke.

At last, even Catholic courts and governments could no longer close their eyes to the backward state of educational methods. Maria Theresa, whose assent to Bourbon plans hostile to the Jesuits was later to deal a fatal blow to the order, approved, in 1752, a reformed scheme of studies, prepared by her government, which attacked "intellectual Jesuitism" at the root; it was there prescribed that the Jesuits must henceforward depart from many important rules of the *Ratio Studiorum*. "No teaching," so this order of the government ran, "shall henceforward be based merely upon the authority of Aristotle or any other author. That abuse shall henceforward be totally discontinued, since many professors endeavor to bring all their teaching of nature by compulsion into agreement with the authority of Aristotle. . ."

In France, the Jesuit educational system, at the time the fathers were about to be expelled from the country, was held up to scorn by the adherents of the Enlightenment. La Chalotais published his *Essay of National Education*, which Alembert joyfully greeted as "the first philosophical work against this rabble." With oratorical astonishment, La Chalotais asks in this pamphlet how civilized humanity could ever have delivered up its youth to a horde of monks, since, as celibates, they could never be in a position to perform any really beneficial educational work. With criminal blindness, he says, the education of French patriots had been left to men who, body and soul, were the minions of a foreign power. A fundamental change must be made; Latin must be replaced by the mother tongue, and the "scholastic hairsplitting of the Jesuits" by the "clarity of Cartesian intelligence." But far greater effects than those which resulted from La Chalotais's pamphlet were immediately produced by Rousseau's *Émile*, that most famous of all educational books, which appeared in 1762, just before the expulsion of the Jesuits from France.

The Power and Secret of the Jesuits

The Freemasons and the Jesuits

In the meantime, all those currents which were opposed to Catholicism, the Society of Jesus and their methods of education, had found in Freemasonry, which had its origin in England at the beginning of the eighteenth century, an extensive organization covering all parts of the world and embracing all classes of society; it was inevitable that a bitter struggle should immediately spring up between the Freemasons and the Jesuits, the "light cavalry of the pope."

The usages handed down from the mediæval "lodges" brought the "Honorable Society and Fraternity of Freemasons," from its very origins, entirely under the intellectual influence of the English Deism of Locke, Shaftesbury and Toland; in the search for a "natural religion," which should draw its truth solely from human reason, the Freemasons were fundamentally opposed to all ecclesiastical dogmatism, and, even though they acknowledged the principle of a supreme being, they would have nothing whatever to do with any dogmatic doctrine concerning the nature of this supreme bring. Within their association, each member had the right to form his own views regarding God, a principle of tolerance which was in flat contradiction to the inflexibility with which the Catholic Church held to revelation in its most literal sense.

The ethics, too, of the Freemasons, quite in accordance with the principles of the Enlightenment, were founded merely on human premises and aims; virtue was to be judged solely according to the natural properties of man, and not from the point of view of "original sin" and "grace"; the moral aim of the Freemason consisted, not in the attainment of heavenly bliss, but in the perfectibility of himself and his fellows during their existence on earth.

The Roman Curia immediately recognized the danger threatening it from this "humanitarian anti-Church," which likewise aimed at superstate and international universality, the purpose of which was the replacement of Catholicism by a "temple of humanity." The Freemasons, too, were well aware of the hostility of the Catholic Church, and in the Jesuits especially the Masonic brothers saw the "sworn enemies of Freemasonry," the "most cunning adversaries of tolerance," and the "worst corruptors of freedom."

Beside the Freemasons there soon rose up a kindred association, the "order of the Illuminati," which, from the very beginning, was intended as an anti-Jesuit organization. Its founder, Weishaupt, a professor of Ingolstadt, heartily hated the Jesuits, and formed his league of Illuminati with the expressed intention "of using for good ends the means which the Jesuit order had employed for bad"; this means consisted mainly in the introduction of an obligation of unconditional obedience, reminiscent of Loyola's *Constitutions*; of a far-reaching mutual surveillance among the membership of the order; and of a kind of auricular confession, which every inferior had to make to his superior.

The Bavarian court confessor, Franck, however, persuaded the Elector Charles Theodore without difficulty to forbid this secret society, which, soon afterwards, was totally suppressed. It was asserted at the time that the Jesuits had prevented the success of the order of the Illuminati by smuggling some of their own people into the fraternity; these managed successfully to confuse the disciples of Weishaupt, and to seduce them from their original fixed principles, thereby bringing about the downfall of the whole association.

Similar assertions have since then continually been made regarding the relations between the Jesuits and the Freemasons. Whenever gross abuses have been found within the lodges, Masonic historians have immediately given vent to the suspicion that the wily Jesuits have once again smuggled their emissaries into the association, and corrupted it in this cunning manner.

Suspicions of this kind are associated with the first beginnings of the lodges in England. The remarkable circumstance that the earliest lists of members contained the manes of several Jacobites is explained by the assumption that the Jesuits had sought to misuse Freemasonry for the restoration of the Catholic Stuarts. When, too, in 1737, Michael Ramsay introduced the so-called "higher degree" into Freemasonry, this soon came to be regarded as a Jesuit intrigue; Ramsay, said many Freemasons, had been bribed by the Jesuits, and had undertaken the task of introducing a Catholic hierarchical spirit into Freemasonry. Even in 1902, the Masonic historian, J. G. Findel, wrote that the Jesuits had succeeded in all parts of the globe in creating strife and confusion among Freemasons by tampering with the rituals and by the introduction of higher degrees.

Many of these statements have, of course, on closer examination, been proved to be merely the outcome of an unmistakable "Jesuit terror." Ignaz Aurelius Fessler, the great reformer of Freemasonry, has poked fun at the "smelling out of Jesuits," remarking that a direct or indirect influence of the Jesuit order on Freemasonry "can neither be proved nor is it probable." In any case, these suspicions sufficiently indicate the deadly hatred which has prevailed, since the eighteenth century, between the Freemasons and the Jesuits.

In spite of the hostility of the Church, which is expressed especially in the papal bulls of condemnation, *In eminenti* and *Providas*, the Freemasons held their ground, and entered into an alliance with the Enlightenment which was as sincere as it was effective. The leaders of the Enlightenment, Montesquieu, d'Alembert, Diderot, Lamattrie, Helvétius, La Chalotais, and, shortly before his death, Voltaire, were members of the Parisian lodge "At the Nine Sisters," and the writings of these men, as well as the teachings of Rosseau, were familiar to every contemporary brother of the lodge. The success of the great *Encyclopædia* was to a considerable extent due to the initiative and support of the Parisian grand lodge.

From now on, the Enlightenment, on the one hand, furnished the Masons with intellectual weapons for the fight against the Church and the Jesuits, while, on the other hand, Freemasonry placed at the disposal of the Enlightenment a powerful organization stretching over the whole world. In this way only did Freemasonry acquire a really important political influence, for in those days the most powerful statesmen of Europe belonged to the Masonic lodges.

Should "Brother" La Chalotais demand in his writings the expulsion of the Jesuits from France, "Brother" Choiseul by his reports to the king, saw to it that the measure was put into effect; and parallel with the intellectual campaign of the Enlightenment, which aimed at the total destruction of the Society of Jesus, ran the edicts, violent measures and counsels of "Brothers" Pombal, Aranda, du Tillot, Kaunitz and van Swieten, the purpose of which was, not only to extirpate the Jesuit spirit, but also the order itself, in Portugal, Spain, Parma, and, finally, even in Austria. With the abolition of the Society of Jesus which was accomplished by Clement XIV, under pressure from "enlightened despots," the Enlightenment and Freemasonry, in close alliance, had won the victory over their most detested opponent.

The Return in Spirit

Just as, however, during the period of the enforcement of the breve *Dominus ac Redemptor*, the fathers had not interrupted their political activities, so now, in the years 1773 to 1814, they continued their intellectual activities. During this period, too, they opposed new tendencies by means of learned writings and pamphlets; as secular priests they maintained a number of their schools, and, although deprived of most of their resources, endeavored under the most difficult conditions to continue their scientific work.

It was at this time that the archbishop of Baltimore, John Carroll, a former Jesuit, established the University of Georgetown, near Washington, the direction of which was given over to the Society of Jesus after its restoration, and which from then on became one of the most important centers of Jesuit research. Soon, also, numerous other Jesuit institutions were founded, for the order, which was now everywhere concerned with winning back its political position, once more spread its scientific outposts over the whole world.

Everywhere, the fathers of the Society of Jesus, as astronomers, physicians, biologists, philosophers, pedagogues, historians, men of letters, moralists, economists and professors of constitutional law, were once again actively engaged in combating, with all the resources of their technical skill and energy and in every sphere, that trend of thought which, originating in the "religion of reason" and the materialism of the period of the enlightenment, still continued to exercise its influence in the nineteenth century, and constituted such a source of danger to the Catholic philosophy.

For wherever the new spirit showed itself, it was almost invariably directed, in some way or another, against the faith of the Church. The rationalism of the nineteenth century, no less than that of the eighteenth century, relied entirely on the reason, and sought to dispense with religion; Darwin and his successors' materialistic theory of evolution denied the existence of any regulating and directing principle in nature, and, moreover, taught that man is not the "image of God," fundamentally different from every other living being, but that he is an organic development from the animal kingdom; this theory, when applied to morals, immediately furnished the basis for the contention that human morals had their origin merely in the adaptation of the gregarious mammals to their material conditions of life, and, accordingly, had nothing whatever to do with "divine ordinances."

The Society of Jesus had made it its task, immediately after its restoration, to combat these materialistic conceptions with all its energy, and here, too, it often, as in earlier times, achieved certain successes, and triumphantly won back a number of strongholds of the scholastic philosophy, which it had previously been forced to abandon under the pressure of the new ideas; over certain fortresses of the new spirit it was able to hoist the "standard of Christ" in place of the "standard of Satan." Now and then, a diplomatic agreement, a peaceable demarcation of the bounds between faith and knowledge was reached with its opponents. Nevertheless, a considerable number of the positions of modern thought proved to be unassailable, and thus the struggle in all its violence continues to be waged even today.

In especial must the Jesuit fighters in the cause of Catholicism have appreciated the necessity for acquiring a command of the natural sciences. Although, in earlier times, the Church had considered itself in a position to adopt a hostile attitude towards the empirical methods of scientific research, to contest its conclusions, and to prohibit their acceptance, or at least to restrict their sphere of application, this procedure would not have been possible in the nineteenth century. Accordingly, after the Jesuits had recognized that empiricism could no longer be resisted they changed their tactics and sought to apply the exact sciences to the service of the faith.

Since the knowledge gained from the study of natural science was primarily utilized by secular science to confirm materialistic and atheistic theses, the only thing for the Jesuits to do was to wrest the weapon from the enemy's hand, and, by empiricism itself, to establish proofs to the existence of God and the truth of revelation. And, just as Thomas Aquinas had fused the heretical theory of knowledge propounded by the Stagirite into one with Christianity, so the Jesuits now sought to turn an exact knowledge of the natural sciences into a supporting pillar of their dogmatic creed, so that it might endure uninjured for centuries to come. For this work, the order had at its disposal a considerable number of prominent scholars, who possessed every qualification for successful scientific activity "to the greater glory of God."

A not unimportant point in favor of the Jesuits in the nineteenth century was the change which had taken place in the official attitude of the papacy towards the altered conception of the universe in the new age. For, some few years after the re-establishment of the Society of Jesus, the Roman Curia had at last decided to repair the "unpardonable error" which it had committed in condemning the Copernican system.

Right up to the year 1822, the papal censorship had been strictly directed towards ensuring that Catholic authors should treat of the heliocentric system as a mere hypothesis; but the cardinals of the Inquisition now decided henceforward to approve also those works "which dealt with the movement of the earth and the fixity of the sun, according to the general views of modern astronomers."

This decision finally removed the obstacle which had hitherto made it extremely difficult for Catholic priests to carry on any form of astronomical research. The fathers of the newly revived Society of Jesus were now free to turn their telescopes towards the heavens without let or hindrance. And it was not long before important discoveries were made, particularly at the observatory of Georgetown. It was here that Father Francesco de Vico, to whom the science of astronomy is indebted for its knowledge of several comets and of the two nearest satellites of the planet Saturn, as well as of numerous new stars, carried on his work; and here also worked for some time Father Angelo Secchi, the most distinguished and celebrated Jesuit astronomer of the nineteenth century.

By his studies of the topography of the moon and its mountain chains, by his discovery of new methods, for the spectrographic investigation of the fixed stars, and by his contributions to the study of nebulæ, Secchi became one of the founders of modern astronomy, and his researches in the sphere of magnetism, meteorology and heat have greatly enriched the science of cosmic physics. The ultimate object of all these labors of Secchi's was however, none other than the production of proofs of the existence of God from empirical science.

This is most clearly apparent from his work, entitled *The Unity of Natural Forces*, in which Secchi expounds in an exemplary manner the principles of the modern theory of heat, thermodynamics, of the kinetic theory of gases, of optics and electricity. Then in his concluding remarks, Secchi endeavors to subordinate the results of the study of nature to faith in God, and to show how all science eventually leads to recognition of the divine principle. The explorable forces and processes in the cosmos, he declares, are merely the "primary material" out of which the great work of creation is fashioned. "The discovery of principles and the knowledge of the immediate causes of natural phenomena do not justify us in ignoring the existence of that First Cause, upon whose will alone depends the first determination of activity in its intensity and direction... If the skill of an artist is all the more dazzling the simpler the principle of activity he employs and the less he needs to apply to the work the hand that has introduced this principle, so, too, is this true in the highest degree of the Eternal Artist..."

Whilst Father Secchi had undertaken the task of incorporating astronomy and physics in the Church's mighty structure of ideas, Father Erich Wasmann bent his endeavor to do the same with biology. The serious threat to the Catholic faith arising out of the biological theories of the nineteenth century, Wasmann seeks to combat on the basis of his studies in entomology and animal psychology, regarding which Wasmann's fundamental rival, A. Forel, wrote that, for genius, "they are one of the most fascinating remarkable chapters of modern times in the history of animal psychology."

From the study of insect life to which he has contributed so much, Wasmann has endeavored primarily to show that the mutability of organic forms is not brought about by chance or by "the struggle for existence," according to the theory propounded by the Darwin school, and that the æsthetic laws which are revealed in the shapes and colorings of the insect world cannot possibly be explained by a purely mechanical conception of nature; indeed, they refute definitely such a theory.

"The philosopher and the theologian," he wrote once, "are not precluded from deducing conclusions of a higher order from the field of entomological knowledge... From the systematic and purposeful ordering which is evident in such a remarkable degree in the instinctive life of the insect world, he may justifiably infer the existence of an infinitely wise Creator. From the palæontological study of insects, he can, finally, show that, from this direction, no valid objection to the acceptance of the Biblical story of the creation can be raised..."

Similarly, when Wasmann proceeds to examine, in accordance with strictly scientific principles, into the origin of the earliest organisms, he arrives at the conclusion that some "extraterrestrial cause" must have brought forth from matter the earliest organisms. "This extraterrestrial, intelligent cause (in spite of being omnipresent in the world, it is substantially different from it) is none other than the Creator Himself."

The traces of divine perfection in the creature world are for Wasmann the "handwriting" which bears witness to the sovereignty of God, and it is particularly in the manifold evidenced of the "golden section" in plants and animals that the Jesuit investigator sees such proof of the existence of a God. Kepler had already expressed the view that the golden section, that celebrated harmonic proportion in which the shorter section of a line divided into two parts is to the greater as the greater is to the whole, appears to play a not unimportant part in the mor-

135. JESUIT BHUECH IN COUTRAY

136. JESUIT CHURCH IN BRUSSELS

137. IGNATIUS HEALING THE POSSESSED

Painting by Rubens, Vienna

phological laws of the vegetable world. Father Wasmann, by numerous measurements, established the fact that in the morphology of insects the *sectio aurea* is often found in the relative proportions of the segments of the body as well as in the proportions of breadth and length.

As regards the significance of these observations from the point of view of natural philosophy, Wasmann holds that they must inevitably "lead every thinking mind to the view that, unless the operation of an influence directed towards an æsthetic ideal is accepted, no satisfactory final explanation can be found for the presence of this morphological conformity to mathematical laws.

The particular feature of the golden section, he declares, lies in the fact that this division is always governed by the "concept of the whole," inasmuch as the relative proportions of the parts are determined by the magnitude of the whole. In this respect, however, the golden section corresponds, in a certain sense, to the *forma substantialis* of scholasticism, since, just as the latter expresses the idea of unity in the substantial existence of the objective world, so does the proportion of the golden section represent the idea of unity in the morphological grouping of organisms. If therefore the golden section appears as a law in nature, this can be attributed only to the dispensation of an "artistic spirit which recognized that proportion as the most complete expressions of unity in multiplicity, and accordingly gave expression to it in the works of nature."

Wasmann concludes his remarks concerning the *sectio aurea* observed in beetles with a sentence which is particularly characteristic of the spirit of Jesuit research work: "The visible form in which the law of the golden section is expressed thus constitute a universal and glorious confirmation of the Christian ideal conception of nature; the laws of the material and spiritual creation blend into a wonderful and rich harmony, sounding forth the praises of its Creator, since it is only a temporal echo of those immutable laws of truth and beauty which from all eternity repose in the spirit of God."

Kant and Neo-Scholasticism

Although even his opponents could not refuse to recognize the value of the work of this Jesuit scientist, yet it was by no means successful in securing the final overthrow of the modern anti-religious school of thought. For, whilst the Jesuit fathers were zealously endeavoring to combat materialism by means of their researches in astronomy, physics and biology, the intellectual development of the age had already outgrown this philosophy, and the belief in the omnipotence of the reason had given place to quite other views. That movement which had once proudly proclaimed that it was possible to explain everything by natural reason and by materialistic laws had, in the meantime, degenerated into a philosophically uninteresting tavern coterie, and the triumphs of the learned Jesuit naturalists over these materialist adversaries were merely "victories" over an assembly of blustering veterans. About disputes in which the one party sought to demonstrate the existence of a God and the other to prove the contrary. Immanuel Kant had already, at the turn of the eighteenth and nineteenth centuries, declared as follows: "Both parties are beating the air and scuffling with their own shadows, since they go outside nature, where there is nothing for their dogmatic clutches which can be seized and held."

The Power and Secret of the Jesuits

For Kant had taught, in his *Critique of Pure Reason*, that all human knowledge is limited to external phenomena in so far as they are accessible to us by experience; any attempt to make any positive or negative assertion that goes beyond these limits, to comprehend the transcendental or to apply rational argument to it, must necessarily lead to "empty and futile speculation." "Objects of the senses," Kant once wrote, "are perceptible by us only as they appear and not as they really are; in the same way, objects which are beyond our apperception are not objects of our theoretical knowledge." The conclusions reached by our reason concerning the immortality of the soul, the origin of the world and the existence of God merely involve thought in "paralogisms, insoluble antimonies and false arguments."

Kant's *Critique of Pure Reason* thus emphatically contradicted the prevailing view of the age of the enlightenment concerning the omnipotence of reason, and at the same time, Catholic theology; it allowed neither the contention that the non-existence of God can be demonstrated by reason, nor the effort to confirm the existence of a Creator by means of intellectual arguments, as Catholic theology had unswervingly endeavored to do since the time of Thomas Aquinas.

Martin Grabmann, the distinguished authority on the intellectual life of the Middle Ages, once defined the aims of scholasticism as consisting in the attempt "to acquire, by the application of reason and philosophy to the truths of revelation, as great an understanding as possible of the content of faith, in order to bring supernatural truth nearer to the thinking from the point of view of reason." As opposed to this scholastic view, in accordance with which the reason cannot rest content with anything less than a clear comprehension of the ultimate universal cause of all things, and therefore of God, Kant demanded that all attempts to obtain a comprehension of the transcendental by means of the reason be definitely renounced.

In this respect, Kant's critique of knowledge represents the culmination of a process initiated by Martin Luther, and it was this fact which caused Treitschke to describe Kant's teaching as "a more mature form of German Protestantism"; Friedrich Paulsen, again, declares that Kant "gave full and clear expression to what was implied originally in Protestantism."

Luther certainly held the passionate conviction that religious truths were entirely outside the scope of reason, that the Catholic Church had made a fatal error in compromising with human reason, and that, in fact, it was the task of the Reformation to free the faith of every form of theological speculation. Thus the Jesuits found in the philosophy of Kant their old traditional enemy, that Protestant spirit which revolted against the attempts of Jesuit theology to establish a union between faith and reason in an all-embracing "Catholicization of thought," and which aimed at excluding the reason from the sphere of religion.

Moreover, all the deductions concerning ethics resulting from Kant's critique were of necessity directly opposed to the Catholic moral philosophy. Whereas the Jesuits had taught that man can achieve complete felicity only in the perfect "possession of the good," Kant denied that it was in any way possible that real "possession of the good" could be attained; no being in the world of the senses, he declares, can be at any time in its existence capable of attaining to such a degree of perfection, which, there, can "be reached in such complete fulfilment only in a progress stretching to eternity." Thus, then, according to Kant, the "possession of the good" is never attainable, but is rather the "eternal aim" of humanity.

Kant and Neo-Scholasticism

Contrary, too, to the moral code of the Catholic Church, which is based entirely on the belief in a divine Ruler of the universe and on His revealed commands, and, accordingly, by its very nature is heteronomous, Kant propounded his theory of the "autonomy of morality," according to which "sins" are nothing more than offences against that "categorical imperative" which every individual human being bears within him, regardless of all written laws.

Since Kant's philosophy rejects every representation of a really existing "ultimate end," and substitutes for it a "direction" towards an infinite never to be fathomed by human understanding, it denies, of course, the existence of an actual hereafter, with its rewards and punishments. It rejects, therefore, both confession and the "direction of conscience" of the Catholic Church, and, in this connection, the Neo-Kantian, Hermann Cohen, declares that autonomous morality, the "veracity of self-knowledge," is "incompatible with the practice of confession, if only for the reason that confession necessarily implies unburdening oneself to another, quite apart from the consequences associated therewith, which are a menace to veracity."

How wide is the gulf between this conception and the aphorism of Alfonso dei Ligouri, the "Prince of Moral theologians," who had declared: "He who would advance along the road to God must place himself under the guidance of a learned confessor and obey him as he would God himself. He who does this need render no account to God of his actions..." No one, perhaps, appreciated more clearly than pope Leo XIII the danger to the Catholic philosophy which the critical philosophy presented; indeed Kant's critique had already penetrated deeply into Catholic circles at the beginning of the nineteenth century. Once again the pope saw the Church confronted with the self-same task which it had had to cope with in the days of humanism, when, for the first time, science began to threaten religious thought in its foundations. And just as the Council of Trent, in the sixteenth century, had evoked the name of the great master of scholasticism to exorcise with it the danger to the faith, so now the magic power of Thomas Aquinas was to show the new spirit of the age its proper limits. In the year 1878, Leo XIII issued his encyclical *Aeterni Patris*, in which he declared anew that the philosophic system of Thomas Aquinas was the basis of all Catholic thought.

This decree by itself would certainly have been even less effective in the nineteenth century than the resolutions of the Council of Trent in the sixteenth century, if the Jesuits had not at once again undertaken the task of upholding the philosophy of Thomas Aquinas against modern views and of adapting and modifying it in all these respects deemed necessary for the purpose of attaining the end in view.

To the activity of the Society of Jesus, above all else, is to be attributed the rapid rise of the neo-scholastic movement, whose task it has been to establish, by research and discussion, as many points of agreement as possible between the new school of thought and the principles of the *philosophia perennis*. By this means, it was to be demonstrated to the world that, notwithstanding everything, the fundamental principles of scholasticism were indestructible and inviolable, and that, as the result, the doctrines of the Catholic Church did, in fact, possess that virtue of infallibility in which secular science was no longer disposed to believe.

The real object of these efforts was the establishment of a synthesis between the Aristotelean-Thomist basic principles of scholastic philosophy and the results of modern scientific research. Had not the pope declared that Aristotelean scholasticism was "the only true and certain system of philosophy," affording "the greatest guarantee of truth"?

A large number of widely distributed Jesuit publications were devoted to the substantiation of this thesis, the most prominent among which is the *Philosophia Lacensis*, published by the Jesuit Fathers Tileman, Pesch, Meyer and Hontheim. While it was the aim of this compilation to revise every branch of philosophy in the spirit of the Thomist philosophy, the *Bibliotheca Scholastica* of Cardinal Franz Ehrle, on the other hand, sought once more to render mediæval sources accessible. Finally, the *Year Book of the Natural Sciences*, published by the Jesuits, was intended to direct attention to those developments in all branches of modern research into the natural sciences which might serve to support the Thomist philosophy, whilst, on the other hand, laying bare the weak points in opposing systems.

When in recent times, the "American Catholic philosopher, J. S. Zybura, endeavored to ascertain, by the issue of a questionnaire, the attitude of modern secular science towards neo-scholasticism, a number of scientists expressed the view that the scholasticism merits a certain degree of consideration even in modern intellectual thought. Professor R.M. Blake of the University of Washington (Seattle), for instance, declares that mediæval philosophy "may well contribute much of value towards thee solution of present-day philosophical problems." He even considers that it is highly desirable "that scholastics and non-scholastics should arrive at a common agreement, particularly just now, when the time appears to be ripe for such an understanding." There exists, in the philosophy of today, strong trends of thought which are closely allied with scholasticism; this applies particularly as regards the tendency towards the adoption of realist views in metaphysics and epistemology. "The scholastic doctrines regarding substance, cause, universal, truth, knowledge, error and many other things seem to be gaining ever wider acceptance." Of particular interest in this connection is the following opinion expressed by a distinguished Viennese philosopher, who, moreover, by personal conviction and scientific training, definitely rejects Catholicism generally and Jesuitism in particular. "even though, at the present day, the majority of scholastic theories appear to be entirely superseded," says Friedrich Eckstein, "on a closer examination it is seen that there are, notwithstanding, an appreciable number of scholastic elements which have not only survived until today, but have even become part of the most important basic conceptions in our present-day scientific life and thought."

Among such scholastic elements in modern science, the most important are the concepts of energy as potential and kinetic, which in the final resort, we owe to Aristotle, and the mediæval philosophers, Scotus Erigena in particular. Similarly, the principle of "organic evolution" is contained in the scholastic conception of the *forma substantialis*, the *essentia, cujus actus est esse;* proceeding from this conception of "substantial form," Descartes and Leibniz evolved their biological theories of "epigenesist" and preformation," which antitheses dominate biological discussions even today.

Hermann Cohen, also a determined opponent of scholastic methods of thought, has pointed out that the fundamental problem in the famous mediæval "controversy regarding universals," viz., whether "universals" are *ante res, in rebus* or *post res*, still plays its part in the difference of opinion over the constancy of biological species, and that, accordingly, the theories of man's descent are closely connected with these old scholastic conceptions.

Kant and Neo-Scholasticism

Many of the most modern scientific systems, such as, for example, Edmund Husserl's "phenomenology," Nicolai Hartmann's "ontology," and "Bergsonism," as well as the investigations carried out by the Meinong school into the "theory of the object," have had the effect of causing many of the most modern philosophers to look around once more for settled objective bases for their system, and thus, in a certain measure, to fall into agreement with scholastic philosophy.

Richard Bie, in his remarkable work, the *Diagnosis of the Present*, rightly observes that the attraction of scholastic philosophy "for frail humanity, stumbling along in doubt and uncertainty through a dreary morass of multifarious knowledge," lies in "the scheme as such, the fixity of a dogmatic tradition, the association, on a higher plane, of reason with the blessing of faith."

The neo-scholastic efforts of the Jesuits appear to touch closely upon the "totality" theory of the latest psychologists; in fact, professor Felix Krueger, Director of the Leipzig institute of Psychology, recently declared that psychology has revealed a number of conceptions and qualities which are "of an entirely different nature" from those with which we are acquainted through the natural sciences. "Man's apperception of objects and his sense of form are not susceptible of any definition of a mechanic-atomistic nature. We meet here with a conception, the fundamental importance of which becomes ever clearer to science, the conception of the world which comprises within itself more than the sum of the individual parts. . . Man's every action arises out of the whole of his being, out of that which, thanks to modern psychology, we now recognize clearly once again to be the primary source of all human feeling, thought and action, viz., the soul."

Nevertheless, the efforts of neo-scholasticism to blend mediæval and modern thought into a new "Catholicity" do not at the present day appear to have been at all successful. This is clearly apparent from the fact that the majority of non-Catholic philosophers and scientists are very skeptical of the prospects of any compromise between secular science and the scholastic philosophy, for, whatever the scholastic philosophy may have in its favor, that which above all else renders it unacceptable to modern scientific thought is its rigid adherence to the doctrines of Aristotle. The twentieth century, which has passed through the school of Kantian criticism, more than any other age emphatically rejects the attempt of Aristotle and his scholastic successors to establish the absolute by reason.

Philosophers of the Marburg school, especially, who have advanced along Kantian lines, have pointed out the incompatibility of modern ideas with the Aristotelean-scholastic philosophy. Hermann Cohen, for instance, describes the "levelling of the idea to a notion" as the "fundamental defect" of the Aristotelean philosophy and of all philosophies based thereon, for the reason that they are, one and all, incapable of apprehending the idea solely as "hypothesis or pure foundation of thought," and not as a real datum.

"In the pursuit of empirical knowledge," also writes Paul Natorp, "it is not possible, nor is it permissible, to conceive of the attainment of complete finality. . . Only the infinitely remote goal towards which our knowledge aspires to approach asymptotically can be indicated. . . the hope of ever arriving at a scientific knowledge of absolute facts disappears, as well as the need for these. For reality is never given, only the eternal problem which, in actual experience, is susceptible of only relative solutions."

The Power and Secret of the Jesuits

Whereas, then the Aristotelean system to a considerable extent is regarded by modern thinking as false and out-of-date, Jesuitism, in its neo-scholastic activities, still clings with the same tenacity as it did in the sixteenth and seventeenth centuries to Aristotle and the scholastic conviction that man is not only inspired by God with the desire, but is also given the power, to apprehend by reason the metaphysical truths and even to penetrate to a knowledge of the Absolute.

The English Jesuit scholar, L. J. Walker, of Campion Hall, Oxford, even goes so far as to attempt to show "that the fundamental principles of the Aristotelean philosophy lead to the same conclusions as those at which modern science has arrived on the basis of more numerous but less coherent hypotheses," and Cardinal Franz Ehrle, one of the eminent exponents of Jesuit scientific thought of our age, simply describes the philosophy of Aristotle as "the most exalted achievement and the most complete compendium of all that has ever been achieved by aided human reason." Every system of philosophy which, "with revolutionary intentions and views, sets itself up against the wisdom of Aristotle," Ehrle declares, is "branded as false with the mark of Cain,"

The Society of Jesus is not indeed, entirely unyielding in its attitude to these questions, but has shown once more that accommodating spirit which has helped it to such success in the past. Just as formerly one Jesuit father, in the guise of a Brahmin, strictly avoided all intercourse with members of lower castes, whilst another, representing himself as a Yogi, was engaged in converting the pariahs; just as one court chaplain, after the manner of Savonarola, publicly denounced the vices of the sovereign, whilst another was indulgent and discreet; just as one Jesuit astronomer violently denounced the Copernican system, whilst another was prepared to admit it as an hypothesis; so, at the present time, side by side with that school of Jesuit philosophy which adheres rigidly to the Aristotelean-Thomist principles, there exists also another school which endeavors to secure recognition, within certain limits, for the Kantian criticism.

Quite recently, Father Erich Przywara has propounded his "polarity philosophy" which departs in a number of material points from the Aristotelean-Thomist philosophy. In this system, he attempts, by basing himself on certain elements of pre-Thomist, Augustinian thought, to reconcile Catholicism with the theories of Descartes, Leibniz and Kant.

Father Bernhard Jansen approaches still more closely to Kantism in the respect that he sharply criticizes the Aristotelean-Thomist "philosophy of existence," and seeks to substitute for it a "philosophy of consciousness" which is unmistakably influenced by Kant. "Jansen's efforts," observed Ernst Karl Winter very appositely in his *Social Metaphysics of Scholasticism*, "are directed towards paving the way for a synthesis of the scholastic theory of existence and the critical theory of consciousness, after the manner of St. Thomas Aquinas, who had similarly made an harmonious synthesis of the Augustinian and Aristotelean philosophies."

This latest phase of the Jesuit effort to establish the "Catholicization of thought" is, perhaps, only in its early stages, and the reconciliation of the two extremes of thought represented by Thomas Aquinas and Kant will no doubt prove to be one of the most difficult tasks the Jesuits have ever undertaken.

Jesuitism and Psychoanalysis

How greatly common sense demands the abandonment of the Aristotelean dogmatic faith in reason is evident from the fact that not only Kantian philosophy and the neo-Kantian Marburg school, but practically all branches of modern thought are unanimous in their view of the limitations of intellectual knowledge. Even those schools of thought which in all other respects are far removed from the Kantian philosophy have espoused its "agnosticism," which denies any possibility of attaining to transcendental truth by means of the reason.

Science in recent times has gone still farther along this road; it is now problematical whether there is such a thing as "ethics," whether we are justified in speaking of "values," and how far any such "evaluation" can be said to have significance. Since, therefore, everything has become uncertain, relative and hypothetical, science and thought are becoming more and more disinclined to accept the conception of an absolute and real truth apprehensible and comprehensible by the reason.

In the same way, Max Scheler's system of "value ethics" combats the overestimation of knowledge based on reason which is the feature common to all Aristotelean thought; Scheler's system is based on the acceptance of an alogical side of the mind, which appreciates values through the senses independently of rational logic. The feelings, preferences, love and hate have nothing at all to do with the inductive experience, and are themselves an approach to reality that no deductive logic can supersede.

Thus, then, the sharp demarcation between the region of the mentally apprehensible and all those spheres which must remain definitely closed to human reason has become the most pronounced characteristic of our age. This modern "irrationalism" has received its strongest scientific support from the science of psychoanalysis, for what the various philosophic systems deduced from speculative considerations has now been confirmed with empirical proofs by this new science.

Thomas Mann, in his recent beautiful and profound study of the position of Freud in the history of modern thought, has shown for the first time how greatly psychoanalysis has contributed towards and justified the modern movement towards the limitation of the materialistic faith in reason. Thomas Man refers to this study to a "general anti-rational scientific movement of today," and shows how psychoanalysis with its "stressing of the daimonic in nature," with its "passion for research" into the mighty realms of the soul, is "as anti-rational as any of the manifestations of the new spirit," which "are successfully combating the mechanic-materialistic elements of the nineteenth century."

Nevertheless, he declares, psychoanalysis has nothing in common with that reactionary movement whose object is to "deride the mind as the most barren of all illusion"; rather is it revolutionary in the true sense of the term, for it must be admitted "that revolutionary movements need not necessarily take the form of the cult of reason and intellectual enlightenment; that enlightenment, in the narrower, historical sense of the word, may represent only one among many of the technical means adopted by the mind for giving to life a new vigor and development, and that even with directly opposite means the greater general enlightenment can be advanced and furthered in the ebb and flow of the tides of mood and thought."

The subject matter of psychoanalysis gives, however, much more than a bare indication of the power of the unknown, the narrow limits of that "little reason" Nietzsche spoke of; the examples adduced by Sigmund Freud from the psychopathology of everyday life and his psychological reflections thereon refute, furthermore, the Aristotelean theory that the will is guided entirely by the conscious reason, the assumption that forms the basis of the whole Jesuit moral theology. With convincing arguments, Freud has shown that human actions are by no means determined solely by conscious intentions freely reached, by are determined to a much greater degree by unconscious desires and strivings; this, however, decisively refutes the whole "system of absolution" which the Jesuits had evolved out of the assumption of the "irresponsibility for involuntary actions."

It would almost seem as if certain passages contained in Sigmund Freud's *Psychopathology of Everyday Life* were put in to contradict the cases of "blameless offences" quoted by the Jesuit moral casuists. While Gury, in the case he quotes of "the servant, Didacus," who let fall a valuable object belonging to his master, exonerates the servant from all sin on the grounds of "absence of intention," Freud holds the view that, "when servants destroy fragile objects by letting them fall," there is always "an obscure contributory motive" to be looked for, "a stupid hostility to works of art," which is a characteristic feature of the servant classes, "particularly in cases where the objects, whose value they cannot appreciate, represent a source of labor to them." Similarly, Freud proceeds, cases of apparently quite involuntary remissness, which gravely imperil the life and health of others, may be explained by an unconscious hostile intention.

Psychoanalysis will not accept even the argument of "forgetfulness," which is so freely exploited by the Jesuits as a ground for exoneration from sin: "the analysis of cases of forgetfulness," declared Freud in his *Psychopathology of Everyday Life*, "shows that the primary motive of the forgetting is always a disinclination to remember something that may give rise to painful feelings." No one, he declares, forgets to do things which seem important to himself, and so cases of forgetfulness, in the last resort, are always to be attributed "to a depreciation of the thing to be remembered" or even to "unconscious opposition." With the assumption of the co-operation of unknown, subconscious desires and aspirations, however, the responsibility of man for his actions is infinitely widened, as result which is diametrically opposed to the fundamental intention of Jesuit moral theology.

In addition to these deductions of a moral order, psychoanalysis presents other points of conflict, of a far more general kind, with the doctrines of the Catholic Church, and this to an extent which scarcely any other scientific system has done since Kant's *Critique*. For Freud and his disciples have utilized the considerable mass of material concerning primitive religious ideas that has been accumulated in the study of folk-psychology, and, by comparisons with the delusions of neurotics, they have traced the origins of the belief in God back to psychopathic conditions.

Whereas the Church in its struggle with atheism had always hitherto been able to fall back on the argument that the uncivilized peoples everywhere and at all times had an innate sense of the existence of a deity, which the Church held could proceed from no other source than God himself, psychoanalysis would have it that these religious ideas have their origin in neurotic feelings of penitence for the first parricide committed by the "primeval horde," and in the efforts of humanity to prevent a repetition of this primeval crime by religious rites and ceremonies.

The Jesuits, of course, could not but reject this doctrine in the most emphatic manner, and, accordingly, those Jesuit fathers who are serving in the "psychoanalytical outposts" are fighting this phase of the Freudian system with the utmost persistence. But the Jesuits, in the course of centuries of struggle in the field of the mind, have learnt how little is achieved by a mere rejection of condemnation of new ideas, and so, just as Fathers Przywara and Jansen endeavored to make peace with Kant, so now Fathers Pichlmayer and Willwoll are endeavoring to bring about a rapprochement with the Freudian theory.

The Catholic teaching of the future, in the view of truly modern Jesuits, must prove its invincibility by its very capacity to assimilate, without any danger to its essentials, even those systems of philosophy which appear to be in contradiction to it.

Accordingly the Jesuit fathers have sought out those elements in psychoanalysis which can be reconciled with Catholic views, and, as a result, it was found that the methods of Freud, if applied in moderation, might offer valuable aid in the Catholic cure of souls.

"It is beyond all doubt," writes one of these Jesuit psychoanalytical experts, "that if an extensive knowledge of the soul and of the laws governing it is recognized as a necessary preliminary to the exercise of spiritual ministrations, then a knowledge of psychoanalytical discoveries must be considered indispensable... The knowledge of the interrelationship between spiritual difficulties and unconscious impulses will enable the father-confessor very much more readily to comprehend all the various elements in the nature and personality of his client and make him very much more cautious in the methods by which he endeavors to influence him. He will be able to recognize in what cases moral exhortation and religious solace alone are insufficient, and also, on the other hand, in what cases a thorough course of psychotherapeutic treatment alone can effect those changes which are a necessary preliminary to the application of the former."

It is true that the Jesuit fathers at the same time emphasize the fact that the priest in one particular respect has a great advantage over the mental physician: "the priest can always say certain words," writes Pichlmayer, "that no expert in psychotherapeutics can ever utter, words that will always exercise an enormously relieving effect; *Ego te absolve!* I absolve thee from thy sins!" The Jesuits have, however, identified themselves much more closely with Carl Jung's efforts to develop the methods of psychoanalytical observation than with Freud's system of psychoanalysis; for, whilst Freud regards all manifestations of religion as being in the last resort "illusions" and the products of neurotic minds, Jung has satisfied himself, as the result of his investigations among the primitive tribes of Central Africa and New Mexico, that in these peoples religious ideas are innate which could not be traced back to psycho-pathological complexes.

Jung's theories are consistent also with Catholic scholasticism in the respect that the Swiss scholar regards synthesis and intuition as essential: "In the nineteenth century, the age of technical development and the exact sciences," he writes, "we left far behind us the intuition of earlier ages. The development of purely intellectualistic, analytical, atomistic and mechanistic thought has, in my view, led us into a blind alley, since, for the purposes of analysis, both synthesis and intuition are essential."

Jung even declares, on another occasion, that, although himself a Protestant, he is satisfied that no other religious faith, from the point of view of its redemptive value, is so congenial to psychoanalysis as is Catholicism. "The symbols of the Catholic liturgy offer the unconscious such ample facilities for self-expression that they act as incomparable dietetics for the soul."

In Alfred Adler's *Individual Psychology* the Jesuits were similarly able to discover many points of contact with Catholicism, particularly in the "demand for the adjustment of the individual in life and in the community in accordance with some absolute truth." Alfred Adler does, indeed, recognize the "welling-up of impulses from below," but, as the fathers emphatically insist, he admits that they may be controlled by "that which essentially determines the moulding of the psychic personality, the guiding thread of the psychic life of the individual."

Thus, although the Jesuits deplore the existence of "one-sided exaggerations and mechanical applications," and find too many "biogenetic principles" in the literature of individual psychology, they, nevertheless, welcome it as "a fruitful attempt, originating in a fine spirit of investigation, not to dissect the structure of the personality scientifically, but to comprehend it as a unity by significant understanding."

The Conflict Over Modern Political Ideals

The emancipation of thought from every association with religious faith, the way for which had been prepared by the natural sciences and systematized by philosophy, necessarily brought it about, in the course of time, that humanity began to draw conclusions affecting its practical life from the new conception of the universe, and to frame its social and political institutions accordingly. In this process, the ideas of the Enlightenment were the first to be turned into new political forms; the great intellectual revolution from rationalism to criticism and to the modern theories of relativity found its expression in politics only quite recently. As is so often the case, political ideas here, too, are seen to lag far behind philosophy.

The French Revolution represented the first attempt to use the religion of reason of the Enlightenment and Rosseau's doctrine of natural right as the foundation of a new order of society. But, after this experiment had failed, the efforts to remodel social conditions according to the new view of life were still continued; it was to this task that liberalism, which during the period of the French Restoration, had espoused the cause of liberty and equality as the ideological heritage of the Revolution, now applied itself. Liberalism did, in fact, succeed, as early as the year 1830, in overthrowing the Bourbons, those stanch upholders of the "theory of divine right," and in putting in their place a "bourgeois king," who occupied the throne by the will of the people. This liberalism, which in France had at first sought to represent only the political interests of the *tiers état*, afterwards found in the works of John Stuart Mill and Herbert Spencer its true ethical program, by which it was first enabled to reach its important position in the intellectual and political life of the nineteenth century.

Out of the "rights of man," ;proclaimed during the French Revolution, was now

The Conflict Over Modern Political Ideals

evolved the claim for the greatest possible degree of individual independence, as formulated by John Stuart Mill in his essay *On Liberty*: "Secondly, the principle requires liberty of tastes and pursuits; of framing the plan of our life to suit our own character; of doing as we like, subject to such consequences as may follow; without impediment from our fellow-creatures, so long as what we do does not harm them, even though they should think our conduct foolish, perverse or wrong. . . Mankind are greater gainers by suffering each other to live as seems good to themselves, than by compelling each to live as seems good to the rest. . .

"The only part of the conduct of anyone, for which he is amenable to society, is that which concerns others. In the part which merely concerns himself, his independence is, of right, absolute. Over himself, over his own body and mind, the individual is sovereign."

If the principle of general tolerance contained in these sentences was in conflict with the views of the Church, a still greater conflict arose out of the moral theories of liberalism. For, according to liberal moral philosophy, nothing more was required of many than that he should encroach as little as possible on the rights and interests of his fellows, and thus promote the general welfare of the community; all actions, according to Mill, are just only to the extent that they are directed towards the promotion of the common weal, and unjust in so far as they are directed towards the opposite end; in this connection Mill's conception of the common weal did not extend beyond earthly well-being and the avoidance of suffering. The "divine laws" which the church laid down as the basis of all morality and the prospect of salvation in the world to come were left entirely out of consideration.

The ethics of liberalism received their clearest expression from Herbert Spencer, who declared that all actions, to be morally good, must be directed towards the expansion of life and the raising of its standards; since, however, life is desirable only in so far as pleasure is derived from it, the expansion of life is synonymous with the increasing of the pleasures of life. The consciousness of a moral duty innate in man, according to Spencer, who was clearly influenced by the materialistic theory of man's descent, can be explained solely by the knowledge, both inherited and acquired from personal experience, that certain actions afford pleasure and are therefore desirable, while others, on the other hand, are unpleasant, and are therefore to be avoided.

It was not until the second half of the nineteenth century that this partly hedonistic moral philosophy of liberalism first came under the influence of Kant's ethical philosophy, and efforts were made to substitute the principle of duty, as defined by Kant, for the simple striving after happiness. Even so, liberalism had approached no nearer to the Catholic philosophy, which was as hostile to the "categorical imperative" as to utilitarian rational morality.

Further, liberal thought evolved principles governing the relationship of the individual to the community, which could not be otherwise than equally unacceptable to the Catholics. Based as it was on the rights of the individual, liberal philosophy denied the right of either the State or the Church to interfere with personal liberty; the State should confine itself to the regulation of the mutual relations of men from the point of view of the promotion of their material welfare, and to the Church a position was granted no different from that accorded to any other private organization of citizens holding common views. The opinions and beliefs of the individual were no concern of the State, and for this reason the education of the young should be free from all religious influences. According to the liberal program, religious instruction in the schools was to be replaced by a "lay catechism," and even marriage was to be a purely civil matter.

The insistence on the individual as opposed to the State was in direct contradiction to the scholastic conception, based on the Aristotelean-Thomist theory of the whole, upheld by the Jesuits, under which the State was regarded not merely as a convenience but as a "substantial living entity," in relation to which all human organizations of lesser scope were merely *societates imperfectae*. Just as Aristotle and Thomas Aquinas had held everything of an individual nature to constitute an element of disunion which must be overcome, and just as the well-being of any part of the human body is of secondary importance to the well-being of the whole, so the interests of the individual are of less importance than the interests of the community, of the State.

It naturally followed that the mediæval philosophers had always thought of the State as in close connection with the Church, and, therefore, it was impossible for Catholicism to accept the insistent demand of liberal philosophers and politicians for the "separation of Church and State." Such a separation must, in fact, inevitably lead to an "indifference of the State towards religion," most reprehensible from the Church's point of view.

The Jesuits accordingly attacked liberalism with the utmost violence throughout the nineteenth century, and attempts on the part of liberal governments to withdraw the schools from ecclesiastical control were the source of repeated conflicts between the two sides.

With equal exasperation, the "pope's light cavalry" turned its attack on the Freemasons; it seemed to them that this movement was almost identical with liberalism, for, although the Freemasons had not adopted the economic program of liberalism their ethical principles and aims for a long time coincided with those of the liberal movement; both movements were striving to secure "toleration," the "independence of the individual" and a deistic religion of humanity.

In the early decades of the nineteenth century, almost every leading personality of the liberal movement in the Latin countries had also been a member of the fraternity of Freemasons, and the July Revolution of 1830, and represented a triumph for both the liberals and the Freemasons.

Thus, it is no matter for wonder that Pope Pius VII, who was friendly towards the Jesuits, issued a bull directed against the Freemasons in the same year that he reinstated the Jesuits; this bull spoke of the "homicidal development" and the "diabolical assemblies" of the fraternity, whose influence is spreading like a "devastating fire." Equally vigorous terms were also used by Pius IX, who, during his pontificate of thirty-two years, issued no fewer than eight condemnations of the Freemasons, and, among other things, described the fraternity as the "synagogue of Satan"; the "Allocution" of 1865 on Freemasonry is said to have been drafted by the Jesuit general, Father Beckx.

As usual, the Jesuits took care that, on this occasion too, the official declaration of the views of the Curia should be accompanied by appropriate propaganda; and a considerable number of Jesuit authors appeared, who made it their special task to attack the Freemasons with all the resources of controversy. Most prominent among them for violence was Father S.H. Pachtler; in his works entitled *The Secret War Against Throne* and *Altar and The Idol of Hu-*

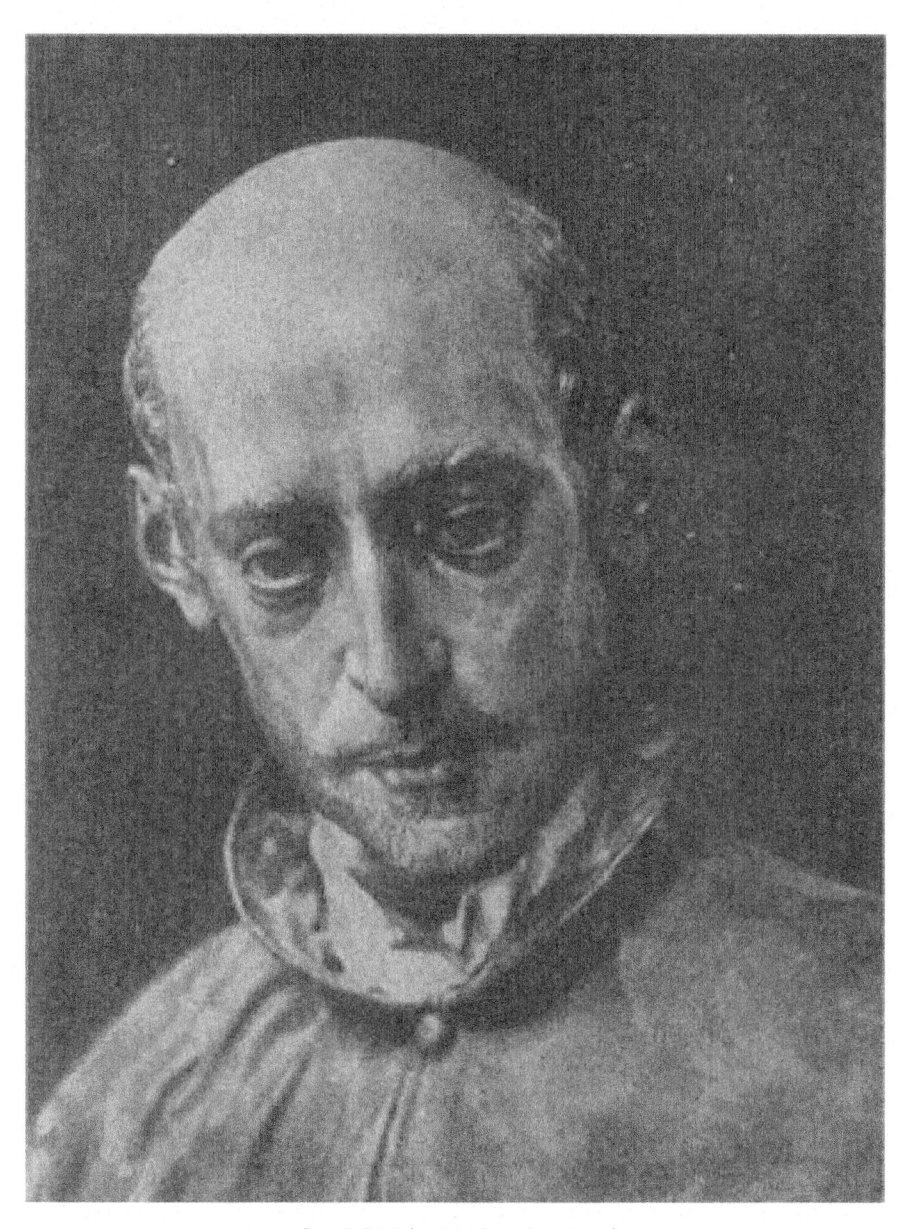

138. IGNATIUS LOYOLA

Bust by Montañes, Seville

130. FRANSCISCO BORGIA

Bust by Montañes, Seville

manity, he endeavored to show that the Masonic fraternity was nothing else than a "dreadful system directed towards the utter perversion of the mind and the heart." On the other hand, the Freemasons did not allow their opponents to have it all their own way, and for their part proceeded to attack, the principles, the practices and the aims of the Society of Jesus.

The Portuguese provincial, Father Ficarelli, issued in the year 1884 a circular letter to all his subordinates, in which he declared that the task confronting them was the overthrow of the "most formidable enemy of the Church," which publicly declares that "nothing can prevent the fulfilment of its sinister plans." Guided by obedience and prudence, the Jesuits were exhorted "to let no single opportunity pass of fostering hatred against the Freemasons, both in their utterances and writings and in their teachings, their preaching and in their spiritual exercises." The Portuguese lodges, however, replied by establishing immediately a special organ, bearing the name *A Luz*, by which to carry on a campaign against the Jesuits.

The fact that the Masonic movement had, during the course of the nineteenth century, identified itself more and more with the ethics of Kant only seemed to remove it still farther from the Catholic Church. "Kant's theory of the autonomy of the moral law," writes Otto Heinichen, a member of the fraternity, "can be described as the basis of all the fundamental principles of Freemasonry. It is to this secret that it owes its success and its enemies."

Pope Leo XIII, the creator of the Neo-Thomist philosophy, supporting his argument on Jesuit anti-Masonic literature, issued in 1884, the encyclical, *Humanum genus*, which, in the style of the *Spiritual Exercises* of Ignatius, began with a dissertation on the "two camps"; in the one was "the true Church of Jesus Christ" and in the other Freemasonry. "It is working openly and freely for the ruin of Holy Church," asserted the pope, "and with the object of depriving Christian peoples of all those blessings which the Redeemer brought them. . . Reason and truth prove to us that this society is inconsistent with righteousness and natural morality. . . ."

It must, therefore, seem all the more surprising at first that in recent times a rapprochement has taken place between the Jesuits and the Freemasons. After a certain disposition towards a reconciliation had been evident for some considerable time on both sides, definite negotiations for an understanding were set on foot in June 1928 between the Freemasons and the Jesuits. At a conference in Aix-la-Chapelle participated, on the one side, Father Hermann Gurber, the most prominent Jesuit authority on Freemasonry and, on the other side, the general secretary of the New York grand lodge, Ossian Lang, the Viennese Freemason philosopher, Dr. Kurt Reichl, and the writer Eugen Lennhoff, the author of a very informative work on the Masonic movement.

As was only to be expected, this discussion revealed fundamental differences of opinion. In particular, Father Gruber referred to the fact that the Church could never adopt the principle of "confessional neutrality and absence of dogma" upheld by Freemasonry and liberalism, and that, furthermore, the "naturalistic ideal of humanity" of the Freemasons was opposed to the principles of Catholicism. Nevertheless, agreement was reached to the extent that both sides showed their readiness to restrict considerably their indulgence in controversy, and, in particular, to refrain from all exaggerated and venomous attacks the one on the other.

As the result, Father Gruber, once the most fervid opponent of the fraternity, in his latest publication directed against the movement no longer charges it with "godlessness," but merely with "Deism," a charge which the Freemasons themselves openly admit.

A clear indication of this complete change of attitude on the part of the Jesuits is afforded by a letter which Father Gruber, as early as the beginning of the year 1927, addressed to the Freemason, Dr. Kurt Reichl, in which he says: "I entirely agree with you in the view that differences between Catholicism and Freemasonry, in which the questions at issue affect the highest interests not only of every individual person, but also of all nations and peoples and of humanity in general, should be discussed with suitable earnestness, in the spirit of true Christian or if you prefer it, humanitarian charity.... with no other object in view than that objective truth may prevail in the interests of all....

"Furthermore, from the truly Catholic standpoint, I regard it as a matter of primary importance, that, under existing conditions, the childish and false ideas regarding Freemasonry which still prevail in wide circles should be combated by discreet, unobtrusive, and therefore all the more effective means...."

In pursuing this line of conduct, Father Gruber stands by no means alone; he is, in fact, actively supported by a number of his fellow-Jesuits, and, in particular, by Father Mace, Father Bonsirven and Father Rosa; the two great Jesuit publications, *civiltà Cattolica* published in Rome and *Études* published in Paris, are working quietly but persistently towards the same end.

Naturally, there are on both sides opponents of such an understanding; the Freemasons of old Prussia, with their rigid protestant views, will have nothing to do with any movement towards a rapprochement with the roman Church, while, in the Catholic camp, the Paris journal, *Revue international*, conducted by Jouin, continues to attack the Freemasons and the Jews from a chauvinistic, nationalist point of view, and goes so far as to accuse the Jesuits of treachery. Father Gruber has, to be sure, replied to such attacks in a dignified manner, declaring that it is the apostolic duty of the Society of Jesus to meet any advances towards a reconciliation with Christian charity and sincere good-will.

This surprising change in the attitude of the Jesuits as well as of a considerable section of Freemasonry is attributable in no small degree to a wise appreciation of the changed circumstances of the present day. It is only necessary to consider to what a negligible extent liberalism and Freemasonry can be regarded as a danger to the Church, as compared with the infinitely greater threat to every religion represented by radical Socialism. The Freemasons, for their part, see in the spread of Marxist views a greater danger to the movement than that arising from Catholicism, for, according as the Socialist elements have adopted more and more advanced views, so have they become more and more hostile to Freemasonry as a "theistic religion of the bourgeoisie." In Hungary and Italy, members of the social-Democratic party had already been forbidden to join the masonic movement; in Austria it is regarded with very considerable disapproval, and in Soviet Russia the movement is entirely banned under severe penalties.

As the spiritual champion of the bourgeoisie, the Masonic movement is, notwithstanding a fundamental divergence of principle, less at variance with Jesuitism than are those radical doctrines which are directed equally against bourgeois ideology and against religion. Accordingly, to both parties it appeared to be only consistent with political prudence to arrive at an agreement with the enemy of yesterday, and to concentrate their energies on a united struggle against the enemy of today.

For while liberalism, like Freemasonry, had confined itself to the principle that the religious convictions of the individual were purely a personal matter and not a matter for criticism, Marxist doctrines are emphatically hostile to every religious faith. According to the materialistic conception of history propounded by Marx and Engels, the economic structure of society is the underlying factor which determines not only every historical occurrence, but also all cultural and religious development. According to this theory, religion is nothing more than an "ideological superstructure," resting on given material and economic conditions, so that "conceptions of "God," "revelations," religious laws governing morality and religious ceremonies are merely symptoms indicative of a certain economic state. Consequently, there are no such things as immutable religious and moral laws but, rather, man, with his "soul," his "moral consciousness" and his conceptions of God, is nothing more than a product determined by his economic environment.

Even though there is at the present time a tendency for Socialism to abandon the purely materialistic philosophy propounded by Marx, in favor of a more Kantian way of thinking, Socialism, nevertheless, still remains in profound opposition to Catholicism in its practical philosophy, not least of all by reason of its aspiration towards a communistic economic system.

The apparent similarity between the socialist programme and numerous sentences in the Gospel at first caused even many "good Catholics" to adopt Socialism, and to regard it as something in the nature of a revival of early Christianity in all its simplicity and purity; many socialist agitators, indeed, had not omitted to brand the principle, accepted and applied by mediæval Catholicism, of private ownership and also of social inequality as "false to the teaching of Christ," and this form of Socialist propaganda could not, therefore, fail to meet with the keenest opposition from the Jesuits.

Once again, they were able to fall back on Thomas Aquinas, who, in his efforts to blend into a harmonious whole all the conflicting elements in the Christian world, had endeavored to reconcile the prevailing economic conditions of his age with the communistic principles of early Christianity. While, before him, the fathers of the Church had upheld the view that poverty alone was consistent with the Christian ideal, and that striving after possession arose from man's imperfection as the result of his fall from grace, Thomas endeavored, with all the arts of scholastic dialectics, to bridge over the contradiction between the evangelical ideal of poverty and the desire for possessions everywhere evident in practical life.

Consistently with Aristotle's teachings, he held that the good Christian may justifiably devote himself to a *liberalitas* which is in the nature of a golden mean between the sinful extremes of avarice and prodigality. The moral worth of man is determined not by poverty or wealth, buy by the wise use to which he puts his worldly goods; for material success of failure is dependent on divine Providence, and man can manifest his true Christian nature only be the manner in which he accepts this Providence and administers his worldly goods for beneficent and charitable purposes.

Even today, the Jesuits endeavor to maintain the Thomist *sociologia perennis*, and, with its aid, to combat Socialism. "Like everything else," writes Victor Cathrein, "property may be, and frequently is, misused. Nevertheless, from the point of view of the purpose of the Creator, it is of considerable moral significance. . . The inequality in the distribution of worldly goods is of exceptional importance as the means by which God is able to try us, and by which we can exercise virtue and thereby attain to everlasting life. By this unequal distribution, both rich and poor are thrown upon each other for mutual assistance in carrying out the divine purpose. . . Man's relationship to God is that of a feofee or steward who is accountable to his master, and who, together with the privileges of his office, has incurred obligations. . . The right of the state to restrict the possession of worldly goods should be conceded only in cases where it can be shown that unrestricted acquisition by the individual would be contrary to the interests of the community as a whole. This has never been demonstrated to be the case, nor can it ever be demonstrated."

Such remarks show clearly enough that Jesuitism is still emphatically opposed to any such radical attacks on the law of private ownership as are contemplated under Socialism; at the same time, however, this attitude should not be interpreted as implying an unconditional approval of the capitalist system. "In so far as Socialism represents a criticism," Cathrein expressly says on one occasion, "it contains much that is true. It has often laid its finger on the open wound and called a spade a spade, while others maintain silence."

It was a principle of Thomist sociology, too, that the carrying on of business for profit and the acquisition of wealth could be justified only in so far as the profits earned were applied to some "necessary or honorable" end, such as, for example, the maintenance of one's family, the support of the needy or the benefit of one's fellow-citizens generally. Furthermore, Thomas, like all other scholastic teachers, held that the making of profit could be justified only when it was the fruit of actual work performed, and, accordingly, the taking of interest for loans was expressly prohibited, in so far as it did not represent compensation for a *lucrum cessans*.

That, in spite of these reservations with which Thomas accepts the principle of private ownership, the prospects of reconciling Catholicism and socialism are remote is clearly shown by Dr. Robert Drill. "Reference is frequently made," he says in an article entitled *Catholicism and Socialism*, "to the adaptability of Catholicism, and undoubtedly Catholicism does possess that quality, but only within certain limits. Catholic ideas about private ownership are not unchangeable and it is not only possible, but probable, that they may be modified in such a way as to embody new ideas on social obligations. But Catholicism will never abandon the principle of private ownership, even the private ownership of the means of production. It cannot do so without falling into an insoluble contradiction with its principles of natural right. Consequently, there exists an antagonism to Marxism which cannot be removed. . . .

"No less important is the antithesis between the principle of the class struggle and the Christian principle of love for one's neighbor, and furthermore the antagonism arising out of the fact that, in the Marxist philosophy, emphasis is laid on the material element, whilst, in Catholicism and Christianity in general, the spiritual element is stressed. It is scarcely to be anticipated that any change in the very foundations of Catholicism will take place. It is always as well to look at things as they are and to cherish no illusions. . ."

Nevertheless as in philosophy, so also in sociology, certain of the most modern Jesuit thinkers have already initiated attempts to compromise with Socialism. Here particular mention should be made of the Jesuit economist, Heinrich Pesch, who, with his system of "solidarism," is endeavoring to establish a synthesis between Capitalism and socialism. Pesch does not hesitate to acknowledge that important human rights of the proletariat are threatened by the capitalist system, and, accordingly, he endeavors to strike a "healthy balance" between the "individualist principle" of capitalistic liberalism and the "social principle" of Marxism. To be sure, Ernst Karl Winter once rightly remarked, Father Pesch's labors represent not so much a sociological study for its own sake, as a fresh attempt to reduce social science to the position of "handmaiden" in the service of religion.

The same may also be said of the attempt to devise a "Catholic religious sociology" on scholastic bases made by Father Gustav Gundlach. While Gundlach sets up the ideal of a "harmonic totality of life," he is at pains to show that such an ideal is possible only within a theocentric world philosophy, and that none more than the Jesuits, with their principle of the "application of all efforts to the utmost advantage" and their "positive valuation of the world," are fitted to establish a truly harmonious sociological system in this age of the "quickened rhythm of life, the most striking manifestation of which is afforded by modern capitalism."

Dostoievsky's Grand Inquisitor

All new ideas which were at variance with Catholic doctrine found in literature a powerful and effective instrument with which to anchor themselves deep in the consciousness of modern humanity. It was the direct, convincing and stirring influence of plays, poems and novels that gave them their real and permanent power over the thought of the age.

The writers of the nineteenth and twentieth centuries, it is true, often enough took their material from the realm of Catholic emotions and ideas and the literary history of all European countries shows "Catholic tendencies" among novelists, dramatists and poets. Nevertheless, although recent times have produced Catholic poets as great as Paul Claudel, as tender and delicate as Francis Jammes, as witty as G.K. Chesterton, yet Francis Thompson was right when he observed that the Church, "once the mother of artists no less than of saints, of Dante no less than of St. Dominic," now preserves for herself merely "the fame of saintliness" and leaves art to the gentiles."

Even the great imaginative writers of the eighteenth century, who largely grew up in the Jesuit schools, for the most part cut adrift from the Church, and in their writings voiced the philosophical and political views of the Enlightenment. The nineteenth century carried this development farther still, and its literature reflected all the problems, passions, conflicts and convictions of humanity, in sole obedience to the law of artistic truth, untroubled by any considerations of "piety." The whole complexity of the human soul, and at the same time, also, the complexity of philosophical and political conceptions, from materialism to psychoanalysis, form the ideas of liberty that grew out of the French Revolution to the communist visions of Bolshevism, found powerful embodiment in the literature of the world during the last hundred years.

So long as it was a question of warring against dangerous scientific discoveries, the Jesuits, as the most zealous defenders of Catholicism, were always able to oppose the inconvenient results of scientific investigation with other results, objectionable philosophical systems with other systems, and either to convict their enemies of drawing "false conclusion," or to twist their views into confirmation of Jesuit dogmas. Moreover, when the need arose for checking hostile political tendencies, the Jesuits were always able to call upon the full resources of controversy. To maintain the strongholds of the Church in these scientific or philosophical polemics required only scholarly diligence, self-sacrificing study and penetrating intelligence, and in these qualities the fathers of the Society of Jesus had never been deficient.

The art of the imaginative writer, however, was not to be "acquired" by even the greatest zeal. What gives art its power over men has always been just its mysterious uniqueness, which defies imitation. The ideas of the powers could not be refuted either by skillful polemic or by convincing dialectic; here proved ineffectual all the powers of controversy and all the weapons of the church, excommunication being as futile as placing on the Index.

What availed it for Jesuit critics to try to depreciate the importance of literature by pointing out that "poetry can never take the place of religion," that "the most beautiful visions of the poets" can only give a "faint idea of heavenly bliss," and that not the masterpieces of art, but only the Church's means of grace can save humanity?

Could Goethe really be measured "by the standards of Christianity," as was attempted by Father Alexander Baumgartner, a man otherwise extremely intelligent and familiar with all the literatures of the world? He also declared that Goethe's best work was derived from his knowledge of Catholic poetry; but this could not undo Goethe's own confession that he was a "decided non-Christian." Again, Goethe's "pernicious and anti-Christian philosophy," of which Father Alois Stockmann speaks, does not influence the thought of the German people any the less because Stockmann declares that "for us Goethe is not an artist of the highest wisdom and the true art of life." There is something of impotent resignation in the remark of Father Stockmann, when he writes that Christ built his church "not on writers and artists of genius," but "on Peter, the uneducated fisherman of Galilee."

It will greatly surprise the worldly reader to learn that Jesuit literary criticism frequently bases its estimate of great imaginative writers not so much on their creative power as on their religious faith and on the "Catholic" or "pagan," "moral," or "immoral" character of their works. Thus Father Baumgartner tries to explain Shakespeare's genius as due to his having been the son of a Catholic; in the case of Schiller, he lays stress on the fact that "after his purification," he devoted himself exclusively to Catholic subjects; Milton and Klopstock are praised because they approached the Church in an orthodox Christian spirit and a theological frame of mind; Lessing receives a word of commendation for his remark that he would rather be subject to the pope than to the little Lutheran popelets; Herder's non-Catholic outlook is explained on the ground that "as superintendent" of a Protestant church he could not do justice to the papacy; of Wieland it is maintained that "he could not have existed without help from Catholic countries"; Molière, Corneille and Voltaire were at least educated in Catholic schools; Byron, Shelley, Heine, Victor Hugo and Leopardi were "nourished on Catholic influences."

On the other hand the greatest minds are rejected in the harshest manner, if the content and spirit of their works are not in harmony with the requirements of the church, Nietzsche, declared Father Sörensen, tried to raise "the gates of hell upon earth"; Ibsen was cast out because "no ray of revealed religion illumines the night of his plays"; Zola and the Italian Verists were reproved for "breaking through the ultimate barriers of morality, decency and propriety." Not even Verlaine, the author of magnificent Catholic poems, escapes this severest judgment from Father Stockmann: "When he was deprived of absinthe in prison, the religious feelings and memories of his childhood awoke for a little space. . . But soon the wretched man relapsed into his vicious life, and in the bawdy poems he produced surpassed even his earlier pornographies." Hence it is only natural to find that "the sultry Dehmel" is one of the most zealous translators of Verlaine.

But little as this division of the poets into good and bad Christians, a labor of love to the Jesuits, availed to remove the embarrassments that literature caused to the defenders of Catholic ideas, the difficulties were most obvious in the case of the greatest imaginative writer of the nineteenth century, Feodor Mikhailovich Dostoievsky. He could not be got rid of by simply casting doubts on his feelings for religion; had he not passionately warred against atheism and the materialistic ideas of the Enlightenment, and exalted Christianity as the only road to the liberation of humanity?

In spite of this, Dostoievsky was the greatest enemy of the Society of Jesus that had arisen since Pascal. All the cherished ideas of the Jesuits, the universal domination of Rome, the power of the human reason to confirm faith, the adaptation of the strict doctrines of the Church to the limited faculties of man, and the expiation of the sins of the world by means of a moral theology devised with the skill of an Aristotle, all these things, to which the disciples of Loyola had for three hundred years devoted all their energy and the most self-sacrificing efforts, had been designated by Dostoievsky, in the "Legend of the grand Inquisitor" in the *Brothers Karamazov*, as the most terrible apostasy from the true teaching of Christ.

In the sketches for the "Grand Inquisitor," only recently discovered among his posthumous papers, Dostoievsky says of Jesuit Catholicism: "The mind which distorts Christianity by bringing it into harmony with the aims of this world destroys the whole meaning of Christianity. . . Instead of the high ideal which Christ set up, we have a second Tower of Babel, and, under the banner of love for humanity, contempt for humanity appears undisguised. . ."

Dostoievsky was, of course, quite aware that no member of the Society of Jesus ever filled the office of Grand inquisitor of Spain; nevertheless, he endowed the figure of this spiritual judge, who in Ivan Karamazov's legend has to justify himself to the returned Saviour, with the characteristic features of a Jesuit. For the novelist regarded the fathers of the Society of Jesus as the most important representatives of the Catholic spirit, the men who by their worldly wisdom, their skill in dialectic and their ethical system were the first to furnish the Catholic aspirations after power with spiritual weapons.

For this reason, however, it seemed to him also that in Jesuitism the contradiction between Catholicism secularized and adopted to the standard of feeble humanity and the strict purity of the Christian idea embodied in Jesus Himself found its most blatant expression. "The Jesuits speak and write like the Grand Inquisitor," Dostoievsky makes Ivan Karamazov say; "I have myself read it all in the writings of Jesuit theologians."

Dostoievsky's "Legend of the Grand Inquisitor" was more dangerous than all previous anti-Jesuit writings put together, for its author had at his command the visionary creative power which alone could give weight and permanence to his indictment. Concerned with something more than malicious attacks, exposures or theological refutation, Dostoievsky's aim was to throw the light of a powerful vision on the tragedy of the secularization by Jesuitical Christianity of a pure conception of salvation, and, while all other theological feuds were bound up with their own age and disappeared with it, Dostoievsky's indictment has, even in our days, lost none of its vital and compelling force.

The "Grand Inquisitor" is, moreover, distinguished from all other polemical writings by its sublime impartiality. In the complete apologetics of Catholicism, it would be difficult to find another work which describes the underlying idea of Jesuitism with such profound understanding as the arguments which Dostoievsky puts into the mouth of his Grand Inquisitor. His powerful, convincing and eloquent defense of the Catholic idea of world power is nowhere interrupted by a single word, a single objection. Christ, the other interlocutor in this unique dialogue, hears the Grand Inquisitor to the end in silence. No opposition, however learned and skilled in controversy, could have annihilated the arguments of the grand Inquisitor with such force as this majestic silence of the Saviour, which puts to flight all arguments founded on reason.

"More than fifteen hundred years have passed," says the Grand Inquisitor to Christ. "Look upon men. Whom has thou raised up to Thyself? I swear to thee, man is weaker and baser than Thou has thought him. Can he do that which thou didst? By setting so high a value on him, thou didst act as if thou hadst no sympathy with him, for thou didst ask too much of him. Respecting him less, Thou wouldst have asked less of him. That would have been nearer to love, for thou wouldst thereby have lightened his burden. . .

"Or is it only the tens of thousands of the great and strong who are dear to Thee? Are all the other millions, who are in numbers as the sands of the sea, all the weak ones, who yet love thee, merely to exist for the sake of the great and strong?

"No, to us the weak ones are also dear. . . how are they to blame if it goes beyond their strength to endure what the strong have endured? Didst Thou then come only to the elect? . . .

"But we, we will forgive them their sins, because they are weak and powerless. . . Even the most painful secrets of their conscience they will bring to us, and we shall have an answer for all. And they will joyfully believe in our answer, for it will save them from the great anxiety and terrible agony they endure at present in making a free decision for themselves and everyone will be happy. . .

"Speak! Were we not right in so acting and teaching? Did we not love mankind so humbly recognizing their feebleness, lovingly lightening their burden and permitting their weak nature every sin with our sanction?"

Unlike most of the other enemies of the Society of Jesus, Dostoievsky never doubted the Jesuits' honest and deep love for humanity, and, although he was the great enemy of Catholicism, he never attempted to dispute that the Catholic Church tries to use its power solely to make men happy. It was the way in which they are to be made happy that seemed to him wrong and opposed to the real teaching of Christ.

For the great Russian novelist did not believe that true Christianity consists in lightening the tasks of man on earth. Anyone who deprives man of his responsibility robs him of his one possibility of appearing before the face of God; to "purge him of sin" with all the aids of dialectic is, therefore, to rob him of true salvation, of his eternal destiny.

For Dostoievsky, suffering was not a painful burden, but a divine mercy, by which alone man can attain to God; the true following after Christ consists, according to him, in man' staking upon himself the guilt of the whole world, in feeling himself responsible before God and suffering for all the sins ever committed on earth. This comic sympathy is for Dostoievsky the love which Christ preached to the world, and, therefore, the work of the Catholic Church, the attempt to relieve the weak of their burden, appears to him like an un-Christian contempt for man., "In truth," says the Starets Zossima, in *The Brothers Karamazov*, "each one is guilty of all, only men do not know it; if they knew it, we should at once have paradise on earth."

Dostoievsky also regards as wrong and mistaken the Jesuit attempt to evaluate sins according to their seriousness: how can a man, even though he be a priest, sit in judgment on another, and acquit him of guilt, "so long as one child weeps on earth"? Thus the Starets Zossima also teaches that no one may judge a criminal until he feels "that he himself is more than all guilty of the deed of the man arraigned before him."

No pamphlet, and not even the most malicious satire, dealt the Jesuit doctrine so hard a blow as this great product of Dostoievsky's imagination with its freedom from polemical harshness. The literary historians of the order had thus a very difficult task, when they undertook to defend themselves against this "mortal enemy." Sensitive Jesuits very soon perceived that the usual method of giving good or bad "marks" to authors according to the piety and morality of their works would be quite out of place here.

Father Friedrich Muckermann made an exhaustive study of the problem of Dostoievsky, and showed a fine understanding of the nature of imaginative writing. He recognizes that, even in non-Catholic artists, "to the subjective honesty and purity of their intention" must be given full value, even if the content of their works arouses opposition in Catholic minds. "As an example, let us take Dostoievsky's 'Grand Inquisitor.'" Writes Muckermann, "unquestionably one of the most powerful visions in literature of the world. Quite apart from the fact that this legend, in spirit of its manifest hostility to Rome, yet expresses a tragic truth beyond all history, it also produces an effect through the inner subjective fire of the writer with his profound conviction of the rightness of his view."

Many another pronouncement from the pen of Father Muckermann makes it clear that in him Jesuit literary criticism underwent a change of attitude to modern views similar to that shown in Father Przywara's and Father Jansen's attitude to Kant, and in Pesch's and Gudlach's attitude to sociology.

The Power and Secret of the Jesuits

PART VIII

THE FOUR HUNDRED YEARS' TRIAL

Gloria Dei and Gloria Mundi

To a far greater extent than any other religious brotherhood, the Society of Jesus had endeavored ever since its foundation to come to terms with all the expressions of the human mind, with theology as well as with natural science, with philosophy, art, politics, economics, constitutional law and jurisprudence. Jesuitism has, accordingly, had to vindicate itself afresh before every new discovery of man, before every change in philosophical outlook and in social institutions, and in this trial, which has lasted for almost four centuries, many harsh accusations have been brought against it.

At the beginning, it was only a handful of Protestant preachers who alleged that the Jesuits were trying "to deceive poor Christians with craft and sophistry and to seduce them into everlasting hell-fire," or a few burgesses of Breslau who testified on oath that they had with their own eyes seen a Jesuit carried off by the Devil during his sermon in the cathedral.

Later, however, innumerable new enemies joined the company of these earliest accusers of the disciples of Loyola, and a medley of accusations arose, which echo from the sixteenth century right into our own time. "Rebels, hypocrites, flatterers, intriguers, enemies of progress, falsifiers of science, corrupters of humanity!" cried European princes and ministers, Asiatic despots, mandarins and Buddhist priests, Protestant theologians and Catholic bishops, slave-dealers and beautiful courtesans, roman inquisitors and American presidents, encyclopædists and educational reformers, astronomers, biologists, psychologists and historians, Kantians and Hegelians, Freemasons, secularists and liberals, democrats and Socialists, who unite in a chorus of indictment in defiance of the limits of time and place.

All along, from the sixteenth century to the present day, the Society of Jesus has been accused of having "betrayed" the supreme good of humanity by their "corrupt doctrine and practice." By their system of exercises, so runs the indictment, faith in the mystical union of the soul with God has been destroyed, and replaced by a mechanical drill, "an ecstasy abased and stifled by arithmetical rules." The Jesuit endeavoring to assign so great a part to the reason and the will in the perfecting of man means that the decisive importance of divine grace is denied, and the omnipotence of the Creator replaced by the alleged omnipotence of His creatures. With these reproaches brought by mystics, Protestants, Dominicans and Jansenists is associated the no less serious accusation that the Jesuit undertaking to adapt the Christian doctrine to secular affairs has led to a revolting degradation of religion. Through their attempt to bring the mysteries of the faith nearer to the limited imagination of the masses by coarse and blatant images, the true inwardness of the life of faith had perished, and an external, formal and superstitious cult of saints had gained the ascendancy.

In its foreign missions, the Society of Jesus has gone to the length of incorporating heathen ideas and ceremonies into its ritual, and thus paganizing Catholicism in a quite inadmissible fashion; they even concealed the crucifixion of Christ merely in order not to shock the heathen, and in order to secure as many apparent conversions as possible.

The Jesuits are also to blame for the fact that the artistic means for the expression of religious feeling have lost all true inwardness; they have reduced the profundity of artistic symbolism to the banality of allegory accessible by the reason, and coarsened the dignity of architectonic and graphic composition into an obtrusive emotionalism and the optical illusions of a mechanical perspective.

This "betrayal of the sublime to the common world," however, reached its zenith in the persistent Jesuitical mixing-up of spiritual aims with political activity, craft and intrigue. For, in their endeavors to gain the favor of kings at court, to deal successfully with the highest dignitaries in parliaments and conclaves of princes, and to settle great political disputes as Rome wished them settled, the fathers all too frequently confused the *Gloria Dei* with the *Gloria mundi*, and were concerned less for the true kingdom of God than for the earthly power and interest of the Church, Thus the Jesuits were responsible for the "substitution of the spirit of political machinations for the spirit of the Gospel."

Do not the letters and instructions of the founder of the order bear witness to the objectionableness of Jesuit methods? Did not Ignatius expressly exhort his subordinates never "either in spiritual talk or in other more indifferent or confidential conversations" to let themselves go entirely, but always to take account of the fact that every word uttered might reach the public? He instructed his disciples, in their intercourse with great and distinguished men, always to win their confidence by adapting themselves to the character of each person, to discover the best ways of flattering them and to keep "a merry countenance and the utmost friendliness of speech." Was not the inventor of that dubious method of correspondence which distinguished between "main letters," with a definite "edifying content," which could be "used for show," and "enclosures," which contained the real and strictly confidential instructions? And what are we to think of those maxims of life which Father Baltasar Gracian, the rector of the Jesuit college at Tarazona, collected together in his *Handbook Oracle*? Are not the most cynical principles of a corrupt worldly wisdom set down in this curious little book?

"What is likely to win favor, do yourself," Baltasar Gracian advises his disciples; "what is likely to bring disfavor, get others to do; know how to dispense contempt; intervene in the affairs of others, in order quietly to accomplish your own ends; trust in today's friends as if they might be tomorrow's enemies; use human means as if there were no divine ones, and divine means as if there were no human ones; leave others in doubt about your attitude; sweeten your 'no' by a good manner; contrive to discover everybody's thumbscrew; trust in the crutch of time rather than in the iron club of Hercules; keep in mind the happy outcome as the victor need render no account; refuse nothing flatly, so that the dependence of your petitioner may last longer; always act as if you were seen; never give anyone an opportunity to get to the bottom of us; without telling lies, do not yet tell all the truth; do not live by fixed principles, live by opportunity and circumstances...."

This is the spirit with which, according to their numerous accusers, the Jesuits have acted since the foundation of the order, and in which they have pursued their course both at courts and among the people, both in Europe and in foreign lands. But they have also educated their young people on these lines and have thus impressed the "Gospel of Loyola," the "most fatal of all time," as Carlyle called it, on each rising generation.

This profound contempt for man, this perpetual readiness to renounce all ideals and reduce the loftiest to the level of our lower nature, also forms the basis of the Jesuit ethic; here, too, the moral ideal means only "a hateful tribunal before which one bows of necessity, or from which one escapes as far as one can by logical dialectic," There is nothing, in the opinion of the Jansenist Pascal, "so lax and wrong that the Jesuits would not contrive to paint it as pious, proper and holy with the brush of their vague and licentious ethical doctrine"; and the Protestant, Adolf Harnack, has maintained that it is the actual aim of the Jesuits "to represent the basest thing as pardonable, and to show the most nefarious criminals a way by which they can still attain to the peace of the Church." Whatever the Jesuits have done whether preaching a way of salvation, setting up moral rules, evolving philosophical systems, explaining the Holy Scriptures, painting pictures, building churches, converting the heathen, engaging in politics, hearing confessions or teaching children, they have always been accused of making too great concessions to the inadequacy of man. Their opponents sadly declare that this is the secret of Jesuit superiority over their enemies, who have always been guided by faith in the noble qualities of man and by the strict principles of pure Christian doctrine.

Even one of Loyola's own disciples, Juan Alvarez of Salamanca, believed that there must be something inconsistent about attaining religious ends by worldly means. He wrote to Father Ignatius to the effect that such conduct was "bowing the knee to Baal." The answer which the founder of the order sent to the anxious priest through his secretary contains everything that Jesuitism can bring forward in justification of its methods.

"You approach the matter from such a lofty standpoint," wrote Ignatius to Father Alvarez, "that you have obviously lost all grasp of reality... If one contemplates your spiritual wisdom, it can hardly be maintained that the use of human means and the employment of earthly patronage for good purposes which are pleasing to God is the same thing as bowing the knee to Baal. On the contrary, anyone who neglects to make use of such means and also to employ this talent given by God, perhaps because he looks upon it as an 'evil leaven' and a 'mischievous confusion of earthly means with divine grace,' has obviously not learnt to direct everything towards the one great end, the glorification of God...

"But he who has set all his hopes on God, and who anxiously employs in His service all the gifts which the Lord has bestowed on him, whether of mind or person, spiritual or physical, in the conviction that the omnipotence of God attains its end by these means or without them, and that in any event human zeal in His service is pleasing to him, that man does not bow the knee to Baal, but to God, by recognizing him as the Creator not only of grace but of nature too... to sum up, it is my belief that the employment of human means at the right time, if they are applied purely to the service of God, is not evil..."

The Power and Secret of the Jesuits

In later times, the Jesuits have always replied to all Catholic attacks by pointing out that it is the task of the Church *communicare orbi terrarium*, to keep in perpetual sympathetic relations with the life and business of humanity as a whole. For this reason, worldly things must not be disregarded; they must rather be followed with interest and skilfully and zealously directed. It is necessary not to "snap the threads" which bind men to this world, but rather "to guide them wisely and to knit them up," which is no way a degradation of high and spiritual things.

But, as the Society of Jesus made it its mission to spread the kingdom of God in this world, in every age and to every civilization, it was bound to come to terms with existing conditions and to take account of them. And, if the Jesuits adapted themselves to all men, in order to win all men, might they not appeal to the words of the Apostle Paul, who taught that the man of spiritual gifts must take account of the weakness of his fellow-men and serve them in their earthly needs with compassionate love? "for though I be free from all men," he writes in the First Epistle to the Corinthians, "yet have I made myself servant unto all, that I might gain the more. And unto the Jews I became as a Jew, that I might gain the Jews; to them that are under the law, as under the law, that I might gain them that are under the law. To them that are without law, as without law... that I might gain them that are without law. To the weak became I as weak, that I might gain the weak: I am made all things to all men, that I might by all means save some. And this I do for the gospel's sake, that I might be partaker thereof with you."

Jesuit Methods in the Light of Modern Times

Nevertheless, again and again, numerous believers will rise up and declare that such an extensive assimilation of divine demands to human weaknesses as the Jesuits have undertaken betokens treason against the true legacy of Christ, and they will prove with many quotations from the writings of the apostles that the Saviour did not intend to found a Church given over to the world, but a community of believers, of elect persons withdrawn within themselves.

The Jesuits, for their part, will always be able to answer that Christianity has maintained its position through the centuries only be reconciling itself with the world, and by its living, apostolic work; by a complete renunciation of the *communicare orbi terrarium*, it would long ago have declined to the creed of a small sect. And the opponents again will thereupon assert that, although the Church may have maintained her existence by such compromises, she is no longer the guardian of the true Christian doctrine.

So the great conflict among believers will continue for ever undecided, the conflict as to whether mystical abandonment or the exercise of the will leads to God, whether man is elected by grace or can work out his own salvation by means of his will, whether "corpse-like obedience" or faith in "the liberty of a Christian man" is the right attitude, whether God requires the stern performance of His commands or mild forbearance, and finally whether the true imitation of Christ consists in a complete renunciation of all temporal activities or in an active, secular apostleship.

Whichever of these combatants may have "theological truth" on his side, it is certain

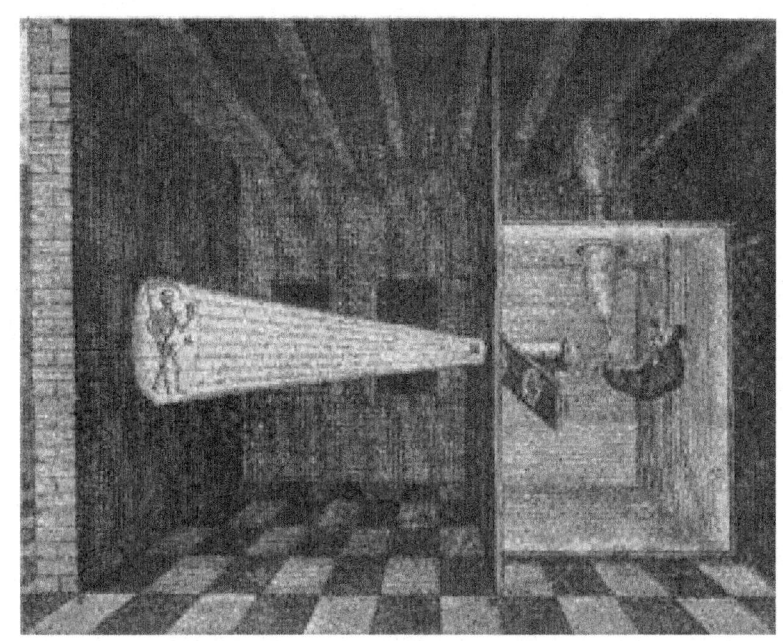

140. THE MAGIC LANTERN INVENTED BY THE JESUIT FATHER KIRCHER

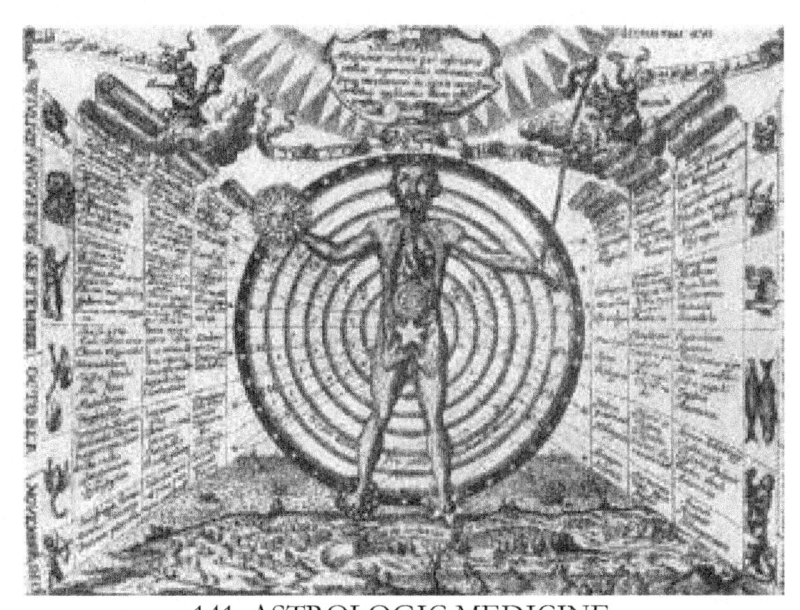

141. ASTROLOGIC MEDICINE
From Ars magna lucis et umbrae by Athanasius Kircher

142. THE GLORY OF ST. IGNATIUS

Painting by Bacicio, l'ome

Jesuit Methods in the Light of Modern Times

that this whole antithesis must remain the concern of believers only. The pros and cons of the controversy are accessible only to religious experience, and are entirely closed against the means of perception of a rational critic. The purely lay observer has no sort of qualification to enable him to judge whether the Jesuits, in accommodating the demands of religion to the level of humanity, and in utilizing worldly means for the attainment of religious ends, are fulfilling or contravening the real spirit of the Gospel.

If the Society of Jesus had merely limited itself within Catholic theology, to ascribing a more important position to the human will, a greater value to "works," to elaborating the apostolic idea, if, in fact, Jesuitism had been nothing but one of those countless interpretations of Christianity which have been essayed at every time by the most diverse creeds, orders and sects, no one outside the Church would have had the occasion or the right to take up the question of all these differences of opinion.

The Jesuits, however, have not limited their service in the "army of Christ" to the stillness of the cloister or to the debates of ecclesiastical convocations, but have extended it to the whole world, to the cabinets of rulers and ministers, to parliaments and universities, to the audience halls of Asiatic despots, to the campfires of the Red Indians, to observatories, physiological and psychological institutes, the stages of theatres, the congresses of learned men and the tribunes of political orators; they have sought to subordinate all man's thoughts and feelings to the Faith, and they have claimed the whole, noisy world, with its wealth of interests and objects, as the sphere of their religious activities.

They have demanded to be accounted men of the world with worldly men, leaned men and with the learned, artists with the artists, politicians with the politicians, and to be regarded as equals in all these circles. Accordingly, in these worldly spheres, they cannot escape criticism of any worldly kind. Moreover, as the Jesuits have had a very considerable influence on the spiritual and material culture of Europe, we are entitled to inquire whether this influence has meant gain or loss, progress or reaction.

If, therefore, for centuries the work of the Society of Jesus in the confessional has been the subject of lay discussion, there seems to be some justification for this. For, while every lay critic might well avoid, as proper to religion, those spiritual conversations of the believer and his confessor which arise from the priest's office of mediator between God and man, on the other hand, with the Jesuits, the confessional is to no small extent connected with the politics, and, the confessors of kings, ministers, generals and sovereigns, they have often determined the history of whole realms. Here too a consideration from the lay point of view may be permitted.

In these days, however, such criticism will be made from standpoints quite different from the earlier ones; if we, today, wish to discover whether the accusations of Pascal and his successors concerning "Jesuit morality" are justified, we shall not be satisfied to attack the "suspicious" tenets of Jesuit moral casuistry; we must rather inquire what the real meaning and end of these maxims were, and by what principles the contemporaries of those casuists judged moral problems. It will then appear that the oft-attacked doctrine of the permissibility of the murder of tyrants was by no means invented by the Jesuits, but that, as early as the twelfth century, John of Salisbury enunciated a very similar doctrine, and that Martin Luther, in one of his speeches, declared that at tyrant might in certain circumstances be killed "like any other murderer or highwayman." In our times, moreover, this principle will no longer elicit the same degree of indignation as in the epoch of absolutism, for, however little deeds of blood and violence may be approved on ethical grounds, we have become accustomed to find the people's right forcibly to remove obnoxious rulers proclaimed in the majority of revolutionary systems of ideas, and the frequency with which this doctrine has been put into practice in recent decades has to a considerable extent dulled our minds to the horror of it.

Today, too, those tenets of the earlier moral-theological literature of the Jesuit order are still called in question which lay down that, in estimating sins, not only moral distinctions, but also social distinctions must be considered. When, however, it is remembered that, at the beginning of the twentieth century, European army officers were still accorded, under law and custom, the privilege of the "defense of their honor," it will be, if not commendable, at least understandable, that in past centuries many Jesuit casuists should have allowed an aristocrat the right to kill an offender of a lower social class.

The consideration of the relationship between the Jesuit order and the inquisition gives rise to similar reflections. Apart from the fact that the Society of Jesus was not in any way, as is frequently assumed, very loosely connected with the Inquisition, and that, with the exception of Portugal, no single country has ever had a Jesuit inquisitor, it must not be forgotten that the Inquisition, according to all the findings of recent investigators, was carried out with relative humanity and justice for the times, and in this respect was far superior to the temporal administration of justice. And although every degree of indignation is justified concerning the forcible suppression of unpopular convictions, it must be remembered, when judgment is passed on the proceedings of the Inquisition that, even in our own days, purely temporal political dictators seek to maintain their authority by means which are not essentially different. "I will permit myself to remark," the Jesuit Naphta says with this in mind in Thomas Mann's *Magic Mountain*, "that every age of torture and the death penalty which does not derive from belief in the future life is bestial madness."

It would certainly be unjust to make the Jesuits alone answerable for barbarous opinions which were characteristic of their age, and from which the present age is weaned to a far less degree than a superficial survey might indicate.

On the other hand, it cannot be denied that many of the Jesuits' moral tenets which at one time were considered "abominable" and "dangerous" have now, in the light of the twentieth century, not only lost their dubious character but actually make a surprisingly modern impression., The old casuists, for example, declared that in great necessity theft is excusable; the civil codes of all civilized lands now admit "irresistible compulsion" as an extenuating circumstance, and hardly anyone nowadays would blame this as Jesuitical laxity.

Even the much-reviled Jesuit maxims of the *reservation mentalis* and "amphibology" appear in these days in a very different light, as the laws of the state themselves expressly admit the criminals' right to lie, and guarantee the inviolability of the professional secrecy of priests, doctors and lawyers. We must, therefore, show some understanding of the seventeenth-century moralists who sought to supply this gap in legal protection.

And must not the modern critic regard the "art of dissimulation," cunning and caution employed in the political and missionary activities of the Jesuits, and expressed in the instructions of the founder of the order and his successors, and perhaps most clearly in the maxims

Jesuit Methods in the Light of Modern Times

of Baltasar Gracian, in a different light from that in which the Dominican, Protestant and Jansenist zealots in their time regarded them? We know today that the view of life termed "Jesuitical" represents an essential traits of post-Renaissance humanity, and that Machiavelli, before the appearance of Loyola, had already propounded the thesis that men must be regarded as they really are, and that this consideration must govern a man's practical dealings with them. The Jesuit order, which was distinguished from all the older religious communities by the very way in which it assimilated the spirit of the Renaissance, could not ignore this fundamental conception of the age concerning the true nature of man; on the contrary, the order had to take cognizance of this in every way, and have regard to it in all its teachings and schemes, in its written orders as well as in its practical performances.

To how great a degree this "Jesuitical spirit" is actually a common property of modern humanity is best expressed perhaps in the words with which Arthur Schopenhauer has prefaced his translation of the *Handbook Oracle* of Baltasar Gracian. He maintained that this book teaches the art to which all people apply themselves, and is therefore of use to every man. It is particularly fitted to be "the handbook of all those who live in the great world, but preeminently of young people who are trying to make their fortunes there, and to whom it gives in advance and once and for all instruction which they could not otherwise obtain without long experience."

In our days, when the whole conception of good and evil has undergone considerable changes, the worldly wisdom and the laxity of which the Jesuits were accused in earlier centuries meet with far more understanding, and the modern reader of the earlier anti-Jesuit polemic literature will feel, more than once, that many of these Jesuit principles, stigmatized as the "product of corruption," are much nearer to our modern ideas than are the stern, mediæval opinions of the Jesuits' enemies.

Finally, it must be taken into consideration that the fathers of the Society of Jesus, in their teaching and works, have always been actuated by an incontestable, true love for humanity. Even Pascal did not deny this, when in his *Provincial Letters* he makes his Jesuit declare that he desires nothing more than to be able "only to teach everywhere the principles of the Holy Gospel in their full severity... We should like nothing better, for the purity of our own morals certainly affords a sufficient proof that it is more from a wise complaisance than from an evil intention that we suffer a greater freedom in other persons. We are compelled to do so, as the world is now so corrupt that men no longer come to us; but we must go to them, otherwise they would forsake us entirely and give themselves up defiantly to sin... For it is the main object of our Society never to repel anybody, whoever he may be, so that the world may not be given over to despair."

Dostoievsky forms the same opinion concerning the attitude of mind and the springs of action of the Jesuits. "I ask you," says Ivan Karamazov to his brother Alyosha, "why do you assume that Jesuits and inquisitors have bound themselves together merely for the attainment of base, material ends? Why do you believe that amongst them there is not a single one who is really tormented by a great passion, by a deep love for humanity?.... Who knows, perhaps this accursed old man, who loves making in so obstinate and peculiar a way, is even now living with a whole crowd of similar old men in a secret league, founded long ago to preserve the secret and protect it from unfortunate and feeble men, and for the purpose of making mankind happy! This unquestionably is the case, So must it be..."

The Power and Secret of the Jesuits

But Jesuit moral theology, independently of the moral evaluation of its individual tenets, invites criticism on philosophical and psychological grounds, for its claims even today, from a purely intellectual point of view, to be the equal of, or indeed superior to, all other doctrines of morality. Thus the philosophical content of Jesuit moral theology must be examined, to see whether it holds its own against modern intellectual conceptions, and this examination undoubtedly gives a negative result.

To begin with, the correctness of the fundamental hypothesis on which the whole system rests must be keenly contested; it is, indeed, more than problematical whether the assertion that the human will is free and controlled simply by intellectual perceptions can still be maintained at the present day. The great contest concerning free will has, indeed, been settled no more decisively by philosophers and psychologists than it was previously by Protestant, Jansenist and Jesuit theologians; whether there really is a will, to what extent it can be free, and what is meant by such "freedom" seems now less clear than formerly, so that the most modern thinkers incline more and more to the opinion that the whole question is contrary to sense, and is an imaginary problem, like so many that have befooled the human intellect through the centuries.

But, in such circumstances, is it still permissible to judge man's moral conduct on such a dubious hypothesis as the assumption of a free will appears, to the modern intellect, to be? This seems the more out of place in view of the fact that, in the administration of temporal justice, which, when it proceeded to model itself on Roman; law, took over at the same time belief in "free will controlled by the intellect," efforts have for a long time been made to assimilate the consequences of the new conceptions, and to do without the problematical "freedom of will." In this sense, the great expert on criminal low, Franz von Liszt, has laid down that jurisprudence must refuse to pass sentence and inflict penalties "in the name of morality"; its task should rather be limited to creating "incentives," which will restrain people from committing crimes, and so to contributing to the safeguarding of social institutions.

Jesuit moral teaching, on the other hand, still persists in the opinion that man is the complete master of his decisions, and, therefore, in every voluntary transgression, he knowingly and willingly commits a "sin" which he must "expiate," according to divine justice. Disregarding the findings of psychoanalysis, which has shown that a great part of human desires and wishes belong to the realm of the unconscious, whence they influence conduct, the Jesuits still claim that every act of will is "conscious"; nowadays, however, this second important fundamental principle of their system seems to be just as seriously shaken as belief in the freedom of the will. A modern scientific examination will not, therefore, be able straightway to approve the philosophical and psychological assumptions of the Jesuit moral doctrine, and will indeed give rise to serious reflection concerning the whole formal conception of the system.

It is true that the moral casuistry of the Jesuits, when it was first formulated, betokened an advance, as it introduced the principle of a finer differentiation, a closer examination of the peculiar circumstance of every transgression. For the Jesuits were the first to recognize that the complexity of life could not be judged by a few inflexible rules, and they took care always to take into consideration to what weaknesses the man was liable, and what conditions should be regarded as extenuating circumstances for his faults. For this purpose they enumerated, in their books on casuistry, thousands of cases laid down exactly in each case how the general rules were to be interpreted here, so that undue harshness should be avoided.

But what was progress in the seventeenth century must be regarded as out-of-date in the twentieth, for, in the meantime, lay thought has arrived at the conclusion that standard rules can never have a constitutive, but only a regulative significance, and that accordingly every attempt to judge human conduct from normative points of view, however finely differentiated, will fail in the last resort.

If the Jesuits had taken to heart the lofty judgment pronounced by Leibniz, that two things discrete in time or place can never be quite "equal" so that each man, and each of his actions, represents something that occurs once only and cannot be repeated, they would have seen that they could no longer draw an analogy between one man and another, one situation and another, and they would have abandoned the attempt to judge deeds which were always committed under their own special conditions according to the pattern of "specimen cases."

From the shortcomings in the method of this moral casuistry arise the absurdities which are so often contained in its precepts. Here even the holy of holies is entered by formal, manufactured, mutually exclusive decisions, and juristic acumen, however great, can no more remove this fundamental evil than can the extension to infinity of the list of "examples."

Now it would not be fair to conceal the fact that, even outside moral theology, the principles of casuistry still persist, since the civil codes of every land seek, by the formulation of legal precedents, to facilitate the judging of events occurring in everyday life. And the judge who finds in the decisions of the supreme court a judgment relating to a previous "similar" case, and gives his judgment in accordance with it, is not so very different from the confessor who in a dubious case appeals to Escobar or Busembaum.

Already, however, the modern representatives of secular jurisprudence have often openly recognized the moral inadequacy of this unsuitable system, and the very modesty with which secular law increasingly professes to be nothing but a practical emergency arrangement for the protection of society indicates greater progress than has been made in moral theology, which still claims to correspond not only to justice but to Divine justice.

True to the Earth

Most of these hypotheses of Jesuit moral teaching which must now be regarded as superseded derive in the last resort, as we know, from the teaching of Aristotle; this is equally true of the belief in the real existence of "free will" and of the claim that this will is under the sole control of the conscious understanding, and no less true of the endeavor to classify and make an inventory of the world and all possible occurrences therein. The Jesuit in Pascal's *Provincial Letters* is, therefore, quite right in saying that the books of Aristotle would have to be burnt, if the fundamental principles of Jesuit morality were proved false.

Indeed, a great thinker of the thirteenth century had already declared that the annihilation of Aristotle's works would be to the great advantage of humanity; the study of these works, wrote Roger Bacon, meant "nothing but a waste of time, the source of errors, and the diffusion of ignorance." And although today men may be lacking in the deep emotion of the

Middle Ages which demanded the burning of books with erroneous contents, yet the present day will agree with old Roger Bacon that the Stagirite is guilty of many important confusions of thought.

This recognition gives rise to the reproach against the Society that it has clung to the teachings of Aristotle as if they were dogmas, although they have already been effectively refuted in many respects, and that it has rejected and suppressed many important intellectual achievements merely because they were not in accordance with Aristotelean physics, metaphysics and ethics.

Modern investigators have shown that it was owing to Aristotle that the conception of a heliocentric universe was not generally accepted as early as four centuries before Christ, although Plato had already recognized and upheld it. For Aristotle, at the celebrated session of the Athenian Academy, spoke in favor of the geocentric system and obtained the victory over Plato's view, a victory which threw back human thought about two thousand years.

Then when in the new era the heliocentric theory was revived, it was due in a large measure to the Jesuits that "the true Copernican theory was rejected, and the false Ptolemaic forcibly maintained. So once more the Aristotelean spirit of reaction inflicted a heavy injury on progress."

It is true that the most recent mathematical and physical theories necessitate a revision of this commonly held opinion, for no longer does the teaching of Ptolemy appear "wholly false," nor that of Copernicus "alone true," as Galileo thought. Rather does it appear that both the systems have fundamentally an equal claim to recognition, and that the superiority of the Copernican system rests solely on the greater simplicity of the astronomical calculations effected with its help. Cardinal Bellarmine had, however, already recognized this when he warned Galileo's pupils to regard the Copernican doctrine only as hypothetical, and not as the sole truth.

But, if it can no longer be flatly stated that the Jesuits, in their campaign against Galileo, were completely in the wrong, nevertheless they were far removed from the spirit of true science, in as much as they supported the Ptolemaic view of the universe not on astronomical grounds, but merely because the "authorities" appeared to support it. Relying firmly on Aristotle, on the Bible and on the Church fathers, they refused to admit the possibility of any other explanation of the universe, and this blind dogmatism, which may be in place in the sphere of religion, can never be approved when it is applied to the findings of scientific inquiry.

In the very same way, the Jesuits, in defiance of all more recent knowledge, have clung to the "authority" of Aristotelean ethics, and here too they must be reproached for not having sufficiently regarded the "Copernican revolution" for which Leibniz and Kant paved the way. For the conceptions initiated by these two thinkers have most clearly shown that in ethics as in astronomy "the eye must be fixed on the sun," if sense and harmony are to be found in the apparent disorder and confusion of human conduct; morality must be judged, not from the standpoint of "attainable virtue," but in relation to the idea of a moral demand which must be regarded as regulative and can never be fulfilled.

But never would the Jesuits condescend to exchange the Aristotelean "virtue attainable on earth" for a "never-ending demand," the Aristotelean "concepts" for the transcendental "ideas" of Plato. Up to the present day, the Jesuit moral philosophers believe with the Stagirite that it suffices to make a careful inventory of the various possible virtues and vices, good deeds and bad, and to pass judgment on them all on the ground of "natural reason." This is the "confusion of tasks" with which Heinrich Gomperz has reproached Aristotelean ethics; it consists in this that "descriptive moral science wishes at the same time to be ethics," while it is obviously impossible, "in describing what is, to determine at the same time what should be." Always and in everything, in ethics as in astronomy, the Jesuits, in the spirit of their old master, have "remained true to the earth" as long as they possibly could. It was a century before they gave up geocentric astronomy, and even yet they have not entirely submitted to the teaching of Kant and Leibniz.

Here must, indeed, be mentioned the efforts of individual modern Jesuit thinkers to get beyond the "Aristotelean barrier"; Father Max Prbilla writes in obvious opposition to the order's former customary belief in authority when he says that "no master of the past" can or should relieve man of the exercise of his own independent power of thought. Nothing could be more preposterous than to attempt to deal with "modern men, so unusually differentiated as they are, by ready-made, rigid formulas. Not the traditional formula, but the seasonable formula must be the decisive one."

The Service of the Order to Civilization

He who wishes to arrive at a just judgment concerning the role of the Jesuits in the intellectual life of Europe must not forget a saying of Chateaubriand, that "the slight injury which philosophy thinks it has suffered from the Jesuits" is scarcely worth consideration in comparison with "the immeasurable services which the Jesuits have rendered to human society."

Even if, regarding the great influence of the spirit of Jesuitism on the whole development of the new era, we do not estimate the harm caused by the philosophical retrogressiveness of the order quite so lightly as did Chateaubriand, we cannot but share this writer's admiration for the many notable astronomical, physical, geographic, ethnographic and other scientific achievements of the Jesuits, or fail to recognize that the order has numbered in its ranks a vast number of unusually gifted inventors.

The name of Father Athanasius Kircher alone is connected with the invention of the magic lantern, the rediscovery of the Archimedean burning-glass, and the speaking-trumpet. He demonstrated the fascination which chalk lines exert on hens, and thereby laid the foundations for inquiry into hypnotic phenomena; he invented a common alphabet for the deaf and dumb, wrote treatises on palæontology, and was one of the first to study the Coptic language and Egyptian hieroglyphics; from him, too, came the first cartographic representation of ocean currents.

Of no less importance was Father Francesco Lana-Terzi, who invented a machine for sowing, worked out methods for teaching those born blind, carried out important investigations into the crystallization of minerals, and who, moreover, in Lessing's opinion, was the creator of the word "ideal." In connection with the invention of the air-pump by Otto von

The Power and Secret of the Jesuits

Guericke, Lana in 1670 first conceived the project of making an air-ship, with the help of vacuum metal balls.

Half a century later, another Jesuit, Father Laurenço Gusmão, accomplished the first balloon ascent at Lisbon, for he, before the Montgolfiers, made a paper balloon go up by means of a fire lighted in the gondola. The severe Portuguese Inquisition saw in this enterprise of Gusmão's a work of the Devil and imprisoned the luckless inventor as a magician; and the other members of the order had to intercede for a long time before Gusmão was released.

Particularly great is the enrichment for which European science has to thank the Jesuit missionaries. For it was they who were the first to undertake adventurous journeys through hitherto untrodden lands and continents, and to report what they had discovered. It was through them that Europe learnt of the conditions in the interior of Canada, Mexico, Brazil, Tibet and Mongolia, and, as they almost always combined their missionary journeys with cartographic surveys, they were of the greatest assistance to later geographers.

The services rendered by the fathers to the study of languages were no less considerable, for, as they always began their missionary work by making the closest study of the idiom of the peoples they hoped to convert, they compiled dictionaries and grammars of almost all the languages of the North and South American Indians, of India and Indochina, and of the Japanese. The Peking missionaries wrote grammars of Chinese and Manchu, and the work of the Jesuit Prémare, *Notitae linguae sinicae*, gave a thorough exposition of all the Chinese styles, proverbs and expressions. That there is today throughout Brazil a *lingoa geral*, which all the Indians understand, and the knowledge of which suffices of travelers all over the immense country, is the work of the Jesuits, and the creations of this language goes back to the enterprise of Father Anchieta.

Among these great services, the smaller services of the Jesuit missions must not be overlooked, for, taken together, they have contributed much to the enrichment of European civilization. It was through the Jesuit Dentrecolles that France, at the beginning of the eighteenth century, learnt of the making of Chinese porcelain, and even the use of the umbrella was first introduced to the West by the Jesuits from China. Moreover, the Jesuit missionaries brought from Asia to Europe plants, spices and medicines such as Peruvian bark, rhubarb and vanilla; the camellia gets its name from the Jesuit Kamel, who sent a specimen of this flower from the Philippines to the great botanist Linnæus.

Finally, the stimulus which European thought received from the knowledge of Indian and Chinese culture imparted by the Jesuits was of the greatest significance. For the father were not only the first to study Sanskrit, they also published translations of the Vedas, and thus directed the attention of the West to Indian philosophy and religion; they must then be regarded as the originators of that great European spiritual tendency which has ultimately led to the theosophical movement of our days.

The opening up of Chinese culture through the Jesuit missionaries, again, not only gave us the writings of Confucius, but also contributed much to the revolution in European taste. The *chinoiseries* of the rococo period are often derived directly from illustrations in Jesuit Chinese publications, whose engravings were copied by the architects of the time with almost pedantic accuracy. Even literature was not untouched by the work of the Jesuit Missionaries:

The Way of Knowledge and the Way of Faith

Voltaire's tragedy, *The Chinese Orphan*, is taken from a translation made by Father Prémare of a Chinese play.

Conversely, the Jesuits were the first to bring to the Chinese a knowledge of European customs and literature, by translating into Chinese the works of the Church fathers and numerous scientific treatises. Father Parrenin, in particular, undertook the translation of the works of French scholars into Manchu, the Emperor K'ang-hi making the necessary corrections in style.

"The Jesuits seized upon the sole and the noblest bond of union between themselves and the emperor and his empire," writes J. G. Herder in his *Adrastea*, "the bond of the sciences and arts. No one can deny them the credit of having sent there an array of learned, worldly-wise, indefatigable men, who moreover brought to Europe the knowledge of the great empire and the surrounding countries, the knowledge of its language and literature, its constitution and customs... We have much for which to thank the French and German Jesuits, through whom the mind and industry of European scholars have been stimulated to the study of the Chinese language and literature, of Chinese chronology, astronomy, history, natural history, and so on. Deguignes alone has done as much in this connection as a Chinese academy... they were accounted learned mandarins; could European missionaries bear a nobler name? If their pure intentions to enlighten the peoples, not to undermine the empire's weal, but through science and morals to establish it on the foundation of true humanity, what name could they bear more nobly, what office fulfil more honorably, than the office of learned, well-mannered mandarins? Then the swan, which the Jesuits, by imperial favor, wear as a sign of honor on their breasts, flies up to heaven, and sings a sweet song to the peoples of earth... Though the name of the Jesuits may be generally hated, the good which humanity has obtained through them must always be worthy of praise, and will certainly benefit the future..."

The Way of Knowledge and the Way of Faith

But, however great the undoubted service of the Jesuits to the sciences and to the progress of civilization may be, their opponents refuse to place their achievements on a level with those of secular research. Whatever the fathers may have undertaken as astronomers, thinkers, inventors geographers or Chinese scholars, their opponents say, has always been done with a preconceived end in view: in all their labors they have followed only one aim, the renewed confirmation of the Catholic idea of God, so that for the Jesuits even science is merely a means "to the greater glory of God."

To start with an established object in view, instead of from purely empirical beginnings, lowers research to the position of the "handmaid of theology," considerably limits its freedom, and is in complete opposition to secular science, which is enabled through freedom from preliminary hypotheses alone to bring the human mind nearer to the truth.

This teleological method of the Jesuits also clearly betrays the Aristotelean spirit, since the fundamental principle of Aristotelean philosophy is that for man's thought as for his deeds and actions, "when he builds a ship or a house, the idea of the whole always appears first as the goal of the activity, and that then this idea is realized through the carrying out of the parts."

Yet even Friedrich Albert Lange, who, in his *History of Materialism*, has directed severe criticism against this, and has accused Aristotle of confusing speculation and investigation in an inadmissible manner, admits that "this system is the most finished example of an effective construction of a uniform and complete view of the universe that history has yet given us. . .

"We have not been created merely to perceive," he says, "but to contrive and construct, and, with more or less mistrust concerning the definitive validity of what our reason and mind may offer us, humanity must always welcome the man whose ingenuity enables him to construct that unity of the world and the intellectual life which is denied to our perceptions. Such a creation will merely be the expression of an age's longing for unity and perfection; but this is something great, and is as important to the maintenance and nourishment of our intellectual life as is science."

Hermann Bahr, who was familiar with all the modern points of view, and who finally returned to the Thomist conception, which regards faith as the highest stage of knowledge, has pointed out that Goethe, in his writings, insists repeatedly on the significance of synthesis, and that he considered that "it was not possible to speak adequately concerning many of the problems of natural science, without enlisting the aid of metaphysics." The "hierarchy of investigators" imagined by Goethe begins at the lowest grade with the "utilizers, the seekers for what is profitable and useful," who "apprehend the practical," while the highest grade enthrones "those who comprehend, who in a nobler sense may be called the creators."

How little, then, it is justifiable in fact to condemn "starting from the idea" as absolutely "unscientific" is testified by one of the greatest natural scientists of the nineteenth century, Justus von Liebig, who in his discourse on Francis Bacon declares that in natural science "all investigation is deductive or of an a *priori* nature"; experiment can never be more than "an aid in the process of thought, similar to calculation." In every case, and of necessity, thought must precede experiment: "Empirical research into nature, in the ordinary sense, simply does not exist. An experiment which is not preceded by a theory, and thus by an idea, stands in the same relation to research as shaking a child's rattle does to music."

Undoubtedly, at present many of Aristotle's opinions can no longer be regarded as valid, and his philosophical methods no less than his physics have for the most part been abandoned by modern research. But, even if it were necessary to reject all Aristotle's teachings, modern criticism could still appropriate one of his sayings, the celebrated statement in the First Book of the *Nicomachean Ethics* that man must not hesitate, in the service of truth, to give up any of his opinions, however dear: "So that, if both Plato and the truth are my friends, it is my bounded duty to give the preference to truth."

In the spirit of this maxim, it must be considered whether—although the Aristotelean methods have become alien to us, although the modern search for knowledge usually takes other ways—in passing judgment on the Aristotelean-Catholic methods, perhaps our "relative" methods ought not to be applied. Just as the geocentric system can be reconciled with the heliocentric, could not the "closed," hierarchical view of the universe which is directed to God be reconciled with the "open" view, which loses itself in infinity, of modern science? Ultimately, perhaps, in both cases the difference exists merely in the method by which the same truth is perceived, so that neither can the Aristotelean-Jesuitical view of the universe, which modern thought has abandoned, be described as "wholly false" nor that of science as "alone true."

Catholicism, in centuries past, has been justly accused of intolerance, in that it would recognize only its own world of ideas and its own terminology as uniquely true, and for a long time refused equal privileges to scientific modes of observation and expression; no less, however, will the present-day view of the universe incur the reproach of being a reprehensible dogmatism, if, forgetful of criticism and relativity, it refuses to admit the way of religion too as an entirely valid form of human aspiration after truth.

The Power and Secret of the Jesuits

BIBLIOGRAPHY

Works frequently used are referred to under the Part for which they were first consulted.

Adam, K.: Das Wesen des Katholizismus. Düsseldorf, 1927.
Amort, E.: De revelationibus, Augsburg, 1714.
Arnold, G.: Historie und Beschreibung der mystichen Theologie, Frankfurt, 1703.
Arsac, J. d': Die Jesuiten, Ihre, Lehre, ihr Unterrichtswesen, ihr Apostolat. Carl Sartori, Vienna, 1867.
Augustine: Works, in: Bibliothek der Kirchenväter, Kempten, 1873ff.
Boeumaker, O.: Beitrâge zur geschichte der Philosophie des Miittelalters, Münster, 1895ff.
Baudouin, C., and Lestchinsky, A.: Innere Disciplin. Nach der praktischen Moral des Buddhismus, des Stoizismus, des Christentums, des Mentalen Heilverfahrens umd im Simme der Psychotherepie. Sibyllen-Verlag, Dresden, 1928.
Baur, F.: Die christliche Kirche des Mettelalters, Tübingen, 1861.
Bellecius, A.: Medulla asceseos seu exercitia S. P. Ignatii de Loyola. Münster, 1846
Benedict of Nursia; Rules, published by the Emaus Abbey, prague, 1914.
Berbière, U.: L'ordre monastique dès origins au 12ᵉ siècle. Bruges, 1924.
Bernard of Clairvaux: S. B. Sermones in Cant. Innsbruck, 1888.
Bernhart, J.: Die phil. Mystik des Mittelalters. Munich, 1922.
Besse, L. de: Die Wissenschaft des Gebets. Regensburg, 1909.
Besse, L. de: Les mystiques bénédictins dès origins au 13ᵉ siècle. Paris, 1922.
Bibliotheca ascetica: 3 Vols. Pustet. Regensburg, 1921.
Birkre: Exercitatorium spiritual cum Directorio horarum canonicarum autore R. P. Garcia Cisnerio. Regensburg, 1856.
Boehmer, H.: Loyola and die deutsche mystic, Teubner, Leipzig, 1921.
Boehmer, H.: Die Jesuiten. Historische Skizze. Leipzig, 1921.
Boehmer, H.: Studien zur Geschichte der Gessellschaft Jesu. Bonn, 1914.
Bolten, J.: Katholisches aus England. Ktholischer Missionverlag, m.-Gladbach.
Bona, J.: De discretion spirituum. Antwerp, 1723.
Bonaventura: Der Lehensbaum. Herder, Freiburg, 1888.
Bouvier, P.: Directoire composé par S. Ign. À l'usage de celui qui donne les exercices etc. Beauchesne, Paris, 1917
Bremer: Kirchliches Handlexikon. Munich, 1907.
Brou, A.: les exercices spirituels de Saint Ignace de Loyola. Pierre Téqui, Paris, 1922.
Brucker, J.: La Compagnie de Jésus. Beauchesne, Paris, 1919.
Calmes, M.: Zur Soziologie des katholischen Ordensstandes. M.-Gladbach, 1927.

Calvin, J.: Works, in; Corpus Reformatorum. 1863ff.
Campbell, T.J.: The Jesuits (1534-1721). London, 1921.
Cassianus: Works, edited by Hurter. Innsbruck, 1887.
Cavaliera, F.: Ascétisme et Liturgie. Paris, 1914.
Cisneros, Garcia de: Schule des geistlichen Lebens. Herber, Freiburg, 1923.
Codina, A.: Los origenes de los Ejercicios de S. Ignacio de Loyola. Barcelona, 1926.
Codina, A.: Studien zu den Exerzitien des hl. Ignatius. Vol. I of Beiträge zur Geschichte und Askese des Exerzitienbuches. Innsbruck, 1925.
Constitutiones Societatis Jesu. Latin-Spanish ed. By Torres. Madrid, 1898.
Daurignoc. J.: Historie de la Compagnie de Jésus. Régis-Ruffet et Cie., Paris, 1862.
Delprat: Die Brüderschaft des gemeinsamen Lebens. Leipsiz, 1840.
Diertins, J.: Historia exercitiorum spiritualium S. P. Ignatii de Loyola, Lille, 1882.
Diertins, J.: Exercitia spiritualia S. P. N. Ignatii cum sensu eorum explanata, Antwerp, 1693.
Dionysius Areopagiticus: Die angeblichen Schriften des D. A. Seidel, Sulzbach, 1823.
Dokumente zur Geschichte. Beurteilung and Verteidigung der Gesellschaft Jesu. Manz, Regensburg, 1841-42.
Döllinger: Handbunch der Kirchengeschichte.
Duhr, B.: Geschichte der Jesuiten in den Ländern deutscher Zunge. Herder, Freiburg i. Br., 1913.
Endres: Thomas von Aquino. Mainz, 1910.
Epistolae Praepositorum Generalium S. J. Gandavi, 1847.
Ersch, J. S., and Gruber, J. G.: Allgemeine Encyklopädie der Wissenschaften und Künste. F. A. Brockhaus, Leipzig, 1838.
Feder, A.: Das geistliche Tagebuch des hl, Ignatius von Loyola. Pustet, Regensburg, 1922.
Fendt, L.: Symbolik des römischen Katholizismus. De Gruyter & Co., Berlin-Leipzig, 1926.
Ferrusola: Commentaria in librum Exercitiorum b. P. Ignatii de Loyola, ed. J. Nonell. Barcelona, 1885.
Freud, S.: Massenpsychologie und Ich-Analyse. Internationaler psychonalytischer Verlag, Vienna, 1923.
Friedell, E.: Kulturgeschichte der Neuzeit. Die Krisis der europäischen Seele von der Schwarzen Pest bis zum Weltkrieg. C. H. Beck, Munich, 1927, 1928.
Friedländler, M. J.: Pieter Bruegel. Propyläen-Verlag. Berlin, 1921.
Cagliardi, A.: (1537-1607) Commentarii seu Explanationes in Exerc. Spirit. Bruges, 1882.
Gonzáles-Serrano, U.: El misticismo, in: Revista de España, Vol. 128, 1890.
Görres, G.: Vier Bücher von der Nachfolge Christi. Schöningh, Münster i. W.
Gothein, E.: Ignatius v. Loyola und die Gegenreformation. Halle, 1895.
Grabmann, M.: Wesen und Grundlagen der Katholischen Mystik. Unich, 1923.
Grabmann, M.: Die Geschichte der scholastischen Methode I-II. Freiburg, 1909-11.
Griesinger: The Jesuits. London, 1885.

Bibliography

Gundlack, G.: Zur Soziologie der katholischen Ideenwelt und des Jesuitenordens. Herder, Freiburg, 1927.

Gutierrez, J.: Manual de los Ejercicios espirituales de S. Ignacio de Loyola. Saragossa, 1912.

Handmann, R.: Exercitia spiritualia. Regensburg, 1904.

Harnack, A. von.: Dogmengeschichte I-III. Tübingen, 1909

Harasser, G.: Exerzitien-Leitung. Vol. I, Tyrolia, Innsbruck, Vol. II, Marianischer Verlag, Innsbruck, 1923, 124.

Heiler, Fr.: Der Katholizismus, scine Idee und seine Erscheinung. Ernst Reinhardt, Munich, 1923.

Heiler, Fr.: Die Mystik im Leben der Kirche. Munich, 1919.

Heiler, Fr.: Das Gebet, eine religionsgeschichtliche und relitionpsychologische Untersuchung. Munich, 1920.

Heiner, Fr.: Die Jesuiten und ihre Gegner. Münchner Volksschriftenverlag, 1906.

Henin de Cuvillers, d': La Monarchie des Solipses. Paris, 1824.

Hettinger. Fr.: Die Idee der geistlichen Übungen nach dean Plane des hl. Ignatius v. Loyola. Manz, Regensburg, 1908.

Holl, K.: Die geistlichen Cbungen des Ignatius von Loyola. Tübingen, 1905.

Holy Scriptures. Ger. tr. By Luther.

Huber. J.: Der Jesuitenorden nach seiner Verfassung und Doctrin. Wirksamkeit und Geschichte. C. c. Lüderitz, Berlin, 1873.

Huizinga, J.: Herbst des Mittelalters. Munich, 1924.

Joussen, J.: Geschichte des deutschen Volkes seit dem Ausgang des Mittelalters. Herder, Freiburg i. Br., 1880-94.

John of the Cross: Works. Lechner, Regensburg, 1859.

Karrer, O.: Der mystische Strom. Von Paulus bis Thomas von Aquin. Jesef Müller, Munich, 1925.

Karrer, O.: Des hl. Ignatius von Loyola Geistliche Briefe und Unterweisungen. Freiburg, 1922.

Karrer, O.: die grosse Glut. Die Mystik im Mittelalter. Jesef Müller, Munich, 1926.

Karrer, O.: Gott in uns. Die Mystik der Neuzeit. Josei Müller, Munich, 1926.

Kassner, R.: Von den Elementen menschlicher Grösse. Insel-Verlag, Leipzig, 1911.

Köhler, B.: Exercitia spiritualia. Berlin, 1907.

Konermann, A.: Exerzitien und Exerzitienorganisation. Aufgaben moderner Seelsorge. Benziger & Co. Einsiedeln, 1925.

Kramer: Die Brüder vom gemeinsaemen Leben. Berlin, 1856.

La Chalotais, de: Compte rendu des Constitutins des Jesuites. 1762.

Landsberg, P.: Die Welt des Mittelalters und Wir. (Ein geschichtsphilosophischer Versuch über den Sinn eines Zeitalters.) Fried. Cohen, Bonn, 1925.

La Gontier, A.: Exercitia tertiac probationis Soc. Jesu. Mainz, 1774.

Lindworsky, J.: wWllenschule. Schöningh, Paderborn, 1927.

Lindworsky, J.: Exerzitien und Charakterbildung. Innsbruck, 1926

Lippert, P.: Zur Psychologie des Jesuitenordens. Kösel, Kempten, 1912.

Lippert, P.: Die Weltanschanung des Katholizismus. Leipzig, 1926.
Loyola, Ignatius: The Spiritual Exercises. Ger. tr. O. C. Recht-Verlag, Munich, 1921.
Maréchal: La psychologie du mysticism. 1902.
Mausbach, J.: Thomas von Aquin als Meister der christlichen Sittenlehre. Munich 1925.
Meschler, M.: Die Gesellschaft Jesu, ihre Satzungen und ihre Erfolge. Herder, Freiburg i. Br., 1911.
Meschler, M.: Das Exerzitienbuch des hl. Ignatius von Loyola. Freiburg, 1925.
Monumenta Ignatiana: S. Ignatii Epistolae et Instructiones 1903ff. Exercitia spiritualia S. Ignatii et eorum Directoria; ed. A. Codina, 1919.
Mörchen, F.: Die Psychologic der Heilgkeit. Carl Marbold, Halle a. S., 1908.
Müller-Reiif, W.: Zur Psychologie der mystischen Persönlichkeit. Berlin, 1921.
Nadal, H.: Epistolae. Madrid, 1898ff.
Nonell, J.: Étude sur la texte des Exercises de S. Ignace. Paris, 1922.
Paufoeder, D.: Die Kirche als liturgische Gemeinschaft. Mainz, 1924.
Peeters, L.: Spiritualité ignatienne et spiritualité liturgique. Tournai, 1914.
Picard, G.: La saisie immédiate de Dieu dans les états mystiques. Paris, 1924.
Poulain, A.: die Fülle der Gnaden, ein Hnadbuch der Mystik. Freiburg, 1910.
Quinet, E., and Michelet, J.: Die Jesuiten. Schweighauser, Basle, 1843.
Ranke, L. von: Weltgeschichte. Part IX. Leipzig, 1888.
Ranke, L. Von: Deutsche Geschichte i. Zeitalter der Reformation. Vols. III-VI. Leipzig, 1881.
Ravignon, P. de: De Pexistence et de l'institut des Jésuites. Poussielgue-Rusand, Paris, 1844.
Reinhardt: Mytik und Pietismus, Munich, 1925.
Ribadeneira: De ratione Instituti S. J. New ed. Rome, 1864.
Richard of St. Victor: De gratia contemplationis libri quinque.
Richstätter, K.: Mystische Gebetsgnaden und Ignatianische Exerzitien. Tyrolia, Innsbruck, 1914.
Rietschel, G. Chr.: Martin Luther und Ignaius von Loyola. Herrosé, Wittenberg, 1879.
Rohr, Erich: Franziskus und Ignatius. Eine vergleichende Studie. F. A. Pfieffer, Munich, 1926.
Rohrbacher: Histoire universelle de l'Église cath. Paris, 1832.
Roothaan, P. J.: Exercitia spiritualia. Regensburg, 1911.
Rosa, E.: Il buono soldato di Cristo e la sua Liliza. Rome.
Rosignioli, C. G.: Noticias memorabiles de los cjercicios espirituales de San Ignacio de Loyola.
Roxas, M.: Meditaciones según las cuatro semanas de los ejercicios de San Ignacio de Loyola.
Schlund, E.: Exerzitien und Exerzitienbewegung. F. A. Pfeiffer, Munich, 1926.
Schlund, E.: Die seraphische Liebe. Franziskanische Exerzitien. Pustet, 1875.
Schmid, F. A.: Manresa oder die geistlichen Übungen des hl. Ignatius in neuer, leichtfasslicher Darstellung zum Gebrauche aller Glaubigen. Pustet, 1875.
Schmitt, C.: Römischer Katholizismus und politische Form, Munich, 1925.

Schoell, E.: Der jesuitische Gehorsam. Eugen Strien, Halle a. S., 1891.

Schumann, Fr. K.: Zur grundwissenschaftlichen Betrachtung des mystischen Erlebnisses. Zeitschrift für Philosophie und philosophische Kritik. Vol. 165, Leipzig, 1918.

Schürmeyer, W.: Hieronymus Bosch. R. Piper & Co., Munich, 1923.

Scoraille, R. de: François Suarez. Paris, 1913.

Sierp, W.: Das Exerzitienbuch des hl. Ignatius von Loyola. Herder, Freiburg, 1925.

Staudlin: Geschichte der christlichen Moral, Göttingen, 1808.

Stöger: Die asketische Literatur über die geistlichen Übungen. Paris-Regensburg, 1850

Stoeckius, H.: Ignatius von Loyolas Gedanken über Auinahme und Bildung der Novizen. Langensalza, 1925.

Sträter, P.: Der Geist der Ignatianischen Exerzitien. Freiburg, 1925.

Suarez, F.: De Spiritualibus Exercitiis S. Ignatii. Paris, 1909.

Suarez, F.: Varia opuscula theological. Mainz, 1600.

Torres, Galeote: La mistica española. Discurso, Sevilla, 1907.

Troeltsch, E.: Gesemmelte Schriften. Soziallehren der christlichen Kirchengruppen. Tübingen, 1912.

Ullmann, C.: Reformatoren vor der Reformation vornehmlich in Deutschland und den Niederlanden. Perthes, Gotha, 1866.

Watrigant: La genèse des Exercices de S. Ignace de Loyola. Amiens, 1897.

Watrigant: Collection de la Bibliothèque des Exercices de Saint Ignace. Paris, 1919.

Weber, The.: Der Gehorsam in der Gesellschaft Jesu. Trewendt, Breslau, 1872.

Weisweiler, H.: Der Jesuitenorden. Germania, Berlin, 1828.

Wetzer-Welte: Kirchenlexikon. Freiburg, 1882.

Ziegler, L: Gestaltwandel der Götter,. Otto Reichl, Darmstadt, 1922.

Zimmermann, Ch.: Beteiligung der Sinnesgebiete an der religiösen Ekstase. Darmstadt, 1914.

Zöckler, O.: Kritische Geschichte der Askese. Frankfurt, 1863.

PART II

Alberola, G.: San Ignacio y los Jesuitas. Madrid, 1897.

Aretina, P.: The conversations of the Divine P. A. Ger. tr. Leipzig, 1903.

Astrain, A.: La conversión de San Ignacio de Loyola. Bilinao, 1921.

Astrain, A.: Der hl. Ignatius v. Loyola, Gründer der Gelellschaft Jesu, Hermann Rauch, Wiesbaden, 1924.

Bartoli, D.: Della vita e dell' istituto di S. Ignatio, fondatore della Compagnia di Giesu. Rome, 1650.

Baumgarten, H.: Geschichte Karls V. Freiburg, 1905.

Baumgarten, H.: Ignatius v. Loyola. Lecture, 1879. Trübner, Strasburg, 1880.

Benrath, K.: Die Reformation in Venedig. Halle, 1887.

Bloch, J., and Loewenstein, G.: Die Prostitution. Marcus, Berlin, 1925.

Block, J.: Das erste Auftreten der Syphilis. Berlin, 1903.
Boehmer, H.: Die Bekenntrisse des Ignatius v. Loyola. Leipzig, 1902.
Boéro, J.: Vie du P. Jacques Laynez, second général de la Compagnie de Jésus, suivie de la biographie du P. Alphonse Salmeron. Lille, 1894.
Braunfeld, L.: Kritscher Versuch über den Roman Amadis von Gallien. Wigand, Leipzig, 1876.
Burckhardt, J.: Die Kultur der Renaissance in Italien. Kröner, Leipzig, 1919.
Chaho and Belsunce: Histoire des Basques. Pau, 1847.
Chapuis: Histoire du royaume de Navarre. Paris, 1616.
Clair, P.: La vie de saint Ignace de Loyola. Plon, Nourrit & Cie. Paris, 1891.
Creixel, J.: San Ignacio. Barcelona, 1907.
Crevier: Histoire de l'Université de Paris. Paris, 1900.
Cros, L. J. M.: Saint François de Xavier, sa vie et ses lettres. Toulouse, 1900.
Dittrich, F.: Regesten und Briefe des Kardinals g. Contraini (1483-1542). Brunswick, 1881.
Dufour, P.: Geschichte der prostitution. Gnadenfeld, Berlin.
Dulaure: Histoire de Paris. Lécrivain & Toubon, Paris, 1861.
Errera: L'epoca delle grande scoperte geographiche. Milan, 1902.
Faber, P.: Cartas, Bilboa, 1894.
Favyin: Histoire de Navarre, Paris, 1612.
Feder, A.: Lebenserinnerungen des hl. Ignatius v. Loyola. Pustet, Regensburg, 1922.
Friedensburg, W.: Die ersten Jesuiten in Deutschland. Halle a. S., 1905.
Fuero general de Navarra. Panplona, 1869.
Fund, Ph.: Ignatius v. Loyola. Berlin 1913.
Füssly, P. and Ziegler, H.: Warhaite reiss gen Venedig und Jerusallem. (In the Zürcher Taschenbuch for the year 1884). Höhr, Zurich, 1884.
Garcia, F.: Vida de San Ignacio de Loyola. Barcelona, 1722.
Godet, M.: La congrégation de Montaigu. Champion, Paris, 1912.
Gomez, A.: Historia de la escultura en España desde principios del siglo XVI hasta fines del XVIII y causas de su decadencia. Madrid, 1885.
Greff: Der hl. Ignatius v. Loyola und seine Zeit. Steyl, 1903.
Groffried, J. L.: Newe Archontologia Cosmica etc. Hoffmann, Frankfurt, 1646.
Haebler, K.: geschichte Spaniens unter den Habsburgern. Gotha, 1907.
Hausen, J.: Rheinische Akten zur Geschichte des Jesuitenordens 1542-1582. Bonn, 1896.
Hefele, C. J.: Der Kardinal Ximenes und die kirchlichen Zustände Spaniens am Endedes 15. und Anfang des 16. Jabrh. Laupp, Tübingen, 1844.
Herrera, O. E.: Vida de San Ignacio de Loyola. Barcelona, 1923.
Histoire de Navarre en quatre livres, Bibliothèque Nationale, Paris, Mss. Fr. 25, 242.
Humboldt, W. von: Der Montserrat bei Barcelona. Reimer, Berlin, 1843.
Kerker, M.: Die kirchliche Reform in Italien unmittelbar vor dem Tridentiuum, in the Tüb. Theol. Quartalsschrift 1859, Tübingen.
Kirch, K.: Ignatius v. Loyola (Religiöse Quellenschriften). Schwann, Düsseldorf, 1926.

Bibliography

Kolb, V.: Leben des hl. Ignatius v. Loyola. Pustet, Regensburg, 1920.

Kretschmer: Die Entdeckung Ameridas in ihrer Bedeutung für die Geschichte des Weltbildes. Berlin, 1892.

Kuypers, F.: Spanien unter Kreuz und Halbmond. Klinkhardt & Biermann, Leipzig, 1917.

La Grèze, Bascle de: la Navarre française. Paris, 1882.

Lamarre, C.: Histoire de Sainte-Barbe. Delagrave, Paris, 1900.

Lanciani, R.: The golden days of the Renaissance in Rome. London, 1907.

Lea, H. C.: A history of the inquisition of the Middle Ages. New York, 1900.

Lemmens: Die Franziskaner im Heiligne Lande. Münster, 1916.

Lomer, Dr. G.: Ignatius v. Loyola. Vom Erotiker zum Heiligen. Barth, Leipzig, 1913.

Loyola, Ignatius: Geistliche Briefe und Unterweisungen. 1922.

Luccis: Vida de San Ignacio de Loyola. 1633.

Lucka, E.: Iabrunst und Düsternis. Ein Bild des alten Spaniens. Deutsche Verlagsanstalt, Stuttgart, 1927.

Maffei, P.: De vita et moribus Ignatii Loyolae, etc. Nat. Cholin, Cologne, 1585.

Maffei, P.: Idem liber ex optimis editionibus repraesentatus. Accessit de D. Ignatii Loyolae Gloria liber singularis. Jos. Roello Vulpio auctore. Padua, 1727.

Marcos, B.: Ignacio de Loyola Biografia, Su doctrina philosophica expuesta en los "ejercicios espirituales," Infuencia da esta en el mundo. Madrid, 1900.

Marx, J.: Das Wallfahren in der katholischfen Kirche. Treves, 1842.

Maruenbrecher, W.: Geschichte der katholischen Reformation. 1870.

Menendez Pelayo, M.: Historia de los Heterodoxos Españoles. Cathólica de San José. Madrid.

Morel-Fatio, A.: L'Espagne au XVIe et aux XVIIe siècle. Henninger, Heilbronn, 1878.

Munster: Cosmographei oder Reschreibung alier Länder etc. Basle, 1550.

Notes géographiques sur les villes d'Espagne et sur les évêques de Pampelune. Bibliothèque Nationale, Paris. Mss. Esp. 344.

Orlandini, N.: Historiae Societatis Jesu pars prima, sive Ignatius. Antwerp, 1620.

Pastor, L. von: Geschichte der päpste. Vol. V. Freiburg, 1925.

Perez, A. J.: San Ignacio de Loyola en Azpeitia—Monografia histórica. Barcelona, 1907.

Perez, R.: La Santa Casa de Loyola. Imprenta del Corazón de Jesú. Bilbao, 1891.

Peschel: Geschiehte des Zeitalters der Entdeckungen. Stuttgart, 1858.

Pluvia: Vida de San Ignacio de Loyola. Madrid, 1753.

Polanco: Vita Ignatii Loyolae et rerum Societatis Jesu historia. Rome, new ed., 1903.

Prat, J. M.: Mémoires pour servir à l'histoire du Père Broet et des origines de la Compagnie de Jésus en France. Le Puy, 1885.

Prat, J. M.: Histoire du P. Ribadeneira, disciple de saint Ignace. Aris, 1862,

Prat, J. M.: Le bienheureux Pierre Le Fèvre, premier compagnon de saint Ignace. Lyons, 1873.

Prescott, W. H.: History of the reign of Ferdinand and Isabella, the Catholic. Ger. Tt. Brockhaus, Leipzig, 1842.

Quicherrat, J.: histoire de Sainte-Barbe. Ilachette & co., Paris, 1860-64.

Ramirez, Arcas D. Antonio: Itinerario descriptivo, geográfico, estadistico, y mapa de Navarra. Pamplona, 1848.
Ramon, G.: Compandio de la vida de S. Ignacio de Loyola. Madrid, 1925.
Reiffenbergins, F.: Historia Socciétatis Jesu ad Rhenum inferiorem. Cologne, 1764.
Renassi, F. M.: Storia dell' università degli studi di Roma, detta le Sapienza. Rome, 1803-1804.
Reumont, A. von: Geschichte der Stadt Rom. Vol. III. Berlin, 1870.
Reynier, G.: La vie universitaire dans l'ancienne Espagne, Paris, 1902.
Ribadeneira: Das Leben des hl. Ignatius v. Loyola. Paderborn, 1887.
Rosa, E.: S. Ignazio di Loyola e le origini della Compagnia di Gesù, Rome, 1927.
Roth von Schrechenstein: Die Rittersürde und der Ritterstand. Freiburg, 1886.
Saeter, J.: Ignatius v. Loyola. Copenhagen, 1911.
Schafer, E.: Beiträge zur Geschichte des spanischen Protestantismus und der Inquisition im 16. Jahrh. Gütersloh, 1902.
Tacchi-Venturi, P.: Storia della Compagnia di Gesn in Italia. Rome, 1910, 1922.
Thompson, F.: Saint Ignatius Loyola. Burns & Oates, London, 1909.
Tschudi, L.: Reys– und Pilgerfahrt zum heyligen Grab. 1606.
Weber, E.: Der hl. Ignatius v. Loyola. Rauch, Wiesbaden, 1924.
Wilkens, C. A.: Geschichte des spanischen Protestationsum in 16. Jahrhundert. Gütersloin, 1888.

PART III

Ach, N.: Über die Bergreffsbildung. Amberg, 1921.
Ach, N.: Untersuchungen zur psychologie, Philosophie und Pädagogik. g. Calvör, Göttingen, 1924-25.
Ach, N.: Willensakt und Temperament. Leipzig, 1920.
Adam, K.: Kirche and Seele. Theol. Quartalschrift, 1925.
Adelung: Versuch einer neuen Geschichte des Jesuitenordens, 1869.
Aristotle: Nicomachean Ethics. Ger. tr. By E. Rolfes. Felix Meiner, Leipzig.
Arnim, H. von: Die drei Aristotelischen Ethiken, publication der Akademie der Wissenschaften, No. 202, Vienna, 1924.
Bach, J.: Dogmengeschichte des Mittlelalters, Vienna, 1875.
Bacon, Francis: Novum Organum, Kirchmann, 1870.
Bellarmine, R.: Disputationes de Controversiis Christianae fidei. Paris, 1620.
Bezold, F. von, Gothein, E., Koser, R.: Staat und Gesellschaft der neueren zeit (his zur französ. Revolution). Teubner, Berlin-Leipzig, 1908.
Binswanger, L.: Einführung in die Probleme der allgermeinen Psychologie. J. Springer, Berlin, 1922.
Boethius: The Consolations of Philosophy. Ger. tr. Reclam. Leipzig.
Bournichon, J.: La Compagnie de Jésus en France, Beauchesne, Paris, 1914.

Bibliography

Brentano, Fr.: Aristoteles. Quelle & Meyer, Leipzig, 1911.

Brodrick, J.: The life and work of Cardinal Bellarmine, S. J. Burns, Oates & Washbourne, London, 1928.

Bühler, K.: Tatsachen und Probleme zu einer Psychologie der Denkvorgänge. Archiv f. d. ges. Psychologie, Vols. IX and XII.

Buss, F. J.: Die Gesellschaft Jesu. Mainz, 1853.

Calot, Fr. And Michon, L. M.: Port-Royal et le Jansénisme. Morancé, Paris.

Cassiodorus: Works.

Cathrein, V.: Moralphilosophie. Vier-Quellen-Verlag, Leipzig, 1924.

Cousin, V.: Madame de Longeuville. Paris, 1859.

Dante: Works. Max Hesse, Leipzig.

Driesch, H.: Grundprobleme der Psychologie. E. Reinicke, Leipzig, 1926.

Duns Scotus: Works, edited by Wadding, 1639, New ed. 1891.

Fischer, K.: Geschichte der neurn Philosophie. Vol. I. Friedrich Bassermann, Mannheim, 1865.

Fonatine, A.: L'esthétique Janséniste, in: Revue de lart ancient et modern. 1908.

Fouqueray, H.: Francis Bacon. London, 1881.

Fröbes, J.: Lehrbuch der experimentellen Psychologie. Herder, Freiburg, 1923.

Gazier, A.: Racine et Port-Royal, in: Revue d'histoire littéraire. Paris, 1900.

Gazier, C.: Pascal et Port-Royal, in: Revue hebdomadaire. Plon, Paris, 1923.

Gazier, C." Madame de Sévigné et Port-Royal, in: Le correspondant. Paris, 1926.

Gazier, C.: Histoire générale du movement janséniste depuis ses origins jusqu'à nos jours. Champion, 1922.

Génin, F.: Les Jésuites et lUniversité. Paulin, Paris, 1844.

Girgensohn, Karl: Der seelische Aufbau des relitiösen Lebens. Leipzig, 1921.

Gomperz, H.: Über die Wahrscheinlichkeit der Willensentscheidungen, in; Sitzungsberichte der k. k. Akademie der Wissenschaften, Vol. 149, No. 3. Vienna.

Gomperz, H.: Das Problem der Willensfreiheit. Diederichs, Jena, 1907.

Gomperz, H.: Die Lebensauffassungen der griechischen Philosophen und das Ideal der inneren Freiheit. Diederichs, Jena.

Gompers, Th.: Griechische Denker. Veit & Co., Leipzig, 1906.

Gruehn, W.: Das Werterlebuis, eine religionpsychologische Studie auf experimenteller Grundlage. Leipzig, 1924.

Gundlach, G.: Zur Soziologic der katholischen Ideenwelt und des Jesuitenordens. Herder, Freiburg, 1927.

Hallays, A.: Les Solitaires de port-Royal. Plon, Paris.

Harenberg, J. Ch.: Pragmatische Geschichte des Ordens der Jesuiten seit ihrem Ursprung bis auf gegenwärtige Zeit. Halle, 1760.

Hartmann, L. M.: Welteschichte in gemeinverständlicher Darsteilung. Vol. III (von K. Kaser). Perthes, Gotha, 1924.

Hempelmann, F.: Teirpsychologie. Akadem. Verlagsges. Leipzig, 1926.

Henning, H.: Psychologie der Gegenwart. Mauritius-Verlag, Berlin, 1925.

Heomigswald, R.: Grundfragen der Denkpsychologie. B. G. Teubner, Leipzig, 1925.

Hume, D.: An inquiry concerning human understanding. Ger. tr. Felix Meiner, Leipzig.
Hume, D.: dialogues concerning natural religion. Ger. tr. Felix Meiner, Leipzig.
Jacobi: Die Lehre des Pelagius. Leipzig, 1842.
James, W.: The varieties of religious experience. Longmans, Green & Co., New York, 1910.
James, W.: Essays in radical empiricism, 1912
James, W.: The principles of psychology, 1890.
Jansen, B.: Wege der Weltweisheit. Herder, Freiburg, 1924.
Jermoe, St.: Works, in: Bibliothek der Kirchevӓter. Kempten, 1872.
Kant, I.: Kritik der praktischen Vernunft. Reclam, Leipzig.
Kant, I.: Kritik der reinen Vernunft. Reclam, Leipzig.
Kellermann, B.: Der ethische Monotheismus der propheten etc. Schwetschke & Sohn, Berlin, 1917.
Keifl: Katholische Weltanschauung und modernes Denken. Regensburg, 1923.
Koyre, A.: Descartes und die Scholastik. Cohen, Bonn, 1923.
Külpe, O.: Über die modern Psychologie des Denkens, Internat. Monatsschrift für Wissenschaft, Kunst u. Technik. Vol. VI. A. Scherl, Berlin, 1912.
Külpe, O.: Vorlesungen über Psychologie, edited by Bühler, Leipzig, 1922.
Lämmer, H.: Die vortridentinisch-katholische Theologie des Reformationszeitalters. Berlin, 1858.
Lämmer, H.: Zur Kirchengeschichte des 16, und 17., Jahrh. Freiburg, 1863.
Leibniz, G. W.: Theodicy. Ger. tr. Dürr, Leipzig.
Leibuiz: System of Theology. Ger. tr. By Dr. Räss and Dr. Weis. Simon Müller, Mainz, 1825.
Lewin, K.: Vorsatz, Wille und Bedürinis. J. Springer, Berlin, 1926.
Lindworsky, J.: Der Willie. J. A. Barth, Leipzig, 1923.
Lindworsky, J.: Das schulssfolgernde Denken, experimentell-psychologische. Untersuchungen. Freiburg, 1916.
Linke, P. F.: Grundfragen der Wahrnehmungslchre. E. Reinhardt, Munich, 1918.
Lipps, G. F.: Das problem der Willensfreiheit. Teubner, Leipzig, 1918.
Loeb, J.: Die Bedeutung der Tropismen für die Psychologie. A. Barth, Leipzig, 1909.
Luther, M.: Works. Erlanger Edition. 1826ff.
Marbe, K.: Experimentell-psychol. Untersuchungen über das Urteil. Leipzig, 1901.
Marbe, K.: Fortschritte der Psychologie und ihrer Anwendungen. B. G. Teubner, Leipzig.
Mausback, J.: Grundlage und Ausbildung des Charakters nach dem hl. Thomas von Aquin. Freiburg, 1920.
Menzer, P.: persönlichkeit und Philosophie. M. Niemeyer, Halle, 1920.
Moog, W.: Eine kritische Übersicht der Philosophie der Gegenwart (Jahrbücher der Philosophie). E. S. Mittler & Sohn, Berlin, 1927.
Müller, G. E.: Abriss der psychologie. Vandenhocck & Ruprecht, Göttingen, 1924.
Oesterreich, T. K.: Das Weltbild der Gegenwart. E. S. Mittler & Sohn, Berlin, 1925.
Petersen, P.: Wilhelm Wundt und seine Zeit. F. Frommann, Stuttgart, 1925.

Bibliography

Pfleiderer, G.: Gottfried Wilhelm Leibniz. 1870.
Pilatus (Viktor Naumann): Der Jesuitismus. Manz, Regensburg, 1905.
Plato: The Republic. (Ger. tr. By O. Apelt.) Felix Meiner, Leipzig.
Pourrat, P.: La spiritualité chrétienne. Paris, 1921.
Quetelet, L. A. J.: Sur l'homme et le développenient de ses facultés. Paris, 1835.
Racine, J.: Abrégé de l'historie de Port-Royal. Soc. Fr. D'Impr., Paris, 1908.
Reik, The.: Dogma und Zqangsidee. Int. psychoanalytischer Verlag, Vienna, 1927.
Reuchlin: Pascals Leben und der Geist seiner Schriften. Stuttgart, 1840.
Riel, C. G. von: Beitrag zur Geschichte der Congregationes de Auxiliis. Constance, 1921.
Russell, B.: Skeptical essays. Norton & Co. New York, 1928.
Russell, B.: The analysis of mind. G. Allen & Unwin, London, 1921.
Sainte-Beuve: Histoire de Port-Royal.
Saupe, E.: Einführung in die neuere Pshchologie. A. W. Zickfeldt, Osterwieck am Harz, 1928.
Schopenhauer, A.: Vierfache Wurzel des Satzes vom zureichenden Grunde. Piper, Munich.
Schopenhauer, A.: Die Welt als Wille und Vorstellung. Piper, Munich.
Schopenhauer, A.: Über den Willen. Piper, Munich.
Selz, O.: Über die Gestze des georgneten Denkverlaufes. Stuttgart, 1913.
Sigwart: Der Begriff des Wollens und scin Verhältnis zum Begriff der ursache. Kleine Schriften, Vol. II.
Sommer,, R.: Tierpsychologie. Quelle & Meyer, Leipzig, 1925.
Strauss, D. Fr.: Voltaire. Six lectures. Alfred Kröner, Leipzig, 1907.
Überweg-Heinze: Grundriss der Geschichte der Philosophie. Berlin, 1915ff.
Voltaire: Correspondance générale.
Voltaire: Siècle de Louis XIV.
Watson, J. B.: Behaviorism. New York, 1925.
Watson, J. B.: Behavoir: an introduction to comparative psychology. New York, 1914.
Weigand, W.: Der Hof Ludwigs XIV. Nach den Denkwürdigkeiten des Herzogs von Saint-Simon. Insel-Verlag, Leipzig, 1913.
Wentscher, E.: Der Wille. Teubner, Leipzig, 1910.
Wessenberg: Die grossen Kirchenyersammhungen.
Wiggers: Darstellung des Augustinismus und Pelagianismus. Hamburg, 1833.
Wolf. P. Ph.: Allgemeine Geschichte der Jesuiten von dem Ursprung ihres Ordens bis auf gegenwärtige Zeiten. Orell, Zurich, 1789-92.
Wörter: Der Pelagianismus. Freiburg, 1874.
Wundt, W.: Grundzüge der phsiologischen psychologic. Vol. I, 7th ed. 1925; Vol. II, 6th ed. 1910, vol. III, 6th ed. 1911, Leipzig.
Wundt, W.: Einführung in die Psychologie. Leipzig, 1920.
Ziehen, T.: Psychophysiolog. Erkenntuistheorie. G. Fischer, Jena, 1898.

The Power and Secret of the Jesuits

PART IV

Arcana Societatis Jesu cum instrucione secreta pro superioribus. Prague, 1635.

Arnim, H. von: Die stoiche Lehre von Fatum und Willensfreihueit, in: Wissenschaftl. Beilage zum 18. Jahresber. D. Philos. Ges. A. d. Universität. Vienna, 1905.

Arnould, M. A.: Les Jésuites depuis seur origine jusqu'à nos jours. Dutertre, Paris, 1846.

Auerbach, E.: die Prophetie. Jüdischer Verlag, Berlin, 1920.

Bar, von: Handbuch des deutschen Strafrechts, 1882.

Basil, St.: Works, in: Bibliothek der Kirchenväter, Kempten, 1873ff.

Beccaria, C.: Über Verbrechen und Strafen. Manz, Vienna, 1876.

Bekker: Theorie des heutigen deutschen Strafrechts, 1857-9.

Bergbohm, K.: jurisprudenz und Rechtsphilosophie. Duncker & Humblot, Leipzig, 1892.

Bergmann, H. A.: Jesuitenpest. 1856.

Berner: Grundlinien der kriminalistischen Imputationslehre. 1843.

Binder, J.: Philosophie des Rechts. Stilke, Berlin, 1924.

Boys, A. du: Histoire du droit criminal des peuples anciens. Paris, 1845.

Brod, M.: Heidentum—Christentum—Judentum. Kurt Wolff, Munich, 1921.

Busembaum, H.: Medulla Theologiae moralis. Leyden, 1686.

Cathrein, V.: Die Grundbegriffe des Strafrechts. Eine rechtsphilosophische Studie. Herder, Freiburg, 1905.

Cathrein, V.: Die Einheit des sittlichen Bewusstseins der Menschheit. Herder, Freiburg, 1914.

Cicero: Works, Vols. 68 to 72, De officiis. Langenscheidtsche Verlagsburchhandlung, Berlin.

Dallas, R. C.: Über den Order der Jesuiten. Beyer & Co. Düsseldorf, 1820.

Deym, F: Beiträge zur Aufklärung über die Gemeinschädlichkeit des Jesuitenordens. J. F. Hartknoch, Leipzig, 1872.

Dreydorff, J. G.: Die Moral der Jesuiten, Dargestellt von einem frommen Katholiken, Blaise Pascal. 1893.

Duhr, B.: Hundert Jesuitenfabeln. Herder, Freiburg, 1913.

Ellendorf: Moral und Politik der Jesuiten. Darmstadt, 1840.

Erb, R.: Vom Wesen des Rechts und der Sittlichkeit. Helbing & Lichtenhahn, Basle, 1925.

Extraits des assertions dangereuses et pernicieuses, en tout genre, que les soi-disants Jésuites ont, dans tous les temps et persévéramment, soutenues, enseignées et publiées dans leurs livres avec l'approbation de leurs supérieurs et généraux. Paris, 1761.

Fichte, J. G.: Machiavellis Politik. Reclam, Leipzig.

Flores, Theologiae moralis Jesuitarum. Celle, 1873.

Frank: Vorstellung und Wille in der modernen Doluslchre. Zeitschr. f. ges. Strair. X.

Frank, E.: Plato und die sogenannten Pythagoreer. Halle, 1923.

Bibliography

Gomperz, H.: Die Lebensauffassungen der griechischen Philosophen und das Ideal der inneren Freiheit. Eugen diederichs, Jena, 1927.

Grassmann, R.: Auszürge aus der vou den Päpsten Pius IX. Und Leo XIII. Ex cathedra als Norm für die römisch-katholische Kirche sandtionierten moraltheologie des heiligen Dr. Alphonsus Maria dei Liguori und die furchtbare Geiahr dieser Mroaltheologie für die Sittlichkeit der Völker. Stettin, 1901.

Gury, J. P.: Moraltheologie, Manz, Regensburg, 1869.

Hammerstein, L.: Die Jesuitenmoral. Paulinus-Druckerei, Treves, 1893.

Hegel, G. W. F.: Works. Vol. VIII. Duncker & Humblot. Berlin, 1840.

Heilig, E. M.: theologia moralis. Le Clerc, Paris.

Heiner, F.: die Jesuiten und ihre Gegner. Münchner Volksschriftenberlag, Munich, 1906.

Henke: Georg Calixtus und seine Zeit. 1853.

Henne am Rhyn, O.: Die Jesuiten, deren Geschichte, Verfassung, Moral, Politik, Religion and Wissenschaft. Max Spohr, Leipzig, 1894.

Huber, F.: Jesuitenmoral. Haller, Bern, 1870.

Jaeger, W.: Aristoteles. Berlin, 1923.

Jansen, J. and Henze: Der hl. Liguori und die S. J. 1920

Jesuiten, Die. Ein Ruf der Warning und Erwechung an alle Freunde der Wahrheit und des Friedens. 1845.

Jesuitismus, Der, getreu nach der Natur gezeichnet und den männern der Kirche, des Staates und des Volkes zur Betrachtung vorgesteilt von einem bekehrten Jesuiten. Otto Wigand, Leipzig, 1872.

Jodl, F.: Geschichte der Ethik als philosophische Wissenschaft. J. g. Cotta, Stuttgart, Berlin, 1920.

Jovy, E.: Pascal et saint Ignace. Champion, Paris, 1923.

Keim, The.: Rom und das Christentum. 1881.

Laistner: Das Recht in der Strafe. 1872.

Lederer, Ph.: Schulchan Aruch. Pilsen, 1900.

Lenz, A.: Ein Strafgesetzbuch ohne Schuld und Strafe. Ulrich Moser, Graz, 1922.

Leu, B.: Beitrag zur Würdigung des Jesuitenordens. Lucerne-Berne, 1840.

Lichtenfels, J.: Lehrbuch der Moralphilosophie oder der Metaphysik der Sitten. J. G. Teubner, Vienna, 1846.

Linss, C. W.: Das Handbuch der theologischen Moral des Jesuiten Gury und die christliche Ethik. Bindernagel & Schimpff, Friedberg, 1869.

Lisst, Fr. Von: Lehrbuch des deutschen Strafrechts, 1894.

Löffler, A.: Die Schuldformen des Strafrechts. Hirschfeld, Leipzig, 1895.

Loiseleur: Les crimes et les peines dans pantiquité et dans les temps modernes. Paris, 1860.

Lorulot, A.: Les secrets des Jésuites. Editions de L'idée. Book XII, May 1928.

Meffert, F.: Der hl. Alions v. Liguori, 1901.

Ménorval, E. de: Bourdaloue, vie d'un Jésuite. Champion, Paris, 1897.

Meyer, H.: Platon und die Aristotelische Ethik. Munich, 1919.

Mischna oder der Text des Talmuds. Jacob Christoph Posch, Onolzback, 1762.
Mix, g.: Aus dem Schuldbuch des Jesuitenordens. 1911.
Monita secreta. (Ger. tr.: Die geheimen Verordnungen der Gesellschaft Jesu.) Paderborn, 1853.
Natorp, P.: Platons Ideenlehre. Leipzig, 1903.
Nippold, F. W. F.: Der Jesuitenorden von seiner Wiederherstellung bis auf die Gegenwart.
Osiander, C. N. von and Schwab, G.: Griechische Prosaiker in neucn Übersetzungen. Aristoteles' Werke. J. B. Metzler, Stuttgart, 1856.
Pascal, B: Pensées. Ger. tr. Reclam, Leipzig.
Pascal: Lettres Provinciales, Paris, 1836.
Pascal: Provinzialbriefe über die Moral und Politik der Jesuiten. G. Reimer, Berlin, 1830
Perrault: La morale des Jésuites. Mons, 1702.
Pilatus (Dr. Viktor Naumann): Quos ego! Fehdebriefe wider den Grafen Hoensbroech. Manz, Regensburg, 1903.
Plato: The Republic (Ger. tr. By Apelt). F. Meiner, Leipzig.
Reichmann, M.: Der Zweek heiligt die Mittel. Ein Beitrag zur Geschichte der christlichen Sittenlehre. Herder, Freiburg, 1903.
Sauer, W.: Gesetz und Rechtsgefühl., Berlin, 1911.
Schilling, Dr. O.: Moraltheologie. Herder, Freiburg, 1922.
Schimberg, A.: L'éducation morale dans les Collèges de la Compagnie de Jésus en France. Champion, Paris, 1913.
Schmidt, I.: Die Ethik der alten Griechen. 1882.
Schmitt, A.: Grundzüge der geschlechtlichen Sittlichkeit. Tyrolia, Innsbruck, 1925.
Smith, Adam: Theory of Moral Sentiments, Ger. tr. Brunswick, 1770.
Sommervogel, C.: Dictionnaire des ouvrages Anonymes et Pseudonymes publiés par des Réligieux de la Compagnie de Jésus. Société Bibliographique, Paris.
Stahl: Philosophie des Rechts. Heidelberg, 1847.
Stammler: lehrbuch der Rechtsphilosophie. De Gruyter, Berlin, 1922.
Thamin, R.: Un problème moral dans l'antiquité. Étude sur la casuistique Stoicienne. 1884.
Thomissen: Études sur l'histoire du droit criminal des peuples ancieens, Paris, 1869.
Viardot, L.: Les Jésuites jugés. Pagnerre, Paris, 1857.
Weber, C. J.: Die Jesuiten, ihre Lehre und ihr Wirken in Kirche, Staat und Familie. E. H. Mayer, Cologne, 1874.
Welcker: Die letzten Gründe von Recht, Staat und Strafe. Giessen, 1813.
Werner, K.: Franz Suarez. Regensburg, 1865.
Westermarck, E. A.: The origin and development of the moral ideas. Ger. tr.
Zeller: Die Philosophie der Griechen. 1892.
Zimmermann, R.: Das Rechtsprinzip bei Leibniz. W. Braumüller, Vienna, 1852.

Bibliography

PART V

Acosta, F. P.: Las Misiones del Paraguay. Castello, Palamos, 1920.

Alegre, F.: Hist. de la Comp. de Jesús en Nueva España.

Alsop, G.: A character of the province of Maryland. London, 1666.

American Archives. Washington, 1837.

Anderson, J. S. M.: The history of the Church of England in the colonies and foreign dependencies of the British Empire. London, 1845-1848.

André, M.: Les missions dominicaines dans l'Extrême-Orient. Paris, 1865.

Apologie des Jésuites, sur leur conduite dans les affaires de la Chine. 1755.

Archives of Maryland. Baltimore, 1883.

Avisi del Giapone. Milan.

Ayres, C.: Fernão Mendes Pinto e o Japão. Lisbon, 1906.

Azara, F. de: Historia del Paraguay.

Bach, M.: Die Jesuiten und ihre Mission Chiquitos in Südamerika. Eine historisch-ethnographische Schilderung. Leipzig, 1843.

Bancroft, G.: History of the United States.

Barreto, F.: Relation des missions de la province de Malabar. Tournay, 1645.

Bartoli: Dell' istoria della Compagnia di Gesù. L'Asia, 1653.

Belevitch-Stanhevitch: La Chine en France au temps de Louis XIV. Paris 1910.

Bellessort, A.: La société japonaise. Paris, 1902.

Bertrand, J.: La mission du Maduré d'après des documents inédits. Paris, 1847-54.

Boéro, J.: Les 205 martyrs du Japon. Paris, 1868.

Bozman, J. L.: the history of Maryland, from its first settlement in 1633 to the Restoration in 1660. Baltimore, 1837.

Braun, B.: Vida, virtudes y santa muerte del P. Fr. H. Glandorff. Mexico, 1764.

Brounsberger, O.: Rückblick auf das katholische Ordenswesen im 19. Jahrhundert. Herder, Freiburg i. Br., 1901.

Brinkley, C.: Japan, its history, arts and literature. 1901.

Brodhead. J. R.: Documents relative to the colonial history of the State of New York. Albany, N. Y., 1856-1861.

Brou, A. and Gilbert G.: Jésuites Missionaires. Spcs, Paris, 1924.

Brou, A.: Saint François Xavier. Paris, 1922.

Burk, J.: The history of Virginia, from its first settlement to the present day. Petersburg, Va., 1804.

Calendars of State Papers: Colonial Series. 1860-1901, London.

Campanella, ein Dichterphilosoph der italienischen Renaissance. Zeitschr. Für Kulturgeschichte, part I, 1893-94.

Campbell, B. U.: Father Andrew White and his companions, the first missionaries of Maryland. Baltimore, 1841.

The Power and Secret of the Jesuits

Carne, J.: Lives of eminent missionaries. London, 1832.

Cartas del Japôn. Alealá, 1575.

Cartas que of padres e irmãos da Companhia de Jesus escreueâro dos Reynos de Japão e China. Evora, 1598.

Chamberlain, B. H.: Things Japanese. Ger. tr. H. Bondy, Berlin, 1912.

Chang Yin Lin: History of the introduction of European science in China during the Ming and Ts'ing dynasties. Ts'ing Hua Journal, Peking.

Charlevoix, F. de: Geschichte von Paraguay und den Missionen der Gesellschait Jesu in diesen Ländern. Mechitaristen-Kongregation, Vienna, 1831.

Charpentier-Cossigny: Voyage à Canton. 1699.

Cordier, H.: La suppression de la Compagnie de Jésus et la mission de Péking. Leyden, 1918.

Cordier, H.: Histoire générale de la Chine et de ses relations avec les pays étrangers. Paris, 1920.

Cottineau de Kloguen: An historical account of Goa. Bombay, 1911.

Criminale, Antonio: Der srste Märtyrer der Gesellschaft Jesu. Herder, Freiburg i. Br., 1918.

Cros, L. J. M.: Saint François de Xavier, Paris, 1894.

Cros, L. J. M.: Saint François de Xavier, sa vie et ses lettres. Toulouse-Paris, 1901.

Cros, L. J. M.: Saint François de Xavier, son pays, sa famille, sa vie (Documents nouveaux). Paris, 1903.

Dohmen: Robert de Nobili, S. J. Ein Beitrag zur Geschichte der Missionsmethode und der Indologie. Münster, 1924.

Delplace: Selectae Indiarum Epistolae. Florence, 1887.

Delplace, L.: Le Catholicisme en Japon, Mechlin, 1908.

Description de l'empire Chinois. 1785.

Dobrizhofer: historia de Abiponibus. Vienna, 1784.

Doyle, J. A.: The English in America. Vol. I. Virginia, Maryland, and the Carolinas. London, 1882.

Dubois, Abbé: Moeurs, institutions et cérémonies des peuples de l'Inde. Paris, 1825.

Duhalde: Description géographique, historique etc. de l'empire de la Chine et de la Tartaric chinoise. Paris, 1735.

Egauer, A.: Die Missiongeschichte späterer Zeiten: Briefe aus Japan. Augsburg, 1795-1798.

Enrich, F.: Historia de la Compañia de Jesús en Chile. Rosal, Barcelona, 1881.

Epistolae Goanae et Malabaricae 1545-60. Coinbra, 1907.

Excerpta ex Diversis Litteris Missionariorum ab Anno 1638 ad Annum 1677. Baltimore.

Fassbinder, M.: Der "Jesuitenstaat" in Paraguay. Halle, 1926.

Florenz, K.: Die historischen Quellen der Shinto-Relition. Göttingen, 1919

Foley, H.: Records of the English Province of the Society of Jesus. London, 1877.

Fonseca, J. N.: An historical and archaeological sketch of the city of Goa. Bombay, 1878.

Forke, A.: Die Gedankenwelt des chinesischen Kulturkreises. Munich-Berlin, 1927.

Bibliography

Frois, P. L.: Die Geschichte Japans. Leipzig, 1925.

Gardiner, S. R.: History of England from the accession of James I to the outbreak of the Civil War, 1603-1624. London, 1883-84.

Genelin, P.: Die Reunionen der Jesuitenn in Paraguay. Leo-gesellschaft, Vienna, 1895.

Geschichte der katholischen Mission im Kaiserreiche China von ihrem Ursprunge an bis auf unsere Zeit. Mechitaristen-Kongregation. Vienna, 1845.

Gothein, E.: Der christlich-soziale Staat der Jesuiten in Paraguay. Leipzig, 1883.

Granet, M.: La religion des Chinois. Paris, 1922.

Greff, N.: Leben des hl. Franz Xaver. Einsiedeln, 1905.

Griffis, W. E.: The religions of Japan from the dawn of history to the era of Méiji. New York, 1896.

Groteken, A.: Die Franziskaner an Fürstenböien bis zur Mitte des 14. Jahrunderts. Buschmann, Münster, 1928.

Groot, J. J. M. de: Universismus. Die Grundlage der Religion und Ethik des Staatswesens und der Wissenschaften Chinas. G. Reimer, Berlin, 1918.

Groot, J. J. M. de: Chinesische urkunden zur Geschichte Asiens. Berlin and Leipzig, 1926.

Haas, H.: Geschichte des Christentums in Japan. Tokio, 1902.

Hamy, A.: Documents pour server à l'histoire des domiciles de la Compagnie de Jésus dans le monde entire de 1540 à 1775. A. Picard, Paris.

Hasse, K. P.: Der kommunistische Gedanke in der Philosophie. F. Meiner, Leipzig, 1919.

Hawks, F. L.: Contributions to the ecclesiastical history of the United States of America. New York, 1836, 1839.

Hayus, J.: De rebus Japonicis. Antwerp, 1605.

Hearn, Lafeadio: Japan, an attempt at interpretation. Ger. tr. Rütten & Leining, Frankfurt a. M., 1911.

Heilige, Der, Franz Xaver in Miyako. Herder, Freiburg i. Br., 1921.

Hermann, H.: Chinesische Geschichte. Stuttgart, 1912.

Hernandez: La Comp. de Jesús en las Repúblicas del Sud de América 1836-1914. Barcelona, 1914.

Hernandez, P.: Organisación social de las doctrinas Guaranis de la Comp. de. J. Barcelona, 1913.

Hinneberg: Die orientalischen Religionen. Berlin, 1906.

Hisho Saito: Geschichte Japans. F. Dummier, Berlin, 1911.

Histoire des differens entre les missionaires Jésuites. 1692-93.

Höver, F.: Der heiligre Pater Claver. Laumann, Dülmen, 1905.

Hughes, T.: Missionary countries, old and new. The American Catholic Quarterly Review, January, 1899.

Humboldt, A. von: Reise in die Äquinoctial-Gegenden des neuen Kontinents. Cotta'sche Buchhhandlung, Stuttgart, 1874.

Huonder, A.: Paraguay, in: Wetzers und Weltes Kirchenlexikon. Freiburg i. Br., 1895.

The Power and Secret of the Jesuits

Huonder, A.: Deutcsche Jesuitissionäre des 17. und 18. Jahrhunderts. Herder, Freiburg i. Br., 1899.

Ibagnez, P.: Jesuitisches Reich in Paraguay. Cologne, 1774.

Informação das cousas de Malauco. Lisbon, 1856.

Jenkins, R. C.: The Jesuits in China and the legation of Cardinal de Tournon. London, 1894.

Jervière, J. de la: Les anciennes missions de la Compagnie de Jésus en Chine. Shanghai, 1924.

Kaempfer, E.: The history of Japan. Glasgow, 1906.

Kempf, K.: Die Heiligkeit der Gesellschaft Jesu. Benziger & Co., Einsiedeln, 1925.

Kip, W. I.: The early Jesuit missions in North America. London, 1847.

Kircher, Ath.: China monumentis qua sacris qua profanes illustrate. Amsterdam, 1667.

Kobler, A.: P. Florian Baucke, ein Jesuit in Paraguay. Regensburg, 1870.

Kobler, A.: Der christliche Kommunismus in den Reduktionen von Paraguay, ein Kulturbild aus dem vorigen Jahrhundert. Würzburg, 1877.

Kraus, J. B.: Der hl. Franz Xaver. Einsiedeln, 1923.

Krose, H. A.: Katholische Missionsstatistik. Herder, Freiburg i. Br., 1908.

Ku Hung Ming: Chinas Verteidigung gegen europäische Ideen. Jena, 1911.

Laske, F.: Der ostasiatische Einfluss auf die Baukunst des Abendlands. Berlin, 1909.

Laures, J.: Der Sklave der Negersklaven. Einsiedein, 1922.

Le Comte, Louis: Das heutige Sina (from the French). Frankfurt a. M. and Leipzig 1699.

Lemmens: Die Heidenmissionen des Spätmisstlalters. Münster, 1919.

Lettre d'un docteur de l'ordre de S. Dominique sur les cérémonies de la Chine. Cologne, 1700.

Lettres édifiantes et curieuses concernant l'Asie, pAfrique et l'Amérique. Société du Panthéon Littéraire. Paris, 1843.

Lettres édifiantes et curieuses, écrites des missions étrangéres. Paris, 1749.

Lettres sur la Morale de Confucius, Philosophe de la Chine, 1680.

Lozano, J. de: Hist. de la Comp. d. J. en la prov. del Paraguay. Madrid, 1639, and Bilbao, 1892.

Mackenzie: Christianity in Travancore. Trivandrum, 1901.

Margraf, J.: Kirche und Sklaverei seit der Entdeckung Amerikas. Tübingen, 1865.

Maso, P. M. S.: Misiones Jesuiticas de Filipinas. Manila, 1924.

Meiner, Ch.: Übersetzungen der Abhandlungen chinesischer Jesuiten über die Geschichte, Wissenschaften und Künste, Sitten und Gebräuche der Chinesen. Leipzig, 1778.

Mergentheim, L., and Louis, P. J.: Priester und mission. Xaveriusverlag. Aix-la-Chapelle, 1918.

Merkel, f. R.: Leibniz' und die Chinamission. Leipzig, 1920.

Missiones, Las, Dominicanas. Avila, 1920.

Missionslage, Die Asiatische, zur Zeit des hl. Franz Xaver. Aix-la-Chapelle, 1918.

Montesquieu: De l'esprit des lois. Geneva, 1748.

Monumenta Xaveriana (Monumenta Historica Societatis Jesu). Madrid, 1900.

Morale, La, de Confucius, Philosophe de la Chine. 1688.

Bibliography

Morris, J. G.: The Lords Baltimore. Baltimore, 1874.

Murdoch, J.: A history of Japan, with maps by Isoh Yamagata. Vol. II. 1909.

Noyaoka: Histoire des relations du Japon avec l'Europe aux seizième et dix-septième siècles. Paris, 1905.

Newhof: L'ambassade vers l'Empereur de la Chine. Paris, 1665.

Noer, von: Kaiser Akbar der Grosse. Leyden, 1880.

Opel, A.: Entstehung und Niedergang des spanischen Wiltreichs. Hamburg, 1897.

Osbeck, P.: Reise nach Ostindien und china. J. Chr. Koppe, rostock, 1765.

Pachtler, G. M.: Das Christentum in tongking und Cochinchina. Chümingh, Paderborn, 1861.

Pagès, L.: histoire de la religion chrétienne au Japon 1598-1651. Paris, 1869.

Parkman, F.: The Jesuits in North America in the seventeenth century. Boston, 1867.

Pastelis, P.: Historia de la Comp. de Jesús en la prov. del Paraguay. Madrid, 1912.

Pastells, P.: Organización de la Iglesia y órdenes religiosas en el virreynato del Peru.

Pastells, P.: Misión de la Compañia de Jesús de Filipinas en el siglo XIX. Carlos Aparici, Barcelona.

Pastells, P.: Labor evangélica, Ministerios apostólicos de los Obreros de la Compañia de Jesús en las Islas Filipinas por el P. Francisco de Colin. Carlos Aparici, Barcelona.

Patiss, P.G.: Das Apostolat und Martyrium der Geselllschaft Jesu in Japan. L. Mayer, Vienna, 1863.

Perrez de Rivas, A.: Crónica y historia religiosa de la prov. de la Comp. de Méjico.

Perry, W. S.: Historical collections relating to the American Colonial Church. (various titles).

Pfotenhauer.: Die Missionen der Jesuiten in Paraguay, 1891-93.

Platel: Memoires historiques sur les affaires des Jésuites avec le S. Siège.

Plaizweg, Lebensbilder deutscher Jesuiten in auswürtigen Missionen. Paderborn, 1882.

Raynal, a.: Histoire philosophique du commerce et des éstblissements des Européens dans les deux Indes. Paris, 1780.

Rebello, G.: Historia das Ilhas de Maiuco, 1561.

Records of the American Catholic Historical Society. Philadelphia, 1884.

Reichwein, A.: China und Europa im 18. Jahrhundert. Oesterheld & co., Berlin, 1923.

Relatio Itineris in marylandian. Declaratio Coloniae Comini Baronis de Baltimore. Excertpa ex Diversis Litteris Missionariorum ab Anno 1635 ad Annum 1638. Baltimore.

Relations des Jésuites, contenant ce qui s'est passé de plus remauquable dans les missions des pères de la Compagnie de Jésus dans la Nouvelle-France. Quebec, 1858.

Relation du bannissement des Jésuites de la Chine. 1769.

Republik, die, der Jesuiten oder das umgestürzte Paraguay. Amsterdam, 1758.

Robertson, W.: History of the Emperor Charles V. London, 1769.

Rochemonteix, P. C. de: Joseph Amiot et les derniers survivants de la mission française de Péking, 1750-1795. Paris, 1915.

Rosa, E.: Los Jesuitas desde sus origins hasta neustros dias.

Rossi, G. M.: Martiri Tonkinesi nel 1723. Festa, Naples, 1914.

The Power and Secret of the Jesuits

Ruis de Montoya: Conquista spiritual hecha por ins relitiosos de la Compañia de Jesús en las provincias del Paraguay, Pariná, Uruguay y Tape. Madrid, 1639.

Russell, B.: the problem of china. Ger. tr. Munich, 1925.

Sainte-Foi, Ch.: Vie du P. Jean d'Almeida, Apôtre de Brésil. Paris, 1859.

Saldamando: Los antiguos Jesuitas del Perú. Lima, 1882.

Satow, E.: The church of Yamaguchi, from 1550 to 1586. Transactions of the Asiatic Soc. of Japan.

Scharf, J. T.: history of Maryland from the earliest period to the present day. Baltimore, 1879.

Schmidt, F.: Der christlich-soziale Staat der Jesuiten in Paraguay in wirtschaftlicher und staatsrechtlicher Bedeutung. Volksverein-Verlag, M.-Gladbach, 1913.

Schurkammer, G.: Der hl. Franziskus Xaverius, der Apostel des Ostens. Aix-la-Chapelle, 1920.

Schurhammer, G.: Der heilige Franz Xaver, der Apostel von Indien und Japan. Herder, Freiburg, i. Br., 1925.

Schurhammer, G.: Franziskus Xaverius. Xaveriusverlag, Aix-la-Chappelle, 1922.

Schurhammer, G.: Shin-To, der Weg der Götter in Japan. K. Schroeder, Bonn-Leipzig, 1923.

Schuster, A.: Paraguay, Land, Volk, Geschichte, Wirtschaftsleben und Kolonisation. Strecker & Schröder, Stuttgart, 1929.

Sepp, A., and Bömn, A.: Reise-Beschreibung. P. N. Führ, Buchdr., Brixen, 1696.

Shea, J. G.: Life of Father I. Jogues. New York, 1885.

Smith, W.: The history of the province of New York, from the first discovery to the year 1732. London, 1757.

Soulié de Morant, G.: L'épopée des Jésuites français en Chine 1534-1928. b. Grasset, Paris, 1928.

Steichen, M. E.: Les daimyo chrétiens. Paris, 1904.

Streeter, S. F.: Papers relating to the early history of Maryland. Baltimore, 1876.

Tanner, M.: Societas Jesu usque ad sanguinis et vitae profusionem militans, in Europa, Africa, Asia et America, contra Gentiles, Mahometanos, Judaeos, hacreticos, impios etc. Prague, 1675.

Taurel: Les Jésuites dans l'América Méridionale.

Techo, N. del: Historia provinciac Paraguaciae S. J. Leodii. 1673.

Trigaultius, N.: De Christianis apud Japonios Triumphis. Munich, 1623.

Vos, E. de: Leben und Briefe des hl. Franz Xaver. Regensburg, 1877.

Voyages et Travaux des Missionaires de la Compagnie de Jésus. Ch. Dounill, Paris, 1861.

Wieger, L.: Histoire des croyances religieuses et des opinions philosophiques en Chine. Paris, 1922.

Wilhelm, R.: Geschichte der chinesischen Kultur. F. Bruckmann, Munich, 1928.

Winterbotham, W.: An historical, geographical, and philosophical view of the Chinese Empire. London, 1795.

Xaveriusforschung im 16. Jahrhundert. Zeitschr. f. Missionswissenschaft, Vol. XII, Münster, 1922.

Bibliography

PART VI

Agricola, I.: Historia Provinciae Societatis Jesu Germaniac superioris. 1727.

Aktenstücke betreff. Die Jesuiten in Deutschland. Mainz, 1872.

Akty istorischeski, St. Petersburg, 1841.

Alegre, F.: Hist. de la Comp. de Jesús en Nueva España.

Apologie générale de l'institut et de la doctrine des Jésuites, 1763.

Argenti, J.: De rebus Societatis Jesu in regno Poloniac ad Sigismundum III. Cracow, 1620.

Arndt, A.: Ein päpstliches Schiedsgericht im 16. Jahrh. (Stimmen aus Maria-Laach, vol. XXXI.) Herder, Freiburg i. Br., 1886.

Arnold, A.: Oratio pro Universitate Parisiensi actrice contra Jesuitas reos. 1594.

Arrêt de la Cour du Parlement, concernant l'abolition de la Société soi-disant de Jésus, du 6. Aoust 1762. Lyons, 1762.

Arrêt du grand Conseil donné en 1625 pour l'Université de Paris, contre les Jésuites, 1625.

Ballester, F.: Histoire de l'Espagne. Payot, Paris, 1928.

Bartoli, D.: Dell' istoria della Compagnia di Gesù. L'Italia, prima parte dell' Europa. Turin, 1825.

Baschet, Armand: La diplomatic vénitienne. Les princes de l'Europe au XVIe siècle . . . D'apprès les rapports des ambassadeurs vénitiens. Paris, 1872.

Bavviere, Pierre: procédure faite contre Jean Chastel etc. 1595.

Bedenken an den König in Frandreich über der Jesuiten Aussöhnung und Wiedereinkomenung in Frankreich. Heidelberg, 1607.

Bellarmine, R. (M. Torti): Responsio Mathaei Torti Presbyteri etc. Cologne, 1608.

Bellarmine, R.: Hieratikon Doron sive modesta et fidelis admonition etc., in: Bachelet's Auctarium Bellarminianum, 1913.

Bellescheim, A.: Geschichte der katholischen Kirche in Irland von der Einführung des Christentums bis auf die Gegenwart. Mainz, 1890.

Bezold, F. von: Geschichte der deutschen Reformation. Berlin, 1890.

Boéro, P. G.: Vita del beato Canisio della Compagnia di Gesù detto l'apostolo della Germania. Rome, 1864.

Bonnerot, Jean: la Sorbonne. Les Presses Universitaires de France, Paris, 1927.

Bournichon, J.: La Compagnie de Jésus en France. Beauchesne, Paris, 1914.

Braunsberger, O.: Entstehung und erste Entwicklung d. Katechismen d. sel. Petrus Canisius, 1893.

Brieger, the.: Contraini und das Regensburger Konkordienwerk des Jahres 1541. Gotha, 1870.

Brosch, M.: Geschichte Englands. Gotha, 1890.

Bruckner, A.: Die Europäisierung Russlands. Gotha, 1888.

Canisius, P.: Epistolae et Aeta. Collegit et adnotationibus illustravit Otto Braunsberger. 1896-1924.

Charke: Life of James II. London, 1816.

Chesterton, G. K.: heretics, Ger. tr. Georg Müller, Munich, 1912.

Clorivière, Pierre de: Gigord. Paris, 1926.

Consiant, P.: Invective contre l'abominable parricide attenté sur la personne du Roy Henry IV etc. Paris, 1745.

Crétineau-Joly, I.: Clément XIV et les Jésuites. Paris, 1847.

Crétineau-Joly: Histoire de la Compagnie de Jésus. Paris, 1846.

Daurignac, J.: Geschichte des seligen Petrus Canisius. Efrurt, 1868.

Daurignac, J.: Geschichte d. Gesellschaft Jesu von ihrer Stiftung bis auf unsere Tage. Regensburg, 1863.

De rebus gestis Stephani I. . . . Contra magnum Moschorum ducem narration. Rome, 1582.

Dorigny, J.: la vie du P. Antoine Possevin de la Compagnie, de Jésus. Paris, 1712.

Dubech, L. and Espezel, P. d': histoire de Paris, Payot. Paris, 1926.

Duhr, B.: Pombal. Sein Charakter und seine Politik. Herder, Freiburg, 1891.

Erinnerung, Der weltberühmten Universität zu Paris treuherzige, an die Königl. Wittib u. Regentin etc. wegen der Jesuiten und ihrer Lehre. Aus dem zu Paris gedruckten Exemplare verteutschet. 1610.

Feidler, J.: Ein Versuch der Vereinigung der russischen mnit der römischen Kirche im 16. Jahrh. (sitzungsberichte d. k. k. Akademie der Wissenschaften, t. XL.) Vienna, 1862.

Foley, H.: Records of the English Province of the Society of Jesus, 1883.

Franzii, W.: Oratio de Jesuitarum cruentis mnachinationibus adversus principes. Wittenburg, 1612.

Freidrich, J.: Beiträge zur Geschichte des Jeuiten-Ordens. Schmidt & günther, Leipzig.

Fuente, v. de la: Colección de los articulos sobre la expulsión de los Jesuitas de España.

Gautier, A.: Étude sur la correspondence de Pierre Canisius de 1541 à 1560. Geneva, 1905.

Geijer, E. G.: Geschichte Schwedens. Hamburg, 1832-36.

Gretserus, J.: Apologia Societatis Jesu in Gallia ad Regem Henricum IV. Scripta. Ratisbon, 1738.

Groeteken, A.: Die Franziskaner an Fürstenhöfen bis zur Mitte des 14. Jahrhunderts. Buschmann, Münster, 1928.

Guggenberger, K.: Geschichte des Staatskirchentums. Ferdinand Schöningh, Paderborn, 1927.

Guggenheim: Geschichte der Jesuiten in Deutschland bis zur Aufhebung des Ordens durch Papst Clemens XIV. Frankfort, 1847.

Guiraud, J.: Histoire partiale, histoire vraie, Beauchesne, Paris, 1917.

Hansen, J.: Rheinische Akten zur Geschichte des Jesuitenordens 1542-1582. Bonn, 1896.

Henri IV et les Jésuites. Adrien Egron, Paris, 1818.

Bibliography

Heppe: Geschichte des deutschen Protestantismus. Marburg, 1858.

Hergenröther: Katholische Kirche und christlicher Staat in ihrer geschichtlichen Entwicklung und in Beziehung auf die Fragen der Gegenwart. Freiburg, 1872.

Hildebrand: Geschichte und System der Rechtsund Staatsphilosophie. 1860.

Histoire du Père La Chaise. Henry Kistenmaeckers, Brussels, 1719-1884.

Huber, A.: Geschichte Österreichs. Gotha, 1888 and 1892.

Hurter, Fr.: Geschichte Kaiser Ferdinands II, und seiner Eltern. Schaffhausen, 1850.

Irance: De la déstruction des Jésuites. Paris, 1826.

James I: Jacobi primi etc. . . . Basilikon Doron etc., London, 1604.

The Works of the Most High and Mighty Prince James etc., Montagu, London, 1616.

Jellinek, G.: Allgemeine Staatslehre. O. Haering, Berlin, 1905.

Jesuitenverfolgung, Die, in England. Geschichtsbilder aus den Zeiten Elisabeths und Jakobs I. Mainz, 1874.

Jésuites, Les, montrés à la France. Guyot, Lyons, 1844.

Karamsin: Istoriya gosudarstva rossyskago. St. Petersburg, 1818-1829.

Keller: Tyrannicidium seu scitum catholicorum de tyranny internecione adversus Calviniani ministry calumnias. Munich, 1611.

Kelsen, H.: Hauptprobleme der Staatsrechtslehre. Mohr, Tübingen, 1911.

Kelsen, H.: Das Problem der Souveränität und die Theorie des Völkerrechts. Mohr, Tübingen, 1920.

Klipffel, H.: Le colloque de Poissy. Étude sur la crise religieuse et politique de 1561, Paris.

Kobler, J.: Die Märtyrer und Bekenner der Gesellschaft Jesu in England während der Jahre 1580-1681, Vereins-Druckerei, Innsbruck, 1886.

Kohler, J.: Lehrbuch der Rechtsphilosophie. Rothschild, Berlin, 1909, 1923.

Krasinski, V. A.: Geschichte der Reformation in Polen. Leipzig, 1841.

Krebs, R.: Bernhard Duhr, S. J., und die Lehre der Jesuiten vom Tyrannenmord. C. Braun, Leipzig, 1892.

Kroess, A.: Gesch. D. böhm. Provinz d. Gesellsch. Jesu. Quellen u. Forschungen z. Gesch. Österreichs u. d. angrenz. Geb. 1927.

Lainii Monumenta. Epistolae et acta patris Jacobi Lainii. Madrid, 1912-15.

Larrey, de: Histoire d'Angleterre, d'Écosse et d'Irlande. Rotterdam, 1707-1713.

Laumier, Ch.: Résumé de Phistoire des Jésuites etc. Dupont & Roret, Paris, 1826.

Laynez, Le P., au colloque de Poissy et à Paris en 1561. (Extrait des Précis historiques, janvier 1889.)

Lerouz: Le père La Chaise Confesseur, 1884.

Leutbecher, J.: Der berühmte Jesuit Juan Mariana über den König und dessen Erziehung. Erlangen, 1830.

Lingard, J.: History of England. Ger. tr. Frankfurt a. M., 1828.

Linguet, S.: Histoire impartiale des Jésuites.

Lutteroth, H.: Russland und die Jesuiten von 1772-1820. Hallberger, Stuttgart, 1846.

Mariana, J.: De rege et regis institutione libri tres. Mainz, 1605.

Martin, J. F.: Gustave Wasa et la Réforme en Suéde. Paris, 1906.

Mayerne, Turquet de: Histoire générale d'Espagne. Paris, 1635.
Mcllwain: Political Works of James I.
Missionaries, arts discovered, The. London, 1688.
Monglave, E. de, and Chalas, P.: Histoire des conspirations des Jésuites. Ponthieu, Paris, 1825.
Mori, H.: Historia Provinciae Anglicanae Societatis Jesu. Audomari, 1660.
Moser, J. J.: Nachr. V. d. Jesuiter-Ordens Aufhebung u. d. darüber entstandenen Streitigkeiten. 1775.
Moses, R.: Die Religionsverhandlungen zu Hagenau und Worms 1540-1541. Leipzig, 1889.
Murr, Chr. G. von: Geschichte der Jesuiten in Portugal unter der Staatsversaltung des Marquis von Pombal. Nuremberg, 1787-88.
Nolhac, P. de: Madame de pompadour et la Politique. Calmann-Lévy Paris, 1928.
Paquiz and Dochez: histoire d'Espagne. Paris, 1855.
Pfülf, O.: Petrus Canisius. Einsiedeln, 1881.
Piaget: Histoire de l'établissement des Jésuites en France, 1540-1640. Leyden, 1893.
Pidal y Mon, A.: El triunfo de los Jesuitas en Francia.
Pierling, P.: Báthory et Possevino, Documents inédits sur les rapports du Saint-Siége avec les Slaves. Paris, 1887.
Pierling, P.: Rome et Démétrius, d'après des documents nouveaux. Paris, 1878.
Pierling, P.: Papes et Tsars. Retaux-Bray, Paris, 1890.
Pierling, P.: Le Saint-Siège, la Pologne et Moscou (1582-1587). Paris, 1885.
Pontat, F.: L'Université et les Jésuites. Deux procès en cour de Parlement au XVI^c siècle. Étude historique. Paris, 1877.
Possevino, A.: Moscovia et alia opera, in officinal Birckmannica, 1587.
Possevino, A.: Livoniae commentaries. Riga, 1852.
Prat, J. M.: Histoire de l'Église gallicane continuée de l'an 1559 à l'an 1563. Paris, 1847.
Prat, J. M.: Recherches historiques et critiques sur la Compagnie de Jésus en France du temps du P. Coton, 1564-1626. Lyons, 1878.
Prat, J. M.: Maldonat et lUniversité de Paris au XVI^c siècle. Paris, 1856.
Ranke, L. von: Englische Geschichte. Berlin. 1859.
Ranke, L. von: Französische Geschichte. Dunker & Humblot. Leipzig, 1868.
Rappel des Jésuites en France. Cologne, 1678.
Reiss, Fl.: Leben d. sel. Petrus Canisius. Freiburg, 1865.
Ribadeneira: Vita P. Iacobi Laynii.
Rochemonteix, P. C. de: Le Père Antoine Lavalette à la Martinique. Picard, Paris, 1907.
Rommen, H.: Die Staatslehre des Franz Suarez, 1927.
Rosenow, E.: Wider die Piaffenherrschaft. Kulturbilder-Verlag, Berlin, 1923.
Saint-Priest, A. de: histoire de la Chute des Jésuites, (1750-1782). D'Amyot, Paris, 1844.
Sander, F.: Alte und neue Staatsrechtslehre. (Zeitschr. f. öffentl. Recht I. Vol. II.) 1921.
Scabra da Sylva, J.: Recueil chronologique et analytique de tout cc qu'a fait en Portugal la Société dite de Jésu. Lisbon, 1769.
Schäfer, H.: Geschichte Portugals. Hamburg, 1836-54.

Bibliography

Schaurie, F.: Christina, Königin von Schweden. 1880.

Schilling: Die Staats– und Soziallehre des hl. Thomas von Aquino. Paderborn, 1923.

Schlosser, F. C.: Geschichte des achtzehnten Jahrhunderts etc. J. C. B. Mohr, Heidelberg, 1865.

Soldan, M. G.: Geschichte des protestantismus in Frankreich. Leipzig, 1855.

Spillmann, J.: Geschichte der Katholikenverfolgung in England 1535-1681. Die engl. Märtyrer der Glaubensspaltung. Freiburg. 1900.

Stoeckins, H.: Forschungen z. Lebensordnung d. Ges. Jesu im 16. Jahrh. 1910-11.

Suarez, F.: Opera Omnia. Ed. Nova a Car. Berton, Paris, 1836-78.

Sugenheim, S.: Geschichte der Jesuiten in Deutschland bis 1773. Frankfurt, 1847.

Tabaraud, M.: Essai historique et critique sur l'état des Jésuites en France. Pichard, Paris, 1828.

Terrien, P. J.: Histoire du R. P. de Clorivière. Poussielgue, Paris, 1892.

Theiner, A.: La Suède et le Saint-Siège. Paris, 1842.

Theiner, A.: Vetera Monumenta Poloniae et Lithuaniae. Rome, 1861.

Tischleder, P.: Sttatsgewalt und katholisches Gewissen. Carolus-Druckerel, Frandfurt, 1927.

Toth, K.: Weib und Rokoko in Frankreich. Amalthen-Verlag, Vienna, 1924.

Turretin, B.: De la déposition des Rois, et subversion de leurs vies et états. Geneva, 1627.

Uspensky, F.: Nakaz tsaria Ivana. Odessa, 1885.

Uxkull, Baronne d': Rome et l'Orient. Publications de documents, d'exposés et de lettres au nom de la justice. Jésuites et Melchites. 1912.

Velics, L.: Vázlatok a Magyar jezsuiták multjából, Budapest, 1912, 1913, 1914.

Vorländer: Geschichte der philosophischen Moral, Rechts– und Stattslehre der Engländer und Franzosen. Marburg, 1855.

Voyer, A.: La Tyrannomanie Jésuitique. 1648.

Walter, F.: Naturrecht und Politik, 1871.

Werner, K.: Franz Suarez. Regensburg, 1865.

Wolf, G.: Deutsche Geschichte im Zeitalter der Gegenreformatica. Berlin, 1898.

Wunster, K.: Loyola und Ganganelli, oder: die Jesuiten im Stande ihrer Erhöhung und ihrer Erniedrigung. J. K. G. Wagner, Neustadt a. d. Orla, 1828.

Zinkeisen, J. W.: Geschichte des osmanischen Reiches in Europa. Gotha, 1846-63.

PARTS VII AND VIII

Allgemeines Handlhuch der Freimaurerei. Second, completely re-edited edition of Leuning's Encyklopädie der Freimaurerei. F. A. Brockhaus, Leipzig, 1863.

Astrain, A.: Histoira de la Compaflia de Jesús en la asistencia de España. Madrid, 1912-1913.

Bahr, H.: Summula. Insel-Verlag. Leipzig, 1921.

Baumgartner, A.: Die Stellung der deutschen Katholiken zur neueren Literatur. Herder, Freiburg i. Br., 1910.
Baumgartner, A.: Geschichte der Weltliteratur. Freiburg, 1807-1906.
Baumgartner, A.: Calderon. Festspiel zum 25. Mai 1881. Mit einer Einleitung über Calderons Leben und Werke. Herder, Freiburg, 1881.
Beaune, H.: Voltaire au collège, sa famille, ses études, ses premiers amis. Lettres et documents inédits. Paris, 1867.
Berge, von den: Theatrum Hispaniae. Amsterdam.
Beyer, G.: Katholizismus und Sozialismus. J. H. W. Dietz Nachf., Berlin.
Bie, R.: Diagnose des Zeitalters. Alexander Duncker, Weimar, 1928.
Bismarck, O. von: Gedanken und Erinnerungen. Cotta, Stuttgart, 1898.
Boscovich, R. J.: Theoria philosophiae naturalis reducta ad unicam legem virium in natura existentium. Venice, 1763.
Bournichon, J.: Histoire d'un siècle. Beauchesne, Paris, 1914.
Boysse, E.: Le théâtre des Jésuites. Henri Vaton, Paris, 1880.
Braun, J.: Die belgischen Jesuitenkirchen. Herder, Freiburg i. Br., 1907.
Brentano, L.: Der wirtschaftende Mensch in der Geschichte. Felix Meiner, Leipzig, 1923.
Brischar: Athanasius Kircher, ein Lebensbild, 1877.
Carlyle, R.: Die Jesuiten, ein Pamphlet. Leipzig, 1869.
Cassirer, E.: Kants Leben und Lehre. Cassirer, Berlin, 1921.
Cassirer, E.: Leibniz' System in seinen wissenschaftlichen Grundlagen. Marburg, 1902.
Cassirer, E.: Naturrecht und Völkerrecht. Berlin, 1919.
Cathrein, V.: Der Sozialismus. 1922.
Caen-Bermudez, J. A.: Dissionario históde los mas illustres professors de las bellas artes en España. Madrid, 1800.
Cohen, H.: Logik der reinen Erkenntnis. Berlin, 1914.
Dingler, H.: Das Experiment, sein Wesen und seine Geschichte. Reinhardt, Munich, 1929.
Dorigny, J.: La vic du P. Edmond Auger, de la Compagnie de Jésus. Lyons, 1716.
Dostoievsky, F. M.: The Brothers Karamazov. Ger. tr. Piper, Munich.
Dostoievsky, F. M.: Die Urgestalt der Brüder Karamasoff. Piper, Munich, 1929.
Duhr, B.: Das Jesuitengesetz, sein Abbau und seine Aufhebung. 1919.
Dunin-Borkowski, S. Von: Pädagogik der Gegenwart in Selbstdarstellungen. Leipzig, 1926.
Ebe, G.: Die Spät-Renaissance. Kunstgeschichte der europäischen Länder von der Mitte des 16. bis zum Ende des 18. Jahrunderts. Berlin, 1886.
Eckart, R.: Die Jesuiten in der deutschen Dichtung und im Volksmund. Handels-Druckerei, Bamberg.
Eckart, R.: Hundert Stimmen atts vier Jahrhunderten über den Jesuitenorden. Wigand, Leipzig.
Eckstein, F.: Comenius. Augewählte Schriften. Insel-Verlag, Leipzig, 1915.

Bibliography

Ehrhard, Dr. A.: Der Katholizismus und das 20. Jahrhundert im Lichte der Kirchlichen Entwicklung der Neuzeit. Jos. Roth, Stuttgart-Vienna, 1902.

Ehrle, F.: Die päpstliche Enzyklika vom 4. 8. 1879 und die Restauration der christlichen Philosophie. (Stimmen aus Maria-Laach, XVIII.) 1880.

Ehrle, F.: Der Augustinismus und Aristotelismus in der Scholastik gegen Ende des 13. Jahrhunderts. (Archiv für Literatur-und Kirchengeschichte des Mittelalters.) 1889.

Eucken, R.: Thomas von Aquino und Kant, ein Kampf zweier Welten. Berlin, 1901.

Ewald, O.: Französische Aufklärungsphilosophie. 1924.

Fechner, G. The.: Über die physikalische und philosophische Atomenlchre. Mendelsohn, Leipzig, 1864.

Findel, J. G.: Geschuchte der Freimmaurerei von der Zeit ihres Entstehens bis auf die Gegenwart. J. G. Findel, Leipzig, 1870.

Findel, J. G.: Schriften über Freimaurerei. Leipzig, 1902.

Flourens: Napoléon et les Jésuites, in: Nouvelle Revue, Feb. 1894. Paris.

Fraschetti: Il Bernini. Rome, 1900.

Freud, S.: Psychopathologie des Alltagslebens. Internationaler psychoanalytischer Verlag, Vienna, 1927.

Freud, S.: Die Zukunft einer Illusion. Internationaler Psychoanalytischer Verlag, Vienna, 1927.

Frias, L.: Historia de la Compaña de Jesús en su asistencia moderna de España. 1923.

Goethe, J. W.: Italienische Reise. Cotta, Stuttgart, 1840.

Gofflot: Le théâtre au collège du moyen-áge à nos jours. Paris, 1907.

Gould, R. F.: The history of Freemasonry. London, 1882-87.

Gracian, B.: Handbook oracle and art of worldly wisdom. Ger. tr. Brockhaus, Leipzig, 1877.

Grainha, E. B.: Histoire de la Franc-Maçonnerie en Portugal. Lisbon, 1913.

Gregor, J.: Wiener szenische Kunst. Wiener-Drucke, 1924.

Grimaldi, F. N.: Physico-mathesis de lumine, coloribus et iride aliisque annexis. Bologna, 1665.

Guldin, P.: Centrobaryca seu de centro gravitatis trium specierum. Vienna, 1635.

Hatzfeld, H.: Geschichte der französicschen Aufklärung. Rösl & Co., Munich, 1922.

Herder, J. G. von.: Adrastea. Begebenheiten und Charaktere des achtzehnten Jahrhunderts. Cotta, Stuttgart, 1829.

Hertling, L. M. von.: Priesterliche Umgangsformen. Rauch, Innsbruck, 1929.

Hessen, J.: Die Weltanschauung des Thomas von Aquino. Stuttgart, 1926.

Hettner, H.: Geschichte der französischen Literatur im achtzehnten jahrhundert. Friedr. Vieweg & Sohn. Brunswick, 1913.

Huonder, P. A.: Zur Geschichte des Missionstheaters. Xaverius-Verlag, Aix-la-Chapelle. 1918.

Hyver: Maldonat et les commencements de l'Université de Pont-à-Mousson, 1572 à 1582. Nancy, 1873.

John, O.: W. A. Mozart. Breitkopf & Härtel, Leipzig, 1889.

Jansen, B.: Die Bedeutung des Kritizismus. (Stimmen der Zeit C VII.)

Jansen, B.: Der Kritizismus Kants, Munich, 1925.

Jansen, B.: Transzendentale Methode und thomistische Erkenntnismetaphysik. (Scholastik III.) 1928.

Jesuiten-Wissenschaft und Gelehrsamkeit, beleuchtet von einen Wahrheitsfreund. Germania, Berlin, 1893.

Jocham, M.: Die sittliche Verspestung des Volkes durch die Jesuiten. Mainz, 1866.

Junghaendel, M., and Gurlitt, C.: Die Baukunst Spaniens in ihren hervorragendsten Werken, J. Bleyl, Dresden, 1893.

Kant, I.: Kritik der reinen Vernunft. Reclam, Leipzig.

Katsch, F.: Die Entstehung und der wahre Endzweck der Freinaurerei. E. S. Mittler & Sohn, Berlin, 1897.

Kehrer, H.: Spanische Kunst von Greco his Goya. Hugo Schmidt, Munich, 1926.

Kelsen, H.: Die Idee des Naturrechtes. (Zeitschrift für öffentliches Recht VII.) 1927-28.

Kirchberger: die Entwicklung der Atomtheoric. 1922.

Kircher, Aik.: Ars Magna Lucis et Umbrae, in X Libros digesta. Apud Joannens Janssonium à Waesberge. Amsterdam.

Kircher, Ath.: Magnes Sive de Arte Magnetica Opus Tripartitum. Cologne, 1643.

Kreitmaier, J.: Die religiösen Kräfte des Barock. (Stimmen der Zeit.) 1926.

Lämmel, R.: Galileo Galilei. Franke, Berlin, 1927.

Landner, J.: Das Kirchliche Zinsverbot und seine Bedeutung. Graz and Vienna, 1918.

Lange, F. A.: Geschichte des Materialismus und Kritik seiner Bedeutung in der Gegenwart. Brandstetter, Leipzig, 1914-15.

Lecky: A history of the rise and influence of Rationalism in Europe. Ger. tr. 1873.

Le Franc, A,.: histoire du collège de France. Paris, 1893.

Lennhoff, E.: Die Freinaurer. Amalthea-Verlag, Vienna, 1929.

Lirac, A.: Les Jésuites et la liberté religieuse sous la Restauration. Victor palmé, Paris, 1879.

Loga: Die spanische Plastik. Berlin, 1911.

Mann, The.: Die Stellung Freuds in der modernen Geistesgeschichte. (Die Psycholanalytische Bewegung.) Vienna, 1929.

Marck, S.: Das Jahrhundert der Aufklärung. Teubner, Leipzig, 1923.

Mill, J. S.: On Liberty. Ger. tr. Reclam, Leipzig.

Mir, M.: Historia enterna documentada de la Compañia Jesús.

Nippold, F.: Die jesuitischen Schriftsteller der Gegenwart in Deutschland. Friedrich Jansa, Leipzig, 1895.

Oldenbourg, R.: Peter Paul Rubens, Berlin, 1922.

Pachtler, G. M.: Ratio studiorum et institutions scholasticae Soc. Jes., per Germaniam olim vigentes. Berlin, 1887.

Pachtler, G. M.: Der Göetze der humanität oder das Positive der Freimaurerei. Freiburg, 1875.

Pachtler, G. M.: Der stille Krieg gegen Thron und Altar oder das Negative der Freimaurerei. Amberg, 1875.

Passavant, J. D.: Christliche Kunst in Spanien. Leipzig, 1883.

Bibliography

Paulsen, F.: Die Geschichte des gelchrten unterrichts. Leipzig, 1896-97.

Paulsen, F.: Kant, der Philosoph des protestantismus, 1899.

Piedad: Jesuitico Teatro. 1654.

Pierron, A.: Voltaire et ses maitres. Didier, Paris, 1866.

Pohle, G.: Angelo Secchi. Cologne, 1883.

Pontal, E.: L'Université et les Jésuites. Deux procès en cour de parlement au XVIe siècle, Ètude historique. Paris, 1877.

Possevino, A,: Bibliotheca seleeta qua agitur de ratione studiorum in historia, in disciplinis, in salute omnium procuranda. Rome, 1593.

Possevino, A.: Tractati de poesi et picture. Lyons, 1594.

Pozzo, A.: Der Mahler und Baumeister Perspectiv, worinnen gezeiget wird, wie man auf das allergeschwindeste und leichteste alles, was zur Architektur u. Baukunst gehört, ins Perspectiv bringen sole. C. F. Bürglen, Augsburg, 1800.

Prat, J. M.: Maldonat et l'Université de Paris au XVIe siècle. Paris, 1856.

Pribilla, M.: Kulturwende und Katholizismus. Dr. F. A. Pfeiffer & Co., Munich, 1925.

Przywara, E.: Kantentfaltung oder Kantverleugnung? (Stimmen der Zeit.) 1923-24.

Reusch, f. H.: Der Prozess Galileis und die Jesuiten. Eduard Weber, Bonn, 1879.

Rhein, P. von.: Jesuiten und evangelischer Bund. Verlag Jägersche Buchhandlung, Speyer, 1892.

Reimann, H.: Musik-Lexikon. Max Hesse, Leipzig, 1900.

Rinaldi, E.: La fondazione del Collegio Romano—Memorie Storiche. Coorperativa Tipografica, Arezzo, 1914.

Rochemonteix, P. C. de: Un collège de Jèsuites au XVIIe et XvIII^e siècles. Le collège Henri IV de La Flèche. Le Mans, 1889.

Rooses, M.: Rubens, sein Leben und Werk. Berlin, 1904.

Rose, H.: Spätbarock. Hugo Bruckmann, Munich, 1922.

Rosenkranz, K.: Diderots Leben und Werke. F. A. Brockhaus, Leipzig, 1866.

Rosenthal, P.: Die "Erudition" in den Jesuitenschulen. Erlangen, 1905.

Rousseau, J. J.: The Social Contract. Ger. tr. Reclam, Leipzig,

Schack, A. F. von: Geschichte der dramatischen Literatur u. Kunst in Spanien. 1845.

Schaub: Der Kampf gegen den Zinswucher, ungerechten Preis und unlauteren Wucher von Karl d. Gr. bis Papst Alexander III. Freiburg i. Br., 1905.

Scheler, M.: Schriften zur Soziologie und Weltranschauung. Leipzig, 1923.

Scheler, M.: Vom Umsturz der Werte. Leipzig, 1912.

Schimnberg, A.: L'éducation morale dans les collèges de la Compagnie de Jésus en France. Honoré Champion, Paris, 1913.

Schmidt, K. A.: Geschichte der Erziehung von Anfang an bis auf unsere Zeit. Stuttgart, 1892.

Schubert, O.: Geschichte des Barock in Spanien. Paul Neff, Esslingen, 1908.

Secchi, A.: Die Einheit der Naturkräfte. Paul Frohberg, Leipzig, 1884.

Secchi: Quadro fisico del Sistema solare secondo le più recenti osservazioni. Rome, 1859.

Secchi: Le soleil. Paris, 1870.

Secchi: Catalogo delle stele di cui is è determinate lo spettro lumninose. Rome, 1867.
Secchi: Sugli spettri prismatici delle stele fisse. Rome, 1868.
Seiller, J. M.: Über die Verdienste der Jesuiten um die Wissenschften und über die Notwendigkeit der Wiederherstellung derselben. 1817.
Serbat: L'architecture gothique des Jésuites au XVIIe siècle. Caen, 1903.
Singer, S.: Der Kampf Roms gegen die Freimaurerei. Ernst Oldenburg, Leipzig, 1925.
Sommervogel, K.: Bibliothèque de la Compagnie de Jésus.
Specht, T.: Geschichte der ehemaligen Universität Dillingen (1549-1804) und der mit ihr verbundenen Lehr– und Erziebungsanstalten. Herder, Freiburg, 1902.
Spengler, O.: Der Untergang des Abendlandes. Munich, 1925.
Steinhuber, A.: Geschichte des Collegium Germanicum Hungaricum in rom. Herder, Freiburg, 1895.
Stirling-Maxwell, W.: Annals of the artists of Spain. London, 1848.
Stockmann, A.: Zum Goethe-Problem. Literarhistorische Studien. Herder, Freiburg, 1920.
Tacchi-Venturi, P.: Storia della Compagnia de Gesù in Italia. Rome, 1922.
Theiner, A.: Geschichte der geistlichen Bildangsanstalten. Mainz, 1835.
Tischleder, P.: Die Staatslehre Leos XIII. Frankfort, 1925.
Tischleder, P.: Staatsgewalt und katholisches Gewissen. Carolus-Druckerei, Frankfurt a. M., 1927.
Villada. P.: El primer centenario del restablecimiento de la Compañia de Jesús en todo el mundo. Administración de razón y fé. Madrid, 1914.
Wasmann, E.: Beiträge zur Lebensweise der Gattungen Atemeles und Lomeclusa. The Hague, 1888.
Waswmann, E.: Der christliche Monismus. Herder, Freiburg, 1920.
Wasmann, E.: Der Trichterwickler. Eine naturwissenschaftliche Studie iiber den Tierinstinkt. Aschendorff, Münster, 1882.
Wasmann, E.: Die Gastpflege der ameisen, ihre biologischen und philosophischen Probleme. 1920.
Wasmann, E.: Die physischen Fähigkeiten der Ameisen. 1909.
Wasmann, E.: Die zusammengesetzten Nester und gemischten Kolonien der Ameisen. Ein Beitrag zur Biologie, Psychologie und Entwicklungsgeschichte der Ameisengesellschaften. Aschendorff, Münster, 1891.
Wasmann, E.: Entwicklungstheorie und Monismus. 1913.
Wasmann, E.: Instinkt und Intelligenz im Tierreich. 1905.
Wasmann, E.: Menschen-und Tierseele. 1910.
Wasmann. E.: Termiten, Termitophilen und Myrmekophilen Ostindiens. 1902.
Wasmann, E.: Vergleichende Studien über die Ameisengäste und Termitengäste. The Hague, 1890.
Wasmann, E.: Vergleichende Studien über das Seelendleben der Ameisen und der höheren Tiere. 1900.
Weber, M.: Wirtschaft und Gesellschaft (Grundriss der Sozialökomik. Vol. III). Mohr, Tübingen, 1925.

Bibliography

Weicker: Das Schulwesen der Jesuiten. 1863.

Weiner, H.: Geschichte der Pädagogik. Walter de Gruyter & Co., Berlin, 1928.

Weingartner, J.: Der Geist des Barock. Augsburg, 1925.

Weisback, W.: Der Barock als Kunst der Gegenreformation. Berlin, 1921.

Wigel, the.: Grundlinien der Erzielungslehre Pestalozzis. Leipzig, 1914.

Winkler: Phänomenologie und Religion. Tübingen, 1921.

Winter, E. K.: Die Sozialmetaphysik der Scholastik. Franz Deuticke, Vienna, 1929.

Witte, L.: Friedrich der Grosse und die Jesuiten. Halle, 1901.

Wittmann: Max Scheler als Ethiker. Düsseldorf, 1923.

Wölflin, H.: Renaissance und Barock. Eine Untersuchung über Wesen und Entstehung des Barockstiles in Italien. Munith, 1888.

Zaorowsky, J.: Vorläufige Darstellung des heutigen Jesuitismus, der Rosenkreuzerey und der Religionsvereinigungen. Frankfort, 1786.

Zeidler, J.: Studien und Beiträge zur Geschichte der Jesuitenkomödie und des Klosterdramas. Hamburg, 1891.

Zimmermann, F. X.: Görz Joh. Leon, Klagenfurt, 1918.

Zirngiebl, E.: Studien über das Institut der Gesellschaft Jesu. Feus, Leipzig, 1870.

Zybura, J. S.: Present-day thinkers and the new scholasticism. Herder, St. Louis, Mo., and London, 1926.

The Power and Secret of the Jesuits

INDEX

Abelard, 166, 173, 395
Abingtons, 313
Abyssinia, 110
Ach, Narziss, 158
Acquaviva, Claudio, 33, 38, 123, 350, 402
Acquaviva, Rodulfo, 239
Acre, 70
Adam (S. J.), 428
Adams, John, 390
Adler, Alfred, 448
Ad majorem gloriam Dei, 21, 30, 38, 45, 105, 214, 428, 435, 477
Adolph, Johann Baptista, 410
Adrastea, (Herder), 477
Æsop, 243
Aeterni Patris (Leo XIII), 441, 453
Africa, 48, 289, 391, 447
Age of Louis XIV (Voltaire), 406
Agra, 240, 405
Aix-la-Chappelle, 453
Akbar the Great, 239-240
Albanel, 284
Albany, 291
Albertus Magnus, 173, 395
Alcalá, 82-4, 89, 405, 421
Alembert, Jean d', 425, 431, 433
Alexander VI, Pope, 215, 281
Alexander VII, Pope, 209, 281
Alexander VIII, Pope, 209
Alexander I of Russia, 389
Alexandre (S. J.), 377
Alexandria, 200, 306
Almanac (Kepler), 400

Almeda (S. J.), 244
Alumbrados, 84
Alvarez, Juan, 465
Amadis of Gaul, 52, 54, 59, 63
Amador, 84
Amaterasu, 228-9
Amazon River, 288
Ambrose, St., 166, 185, 402
America, 5, 48, 160-4, 282, 284-5, 288-9, 291-2, 297, 301-2, 305-6, 377, 391, 403
Amigant, Angelica de, 64
Amphibology, 175, 470
Amyot (S. J.), 276
Analysis of Mind (Russell), 161
Anchieta (S.J.), 288, 291, 476
Andrada, Antonio, 240
Andrade, gen. Gomez F. d', 304
Angelo, Fra, 78
Angoulême, 362
Anjiro, 222-225, 231
Annat (S. J.), 144, 366
Anselm of Canterbury, 25
Anthony of Florence, St., 289
Antipater of Tarsus, 200-202
Antoninus, St., 185
Antonio, Aleixo, 305
Antwerp, 419, 421
Apollo et Hyacinthus (Mozart), 413
Apostolicum pascendi (Clement XIII), 383
Aquinas, Thomas, 25, 29, 113-4, 122, 130, 156, 167, 173, 203, 289, 320, 395, 435, 440-1, 444, 450, 455

INDEX

Aranda Count de, 306, 382, 433
Aretino, Pietro, 99
Arevalo, 49-50, 53, 55, 362
Argenson, Marquis d', 374
Argentina, 294
Arian controversy, 121
Arima, 405, 409
Aristotle, 41, 87, 115, 147, 153, 156, 166, 168-171, 176-180, 183, 186-7, 200-201, 203-206, 333, 336, 392, 395, 397-8, 406, 431, 443-4, 450, 455, 459, 473-4, 478
Arizona, 287
Arma Austriaca, 409
Arnauld, Angélique, 128-9, 136, 141
Arnauld, Antoine jun., 134, 137, 150, 281
Arnauld, Antoine, sen., 128-9
Arnauld, Robert, 129
Arnoux (S. J.), 363
Arsenin, Igumen, 341
Art, Jesuits in, 47, 272-277, 286, 293-299, 304, 306, 417-422, 463-4, 465, 468, 476-7
Arteaga, Juan de, 83-4
Asceticism, 69, 103, 333
Astrakhan, 389
Athalie (Racine), 132
Athanasius, 338, 415, 417, 467, 475
Attiret (S. J.), 274-5
Aubigny, d' (S. J.), 362
Auerbach, 184
Augsburg, 298, 330, 339, 352, 404
 Bishop of, 404
 College of, 404
 Confession, 330
 Peace of, 352
Augustine, 29m, 39, 113-114, 116, 118, 124, 127, 130-1, 138, 143, 150, 173, 176, 289, 392, 396

Augustinians, order of, 100, 147,
Augustinus (Jansen), 127, 132, 137-8, 141
Aumont, Marquise d', 130
Austria, 123, 329, 383, 388, 401, 434, 454
 Archduke Albert of, 123
 Archduke Charles of, 358
 Archduke Ernest of, 331, 358
 Archduke Ferdinand of, 409
 Archduke Leopold of, 358
Avancini (S. J.), 417
Aveiro, Duke of, 377
Aylworth (S. J.). 314
Azpeitia, 53
Aztecs, 409
Azuchi, 244
Bach, M., 294, 298, 300
Bacon, Francis, 422, 478
Bacon, roger, 395, 473-4
Bahr, Hermann, 478
Baius, Michael, 118, 121, 127, 137
Balbach (S. J.), 358
Balde, Johann Jakob, 417
Baldinucci, Filippo, 419
Ballets, Jesuit, 414, 422
Balley, College of, 406
Baltimore Archbishop of
 (See Carroll, John)
 (See Calvert, Sir George)
Bamberg, 420
Bancroft, George, 284
Banez (S. J.), 197
Barberini, Cardinal, 358
Barcelona, 71-3, 76, 81, 169
Baroque, 47, 419-422
Barreto (S. J.), 248-9
Barriere, 325
Barshch (S. J.), 342

INDEX

Barzæus, Gaspar, 217, 236
Basil, St., 338
Basilius (Capuchin), 128, 198
Bassano, 101
Bassein, 222, 405
Báthory, Stephen, 330-333, 339-341
Battle of the Maccabees, The, 409
Baucke, Florian, 306
Baumgartner, Alexander, 458
Baunius (S. J.), 176-7, 179, 208
Bavaria, 355-6, 358-9, 385, 408, 432
  Duke Albert IV of, 355
  Elector Charles Theodore of, 432
  Duke Maximillian of, 358
  Duke William V of 356
Becan (S. J.), 358
Beckx, Pierre Jean, 450
Behaviorism (Watson), 162
Behaviourism, 160-164
Belgium, 34, 391, 421
Bellarmine, Roberto, 237, 319-320, 351, 356, 361, 385, 397-9, 419, 426-7, 474
Bellomont, Lord, 286
Benavente, Ana de, 83
Benedictines, order of, 39, 100
Benedict of Nusia, 39, 239
Bengal, 240
Benoit (S. J.), 265, 275
Bergson, Henri, 157, 443
Bernard of Clairvaux, 19, 25, 19, 39, 166173, 395
Bernini, Lorenzo, 419
Bernis, Cardinal de, 376
Berry, Duchese de, 373
Berthier (S. J.), 425
Bérulle, Cardinal de, 128
Bethlehem, 26

Bianchi (S. J.), 99, 209
Bibliotheca Scholastica (Ehrle), 442
Bidermann (S. J.), 417
Bie, Richard, 443
Bilbao, 390
Bilke, Gunnila, 329
Billom, 182, 405
Bismarck, Otto von, 389
Blake, R. M, 442
Blÿenbeck, 33
Blount (S. J.), 282
Blyssem, Heinrich, 357
Bobadilla, Nicholas, 214, 349, 352, 355
Bodkin, Provincial, 390
Boehmer, Heinrich, 32, 48
Bohemia, 337, 357-8
Bohemian Brethren, 337
Boleyn, Anne, 317-8
Bolivia, 287, 294
Bonaventura, 402
Bonsirven (S. J.), 454
Book of Exercises
  (See Cisneros, Garcia de)
Book of Indications for the Seansons
(Yao), 258
Book of Spiritual Exercises
  (Loyola, See spiritual exercises)
Borghese, Camillo
  (See Paul V, Pope)
Borgia, Francisco, 103, 405, 419, 452
Boscovich, Roger Joseph, 403
Bourdaloue, Louis, 366, 369
Bourdin, Pierre, 150
Bourne, Cardinal, 390
Bouvet (S. J.), 267-8
Brabant, 298
Brahe, Tycho, 261
Brahmins, 235-240, 247, 391

INDEX

Braun, Joseph, 421
Brazil, 288, 294, 303, 309, 408, 476
Brébeuf, Jean de, 280, 285
Breslau, 404, 463
 Bishop of, 404
Bressani (S. J.), 286
Breughel, Jan, 420
Brossard (S. J.)
Brothers of Common Life, 19, 40, 69
Brouet, Pasquier, 317
Bruges, College of, 421
Brussels, College of, 421
Buddhism, 221-3, 223, 225-7, 231-2, 239, 244-5, 250-2, 262, 463
Buenos Ayres, 300, 305
 Governor of, 305
Bungo, 230-1, 409
Burgo, Juan de, 185
Busembaum, Hermann, 168-9, 171, 175, 197, 208, 473
Business, Jesuits in, 198-302, 305-6, 378-9
Byron, Lord, 458
Caceres, Lope de, 83-4
Cadière, la belle, 194, 378
Calais, 311
Calderon, Pedro, 417, 428
California, 287
Calixtus, Georg, 203
Calles, Plutarco E., 391
Calmette (S. J.), 238
Calvert, Sir George, 282
Calvin, John, and Calvinism, 30, 111-13, 114, 117-18, 133-35, 154, 340, 348-51, 400, 418
Cambridge, University of, 185, 347
Campenella, Tommaso, 309
Campion, Edmund, 311-12
Canada, 284-5, 290, 476

Canisius, Peter, 350, 354-5, 404
Canton, 235, 248-50, 253-4, 389, 404
Caraffa, Cardinal
 (See Paul IV, Pope)
Carinthia, 357
Carlyle, Thomas, 465
Carmelites, order of, 39
Carneades of Cyrene, 200, 203-4, 206
Carniola, 357
Carroll, Bishop John, 284, 434
Cartegena, 289
Carthusians, order of, 39
Cassianus, Joannes Eremita, 116, 124
Cassiodorus, 25
Castelli, 398
Castiglione (S. J.), 274
Castile, 55
Castillo, Juan de, 172
Castro, Cardinal de, 123
Castro, Dr. de, 84
Casuistry, 168-9, 172, 175, 184-7, 200, 205-6, 210, 469, 472-3
Catesby, Robert, 318
Catherine of Aragon, 317
Catherine II of Russia, 387, 389
Catholic Evidence Guild, 34
Catholicism and Socialism (Drill), 456
Catholic Workers' College, 34
Cathrein, Victor, 155, 170, 174, 183, 204-6, 455-6
Caussin (S. J.), 363-5
Cavour, Count, 389
Cenodoxus, 408
Censor, 268, 351, 397, 418, 435
Cerularius, Michael, 338
Cervantes, Miguel de, 54
Cesi, Prince, 397
Ceylon, 221
Champaigne, Philippe de, 136, 144

INDEX

Chang-chuen-shan, 235
Chantelou, Chevalier de, 419
Chapelain (S. J.), 425
Chaprang, 240
Charlemagne, 74
Charles V, Emperor, 112, 352, 355
Charles I of England, 318
Charles II of England, 318, 344
Charles X of France, 390
Charles II of Spain, 381-3
Charles III of Spain, 381-3
Charlet (S. J.), 148
Charlevoix, F. de, 297
Chastel Jean, 326
Chateaubriand, Vicomte de, 293, 475
Châteauroux, Duchesse de, 374
Chaynim, Bartolomeo de, 185
Cherubinische Wandersmann, Der (Scheffler), 417
Chesterton, G. K., 457
Chicago, 163-4
Child, Charles M., 163
Chili, 294
China, 155, 222-3, 229, 232, 235, 247-278, 281, 333, 346, 391, 400, 405, 420, 426, 476
China and Europe in the Eighteenth Century, (Reichwein), 426
Chinese Orphan, The (Voltaire), 477
"Chinquinquo,", 222-228
Chioggia, 73
Chiquitos, 293
Chitomachon, King, 282
Choiseul, Duc de, 274, 381, 385, 433
Christ, order of, 278
Christina of Sweden, 330, 348
Chrysippus, 187

Chrysostom, 113-4, 166, 173, 185, 338
Church Peace of 1668, 142
Cicero, 184, 200-2, 207, 406
Ciermans, Jean, 150
Cisneros, Francisco Jimenez de, 50
Cisneros, Garcia de, 25, 39, 69
Civiltà Cattolica, 454
Claudel, Paul, 457
Claver, Petrus, 289-90
Clavius, Christoph, 250, 254, 397-98
Clément, Jacques
Clement V, Pope, 320
Clement VIII, Pope, 123-4, 143, 266
Clement IX, Pope, 141, 291, 383, 393
Clement XI, Pope, 143, 291
Clement XIII, Pope, 383
Clement XIV, Pope, 383-4, 393, 434
Clementia Croesi, 412
Clermont, college of, 131, 134, 138, 363, 373, 405-6, 408, 411-2, 414, 426-8
Clorivière, Pierre de, 388
Cochin, 222-3, 405
Cochin China, 248
Cochlæus, Johann, 32
Coello, Alonso Sanchez, 106-7
Cohen, Hermann, 441-3
Cohort, The, 390
Coimbra, College of, 104, 320, 405
Collegium Germanicum, 404
Collegium Regium, 421
Collegium Romanum, 398, 405
Collins, Anthony, 425
Cologne, 102, 404
Colorado river, 287
Comenius, Johana Amos, 431
Comitolus (S. J.), 209
Comorin cape, 218, 222
Concordia liberi arbitrii cum gratiae donis (Molina), 122, 124

INDEX

Condé, Prince Louis de, 130
Confession, 185-198, 217, 237, 312, 330, 341-2, 355-6, 360, 362, 381, 420, 427-8, 432, 441, 453, 458, 465, 469
Confessionale (Chaymin), 185
Confucius, 243, 252, 254, 257, 259, 277, 426, 476
Congo, 391
Congregationes de auxiliis, 124
Constance, College of, 421
Constantine, 416
Constantine, Emperor, 239-40
Constantine, Chinese Emperor, 260
Constantinople, 331-2
Constitutions (S. J.), 34-5, 38, 40, 42, 48-9, 103, 378, 388, 406, 432
Contarini, Cardinal, 100
Conte, Jacopin' del, 105
Conti, Princesse de, 130
Contzen (S. J.), 356, 358-9
Copernicus, Nicolaus, 256, 397, 399, 401, 474
Corneille, Pierre, 47, 131-2, 416, 428, 458
Cortese, Abbot, 100
Cortese, Jacopa, 420
Cortona, Pietro da, 420
Costa, Da (S. J.), 238, 426
Costa, Francis, 351
Coton, Pierre, 361-3
Counter-Reformation, 185, 317, 340, 350-1, 357, 408, 418, 420
Couplet (S. J.), 426
Courtois Jacques
 (See Cortese, Jacopo)
Cracow, 342
Crécy, 374
Critique of Judgment (Kant), 156
Critique of Pure Reason (Kant), 440

Crusades, 70, 74
Cuellar, Juan Velasquez de, 49-50
Cuellar, Maria Velasquez de, 53-4
Cum occasione (Innocent X), 138
Curia, papal (See papacy)
Curtius (S. J.), 401
Cuzco, 287
Cyprus, 74
Czyrzowski (S. J.), 343
Dainichi, 230-1
Dames du Sacré Coeur, 388
Damocles, 410
Dandini, Ottaviano, 420
Daniel, Antoine, 286
Dante, 317, 457
Darwin, Charles, 434, 436
Davila, Beatriz, 82
Decisions of Cases of Conscience (Perkins), 185
Decker (S. J.), 400
De dono perseverantiae (Augustine), 116
De gratia contra Pelagium (Augustine), 116
Deguignes (S. J.), 477
Dehmel, Richard, 459
Delaware, 284
Delhi, 405
Demetrius, the "false", 340-44
Democritus, 166
Denmark, 359
Denonville, Marquis de, 285
Dentrecoiles, (S. J.)
De officiis (Cicero), 201
De praedestinatione Sanctorum (Augustine), 116
De rege et regis institutione (Mariana), 325
De revolutionibus orbium coelestium (Copernicus), 397
Derkennis (S. J.), 149

518

INDEX

Descartes, René, 47, 148-154, 157, 210, 348, 403, 422, 427, 442, 444
Description de l'empire chinois (Duhalde), 426
De servo arbitrio (Luther), 112
Desmarets (S. J.), 375
Deusto, College of, 390
Diagnosis of the Present (Bie), 443
Diaz, Ana, 83
Dichtung and Wahrheit (Goethe), 131
Diderot, Denis, 47, 416, 425-6, 428, 433
Dillingen, College of, 404, 421
Dimitri, Tsarevich (See Demetrius, the "false"
Dinet, Provincial, 148-50
Diogenes the Babylonian, 200-2
Dionysius, Henry, 351
Dionysius the Areopagite, 20, 42
Directorium in exercitia spiritualia (S. J.), 33
Dissertatio de actione scenic (Lang), 416
Divine Comedy (Dante), 117
Dogma and Compulsory Doctrine (Reik), 121
Dolbeau (S. J.), 284
Dominic, St., 457
Dominicans, order of, 118, 122-4, 150, 204, 209, 211, 213, 277-8, 281, 401, 463, 471
Dominus ac Redemptor (Clement XIV), 383-5, 387, 434
Dorat, Abbé, 369
Dostoievsky, Feodor, 457-61, 471
Douai, 317
Dover, 311
Drill, Robert, 456
Dubois, Cardinal, 373
Ducerceau (S. J.), 410, 417
Duhalde, Jean Baptiste, 426
Duns Scotus, John, 173
East Indies, 110

Eckhart, Master Johannes, 205
Eckstein, Friedrich, 442
Education, Jesuits, 134, 201, 262, 284, 300-1, 343, 350, 365, 387, 389-90, 403-8, 414, 416, 422, 431-2
Eguia, d' (S. J.), 405
Ehrle, Cardinal, 442, 444
Eichstätt, College of, 421
"election," the, 24
Elements of Human Greatness (Kassner), 32
Elizabeth, Queen, 311, 318
Elizalde, de (S. J.), 209
Emancipation Act., 389
Emanuel I of Portugal, 387
Embrun, Council of, 143
Emile (Rousseau), 431
Encomiendas, 291, 302
Encyclopædia, 425, 428, 433
"end justifies the means,", 172-7, 428
Engels, Friedrich, 455
England, 34, 213, 282, 285, 311-5, 317-8, 320-22, 344-48, 358, 362, 366, 388-90, 408, 432-33
Enlightenement, 20, 104, 238, 257, 377, 382, 396, 422, 425-28, 431-34, 440, 445, 448, 457, 459
Ensayalados, 83
Enzenberg, Countess, 384
Ephesus, Council of, 116
Equiprobabilism, 203
Erasmus, Desiderius, 112
Erigena, John Scotus, 442
Escobar y Mendoza, Antonio, 181, 191, 195, 197, 202, 207-9, 473
Esprit des lois (Muntesquieu), 309
Essai sur les mœurs (Voltaire), 426
Essay of National Education (La Chalotais), 431
Esther, 410

INDEX

Esther (Racine), 132
Estrada, Sor Antonia, 71, 81
Étioles, Le Normant d', 375
Études, 454
Evora, University of, 122
Exaeten, 33
Examen particulare, 31, 87
Explanation of Nature (Diderot), 425
Faber, Peter, 32-3, 87-89, 222, 349-50, 354
Fabri, Honoré, 153
Fan, Chinese censor, 268
Fatehpur Sikri, 239
Faustus of Mileve, 176
Fechner, Gustav Theodor, 158, 403
Fénélon, Bishop François, 142
Feodor, Tsar, 341
Ferdinand I, emperor, 358
Ferdinand II, Emperor, 360
Ferdinand III, Emperor, 409
Ferdinand the Catholic of Spain, 49
Fermat, Pierre de, 403
Ferney, 428
Ferrier (S. J.), 366
Fessler, Ignaz Aurelius, 433
Ficarelli (S. J.), 453
Fillucius (S. J.), 167
Findel, J. G., 433
Flor, Maria de la, 82-3
Flowers of the Saints, The, 59
Foix, Germaine de (See Germain, Queen)
Fonteney (S. J.), 268
Forel, A., 436
Forer (S. J.), 351
Foscarini, 399
Fouché, Joseph, 388
France, 33, 55, 93, 98, 130, 133-34, 138, 262, 267, 275, 278, 284-85, 290, 318, 320-22, 325-26, 347-48, 352, 354-65, 370-73, 376-78, 381, 384, 388, 390, 403, 405, 410, 417, 431
Franciscans, order of, 39-40, 50, 77-78, 100, 211, 213, 277-78
Francis of Assisi, 29, 39, 59-60, 64, 82
Francis I of France, 55, 93
Francis of Sales, 20, 128
Franck (S. J.), 432
François de Paris, 144, 151-52
Frangipani, Antonio, 98
Franklin, Benjamin, 31, 284, 428
Frederick V of the Palatinate, 358
Frederick the Great, 387, 389
Freemasonry, 432-34, 450, 453-55
Free will, 35, 111-164, 165, 167, 177-78, 320, 414, 472-73
Freiburg, College of, 350, 404
Freud, Sigmund, 41, 445-47
Frontenac, Comte de, 290
Fulda, College of, 404
Funai, 231
Fundamentum theologiae moralis (Gonzalez), 209
Galilee, Galileo, 150, 154, 394, 397-402, 422, 474
Galitsin, Prince, 389
Gallicanism, 321, 349
Gama, Vasco da, 213
Ganganelli, Cardinal (See Clement XIV, Pope)
Ganges, 240
Garibaldi, Giuseppe, 389
Garnet, Henry, 318
Gaultier (S. J.), 428
Ge-hol, 274
Geneva, 20, 30, 112
Gennadius, 339

INDEX

Georgetown, University of, 284, 434-35
Gerard (S. J.), 314
Gerbillon (S. J.), 265, 267-68
Germaine, Queen, 50-51, 59
Germanus, 166, 173
Germany, 33, 213, 348-52, 354-56, 359-60, 366, 389-90, 404, 407, 417, 421
 Bundesrat of, 174
 Reichstag of, 389-90
Gestaltwandel der Götter (Ziegler), 41
Ghent, 421
Gilbert, 312
Girard, 194, 378
Glandorff (S. J.), 287, 391
Goa, 214-18, 220, 222, 226, 228, 230-32, 239, 278, 405, 409
Gobi desert, 240
Godfrey de Bouillon, 416
Godinez (S. J.), 20
Godunov, Boris, 341-43
Goes, Benedict, 239-40, 248-49
Goethe, Johann Wolfgang von, 131, 416, 422, 458, 478
Gomperz, Heinrich, 475
Go-Nara, Great Voo, 228-29
Gonzales, Luis, 64, 68
Gonzalez, Tirso, 209
Good Hope, Cape of, 214
Görz, 415
Gothein, Eberhard, 31, 48
Grabmann, Martin, 440
Grace (See Free will)
Gracian, Baltasar, 464, 471
Granada, 50
Gran Chaco, 306
Graz
 Archduke of, 330, 357
 University of, 123, 355, 404
Great Prince of Fez, The (Calderon), 417

Greece, 134, 166, 177-79, 183, 186-87, 200, 205, 236, 338
Greenway (S. J.), 318
Gregory VII, Pope, 70, 319
Gregory XIII, Pope, 330, 334
Gregory of Nazianzus, 205
Gregory of Nyssa, 185
Gresset, Louis, 428
Gretser (S. J.), 351
Grienberger (S. J.), 398, 400
Grimaldi (S. J.), 155
Grimaldi, Francesco, 403
Gruber, Hermann, 453-54
Guaranis, 293
Guéménée, Princesse de, 130
Guéret (S. J.), 326
Guericke, Otto von, 476
Guignard (S. J.), 324, 326
Guipuzcoa, 54
Gujarat, 214
Guldin, P., 400-401
Gundlach, Gustav, 457
Gunpowder Plot, 318
Gury, J. P., 169, 171, 174, 195-99, 205-6, 446
Gusmão, Lourenço, 476
Gustavus Alolphus, 330, 348, 359
Hagenbrunn, 388
Halle, College of, 421
Hamon, 129-30
Handbook Oracle (Gracian), 464, 471
Han-gai-ti, Emperor, 268
Harnack, Adolf von, 465
Haroun al-Raschid, 74
Hartmann, Nicolai, 443
Hecato, 200
Hegel, G. W. F., 209, 463
Heidelberg, University of, 404
Heine, Heinrich, 458

INDEX

Heinichen, Otto, 453
Hell, Maximilian, 403
Helvetius, Claude, 425, 433
Hémon, F., 133
Henley, 312
Henry VIII of England, 317-19, 362, 366
Henry II of France, 321-22
Henry III of France, 322, 324-26, 360
Henry IV of France, 325-26, 360-63,, 367
Herder, Johann G. von, 417, 458, 477
Herrick, C. Judson, 163
Hesse, Landgrave of, 173
Hideyoshi, Daimyo Toyotami, 242, 247
Hildesheim, 408
Hillel, House of, 199
Himalayas, 240
Hindlip Hall, 313-14
History of Materialism (Lange), 403, 478
History of Port Royal (Racine), 132
History of the United States (Bancroft), 284
Holbach, Baron d', 425
Holland (See Netherlands)
Holland, Thomas, 313
Homoro, 221
Hontheim (S. J.), 442
Hradcany, 331
Hudson's Bay, 284
Hugo, Victor, 458
Huguenots, 325, 362, 370
Humanum genus (Leo XIII), 453
Humboldt, Alexander von, 288, 306
Hume, David, 154-55
Hungary, 340, 454
Hurons, 285-86
Hurtado (S. J.), 197
Husserl, Edmund, 443

Ibsen, Henrick, 458
Idol of Humanity, The (Psachtler), 450
Ignatius Cures One Possessed (Rubens), 419
Illuminati, order of, 432
imitatio Christi, 29, 69
Imitation of Christ(See Thomas à Kempis)
Incas, 288, 409
Inchhofer (S. J.), 400
Inconveniences of Greatness, The, 410
India, 88, 101, 191, 213-222, 226-27, 231-32, 236-40, 267-68, 272, 391, 405, 408, 417, 476
Individual Psychology (Adler), 448
Indo-chino, 221, 476
In eminenti (bull), 433
Ingolstadt, University of, 123, 350, 356, 400, 404, 432
Iñigas, 72, 82
Innocent X, Pope, 138, 281
Innocent XI, Pope, 209
Innocent XIII, Pope, 143
Innsbruck, College of, 404, 421
Institutes of the Christian Religion (Calvin), 112
Institutio oratoria (Quintilian), 341
Ireland, 317
Irkutsk, 389
Iroquois, 285-87
Isabella of Spain, 50, 53
Isidro, 82
Italian Journey (Goethe), 416, 422
Italy, 71-72, 100, 454
Itapua, 294
Ivan the Terrible, 330-32, 334-342
Iyeyasu, Daimyo, 247
Jaeger, Werner, 183
Jaffa, 74, 81

INDEX

Jagiellonika, Princess Anne, 327, 329
Jakielonika, princess Catherine, 332
James, William, 160
James I of England, 315-16, 318-20
James II of England, 283, 344-45, 347
Jammes, Francis, 457
Jam Zapolski, Treaty of, 336
Jansen, Bernhard, 153, 444, 447, 461
Jansen, Cornelius, 125, 127, 137, 141, 144
Jansenist controversy, 111, 116, 129-32, 134, 137-38, 141-44, 147-48, 150, 154, 157, 164, 174, 179, 209-10, 277, 369, 373, 378, 414, 425, 427, 463, 465, 471-72
Janua linguarum reserata (Comenius), 431
Japan, 88, 101, 110, 222-232, 235-36, 241-48, 272, 366, 391, 405, 408-9, 476
Jefferson, Thomas, 390-91
Jena, University of, 404
Jerome, St., 205, 239
Jeronimas, Cloister de las, 71, 81
Jerusalem, 30, 65-66, 70-71, 73-74, 77-78, 81, 89-90, 93
Jogues, Isaat, 286
John II Casimir of Poland, 344
John III of Portugal, 110, 213
John of Salisbury, 469
John III of Sweden, 327-30
John of the Cross, 35
Joliet, Louis, 284
Joseph II, Emperor, 385
Joseph I of Portugal, 376-77
Jouin, 454
Journal des Débats, 388
Journal des Trévoux, 425
Jouvancy (S. J.), 410, 414
Judaism, 184, 200
Jung, Carl, 447-48

Jurieu, Pastor, 370
Kabul, 240
Kagoshima, 222, 224-25, 227
Kamel, George Joseph, 476
Kandy, 221-22
K'ang'hi, Emperor, 260, 262, 265-68, 281, 477
Kant, Immanuel, 156-57, 206-7, 209, 439-47, 449, 453, 455, 461, 463, 474-75
Kareu, F. X., 387
Kassa, 339
Kassner, Rudolf, 32
Kaunitz, Prince von, 384, 433
Keller (S. J.), 351
Kepler, Johann, 397, 400-402, 436
Kia-k'ing, Emperor, 391
K'ien-lung, Emperor, 271-75
Keiv, 341
Kircher, Athanasius, 467, 475
Klopstock, Gottlieb, 458
Koffler, I(S. J.), 384
Koran, 239
Krasnoie Selo, 343
Kremlin, 336, 339, 343-44
Krueger, Felix, 443
Kublai Khan, 261
Kühn (S. J.), 287
Külpe, Oswald, 158
Kulturkampf, 389-90
Kwang-si, Viceroy of, 254
Kyoto, 228
La Chaise, François, 369
La Chalotais, Louis de, 431, 433
Lacroix (S. J.), 197
Lætus, Pomponius, 90
La Fléche, College of, 148, 367, 380, 427
Laibach, 420
Lalement, Gabriel, 286

INDEX

Lamartine, A. M. de, 406
Lamettrie, Julien de, 433
Lamormaini, William, 358-61, 363
Lana-Terzi, Francesco, 475
Lang, Franz, 400, 416
Lang, Ossian, 453
Lange, Friedrich Albert, 403, 478
Langres, College of, 428
La Plata, Archbishop of, 288
 Governor of, 302
La Plata river, 304
Lasso, Oriando di, 413
Last Judgment (Michelangelo), 418
Last Judgment (Rubens), 419
La Storta, 67, 85
Latour (S. J.), 276
Latri, Pietro, 420
Lavalette (S. J.), 378
La Vallière, Louise de, 366, 371
Laws (Plato), 166
Laxism, 209
Laymann, Paul, 174
Laynez, Diego, 47, 89, 93, 322, 325, 426
Lazarists, order of, 391
League, the Catholic, 325, 361
Lebzeltern, von, 383
Leibniz, Gottfried Wilhelm, 153-156, 161, 442, 444, 473-75
Leipzig Institute of Psychology, 158, 443
Le Jay (S. J.), 349, 355, 410, 417
Lemaistre, Antoine, 128-29
Le Moyne, Simon, 286
Lenin, Nicolai, 48
Lennhof, Eugen, 453
Leo X, Pope, 213
Leo XIII, Pope, 441, 453
Leopardi, Giacomo, 458

Leopold of Belgium, 358, 391
Lespinasse, Mlle. De, 425
Lessing, Gotthold, 458, 475
Lessius, Leonhard, 191, 197
Le Tellier, Michel, 142-43, 147, 373
Letter on Obedience (Loyola), 42
Liancourt, Duc de, 134
Liancourt, Duchesse de, 130
Liberalism, 448-50, 453-55, 457
Liebig, 478
Liege, College of, 346
Life of Christ (See Ludolphus of Saxony)
Liguori, Alfonso dei, 186, 198
Lima, 287-88
Lindworsky, Johann, 159-60
Linnæus, Carl, 476
Li Pu, 256
Lisbon, 102, 104, 167, 213-15, 278, 303-305, 317, 383, 476
Liszt, Franz von, 472
Literature, Jesuit, 457-61
Lithuania, 340-41
Livonia, 335, 342
Locke, John, 425, 431-32
Loeb, Jacques, 162-64
London, 34, 311-12, 314, 347, 389
Longueville, Duchesse de, 130, 137
Lopez, Carlos Antonio, 306
Loreto, 298
Loretto, 356
Louisiana, 390
Louis XIII of France, 362-64, 376, 412
Louis XIV of France, 131, 142, 147, 278, 347, 365-373, 408, 413
Louis XV of France, 147, 372-74, 378
Louis XVI of France, 384
Louis Philippe of France, 390

INDEX

Louvain, University of, 118, 121, 127, 421
Lower California, 287
Loyola, 56, 77, 171, 421
Loyola, Ignatius
2, 20-21, 24-26, 29-38, 41-42, 45
 Part II (47-110)
111, 130, 160, 167, 169, 171-78, 180, 207, 214-15, 217, 222, 305, 317, 321, 349, 352, 356, 387, 404-407, 413, 417-20, 425, 438, 451, 453, 464-65, 468
Lucerne, 404, 409
Ludolphus of Saxony, 59, 69-70
Lugo (S. J.), 197
Luther, Martin, 29, 32, 111-13, 134, 154-55, 172, 203, 213, 321, 327, 329, 349-52, 355, 396, 400-401, 407, 440, 458, 469
Luxemburg, 33
Luynes, Duc de, 129, 363
Luynes, Duchesse de, 130
Luz, A, 453
Lyonne, Hugues de, 291
Lyons, 425
Macao, College of, 249, 405
Macaulay, Thomas B., 347
Mace (S. J.), 454
Macedo, Antonio, 348
Machault d'Arnouville, J. B., 375
Machiavelli, Nicolo, 173, 471
Madagascar, 391
Madrid, 67, 75, 291-92, 301, 303, 305, 317, 325, 381-84, 421
Madura, 237-38, 391
Maggio, (S. J.), 355
Magic Mountain (Mann), 470
Mahony, 384
Maintenon, Marquise de, 369-70

Mainz, College of, 123, 404
 Elector of, 385
Maistre, Joseph de, 306
Malacca, 222-23, 232, 235
Malagrida (S. J.), 377
Mamelukes, 302-303
Manares, 20
Mandavi river, 214
Manila, 268
Mann, Thomas, 445, 470
Manresa, 6, 7, 57, 63-4, 67-9, 71, 81-3, 94, 101
Manu, 101
Marburg, University of, 404, 443, 445
Maria, Empress of Austria, 123
Mariana, Juan de, 325-26, 356
Maria Theresa, Empress, 383-84, 431
Marie Antoinette, Queen, 384
Marie Thérèse, Queen, 384
Marquette, Jacques, 279, 284-87
Marseilles, 378
Martinique, 378
Martorell, Johanot, 54
Marx, Karl, 454-57
Maryland, 282-84, 390
Mary I of England, 317
Mary II of England, 348
Mary of Modena, 344-45
Massenpsychologie und Ich-Analyse, 41
Matthias, Emperor, 357
Mattos (S. J.), 377
Maximilian II, Emperor, 339, 355-56, 358-59
Maxwell, James Clerk, 403
Mayrhofer (S. J.), 351
Mazarin, Jules, 365-66, 408
Méchant, Le (Gresset), 428

INDEX

Medici, Catherine de', 322
Medici, Marie de', 362-63
Medina, Bartholomues de, 203-204
Meditationes de prima philasophia (Descartes), 150
Meinong, Alexius, 443
Melanchthon, Philipp, 401, 404
Méland (S. J.), 149
Mena, Pedro de, 419
Mengin (S. J.), 356
Mental reservation, 141, 175-76
Mercure de France, 388
Mersenne, Marin, 402
Mesnil, Advocate-general du, 321
Metternich, Prince, 389
Metz, 374
Mexico, 287, 391, 408-09, 447, 476
Meyer (S. J.), 442
Michelangelo, 418
Michelet, Jules
Micholte, 390
Milet (S. J.), 286
Military affairs, Jesuit, 259-60, 262, 285, 297, 299-302
Mill, John Stuart, 448-49
Milton, John, 458
Miron, Provincial, 102, 104
Mirror for Preachers (Mayrhofer), 351
Missions, Jesuit, 155,
Part V 213-310
390-92, 400, 404-405, 408, 425, 463, 466, 470-71, 476-77
Mississippi river, 279, 284
Missouri, 390
Missouri river, 284
Miyako, 228, 230, 244, 405, 409
Mniszek, George, 342
Mniszck, Marina, 342

Mohammed, 74, 77, 81, 90, 93, 217-18, 221, 236, 239-40, 259, 261, 330
Molière, 47, 132, 410, 416, 428, 458
Molina, Luis, 120, 122-24, 148, 196-97
Molinist controversy, 124, 143, 150, 154, 211, 277
Molino, tirso de, 417
Moluccas, 222
Monfelice, 101
Monita secreta, 210
Mons, 421
Montaigu, College of, 69, 79, 84
Montañes, Juan Martinez, 419, 451-52
Monteleone, duke of, 404
Montespan, Marquise de, 366, 371
Montesquieu, Baron de, 309, 433
Montgolfier brothers, 476
Montoya (S. J.), 303
Montserrat, 6, 61-3, 69, 71
Montalvo, Garcia Rodriguez de, 54
Moralez (P. F.), 281
Moral philosophy, Jesuit
 part III (111-164)
134, 217, 356, 446, 459-62, 464-65, 469, 471-73, 474
Moral Theology (Liguori), 186
Moravia, 357, 431
More, Sir Thomas, 309
Moroni, giambattista, 109
Moscow, 330-32, 336-38, 340, 343, 388-89
Mozart, Leopold, 413
Mozart, Wolfgang Amadeus, 413
Muckermann, Friedrich, 461
Munich, 7, 33, 351, 355-56, 358-59, 400, 421
 College of, 404, 408, 410, 413-14, 416
Münster, College of, 404

INDEX

Musical Comedy of the Liberation of Ignatius Loyola, 413
Mysticism, 19-21, 29, 32, 35, 69, 84, 101, 184, 205, 377, 417, 463, 466
Nagasaki, 409
Najera, 54-5
Namur, College of, 421
Nantes, Edict of, 362, 370
Naples, 383-84, 389
Napoleon, 388, 390
Natorp, Paul, 443
Navarette, Father, 281
Navarre, 54-5, 83, 88, 227, 325
Nazareth, 26
Negro river, 304
Neidhart (S. J.), 381
Neo-Kantian, 441, 445
Neo-Platonists, 116
Neo-scholasticism, 438-444
Nepal, 240
Netherlands, 33, 69, 110, 247, 362, 365, 388
Neuchâtel, Princesse de (See Longueville, Duchesse de)
Newcomb, Simon, 403
New Jersey, 284
Newman, Cardinal, 389
New Mexico, 287, 447
New Orleans, 284
Newton Isaac, 403, 422, 425
New York, 163-64, 283-84, 286, 390, 453
Nice, 93
Nicholas of Cusa, 148, 396
Nicolai, Lorenz, 327-29
Nicole, 129, 132, 141
Nicomachean Ethics, 115, 166, 177-80, 183, 186, 204, 478
Nieburg, 419

Nietzsche, Friedrich, 446, 458
Nile, 40
Noailles, Cardinal de, 142-43, 147, 373
Nobili, Robert de, 237-38, 251, 391
Nobunaga, Daimyo Oda, 244, 247
Nola, Roberto de, 50
Nostitz, Robert von, 34
Notitae linguae sinicae (Prémare), 476
Novgorod, 336
Novum Organum (Bacon), 162
Nuremberg, 298
Nymwegen, Treaty of, 414
Obedience, 29, 34-42, 48, 105, 224, 258, 304-5, 320, 381, 432, 453, 457, 466
Of Duty (Hecato), 200
Of the Two Chief World Systems (Galileo), 399
Old Catholicism, 174
Olive, Giovanni Paolo, 427
Olivet (S. J.), 427
Olmütz, Bishop of, 404
Omar, Caliph, 306
Omsk, 389
On Frequent Communion (Arnauld), 137
On Liberty (Mill), 449
Onuphrius, St., 60
Opinionum praxi (Bianchi), 209
Orban (S. J.), 155
Orbis pictus (Comenius), 431
Organtino (S. J.), 243
Orinoco river, 306
Orleans, Duke of, 147, 284, 373
Ormuz, 214, 236
Orosius, 306
Ortiz, Pedro, 90, 349
Osaka, 409
Otrepiev, Grishka (See Demetrius, the "false.")
Oven (S. J.), 314

INDEX

Oxford, 312
 University of, 34, 347, 444
Paccanari (S. J.), 388
Pachtler, G. M., 450
Padua, 73
Pamir plateau, 240
Pamplona, 53-5
Panætius, 201
Panzi, 274
Papacy, 317, 338, 342, 352, 370, 385, 392, 435, 458
Para, bishop of, 304
Paraguay, 293-98, 300-303, 305-306, 308-310
Parana river, 294, 302
Paravas, 217-18, 221
Paris, 5-7, 69, 79-80, 84, 87, 89-90, 93, 100, 103, 126-28, 130, 132-34, 137, 142-44, 147, 151-52, 226, 228, 276, 278, 285, 290, 321, 325-26, 360, 364, 267, 373-74, 378, 383, 388, 405
Parma, 383-84
Parrenin, 271, 477
Parsons (S. J.), 282, 311
Parsons, Robert, 311
Pascal, Blaise, 111, 131-33, 140-41, 143-44, 174, 176-77, 179, 208-22, 459, 465, 469, 471, 473
Pascal, Jacqueline, 132, 141
Pascual, Inez, 71
Pasquier, Étienne, 321
Passau, Bishop of, 404
Patristic philosophy, 113-14, 118-19, 123-24, 129, 138, 147, 159, 166, 176, 184-85, 204-5, 398, 455, 474, 477
Paul, St., 112-13, 156, 161, 169, 174, 176, 289, 466
Paul III, Pope, 90, 92-93, 95
Paul IV, Pope, 100
Paul V, Pope, 124, 281

Paulsen, Friedrich, 440
Pavlov, I, P, 160-64.
Pázmány, Peter, 340, 357
Perchersk, 336
Peking, 232, 235, 241, 255, 257, 260, 261-68, 271-73, 275-78, 476
Pelagius, 116-18
Pennaforte, Raymund de, 185
Pennsylvania, 284
Peralta, 84
Peramas (S. J.), 301
Pereira, Diogo, 232, 235
Périer, Florin, 132
Perkins, William, 185
Perra, Juan de la, 82
Persia, 214, 236, 342
Peru, 101, 287-88, 374, 408-9, 476
Perusscau (S. J.), 372, 374-75, 381
Pesch, Heinrich, 442, 457, 461
Peter, St., 60, 113, 138, 169, 319, 334, 383, 419, 458
Peter Lombard, 25, 395
Petre, Edward, 347
Phédre (Racine), 131
Philip IV of France, 320
Philip II of Spain, 328
Philip III of Spain, 292, 315, 325
Philip IV of Spain, 292, 404
Philip V of Spain, 303
Philochrysus, 410
Philosophia Lacensis, 442
Philosophy of Right (Hegel), 209
Philothea, 413
Photius, 338
Pichlmayer (S. J.), 447
Pietas victrix, 417
Pinheiro, Emanuel, 239
Pius V, Pope, 118
Pius VII, Pope, 387-88, 450

INDEX

Pius IX, Pope, 450
Plato, 115-16, 156, 166, 178-79, 183, 204-7, 474-75, 478
Plautus, 428
Poirot I(S. J.), 274
Poissy, 322
Polanco (S. J.), 81, 110
Poland, 329-333, 335-39, 340-42, 344, 347, 366, 387, 427
Polo, Marco, 222
Polotsk, 331
Pombal, Marquis of, 376-78, 383, 433
Pompadour, marquise de, 372-76, 381
Pontcarré, Mme. De, 130
Pontchâteau, Baron de, 129
Porée (S. J.), 410, 416-17, 427
Porta, Jocomo Della, 420
Port Royal de Paris, 126-37, 139-44, 150
Portugal, 42, 104, 110, 122, 213, 222, 232, 244, 248, 278, 282, 303-4, 306, 376-79, 381, 390, 433, 470
Possevino, Antonio, 328-340, 342, 361
Potomac river, 282
Pozzo, Andrea del, 420, 430
Pragmatism, 160
Prague, 331, 350, 357-58, 404
 Defenestration of, 357
 University of, 404
Prat, Guillaume du, 405
Predestination (See free will)
Prémare, Joseph Henry (S. J.), 476-77
Prescott (S. J.), 317
Pribilla, Max, 475
Priero, Sylvester de, 185
Prince, The (Machiavelli), 173
Probabiliorism, 204
Probabilism, 202-9, 378
Prophetie, Die (Auerbach), 184

Providas (bull), 433
Provincial Letters (Pascal), 133, 174-76, 179, 209-11, 471, 473
Prussia, 156, 389, 454
Przywara, Erich, 447
Psychoanalysis, 121, 445-48, 457, 472
Psychopathology of Everyday Life (Freud), 446
Ptolemaic system, 400, 474
Pupilla oculi, 185
Puritans, 31, 282, 318
Quebec, 284-85, 290
Quesnel, Pasquier, 142-43
Quilon, 405
Quinet, Edgar, 32, 42, 113, 390
Quintilian, 343
Racine, Jean, 131-32, 140
Ramleh, 77
Ramsay, Michael, 433
Rann Yu, 256
Rapin (S. J.), 428
Ratio atque Institutio Studiorum Societatis Jesu, 405
Ratio docendi et discendi (Jouvancy), 410
Ravaillac, François, 362
Ravenna, 94
Redemptorists, order of, 186
Regensburg, College of, 416, 421
Regicide, 210, 324, 326
Reichl, Kurt, 453-54
Reichwein, Adolf, 426
Reign of Terror, 388, 414
Reik, Theodor, 121
Reinalde, Juan de, 83-4
Rejadella, Theresa, 169
Religion within the Bounds of Reason Only (Kant), 206
Reni, Guido, 420

INDEX

Rennes, 364
Responsa moralia (Comitolus), 209
Revue Internationale, 454
Rheims, 317
Rhine, 421
Rhodes, Alexander de, 248
Rhodesia, 391
Ribadeneira, Pedro, 49, 65, 68, 76, 106, 109
Ricci, Matteo, 248-57, 402
Riccioli, Giovanni Battista, 402
Richelieu, Cardinal de, 363-66, 373, 376
Rimel, Stephan, 357
Rio de Janeiro, 291
Robespierre, Maxmillen, 388
Rodriguez, Francis, 355
Rodriquez, Simon, 89, 94, 104, 167
Rome, 36-7, 73, 85-6, 90, 93-4, 98, 101-2, 104, 110, 118, 121, 123, 137, 153, 205, 209, 213-14, 223, 234, 236, 238, 243, 245-46, 249-50, 253-54, 275, 278, 311-12, 318-18, 320-21, 326, 328-31, 333, 337, 339, 340, 342, 344, 348-50, 352, 355-56, 358-62, 364, 366, 370, 383, 385, 388, 392, 397-98, 400, 404-5, 410, 413, 418-21, 454, 459, 461, 464
Rosa, (S. J.), 454
Rosa Ursina (Scheiner), 402
Roser, Doña Isabella, 71-2
Rouen, 132
Rousseau, Jean Jacques, 426-27, 431
Rubens, Peter Paul, 2, 418-20, 438
Rubio (Franciscan), 6, 82
Rudolph II, Emperor, 331, 339, 355
Ruga (S. J.), 344, 347
Russell, Bertrand, 161, 163
Russia, 162-63, 267, 271, 310, 330-44, 347, 387, 389, 454, 460
Ruthenia, 340

Sa, Calixto de, 83-4
Sablé, Marquise de, 130
Sacy, de (S. J.), 129-30, 375-76
Saint-Cyran, Abbé de (See vergier de Hauranne, Jean du)
Sainte-Barbe, College of, 87, 405
Saint-Jacques, Hôpital, 79, 84
St. John's Island (See Chang-chuen-shan)
St. Lawrence river, 284
St. Mary (Maryland), 282
Saint Mary Magdalene, 410
St. Mary of the Hurons, 285
St. Omer, 317, 421
St. Paul's College, 405
St. Petersburg, 163-64, 271, 388-89
Saint-Simon, Duc de, 366, 370
St. Thomé, 405
Saint-Vincent, Grégoire de, 403
Salamanca, 75, 83-4, 405, 421, 465, 475
Sallusti (S. J.), 274
Salmeron, Alfonso, 89, 317
Salzburg, Bishop of, 404
 College of, 413
Samson, 413
Sanchez, Isabel, 82
Sanchez, Tomas, 197, 202, 207
Sandãus, Maximilian, 417
Sandomir, Palatine of (See Mniszek, George)
San Iago, order of, 84
San Isidro, College of, 404, 421
San Jose, 300
San Juan Bautista, 298, 421
San Sacramento, 303
Santa Ana, 294
Sante Fe, 300, 306
Santo Corazon, 300

INDEX

San Xavier, 300
São Pedro do Rio Grande, 304
Sarasa (S. J.), 155
Sardinia, 389
Savonarola, Girolamo, 444
Sawicki (S. J.), 342-43
Saxony, 59, 69-70, 359
Schall, Adam von, 259-62
Scheffler, Johann, 417
Scheiner (S. J.), 358
Scheiner, Christoph, 401-2
Scheler, Max, 445
Scherer (S. J.), 355, 358
Schiller, J. C. Friedrich von, 458
Scholasticism, 24-5, 41-2, 112-13, 114, 116-17, 123, 147, 149-52, 156, 158, 164, 166-67, 172-73, 177-78, 184-85, 203, 205, 210, 226, 319-20, 392-94, 396, 403, 405, 423, 426-29, 434, 437, 440, 441-45, 447, 449, 455-57, 473
Schopenhauer, Arthur, 157, 471
Science, Jesuits in, 113, 153, 155, 157-58, 177, 210, 225, 248-65, 267-72, 275, 278, 282, 287-88, 370, 395-403, 406, 422-23, 433-39, 441-48, 457-58, 463, 473-79
Secchi, Angelo, 435-36
Secret War against Throne and Altar, The (Pachtler), 450
Séguier, Pierre, 133
Seguiran, de (S. J.), 363
Semi-Pelagianism, 116
Seneca, 101, 184
Sepp (S. J.), 293, 297
Serma de institutione monachorum (Basil), 39
Sesmaisons, de (S. J.), 134
Seven Years' War, 387
Sévigné, Mme. De, 130

Seville, 6, 50, 317, 451-52
Shaftesbury, Earl of, 432
Shakespeare, William, 407, 413, 458
Shammai, House of, 199
Shelley, Percy, 458
Shinto, 231
Shun-chi, Emperor, 260
Sicily, 389
Sickelpart (S. J.), 274
Sigismund III of Poland, 341-42, 344
Sigmund (S. J.), 276
Silesia, 357, 387
Silesius, Angelus (See Scheffler, Johann)
Sin-ching, 255
Singlin, Father, 129
Skarga, Peter, 340, 342
Smolensk, 332
Social Contract, The (Rousseau), 426
Socialism
Social Metaphysics of Scholasticism (Winter), 444
Södermanland, Duke Charles of, 330
Sokotra island, 222
Sollicitudo omnium Ecclesiarum (Pius VII), 388, 390
Sonderbund, 389
Sörensen (S. J.), 458
Sosan, Prince, 267
Soto Ferdinando de, 284
Spain, 6, 50, 54, 83-4, 98, 105-6, 109-10, 123-24, 222, 247, 282, 288, 292, 303, 306, 315, 328, 358, 360-63, 365, 379, 381-84, 388-90, 404, 417, 421, 433, 459
Spee, Friedrich von, 417
Spencer, Herbert, 448-49
Speyer, College of, 404
Spinoza, Benedict, 153-55
Spirit of Christianity (Chateaubriand), 293

INDEX

Spiritual exercises, 19-34, 39, 48, 68-9, 81-4, 87, 89, 103, 111, 113, 305, 348, 350, 351, 377, 380, 405, 407, 418-420, 441, 463-64
Stagira, 114-18, 179, 183, 186-87, 189, 395
Stanislaus of Poland, 327, 427
Staritsa, 334
Stephen of Poland (See Báthory, Stephen)
Stevenson, Robert Louis, 287
Steyl, 33
Stockholm, 327-30
Stockmann, Alois, 458-59
Stoicism, 21, 166, 184, 198-201, 205
Stuart, Mary, 318
Sturm, Johann, 404
Styria, Archduke Charles of, 331, 355
 Archduke Ferdinand of (See Ferdinand II, Emperor);
 Archduke Maria of, 331
Suarez, Francisco, 20, 35, 38, 122, 319-20, 356, 426
Sue, Eugène, 390
Suffren (S. J.), 363
Sully, Duke of, 319, 361
Summa de poenitentia et matrimonio (Pennaferte), 185
Summa Silvestrina, 185
Summa Theologiae (Aquinas), 395
Summula confessorum (Antoninus), 185
Superior, Lake, 284
Suso, Heinrich, 29
Sweden, 213, 327-31, 341-42, 348, 359, 365-66
Swieten, Gerard van, 385, 433
Switzerland, 388-89, 404, 409, 421
System of Theology (Leibniz), 154
Szatmár Németi, 339
Tacchi-Venturi, P., 6

Tacquet (S. J.), 149
Tagus river, 376
Takahisa, Daimyo Shimatsu, 224-25
Talmud, 172, 198-202, 236
Talon, Advocate-General, 129
Tamuyos, 291
Tanner, Adam, 402
Tao, 257-60
Tapajos river, 304
Tarahumares mts., 287
Tarazona, College of, 464
Tartuffe (Moliere), 428
Tashiteru, Shogun Ashinaka, 229
Tatary, 223, 265, 274
Tavora, Marquis of, 376-77
Templars, order of, 74
Tencin, Mme. De, 425
Terence, 428
Tertullian, 184, 402
Texas, 287
Thames, 282
Theatines, order of, 93-4, 100
Theatre, Jesuit, 47, 407-17, 422, 428
Thébaide, le (Racine), 131
Theodicy (Leibniz), 154-55
Theodosius, Emperor, 306
Theophilus, 413
Theosophy, 476-77
Thibault (S. J.), 276
Thirty Years' War, 351-60, 363
Thomas à Kempis, 25, 40, 69
Thompson, Francis, 457
Thoughts (Pascal), 131, 210-11
Tibet, 240, 476
Tileman (S. J.), 442
Tillemont, Sébastien de, 129
Tillot, Minister du, 433
Timur, Lenk, 239
Tirant lo blanch, 54

INDEX

Tokio, 391
Toland, John, 432
Toledo, 222, 421
 Archbishop of, 222
Tolemei (S. J.), 155
Tonking, 234, 248
Torres (S. J.), 225-26
Tournai, 421
Tournemine (S. J.), 427
Transylvania, 332, 339-40
 Voivode of (See Báthory, Stephen)
Treitschke, Heinrich von, 440
Trent, council of, 114-19, 322, 396-97, 441
Treves, University of, 123
Trevisano, Senator, 65, 74
Treviso, 101
Trieste, Bishop of, 404
Trutz-Nachtigall (Spee), 417
T'ung-chih-kang-mu, 254
Turkestan, 240, 275
Turkey, 332
Tuscany, 384
Tuticorin, 218, 405
Tutiorism, 203
"two standards,", 27, 30
"two swords,", 319-20
Unam sanctam (Clement V), 321
Unigenitus (Clement XI), 144, 147, 373
United States, 284, 390
Unity of Natural Forces, The (Secchi), 436
Universae theologiae moralis problemata (Escobar), 195
Upsala, 330
Urban VIII, Pope, 281
Uruguay, 294
Uruguay river, 292-93, 304
Utopia, 301-2, 305-310
Valdelirios, Marquis of, 304

Valencia, 50
Valentia (S. J.), 122
Valera, Blas, 287, 420
Valeriani, Giuseppe, 420
Valignami, Alessandro, 249
Valkenburg, 33
Valois, Marquerite de, 362
Van Dyck, Anthony, 419
Vannes, 33
Vasquez (S. J.), 204, 208
Vatier, de (S. J.), 149
Vavasseur (S. J.), 428
Vedas, 237, 239, 476
Vega, Lope de, 417
Venice, 73-4, 90, 93-4, 100-101, 330-331, 336, 339
 Great Council of, 330
Verbiest, Ferdinand, 261-62
Vergier de Hauranne, Jean du, 125, 127, 129
Verjus (S. J.), 155
Verlaine, Paul, 459
Verona, 101
Vetter (S. J.), 351
Vicenza, 101
Vico, Francesco de, 435
Vienna, 6, 7, 123, 330-31, 333, 350, 353, 355, 357-59, 380, 383-84, 388, 404, 408-9, 415-17, 420, 423-24, 438
Vignola, da, 420
Villagarcia, 124
Villler, Bartholomæus, 357, 360
Vilna, 330, 331, 333
Vincent de Paul, 20, 128
Virgil, 406
Virginia, 282, 284
Visdelon (S. J.), 268
Vitelleschi, Mutio, 358-60, 365
Vocation of Francis Xavier, The, 416

533

INDEX

Volga river, 334
Voltaire, 47, 111, 116, 127, 130, 132, 137, 141-42, 144, 211, 309, 370, 377, 387, 406, 416, 425-28, 433, 458, 477
Vorarlberg, 33
Walker, L. J., 444
Wallenstein, Albrecht von, 359
Wan-li, Emperor, 258
Warner, Provincial, 283
Warsaw, 340
Warsewicz, Stanislaus, 327, 329
Washington, D. C., 282, 284, 434
Washington, University of, 442
Wasmann, Erich, 164, 436, 439
Watrigant, J., 34
Watson, John B., 162-63
Wegen der Weltweischeit (B. Jansen), 153
Weishaupt, Adam, 432-33
Wentscher, Else, 160
White, Andrew, 282
White, Russia, 387
Wiegand, 350
Wieland, Christoph, 458
William of Orange, 284, 384
Willwoll (S. J.), 447
Winter, Ernst Karl, 444, 457
Wisniwiecki, Prince Adam, 341
Wladislaus IV of Poland, 344
Worcester, 313
Worms, Diet of, 349
Wundt, Wilhelm, 158, 160, 162
Würzburg, Bishop of, 404
 College of, 123, 158-59, 404
Xavier, Francis, 87-9, 214-19, 221-32, 235-37, 240
Xavier, Jerome, 239
Yamaguchi, 227, 230, 391

Yam-kam-siem, 261
Yao, Emperor, 258
Yaqui river, 287
Year-book of the Natural Sciences (S. J.), 442
Yellowstone river, 284
Yoen-ming-yoen, 272, 275-76
Yogis, 235-38
York, Duke of (See James II of Egland)
Yoshishige, Dainmyo Otomo, 230-31
Yoshitaka, Daimo Uchi, 230
Ypres, Bishop of (See Jansen, Cornelius)
Yei'-ling, 258
Yung-chêng, Emperor, 268, 271
Zamoyski, Jan, 335-36, 342
Zeeghers, Daniel, 420
Zephyris, Francis of, 297
Ziegler, Leopold, 41
Zimmermann, F. X., 6, 415
Zola, Émile, 459
Zoroaster, 239
Zucchi (S. J.), 400
Zybura, J. S., 442

Sun	M	T	W	Th	F	S
						18
19	20	21	22	23	24	25
26	27	28	29	30	1	2
3	4	5	6	7	8	9
10	11	12	13	14	15	16
17	18	19				